THE WORLD WILDLIFE GUIDE

The
World
Wildlife
Guide

Foreword by Her Royal Highness
Princess Beatrix
of the Netherlands

Edited by
Malcolm Ross-Macdonald

THE VIKING PRESS · NEW YORK

Devised by Barbara Cooper

Original research: Barbara Cooper, Susan Craig,
Marianne Eastgate, Patricia Quick
Format and graphics: Bruce Robertson, Edward Price
Further and pictorial research, writing, layout, maps:
Malcolm Ross-Macdonald

Published in 1972 by The Viking Press, Inc.
625 Madison Avenue, New York, NY 10022

SBN 670–79018–4
Library of Congress catalog card number: 77–163977
Printed and bound in Great Britain by the Westerham Press

Foreword

Pollution of the air, the soil, and the waters now means that virtually no living plant or animal anywhere on earth can be said to be altogether unaffected by the activities of man. Natural habitat and renewable resources continue to disappear, and plant and animal forms are becoming extinct at a disastrous and still increasing rate. Fall-out even descends on the penguins in the Antarctic and on the lichens which feed the caribou in the Arctic.

There is reason to doubt whether, in due course, there will be any wildlife or wild country left outside National Parks, Nature Reserves and Sanctuaries. Certainly the areas so far set aside will be inadequate to preserve even the main types of wildlife habitats or to accommodate all the people who will want in the future to enjoy the beauty and fascihation of wilderness. Much more land in many parts of the world will need to be devoted to this kind of spiritual refreshment: and to make this possible, existing wild areas must be seen to be a valuable form of land use.

This is where, I am convinced, *The World Wildlife Guide* can play an important part, for the National Parks and Reserves will prosper only if they are visited; indeed they will continue to exist in newly developing countries only if they pay their way.

Designed principally for the traveller, it shows that every continent has its share of accessible and organized places where there is rewarding wildlife-viewing in natural surroundings. By encouraging people to visit such areas, this book will inevitably encourage a trend towards the setting up of more and yet more of them. To every country it offers the encouragement that money invested in sound conservation is money well spent. To many endangered animals it offers the most precious hope of all: survival. To all who care about such things—whether they are conservationists or tourists—I am happy to recommend *The World Wildlife Guide*.

How to use this book

The countries represented are indexed on page 9. The world map on pages 10–11 is a key to all the other major maps in the book. Each major map, in turn, shows every park, reserve, or other site within its boundaries and refers you to the page on which it may be found.

The standard format for each major site is self-explanatory – except for the symbols that introduce semi-tabular matter. Not all of them are used for each entry; an omission means that information was scant, or suspect, or simply not interesting enough. The symbols are as follows:

Fauna Here are listed the main animals (especially mammals and birds) of the park or reserve – also noteworthy rarities such as leopard and tiger. Officially a listing means no more than that an animal is sighted at least once every 12 months. A plural in this list shows that more than one species is intended.

Flora A list of the main or noteworthy plants of the park.

Accommodation Here we list hotels, lodges, campsites, and other accommodation in or near the site. The rates quoted (in local currencies) are current for spring 1971, but world-wide inflation is so rampant that intending visitors should mentally add, say, 10 per cent to rates given here so as to keep the surprises on the pleasant side.

Access Here we describe the major land, air, and water routes to the park or reserve, together with notes on road conditions, car hire, seasonal factors, and so on.

Internal transport Here are described the trails, tracks, roads, or rivers within a particular park or reserve, plus notes on horse, car, or boat hire, fuel stations, breakdown facilities, and organized internal tours.

Season The months when the park is open, followed by the months when it is most rewarding to visit for wildlife viewing.

Time needed This is generally the maximum and minimum time an ordinary, non-specialist traveller should aim to devote to the park or reserve. It does not include travel time to and from the site.

Entry fees Fees for pedestrians, vehicles, and passengers.

Guides or rangers Their availability, and rates charged.

Other notable features Here we list places in or near the park likely to interest travellers – archaeological ruins, museums, historic sites, and so on.

Information This is the nearest source of information to the site; usually it is the park or reserve authority itself, sometimes the local administering body; occasionally we have referred the reader to the local or overseas tourist office.

Many sites are not accorded this full tabular treatment. In general, this means that they are of lesser interest *to the traveller* – however important their conservation role; but it may also mean that the information was too sparse to justify tabulation. For a few areas a brief essay was more appropriate to the material.

The species lists that conclude each section index the animals in alphabetical order and list the sites reporting them in the order in which they occur in the book.

Contents

Preface

Several years ago, when this book was first conceived, we were exclusively concerned with travel literature – producing guides to the world's most visited countries. In making such guides, the first step is to look at the existing literature so that intelligent and searching questions can be asked of the agents and correspondents in the countries concerned. Again and again we found ourselves framing lengthy question-sheets on the national parks and wildlife-viewing facilities of widely differing countries. With the obvious exceptions of East and Southern Africa, these attractions were universally ignored by the standard reference works – which, at best, mentioned and dismissed them in a few lines. We decided to remedy this deficiency by producing a traveller's guide exclusively devoted to wildlife.

Our first step was to approach the London offices of the World Wildlife Fund (WWF) and the International Union for the Conservation of Nature (IUCN). Their encouragement and interest was immediate and has never since wavered. (In return for such help, the WWF in Britain, the USA, and other countries where this book is sold will benefit substantially from such sales). As a first step we drew up a list of about 180 major parks and sanctuaries in every continent. Sir Hugh Elliott, editor of the English-language edition of the official UN list of parks and sanctuaries* was especially helpful, and, despite his own commitment to that and other IUCN business, has given us splendid help at various stages of preparation since.

We started to research our original list with the assistance of BOAC offices around the world. Very soon the project took on an independent life. Most books accept their initial outlines and grow respectably to fill them; this one has steadfastly refused to do any such thing. Word of our project spread quickly, and all sorts of people with interests in travel or wildlife wrote or sent indirect word exhorting us not to omit this or that park or reserve. Our own efforts, too, provoked unaccustomed partnerships between national agencies for tourism and those for conservation – resulting in lists of parks never before published in a form accessible to the average traveller. The section on Australia is one example of this happy union, and owes a great deal to the skilful co-ordination of Roger Clarke of the Australian Tourist Commission.

Across the Atlantic we had generous help from Philip A. Dumont of the Division of Wildlife Refuges, Edwin N. Winge of the National Park Service (both USA), and Darrell Eagles of Canada's Department of Indian Affairs and Northern

---

United Nations List of National Parks and Equivalent Reserves by Jean-Paul Harroy (Hayez, Brussels) US$19.00.

Development. To their unstinted efforts we owe the completeness of our coverage of *national* sites in North America. Michael Blackmore of Britain's Nature Conservancy gave help of a similar high order for the British sites. Further help is acknowledged on page 416.

All these people, and others in many different countries, suggested places omitted from our original list. And so, in an appropriately organic fashion, the book grew beyond its early confines. Naturally there came a moment when we had to stay 'Stop!' – at least for this first edition. Naturally, too, such a decision (plus, it must sadly be recorded, the sloth or indifference of some authorities) has produced some rather arbitrary results. Thus there are few or no listings for Madagascar, Indonesia, and parts of South America and Northern Africa. We know that there are parks in these areas, but we have been unable to assure ourselves of their accessibility or of the quality of their facilities for visitors. Similarly, the state parks in the USA are under-represented, either because the state authorities did not reply at all to our repeated letters or because they replied too late for inclusion.

With the benefit of hindsight we can discern another under-represented area: reserves and sanctuaries financed by private or semi-official bodies. Examples in the USA are the National Audubon Society's Big Cypress and their Rainey Sanctuary, Stone Harbor City's heronry, and the Pacific Grove Butterfly Sanctuary, California. The US National Appeal of the WWF has helped to save other important areas: the best marshlands in southern New Jersey, the Texas habitat of Attwater's prairie chicken, and critical breeding grounds for the white-winged dove. In Britain, too, there are a dozen such places, only two of which are represented in these pages. We very much hope that readers who know of such sites – particularly those involved in their founding and running – will send us details so that we can cover this important part of the conservation movement more adequately.

Fault may be found with the species lists. In compiling these lists we have generally relied on first-hand evidence – information from wardens, administering authorities, and trustworthy visitors. Unfortunately this has resulted in a somewhat uneven standard of reporting from section to section. African birds, particularly, are here under-represented. Such variation is, perhaps, unavoidable until publication sets a standard that all can see and follow.

In spite of inevitable omissions, with its coverage of more than 600 sites in all the continents, the book can claim to be the most complete guide to the world's important parks, reserves, and sanctuaries. We hope it will quickly become the standard nonacademic reference for thousands of travellers (armchair and otherwise) interested in conservation.

Barbara Cooper, Malcolm Ross-Macdonald, 1971

Master Key to the Maps

The squares on the map relate to the parts of the world covered in this book. In the USA, for instance, M92 and M93 refer you to maps on pages 92–3 where the location of each American park in the text is given together with its page; S181 refers you to a species list on page 181. Page numbers without an M or S prefix refer to text pages (e.g. the Caribbean on pages 407–10).

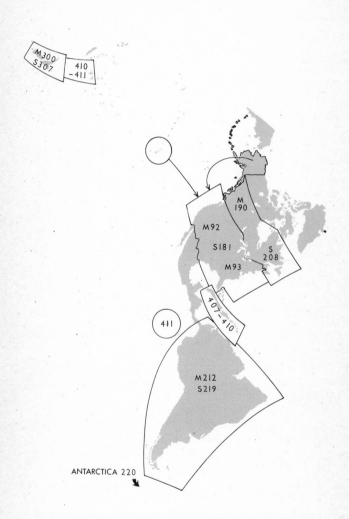

M300
S307

410
–411

M
190

M92

S181

S
208

M93

407–410

411

M212
S219

ANTARCTICA 220

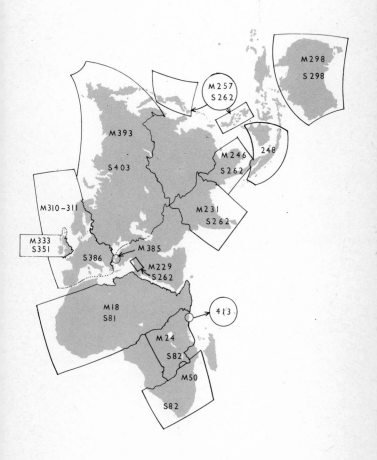

AFRICA

Introduction by
Rennie Bere

Africa stretches across the equator from the Mediterranean to the Cape of Good Hope and includes almost every type of country imaginable: coral beaches, swamps, deserts, tropical rain-forest and high mountains covered by perpetual snow and ice as well as the grasslands which support so many wild grazing animals. Even so, there is a pattern in all this variety. The heart of the continent is the evergreen rain-forest; it spreads along the equator from West Africa to the great lakes. North, south and east of the forest are the savanna woodlands: the Guinea savanna, the Nile basin and the southern woodlands which are generally known as *Miombo*. Between these woodlands and the deserts – Sahara in the north and Kalahari in the south – is the dry savanna, most of which is dominated by acacias and baobab trees; it includes the Sudanese steppe, the thorn bush country of the Horn of Africa and the southern bushveld. Small areas of rain-

Elephants and cattle egrets on the Nile banks in Murchison NP.

forest intrude into the savannas as do the main highland areas of which the most important are the mountains of East Africa and Ethiopia, the East African grasslands and the highveld of South Africa. Mediterranean Africa and the Cape, the sub-tropical extremities of the continent, are the regions most influenced by man.

There is a comparable pattern in the distribution of wildlife. Some highly adaptable species, such as the elephant, can live in several different habitats; hippos also thrive almost anywhere, provided that there is warm water and enough grass for them to eat. Most species, however, are limited to a relatively small range of habitats: blue duikers, for example, live only in the forests, oryx on the steppes and wildebeest on the grassland plains. This means that the same kinds of animal, though not necessarily the same species, are found throughout the woodlands and that, for instance, animals living on the Sudanese steppes have their counterpart in the southern bushveld. There are both northern and southern forms of giraffe, wildebeest, hartebeest, eland, roan antelope and several others; the northern gazelles and oryx are replaced by the springbok and the gemsbok. Zebra occur in almost all the dry savanna regions. Leopards are found in thick bush throughout much of Africa; lion, cheetah and wild dog hunt for prey on the open plains.

A few generations ago these various animals were plentiful and generally distributed. Today they are largely limited to national parks, reserves and a few other wilderness areas. Unless these remain intact there is little future for their wildlife.

Most of the more important and better known reserves are in the savannas; other habitats, except perhaps the mountains, are much less well served. In the forest regions – where animals are difficult to see and, for this reason, of little interest to tourists – there are no properly established national parks with the result that many fascinating creatures, notably monkeys and other primates, are becoming increasingly scarce. Animals of the Sahara desert have been decimated by man, one example being the addax (a beautiful oryx-like antelope with spirally twisted horns) which is facing extinction because insufficient provision has been made for it. Fortunately, however, the wildlife of the southern deserts is well protected in the Kalahari-Gemsbok National Park. Little is now left of the formerly abundant wildlife of the Cape; and few animals survive in north Africa though recently established parks in Tunisia and Morocco should assure a future for at least a few Atlas gazelles and the Barbary stag, the only member of the deer family to occur anywhere in Africa.

The island of Madagascar, which has probably been separated from continental Africa for sixty million years, still supports one of the world's most distinctive faunas, including twenty unique species of lemur and the insectivorous tenrecs, but the giant tortoises which once astonished travellers are no longer there. The forests, which used to be continuous, have mostly been cut down so that the reserves now established on the island are of outstanding importance.

Several unusual species live in the Ethiopian highlands, the largest mountain bloc in Africa, and game parks have been created for their protection: walia ibex, gelada baboon and the rare Simien fox – all in the Simien mountains; and the mountain nyala, which lives in the mist forest at over 11,000 ft, in the Bale mountains south of Addis Ababa. Unfortunately, however, the Ethiopian government seems to have difficulty in making a reality of conservation; frequent forest fires as well as illegal cutting of timber is steadily destroying the habitats occupied by these animals. The Aberdare mountains in Kenya are, by contrast, well protected so that the colourful bongo antelope should be safe; and the national park which includes the highest peaks of Mount Kenya guards the finest mountain architecture in Africa and incidentally provides incomparable opportunities for mountaineering.

The greater part of the Birunga volcanoes, which stretch across the western rift valley in an unbroken chain, are divided between the Parc National Albert and the Parc des Volcans, the Uganda slopes of the more easterly of these mountains being protected by the small Muhavura Gorilla Sanctuary in which gorillas are not now permanently resident. As yet the mountain gorilla seems reasonably secure among the volcanoes though there is a constant threat of encroachment mainly by cattle-keepers from Rwanda. Meanwhile the great apes roam peaceably through their wild and incredibly beautiful homeland, rich with colourful flowers and trees, and I know of no greater natural thrill than a face-to-face encounter with a big male silver-back in these idyllic surroundings.

There is nothing in West Africa to compare with the famous game parks of the East and the South, though several areas, such as the Mole reserve in Ghana, have considerable potential and all play their vital role in conserving the flora and fauna of the region; without the Nikola-Koba National Park in Senegal, for instance, the western giant eland would now be extinct. But between Senegal and Lake Chad, country once famous for its wildlife, reserves are generally too few and too small. The Dinder National Park in the Sudan, a remote undeveloped area to the east of the Blue Nile, and Awash National Park in Ethiopia protect the wildlife of the Sudanese steppe; both areas have great possibilities. The Nimule Park in southern Equatoria is a gem in which the northern white rhinoceros still occurs. I recollect a mother elephant in this park concernedly steering her calf along a mile or more of rocky ground while my companions and I walked alongside her, seldom more than fifty yards away.

Uganda's Murchison Falls and Queen Elizabeth National Parks lie in the great basin of the Nile and support what is probably the highest biomass in Africa: mainly elephants, hippopotamuses, buffaloes and antelopes. This huge number of very large animals requires strict and careful management if they are to be prevented from doing excessive damage to the vegetation, and this is being carried out under expert scientific direction. Another problem of these parks is poaching, a direct result of the high human population in what is one of the most fertile regions in Africa. Nile crocodiles have suffered intolerable persecution and are severely reduced in number. They also suffer from over zealous visitors; as tourist launches approach the sand-banks, the basking saurians slither into the water, exposing their eggs to the attentions of hungry baboons, monitor lizards and storks. A problem of an entirely different order is the threat of a hydro-electric power station at Murchison Falls. Not only would this project interfere with the flow of water, it would destroy for ever the solitude of one of the world's great beauty spots.

The great parks of Kenya and Tanzania deserve every bit of their worldwide reputation. Each park has its individuality as a glance at the descriptions below will show. Northern Kenya and parts of Tsavo, where the elephant population is even greater than in Uganda, are arid areas where there is often a shortage of water. The Serengeti in Tanzania supports the world's most fabulous concentration of wild animals, with lions, leopards, cheetahs, wild hunting dogs and hundreds of thousands of antelopes. At certain seasons the wildebeest, gazelle and zebra migrate right across the plains, probably the most exciting event in the whole of Africa's wildlife calendar. The Masai Mara Reserve in Kenya and the Ngorongoro Conservation Area in Tanzania are parts of this same grassland region. The major problem, apart from the perennial one of poaching, is to reconcile the wild animals with the demands of the Masai herdsmen and their cattle which, for generations, have shared the grazing with the antelopes. Amboseli, which is also part of Masailand, has given me the wonderful memory of a lioness leaving a young lion on guard and then trotting off for several miles to collect her cubs before starting to feed on a zebra kill. Lake Nakuru National Park, in the rift valley, is one of the very few African reserves to be established for its birdlife alone though the birds are exciting and varied everywhere. The lake supports an astonishing collection of water birds, among them thousands of flamingoes which give a marvellous pink glow to the scene.

Kafue and the Luangwa valley in Zambia and the fine new parks in Botswana are comparable to East Africa's best. But many of the Rhodesian reserves, including the famous Wankie National Park, are deteriorating fast owing to inadequate management. Where man once played a dominant part as hunter or cultivator, it is rarely sufficient just to eliminate this influence. The park authorities must be prepared to involve themselves actively or else, as in Rhodesia, the habitat will deteriorate and the animals – in this case the species involved are mainly antelopes, rhinos and giraffes – will suffer more or less severely from malnutrition if they do not actually die of starvation. There is, in fact, a regular cycle which is only too common in low rainfall areas in Africa. Overgrazing first destroys the palatable grasses and this leads to an increased growth of woody shrubs which are browsed by an entirely different range of animals; ultimately even the shrubs are destroyed and conditions then approximate to desert.

Although the early settlers in South Africa made a more violent assault upon the wildlife than anybody else on the continent, later generations have made notable amends. The famous Kruger National Park was the first of its kind in Africa – it is still among the finest as well as being the most visited. Almost all the bushveld animals are found there, greater kudu and impala (respectively the most finely horned and the most graceful of the antelopes) being particularly numerous and impressive. Elephants, of which there were only about one hundred in 1930, now number over seven thousand chiefly because of the large influx of these animals from Rhodesia and Mozambique; the resulting management problem is caused by lack of water and not, as in Uganda, insufficient food. The recently established William Pretorius reserve in the Orange Free State provides a home for the strange white-tailed gnu whose aggressive habits are in keeping with its formidable forward-thrusting horns. In the Hluhluwe and Umfolozi reserves in Natal there are rhinos, both black and white, as well as the uncommon lowland nyala. The white rhinos have thrived to such an extent that it has become possible in recent years to transfer surplus animals to other parts of Africa to restock areas where they have become extinct. Relic populations of mountain zebra and bontebok have been saved from following the quagga and blawbok or blue antelope (a smaller relative of the roan antelope) into extinction by the small national parks which bear the names of these animals.

Africa is changing rapidly under the pressure of an expanding and developing human population. The game parks are enclaves in this environment and they give some idea of what Africa must have been like before man took control and started to play havoc with the natural order. They provide incomparable opportunities for scientists as well as for the edification and enjoyment of ordinary visitors. But they will continue to do so only while governments throughout the continent support the park authorities in their never-ending struggle against poaching and encroachment. Politicians are often reluctant to take the unpopular decisions and even more unpopular actions that this requires. The wildlife has no vote.

Northeast and Northwest Africa

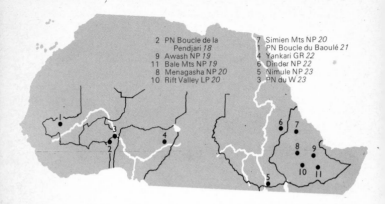

2 PN Boucle de la Pendjari *18*	7 Simien Mts NP *20*
9 Awash NP *19*	1 PN Boucle du Baoulé *21*
11 Bale Mts NP *19*	4 Yankari GR *22*
8 Menagasha NP *20*	6 Dinder NP *22*
10 Rift Valley LP *20*	5 Nimule NP *23*
	3 PN du W *23*

The tourist potential of northern Africa's wildlife areas is very much underdeveloped. In the following pages there are entries for a mere 11 parks. Those for Ethiopia owe their completeness to Jeffrey Boswall, whose television films about his recent wildlife safari to that astonishing country have delighted viewers in many countries. His generous help in augmenting and rearranging our original entries for Ethiopia was of great value. The entries for the Sudan owe their completeness to similarly generous help from Sir Hugh Elliott, who had recently returned from a visit to the parks here listed. Entries for the remaining parks were completed with the help of conservation and tourism agencies in the six countries involved. Since our firmest information has come from people who have visited the areas, we would welcome first-hand and detailed accounts from readers returned from visits to reasonably accessible parks in northern Africa.

Dahomey

Parc National de la Boucle de la Pendjari 1,076 square miles; around 580 ft above sea level. The park lies on the alluvial plain of the Pendjari river in northwestern Dahomey; it is named for the large loop (hence *boucle*) that the river makes in that region. It consists mainly of savannah and bush, well forested near the river and its tributaries; it has many marshes that persist throughout the dry season.

- Elephant, hippo, crocodile, many antelope species, kob, waterbuck, lion, leopard, cheetah, warthog. Birds include crested crane, marabou, heron.
- Camp with 30 beds at Porga; rates from 400 Fr CFA (dormitory) to 1,300 Fr CFA (twin bedroom).
- The main road from Dahomey to Volta, via Natitingou and Porga, leads to the park; minimum distance 422 miles, Cotonou to Porga. Nearest airport at Parakou, 186 miles from Porga by motorable road.
- 155 miles of track within the park; passable to jeeps.

☀ Open October to June; best time January to April.

🕐 2 to 5 days.

☞ None available.

⇨ Office Dahoméen du Tourisme, BP 89, Cotonou, Dahomey.

Ethiopia

Awash National Park 468 square miles; about 3,000 to 6,000 ft above sea level. The park (pronounced 'Ah-wash') lies in the valley of the Awash river, at the eastern foot of the Shoa escarpment. The Awash, which breaks into a five-fingered cascade within the park, is most picturesque. This is where the Rift Valley joins the semi-desert plains of Danakil before reaching north into the Red Sea. In the park, grassy plains alternate with stretches of thorny bush. Dominating all is the spectacular volcanic cone of Mt Fentale (6,000 ft).

🐾 Oryx, Grévy's zebra, Soemmering's gazelle, greater and lesser kudu, Chanler's reedbuck, waterbuck, hippo. Birds include ostrich, carmine bee-eater, Kori bustard, Abyssinian roller.

🛌 Caravan (trailer) accommodation is available on the rim of Awash Canyon. Camp Awash, near the falls, offers first-rate tented accommodation with meals in a dining marquee.

✈ About 3 hrs drive by good road from Addis Ababa. Awash rail station is a few miles from the park and is served by park transport. The park has an airstrip for light charter aircraft.

🚐 There are a number of good roads, suitable for saloon cars; many more miles of track are accessible to 4-wheel-drive.

☀ Open and pleasant all the year.

🕐 2 to 5 days.

✉ $E2 per person.

⌷ *Awash National Park* by John Blower; Ethiopian Tourist Organization.

☞ No guides available but wardens will give advice.

⇨ Wildlife Conservation Dept, PO Box 386, Addis Ababa.

Bale Mountains National Park (proposed). A park of yet-to-be determined area is proposed in this region, 250 miles southeast of Addis Ababa to protect the unique mountain nyala, a kind of mountain kudu that lives only in the Bale and Arussi mountains of south-central Ethiopia. At one time it was on the list of endangered species, but recent surveys have indicated a population of about 5,000 and it has been removed from that list. Apart from its value in conservation the park-designate is increasingly popular for its magnificent and completely unspoiled mountain scenery. Its most notable bird is the Abyssinian blue-winged goose.

🛌 The situation is identical with that at the proposed Simien Mountains park: you hire your own horses, mules, guides, and bearers locally, and take for all your needs except water. The Wildlife Conservation Department may allow a temporary stopover in its house at Dinchu.

☀ Open all year; avoid the local rainy season, July–August.

🕐 Minimum 7 days; preferably 10 to 14.

✉ Free.

⇨ Wildlife Conservation Dept, PO Box 386, Addis Ababa.

Menagasha National Forest 11 square miles (but contained within a larger reserve of 94 square miles); 8,116 to 10,416 ft above sea level. This is more of a botanical reserve than a wild-life area, since the animals – though fairly abundant – are less easily glimpsed in a forest than on an open plain. It stands on the slopes of an extinct volcano (Mt Wochacha) and its chief attractions are the fine stands of podocarpus, juniper, and hagenia. Above the forest line there are banks of tree heather, Abyssinian rose, giant lobelia, and giant St John's wort.

- Black-and-white colobus monkeys, olive baboon, Meneliki bushbuck. Many birds, including the white-cheeked turaco.
- None (too close to Addis Ababa, where accommodation is plentiful).
- The village of Menagasha is about 20 miles west of Addis; drive on for a further 2 miles then take the left turn at the sign marked 'Spring Farm'.
- Foot.
- Open all year; rains in July–September can make going difficult.
- Day trip from Addis Ababa.
- Free.
- Not necessary.
- Wildlife Conservation Dept, PO Box 386, Addis Ababa.

Rift Valley Lakes Park (proposed) When it is established, this park will embrace two of the lakes, Shala and Abyata, on the floor of the Ethiopian Rift, about 6,000 ft above sea level. Lake Abyata is about 120 miles south of Addis Ababa; Shala, the next lake downstream, is close by. Both are to the west of the road. For visitors Abyata is the more interesting – indeed, it has been described as one of the best birdwatching sites in the world. Nearly 100 different water and shore birds have been identified here.

- Great white and pink-backed pelicans, greater and lesser flamingos, marabou stork, and numerous cormorants, ducks, geese, ibises, gulls, terns, and waders.
- There is a modern hotel and campsite on the shore of Lake Langano, 7 miles back toward Addis and on the east of the road.
- At the 190 km stone turn right on to the tracks that skirt either bank of the Horakalla river. The lakeshore is only 2 miles from the main road and the tracks are suitable for saloon cars.
- On foot.
- Open and pleasant all year.
- 1 to 3 days.
- Free.
- Not needed.
- Wildlife Conservation Dept, PO Box 386, Addis Ababa.

Simien Mountains National Park (proposed) 391 square miles; 8,000 to 12,000 ft above sea level. The Simien mountain scenery is easily the most dramatic in all Africa. The main object of the proposed park is to provide a refuge for the

Walia ibex, which inhabits the northern ramparts of the Simien massif – a 20-mile stretch of cliffs that rear 3,000 to 5,000 ft. This animal is found nowhere else in the world, and the total population is less than 150. Another rare and threatened species is the Simien fox, which hunts among the arboreal heather and giant lobelia of the Afro-alpine meadows. The Gelada baboon, which lives in troops several hundred strong in these ranges, is common and approachable. All three mammals are unique to this region, which, despite its 'national-park' designation is steadily being ruined by forest clearance and the ploughing up of the unique meadows. Conservationists are unanimous in urging the Imperial Ethiopian Government to act against this destruction before it is too late.

🏃 Walia ibex, Simien fox (sometimes misleadingly called 'Abyssinian wolf'), Gelada baboon. Birds include lammergeyer, thick billed raven, wattled ibis, chough.

🛏 None. A visit to the High Simien is an expedition and calls for careful planning. There are no extraordinary hazards, and the trip is one of the most rewarding in the world.

🚩 Horse or mule (both of which can be hired at Debarek) or on foot – a 2- or 3-day journey, depending on conditions.

☀ Open all year; avoid July–September.

⏱ At least 7 days, preferably 10 to 14.

🎫 Free.

📖 *Simien, the Roof of Africa* by John Hurrell Crook; Ethiopian Tourist Organization.

🔭 Bearers and muleteers for hire at Debarek.

➡ Wildlife Conservation Dept, PO Box 386, Addis Ababa.

Mali

Parc National de la Boucle du Baoulé 1,367 square miles (makes 2,700 square miles with neighbouring Badinko and Fina game reserves); about 1,000 ft above sea level. Most of the park consists of sandstone plateau crossed by a chain of mountains flanked by long parallel rows of hills. The south is flatter, with large plains of sand and clay and a few areas of red laterite soil. Scattered trees include pterocarpus, gardenia, bauhinia, dialim, and, in the east, kapok.

🏃 Gazelles, kob, hippo, Derby's eland, giraffe, lion, elephant, African buffalo, topi, antelopes and numerous duikers.

🛏 At Baoulé, 6 bedrooms, 1 common room with refrigerator, bathroom, wc, kitchen; at Madina, 3 bedrooms, bathroom, wc, kitchen; at Missira, 3 bedrooms, 1 common room with refrigerator, bathroom, wc, kitchen, self-catering at each camp with advice (but not full service) from a 'boy-cuisinier'. Rates from 1,500 Mali Francs per room per day. Bookings via Office Malien de Tourisme, BP 222, Bamako, Mali.

🚩 By road from Bamako, 62 miles; no rail or air access.

🚗 250 miles of internal road; suitable for cars, best for jeeps.

☀ Open October to June; best time January to April.

⏱ 2 to 4 days.

➡ Office Malien de Tourisme, BP 222, Bamako, Mali.

Nigeria

Yankari Game Reserve Just over 800 square miles; 700 to 1,200 ft above sea level. The reserve stands in hilly wooded savannah, dense in some parts, in others broken by stretches of grass and marshy forest. The region is well furnished with water. In places there are hot springs and you may come across the remains of old wells dug into sandstone outcrops.

- Elephant, hippo, roan antelope, waterbuck, bushbuck, lion, giraffe, leopard, crocodile, cheetah, warthog, hartebeest, jackal, hunting dog, buffalo, many species of monkey; wide range of birdlife.

- Rondavels and tents at Wikki Warm Springs (selfcatering and restaurant facilities). Bookings through the Regional Game Warden, Bauchi. Rates from £2 per night; full board and tea £2 extra.

- The reserve is in Bauchi Province of Nigeria's North Eastern State and 75 miles southeast of Bauchi town. The nearest airport is at Jos, 82 miles away. There is an airstrip at Bauchi. Return road trip from Bauchi 67/6.

- 125 miles of road suitable for saloon cars. Daily tours are organized from the camp. Breakdown recovery 25/– to 47/6 within park; 67/6 to Bauchi.

- Open 1 November to 30 June; best time January to April.

- 2 to 4 days.

- 17/6 per person; 10/– under 15 years old; free under 4.

- 12/6 per vehicle and 4 passengers; 5/– each additional passenger (not counting the guide himself).

- Nigerian Tourist Association, PO Box 2944, Lagos.

Sudan

Dinder National Park 2,750 square miles; 2,300 to 2,600 ft above sea level. Created in 1935 the park enforces total protection (though rubber extraction, under supervision, is allowed in the western sector). Unfortunately the animals are not protected during annual migrations that take them outside the park boundary, so their survival is not ensured. The park consists mostly of thick savannah bush, well watered by the Dinder river.

- Giraffe, reedbuck, hartebeest, roan antelope, bushbuck, oribi, dikdik, several gazelle species, lion, buffalo, waterbuck, greater kudu, ostrich, black rhino, elephant, hyena, jackal.

- Tourist camp (50 beds) at Galegu, in the eastern sector. Three smaller camps elsewhere in park.

- By road south from Khartoum through Wad Medani to Sennar; turn left on road to Kassala, then right at Dinder town on road to Galega; total distance 290 miles. The road may become impassable during the wet season in July–August (when the park is, in any case, closed). No convenient air access. Rail access to Dinder, 60 miles from park.

- A good, surfaced road crosses the park and sprouts a dozen branches to the camps, populous waterholes, and constructed hides.

- Open part-August to June; best time November to March.

ⓘ   2 to 5 days.

⇒   Tourist Dept, Ministry of Communications and Tourism, Khartoum.

Nimule National Park 61,750 acres; 1,650 to 2,600 ft above sea level. A reserve since 1946 and a park since 1954, Nimule stands on a hilly plateau near the Nile in southern Sudan. The Ilingua Mountains form a barrier on its western edge, and from their foothills run valleys (or khors) cut by rushing torrents, the most spectacular of which forms the Fula Rapids. The landscape is of open savannah with bush and scattered tamarind trees. There are no specific tourist facilities but the park is popular because the animals are both accessible and approachable.

↢   White rhino, elephant, buffalo, waterbuck, hippo, reedbuck, hartebeest, kob, warthog, oribi, eland, bongo, Nile lechwe, yellow-backed duiker.

↤   Hotel in Juba; rates from 200 PT without airconditioning, private bath and in shared room, up to 500 PT for single room with those amenities. Five per cent service charge.

↦   By road from Khartoum via Kosti, Malakal, and Juba; total distance about 900 miles. Roads south of Malakal are generally passable only between mid-December and mid-April. From Masindi in Uganda the park is only 150 miles by road.

🚗   Rough tracks suitable to 4-wheel drive.

☀   Open August to May; best time winter.

ⓘ   2 to 4 days.

⇒   Tourist Dept, Ministry of Communications and Tourism.

Upper Volta, Niger, Dahomey

Parc National du W 6,534 square miles; 583 to 1,246 ft above sea level. The park is shaped like a letter W and lies across the borders of Dahomey, Volta, and Niger. Over half of it (3,910 square miles) is in Dahomey; of the remainder 1,350 square miles are in Volta and 1,274 square miles are in Niger. The lusher parts of the park are generally in the south, where tall, cathedral-like forests form along the banks of the seasonal rivers. Northwards the terrain gives way to savannah and bush, and in the far north it becomes almost saharan. In the Dahomey part the park is crossed by the Atacora 'mountains' (highest point 1,246 ft). Most of the soil is red laterite, rich in iron and aluminium, sharply eroded in places.

↢   Elephant, kob and many antelope species, monkeys, lion, cheetah, jackal, hippo, crocodile, warthog, African buffalo.

↤   Camps at Tapôa (Niger); Diapaga (Volta); and Keremou (Dahomey).

↦   Airports at Ouagadougou (Volta) and Niamey (Niger). Roads from Niamey to Tapoa (96 miles); Niamey to Diapaga (120 miles); Ouagadougou to Diapaga (280 miles).

🚗   125 miles of fair-weather track within the park connects the camps and game viewing sites.

☀   Open all year; best time February to April.

East and Central Africa

CONGO
1 Albert NP *25*

KENYA
5 Aberdare NP *26*
2 Isiolo GR *27*
4 L Nakuru NP *27*
3 Marsabit NP *28*
8 Mara NP *29*
10 Amboseli NP *29*
7 Meru NP *30*
1 Mt Elgon NP *31*
6 Mt Kenya NP *31*
9 Nairobi NP *32*
2 Samburu GR *32*
11 Tsavo NP *33*

TANZANIA
3 Arusha NP *36*
6 Gombe Stream GR *41*
4 L Manyara NP *37*

8 Mikumi NP *37*
2 Ngorongoro CA *38*
7 Ruaha NP *39*
1 Serengeti NP *40*
5 Tarangire GR *41*

UGANDA
4 Kidepo Valley NP *42*
1 Mt Muhavura GS *42*
3 Murchison Falls NP *43*
2 Q Elizabeth NP *44*

MALAWI
2 Kasungu NP *45*
3 Lengwe NP *46*
1 Nyika NP *47*

ZAMBIA
1 Kafue NP *47*
2 Luangwa NP *48*
3 Sumbu GR *49*

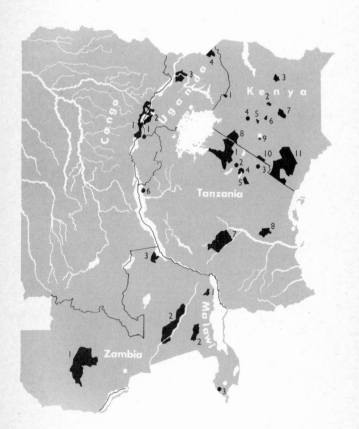

Large herds of brindled gnu and common zebras graze the open grasslands in many African parks – like these in the Serengeti.

Congo

Albert National Park 3,124 square miles; 3,000 to 14,786 ft above sea level. Founded in 1929 this is the oldest and most famous of the Congo's parks. It joins up with the Queen Elizabeth National Park in Uganda and stretches 150 miles from the Mountains of the Moon (Ruwenzori) in the north to Lake Kivu in the south; its average width being about 50 miles. South-north flowing rivers drain most of the park and the steep escarpments of their valley form a natural barrier around the area. There are 7 distinct zones within the park. In the southwest are active volcanoes, with lava flows and hot springs. Topsoil is thin here so the forest is sparse – though still thick enough to support fair numbers of tree hyrax and chimpanzees; there is also a herd of small long-haired buffalo. To the southeast the volcanoes are extinct, and their rich lava soil supports great forests of bamboo, home of the elusive mountain gorilla. North of the volcanic regions lies the alluvial plain of the Rwindi-Rutshuru sector, once part of Lake Edward. As the lake shrinks the plain is changing character from open to wooded savannah; as a result the antelope are decreasing while buffalo, elephant, and lion are increasing. Lake Edward fills most of the centre of the park; it is better stocked with wildlife than any other lake in the world – hippos (but no crocodiles), a huge variety of fish and waterfowl, and (in the Tshiaberimu Mountains) a rare type of gorilla. The Semliki river drains Lake Edward into Lake Albert. The upper Semliki zone is a tree-covered plain whose vegetation grows denser the nearer you get to the river bank; here are plenty of elephant, buffalo, and antelope. The middle Semliki is covered by impenetrable tropical jungle, where okapi have recently been found. The seventh zone is that of the Ruwenzori (for description see under Queen Elizabeth National Park, Uganda).

🐃 Mountain gorilla, chimpanzee, tree hyrax, elephant, hippo, buffalo (red and black), antelopes (including topi and kob), lion, leopard, okapi, hunting dog, aardvark.

🛏 Rwindi Hotel has 35 beds (20 first class), restaurant, and service. Its reopening after the park's recent chequered history was not confirmed at time of going to press, so check with any Congolese tourist office before visiting.

✈ The 'Interlake Road' leads from Kisangani via Beni and Butembo to Rwindi in the park. From Tanzania you can enter via Goma and Rutshuru. From Queen Elizabeth NP you can go to Kasese and then either west to Beni or south to Rutshuru. Nearest airport to Rwindi is at Goma on Lake Kivu. Kasese in Uganda is near the northern end of the park and has air and rail connections.

🚙 Some well kept roads allow saloon-car access to the most popular parts of the park, but most of it is accessible only to 4-wheel drive.

☀ Open all year; best time winter.

🕐 2–5 days.

⇨ Congolese tourist offices.

A note on East African prices

Unless otherwise stated the following rates apply in all National Parks and Reserves in Kenya, Tanzania, and Uganda: Entry fee 20/- each adult (5/- children under 14); 10/- per car; each country has lower concessionary rates for its own citizens. At many parks there are ranger-wardens who will act as guides for a fee of 5/- per half day (in some cases 5/- per day). At most parks in Kenya and Tanzania the do-it-yourself camping fee (bring for all your needs except water and firewood) is 5/- per person per night, with reduced fees for children.

Kenya

Aberdare National Park 228 square miles; 6,600 to 13,000 ft above sea level. The park lies in the forests and moors of the Aberdare mountains. It is crossed by numerous streams, many of which fall in 100 ft cascades to the bamboo forests in the foothills. Much of the wildlife consists of shy forest species and, except for the floodlight waterhole at Treetops, is not easily seen. The area is almost unique in the tropics for its rich alpine and subalpine flora. It can be cold at night.

🐃 Elephant, buffalo, black rhino, bongo (rare antelope), water-buck, bushbuck, leopard, duiker, and giant forest hog. Among some 200 species of birds are double-collared, malachito, tacazze and golden-winged sunbirds, hawk eagles, green ibis, Egyptian goose, golden-rumped tinker bird, crowned hornbill and red-naped widow bird.

🛏 Treetops 'Hotel', 12 miles from Nyeri, is actually a hide built high in the branches of a number of Cape chestnut trees overlooking a well frequented waterhole, where big animals, no longer disturbed by the floodlighting, come nightly to drink and to scratch for salt. All inclusive round trip from

Nairobi costs 300/– per person (children under 12 not accepted). Full board at The Ark hotel costs 200/– per person per day; bookings through Forest Lodges, PO Box 8559, Nairobi. There are four campsites (bring for all your needs) at Karimu, Magura, Gikururu, and Chania; 5/– per person.

🛬 From Nairobi by hard surfaced road 100 miles north to Nyeri, which is a few miles outside the park's eastern edge. There is a longer but more scenic route via Naivasha, in the Rift Valley, which is to the west of the park. Nearest rail points are Nyeri and Naivasha. Nearest airport Nairobi.

🚐 A new all-weather road runs through the park, crossing many streams and rising to over 10,000 ft in places.

🌤 Open all year; best time January to February.

🕐 1 day.

⇥ Kenya Tourist Offices.

Isiolo Buffalo Spring Game Reserve 75 square miles; 3,000 ft above sea level. This reserve lies on the opposite bank of the Uaso Nyiro river from the Samburu reserve (see p. 32).

Lake Nakuru National Park 11,650 acres; 5,830 ft above sea level. The park was created in 1960, chiefly as a sanctuary for the vast population of flamingoes – between $1\frac{1}{2}$ and 2 million – that inhabit it and nearby sodium lakes. Some 403 other species of birds also occur here. Roger Tory Peterson called it an ornithologist's paradise, 'the most staggering bird spectacle in 38 years of bird watching'. The lake is some 8 miles long by 4 wide; its north and eastern approaches are mostly of sedge, while the south is chiefly surrounded by spiky Pa grass. Fever trees dot its shores. The big congregations of greater and lesser flamingo are on the west side, where the margins are firm and the water only inches deep.

A crested crane, one of the 403 recorded species at Lake Nakuru.

🛏 None in the park; nearest hotel (the Stag's Head) is at Nakuru township, 2 miles away; daily inclusive rates from 80/– single, 105/– double. Camping is allowed on Nakuru showground if no show is in progress.

🛬 By road, signposted from the hotel. The hotel also organizes regular daily trips to the park. Nakuru is just under 100 miles by road and rail northwest of Nairobi. Many tour operators run day-trips from the city.

🚗 By road around the lake.

🌄 Open all year; best time January to March and June to September.

🕐 Day or half day from Nakuru.

🗎 A booklet published by Nakuru Chamber of Commerce has an extensive description of the lake and district and includes a complete list of all 370 bird species recorded in the park.

👁 Just outside Nakuru township is the Menengai Crater, a fine example of an extinct volcano. The thickly wooded floor is 1,450 ft deep, and the cone 7 miles across. From the rim there are spectacular views of Lake Nakuru, the town, and the Solai Valley.

⇨ Kenya Tourist Offices.

Marsabit National Park 10,615 square miles; 1,980 to 8,000 ft above sea level. Semi-desert thorn scrub country crossed by the Matthews and Ndotos mountains. Until mid-1970 the north of Kenya was closed to visitors, but the whole area is now reopened. Marsabit is for people used to rough safari and camping – also for photographers who want unusual desert scenery. Warning: do not attempt to photograph the desert tribespeople without express permission from them; it violates their religious taboos.

🦌 Elephant (rare large tuskers), greater kudu, beisa oryx, reticulated giraffe, black rhino, Grévy zebra, striped hyena, Cape buffalo. Birds: ostrich, water birds (to be seen around Lake Paradise, a volcanic crater, and the swamp near the lodge) and an uncommon number of birds of prey are the main feature. (Some tribes have grazing rights at Marsabit, so there is strong competition for good pasture.)

🛏 Marsabit Lodge: a small log cabin which takes 6 people (4 in comfort). Reservations through Bunson's Travel Service, PO Box 5456, Nairobi/tel: 20625 and 25400. A campsite is also available; apply to the Government Agent, Marsabit. Rates from 5/–.

🛬 Nairobi to Isiolo (see under Samburu GR) thence by secondary road north to Marsabit; total 250 miles. But most visitors go by air. There is a landing strip at Marsabit. Nearest airport with scheduled services is Nairobi. No rail access.

🚗 Rugged 4-wheel-drive roads; Marsabit is really for seasoned travellers. A minimum of two cars is allowed to travel from Archer's Post to the log cabin.

🌄 Open all year; best time June to August but humidity is low all year.

🕐 2 to 5 days.

🗎 *Out of the Blue*, by Viven de Wattville.

🗺 Hire through Bunson's Travel Service (address above).

⇨ Kenya Tourist Offices.

Masai Mara Game Reserve 700 square miles; 5,000 to 5,500 ft above sea level. Set on the southwest frontier of Kenya, between the Rift and Lake Victoria, the Mara reserve is made up of unspoiled open jungle plain, and is notable for its huge herds of plains game. It is continuous with the Serengeti National Park in Tanzania. To the west is a ridge of hills, clad with acacia. The Mara river runs north-south through the middle of the reserve. Some 160,000 acres are under total protection (no grazing or rearing of domestic species). The remainder is not strictly reserved, though wildlife *is* strictly protected.

Lion (the largest number to be found in Kenya), topi and roan antelope (confined to this reserve in Kenya), Thomson's gazelle and Grant's gazelle (both abundant), elephant, giraffe, buffalo, black rhino, Burchell's zebra, hippo, leopard, cheetah, bushbuck, eland, duiker, Bohor reedbuck, gnu, Coke's hartebeest, warthog, hunting dog. Birds are abundant.

In central section: Keekorok Lodge (40 beds), cabins of cedar and local stone, private baths, swimming pool, restaurant; provisions and petrol. Inclusive daily rate from 168/– single, 231/– double. Reservations through East African Wildlife Lodges, PO Box 7557, Nairobi/tel: 22860. In remainder of park: camping for up to 7 parties in various designated areas. Nightly rates per person: 30/– for visitors to Kenya, 10/– for residents (children under 10 half rate); payment in advance to Game Department, PO Box 241, Nairobi.

164 miles over roads of varying quality from Nairobi on the Naivasha road to Keekorok Game Lodge, which is also connected by road with Seronera in the Serengeti. Nearest point with scheduled air services is Seronera; airstrip near main lodge. No rail access.

100 miles of fairly good road within the park.

Open all year; best time July to March, especially December.

2 to 5 days.

Kenya tourist offices.

Masai Amboseli National Park Over 1,000 square miles; some 4,000 ft above sea level. Dry, volcanic ash country with a few swamps and springs and one big 'lake' (Lake Amboseli), which is usually dry. The land is owned by the Masai, who operate the reserve and have extensive grazing rights there. The reserve is not included in the official lists of conservation areas because, in the recent past anyway, concessions made to the tribe were incompatible with conservation – particularly with regard to competition for water. However, Amboseli has recently been enlarged from its original 87 square miles and this has made it easier to accommodate conflicting demands. Today, with its controlled wildlife population, its idyllic setting at the foot of Kilimanjaro, and its easy access from Nairobi, the reserve is one of the most popular and rewarding in Kenya.

Rhino (the principal attraction), elephant, buffalo, leopard, cheetah, Masai giraffe, oryx, kongoni, eland, zebra, lion, brindled gnu, Thomson's and Grant's gazelles, giraffe-necked antelope. Bird life is prolific and includes Masai ostrich, golden weaver, glossy starling, Madagascar squacco heron, scarlet-chested sunbird and Kenya violet-backed sunbird.

Amboseli New Lodge, hotel type accommodation with licensed restaurant; nearby is a permanent tented safari camp luxuriously appointed; nightly campfire. Rates for both are from 168/– single, 231/– double, inclusive, daily. Bookings via East African Wildlife Lodges, PO Box 7557, Nairobi/ tel: 22860. Ol Tukai Lodge (tented camp, self-catering) 40/– per person, children 10/–. There is also an attractive hotel at the Namanga entrance.

There are two routes from Nairobi: the first (155 miles) is to Athi River and along the Kajiado-Namanga-Arusha road; Ol Tukai Lodge is some 50 miles off this road, through the main gate. The second (145 miles) is along the Mombasa road to beyond Emali, then on the main Loitokitok road until it branches off to the Lodge. There is an airstrip in the reserve.

The principal area for wildlife viewing is in the eastern part of the reserve, where unsurfaced internal roads are suitable for family cars; the usually dry bed of Lake Amboseli also gives a good motoring surface.

Open all year; best time July to March, especially December.

2–5 days.

There is a meerschaum mine on the lake: the only one of its kind in the world. Pipe-smokers may be interested to know that pipes bearing the distinctive elephant motif are manufactured (at Arusha) from Amboseli meerschaum.

Kenya Tourist Offices.

Meru National Park 700 square miles; 1,000 to 4,400 ft above sea level. Set in plains of fairly dense bush, with large stretches of grass and a few patches of forest. Less accessible than the most popular parks, but not so inaccessible that only seasoned travellers need apply. The equator runs through the south of the reserve; this area was the birthplace of Elsa, the *Born Free* lioness. The Adamsons' camp was on the Ura River.

White rhino (the only ones to be found in Kenya's parks), lesser kudu, bushbuck, eland, duiker, beisa oryx, waterbuck, reedbuck, impala, and other antelopes, Burchell's zebra, Grevy's zebra, giraffe, reticulated giraffe, black rhino, lion, leopard, cheetah, hippo, warthog, buffalo. Over 250 different kinds of birds are listed.

Leopard Rock Lodge (20 beds), bring own bedding and food, cook for yourself. Rates from 12/– per person per night; reservations to Wildlife Department, PO Box 41, Nairobi/ tel: 20672. Kenmare Lodge (12 beds), same facilities, rates, and address.

From Meru about 50 miles of secondary road lead to the park. There are two routes from Nairobi to Meru: the direct one via Embu (166 miles), and a more scenic one via Nyeri and Nanyuki, between the Aberdares and Mt Kenya (181 miles). The reserve has two landing strips; nearest airport Nairobi. No rail access.

A good tourist road runs down the whole eastern side of the park, where the lodges are. Parts of the park are accessible only to 4-wheel drive. There is an airstrip near Kenmare

Lodge. Launch trips on Tana river; rates from 30/– per adult. For adventurous visitors there is a 'wilderness area' in the north of the reserve which – with an experienced ranger guide and porters – offers the opportunity of a safari on foot.

☀ Open all year; best time July to March, especially December.

🕐 2–5 days.

👁 The Nkeri Falls, 5 miles from Meru, are the most spectacular in Kenya.

⇨ Kenya Tourist Offices.

Mount Elgon National Park 37,500 acres; 5,000 to 8,300 ft above sea level. A new and unspoiled park on the lower eastern slopes of Mt Elgon (14,178 ft), particularly interesting for its vegetation, birdlife, and butterflies.

🐾 Forest elephant, buffalo, leopard, waterbuck, oribi, bushbuck, red forest and grey duiker, colobus and blue monkey, baboon, giant forest hog, pangolin, porcupine, hyena, giant rat, fruit-eating bat.

🌿 Cedar, olive and podocarpus forest; orchids, giant groundsel, giant lobelia, acanthus, bamboo; a great variety of moorland species (e.g. giant heather).

🛏 Camping allowed in park. Good accommodation at Kitale Club (from 80/– double bed and breakfast).

✈ Kitale, 236 miles from Nairobi and 44 miles from the main Nairobi–Kampala road, is 13 miles from the park.

🚗 A track at present suitable only for 4-wheel-drive vehicles runs through the park. Land Rover trips with knowledgeable guides (about £5 for a day) can be arranged through the Kitale Club, P.O. Box 30.

☀ All year. Afternoon rains April–August. Higher parts of park best from October to March.

🕐 1 day minimum.

🎟 Free.

⇨ Kenya Tourist Offices.

Mount Kenya National Park 227 square miles; 11,000 to 17,000 ft above sea level. This is not one of Kenya's great animal viewing parks, but it offers spectacular mountain scenery and flora – with the chance of seeing several of the smaller and fleeter-footed mammals. The vegetation varies with the altitude: first a belt of rainforest and bamboos; then, at 14,000 ft begin forests of camphor and giant lobelias, with clearings of giant groundsel; and below the snowline grow forests of conifer and cedar. In the craggy valleys of Batian and Nelion, which rear to 17,300 ft, grow many alpine and subalpine species – despite the fact that the park lies on the equator.

🐾 Elephant, buffalo, black rhino (all at lower altitudes), bongo antelope (rare), bushbuck, common duiker, black-fronted duiker (local), leopard, colobus monkey, giant forest hog. Bird life is interesting but not as rich as in other parts of the country.

🛏 The only accommodation actually within the park consists of three huts belonging to the Mountain Club of Kenya. Though the peaks are accessible only to skilled climbers, most healthy people should have little difficulty in reaching the lower summits – for instance, Point Lenana (16,355 ft). Details of hut bookings, equipment, vehicle hire, or mules and guides from the Secretary, Mountain Club of Kenya, PO Box 5741, Nairobi. It is also possible to make saloon car trips to parts of the park from Nyeri, Meru, Chuka, and Nanyuki, all of which lie on the road that encircles the mountain.

⇥ By road and on foot.

☀ Open all year, subject to sudden closure in unfavourable weather; best time December.

⏱ 1–2 days.

☞ See above.

⇨ Kenya Tourist Offices.

Nairobi National Park 44 square miles; 5,000 to 6,000 ft above sea level. The boundary of the park is a mere five miles from the centre of Nairobi. Despite its small size it contains three different zones. The western zone, which is continuous with the Nairobi suburbs, is thickly wooded, with groves of Kenya olive, flowering Cape chestnut, and muhugu trees. The central zone is a broad plain of grass and flowering shrub dotted with shady acacia thorns of varying height. The eastern zone provides drainage for the whole region and is well furnished with rivers and waterholes. The shelter of the forest, the pasture on the plain, and the water of the drainage zone make this the centre of a migration area that extends for 100 miles beyond the park boundaries. The popularity of the park (almost 200,000 people visit it each year) has made it more like a huge open zoo than an African wildlife park – though by European standards it is pretty untramelled.

⚐ Lion, leopard, black rhino, buffalo, zebra, impala, kongoni, eland, gnu, Thomson's gazelle, Grant's gazelle, waterbuck, giraffe. Birds include Masai ostrich, secretary bird, Hartlaub's turaco, crowned crane, speckled and blue-naped colies, marabou stork, and Kori bustard.

⇤ None in park.

⇥ The main gate is on the Langata road, 5 miles south of Nairobi. Being next door to the airport, the park is handy for a short visit by passengers in transit.

⇥ Good surfaced roads (the only permissible routes) run through the park.

☀ Open all year, 6.30 am – 7 pm daily. Best time to visit the park: just after sunrise.

⏱ A few hours to one day.

🎫 Visitors: 10/– per vehicle plus 20/– per adult (children under 14, 1/–). Also yearly and half-yearly season tickets.

⌂ Caltex map available at gates, 2/–.

◎ At the main entrance is the popular animal orphanage for orphaned and semi-tame animals. Fine specimens of lion, rhino, warthog, etc, can be inspected at close quarters. Admission 2/–, children 50c.

⇨ Kenya Tourist Offices.

Samburu Uaso Nyiro Game Reserve 40 square miles; around 3,000 ft above sea level. Generally known as the Samburu reserve, it lies in arid open savannah plains on the north bank

The white rhino has a wide mouth for grazing (in Dutch, wide is 'weid' – hence 'white'). It is next to the elephant in bulk (3 or more tons). Its sight is weak, but its hearing and smell are acute.

of the Uaso Nyiro river, which is narrow enough for animals to ford. On the other bank across a causeway is the Isiolo Buffalo Springs reserve (listed earlier).

- Spotted and striped hyenas, leopard, elephant, Grévy's and Burchell's zebras, black rhino, giraffe, reticulated giraffe, bushbuck, eland, buffalo, waterbuck (2 species), beisa oryx, klipspringer, dikdik, impala, Grant's gazelle, crocodile, gerenuk, hunting dog, warthog, serval cat, cheetah, lion. Birds include Somalian ostrich (blue necked) and vulturine guinea fowl. (This list applies also to the Isiolo reserve).

- Samburu Lodge (34 beds), built of cedar and stone on the banks of the river; electric light, private baths with h&c, swimming pool, refrigerators, bar, lounge, restaurant, radio telephone. Rates from 168/– single, 231/– double, full board. Reservations through East African Wildlife Lodges Ltd, **PO** Box 7557, Nairobi/tel: 22860 & 22869. Booking office for callers in York St, Nairobi.

- The road leads 213 miles (6 hrs) from Nairobi, crossing the equator; it passes Mt Kenya and drops over a mountain escarpment in thick cedar forest down to Isiolo, from where it leads through the Isiolo reserve to the river crossing.

- 100 miles of road within the park are passable to safari cars, which, with guides, can be hired at the lodge from 3/– a mile.

- Open all year; best time June to August, but humidity is low most of the year.

- 2–5 days.

- Kenya Tourist Offices.

Tsavo National Park 8,034 square miles; 800 to 2,000 ft above sea level. One of the largest national parks in the world and the main stronghold and reservoir of Kenya's wildlife. It lies on the Tanzania border, in the eastern foothills of Kilimanjaro, half way between Nairobi and Mombasa. The main highway and railway from the coast run through the middle of the park. The area north and east of the road is Tsavo Park East; that the south and west is Tsavo Park West. The range of

33

climate matches the range of altitude – from the arid eastern section, with 16 in. rainfall a year, to the lush Chyulu hills, with over 80 in. a year. Two permanent rivers, the Tsavo and the Athi (which converge in the park to form the Galana), run through the region; from the roads that skirt their banks you can always be sure of seeing wildlife. Most of the plains are open grassland, sprinkled with acacia thorns, prehistoric looking baobabs, many succulents – including four species of aloe – and candelabra trees. The plains respond to the slightest rain; shrubs and flowers that seemed dead or dormant suddenly burst into flower, turning its sere browny green into a luxuriant display of colour. The living rock of the plains, best seen in the Ngulia and Ndi hills, is around 600 million years old. Yesterday (geologically speaking) a series of volcanic eruptions in the west of the park pushed a thick layer of volcanic lava over this bedrock. The older cones are now green hills; the younger ones are still stark and marked by black lava flows.

This is by far the best area in Kenya for seeing elephant; there are some 20,000 in the park and surrounding country. Other animals: giraffe, buffalo, black rhino, lion, leopard, hippo (at Mzima Springs near Kilaguni there is an underwater tank from which hippo can be viewed), zebra, monkeys, hartebeest, gerenuk, fringe-eared oryx, and numerous other species of antelope.
Bird life is wonderfully varied and colourful: well over 250 different kinds being listed.

The two newest lodges, in the luxury category, are at Voi and Ngulia. Both are in spectacular settings and offer every modern amenity. Rates from 160/– single, 220/– double, full board. Kilaguni Lodge offers full hotel-style accommodation, 22 miles from the northwest gate at Mtito Andei. Recently installed floodlighting creates artificial moonlight for night-time wildlife viewing. Full amenities and swimming pool. Rates from 140/– single, 200/– double, full board. Reservations to African Tours and Hotels, PO Box 30471, Nairobi/tel: 23316 & 23317. Kitani Lodge, 17 miles farther from Mtito Andei, offers self-catering facilities in double bandas with private baths; bedding, crockery, cutlery for hire. Rates 30/– per person (15/– children under 15). Reservations to Bunson's Travel Service Ltd, PO Box 5456, Nairobi/tel: 20625 & 25400. Aruba Lodge, in the eastern section 22 miles from Voi, offers full catering facilities; rates 30/– per person (15/– children under 15). Reservations to Sea, Sun & Game Safaris, PO Box 52, Malindi. Nearby is a pitch-your-own-tent campsite with communal showers, latrines, and catering facilities; enquiries also to Sea, Sun, & Game Safaris. Both campsite and lodge are built on the banks of a large dam on the Voi river – a favourite watering place of elephants and other animals. You can also stay at the Tsavo Inn at Mtito Andei/tel: Mtito Andei 1Y1 or the Park Inn, PO Box 28, Voi/tel: Voi 4. Daily rates per person from 50/– b&b to 75/– inclusive. Reservations to Inns of Africa Ltd, PO Box 1333, Nairobi/tel: 27938, or direct to hotels. There is also a campsite (bring your own tent) at the Mtito Andei gate; showers and latrines; 5/– a night.

By all-weather road 150 miles from Nairobi to the park boundary at Mtito Andei. Voi, near the other end of the park, is about the same distance from Mombasa. Rail stations at Mtito Andei, Voi, and Tsavo. Airstrip at Kilaguni Lodge; nearest airports Nairobi and Mombasa.

🚐 Over 1,000 miles of roads and tracks have been developed through the park. On some you can drive for hours without meeting a soul or seeing the dust of another vehicle; you can see Eastern Africa very much as the early European explorers must have seen it. The most popular roads are those that follow the permanent watercourses.

☀ Open all year; January to March is hot and dry (also dusty); June to September is warm, humid, often overcast.

🕐 3–14 days.

🛢 Caltex map, available at gates, 2/–. *The Maneaters of Tsavo* by Colonel Patterson.

⇨ Kenya Tourist Offices.

Note: Two new lodges have opened as this book goes to press. The Mountain Lodge, Mt Kenya NP, is built alongside a traditional game-migration route and overlooking a floodlit waterhole; K Shs 200 single, 320 double plus 5 per cent service. The Ark, Aberdare NP, is an ideal spot for viewing (including night viewing) both forest and plains species; bookings through Forest and Frontier Lodges, Nairobi.

The sable antelope, a forest-living species found from Kenya to the Transvaal. They drink at morning and evening, often graze with zebra and kudu, both of which have better hearing and scent.

Tanzania

Arusha National Park 45 square miles; 5,000 to nearly 15,000 ft above sea level. The park includes all of the former Ngurdoto Crater National Park and Momela lakes as well as the newly designated Mt Meru (14,979 ft). The crater and lakes are the wildlife-rich area of the park; the western, Mt Meru, end is more scenic. A well-surfaced road leads from 5,000 to 8,000 ft in 6 miles – the last two being fairly steep; and offers spectacular views most of the way. By prior arrangement you can walk with a ranger to the summit, where the precipices are sheer and majestic. The Ngurdoto crater is a caldera, or sunken crater of an extinct volcano. Its average diameter is between 4 and 6 miles and the floor is about 1,000 ft below the rim. Visitors are not allowed to enter the bowl but a number of superb viewpoints have been set up along the crater rim, which is thickly clad with rainforest. From these points you can look down on acacia groves and the grassy shores of the Momela lakes, outside the crater where the wildlife concentrates at evening time. (In the recent geological past the crater was a lake; but its wall broke at one point, creating what must have been one of the most spectacular floods in history. The Momela lakes are a remnant of the cataclysm). Although you cannot get near to the animals within the park, they wander in and out quite freely, so there is a good chance of meeting them in the forest around the crater rim.

Elephant, buffalo, black rhino, giraffe, waterbuck, lion, eland (occasional visitors), baboon, bushbuck, bushpig, civet, duiker, genet, hippo, leopard; colobus, vervet, and Sykes monkeys; mongoose, reedbuck, suni, warthog, hunting dog. The area is notable for waterbirds–among them greater and lesser flamingo–which congregate round the lakes.

Momela Game Lodge, near northern entrance to park. Thatched rondavels, restaurant, lounge, open log fire in cool season, hotel-like amenities; rates from 65/– full board; bookings through United Touring Company, PO Box 3173, Arusha. You can also stay at hotels in Arusha; rates from 60/– double (Travelodge) to 80/– single (New Arusha). Camping on Meru mountain sites 5/– per adult, children half rate; book in advance through Park Warden.

From Arusha take the tarmac Moshi road, turn left at mile 13 on to an all-weather gravel road; after 9 miles turn right and the Crater Gate is about a mile away. From Nairobi turn left 24 miles before Arusha and follow signs to Momela Game Lodge (169 miles). Many people leave Arusha in mid-afternoon and drive to Crater Gate for a picnic on the rim, then motor slowly down to the lakes and leave by the Momela Gate at nightfall (gates close 7 pm).

About 30 miles of all weather road run around the crater between the two entrance gates. The Mt Meru road is described in the opening paragraph above.

Open all year; best time July to March, especially December.

Day or half day for game; two days for game and mountain.

Park Warden, Arusha National Park, PO Box 3134, Arusha/ tel: 2335 & 6.

Lake Manyara National Park 123 square miles (21,120 acres of land and 64,000 acres of water); 3,160 to 6,000 ft above sea level. The large salt lake lies in the northern part of the Rift Valley, between Arusha and the Serengeti. As the ground rises up to the western escarpment of the Rift, it passes through five zones of vegetation, beginning with a groundwater forest of soaring mahogany and fig with plenty of open glades, then extensive reed marshes fringed by open grassland, which gives way to park-like groves of acacia before rising to the scrub and scree of the escarpment.

Elephant, buffalo, black rhinoceros, zebra, lion (this is one of the very few areas of Africa where they can be seen lying up in the trees), leopard (also to be seen in the trees), hippo, impala, baboon, bushbuck, bushbaby, bat-eared fox, civet, dikdik, giraffe, hyena, jackal, klipspringer, mongoose, reedbuck, Sykes monkey, vervet, waterbuck, warthog. Birds near water include flamingo, pelican, many ducks and waders, jacana, egret, ibis, stork; birds on open lands and in acacia groves include plovers, coursers, larks, kingfishers, and wagtails.

Lake Manyara Hotel, 6 miles from park gate, has swimming pool and car-service facilities; built on the escarpment overlooking the park. Rates from 140/– single, full board. Bookings through Hallmark Hotels, PO Box 348, Dar es Salaam. Land Rovers for hire. You can also stay at the New Arusha Hotel (convenient for Ngorongoro and Serengeti, too); swimming pool; most rooms with private baths. Inclusive rates from 60/– single, 120/– double. There is a campsite in Arusha with wc and shower facilities only; rates from 5/– per adult; call at Information Bureau, Uhuru Rd for directions. Campsites are also available near the park boundary – the park warden will point them out. No facilities whatever.

75 miles southwest of Arusha. Take the Great North Road south from Arusha as far as Makuyuni, then the all-weather road west as far as the village of Mto-wa-Mbu; the entrance of the park is almost 2 miles beyond (open 6 am to 6.30 pm). Nearest airport with scheduled services at Arusha. Un-licensed airstrip in park. Nearest rail point at Arusha.

The main all-weather track runs south from the entrance gate to the hot springs at Maji Moto at the other end of the park. Several circuit loops lead from and to this track, but they are often closed in the rainy season. Land Rovers can be hired.

Open all year; best time December.

1–2 days.

Available at 5/– a day.

There is an interesting museum near the park gate – popular with children.

Tanzania Tourist Offices.

Mikumi National Park 450 square miles; 1,800 ft above sea level. Founded in 1964, a recent addition to Tanzania's national parks and the one most accessible from Dar es Salaam. It consists mostly of open plains with wooded hills – typical of East African savannah country. 8,000 ft mountains, well outside the park boundary rise up on both eastern and western sides, making a good background for photos. The flood plain of the Mkata river lies in a horseshoe ring of hills and supports large herds of buffalo and elephant.

🐾 Elephant, buffalo, lion, zebra, gnu, giraffe, hippopotamus, impala, baboon, warthog, jackal (all common), rhino, cheetah, greater kudu, hartebeest, hunting dog, waterbuck, hyena, mongoose, duiker, bushbaby; colobus, vervet, and other monkey species; leopard and sable antelope are rare. A good variety of birds.

🛏 Tented lodge (16 beds) at Kikoboga, near park HQ; inclusive daily rates from 70/-. Bookings through Oyster Bay Hotel, PO Box 1907, Dar es Salaam. Campsites are also available at 5/- daily per adult; bookings through Chief Park Warden, Mikumi NP, PO Box 642, Morogoro. For hotel-style comfort the Mikumi Wildlife Lodge, 140/- full board, is bookable via Hallmark Hotels, PO Box 348, Dar es Salaam.

✈ By road 160 miles from Dar; best conditions during June to November dry season (there is sometimes a short dry spell in January to February). Nearest airport at Iringa, about 50 miles away. Tim-Air charters operate inclusive flights from Dar with one-night stopover.

🚙 A good network of all-weather roads spans the park. Some remote regions need 4-wheel-drive in the rainy season. Check on roads at the gate and take a guide. The most scenic route goes up through forest and hills to the Mkata river watershed. Land Rover trips available at 40/- per person.

☀ Open all year; the most comfortable time is during the dry season (June to November), but when the November rains come the buffalo form large herds on the plains – and only during the rainy periods can you see the large herds of bulls in the mud wallows.

🕐 2–5 days.

📷 Available at 5/- a day.

➡ Chief Park Warden, Mikumi National Park, PO Box 642, Morogoro; or Tanzanian Tourist Offices.

Ngorongoro Conservation Area 102 square miles (area of actual caldera); 5,500 to 7,500 ft above sea level. The caldera is one of the wonders of the world – the sunken cap of what must have been a truly stupendous volcano when active, it averages between 10 and 12 miles across and its rim soars 2,000 ft above the floor. From a lake at the centre the land spreads out through bamboo and humid tropical forest to dry plain and bush. The caldera is the hub of a much larger (3,200 square miles) conservation area in which wild animals and Masai grazing flocks co-exist. Unlike Ngurdoto, visitors are not barred from the floor since it is large enough for their cars not to disturb the game.

🐾 Black rhinoceros, buffalo, elephant, lion, leopard, gnu, zebra, cheetah, hunting dog, hyena, jackal, Grant's gazelle, hippo, baboon, bushbuck, eland, waterbuck, reedbuck, klipspringer, steenbuck, dikdik, Thomson's gazelle, impala, vervet monkey, genet, mongoose. Birds of prey (Verreaux's eagle, steppe eagle, tawny eagle, etc) range the high cliffs of the crater, and there are many other species of birds in the area.

↤ Ngorongoro Crater Lodge (105 beds) has full hotel type facilities; rates from 75/– to 140/– (single, private bath), 120/– to 180/– (double, private bath), 60/– to 90/– (single, share bath), 100/– to 140/– (double, share bath) – variations depend on season; bookings via Tanzania National Parks, Private Bag, Arusha. The new Ngorongoro Wildlife Lodge, on the crater rim, charges from 140/– single, full board; book via Hallmark Hotels, Box 348, Dar es Salaam. Dhillon's Forest Resort (a small guesthouse) 30/– per day single, 50/– double, under twelves 15/–; meals a la carte; bookings through Ngorongoro Forest Resort Ltd, Barclays Bank Bld, PO Box 729, Arusha/tel: Arusha 2694. At both places Land Rovers with driver guides can be hired at 50/– a seat or 200/– to 250/– a day. Camping is allowed near the lodge at 5/– per person per night; bookings as for the Lodge. Camping at Kimba tented camp (30 beds) on crater rim; 70/– full board, 35/– children up to 16, children up to 3 free; landrovers for hire at 240/– a day; bookings through Shields, India Rd, PO Box 284/602, Arusha/tel: Arusha 2147 & 2706. There is a youth hostel for organized educational parties; details from Regional Office, PO Box 3050, Arusha/tel: 2704 and 2381.

↦ 112 miles from Arusha (nearest suitable township), 290 miles from Nairobi, 87 miles from Seronera in Serengeti, 37 miles from Lake Manyara. All local roads (the approach road is 7,500 ft up) are passable to saloon cars, but to go down on to the crater floor via the Lerai Descent you will need a 4-wheel drive vehicle. Scheduled air services to Arusha and Seronera; airstrip for light charter aircraft up to Aerocommander weight. Nearest rail point is Arusha.

🚘 Tracks on the crater floor are passable to 4-wheel drive vehicles only – and even then you should inquire about passability before you set out. At Crater Lodge there is a fully equipped garage for all classes of repair (spares limited); all grades of automotive fuel on sale.

☀ Open all year; best time December.

🕐 1–2 days.

🛢 Ngorongoro Bulletin (free at lodges and gates). The Conservator, PO Box 6000, Ngorongoro Crater, has published four numbered booklets at 3/– each. (1) deals with early history, (2) with geological history, (3) contains a complete species list for birds, (4) a complete species list of wild mammals.

◎ Olduvai Gorge (also spelled Olduwai and Oldupai on signs) is 32 miles from the Lodge, on the road to Serengeti. It was here that Dr Leakey found the skulls of *Zinjanthropus boisei* and *Homo habilis*, which pushed our knowledge of man's prehistory back to 2 million years before the present. There is a day shelter for tourists, who are shown around by an English speaking guide; entry 3/–.

⇨ Conservator's Office, India Road, PO Box 3102, Arusha/tel: 2304; or Tanzanian tourist offices.

Ruaha National Park 5,000 square miles, 2,500 to 5,250 ft above sea level. Established in 1964, the park is one of the most recent additions to the enlightened Tanzanian conservation programme. Although it lies in the Rift, it is mostly rolling plains country with plenty of rocky outcrops. The biggest attraction is the Great Ruaha river, which forms its eastern border; the smaller Njombe river is the western boundary. The wooded fringes of the river offer plenty of shade from the dazzling sun. The other areas opened up for wildlife viewing are the Mdonya woodlands and the Mbage-Mwagusi track.

⌐ Elephant (best seen in Mbage-Mwagusi area), black rhino, buffalo, lion, sable and roan antelopes (mostly in the Mdonya woodlands areas), greater and lesser kudus, impala. Fish eagle are numerous along the river.

⇦ Two good hotels at Iringa, 75 miles away: White Horse Inn, PO Box 48 and Iringa Hotel, PO Box 46. Mkwaya Camp, near the park ferry has 6 double rondavels with bedding, h&c, and drinking water; in all other respects visitors must be self-contained. Bookings through Mr G. E. Scott, PO Box 212, Iringa, or through the Tanganyika (*sic*) Farmers Association, PO Box 230, Iringa. Camping is also allowed at Mkwaya for 5/– per adult per night; bookings through Mkwaya Game Camp, PO Box 204, Iringa; occasionally camping is permitted at other sites; contact the park warden, PO Box 369, Iringa or the Tanganyika Farmers Association.

⇨ About 290 miles from Dar es Salaam via Iringa; the road is often poor in the wet season. At all times take the right fork at Mloa to avoid low, swampy ground around Tungamu-lenga. There is a landing strip for light aircraft at Msembe, or you can fly to Iringa and drive the remaining 70 miles.

⇦ Tracks to the Mdonya woodlands, the Ruaha riverside drive, and the Mwagusi track, though all are sandy, are usually passable to saloon cars. Ask at the gate and take a guide with you.

☼ Open all year; avoid January to March.

⌐ Often available at 5/– a day.

◉ There are photographic hides and tree-houses overlooking several of the water-holes.

⇨ Warden, Ruaha National Park, PO Box 369, Iringa; or Tanzanian Tourist Offices.

Serengeti National Park Over 5,700 square miles; 3,000 to 6,000 ft above sea level The Serengeti has the largest and most spectacular concentration of plains animals in the world. Recent censuses give a population of over 1,250,000 animals, of which some 300,000 are gnu. For most of the year these animals roam the vast, treeless expanse of the plain, but with the start of the dry season, in late May or early June, they begin their famous migrations to the western corridor of the park, where the rivers run down to Lake Victoria (the corridor ends some 5 miles from the lakeshore). These migrations are one of the most remarkable sights in Africa: processions of animals, six or seven abreast, stretching almost from horizon to horizon, all plodding steadily westwards. The sick and aged, who fall steadily back, attract prides of the black maned lion for which the park has long been famous. Wildlife viewing in the north is less easy since the tree thickness steadily increases in that direction. At 80°F, midday temperatures are not as high as you might expect – until you remember that the entire park is above the average altitude for most European or American mountains. Night temperatures are 60° or less, so you will need warm clothing.

⛢ Gnu (about 350,000), zebra (180,000), Thomson's and Grant's gazelles (500,000), lion (one of the largest populations in Africa), leopard, hyaena, hunting dog, cheetah, giraffe, black rhino, eland, roan antelope, buffalo, Coke's harte-beest. A rich variety of birds (over 300 kinds listed).

🛏 Seronera Old Lodge has 6 furnished rondavels (maximum 4 beds each) with wash basin, electricity, and half-share of a servant and bathroom. Seronera New Lodge has 16 two-bed cubicles and tented accommodation up to 34 more beds; some of these are available to self-caterers; communal ablutions and wcs. Daily rates per person with full catering 95/– (83/– for double occupancy), children 40/–; without catering 30/– (double or single occupancy), children 14/–. A government levy of 2/– is added to all rates. Reservations through East African Wildlife Lodges (T) Ltd, PO Box 3173, Arusha/tel: Arusha 2369. Lobo Wildlife Lodge, Keekorok, 140/– full board (book through Hallmark Hotels); Ikoma Fort Lodge, northwest of Seronera, 140/– full board (PO Box 751, Arusha). Non-bookable accommodation (2 double cabins, furniture, cutlery – bring own bedding, servants, and drinking water) at Ndabaka entrance; 15/– single, 30/– double, 2/– servants.

✈ By road: Nairobi via Arusha 379 miles (takes in Lake Manyara NP; and Ngorongoro Crater NP; Nairobi via Narok 295 miles (takes in Mara GR). These routes use the gates at Klein's Camp, Soitayai, and Naabi Hill – none of which is easy for saloon cars. Nor is any route via the Simuyu gate in the southwest. The other gates – Ndabaka, Banagi, Tabora (all west of the park) and Sand River (on the Mara boundary with Kenya) are suitable for saloon cars. There is a good airstrip at Seronera, which takes scheduled tours from Nairobi daily. No convenient rail access.

🚗 During dry weather the main roads will take the sturdier types of saloon car but 4-wheel drive cars are, in general, much more suitable. Saloon car drivers should always check on the roads with the Parks Director in Arusha before going in. Land Rovers and drivers can be hired at Seronera for 2/80 a mile. Seronera is equipped for light repairs and petrol, oil, and diesel sales. Travel prohibited 7 pm to 6 am.

☼ Open all year; best time late May for migrations.

🕐 Scheduled day tour from Nairobi; up to 14 days in own or hired transport.

📘 Brochure and map at all Tanzanian tourist offices; *Serengeti Shall Not Die* by Bernhard Grzimek.

📷 Available for hire at Seronera and Ndabaka Gate; 10/– per day; strongly recommended.

👁 Olduvai Gorge lies between The Serengeti and Ngorongoro Crater (full details under Ngorongoro Crater).

⇨ Tanzanian Tourist Offices.

Note: Two new Tanzanian parks have been gazetted as these pages go to press; both are shown in the map on page 24. The Tarangire NP (1,000 square miles) is 80 miles from Arusha and 5 miles off the main Cape-Cairo road. Wildlife is comparable to the Serengeti and other prime parks. Facilities are still being developed. Inquire at Arusha before you visit. Gombe NP (60 square miles) is accessible by boat from Kigoma. It protects about 200 chimpanzees (also red colobus, buffalo, defassa waterbuck, bushbuck, leopard); the world's best site for seeing chimpanzees. The nearest tourist facilities are at Kigoma.

Uganda

The following scale of charges applies to all three of Uganda's parks:

Launch hire: 1st hour 15/– (children 5/–); for each subsequent hour or part 10/– (children 5/–); minimum charges 45/– 1st hour, 100/– 2nd hour, 140/– 3rd hour. Scheduled services have priority over launch hires, which are offered subject to availability of boats.

Camping fees Do it yourself 10/– (children 5/–); organized camp-site 5/– (children free).

Transport hire Transport suited to the terrain is available in all parks at 2/50 per mile, including the cost of a driver-guide.

Kidepo Valley National Park 556 square miles; 3,500 to 9,000 ft above sea level. The newest, least developed and scenically the most beautiful of Uganda's parks, Kidepo lies in the rugged mountains that border the western flank of the main Rift, up near the border with Sudan. The landscape is dry savannah and mountain scree.

⚜ Elephant, buffalo, black rhinocerus, Rothschild's giraffe, lion, leopard, cheetah, waterbuck, and species not found in the other two big parks such as zebra, roan antelope, greater and lesser kudu, ostrich, eland, and hartebeest. A rich variety of birds, including Abyssinian scimitar bills and hornbills, golden oriole, scarlet-chested sunbird, rose-ringed parakeet and blue quail.

🛏 The Apoka Lodge (10 double bandas, serviced, private baths and wcs, lounge, bar, dining room, kitchen) offers self-catering facilities; non-perishable and tinned (canned) provisions on sale. Full catering facilities are planned; 40/– per bed per night. Booking well in advance through Warden. Campsites with water and firewood but no latrines, 5/– per adult per night. Laundry service available at nominal charge.

✈ By road from Kampala via Masindi, Gulu and, Kitgum, 375 miles; you could do side trips to Lake Albert, the Budongo Forest, and Murchison Falls NP from this route. Landing strip for light aircraft in park; nearest scheduled air services at Gulu, nearly 150 miles away. Nearest rail point at Gulu. 1,000 yard airfield (marked Kidepo Lomej) $1\frac{1}{2}$ miles from camp; 900 yard airstrip (Kidepo–Apoka) at camp HQ, where limited stocks of 100/130 and 80/87 fuel and 100 oil are kept.

🚐 Land Rovers (at 2/50 a mile) help you see the best of the park, though much is suitable for saloon cars.

☀ Open all year; best time during the dry season, December to early April.

🕐 2–5 days.

📷 Available (and advisable) at 5/– per half day.

🏠 Warden, Kidepo Valley National Park, Private Bag, Kitgum; or Uganda Tourist Associations.

Mount Muhavura (Kigezi) Gorilla Sanctuary 17 square miles; 6,000 to 13,500 ft above sea level. This is one of the last remaining haunts of the rare mountain gorilla. The volcanic peaks of the region offer no real challenge to any fit person with good legs and lungs. The views across the plains to the lakes and the Mountains of the Moon are superb. The Travellers Rest at Kisoro (11 beds with private bath) has a staff of guides who know the movements of the gorillas – but even this does not guarantee that you will see one. Fearsome though they look they are, in fact, very shy. And they can move easily through thickly tangled brush that takes humans hours to negotiate. You might be lucky and see one on your first excursion; or you could climb for a week and not even hear one. Kisoro is nearly 300 miles by road from Kampala.

Murchison Falls National Park 1,550 square miles; 1,600 to 5,000 ft above sea level. The park contains one of the wonders of Africa – the Murchison Falls, where the entire output of Lake Victoria crashes and thunders through an echoing gorge, plunging 140 ft to a huge river pool. At one time the gorge was a mere 20 ft wide at the top, but colossal rains in 1961 opened up two lesser falls alongside the main one – making the falls even more impressive than before. Launches ply to the huge pool at the foot of the falls, passing through areas rich in elephant, kob, buffalo, crocodile, and birdlife; adults 30/- (children under 14, 10/-). From there you can climb up beside the falls. In the country above there is plenty of rhino and giraffe. Two well-known salt licks are now the favourite places for viewing animals. The elephants have multiplied beyond their natural limits and have threatened the ecology of the whole park; some culling has been done.

ᕁ Elephant (there are thought to be over 12,000), buffalo, Rothschild's giraffe, hippopotamus, lion, leopard, crocodile (the biggest concentration in Africa), chimpanzee, baboon, oribi, kob, black rhino, white rhino (introduced from left bank to right) and many species of buck. Birds include goliath heron, saddle-billed and whale-headed stork.

ᕍ Paraa Safari Lodge (100 beds), private bath and wc, full hotel type facilities; built on the Victoria Nile below the falls, daily launch trips; ranger-guides available for overland trips; museum. Rates from 90/- single, 170/- double, Full board. Chobe Safari Lodge (70 beds), newly built in the less well known eastern end of the park; full hotel facilities; all rooms face the Nile. Rates as for Paraa. Camping and hotel bookings as at Queen Elizabeth NP.

ᕝ By road 190 miles from Kampala via Nakasongola and Masindi; 300 miles from Queen Elizabeth NP via Fort Portal and Masindi. Travellers beyond Masindi should remember that the Nile ferry closes at 6.30pm. The Masindi Hotel is a convenient stopover from which you can make excursions to Lake Albert and to the Budongo Forest (superb mahogany trees and wild orchids). Thrice weekly flights from Entebbe to a landing strip in the park, met by park transport. Nearest rail point at Gulu, 73 miles away.

ᕬ 150 miles of track, passable to saloon cars. Launch trips (see opening paragraph above).

☀ Open all year; best time December to April.

◔ 2–3 days.

⌂ Uganda Tourist Associations.

Queen Elizabeth National Park 860 square miles; 3,050 to 4,500 ft above sea level. The park lies in the Rift, in south-western Uganda. Parts of lakes George and Edward come within its boundary, together with the 20-mile-long Kazinga channel, which joins them. Northwest stand the lofty peaks of the Mountains of the Moon (or Ruwenzori), parts of whose foothills nudge into the park – in an area pockmarked with ancient volcanic craters and known as the 'explosion area'. In the south are open plains where big herds of topi, kob, and buffalo graze; here the lions of Kigezi are famous for their habit of climbing trees. Moving northward you pass through the Maramagambo Forest, sanctuary for chimpanzees, baboons, and colobus monkeys (all of which you are more likely to hear than to see). North of the forest the animals are famed for their lack of fear. Hippos, shy nocturnal creatures in other parks, here wander by day far from their lakes and mud pools. Buffalo will not stir as you pass – nor, of course, will the elephants.

⚐ Topi (found only here in Uganda), kob, buffalo and elephant (large herds of plains species and species more common in the Congo jungles), lion (as in Lake Manyara NP, Tanzania, they are tree-climbing), hippo, waterbuck, bushbuck, warthog, giant forest hog; leopard (now quite common). *Note* There are no giraffe, zebra or rhino in the park. Birds include whale-headed stork, malachite kingfishers, bee-eaters, sunbirds, geese, ducks, waders, jacana, honey guide.

⇌ Mweya Safari Lodge (100 beds) in the centre of the park has full hotel facilities; animals pass close to the lodge on their way to water; rates from 90/– single, 170/– double, full board, Bookings through Lodge Booking Office, **PO Box 3473**, Kampala/tel: 3822. Game ranger escorts for overland trips available at lodge; rates from 5/– per half day. Launch trips operate from the lodge along the Kazinga channel; 30/– single (10/– children under 14. The Hotel Margherita (50 beds), operated by the same company, stands at the foot of the Mountains of the Moon, an hour's drive from the lodge; rates from 50/– single, b.&b. 84/– full board. Camping is allowed by arrangement at certain sites; charges vary according to party and accommodation up to a maximum 20/– per person per night; apply to the Warden.

⇒ By good road 272 miles from Kampala via Masaka and Mbarara. 300 miles from Murchison Falls NP via Masindi and Fort Portal. 142 miles from Kabale. Nearest airstrip at Kasese, 40 miles from the lodge; has thrice weekly service from Entebbe by E African Airways (who operate 3 and 4 day package tours of the park). Comfortable thrice weekly overnight rail journey from Kampala to Kasese. Lodge transport meets both services.

⛟ By saloon car overland; by launch along the Kazinga Channel and on the lakes.

☀ Open all year; there is no month when a visit is not recommended – in fact during the Oct-Nov and Mar-Apr rains the park is often at its best (the 'rains' are really torrential showers).

◔ 3–7 days (longer if you include trips to the Mountains of the Moon).

⌂ Uganda Tourist Associations.

The nyala, a shy and mainly nocturnal relative of the bushbuck is at the northern end of its range in Malawi – best seen at Lengwe NP.

Malawi

Malawi Kasungu National Park Over 800 square miles; averaging about 3,300 ft above sea level. The terrain consists of gently rolling wooded hills with scattered rocky outcrops. The Dwangwa, Lingadzi, and Lifupa streams rise in the park, and their wide, grassy valleys make for easy game viewing. During the open season the area is dry and hot, with cold nights.

Animals are similar to those in the Luangwa valley, except for giraffe, which are absent here. So, too, are hippos, though in time they may be attracted to the dams being built within the park. Species you will see include: elephant, buffalo, zebra, hartebeest, kudu, eland, roan, sable, reed-buck, waterbuck, oribi, occasional rhino: lion, leopard, cheetah. Birds include many eagles, vultures, and carmine bee-eater.

At Lifupa game camp there are 12 rondavels with accommodation for 24 people: each has basic furniture, foam-rubber mattresses, bedclothing, mosquito nets, lamps, shower, basin, and wc; K4 each per night or K2 per adult, K1 children 2–12. There is a communal dining room with 2 refrigerators. The stores have basic dry goods and beer. The camp has a petrol pump.

There is an airfield for light aircraft near the camp. Nearest town is Kasungu, 30 miles away by good road; 86 miles farther away, is the regional capital, Lilongwe, which has scheduled air connections. The park is also within easy reach of the Salima Lakeshore resort on Lake Nyasa.

Over 300 miles of good road run within the park. No foot travel is permitted. The best view is from the Black Rock summit.

Open May 1 to December 31; best time June to October.

2–5 days.

K1.50 per car plus 25t per passenger. If you are carrying more than the licensed number of passengers, a double car fee is charged; if more than three times (say, a party of 13 school-children in a Land Rover licensed for 6 adults) a triple car fee is charged. Children under 2 are free but there are no cots at the camps.

☞ Always ask the guards which tracks are the best for viewing at the time of your visit; the best area changes from week to week.

👁 A guard will gladly escort you to see the ancient rock paintings at Wangombe Rume hills.

⇨ Assistant Commissioner of Forests, PO Box 65, Lilongwe/tel: 2272.

Malawi Lengwe National Park about 50 square miles; about 2,000 ft above sea level. Much of the park is covered with large stands of dense thicket – cover for the rare and beautiful nyala antelope, here found at the northernmost end of its range in Africa. Elsewhere are open grassy glades and fairly thin deciduous forest. The nature of the country makes game viewing less easy than in other parks; but when you do see an animal it is that much more of a surprise and the circumstances that much more intimate. For many visitors this makes the park more, rather than less, rewarding.

🐾 Nyala antelope, bushbuck, kudu, hartebeest, impala, duiker; Samango monkey, Livingstone's suni, buffalo; lion, leopard. Birds include bee eater, sunbirds, weavers, roller (especially lilac-breasted roller), parrots; ibis, marabou stork, and many other water birds: guinea fowl, francolin, fish eagle, vultures, bustard.

🛏 At Lengwe game camp are two double-bedroomed guest houses, each with basic furniture, foam mattresses, mosquito nets, bedding, lamps, and verandahs. Ablutions are in a separate block. There is a fully-equipped kitchen and a cook's services are included in the charges: K2 per person, K1 per child between 2 and 12 (no cots provided), or K4 per room, or K8 per chalet. Servants sleep in a separate room for 10t. Car entrance fees are £1.50. Accommodation bookings confirmed in advance via United Touring Company Ltd, PO Box 176, Blantyre/tel: 30122 ext 27 and 28.

✈ The nearest town is Chikwawa (15 miles), where you can buy petrol and a very limited range of stores. Blantyre, the capital, serviced by scheduled international air connections, is only 31 miles farther north from Chikwawa, so the park is easily accessible to day visitors from Blantyre.

🚐 A circular drive within the park feeds a number of crescent branches; total length of park roads is 40 miles. A short walk from the camp is a well-constructed hide (the only one in the park). It looks out over a much frequented waterhole.

☀ Open all year; best time June to October.

🕐 1–3 days.

🗺 As for Malawi Kasungu.

☞ Rangers will act as guides, free, unless other duties prevent them.

⇨ United Touring Company Ltd, PO Box 176, Blantyre/tel: 30122 ext 27 and 28.

Malawi Nyika National Park 360 square miles; averaging 7,000 ft with occasional peaks rising to above 8,000 ft above sea level. The park is divided by ridge upon ridge of mountain grassland scored by deep valleys, clad here and there with evergreen forest. The views from some of the higher valley slopes are stupendous. The headwaters of three rivers – Chelinda, North Rukuru, and Runyina – are within its borders. Because of the altitude, nights can be very cold, with frosts in June to August.

> Eland, zebra, roan antelope, reedbuck, duiker, bushbuck, hyena, genet, serval, caracal, lion, leopard, cheetah. Near Chelinda camp there are three dams where there is good bird viewing. The park's most attractive species include secretary bird, wattled crane, and Stanley's bustard; other avifauna similar to Lengwe.

> At Chelinda camp 18 visitors can stay in 4 self-contained chalets, each with living room, fireplace, 2 or 3 double bedrooms, own shower and wc, fully-equipped kitchen. Room for 8 more visitors in 4 double bedrooms near the communal lounge (which has a large refrigerator). The camp has basic provisions; paraffin (kerosine), firewood, and the services of a cook are included in the basic charges, which are the same as for Malawi Lengwe.

> Nearest airport at Mzuzu, 117 miles away by surfaced road via Rumpi. There are two airfields for light aircraft near by, one at Katumbi, and one just over a mile from Chelinda camp.

> 106 miles of good road form a network that takes in most of the park. This is the only park in Malawi where you are allowed to tour on foot.

> Open all year; best time June to October.

> 3–5 days.

> As for Malawi Kasungu.

> Rangers will act as guides, free, unless other duties prevent them.

> At Finigra, just outside the southern boundary, is an ancient rock shelter decorated with paintings made some 3,500 years ago. Park guards will take you to this historic monument.

> Director of Forests and Game, PO Box 182, Zomba/ tel: 797.

Zambia

Kafue National Park 8,650 miles at an average 3,300 ft above sea level. A vast plateau, half the size of Switzerland, watered by tributaries of the Kafue river, which forms part of its eastern boundary. The vegetation, always lush and green, varies from mixed forest, thicket, woodland, and grass in the south to broad, alluvial grassland and patches of evergreen forest in the north. (The town of Kafue lies over 150 miles eastwards, which can be confusing when you first look for the park on a map).

> Hippo, buffalo, zebra, elephant, black rhino, lion, sable, oribi, kudu, impala, roan antelope, eland, lechwe, gnu, sitatunga, duiker, crocodile. Birdlife is rich especially in the

Busanga flood plain: openbills, saddlebills, wattled crane, crested crane, jacanas, cormorants, Ross's lourie, Boehm's bee eater, black-backed barbet; martial, bataleur, long-crested, and fish eagles; marabou stork; and white-backed, hooded, white-headed, and lappet-faced vultures.

⇌ Main camp at Ngoma in southern part of park; hotel, standard chalets with h&c, electricity, private baths and wcs, licensed restaurant; petrol and limited provisions on sale; minor motor repairs; motor boat and guide for hire; airstrip; servant's accommodation. Other camps (cooking utensils, crockery, cutlery, refrigerators, beds and linen, mosquito nets, lamps, cook and hut attendant all provided, but bring your own food) at: Katala (on island, easy reach Ngoma game viewing roads), Nanzhila (40 miles south from Ngoma, excellent game viewing), and, in the north of the park: Chunga (petrol and food, good fishing and boating), Kafwala (reserved for members of Zambia's Wild Life Conservation Society), Lufupa, Moshi (airstrip, game viewing centre for north, petrol), Ntemwa (easy reach Busanga flood plain and birdlife). There is also a school camp where children of school age can attend a course on wildlife conservation. Caravans allowed at camps for 20/- a night; camping forbidden.

✈ From south by good surfaced road via Kalomo to Dundum-wenzi gate. From copperbelt and Lusaka (3 hrs away) via Mumbwa and Nalusanga gate; since the gate is 60 miles from the nearest camp (Chunga), many break the journey at Mumbwa. Nearest airport at Mumbwa; Lusaka and Living-stone also feasible; airstrips at Ngoma, Chunga and Moshi. No feasible rail access.

🚐 By car over unsurfaced roads and by boat (for rent).

☀ From about mid-June (depending on when the rains end) to early November.

🕐 3 days to 2 weeks.

📖 The tourist bureau publishes two good brochures, one on the geography, geology, game, and history of the park, the other on the attractions, accommodation, and rules.

👁 There is a lookout tree platform in front of the hotel at Ngoma; chairs and a telescope provided; take a book, blanket (in evenings), and binoculars. Other places of interest in the area: Sacred Tree (near Ngoma); ruins of old Nkala Fort (near Ngoma); rainmaking ceremonies at Kaindabaila hill (north of Ngoma).

⇨ Zambia tourist bureau.

Luangwa Valley National Park 6,000 square miles; 1,000 to 2,000 ft above sea level. The park centres along a 120-mile stretch of the long and tortuous valley of the Luangwa river in the northeastern part of Zambia. It holds what is probably the heaviest balanced concentration of game in the whole of Africa and is one of the continent's most rewarding parks to visit. Much of the landscape is truly parklike, with broad grassy stretches broken by mopani woodland, all nestling between high ranges of mountains. The meandering river has changed course many times and has left many beds and oxbow pools rich in vegetation. You can join special Wilderness Trails – parties of up to 6 with an armed guide – to follow the game on foot. Luangwa is Africa's only major reserve where you can take these daily walking camera safaris throughout the dry season – thanks to its abundant waters, which act like a magnet to animals throughout the region. One of the most fascinating sights is the 'elephant crossing'; elephants maraud the surrounding country (where they are not protected) at night, returning to the safety of the park just before sunrise.

🦌 Elephant, hippo, buffalo, impala, kudu, eland, zebra, Thornicroft's giraffe (unique to the valley), lion, leopard, crocodile, black rhino (Zambia's largest concentration), puku, Cookson's brindled gnu, antelope, waterbuck. Oribi, grysbok, and bushpig are rarer here. Birds include many species of eagle and vulture and the carmine bee eater.

🏠 Main camp at Mfuwe; modern chalets, private bath, electric light; restaurant; airstrip takes up to DC3s. Other camps with bedding, cutlery, crockery, refrigerators, staff, but no food, at Big Lagoon, Nsefu, Lion, Luambe, Luamfwa and Lusingazi.

✈ By air to Mfuwe or Fort Jameson (85 miles away). By road via Fort Jameson.

🚗 The longest section of road (surface of varying quality) runs north and south from Mfuwe on the western bank; from it there are pontoon crossings to Luambe in the north and Luamfwa in the south. Nsefu is a 50-mile detour from the Ft Jameson-Mfuwe road. Petrol at Luambe, Big Lagoon, Nsefu, Mfuwe, and Luamfwa. Provisions at Mfuwe and Luamfwa. More than 30 detours, many of them loops, lead from the main camp road to well frequented fords, grazing grounds, and waterholes.

☼ Open all year; best time June to October.

🕐 3–7 days.

➪ Zambia Tourist Bureau.

Sumbu Game Reserve 500,000 acres; between 2,600 and 3,300 ft above sea level. On the southwestern shores of Lake Tanganyika, the landscape rises from acacia covered deltas through low thicket-clad foothills to higher hills where the forest is broken by small grassy stretches.

🦌 Elephant, hippo, buffalo, warthog, eland, zebra, sable and roan antelopes, waterbuck, bushbuck, puku, klipspringer, Sharpe's grysbok, duiker and hyrax. Vulturine fish eagle and waterbirds abundant.

🏠 Main rest camp at Kasaba Bay; 20 thatched double cottages with bathrooms; restaurant; open all year; airstrip. Nkamba Bay has thatched accommodation for 14; all facilities including cooks and servants, but bring your own food. Nonda Point has same facilities as Nkamba Bay.

✈ By good surfaced road from Abercorn, near Kasaba Bay. You can break your journey at the hotel at Abercorn. Nearest airport is at Abercorn; Lusaka also feasible; airstrip at Kasaba Bay. No rail access.

🚗 By boat on lake; hire fees from 20/– per hour.

☼ Open all year; best time June to October.

🕐 3 to 7 days.

◉ The Kalambo Falls, at 1,400 ft, are the second longest single-drop falls in Africa; they are on a feeder river about 60 miles across the lake from Kasaba Bay.

➪ Zambia Tourist Bureau.

Southern Africa

Mozambique

Gorongoza National Park 2,300 square miles; 300 to 650 ft above sea level. One of the most rewarding wildlife areas in Central Africa, the park encloses four major types of land-scape: subtropical palm jungle; thorn scrub of varying density; wide, open grassland; and marshy land teeming with waterholes. It is rich in all the African animal and bird life that thrives in these habitats. The camp area is set amid sparse thorn scrub, and from it a sandy track opens out into a broad, grassy plain rich in game and predators. The major

Lions, once common in Europe, Africa, and Asia (see page 239), now flourish only in central and southern Africa. They are the only true social cats, living in prides of about eight (but exceptionally up to thirty) and hunting any herbivore except elephant, hippo, and rhino. Their territory varies from 15 to 50 square miles and they kill and feed, on average, only once a week. Females, as the one above shows, lack the manes that characterize the males.

attraction is an abandoned rest camp that has been taken over by lion. Behind the camp is a tree-lined stream whose banks swarm with baboons. The whole area is well watered.

⚐ Elephant, buffalo, zebra, brindled gnu, hartebeest, impala, bushbuck, duiker, eland, kudu, sable, nyala, lion, leopard, lots of monkeys; stork, vulture, African rollers, and spoonbills and other waterbirds around the waterholes. In one particular area of tall acacia thorns is a collection of waterholes noted for their hippo and crocodile populations.

🏠 There is one small rest camp in pretty surroundings. Rondavels (2 to 1 bath) 220 escudos (note: escudos is abbreviated $), child 150$; bungalows (2 to 1 bath) 200$ adult, 140$ child; rooms with running water and communal bath 180$ adult, 120$ child. Basic necessities, including mosquito nets, provided. Cooked breakfast 25$ adult, 16$ child; lunch 50$ and 30$; dinner 60$ and 40$. There is also a curio shop. Petrol pumps supply two grades of fuel.

🡺 The camp is about 20 miles north of Vila Machada on the main Beira–Umtali road. Turning is on right, but signpost is easy to miss – look out for a cafe on the corner as a more obvious landmark. From there on the road is a sandy track through scrub and tall grass. From Umtali a total 130 miles; from Beira 90 miles. Vila Machado is also on the Beira–Umtali railway; a tourist bus from the park meets trains. There is an airstrip for light aircraft near the rest camp.

🚙 There is no safe foot access within the park. The tracks are suitable for private cars, and camp buses run regular trips. There are 24- and 36-hour tours from Beira which include a brief visit to the park.

☀ Closed during October to April rains.

🕐 4–5 days.

🎫 100$ adult, 40$ child, 40$ car.

🎟 Available for advance booking.

🡆 Tourist Information Office, Beira.

Rhodesia

Rhodesia has 25 national parks and game reserves devoted to wildlife conservation. The oldest is Wankie National Park, founded in 1929, the newest is Kyle, created in 1967. They afford total protection to approximately 75 major species. The administering authority is the Department of National Parks and Wild Life Management, PO Box 8365, Causeway, Salisbury, Rhodesia.

Unless otherwise stated the following schedules of charges apply within all Rhodesian parks and reserves. *Entry* 15/– per person for 1–7 days; 2/6 for those aged 3–16; younger children free. *Accommodation* Chalet (basic furniture, bedding, external cooking facilities, cooking utensils, communal ablutions) 12/6 per person per night or 15/– for single occupant of two-bedroom chalet; weekly 75/– and 90/– respectively. Cottage (basic furniture, bedding, internal cooking facilities, cooking utensils, individual ablutions) 17/6 or 25/– for single occupancy; weekly 105/– or 150/– respectively. Lodge (basic furniture, bedding, internal cooking facilities, ablutions, cutlery, crockery, cooking utensils, servant) 22/6 or 35/– for single occupancy; weekly 135/– or 210/– respectively. Mountain cabin (communal beds, cooking, and ablutions) 7/6 per person per night. Camp site or caravan site 2/6 per person per night or 2/6 per vehicle for daytime stay. For night use (must be arranged in advance with warden) of permanent lookout in certain parks 5/– per person. For emergency assistance 2/– per mile travelled by warden or deputy (minimum 20/–) or 20/– per boat hour (minimum 20/–). Guide fees: park officer 15/– per hour; park servant 3/6 per hour.

Chete Game Reserve 323,000 acres at an altitude of 1,500 to 2,500 ft on the southern shores of Lake Kariba, about 60 miles west of the Matusadona Reserve. Visits should be arranged with the administering authority.

↝ The reserve is largely stocked with game rescued during the 1963 Operation Noah, when animals trapped by the rising waters of the Kariba dam were ferried from the islands to the lake shores. Hippo, elephant, buffalo, kudu, waterbuck, impala, lion, leopard, hyena, jackal, crocodile, and many birds.

↜ None in the reserve. At Binga there are self-contained chalets at 60/– a day, double rooms with communal facilities but no cooking or eating utensils at 15/– a day, and camp or caravan sites with communal ablutions at 3/– a day. Here you can hire 6-passenger steel boats plus guide at 50/– a day. There is similar accommodation at M'libizi, about 40 miles away at the western end of the lake. Bookings via The Manager, P/Bag 5, Dett/radio tel: ZEE 12 for Binga; Mr & Mrs F. Johnson P/Bag 927, Bindura/tel: 1904 for M'libizi.

↝ By road to Binga (406 miles from Salisbury), then by boat.

↜ Only by boat. The inland parts are deliberately preserved as wilderness to allow the hippos to breed in peace. A few trails are passable to 4-wheel-drive vehicles.

☼ Open all year; best time May to October.

🕐 1–2 days.

▨ Free.

⇨ From Rhodesia Tourist Board (RTB).

Chewore Game Reserve 809,000 acres about 2,000 ft above sea level. Chewore lies in uninhabited country on the banks of the Zambezi, in the far north of Rhodesia. There is no resident warden but the area is well policed and strictly protected. Visits should be arranged with the administering authority.

↝ Chewore has the greatest concentration of black rhino in the whole of central and southern Africa. Buffalo, sable and roan antelope, kudu, bushbuck, waterbuck, nyala, impala, baboon, crocodile, hippo, and interesting bird life.

🜋 Chief feature is the acacia, which covers most of the hills in the reserve.

↜ There is a camping place, without facilities, in the reserve, but no other accommodation – the nearest being at Mana Pools. It is possible to visit Chewore in a side trip from the Mana Pools reserve.

↝ By road between May and October. There is no internal road network as the reserve is a wilderness area. But you can move about in 4-wheel-drive vehicles or on foot.

☼ May to October.

🕐 7 days.

⇨ 20/– a vehicle; note that the entry road to Chewore crosses the Mana Pools reserve, so you pay a further 20/– per vehicle at the Mana Pools gate.

⇨ From RTB.

Chizarira Game Reserve 360,000 acres about 3,700 ft above sea level. The reserve is named after the Chizarira mountains; it is a wooded plateau with wide grassy plains crossed by swiftly flowing streams. Though this is scenically one of the most attractive of Rhodesia's northern reserves and has a good tourist potential, the area is to be left undeveloped so as to preserve the wilderness and give total protection to the animals – particularly the hippos. It lies about 30 miles south of the Chete reserve. Visits should be arranged with the administering authority.

⇾ Hippo, elephant, lion, leopard, sable, kudu, roan, sassaby, impala, buffalo, zebra, warthog, bushpig, bushbuck, hyena, jackal, and a rich birdlife.

⇾ As for Chete reserve.

⇾ By road only; turn right 5 miles from Binga.

⇾ By 4-wheel-drive vehicle only. Unsurfaced roads throughout; vary from reasonable to poor. No petrol pumps so vehicle must have a minimum 300-mile range. Not for novices.

⇾ May to October.

⇾ 7 days – including travel from main centres.

⇾ Free.

⇾ By special arrangement with Chete reserve warden.

⇾ From RTB.

Inyanga National Park 85,000 acres between 6,000 and 7,000 ft above sea level. A grassy plateau, sloping upwards to the east, in Rhodesia's lovely eastern highlands. The slopes of Mount Inyanga are lightly forested. There are spectacular gorges and falls at Pungwe, Nyamziwa, Inyangombwe, and – greatest of all – Matarazi (about 2,000 ft). The Matarazi Falls are in a high plateau with an evergreen forest. Game viewing is less exciting here than elsewhere in Rhodesia, but the park has a lot to offer the less energetic tourist; its high altitude is bracing and the air is free of mosquitoes and midges.

⇾ Kudu, waterbuck, reedbuck, blue duiker, klipspringer, hyena, jackal, leopard, bushpig, secretary bird, and francolin.

⇾ Lodges and huts are more widely scattered than in other parks. The warden's office is about 6 miles south of Inyanga Village. A half mile away, at Marora Drift, there is a one-acre caravan and camping site. Two miles away, near Rhodes' Hotel, there is a two-bedroom lodge (6 beds). At Inyangombwe, also 2 miles from the office, is a 25-acre caravan and camping site. At Nyamaziwa Falls, 3 miles from the office, is a two-bedroom lodge (4 beds). At Mare Dam, 4 miles from the office, are 2 one-bed and 11 two-bed cottages (9 with bathrooms). And at Pungwe Drift, 16 miles from the office, there are 2 two-bedroom lodges. There is a new caravan and camping site at the confluence of the Inyangombwe and Marora rivers. All bookings via the warden. There are eight hotels within 20 miles of the park; daily minimum rates per person vary from 17/6 for a room to 75/- for a cottage. Rhodes's original homestead now forms part of the Rhodes' Inyanga Hotel; his study is preserved.

⇾ Nearest airport is at Umtali, 75 miles away; Salisbury is 169 miles away. Road access is via Rusape, 64 miles away.

Rusape is also on the Salisbury–Umtali railway line; buses connect for Inyanga on Tues, Thurs, and Sats.

🚌 There is a good road network within the park.

☼ Open all year; best time April to November.

🎫 Free.

🎟 Not needed.

👁 A forgotten Iron Age people once flourished in this region. They have left behind them a vast complex of forts, redoubts, terraces, pits, and water furrows. The 'slave pits' (which were probably cattle kraals) are within walking distance of the Rhodes' Hotel on the Inyanga downs. The most accessible concentration lies about 10 miles northwest of Inyanga Village; known as the van Nierkerk and Nyahokwe ruins, they cover over 50 square miles. There is a 9-hole golf course in the park as well as a private 18-hole course belonging to the Troutbeck Inn. Swimming is safe in lakes and streams as well as in a natural pool at the confluence of the Inyangombwe and Nyanora rivers.

⇨ The Warden, P/Bag 2, Juliasdale/tel: 1211.

Lake Kyle Game Reserve 40,500 acres (much of it water), 4,000 ft above sea level. This small diamond shaped reserve is tucked into the V of Lake Kyle and is bounded by water on three of its sides. The terrain is highveld grassy plains broken by scattered copses and densely wooded ravines.

🐾 Many species are reintroductions. White rhino, giraffe, buffalo, kudu, gnu, nyala, reedbuck, bushbuck, impala, sable, zebra, eland, oribi, ostrich, duiker, steenbuck, hippo, crocodile, warthog, Lichtenstein's hartebeest, and numerous birds.

🛏 There are 6 one-bedroom lodges and 3 two-bedroom lodges with gas lamps. Bookings via the warden. It is also possible to stay at Zimbabwe NP, just across the lake.

✈ By road from Fort Victoria, about 30 miles away. There is also an airport and railhead at Fort Victoria (190 miles from Salisbury). You must arrive during daylight hours. You can reach the shores of the reserve by boat from Zimbabwe and Kyle view.

🚌 By car on all-weather roads; no driving during hours of darkness.

☼ Open all year; best time May to November.

🕐 1–2 days.

🎫 5/- per vehicle.

🎟 Not necessary.

⇨ The Warden, PO Box 393, Ft Victoria/tel: 68122.

McIlwaine National Park 18,200 acres (much of it water); 4,500 ft above sea level. A wooded park stretching around the shores of the 9-mile-long shores of Lake McIlwaine, only 18 miles from Salisbury.

🐾 On the southern shores of the lake there is an enclosure for species introduced from Wankie NP. Giraffe, zebra, buffalo, eland, sable, brindled gnu, impala, oribi, kudu, waterbuck, reedbuck, steenbuck, duiker, sassaby, leopard, monkeys, baboon, crocodile, warthog, and 250 species of bird, including ostrich.

🛏 Twenty-one chalets with electricity and 3 lodges with paraffin lamps; swimming pools, on south side of lake. To the north of the lake are 5-acre caravan and camping sites with communal facilities (including laundry). Bookings through warden. The Hunyani Hills Hotel overlooks the lake; private harbour, pools, and miniature golf; chalets with private baths cost from 44/– per person per day. Reservations to PO Box 2852 Salisbury/tel: 2642683, telegrams Trebelaitch,

By road and air from Salisbury. Nearest railway station is at Norton, a few miles from the gates.

By road; in the game area visitors may only get out of their cars in the enclosed picnic areas.

Open all year; best time April to November.

1 day.

5/– per vehicle, including lakeside areas.

Not necessary.

There are water skiing facilities on the lake, also tennis courts and croquet lawns. Bushman paintings are common in the park; the finest are at Bushman's Point picnic area, inside the game area.

The Warden, P/Bag 62, Norton/tel: 229.

Hippos, once widespread, are now confined to the rivers and lakes of tropical Africa. The herds bask in water or mud by day and go ashore to graze near by at night. They are placid unless disturbed.

Mana Pools Game Reserve 575,000 acres; 1,200 ft above sea level. The area is very similar to Chewore – in fact, the two reserves are joined near their southern ends. Mana is noted for the groups of pools formed by the flooding of the Zambezi; during dry months the pools attract large herds – buffalo herds up to 700 head have been counted. But despite its riches, Mana is only for the more adventurous visitor. Take mosquito nets and insect repellent; this is a tsetse fly area.

Elephant, buffalo, black rhino, sable, eland, zebra, waterbuck, impala, lion, leopard, hyena, crocodile, hippo, warthog, kudu.

Mana Tree Lodge is a 16-bed game viewing hotel; it has a high tree platform overlooking the banks of the Zambezi; there are also minibus tours of the pools. Rates (incl.)

around 105/– daily; reserve well in advance via Makuti Motel, P/Bag 96, Karoi/tel: 2830; no casual visitors, no children under 12. There is also a 10-acre camping and caravan site at Nyamepi, 42 miles from the turnoff (see access). Camping fee 2/6 per person per night; 1/3 under 16.

By road 14 miles north of Makuti via Marangora (where the warden has his office), then turn off right; bear left at Chewore turn. Nearest airport is at Lusaka in Zambia; Salisbury is 300 miles away. Nearest food and petrol is at Makuti.

By car on good-weather roads; no restrictions on dismounting but some of the animals are dangerous.

1 May to 30 November depending on rains and road conditions; best time August to November.

1–2 days.

20/– per vehicle.

Not necessary.

The Warden, P/Bag 62, Karoi/tel: 2812.

Matusadona Game Reserve

Matusadona Game Reserve 522,000 acres; 1,500 to 2,500 ft above sea level. The landscape is very similar to that of the Chete GR, some 60 miles farther up the shore of Lake Kariba. The reserve is a haven for animals that fled from the rising floodwaters of the lake; here they enjoy total protection. Visits should be arranged with the administering authority.

Black rhino, elephant, buffalo, sable and roan antelope, kudu, bushbuck, waterbuck, hippo, crocodile, lion, leopard, hyena, pig, and many birds.

Camping only; no facilities whatever provided. It is also possible to stay at Bumi Hills, across the creek of the Bumi river, which forms the reserve's western boundary. There are eight chalets at rates from 40/– per person per day; landing strip for light aircraft. Reservations via P/Bag 6/tel: 353.

By regular boat service from Kariba, which is 229 miles by road from Salisbury. Land access by 4-wheel-drive vehicles only; improved road system under construction (1968).

On foot near lakeshore or by 4-wheel-drive vehicle.

May to October; best time May to October.

7 days, including travel to and from; visits must be pre-arranged with warden.

Free.

The Warden, PO Box 76, Kariba.

Mushandike National Park

Mushandike National Park 32,000 acres; 3,900 ft above sea level. An area of densely wooded hills surrounding a 1,000-acre man-made lake.

Sable antelope, kudu, waterbuck, reedbuck, steenbuck, klipspringer, duiker, leopard; rich birdlife includes heron, flamingo, egret, and tern.

Brachystegia spiciformis, Balusanthus speciosus, Colophospermum mopane, Afzelia quanzensis, and acacia.

Three one-room, 2 two-room chalets, a cottage, and a lodge – all near warden's camp; paraffin and gas lamps. Also a 5-acre caravan and camping site with communal facilities, incl. h/c water. Reservations through the warden. Nearest petrol and stores at Mashaba, 16 miles away. There is a swimming pool for residents in the park.

⇥ A good gravel road leads from Ft Victoria–Beit Bridge road.

🚗 By car; good roads.

☀ Open all year; best time April to November.

⏱ 1–4 days.

▨ Free.

⌐ Not necessary.

⇨ The Warden, P/Bag 9036, Ft Victoria/tel: 0–9603.

Rhodes Matopos National Park 2,500 acres (game park only); 4,500 ft above sea level. The Matopos is an area of massive hills and fantastic granite formations beginning about 20 miles south of Bulawayo (which is 277 miles from Salisbury). It has great religious importance for the Matabele. Cecil Rhodes chose the hills for his burial place. His friend Sir Leander Starr Jameson is buried nearby, as is Sir Charles Coghlan, the colony's first prime minister. This natural mausoleum, known as View of the World, actually lies just outside the borders of the park. The game park proper is a small enclave in the western end of the national park; it is traversed from north to south by the Ove River and its tributaries, one of which has been dammed. A loop on the Antelope Mine–Bulawayo road runs east-west through the park.

⇶ Indigenous species include impala, kudu, bushbuck, sable antelope, duiker, steenbuck, klipspringer, rock rabbit, monkeys, baboons, and leopard; the park is also rich in birdlife, especially black eagle (largest colony in southern Africa). Species imported from Wankie NP include giraffe, buffalo, black and white rhinoceros, eland, brindled gnu, reedbuck, and ostrich.

⇥ Nearest accommodation to the game park is at Mpoma Dam, just beyond its western boundary on the loop road mentioned above; it consists of a 5-acre camping and caravan site. A few miles to the east of the game park is the main camp and warden's lodge: Maleme Camp. Maleme is the most beautiful of many man-made dams within the national park. The camp has twenty chalets; cooking utensils and h/c water included. Bedding and refrigerators for hire. There is also a caravan and camping site here. Toward the eastern end of the national park there are two more caravan and camping sites – at Mtshelele Dam (10 acres) and Toghwana Dam (5 acres). Reservations through the warden. There are two hotels in the region north of the park: the Matopos Dam Hotel, 12 doubles, 4 singles, bed and breakfast from 22/6; reservations to P/Bag 131K, Bulawayo/tel: 88044–12; and the Hermits Peak Guest House, 10 doubles, swimming pool, bed and breakfast from 22/6; reservations to P/Bag 218K, Matopos/tel: 0–1923.

⇥ By road; Maleme Camp is 34 miles from Bulawayo just off the Antelope Mine road. The other camps are farther within the park. The nearest airport is at Bulawayo. The nearest railway station is at Figtree, about 10 miles from Matopos.

🚗 An all-weather road meanders through the park, passing through or near all the camps listed above.

☀ Open all year; best time April to November.

⏱ 1 day (game park only).

▨ 5/– per vehicle in game area.

The sacred ibis is widespread in Africa south of the Sahara. (This one, carrying nesting materials was photographed in Uganda.) Like all ibises it is a wader; often it coexists with spoonbills (close relatives), cormorants, and snake birds – with which it is not in direct competition. To ancient Egyptians it was the scribe-god Thoth.

👁 Some of the finest Bushman paintings in Africa are to be found in the Matopos. Among the best: Pomongwe cave and Nswatugi cave, both near Maleme; Bambata cave, near Hermits Peak; and Silazwane cave, near Mtshelele. Rowing and sailing is allowed on some of the dams; power boats on Mpopoma dam only. Rhodes's summer house, the arboretum started by Rhodes, and the Shangani Patrol Memorial are all near by.

⇨ The Warden, P/Bag 42K, Bulawayo/tel: Matopos 0–1913.

Ngezi National Park 25,000 acres; 3,900 ft above sea level. Set in the Mashaba mountains, just over 30 miles north of Sebakwe NP, on the slopes surrounding the 1,500-acre Ngezi dam. On the western slopes the vegetation, chiefly *Brachystegia boehmii*, is dense; on the eastern slopes the trees are less dense and more varied – *Faurea saligna*, *Kirkia acuminata*, *Sterculia quinqueloba*, and *Adansonia digitata*.

🐾 Sable antelope, duiker, kudu, waterbuck, bushbuck, leopard, zebra, impala, hippo, crocodile; among many birds the pygmy goose is notable as this is its only known nesting place in the country.

🛏 Two cottages and one lodge, paraffin lamps; also a caravan and camping site with communal facilities. Reservations through the warden. There is a nearby store. Nearest townships are Featherstone (39 miles) and Battlefields (42 miles). There are three hotels at Que Que, 50 miles away.

✈   The only all-weather road to the park is a 35 miles turnoff just 4 miles south of Featherstone on the Salisbury–Ft Victoria road. The minor road linking Hartley with the Que Que–Umvuma road runs near the park.

🚗   By car.

☼   Open all year; best time April to November.

⏱   1–2 days.

🎫   Free.

🛏   Not necessary.

➪   The Warden, P/Bag 7, Featherstone/tel: Umniati 626.

Sebakwe National Park 6,600 acres; 4,500 ft above sea level. Set near the geographical centre of Rhodesia, around the shores of the large Sebakwe dam, which takes up much of the park. The dam is edged by low sandveld hills covered in *Brachystegia boehmii* and *Faurea saligna*. Other flora includes *Julbernardia globiflora*, *Terminalia sericaea*, and *Burkea africana*.

🐾   Zebra, impala, reedbuck, duiker, baboon, leopard, kudu, jackal, and many birds, including migratory species from Europe (September to April).

🛏   Three cottages with paraffin pressure lamps and a 2-acre caravan and camping site with communal facilities.

✈   34 miles east of Que Que on the Umvama road. Que Que is 134 miles from Salisbury and 143 miles from Bulawayo; it is also the nearest railway station. The nearest airport, Ft Victoria, is about 100 miles away.

🚗   By car.

☼   Open all year; best time April to November.

⏱   1–4 days.

🎫   Free.

🛏   Not necessary.

➪   The Ranger, PO Box 454, Que Que/tel: 39829.

Victoria Falls National Park 146,000 acres; 3,200 ft above sea level. The park's northern border (it is also Rhodesia's border with Zambia) is the 35 miles of meandering shore of the Zambezi above the Victoria Falls. It stretches inland between 10 and 30 miles. Immediately surrounding the falls the landscape is humid and luxuriant; farther away it is drier and sparser.

🐾   Elephant, buffalo, zebra, giraffe, eland, kudu, waterbuck, impala, bushbuck, sable antelope (particularly fine), baboon, hippo and crocodile; cheetah, leopard, and lion are occasionally seen. A great variety of birds.

🌿   In the humid rainforest: *Diospyros mespiliformis*, *Ficus mallotocarpa*, *Ficus ingens;* elsewhere: *Baikiaea plurijuga*, *Burkea africana*, *Afzelia quanzensis*.

🛏   In main camp a mile from the falls: 22 two-bedroom and 12 one-bedroom chalets; illuminated caravan site with communal facilities, including laundry; illuminated camping site with similar facilities; licensed restaurant. At Zambezi camp 4 miles upstream: twenty self-contained lodges along the river bank. At Kandahar fishing camp 5 miles upstream: half-acre campsite with communal facilities. Reservations through warden. There are two hotels near the falls: the colonial style Victoria Falls and the modern Casino; both have pools as well as banks, salons, shops, etc. The National Parks Reception Office has an information bureau at the main camp.

There are daily flights from Salisbury and Kariba as well as from Bulawayo, Wankie, and Johannesburg. Livingstone international airport, in Zambia, is just 10 miles away. By road Victoria Falls is 423 miles from Salisbury, 231 from Bulawayo, and 352 from Lusaka, in Zambia. There is a daily rail service from Bulawayo and rail connections to Livingstone and Lusaka, in Zambia.

Almost 50 miles of internal road are open May to December depending on rains. The Zambezi Drive follows the river; game can be seen on the land side, elephants, hippos and crocodiles on the river side; parts of the drive follow the old pioneer wagon road to Kazungula. The Chamabonda drive skirts the southern side of the park; it runs near the water pans of the Chambonda Vlei; viewing here is especially good from September to December. The main road to Kazungula and Kasane runs through the centre of the park. Cars can be hired at the main camp. Outboard motorboats are also for hire.

Open all year, but game area closed December to March, subject to rains; best time April to November.

1–3 days.

Free.

Not necessary.

There are upriver launch trips from a landing stage on the way to Zambezi camp; they go about 12 miles and stop off for tea at Kandahar island. About 3 miles up the road to Livingstone there is an African craft village where masked Makishi dancers periodically dance to tribal music. And upriver from the statue of Livingstone (who discovered the falls) there is a baobab tree almost 67 ft in circumference.

The Warden, P/Bag 8, Victoria Falls/tel: 210.

Wankie National Park Over 5,000 square miles; 2,900 ft above sea level. Rhodesia's premier national park. The northern third of the park is open to visitors, the rest being devoted to conservation. There are excellent facilities for viewing and photography. A number of water holes have been set up artificially, and they provide gathering points for game and for many species of birds. The park lies on the eastern fringes of the Kalahari sands, but it is not as arid as the Kalahari proper; there are extensive forests of teak, umtshibi (*Guibortia soleosperma*) and mukwa (*Pterocarpus angloensis*). In the parts open to visitors the authorities have set up a number of observation platforms; the one at Nyamandhlovu Pan is the most rewarding.

Elephant (about 7,000), buffalo (herds of 400+), white rhino (reintroduced), black rhinoceros (zealously protected), leopard, hyena, cheetah, jackal (black backed and side striped), crocodile, ostrich, mongoose, baboon, vervet monkey, kudu, brindled gnu, eland, roan and sable antelope, waterbuck, impala, steenbuck, gemsbok, sassaby; hippos, giraffe, zebra, and lion are commonest in the Robins basalt area.

The African buffalo, which suffered heavily in the rinderpest epidemics of the 1890s, is now common only in reserves and near thick bush between Natal and the Sudan. By day they shelter under close-canopy bush or forest, coming out to graze in large (100 plus) herds by night, drinking, on average, twice before lying up again. Their weight (up to 1,500 lb) and the massive horns make them difficult prey; even lions hunt them warily. They are strong swimmers, too. A rare relative is the dwarf forest buffalo of Central and West Africa.

⇐ Three rest camps can house 200 people; lodges for a further 50 are under construction. All chalets and lodges have furniture, drinking water, hot baths, and wcs in or near by. Bedding, refrigerators, cooking utensils, and fuel can be hired or bought. At all camps there are: petrol station; stores selling food, liquor, toiletries, and film; licensed restaurant; caravan and camping sites. Reservations through the warden. The main camp, in the east of the park, is open all year; others open 1 June to 30 November, subject to road conditions. Robins camp and its satellite Nantwich camp are respectively 90 and 95 miles west of the main camp. There are eight hotels within reach of the park; some are also conveniently sited for visits to the Victoria Falls NP.

⇒ Airfield at main camp; eight scheduled flights a week from Victoria Falls and from Salisbury via Kariba; extra flights between June to October. The daily rail service Bulawayo–Victoria Falls stops at Dett, where transport connects for the 14-mile journey to the main camp. Rhodesian railways run 'Gametrail' package tours to Wankie and 'Rainbow' tours to Wankie and Victoria Falls. There is separate road access to each of the three larger camps – all turnoffs from the Victoria Falls–Bulawayo road. Robins Camp is 44 miles from Matesi, which is 32 miles from Victoria Falls. Sinamatella camp is 30 miles from Wankie, which is 70 miles from Victoria Falls. The main camp, which can be reached via Dett or Gwaai River, is 160 miles from Bulawayo, 120 miles from Victoria Falls, and 321 miles from Salisbury.

🚗 A large network of good weather roads connects the main camps and the various pans; only the 5 miles between Nantwich and Robins camps is open during darkness. Regulations about speed and dismounting are strictly enforced, with on the spot fines. Maps are available at all camps and gates. Between the Main and Sinamatella camps is a fenced picnic site.

🌅 Open all year; best time August to November.

🕐 4–7 days.

☞ Not usually necessary.

⇨ The Regional Warden, Wankie National Park, PO Dett.

Zimbabwe National Park 1,786 acres; 3,800 ft above sea level. Set in wild bush country and rolling hills on the western shore of Lake Kyle – opposite the Kyle game reserve.

🐾 Kudu, duiker, steenbuck, bushbuck, klipspringer, leopard, baboon; rich birdlife includes hornbill, green pigeon, freckled nightjar, and purple crested lourie.

🌿 Senecio and *Albizia adianthifolia*.

🛏 Eight one-roomed rondavels, 3 two-bedroomed chalets, and one fully equipped cottage; a 10-acre camping and caravan site with communal facilities – all with electric light and hot water. Reservations via the warden. Near by is a tearoom, a store, and a 9-hole golf course. Nearest service station and store is 8 miles along the Ft Victoria road. Other accommodation in the area includes the Great Zimbabwe Ruins Hotel, Sheppards Hotel, and Kyle View Chalets. All have swimming facilities.

✈ Nearest airport is at Ft Victoria; Rhodesian Air Services will arrange transport to Zimbabwe for their passengers. By road the park is 18 miles from Ft Victoria, 212 miles from Salisbury, and 199 miles from Bulawayo. Nearest rail station is at Ft Victoria. The park is only 40 miles from the Kyle reserve.

🚗 On foot; though the site itself can be visited by car.

🌅 Open all year; best time April to November.

🕐 1–2 days.

☞ Not necessary.

👁 Considered purely as a game park Zimbabwe is less rewarding than other parks, but it has a number of attractions for family people (compactness, safe swimming, etc). Its chief feature is, of course, the famous Zimbabwe ruins, which cover over 70 acres. The chief building is the 'temple', which was probably a palace. In places its outer wall rises to 30 ft; within is a maze of passages and enclosures and a strange conical tower which has never been properly excavated. A few hundred yards away, on top of a rocky hill, stands the 'Acropolis' – a series of terrace platforms held in by retaining walls that skilfully incorporate some of the rock outcrops. The two buildings are separated by a number of smaller enclosures known as the 'Valley Ruins'. The site was first occupied around the 8th century AD, but most of the buildings were erected during or since the 15th century by a Bantu people. It formed the inspiration for the Dead City in Rider Haggard's *She*. Objects recovered from digs at the ruins are displayed in a museum on the site.

⇨ The Warden, P/Bag 9087, Ft Victoria/tel: 0–8903.

South Africa

South Africa led the conservationist movement in Africa. In 1897 she established the Umfolozi Game Reserve and, a year later, the Sabie Game Reserve (since enlarged and renamed Kruger National Park). At that time the human exploitation of the open savannah that covers much of the eastern and southern continent had gone farther in South Africa than elsewhere; and the need for conservation was greater. Even so the whole idea of closing off large areas of fertile country and allowing wild beasts to multiply there was widely challenged. And without the enthusiastic support of farsighted statesmen like Kruger and the determined efforts of conservationists like Colonel J. Stevenson-Hamilton (warden of the Sabie Reserve), South Africa today might have no wildlife to speak of.

Thanks to such determination South Africa now has over 20 protected areas. Some are aimed at preserving single species, such as the Mountain Zebra Game Reserve or the Addo Elephant National Park (though, of course, other species flourish there too). Others aim at preserving something like an ecological balance, such as the Kruger National Park and the St. Lucia Game Reserve. Some fulfil both functions, such as the Kalahari Gemsbok National Park.

Their variety extends well beyond their function. From the parched heat of the Kalahari Gemsbok in January to the snow-filled valleys of Golden Gate Highlands in July; from the humid swamps of Ndumo in June to the cool green pastures of Kamberg in May – by picking your time and location you can choose among an enormous ecological range, from semitropical to alpine.

Admission unless otherwise stated the following rates apply: 75c per car and 5 passengers; additional passengers 35c (20c under 16; free under 6).

Accommodation In the following notes on South African parks these daily rates apply for accommodation unless otherwise stated: *Luxury rondavels* R5 each for first two people; R1.25 for each extra person. *Rondavels and 'square-davels'* R2.50 each for first two; R1 for each extra person. *Ordinary huts* R2 each for first two; 75c for each extra person. *Dormitories* R2 for six or fewer; 75c for each extra person. *Ordinary room (Nammuteri)* R2 each for first two; 75c each extra person. *Rooms with running water (Nammuteri)* R2.75 each for first two; R1 each extra person. *Tents* R1 a night. *Campsites* 75c for five or fewer; 15c each extra person.

When you book state: the number of nights to be spent at each camp – with dates; the members of your party and how they are to be split up; the type of accommodation required; and acceptable alternatives (both for camps and accommodation). If you wish, the reservations people will propose an itinerary for your approval.

The leopard, a long-tailed cat, is an expert climber and preys from trees.

Addo Elephant Park Nearly 50,000 acres of luxuriant en-
tangled bush, 45 miles north of Port Elizabeth, in the foothills
of the Zuurberg Mountains. During the first part of this
century the elephants in the area were all but wiped out by
angry citrus farmers whose crops they destroyed. Between
the wars the few remnants – who were also the shyest, fiercest,
and most cunning – were herded into the present park and, in
1945, enclosed behind the toughest steel fence ever built. The
bush is too thick to enable them to be seen during most of the
day but at 5pm they are lured out into special feeding places
by meals of oranges, pineapples, and oat hay.

🐾 Elephants apart there are also springbuck, grey rhebuck,
mountain reedbuck, duiker, steenbuck, red hartebeest,
eland, cape buffalo (rare), black rhino, and hippo – all of
whom would have been wiped out but for the enclosure.

🌿 A huge concentration of drought-adapted plants, including:
cotyledons, aloes, creepers, and mesembryanthemums,
spekboom, boerboom, melktou, ghwarrie, acacia, and
sneezewood.

🛏 None within the park. There are nearby hotels at Uitenhage
and Port Elizabeth.

🚗 By own car from Port Elizabeth via Coega and Addo; by
guided limousine or SA Railway bus – also from PE.

🚙 The elephant enclosure takes up about a third of the actual
park. The road, which is surfaced, skirts its edge; there is no
public access to the enclosure. There are 10 observation
mounds on this road. Other roads open to the public pass
near specially equipped picnic spots where you can buy
firewood. There is also a restaurant and a cafe.

☀ All year. Summer is very hot, winter is cold.

🕐 1 day (whole park); ½ day (elephant-feeding only).

🗒 Maps free from Satour offices. The book *The Addo Elephants*
is on sale at the gate – chiefly history and anecdotes.

➡ The Tourist Officer, Addo Elephant National Park, PO
Coerney/tel: Addo 140 (telegrams Natpark, PO Coerney).

Bontebok National Park A small, sandy depression in a rocky plateau at the foot of the Langeberg mountains and along the banks of the Breede river; 300 ft above sea level. Until 1931 the bontebok was one of the rarest of antelopes; only 17 existed in the south western Cape. Early attempts to revive the species failed because of unsuitable land. Then in 1960 they were moved here – their original home. Obviously conditions here were much more favourable and those few survivors have multiplied and flourished. Now they number over 150.

⚞ Bontebok, grey rhebuck, springbuck, red hartebeest, eland, grey duiker, steenbuck, Cape grysbok, Cape buffalo, and around 170 bird species.

⚜ Scrub veld with stretches of grass; also karoo thorn, white milkwood, turkey berry, dune taaibos, cherrywood, Breede river yellowwood, bastard olive, taaibos, and aloe.

⇌ None in the park. Nearest hotels are in Swellendam, 2 miles away. There is also a nearby campsite.

⇥ By road 2 miles south of Swellendam, 150 miles from Cape Town. Nearest station is at Swellendam. There is an airstrip for light charter aircraft on the northern perimeter. Nearest airport Cape Town.

🚐 Own car. There are scheduled picnic sites within the park, and they are the only places where you may get out of your car. Firewood is available there at 10c a bundle.

🔆 Open all year; no particular best time.

🕐 1 day.

🛈 Brief guide (including map) free at gate.

👁 The Old Swellendam Racecourse, some Hottentot graves and remnants of kraals, and an old wagon trail are all within the park.

⇨ Tourist Officer, Bontebok National Park, Swellendam/tel: Swellendam 3313 (cables Natpark Swellendam).

Coleford Nature Reserve A small (3,160 acre) reserve, 1,000 ft above sea level in the southeastern foothills of the Drakensberg range. It consists mainly of lightly undulating grassy stretches; established mainly to protect a small nucleus herd of white-tailed gnu and blesbok – its only notable wildlife.

⇌ Rest camp of 6 'squaredavels' and 5 other rooms with communal lounge, kitchen, and ablutions; h&c, bedding, cutlery, crockery, and servants provided, but no food. No store. Three miles from the camp there is a cottage with 2 three-bed rooms. Reservations Officer, PO Box 662, Pietermaritzburg, Natal.

⇥ By road 21 miles from Underberg on the Bulwer–Swartberg road. Underberg is 128 miles from Durban via Pietermaritzburg and 348 miles from Johannesburg via Ladysmith and Nottingham Road. Nearest station is at Underberg. Nearest airport is Durban.

🚐 On horseback; horses for hire at R2.50 per ½ day.

🔆 Open all year; no particular best time.

🕐 1–2 days.

👁 There is a tennis court near the camp.

⇨ National Parks Board, Pietermaritzburg, Natal.

Giant's Castle Game Reserve 90,000 acres of grassy plateaux and ravines nestling 5,000 to 11,000 ft up in the eastern face of the Drakensberg. The reserve is visited as much for its superb scenery as for its game.

Eland (one of SA's largest herds), oribi, grey rhebuck, reedbuck, mountain reedbuck, white-tailed gnu, black backed jackal, baboon, bushbuck, grey duiker, klipspringer; the last six named are difficult to find. Birds include black stork, black eagle, martial eagle, lanner falcon, lammergeyer, orange breasted rockjumper, giant kingfisher, and Natal sugarbird.

A superb rest camp with beds for 40, set in a well tended wildflower garden and lawns; bedding, cutlery, crockery, cooks provided but not food. No store in reserve. Reservations Officer, PO Box 662, Pietermaritzburg, Natal.

By road 138 miles from Durban via Mooi Rivier; 246 miles from Johannesburg via Harrismith and Bergville. Nearest station is at Loskop, 17 miles away, but Estcourt, a further 12 miles, is more frequently served. Nearest airport is at Durban.

Own car on the reserve's one road, which is sometimes difficult in the rains. All travel off this road is on foot; guides are needed for journeys of any length. There is plenty of swift climbing for the energetic.

Open all year; best time September to May.

3 days minimum.

National Parks Board, Pietermaritzburg, Natal.

Golden Gate Highlands National Park 10,500 acres; 6,000 to 9,000 ft above sea level. As much a scenic reserve as a National Park, Golden Gate Highlands has a different climate, vegetation, and wildlife from other SA parks. Summers are invigorating and without a dry season; winters are cold – snow usually lies on the mountains and sometimes carpets the valleys, too. Waterfalls have been known to freeze. In autumn the colours are unrivalled. Geologically the park is unique in Southern Africa. The chief rocks are sandstone, which rise in deeply eroded yellow, red, and purple bluffs at the valley edges. The sandstone beds are often topped with peaks and outcrops of Drakensberg basalt.

Eland, red hartebeest, white-tailed gnu, blesbok, springbok, zebra, grey rhebok, mountain reedbuck, duiker, klipspringer. Birds include the rare black eagle.

Highveld grassland with an assortment of shrubs and bulbous plants. Roads are lined with planted willows and poplars. Indigenous trees cling to the mountain slopes: mountain sage, wild olive, protea, and oudehout.

Hotel rooms with private bath R2.50 per person per night, with shared bath R1.90, with public bath R1.60 (75–50c cheaper under 16); nonwhite servants 25c. Meals add R2.20 to above rates. Camping and caravan sites (bring own equipment) 25c per person per night. There are also hotels at Clarens, Kestell, and Bethlehem.

By road 12 miles from Clarens, 26 miles from Kestell, 36 miles from Bethlehem, 52 miles from Harrismith. Gates close 30 mins after sunset, reopen 30 mins before sunrise. Nearest railway stations are at Bethlehem and Harrismith.

Nearest airports (scheduled services) at Bloemfontein and Welkom.

🚐 By own car. Some roads within the park are surfaced. Petrol is on sale at the hotel. Saddle horses can be hired at 30c an hour. Short excursions on foot from the hotel are permitted.

🌤 Open all year; best time summer and autumn.

🕐 2–7 days.

🗋 Small illustrated brochure free from Satour.

⇨ The Tourist Officer, Golden Gate Highlands National Park, PO Golden Gate, Orange Free State/tel: Golden Gate 2. Reservations to same address. Urgent reservations wire Natpark, Golden Gate.

The pangolin, or scaly anteater, has scales everywhere except on its belly. By day it sleeps in a sealed burrow; by night it attacks termite heaps, licking them into a toothless mouth with a foot-long tongue.

Hluhluwe Game Reserve Hluhluwe (pronounced shloo-shloo-wee) means 'sweet waters' in Zulu. Its 57,000 acres cover the wide, green hills of Zululand. In the steeper northern regions the river banks are densely forested. In places the open grassland gives way to sparser bushveld.

🗢 The chief attraction of the reserve is its numerous black and (rare) white rhinos. The names are misleading; 'white' is a misreading of 'wide' – referring to the squarer face and wider mouth of the 'white' rhino. The animals are active in the evening, night and early morning, which makes it advisable to arrive in broad daylight. Hluhluwe differs from other game reserves in that you are allowed to leave your car (in the company of a Bantu guide) and approach the animals. They see poorly, but hear and smell very distinctly. Other animals: buffalo, zebra, kudu, brindled gnu, impala, water-buck, bushbuck, steenbuck, reedbuck, red duiker, blue duiker, grey duiker, giraffe, warthog, bush pig, leopard, baboon, crocodile, nyala; birds include hornbill, bustard, francolin, guinea fowl, bee eater, tawny eagle, and fish eagle.

🞂 The common savannah and veld species as well as acacia, wild pear, and the Umhluhluwe creeper.

🛏 One rest camp with furnished cottages and thatched rondavels with electric light, h&c, bedding, towels, crockery, and service – but no food (except on organized tours). Nearest stores at Mtubatuba and Hluhluwe. Rates are approximately R2 per person per day.

🛬 182 miles from Durban via Mtubatuba (take the Golela Road and branch off at Hluhluwe Station). There are rail stations at Mtubatuba and Hluhluwe. Nearest airport is at Durban; the reserve is also within reach of Johannesburg.

🚐 No scheduled internal tours but SA Railways operate coach tours between Johannesburg and Durban which stop 2 nights in Hluhluwe. Private operators and safari companies in both cities also operate tours by car and coach. Petrol is on sale in the camp. Tyre chains advisable in wet summer season. Head and neck covering for strong sun; warm clothing for mornings and evenings.

🌤 The reserve is open all year. Best season is May to August.

🕐 2–3 days.

👉 Bantu guides cost 50c a day.

⇨ Camp Superintendent, Hluhluwe Game Reserve, PO Box 25, Mtubatuba, Zululand, Natal, or any Satour office.

Kalahari Gemsbok National Park 3,700 square miles of arid sand dunes and sparse vegetation, sandwiched between SW Africa and Botswana in the northernmost reaches of Cape Province (altitude 4,000 ft). It is crossed by two watercourses, the Auob and the Nossob, which flow only once or twice a century. These watercourses provide the only roads across the park.

🦌 Gemsbok, springbuck, gnu, red hartebeest, eland, lion, hyena, duiker, steenbuck, ant bear, warthog, honey badger, meerkat (mongoose), camel (imported and escaped), ostrich, kudu, leopard, cheetah, jackal, wild dog; birds include secretary bird, giant bustard, namaqua dove, francolins, lammergeyer, vultures, and eagles.

🌿 Saltbush, camelthorn, tsama melon, various bulbs, and trees along the dry watercourses.

🛏 At Twee Rivieren there is a family cottage and 2-, 3-, and 4-bed huts; at Mata Mata and Nossob Camp there are 3-bed huts. R9 per night for the cottage; R1 per night for hut accommodation per person, 75c children under 16. Bedding costs 35c a night (maximum 4 nights); towels 5c a day. Bring your own crockery and utensils. There is no restaurant and the shop sells only nonperishable food. Reservations to The Director, National Parks Board, PO Box 787, Pretoria/tel: 3–5611 or 3–5618.

🛬 By road 200 miles from Upington, 650 miles from the Reef and Pretoria, and 690 miles from Cape Town. Nearest stations are at Upington and Keetmanshoop. Nearest airfield at Upington. Consult the town clerk of Upington about scheduled tours of the park by bus and air; rates around 30c a mile for 5 passengers.

🚐 Own car or scheduled tours from Upington. Roads are unsurfaced. Petrol on sale at all three camps. To reach Nossob Camp in time you must start from Twee Rivieren or Mata Mata before noon.

🌤 Open all year but only between March to October will most people find the heat bearable. In December to January the heat is extreme. Nights can be extremely cold.

🕐 You can drive through the park in 2 fairly leisurely days; you will need 3–4 days just to visit the three camps.

🚗 R1.25 per person (30c under 16, free under 6) and R1.25 per car. Vehicles over 2 tons R2.50, mobile homes R3.75, trailer caravan R2.50, luggage trailer R1.25.

🛗 Small brochure (including map) at entrance or from Satour.

👁 The park lies across part of the Kalahari home of the Bushman. There is a Bushman settlement within walking distance of Twee Rivieren.

⇨ The Nature Conservator, Kalahari Gemsbok National Park, PO Gemsbokpark (via Upington)/tel: Gemsbokpark (urgent reservations also to this address).

Kamberg Nature Reserve 5,500 acres of well-watered green country, 4,000 ft up in the Drakensberg foothills; resembling open prairie.

🐃 Oribi, eland, reedbuck, grey rhebuck, grey duiker, mountain reedbuck. The reserve's chief attraction is the herd of Zulu royal cattle or Inyonikaipumuli. The name actually means 'the birds have no rest' and refers to times when the cattle were so plentiful that the tickbirds following them had no time to rest. The shields of the famous Zulu impis (crack warriors) were made of the hides of these white cattle.

🏠 Hutted camp with 5 'squaredavels', communal lounge, kitchen, and ablutions; bedding, crockery, cutlery, cooks, and servants included, but no food. No store. Reservations Officer, PO Box 662, Pietermaritzburg, Natal.

✈ By road 25 miles from Rosetta, which is about 80 miles from Durban on the main Johannesburg road. The nearest station is at Mooi Rivier, which is a few miles from Rosetta, and on the main Durban–Johannesburg line. Nearest airport at Durban.

🚗 Own car and on foot.

☀ Open all year; best time summer and autumn.

🕐 1 day or short vacation.

👁 The rocky cliffs on the edges of the reserve hold some interesting rock paintings.

⇨ Camp Superintendent, Kamberg Nature Reserve, PO Rosetta, Natal.

Hunting-dog packs (up to 60 members) hunt around dawn, resting by day and sleeping or moving by night over vast areas.

The Kruger National Park This is South Africa's greatest park and one of the finest of the world's accessible wildlife areas. Its 8,000 square miles lie in the extreme north east of the country, along the Mozambique border, and run from the Limpopo in the north to Komatipoort, 200 miles to the south. The wide, grassy plains of the southern section, crossed by meandering rivers, slowly merge with the more rugged bush of the centre and north. The main rivers – the Sabie in the south and the Olifants in the north – cross the park from the east; here and there they and their tributaries run through deep gorges. There are also some densely wooded slopes. In general, however, the landscape is open and is ideal for watching game.

⇨ African buffalo, brindled gnu, bushbuck, cheetah, crocodile, duiker, elephant (more to the north), giraffe, hippo, klipspringer, kudu, leopard, lion, monkeys, ostrich, polecat, quagga, red jackal, roan antelope, spotted hyena, steenbuck, vervet monkey, warthog, waterbuck, white rhino, wild dog. There are no springbuck.

🕄 Numerous flowering plants and shrubs. Noteworthy trees include baobab, bluegum, fever tree, wild fig, strangling fig, sausage tree, kiaat, knobthorn, and Transvaal ebony.

🛏 Ordinary huts with shared facilities range from R1.60 a day at Letaba, Lower Sabie, Olifants, Pretoriuskop, and Skukuza, through R1.40 at Orpen, Satara, and Shingwidzi, to R1.25 at Crocodile Bridge, Malelane, and Punda Milia. Rates at Nwanedzi Rest Camp vary between R1.40 and R2.50 per person. Some of the camps also have self-contained family accommodation at rates around R2.50 per person. Camping is allowed only at Pretoriuskop at 50c per person (25c if you bring your own tent). Three daily meals add R2.40 to the above rates. Stores at main camps sell food, cigarettes, books, photo supplies, and souvenirs. Visits during school holidays and long weekends require advance booking – it is, in any case advisable to book well in advance. Reservations for summer season begin June 1; for winter October 15. Reservations by letter to The Director, National Parks Board, PO Box 787, Pretoria (cables Natpark Pretoria); phone (urgent cases only) Pretoria 3–5611 or 3–5618 Monday to Friday; or call at Room 235, 2nd Floor, Sanlam Building, cnr Andries and Pretorius Streets, Pretoria. During the summer season accommodation is available at Olifants, Pretoriuskop, and Skukuza only.

⇨ By road during the winter season, reading clockwise from southeast: Crocodile Bridge (rail also), Malelane (rail also), Numbi, Skukuza (rail also), Orpen, Phalaborwa, and Punda Milia. During the summer season only the Crocodile Bridge, Numbi, and Skukuza gates are open. Pretoriuskop is 220 miles from Johannesburg, which has the nearest airport.

🚐 No scheduled internal services, but outside operators run bus and limousine tours with guides – details from Satour. There are more than 1,000 miles of internal road, some surfaced. Motor workshops at Letaba and Skukuza.

🌅 Summer October 15 to May 1; winter May 1 to October 15. August to October are the best months since the dry weather forces the animals to concentrate near the water holes. Note: Kruger is a malaria area (in summer); prophylactics on sale at camps. Bring a torch – nights are dark and sudden. Head and neck protection essential. Take summer clothing for the day, something warmer for mornings and evenings; a rug in June.

🕐 2–15 days; the reservation office will gladly help plan an itinerary to suit you.

✉ R1.25 per person per visit, children 6–16 30c, children under 6 free. R1.25 per vehicle plus 65c per day, mobile homes R1.25 per day, caravans 65c plus 65c a day, luggage trailer 30c plus 30c per day. Minimum entry R3.75.

🛢 Free guide from Total, the petrol company who operate the petrol concession within the park. Map 30c from National Parks Board of Trustees.

🗺 No official guides, but see 🛢 above.

👁 From Pretorius you can take day trips to such outside beauty spots at Barberton, Graskop, Nelspruit, Sabie, and White River; as long as you spend the night in camp you need not renew the entry fee.

⇨ The Director, National Parks Board, PO Box 787, Pretoria or any Satour office.

Loteni Nature Reserve 5,300 acres of open prairie; 4,600 ft up in the shadow of the Drakensberg. Close by and very similar to the Kamberg reserve.

🦌 Reedbuck, mountain reedbuck, grey rhebuck, eland, grey duiker, oribi, and bushbuck. Birdlife is montane: black stork, black eagle, martial eagle, lanner falcon, lammergeyer, orange-breasted rockjumper, giant kingfisher, and Natal sugarbird.

🏕 Rest camp with 12 'squaredavels'; communal lounge, kitchen, and ablution blocks; bedding, cutlery, crockery, cooks, and servants included, but no food. No store. Reservations Officer, PO Box 662, Pietermaritzburg, Natal.

🛣 By road 9 miles west of Loteni Store, which is 49 miles from Nottingham Road on the way to Himeville. Nottingham Road is 86 miles from Durban, 318 miles from Johannesburg. Nearest station is at Mooi Rivier, 12 miles from Nottingham Road. Nearest airport is at Durban.

🚗 Own car and on foot.

🌞 Open all year; best time September to May.

🕐 1 day or short vacation.

⇨ National Parks Board, Pietermaritzburg, Natal.

Mkuzi Game Reserve 61,500 acres, 2,600 ft up in northern Natal. The reserve contains both thick bush and open grassy plains. There are towering forests of sycamore figs and a large aloe forest near the camp. The climate is often hot. There are three large waterholes which permanently support thousands of head of game. Nhlonhlela Pan is an eerie expanse of khaki water edged by tall fever trees – the home of many crocodiles. Bube Pan has a unique hide from which you can watch animals at very close quarters.

🦌 Impala, black rhino, brindled gnu, nyala, kudu, reedbuck, red duiker, grey duiker, Burchell's zebra, steenbuck, suni, bush pig, warthog, jackals, leopard, crocodile. Birds include the white-backed vulture, stilt, crested guinea fowl, Natal francolin, black cuckoo, green-spotted wood dove, violet starling, greater honeyguide, white-fronted bee eater, and (in Nsumu Pan) pelican and Egyptian geese.

🏠 Rest camp with 6 huts, ablution and kitchen blocks; bedding, cutlery, crockery, and servants provided, but no food. No store. Also three rustic huts with beds, mattresses, and cold water; nothing else provided. Reservations Officer, PO Box 662, Pietermaritzburg, Natal.

✈ By road 250 miles northeast from Durban along the main coast road via Hluhluwe station; the turn off through the Lembobo hills is 50 miles north of Mtubatuba, from where the reserve is 10 miles farther east. There are no bus tours. Nearest station is Mkuze. Nearest airport is Durban; Lourenço Marques also feasible.

🚗 Own car or short excursions on foot – in either case it is obligatory to carry a Bantu guide. Car chains are advisable in summer. Petrol on sale in reserve.

☀ Open all year; best months September to May.

⏱ 3–5 days.

⇨ National Parks Board, Pietermaritzburg, Natal.

Mountain Zebra National Park An area of some 46,000 acres in the middle of the Great Karoo on the northern slopes of Bankberg mountain. In 1937 this was the home of the last herd of mountain zebra in the Cape Province. In that year the National Parks Board bought a farm there and turned it into a sanctuary for them. The farm, and others that have since been added, make up the Mountain Zebra Park. The mountain zebra, at 12 hands, is the smallest of all zebras; the body stripes do not meet on the stomach, though they do go right around the legs. It has no shadow stripes and its face is a chestnut brown.

🦓 Apart from the zebra, the Board has reintroduced other indigenous species – mountain reedbuck, grey rhebuck, klipspringer, steenbuck, duiker, eland, white-tailed gnu, blesbuck, springbuck, gemsbok, red hartebeest, and ostrich. Wild birds have also taken to the sanctuary; among 146 recorded species are Stanley cranes, secretary birds, bustards, plovers.

🌿 Typical karoo landscape of semi-arid veld; bitterkaroo, koggelmandervoet, pentzia, raisinbush, tolbos, dgom bush, turpentine grass, stick grass, assegai grass, buffalo grass, salt bush, broom bush, aloes, cotyledons, mesembrian-themums, karee, acacia, wild olive, white stinkwood, and kiepersol trees.

🏠 Limited accommodation at a rest camp (a modified farm-house) in the centre of the park. R1.80 per person per night (R1.25 under 16); bedding, towel, crockery, cutlery, cooking utensils included. Bring own food – no perishables on sale within camp. There are also camping and caravan sites at 25c per person per night. Nonwhite servants' rooms 25c (no bed or bedding). Refrigeration facilities at 35c a day. Bookings via The Director, National Parks Board, PO Box 787, Pretoria/tel: Pretoria 3–5611 or 3–5618.

✈ 4 miles north of Cradock on the Middleburg road take the Graaff Reinet turn, go 3½ miles, where the park turn is signposted; thereafter follow the signs. Total distance 17 miles. Cradock is also the nearest rail point.

🚗 Own car or horse (30c per hour). Excursions on foot are permitted. No petrol in park. No surfaced roads.

☀ Open all year; summers are hot, winters are cold.

🕐   1 energetic day or 3 lazy ones.

🎫   Standard fees. Travelling times 8am–6pm (October 1 to April 30), 9am–5pm (May 1 to September 30).

🏠   Free brochure, including map, from Satour.

⇨   The Nature Conservator, Mountain Zebra National Park, Cradock/tel: Cradock 2113 (urgent bookings wire Natpark Cradock).

The impala, one of the most graceful of all antelopes, is common both in thick scrub and open savannah. Alarmed, it can leap 10 ft high over a distance of up to 30 ft. It is often found with zebra and gnu.

Ndumu Game Reserve 25,000 acres of subtropical bush and savannah, scored by lakes and streams in the alluvial plain of the Pongolo River, 2,600 ft above sea level. The chief feature of the park is its large crocodile population. Entomologists also find the park rewarding.

🦌   Hippopotamus, nyala, bushbuck, impala, bush pig, grey and red duiker, reedbuck, suni, and crocodile. Rhinos have been reintroduced. The birdlife is unique in Natal since it includes many tropical species at the southern end of their range. Listed birds include black heron, dwarf goose, fish eagle, bat hawk, crested guineafowl, water dikkop, jacana, fishing owl, white-eared barbet, broadbill, nicator, and sometimes flamingo (in Inyamiti Pan).

🛏   Rest camp with 7 two-bed huts, kitchen, ablutions; h&c, electric light, bedding, cutlery, crockery, cooks, and servants included but no food. The nearest store is at Ndumu, a mile from the reserve (and 5 miles from the camp).

🚗   By road from Durban 331 miles; turn off about 5 miles after Mkuze and take the road to Jozini Dam; follow sign to Otobotini Store, from where the reserve is signposted. If you have a valid passport you can go on from Mkuze to Golela and into Swaziland, turning off for the reserve at Ingwavuma. From Johannesburg 350 miles via Standerton and Golela. Stations at Golela and Mkuze are served from Durban. Nearest airport is about 100 miles away at Lourenço Marques; otherwise Durban.

🚐 Own vehicle or National Parks transport; all trips in company of European ranger – to avoid trouble with crocodiles. Those wishing to walk must have a Bantu game guide. Petrol on sale at camp. Tours extend out of the park, right up to the Mozambique border.

🌤 Open all year. Summer is hot and steamy – malarial precautions needed; best time May to September.

🕐 3–5 days.

🎫 R1.25 per person (30c under 16, free under 6) and R1.25 per car.

⇨ National Parks Board, Pietermaritzburg, Natal.

Oribi Gorge Nature Reserve 4,412 acres of forested slopes along the Oribi Gorge; 1,680 ft above sea level. The camp is on the tableland at the head of the Gorge and commands a superb panorama. There are several good walks in the reserve.

🐾 Leopard, bushbuck, blue duiker, grey duiker, oribi.

🏠 Rest camp with 6 'squaredavels'; communal kitchen, ablutions, and lounge; bedding, cutlery, crockery, and cooks and servants included but bring your own food. No shop. Reservations Officer, PO Box 662, Pietermaritzburg.

✈ 13 miles west of Port Shepstone, which is 80 miles from Durban along the main coast road. Nearest station is at Port Shepstone. Nearest airport at Durban.

🚐 Tours can be arranged by car from Durban or by bus from Margate. Walking is permitted.

🌤 Open all year.

🕐 2–5 days.

⇨ Ranger-in-Charge, Oribi Gorge Nature Reserve, PO Plains, Natal.

Royal Natal National Park and **Rugged Glen Nature Reserve** Together these parks comprise some 20,000 acres of rugged Drakensberg landscape, deeply scored with ravines. Waterfalls are plentiful and there are numerous ancient rock paintings in a reasonably good state of preservation. From the summits, on a clear day, you can see a fair part of Natal. (The film 'Zulu' was shot in this area.)

🐾 White-tailed gnu, grey duiker, grey rhebuck, mountain rhebuck, reedbuck, bushbuck, klipspringer, hyrax, and baboon. Birds are less numerous than in the lowveld; they include secretary bird, black eagle, white-necked raven, malachite sunbirds, familiar chat, pipits, and grass warblers.

🏠 Royal Natal National Park Hotel (60 rooms), fully licensed; reservations to The Lessee, Royal Natal National Park Hotel, PO Mont-aux-Sources/tel: M-aux-S 1. Tendele Camp has 13 'squaredavels' with 2 kitchens, communal ablutions and lounge; bedding, crockery, and cutlery supplied but no food. Royal Natal National Park Campsite has hedge-separated but open sites, kitchen, ablution block, and lounge. Bring your own equipment; no food. Reservations Officer, PO Box 662, Pietermaritzburg.

✈ By tarred road 155 miles from Durban to Bergville, then 26 miles of hard dirt road to the park. The scheduled 2-day SA Railways coach tour between Johannesburg and Durban includes an overnight stop in the park, where the journey may be broken. Nearest railway stations are at Bergville (from Durban) or Harrismith (from Johannesburg). Nearest airports at Durban and Welkom.

🚐 On foot or on horseback. Guides are advisable on long trips; they are available at Tendele Camp.

☀ Open all year.

🕐 From 3 days to a full vacation.

🔖 Map and descriptive booklet – including species lists – at the Warden's Office.

⇨ The Warden, Royal Natal National Park, PO Mont-aux-Sources, Natal.

St Lucia Game Reserve An area of 31,000 acres at sea level in northern Natal. Early hunters practically exterminated the wildlife in this area – particularly the hippos and crocodiles. In the 1940s sugar farmers cleared the swamps, as a result of which silt flowed down and blocked the estuary mouth, preventing the entry of marine life into the marshes. Between 1948 and 1960 the mouth was unblocked and the original conditions were re-established. As a result more than 350 species of coastal birds now inhabit the reserve and its many islands.

🐦 Pelican, gulls, ibis, ducks, geese, flamingo, narina trogons, white crested guineafowl, Reichenow's louries, bush shrike, pink-throated longclaw, goliath heron, saddlebill, spoonbill, white-bellied bustard, jacana, avocet, caspian tern, green coucal. Mammals include nyala, bushbuck, reedbuck, suni, grey and red duiker, steenbuck, and bush pig.

🌿 Many orchids. The Barringtonia tree sheds creamy-white blossom like a carpet over the lakes.

✈ 170 miles from Durban by road or nearly 390 miles from Johannesburg via Standerton and Utrecht. Both roads

The white pelican's range covers the whole of Africa. It is remarkable for its communal fishing, which has an unusual military precision.

merge at Mtubatuba. Do *not* take the St Lucia road from Mtubatuba – it goes only to the estuary; instead take the Mkuze road for 10 miles, then turn off to Charters Creek. Nearest railway station is at Mtubatuba. Light charter aircraft can land near the reserve.

At Charters Creek there are 15 2-bedded rondavels, communal lounge, kitchen, and ablutions. Bedding, cutlery, crockery, and servants supplied but visitors bring their own food. Also an open campsite with latrines and tap; bring all own equipment. At Fanies Island, 7 miles to the north, there are 12 2-bedded rondavels and a campsite; same facilities and conditions as for Charters Creek. At St Lucia (reached directly from Mtubatuba – see ⇨) there is an open campsite with latrines and tap; bring own equipment and food. Reservations to Reservations Officer, PO Box 662, Pietermaritzburg/tel: 4–1441 (telegrams Fauna, Pietermaritzburg).

Ranger-guided launch tours from Charters Creek and St Lucia. Rowboats for hire at all three camps. Between April and September there are 3-day Wilderness Trails – 1 day by launch, 2 days on foot, accompanied by a ranger; price R12.50 per person per day. Tours and boat bookings to Ranger-in-Charge, PO St Lucia Estuary, Natal/tel: St Lucia 20; Camp Superintendent, Fanies Island, PO Nyalazi River, Natal/tel: Mtubatuba 1103.

Open all year; best time summer and autumn.

2–7 days.

R1.25 per vehicle and 5 passengers; additional passengers 35c (20c under 16, free under 6).

From offices named under ⌷ above.

Umfolozi Game Reserve 72,000 acres; around 1,500 ft above sea level. Umfolozi is only 15 miles from Hluhluwe Game Reserve; landscape, flora, and fauna are very similar. The great attraction of Umfolozi are the Wilderness Trails – 2-, 3-, 4-, or 5-day hikes, with guides, through areas where cars are forbidden. Trails should be booked in advance through the Wilderness Trails Officer, Umfolozi Game Reserve, PO Box 99, Mtubatuba, Natal; prices between R4 and R5.75 per person, per day. Head and neck covering for strong sun and warm clothing for mornings and evenings are advisable.

White rhino, black rhino, red and grey duiker, bushbuck, warthog, brindled gnu, zebra, waterbuck, reedbuck, impala, klipspringer, mountain reedbuck, kudu, nyala, buffalo, leopard, baboon, crocodile. Birds include: night heron, yellow-billed stork, Wahlberg's eagle, martial eagle, Shelley's francolin, black-bellied bustard, Temminck's courser, Klaas's cuckoo, little bee eater, crested barbet.

As Hluhluwe, plus acacia and sycamore fig.

A rondavel rest camp with communal facilities. Each rondavel has a cook, who will prepare food supplied by visitors (on Wilderness Trails food is supplied). Food can be bought on the way or at Mtubatuba station; a thrice-weekly lorry goes to Mtubatuba, and the driver will make urgent purchases for visitors. Electric light 5 am to 10 pm. Crockery, cutlery, and bedding included. Reservations to Reservations Officer, PO Box 662, Pietermaritzburg/tel: 4–1441 (telegrams Fauna, Pietermaritzburg).

By road 182 miles from Durban via Mtubatuba, which is 32

miles from the reserve. Nearest station is at Mtubatuba.
Nearest airport at Durban.

🚐 Own car; chains necessary in wet summer months. Private
operators run limousine tours from Durban; details from
Satour. Petrol available at camp.

🔆 Open all year. Best months are May to August.

🕐 2–3 days.

🛏 As for Hluhluwe.

⇨ Camp Superintendent, PO Box 25, Mtubatuba, Natal or any
Satour office.

Willem Pretorius Game Reserve A compact 26,000-acre
reserve bordering the Allemanskraal Dam in the Orange
Free State. Alongside, but completely separate, is a rest camp
and holiday resort. The scenery varies from the mountain
slopes of the Doringberg through wooded gorges to the flat
grassy plains around the dam.

🦒 Giraffe, white rhino, blesbok, white-tailed gnu, red hartebeest, eland, zebra, impala, springbuck, reedbuck, steenbuck, rhebuck, duiker. Most of the animals are descendants
of those that once roamed the now defunct Somerville Game
Reserve. There are no lions in the area, so the antelope are
more relaxed than elsewhere. Breeding is so successful that
the herds are now being culled.

🏠 40 thatched rondavels with fridges, showers, bedding, and
mattresses. Food and cooking facilities available; also a good
restaurant. Caravan and camping site. Book well in advance
from The Provincial Secretary, PO Box 517, Bloemfontein.

✈ By road 96 miles north of Bloemfontein on the Johannesburg
road; 181 miles south of Johannesburg. Nearest railway
station is at Henneman, 29 miles away, on the Johannesburg-
Bloemfontein line. Nearest airport is at Bloemfontein.

🚐 Own car; 30 miles of made up road lead to good vantage
points over drinking places; best times for viewing are early
morning and evening.

🔆 Open all year; best months October to January; best
autumn month May.

🕐 1–3 days in park.

👁 By the main road through the reserve there are some
interesting prehistoric huts of unmortared stone.

⇨ The Director, The National Parks Board of Trustees, **PO**
Box 787 Pretoria/tel: 3–5611 or 3–5618.

Southwest Africa

Etosha National Park 16,250,000 acres; 4,000 ft above sea
level. Thousands of years ago the Kunene river ran through
this region, feeding what was then the Etosha lake; but the
river, and then the lake, ran dry, leaving the present pan – a
flat, semi-arid stretch about 80 miles long. Even today after
heavy rains some 3,200 square miles of the pan are flooded to
a depth of about 3 ft, but the water seeps away within weeks
eventually to reappear in one or other of the waterholes that
support so many thousands of animals.

The region was the last to be occupied by Europeans, and it still cannot be called anything but primeval. It has never been densely populated and when the game was practically exterminated by rinderpest around the turn of the century, the local tribesmen wandered off to other game areas. The German governor of the time, von Lindequist, declared the area a game reserve. The game slowly recovered but little was done to develop the area until the 1950s. Since then the park has steadily increased in popularity.

⚐ Springbok, Burchell's zebra, brindled gnu, gemsbok (to the west), kudu (to the southeast), hartebeest (between Okaukuejo and Namutoni), eland (rare), steenbuck, duiker (shy), damara dikdik (near Namutoni early morning and late evening), giraffe, elephant, rhino (very rare and only in west), lion, cheetah, leopard and hyena (both shy), bat-eared fox, lynx, aardwolf, honeybadger, squirrel, mongoose, python. Birds include ostrich, giant and other bustards, guineafowl, francolins, cranes, secretary bird, hornbills, lourie, hawks, eagles, and all kinds of waterfowl.

⌘ The park covers the coastal desert of the Namib and extends into the semi-arid regions of the interior. The flora is unremarkable – thorn, low bush, occasional grassy stretches, and mopane trees. The farther east you go, the richer the vegetation, which includes tambotie, deurmekaar, wolf's thorn, wild fig, date palms, appelblaar, marula and makalanie palm.

⇦ There are three rest camps: Okaukuejo, Halali, and Namutoni. *Okaukuejo*, at the western edge of the pan, offers luxury 5-bed rondavels, h&c, own wc, shower, gas stove at R3.75 for 2 plus R1.25 for each extra person. Self-contained bungalows, 6 beds, h&c, own wc, shower, R2.50 for 2 plus R1 for each extra person. Bungalows, 3 beds and communal amenities, R1.80 for 2 plus 75c for each extra person. Dormitories, 8 beds, communal amenities, R1.85 for 6 plus 30c for each extra person. Tents, 3 beds, communal amenities, R1 a night.
Halali, near the middle of the southern edge of the pan: luxury bungalows, bungalows, dormitory, and tents – same prices as Okaukuejo.
Namutoni, at the western outlet to the pan: luxury rooms, 3 beds, washbasin, and communal facilities, R2.50 for 2 plus R1 for each extra person. Rooms, 2 to 6 beds, communal amenities, R1.85 for 2 plus 65c for each extra person. Dormitories, 6 or more beds, communal amenities, R1.85 for 6 plus 30c for each extra person. Ordinary rooms, 2 beds, communal facilities, R1.85 for 2.
Namutoni is a picturesque old fort built by the Germans in 1904; 7 soldiers once withstood over 500 Ovambos there. Okaukuejo is another old German fort. Halali was opened in 1967; its name denotes the sound blown in German hunts when (strangely enough in this context) the hounds draw in for the kill. Each camp has a swimming pool and a shop that sells fresh meat, beer, canned food, cooking utensils and cutlery, eggs, bread and butter, films, and souvenirs, but no fresh fruit, milk or vegetables. Petrol stations at each camp sell cold drinks, petrol, diesel fuel (but not avgas); no vehicle servicing. Breakdowns are towed at 20c a mile to Okaukuejo for repair. There are no servants at any of the camps. Sheets, blankets, pillows, and towels can be hired (except by campers) at 15c each per night. No cots for hire. All camps

Greater Kudu at Etosha NP. Among the most striking of all antelopes, it has spiral horns that can reach up to 5 ft. Bulls are solitary except in the mating season. Kudu prefer broken, hilly country.

have camping sites with communal facilities, 70c for 5, 15c for each extra person. There is a post office at each camp. Reservations to Senior Tourist Officer, Nature Conservation and Tourist Branch, Private Bag 13175, Windhoek; cables Swasec, Windhoek/tel: 7657 or 7941. Reservations up to a year in advance.

 By road from the south – via Outjo for Okaukeujo and Tsumeb for Namutoni and Halali. Okaukuejo is 272 miles from Windhoek; Namutoni is 341 miles. South African Airways operate scheduled flights from Johannesburg and Cape Town to Windhoek, where you can hire a car. SW African Transport hire light aircraft for flights to landing strips at each of the camps. SA Railways operate a scheduled bus service to the park and back; total trip of 5 days costs R90, including food and accommodation.

Own car; one car for hire at Okaukuejo and Namutoni – book well in advance.

Okaukuejo and Halali are open May 1 to October 15; Namutoni is open April 1 to November 30. Travel along the road between Namutoni and Okaukuejo is prohibited in the wet seasons April 1 to 30 and October 16 to November 30; during April, too, there is no camping at Namutoni. The best time for a visit is September to August. Avoid school holidays. During opening season the climate is moderate to cool, and dry.

4–10 days.

R1.25 per vehicle plus 70c per person over 12 years old.

Road maps, route suggestions and other information from AA of South Africa. Shell Company of SW Africa publish a free map of the park with helpful drawings of the animals and a keyed route indicating those you are most likely to see at any one point.

Director of the Nature Conservation and Tourism Branch, Private Bag 13186, Windhoek, SW Africa.

Africa: Species Lists

(NORTHEAST AND NORTHWEST)

ANTELOPES Pendjari; Baoulé; P N du W
— **Mountain Nyala** Bale Mts
— **Roan** Yankari; Dinder
BABOON, Gelada Simien Mts
— **Olive** Menagasha
BEE-EATER, Carmine Awash
BOAR Tazekka
BONGO Nimule
BUFFALO, African Bamingui-Bangoran; Baoulé; Yankari; Dinder; Nimule; P N du W
BUSHBUCK Dinder
— **Meneliki** Menagasha
BUSTARD, Kori Awash
CHEETAH Pendjari; Yankari; P N du W
CHOUGH Simien Mts
CORMORANTS Rift Valley
CRANE, Crested Pendjari
CROCODILE Yankari; P N du W
DIKDIK Dinder
DOG, Hunting Yankari
DUCKS Rift Valley
DUIKERS Baoulé
— **Yellow-Backed** Nimule
ELAND Bamingui-Bangoran; Nimule
— **Derby's** Baoulé
ELEPHANT Bamingui-Bangoran; Pendjari; Baoulé; Yankari; Dinder; Nimule; P N du W
FLAMINGO, Greater Rift Valley
— **Lesser** Rift Valley
FOX, Simien Simien Mts
GAZELLES Baoulé; Dinder
— **Soemmering's** Awash
GEESE Rift Valley
GIRAFFE Bamingui-Bangoran; Baoulé; Yankari; Dinder
GOOSE, Abyssinian Blue-Winged Bale Mts
GULLS Rift Valley
HARTEBEEST Yankari; Dinder; Nimule
HERON Pendjari
HIPPOPOTAMUS Bamingui-Bangoran; Pendjari; Awash; Baoulé; Yankari; Nimule; P N du W
HYENA Bamingui-Bangoran; Dinder
IBEX, Walia Simien Mts
IBISES Rift Valley
— **Wattled** Simien Mts
JACKAL Bamingui-Bangoran; Yankari; Dinder; P N du W
KOB Pendjari; Baoulé; Nimule; P N du W
KUDU, Greater Awash; Dinder
— **Lesser** Awash
LAMMERGEIER Simien Mts
LECHWE, Nile Nimule
LEOPARD Yankari
LION Bamingui-Bangoran; Pendjari; Baoulé; Yankari; Dinder; P N du W
MARABOU Pendjari
MONKEYS Yankari; P N du W
— **Black and White** Menagasha
ORIBI Dinder; Nimule
ORYX Awash
OSTRICH Bamingui-Bangoran; Awash; Dinder
PELICAN, Great White Rift Valley
— **Pink-Backed** Rift Valley
RAVEN, Thick-Billed Simien Mts
REEDBUCK Dinder; Nimule
— **Chanler's** Awash
RHINOCEROS, Black Bamingui-Bangoran; Dinder
— **White** Nimule
ROLLER, Abyssinian Awash
STORK, Marabou Rift Valley
TERNS Rift Valley
TOPI Baoulé
TURACO, White-Cheeked Menagasha
WADERS Rift Valley
WARTHOG Bamingui-Bangoran; Yankari; Nimule; P N du W
WATERBUCK Bamingui-Bangoran; Pendjari; Awash; Yankari; Dinder; Nimule
ZEBRA, Grévy's Awash

A black-headed heron, common south of the Sahara. Like other herons it has long legs and a long bill adapted to life in marshes and shallow water. Its neck-vertebrae are of unequal length, resulting in the characteristic S-shape, especially in flight.

AARDVARK Albert
AARDWOLF Etosha
ANT BEAR Kalahari Gemsbok
ANTELOPES Albert; Meru; Tsavo;
Luangwa
— **Giraffe-Necked** Amboseli
— **Nyala** Lengwe; Gorongoza; Chewore;
L Kyle; Hluhluwe; Mkuzi; Ndumu; St
Lucia; Umfolozi
— **Roan** Mara; Ruaha; Serengeti; Kidepo;
Kasungu; Nyika; Kafue; Sumbu;
Chewore; Chizarira; Matusadona; Wankie;
Kruger
— **Sable** Mikumi; Ruaha; Kasungu; Kafue;
Sumbu; Gorongoza; Chewore; Chizarira;
L Kyle; McIlwaine; Mana; Matusadona;
Mushandike; Matopos; Ngezi; Victoria
Falls; Wankie
AVOCET St Lucia
BABOON Mt Elgon; Arusha; Manyara;
Mikumi; Ngorongoro; Murchison Falls;
Chewore; McIlwaine; Matopos;
Sebakwe; Victoria Falls; Wankie;
Zimbabwe; Giant's Castle; Hluhluwe;
Royal Natal; Umfolozi
BADGER, Honey Kalahari Gemsbok;
Etosha
BARBET, Black-Backed Kafue
— **Crested** Umfolozi
— **White-Eared** Ndumu
BAT, Fruit-eating Mt Elgon
BEE-EATERS Q Elizabeth; Lengwe;
Hluhluwe
— **Boehm's** Kafue
— **Carmine** Kasungu; Luangwa
— **Little** Umfolozi
— **White-Fronted** Mkuzi
BLESBOK see also **BONTEBOK**
Colesford; Golden Gate Highlands;
Mt Zebra; Wm Pretorius
BONGO Aberdare; Mt Elgon; Mt Kenya
BONTEBOK Bontebok NP
BROADBILL Ndumu
BUCK Murchison Falls
BUFFALO, African (or Cape) Albert;
Aberdare; Marsabit; Mara; Amboseli;
Meru; Mt Elgon; Mt Kenya; Nairobi;
Samburu; Tsavo; Arusha; Manyara;
Mikumi; Ngorongoro; Ruaha; Serengeti;
Kidepo; Murchison Falls; Q Elizabeth;
Kasungu; Lengwe; Kafue; Luangwa;
Sumbu; Gorongoza; Chete; Chewore;
Chizarira; L Kyle; McIlwaine; Mana;
Matusadona; Matopos; Victoria Falls;
Wankie; Addo; Bontebok; Hluhluwe;
Kruger; Umfolozi
BUSHBABY Manyara; Mikumi
BUSHBUCK Aberdare; Mara; Meru; Mt
Elgon; Mt Kenya; Samburu; Arusha;
Manyara; Ngorongoro; Q Elizabeth;
Lengwe; Nyika; Sumbu; Gorongoza;
Chewore; Chizarira; L Kyle; Matusadona;
Matopos; Ngezi; Victoria Falls;
Zimbabwe; Giant's Castle; Hluhluwe;
Kruger; Loteni; Ndumu; Oribi Gorge;
Royal Natal; St Lucia; Umfolozi
BUSHPIG Arusha; Luangwa; Chizarira;
Inyanga; Matusadona; Hluhluwe; Mkuzi;
Ndumu; St Lucia
BUSTARDS Lengwe; Hluhluwe; Mt Zebra;
Etosha
— **Black-Bellied** Umfolozi
— **Giant** Kalahari Gemsbok; Etosha
— **Kori** Nairobi
— **Stanley's** Nyika
— **White-Bellied** St Lucia
CAMEL, Feral Kalahari Gemsbok
CARACAL Nyika
CAT, Serval Samburu; Nyika
CHAT, Familiar Royal Natal
CHEETAH Mara; Amboseli; Meru;
Samburu; Mikumi; Ngorongoro;
Serengeti; Kidepo;
Kasungu; Nyika; Victoria Falls; Wankie;
Kalahari Gemsbok; Kruger; Etosha
CHIMPANZEE Albert; Murchison Falls
CIVET Arusha; Manyara
COLY, Blue-Naped Nairobi
— **Speckled** Nairobi
CORMORANT Kafue
COUCAL, Green St Lucia
COURSERS Manyara
— **Temminck's** Umfolozi
CRANES Etosha

— **Crested** Kafue
— **Crowned** Nairobi
— **Stanley** Mt Zebra
— **Wattled** Nyika; Kafue
CROCODILE Samburu; Murchison Falls;
Kafue; Luangwa; Gorongoza; Chete;
Chewore; L Kyle; McIlwaine; Mana;
Matusadona; Ngezi; Victoria Falls;
Wankie; Hluhluwe; Kruger; Mkuzi;
Ndumu; Umfolozi
CUCKOO, Black Mkuzi
— **Klaas's** Umfolozi
DIKDIK Samburu; Manyara; Ngorongoro
— **Damara** Etosha
DIKKOP, Water Ndumu
DOG, Hunting (or **Wild**) Albert; Mara;
Samburu; Arusha; Mikumi; Ngorongoro;
Serengeti; Kalahari Gemsbok; Kruger
DOVE, Green-Spotted Wood Mkuzi
— **Namaqua** Kalahari Gemsbok
DUCKS Manyara; Q Elizabeth; St Lucia
DUIKER Aberdare; Mara; Meru; Mt Elgon;
Mt Kenya; Arusha; Mikumi; Lengwe;
Nyika; Kafue; Sumbu; Gorongoza; L Kyle;
McIlwaine; Mushandike; Matopos;
Ngezi; Sebakwe; Zimbabwe; Addo;
Golden Gate Highlands; Kalahari
Gemsbok; Kruger; Mt Zebra; Wm
Pretorius; Etosha
— **Black-Fronted** Mt Kenya
— **Blue** Inyanga; Hluhluwe; Oribi Gorge
— **Grey** Mt Elgon; Bontebok; Giant's Castle;
Hluhluwe; Kamberg; Loteni; Mkuzi;
Ndumu; Oribi Gorge; Royal Natal;
St Lucia; Umfolozi
— **Red** Mt Elgon; Hluhluwe; Mkuzi;
Ndumu; St Lucia; Umfolozi
EAGLES Kasungu; Luangwa; Kalahari
Gemsbok; Etosha
— **Bateleur** Kafue
— **Black** Matopos; Giant's Castle; Golden
Gate Highlands; Loteni; Royal Natal
— **Fish** Ruaha; Lengwe; Kafue; Hluhluwe;
Ndumu
— **Hawk** Aberdare
— **Long-Crested** Kafue
— **Martial** Kafue; Giant's Castle; Loteni;
Umfolozi
— **Steppe** Ngorongoro
— **Tawny** Ngorongoro; Hluhluwe
— **Verreaux's** Ngorongoro
— **Vulturine Fish** Sumbu
— **Wahlberg's** Umfolozi
EGRET Manyara; Mushandike
ELAND Mara; Amboseli; Meru; Nairobi;
Samburu; Arusha; Ngorongoro;
Serengeti; Kidepo; Kasungu; Nyika;
Kafue; Luangwa; Sumbu; Gorongoza;
L Kyle; McIlwaine; Mana; Matopos;
Victoria Falls; Wankie; Addo; Bontebok;
Giant's Castle; Golden Gate Highlands;
Kalahari Gemsbok; Kamberg; Loteni;
Mt Zebra; Wm Pretorius; Etosha
ELEPHANT Albert; Aberdare; Marsabit;
Mara; Amboseli; Mt Elgon; Mt Kenya;
Samburu; Tsavo; Arusha; Manyara;
Mikumi; Ngorongoro; Ruaha; Kidepo;
Murchison Falls; Q Elizabeth; Kasungu;
Kafue; Luangwa; Sumbu; Gorongoza;
Chete; Chizarira; Mana; Matusadona;
Victoria Falls; Wankie; Addo; Kruger;
Etosha
FALCON, Lanner Giant's Castle; Loteni
FLAMINGO Nakuru; Manyara;
Mushandike; Ndumu; St Lucia
— **Greater** Arusha
— **Lesser** Arusha
FOX, Bat-Eared Manyara; Etosha
FRANCOLIN Lengwe; Inyanga; Hluhluwe;
Kalahari Gemsbok; Etosha
— **Natal** Mkuzi
— **Shelley's** Umfolozi
GAZELLE, Grant's Mara; Amboseli;
Nairobi; Samburu; Ngorongoro;
Serengeti
— **Thomson's** Mara; Amboseli; Nairobi;
Ngorongoro; Serengeti
GEESE Q Elizabeth; St Lucia
GEMSBOK (Cape Oryx) Wankie; Kalahari
Gemsbok; Mt Zebra; Etosha
GENET Arusha; Ngorongoro; Nyika
GERENUK Samburu; Tsavo
GIRAFFES Mara; Meru; Nairobi; Samburu;
Tsavo; Arusha; Manyara; Mikumi;

AFRICA: SPECIES LISTS (EAST, CENTRAL, SOUTHERN)

Serengeti; Murchison Falls; L Kyle;
McIlwaine; Matopos; Victoria Falls;
Wankie; Hluhluwe; Kruger; Wm
Pretorius; Etosha
— **Masai** Amboseli
— **Reticulated** Marsabit; Meru; Samburu
— **Rothschild's** Kidepo; Murchison Falls
— **Thornicroft's** Luangwa
GNU Kafue; L Kyle; Kalahari Gemsbok
— **Brindled** Mara; Amboseli; Nairobi;
Mikumi; Ngorongoro; Serengeti;
Luangwa (Cookson's); Gorongoza;
McIlwaine; Matopos; Wankie;
Hluhluwe; Kruger; Mkuzi; Umfolozi;
Etosha
— **White-Tailed** Colesford; Giant's Castle;
Golden Gate Highlands; Mt Zebra; Royal
Natal; Wm Pretorius; Etosha
GOOSE, EGYPTIAN Aberdare; Mkuzi
— **Pygmy** (or **Dwarf**) Ngezi; Ndumu
GORILLA, Mountain Albert;
Mt Muhavura
GRYSBOK Luangwa
— **Cape** Bontebok
— **Sharpe's** Sumbu
GUINEA FOWL Lengwe; Hluhluwe; Etosha
— **Crested** Mkuzi; Ndumu
— **Vulturine** Samburu
— **White-Crested** St Lucia
GULLS St Lucia
HARTEBEEST Tsavo; Mikumi; Kidepo;
Kasungu; Lengwe; Gorongoza; Etosha
— **Coke's** Mara; Serengeti
— **Lichtenstein's** L Kyle
— **Red** Addo; Bontebok; Golden Gate
Highlands; Kalahari Gemsbok; Mt Zebra;
Wm Pretorius
HAWKS Etosha
— **Bat** Ndumu
HERONS Mushandike
— **Black** Ndumu
— **Goliath** Murchison Falls; St Lucia
— **Madagascar Squacco** Amboseli
— **Night** Umfolozi
HIPPOPOTAMUS Albert; Mara; Meru;
Tsavo; Arusha; Manyara; Mikumi;
Ngorongoro; Murchison Falls;
Q Elizabeth; Kafue; Luangwa; Sumbu;
Gorongoza; Chete; Chewore; Chizarira;
L Kyle; Mana; Matusadona; Ngezi;
Victoria Falls; Wankie; Addo; Kruger;
Ndumu
HOG, Giant Forest Aberdare; Mt Elgon;
Mt Kenya; Q Elizabeth
HONEY GUIDE Q Elizabeth
— **Greater** Q Elizabeth
HORNBILLS Kidepo; Zimbabwe;
Hluhluwe; Etosha
— **Crowned** Aberdare
HYENA Mt Elgon; Manyara; Mikumi;
Ngorongoro; Serengeti; Nyika; Chete;
Chizarira; Inyanga; Mana; Matusadona;
Wankie; Kalahari Gemsbok; Etosha
— **Spotted** Samburu; Kruger
— **Striped** Marsabit; Samburu
HYRAX Sumbu; Royal Natal
— **Tree** Albert
IBIS Manyara; Lengwe; St Lucia
— **Green** Aberdare
IMPALA Meru; Nairobi; Samburu;
Manyara; Mikumi; Ngorongoro; Ruaha;
Lengwe; Kafue; Luangwa; Gorongoza;
Chete; Chewore; Chizarira; L Kyle;
McIlwaine; Mana; Matopos; Ngezi;
Sebakwe; Victoria Falls; Wankie;
Hluhluwe; Mkuzi; Ndumu; Umfolozi;
Wm Pretorius
**INYONIKAIPUMULI (Zulu Royal
Cattle)** Kamberg
JACANA Manyara; Q Elizabeth; Kafue;
Ndumu; St Lucia
JACKAL Manyara; Mikumi; Ngorongoro;
Chete; Chizarira; Inyanga; Sebakwe;
Wankie; Kalahari Gemsbok; Mkuzi
— **Black-Backed** Giant's Castle
— **Red** Kruger
KINGFISHERS Manyara
— **Giant** Giant's Castle; Loteni
— **Malachite** Q Elizabeth
KLIPSPRINGER Samburu; Manyara;
Ngorongoro; Sumbu; Inyanga;
Mushandike; Matopos; Zimbabwe;
Giant's Castle; Golden Gate Highlands;
Kruger; Mt Zebra; Royal Natal; Umfolozi

KOB Albert; Kidepo; Murchison Falls;
Q Elizabeth
KONGONI Amboseli; Nairobi
KUDU Kasungu; Lengwe; Kafue;
Luangwa; Gorongoza; Chete; Chewore;
Chizarira; Inyanga; L Kyle; McIlwaine;
Mana; Matusadona; Mushandike;
Matopos; Ngezi; Sebakwe; Victoria Falls;
Wankie; Zimbabwe; Hluhluwe;
Kalahari Gemsbok; Kruger; Mkuzi;
Umfolozi; Etosha
— **Greater** Marsabit; Mikumi; Ruaha;
Kidepo
— **Lesser** Meru; Ruaha; Kidepo
LAMMERGEYER Giant's Castle; Kalahari
Gemsbok; Loteni
LARKS Manyara; Ngorongoro
LECHWE Kafue
LEOPARD Albert; Aberdare; Mara;
Amboseli; Meru; Mt Elgon; Mt Kenya;
Nairobi; Samburu; Tsavo; Arusha;
Manyara; Mikumi; Lengwe; Nyika;
Serengeti; Kidepo; Murchison Falls;
Q Elizabeth; Kasungu; Lengwe; Nyika;
Luangwa; Gorongoza; Chete; Chizarira;
Inyanga; McIlwaine; Mana;
Matusadona; Mushandike; Matopos;
Ngezi; Sebakwe; Victoria Falls; Wankie;
Zimbabwe; Hluhluwe; Kalahari
Gemsbok; Kruger; Mkuzi; Oribi Gorge;
Umfolozi; Etosha
LION Albert; Mara; Amboseli; Meru;
Nairobi; Samburu; Tsavo; Arusha;
Manyara; Mikumi; Ruaha; Serengeti;
Kidepo; Murchison Falls; Q Elizabeth;
Kasungu; Lengwe; Nyika; Kafue;
Luangwa; Gorongoza; Chete; Chizarira;
Mana; Matusadona; Victoria Falls;
Wankie; Kalahari Gemsbok; Kruger;
Etosha
LONGCLAW, Pink-Throated St Lucia
LOURIES Etosha
— **Purple-Crested** Zimbabwe
— **Reichenow's** St Lucia
— **Ross's** Kafue
LYNX Etosha
MALACHITO, Double-Collared
Aberdare
MONGOOSE Arusha; Manyara; Mikumi;
Ngorongoro; Wankie; Kalahari Gemsbok;
Etosha
MONKEYS Tsavo; Mikumi; Gorongoza;
McIlwaine; Matopos; Kruger
— **Blue** Mt Elgon
— **Colobus** Mt Elgon; Mt Kenya; Arusha;
Mikumi
— **Samango** Lengwe
— **Sykes** Arusha; Manyara
— **Vervet** Arusha; Manyara; Mikumi;
Ngorongoro; Wankie; Kruger
NICATOR Ndumu
NIGHTJAR, Freckled Zimbabwe
OKAPI Albert
OPENBILLS Kafue
ORIBI Mt Elgon; Murchison Falls; Kasungu;
Kafue; Luangwa; L Kyle; McIlwaine;
Giant's Castle; Kamberg; Loteni; Oribi
Gorge
ORIOLE, Golden Kidepo
ORYX Amboseli; Tsavo
— **Beisa** Marsabit; Meru; Samburu
— **Cape** see **GEMSBOK**
— **Fringe-Eared (?)** Tsavo
OSTRICH Marsabit; Amboseli; Kidepo;
L Kyle; McIlwaine; Matopos; Wankie;
Kalahari Gemsbok; Kruger; Mt Zebra;
Etosha
— **Masai** Nairobi
— **Somalian** Samburu
OWL, Fishing Ndumu
PANGOLIN Mt Elgon
PANTHER Wankie
PARAKEET, Rose-Ringed Kidepo
PARROTS Lengwe
PELICAN Manyara; Mkuzi; St Lucia
PIGEONS, Green Zimbabwe
PIPITS Royal Natal
PLOVERS Manyara; Mt Zebra
POLECAT Kruger
PORCUPINE Mt Elgon
PUKU Luangwa; Sumbu
PYTHON Etosha
QUAGGA Kruger

QUAIL, Rose-Ringed Kidepo
RABBIT, Rock Matopos
RAT, Giant Mt Elgon
RAVEN, White-Necked Royal Natal
REEDBUCK Meru; Arusha; Manyara;
Ngorongoro; Kasungu; Nyika; Inyanga;
L Kyle; McIlwaine; Mushandike;
Matopos; Sebakwe; Giant's Castle;
Hluhluwe; Kamberg; Loténi; Mkuzi;
Ndumu; St Lucia; Umfolozi;
Wm Pretorius
— **Bohor** Mara
— **Mountain** Addo; Giant's Castle;
Golden Gate Highlands; Kamberg;
Loteni; Mt Zebra; Royal Natal; Umfolozi
RHEBUCK, Grey Addo; Bontebok;
Giant's Castle; Golden Gate Highlands;
Kamberg; Loteni; Mt Zebra; Royal Natal;
Wm Pretorius
RHINOCEROS Kasungu; Ndumu; Etosha
— **Black** Aberdare; Marsabit; Mara;
Amboseli; Meru; Mt Kenya; Nairobi;
Samburu; Tsavo; Arusha; Manyara;
Mikumi; Ngorongoro; Ruaha; Serengeti;
Kidepo; Murchison Falls; Kafue;
Luangwa; Chewore; Mana; Matusadona;
Matopos; Wankie; Addo; Hluhluwe;
Mkuzi; Umfolozi
— **White** Meru; Murchison Falls; L Kyle;
Matopos; Wankie; Hluhluwe; Kruger;
Umfolozi; Wm Pretorius
ROCKJUMPER, Orange-Breasted
Giant's Castle; Loteni
ROLLERS Lengwe; Gorongoza
— **Lilac-Breasted** Lengwe
SADDLEBILLS Kafue; St Lucia
SASSABY Chizarira; McIlwaine; Wankie
SCIMITAR BILL, Abyssinian Kidepo
SHRIKE, Bush St Lucia
SECRETARY BIRD Nairobi; Nyika;
Inyanga; Kalahari Gemsbok; Mt Zebra;
Royal Natal; Etosha
SITATUNGA Kafue
SPOONBILLS Gorongoza; St Lucia
SPRINGBUCK Addo; Bontebok; Golden
Gate Highlands; Kalahari Gemsbok;
Mt Zebra; Wm Pretorius; Etosha
SQUIRREL Etosha
STARLING, Glossy Amboseli
— **Violet** Mkuzi
STEENBUCK Ngorongoro; L Kyle;
McIlwaine; Mushandike; Matopos;
Wankie; Zimbabwe; Addo; Bontebok;
Hluhluwe; Kalahari Gemsbok; Kruger;
Mkuzi; Mt Zebra; St Lucia; Wm Pretorius;
Etosha
STILT Mkuzi
STORK Manyara; Gorongoza
— **Black** Giant's Castle; Loteni
— **Marabou** Nairobi; Lengwe; Kafue

— **Saddle-Billed** Murchison Falls
— **Whale-Headed** Murchison Falls;
Q Elizabeth
— **Yellow-Billed** Umfolozi
SUGARBIRD Giant's Castle; Loteni
SUNBIRDS Q Elizabeth; Lengwe
— **Golden-Winged** Aberdare
— **Kenya Violet-Backed** Amboseli
— **Malachite** Royal Natal
— **Scarlet-Chested** Amboseli; Kidepo
— **Tacazze** Aberdare
SUNI Arusha; Mkuzi; Ndumu; St Lucia
— **Livingstone's** Lengwe
TERN Mushandike
— **Caspian** St Lucia
TINKER BIRD, Golden-Rumped
Aberdare
TOPI Albert; Mara; Q Elizabeth
TROGON, Narina St Lucia
TURACO, Hartlaub's Nairobi
VULTURES Kasungu; Lengwe; Luangwa;
Gorongoza; Kalahari Gemsbok
— **Hooded** Kafue
— **Leppet-Faced** Kafue
— **White-Backed** Kafue; Mkuzi
— **White-Headed** Kafue
WADERS Manyara; Q Elizabeth
WAGTAILS Manyara
WARBLER, Grass Royal Natal
WARTHOG Mara; Meru; Samburu; Arusha;
Manyara; Mikumi; Q Elizabeth; Sumbu;
Chizarira; L Kyle; McIlwaine; Mana;
Hluhluwe; Kalahari Gemsbok; Kruger;
Mkuzi; Umfolozi
WATER BIRDS Marsabit; Lengwe;
Sumbu; Gorongoza; Etosha
WATERBUCK Aberdare; Meru; Mt Elgon;
Nairobi; Samburu; Arusha; Manyara;
Mikumi; Ngorongoro; Kidepo;
Q Elizabeth; Kasungu; Luangwa; Sumbu;
Chete; Chewore; Inyanga; McIlwaine;
Mana; Matusadona; Mushandike; Ngezi;
Victoria Falls; Wankie; Hluhluwe;
Kruger; Umfolozi
WEAVERS Lengwe
— **Golden** Amboseli
WIDOW BIRD, Red-Naped Aberdare
WILDEBEEST see **GNU**
ZEBRA Amboseli; Nairobi; Tsavo;
Manyara; Mikumi; Ngorongoro
Serengeti; Kidepo; Kasungu; Nyika;
Kafue; Luangwa; Sumbu; Gorongoza;
Chizarira; L Kyle; McIlwaine; Mana;
Ngezi; Sebakwe; Victoria Falls; Wankie;
Golden Gate Highlands; Hluhluwe;
Umfolozi; Wm Pretorius
— **Burchell's** Mara; Meru; Samburu;
Mkuzi; Etosha
— **Grévy's** Marsabit; Meru; Samburu
— **Mountain** Mt Zebra NP

A dikdik, seven species of which are found in Africa south of the Sahara. Among the smallest of all antelopes, they have straight horns.

NORTH AMERICA

Introduction by
Roger Tory Peterson

Unlike the Old World where the evolution of civilization was
slow enough to allow a kind of equilibrium to exist – albeit
much modified from its primeval state – the wildlife of North
America suffered the burgeoning impact of Europe's migrant

American elk, or wapiti, on a headland at Ecola SP, Oregon. The elk is not to be confused with the European elk, a relative of the moose.

millions in much too short a span of time for some species to adapt and survive. Some of the larger mammals were extirpated from much of the continent and birds such as the passenger pigeon, Carolina paroquet, Labrador duck and heath hen became extinct.

The shock effect of this had its compensating reaction and today North America enjoys some of the world's most enlightened wildlife legislation and a very extensive network of parks, refuges, reserves and sanctuaries.

When and where did the National Park idea originate? Some conservation historians insist that it was in 1864 when Abraham Lincoln, then president of the USA, signed the act that set aside the incomparable Yosemite Valley and the nearby Mariposa Grove of Sequoias in California 'for public use, resort, and recreation.' It was elevated to National Park status in 1890.

However, the Yellowstone, 3470 square miles in north-western Wyoming was actually the first area in the world to be designated a 'National Park' by legislative action. The bill was passed after some of the most altruistic lobbying in US history and was signed into law by President Ulysses S. Grant on March 1, 1872. Judge Cornelius Hedges in his plea to the Congress of the US stated:

'It seems to me that God made this region for all the people and all the world to see and enjoy forever. It is impossible that any individual should think that he can own any of this country for his own in fee. This great wilderness does not belong to us. It belongs to the Nation. Let us make a public park of it and set it aside ... never to be changed but to be kept sacred always.'

This statement was made a century ago by a man of vision during the era of western land grabbing. He and an exploratory party with commercial exploitation on their minds had spent a month mapping the geysers, waterfalls and canyons of this primeval montane region. As they sat around the camp-fire one night, the phrase 'national park' entered into their conversation. It would be criminal, they concluded, to carve up this awe-inspiring wilderness for money – an extraordinary verdict for a group of 'practical' men, which included a sur-veyor, an army officer, a banker and a judge. But they were men of sophistication; most of them (as James Fisher pointed out) were New England educated during the period when Thoreau was preaching his philosophy of wilderness values and when Emerson, Hawthorne and Longfellow were widely read 'romantics in the presence of nature.'

Once the seed was planted national parks sprouted all over the world. The second was Australia's Royal National Park, designated a public reserve in 1879 and formally dedicated as a park in 1886.

The US, as of 1970, has more than 280 areas within its national park system (which, in addition to wilderness areas, includes 'National Monuments' such as prehistoric Indian sites, and historic landmarks, and also national seashores, scientific reserves, etc). The gross acreage is nearly 30 million, an area half again as large as Scotland or larger than Den-mark, the Netherlands, and Belgium combined.

The number of visitors (or rather, visits) to the national parks of the US now exceeds 170 million annually. The sup-port as well as the pressures of a public hungry for outdoor experience makes it essential to plan for the future. The

National Park network of the USA continues to grow, as it does in Canada and in most other countries of the world. Six or seven new areas of great beauty and wilderness have been proposed, and it will be just a matter of time, financing and legislative action before they also become parks.

In addition to the National Parks of the US most of the 50 states also have parks where wild land has been set aside. These are administered by the state governments. In Canada they have their counterpart in the Provincial parks.

Canada, the United States' neighbour to the North, has a splendid system of parks and refuges, some of them very large, such as Banff, Canada's oldest park, established in 1887. It embraces 1,600,000 acres. Even larger is Jasper, also in the Rocky Mountains, covering 2,750,000 acres. Largest of all is Wood Buffalo Park in Alberta, the last breeding stronghold of the Whooping Crane, embracing 11 million acres (an area larger than Denmark). Some of the Provincial parks are also very extensive – such as Algonquin in Ontario, nearly 2 million acres of forest and lakes where the cry of the loon and the howl of wolf thrill the camper. Canada is now considering parks and tourism in its Arctic far north, a harsh but vulnerable environment worth safeguarding.

Just what is a park? My new dictionary defines a park as 'A tract of land set aside for public use; as (*a*) an expanse of enclosed grounds for recreational use within or adjoining a town, (*b*) a landscaped city square, (*c*) a tract of land kept in its natural state.'

A national park, as we conceive it, fits the latter category. But even when men of good will get together at international conferences to discuss national parks it soon becomes apparent that they do not always mean the same thing. Some still think in terms of manicured recreation grounds, tidied up like a country club complete with golf course and swimming pools. That kind of contrived recreational park, though agreeable enough and serving a purpose, is monotonously the same the world over. It does not reflect the national heritage, the natural landscape – the wilderness – that has evolved over the millennia and which cannot be duplicated precisely in any other country. Every nation has something of value to offer its citizens and to the rest of the world in its national parks. They are the soul of the land, showplaces to be preserved, to be guarded against attrition.

This does not mean that they are not to be used. But an anomalous situation exists in some of the world's most popular national parks and reserves. They are literally being loved to death. In the Yellowstone and Yosemite during the months of July and August, cars are often bumper to bumper on the main roads.

This is the dilemma faced by park administrators: to provide for a proliferating public who are attracted to the parks in ever greater numbers and, at the same time, to protect the biota – the plants, animals, soil and water – from the tramp of too many feet. Too many boots can be as destructive as too many motorcars or too many small boats. In Rocky Mountain National Park in Colorado ecologists estimated that 25 years of walking over the lichen- and flower-covered rocks near the high lookouts and parking places could deteriorate the alpine tundra to a point where it would take 500 years for its full recovery. The solution was to provide a few inconspicuous asphalt paths to channelize the flower gazers, bird watchers and other tourists.

Park management is primarily the management of people, but there are also times, even in the most spacious of parks, when the animals for which they were set aside slip out of balance and seriously damage the environment. Examples: too many elk in the Yellowstone; too many hippos in Uganda's Queen Elizabeth Park; too many elephants at Murchison. There are reasons for these maladjustments which I won't go into here, but in such instances qualified biologists have recommended and carried out control programmes. It would be contrary to the National Park concept to allow public hunting as a remedy.

Fully as important to wildlife as the parks are the refuges (around 330) embraced in the National Wildlife Refuge system of the US. These range from small areas to refuges of more than 4000 square miles. The total acreage approximates that of the National Park System, nearly 30 million acres. More than two-thirds of the refuges (about 260) are primarily for waterfowl. These fall into three basic categories: (1) those in the north for nesting; (2) those along migration routes: and (3) those in the south for wintering. These are intensively managed by water control structures which include hundreds of miles of dykes, spillways, etc. Waterfowl food plants are cultivated. The refuge effort is financed in part by the federal treasury (about 30 million dollars annually) and in part by the sale of the 'duck stamp' to citizens and other sources. Men, women and children flock to these refuges to see the wildlife, to picnic, to fish, to bird watch and to photograph. Controlled waterfowl shooting is permitted on limited sections of some refuges, but the number of persons who pursue waterfowling amounts to only about 4 per cent of the human visitation which is now about 17 million annually.

The Federal refuge system in the United States began at the beginning of the century when President Theodore Roosevelt, by executive order established the Pelican Island Refuge in Florida to protect breeding brown pelicans and other colonial waterbirds. This was in 1903 and during his tenure this conservation-minded president put his pen to forty such executive orders, mostly for the protection of heron rookeries and tern colonies that were threatened by the plume trade. From this modest but urgent beginning the refuge system grew to its present dimension.

Looking at a map of North America on which the parks and refuges have been plotted, one is aware that the majority and also the largest ones are in the West. This is understandable when one realizes that in relatively young countries, such as the US and Canada, more unpopulated or thinly populated land was available in the West than in the thickly populated East, where colonization by Europeans had a longer history. Furthermore, rugged mountain country, canyons and alpine meadows are not as suitable for agriculture. Nor are most deserts. There are not as many vested interests involved and thus it becomes relatively easy to set such land aside in perpetuity.

The mountain areas offer more scenic grandeur – waterfalls, high peaks, tumbling streams – the kind of scenery the travelling public expects in a park. It is only recently that planners have come to grips with the urgency of saving beaches, shorelines, and coral reefs. The most neglected environment of all is the original prairie which is now almost non-existent. Grass is humble and less easy to dramatize than trees. Fortunately, the original prairie biota (except for the larger predators) can be re-created through management.

Most National Parks and wildlife refuges offer the visitor up-to-date lists of the birds and mammals and guide sheets or guide books to the area. Many offer a variety of interpretative services, including ranger-naturalists, nature trails and even small museums. Some put on excellent lecture programmes; in Grand Canyon the emphasis is on geology; at Yellowstone, geysers and the large mammals; at Everglades, birds; and at others it may be botany. The interpretative service of the US National Parks which reaches millions, is, in my opinion, the most massive and most effective attempt to bring sound nature education to the public.

Supplementing the parks and refuges, there are also vast acreages of national forests and other lands under federal jurisdiction. Under the recent Wilderness Act of the US certain primeval areas and other wild sections have been set aside never to be violated by roads or buildings but, instead, to be visited only by trail, horse or canoe.

In addition to the network of national, state and provincial lands there are several hundred natural areas, principally of botanical interest, acquired by the Nature Conservancy, a fund-raising organization with extensive land holdings.

Many other conservation organizations – from the National Audubon Society and the North American sections of the World Wildlife Fund right down to individual cities and groups of private citizens – also own sanctuaries or support their establishment and fund their operations. In the pages that follow we cannot touch on all of the parks, reserves, refuges and sanctuaries of North America. Indeed, no complete directory of these has ever been attempted nor has anyone ever visited them all.

United States of America

UNITED STATES OF AMERICA

Michigan
1 Isle Royale NP *135*
3 Kirtland's Warbler MA *136*
2 Seney NWR *137*
4 Shiawassee NWR *137*
Minnesota
1 Agassiz NWR *138*
3 Rice Lake NWR *139*
4 Sherburne NWR *140*
2 Tamarac NWR *140*
5 Upper Mississippi W&FR *140*
Missouri
3 Mingo NWR *141*
1 Squaw Creek NWR *141*
2 Swan Lake NWR *142*
Nebraska
1 Crescent Lake NWR *142*
1 Ft Niobrara NWR *142*
2 Valentine NWR *144*
North Dakota
12 Arrowwood NWR *144*
4 Audubon NWR *144*
1 Des Lacs NWR *144*
7 Ft Lincoln SP *145*
10 J Clark Salyer NWR *146*
3 Lake Ilo NWR *146*
6 Lake Metigoshe SP *146*
8 Long Lake NWR *147*
2 Lostwood NWR *147*
9 Slade NWR *147*
11 Sully's Hill NGP *147*
13 Tewaukon NWR *147*
14 Turtle River SP *147*
1 Upper Souris NWR *148*
Ohio
1 Ottawa River NWR *148*
South Dakota
1 Custer SP *148*
1 Lacreek NWR *149*
5 Lake Andes NWR *149*
4 Sand Lake NWR *149*
2 Wind Cave NP *150*
Wisconsin
2 Horicon NWR *151*
1 Necedah NWR *151*

THE SOUTH
Alabama
2 Eufaula NWR *152*
1 Wheeler NWR *152*

Arkansas
2 Big Lake NWR *152*
1 Holla Bend NWR *152*
3 Wapanocca NWR *152*
4 White River NWR *152*
Florida
2 Chassahowitzka NWR *153*
10 Everglades NP *153*
12 Florida Keys Rs *155*
5 Highlands Hammock SP *156*
8 Jack Island SP *156*
7 J N 'Ding' Darling NWR *156*
11 John Pennekamp Coral R *157*
3 Lake Woodruff NWR *157*
9 Loxahatchee NWR *157*
6 Merritt Island NWR *158*
4 Myakka River SP *158*
1 Saint Marks NWR *159*
Georgia
3 Blackbeard Island NWR *160*
2 Okefenokee NWR *160*
1 Piedmont NWR *161*
Louisiana
1 Chicot SP *161*
5 Delta NWR *161*
4 Lacassine NWR *161*
3 Sabine NWR *162*
2 Sam Houston SP *162*
Mississippi
2 Noxubee NWR *163*
1 Yazoo NWR *163*
North Carolina
2 Mattamuskeet NWR *164*
3 Pea Island NWR *164*
1 Pungo NWR *164*
South Carolina
4 Cape Romain NWR *165*
1 Carolina Sandhills NWR *166*
2 Santee NWR *167*
3 Savannah NWR *167*
Tennessee
4 Cross Creeks NWR *167*
5 Gt Smoky Mts NP *167*
2 Hatchie NWR *170*
1 Reelfoot NWR *170*
3 Tennessee NWR *170*

Virginia
10 Back Bay NR *170*
7 Chincoteague NWR *170*
2 Fairy Stone SP *171*
1 Hungry Mother SP *171*
4 Parker's Marsh NA *171*
4 Pocahontas SP *172*
5 Presquile NWR *172*
9 Seashore SP *172*
3 Shenandoah NP *173*
8 Wreck & Bone Is NA *174*

THE NORTHEAST
Delaware
1 Bombay Hook NWR *175*
Maine
1 Moosehorn NWR *176*
Maryland
2 Blackwater NWR *177*
1 Eastern Neck NWR *177*
Massachusetts
1 Parker River NWR *177*
New Jersey
2 Brigantine NWR *178*
1 Great Swamp NWR *179*
New York
1 Iroquois NWR *180*
2 Montezuma NWR *180*
3 Morton NWR *180*
Pennsylvania
1 Erie NWR *181*
Vermont
1 Missisquoi NWR *181*

93

USA: Pacific States

Alaska

Aleutian Islands National Wildlife Refuge 2,720,235 acres, 70 treeless, windy mountainous islands, some volcanic. Fauna typical of Alaskan mainland: sea otter, sea lion, brown bear, foxes, reindeer, caribou, wolf. Usual northern water and land birds, also less usual varieties: guillemot, murre, emperor goose, oldsquaw, whooper swan. Salmon in streams. No commercial transport service. Hotel accommodation at Cold Bay. Refuge Manager, Cold Bay, Alaska 99571. Best June to September.

Clarence Rhode National Wildlife Range 1.8 million acres of rugged, windswept Alaskan tundra containing 50,000 lakes. The USA's second largest National Wildlife Refuge. Waterfowl, sandpiper, plover, curlew, arctic tern, glaucous mew, snipe. Nearest town is Bethel, then one hour by 'bush plane' to Old Chevak field station. Refuge Manager, Box 346, Bethel, Alaska 99559. Best June to August.

Kenai National Moose Range 1,730,000 acres, between sea level and 6,612 ft altitude. This wildlife refuge was established in 1941 on the Kenai peninsula. Its only coastal stretch lies in the Turnagain Arm of the Cook Inlet, opposite Anchorage. From there it reaches 100 miles southward across lake-mottled muskeg country to the scattered ranges of the Kenai mountains. Two of the lakes are large: Skilak, in the centre (24,000 acres) and Tustumena, near the southwest border (73,000 acres); in all there are over 1,200 lakes. Kenai river and Skilak lake were important arteries in the Gold Trail of the 1880s.

🐾 Moose (7,500 in the range), dall sheep, Rocky Mountain goat, brown bears (rare, in the mts), black bears (common), beaver (not protected), muskrat, mink, tree squirrel, lynx, coyote, marmot and wolverine (in the mts). Over 160 bird species include waterfowl (Moose river, outlet to Skilak lake, and Chickaloon flats) – mallard, goldeneye, teal, scaup, and the rare trumpeter swan – bald eagle, hawks, gulls, common loon, and cormorants (Skilak lake), spruce grouse, ptarmigan; songbirds include redpoll and chickadee as winter residents; sparrow, golden-crowned swallow, robin, golden plover, wandering tattler, northern phalarope, and sandpiper are all summer visitors.

🌿 The lowland is mostly forest with harvested and burned clearings; here grow dogwood, azaleas, shooting star, willowherb, and blue lupine. Trees include spruce, aspen, willow, and birch. Above the timberline, in the short alpine summer, grow cushion pink, daisies, columbine, and forget-me-not.

🏕 Camping (60-day limit) throughout the range; at the 13 public camp-grounds the limit is 2 consecutive weeks. There are motels at nearby Soldotna and Kenai – both outside the refuge border.

⇥ 112 miles from Anchorage via Sterling Highway. Light aircraft may land anywhere north of Kenai river, but south of it may land only on lakes and designated strips.

🚐 Foot and horse trails. There is a portage system between many lakes and rivers – maps from range HQ at Kenai or Skilak lake guard station.

☀ Open all year; best time June to September.

◷ 3 days.

✉ Free.

⇨ The Refuge Manager, PO Box 500, Kenai, Alaska 99611/tel: (907) 283–7563.

Mount McKinley National Park 3,030 square miles, 1,400 to 20,320 ft above sea level (the highest point on the North-American continent). Most of the park lies above the timberline, an ill-defined region between 2,500 and 3,000 ft above sea level. Below is spruce forest, thickest in the river valleys and floored with a springy carpet of lichen and moss. Above, the trees give way to wet alpine tundra – scattered ponds and dense plant growth (not good hiking country). Gravel bars left by departed glaciers, whose handiwork is evident throughout the park, are scored by multiple parallel streams known as 'braided' streams. The uplands, below the snowline, are dry alpine tundra, with matted hummocks of dwarf plants (heather, rhododendron, fireweed).

⇢ Dall sheep, barrens caribou, grizzly bear, moose, red fox, porcupine, beaver, red squirrel, arctic ground squirrel, hoary marmot, snowshoe rabbit, cony. Over 130 bird species include golden plover, kinglet, golden eagle, ptarmigan, and long-tailed jaeger.

🏠 McKinley Park Hotel, closed during winter; rates (b & b only) from $14–20. Bookings via Manager, McKinley Park Hotel, McKinley Park, Alaska 99755 (May 26 to September 10) or Mt McKinley National Park Co, 149 North Stone Ave, Tucson, Arizona 85701 (October 1 to May 25). There are 7 camp-grounds along the only road through the park; all have water, tables, tent sites, hearths for fires, and ablutions but no trailer (caravan) utilities. At the far end of the road near Kantishna ghost town and just outside the park border, lies Camp Denali; bed and full board available. Bookings via Camp Denali, McKinley Park, Alaska 99755 (June 1 to September 10) or Camp Denali, Box D, College, Alaska 99735 (September 11 to May 31).

⇥ Denali Highway, 160 miles between Paxson and entrance, gravel surface, passable June 1 to September 15 approx. Alaska Railroad offers daily trips from Fairbanks (4 hrs) and Anchorage (8 hrs). The hotel has a 3,000-ft airstrip for private and nonscheduled aircraft and rents cars.

🚐 A single road, 88 miles long and parallel to the Alaska Range, runs through the north of the park; open June 1 to September 10 only. Several short, self-guiding trails start from the park hotel, from where there are also guided walks with a park ranger. For details of longer trails (and cautions about grizzlies and moose) consult the park HQ.

☀ Open May 26 to September 10; best time mid-June to end of July (though these are the months most favoured by mosquitoes).

◷ 1–14 days.

✉ $1 per car and occupants per day; or 50c per individual hiker, rider, party-tourist.

🗋 Seven guide books, maps, etc, on sale in the park or send for price list from Mt McKinley Natural History Association, McKinley Park, Alaska 99755.

☞ Nature walks led by ranger–naturalists; slide show and film – all daily.

⇨ The Superintendent (address as above).

Dall sheep rams in Mount McKinley NP, Alaska.

California

Havasu Lake National Wildlife Refuge 22,007 acres on the Colorado River, marshes, lakes, deep canyons, mud and lake deltas. Refuge for wintering waterfowl: pintail, teal, mallard, geese. Avocet, sandpiper, heron, Harris hawk (rare). Bighorn sheep, wild burro, feral horse. Camping, picnicking, boating, horse trailer spaces, meals. Nearest town Needles. Refuge Manager, PO Box A, Needles, California 92363. Good all year.

Kern-Pixley National Wildlife Refuge 14,789 combined acres, where deep wells were drilled to provide necessary water, channels and dikes constructed for ponding. Provides habitat for several thousand migrating and wintering ducks, geese, including Canada and Ross' geese. Near town of Delano. Refuge Manager, PO Box 219, Delano, California 93215. Best October to March.

Klamath Basin National Wildfowl Refuges 5 waterfowl areas, ranging in size from 12,700 to 37,300 acres, straddling the California–Oregon border, about 4,000 ft up, to the east of the Cascade Range of the Rockies. These 5 lakes are all that remain of what was once nearly a million acres of water and marsh. They are both an important breeding ground and a regular stopover for migrants in the Pacific flyway – it is estimated that over 80 per cent of all the birds in the flyway, amounting to 7 or 8 million birds at any one time, concentrate at the basin. From north to south:

Klamath Forest National Wildlife Refuge, Oregon (15,226 *acres*) Nesting ground for Canada geese, sandhill cranes, diving ducks. Dirt road access.

Upper Klamath National Wildlife Refuge, Oregon (12,698 *acres*) Unique for its vast tule marsh – drowned stream beds fringed with willow banks; the mountainous western slopes of the refuge are thickly forested. Double-crested cormorants, great blue herons, black-crowned night herons, common egrets. Dirt road access, liable to snow blockage.

Lower Klamath National Wildlife Refuge, California (21,459 *acres*) The first US refuge for waterfowl, established by Teddy Roosevelt in 1908; lake, marsh, and upland. The area dried out in 1921 but since 1942 the marshes have been artificially re-established and maintained. Has vast numbers of waterfowl and waterbirds, including three grebes (eared, western, pied billed). Paved road access.

Tule Lake National Wildlife Refuge, California (37,336 *acres*) Marsh and lake amid fertile grainfields. Grebes (eared, western, pied billed); together with Lower Klamath has the largest concentration of waterfowl in North America. Paved road access.

Clear Lake National Wildlife Refuge, California (33,440 *acres*) Open lake amid sagebush uplands; windy. White pelican (major US colony), pronghorn, sage grouse, California and ring-billed gulls, Caspian tern, cormorant, great blue heron.

🏳 Apart from birds mentioned above the following may be seen at any of the refuges, especially during the fall migrations: pintail, mallard, American widgeon, geese (white fronted, cackling, Ross, snow, Canada), many species of duck, shoveler, scaup, canvasback, blue-winged teal, cinnamon teal, and gadwall. Also hawks, owls, herons, rails, and shore birds.

🛏 Hotels and motels in Klamath Falls, Oregon, and hotels in Tulelake, California.

✈ Nearest airport at Klamath Falls from where there are surfaced roads to the refuge.

🚗 None of the internal roads is paved; always check with refuge HQ before starting a trip.

☼ Open all year; best time May–November.

▨ Free.

⇨ Refuge HQ, Box 74, Route 1, Tulelake, California 96134/ tel: (916) 667–2231.

Merced National Wildlife Refuge 2,562 acres of flat grasslands, marsh and slough areas in the Pacific Flyway. Wintering habitat for 100,000 geese (about 20,000 from the Arctic Circle) and 350,000 ducks daily. Near town of Merced. Refuge Manager, Box 854, Merced, California 95341. Best October to March.

Modoc National Wildlife Refuge 6,016 acres consisting of 3 tracts lying at the base of the beautiful Warner Mountains, being developed for nesting and migrating ducks and geese. Whistling swan, sandhill crane, white pelican. Bird list contains more than 100 species. Mule deer, pronghorn, bobcat, badger, skunk, ground squirrel, coyote. Swimming, boating, picnicking, ice skating. Near town of Alturas. Refuge Manager, PO Box 1439, Alturas, California 96101. Best September to November, April to June.

Sacramento National Wildlife Refuge 10,775 acres; all around 75 ft above sea level. Since prehistoric times the Sacramento valley has been the winter home of vast concentrations of waterfowl. With the coming of man and the confining of the river grew the need for this special refuge. One of its main functions is to provide cultivated feeding grounds that will keep the birds off the nearby farmland until after harvest. Three nearby refuges are Delevan (no visitors), Colusa (self-guided tours), and Sutter (limited visitor access).

- Pintail, mallard, American widgeon, teals (green-winged and cinnamon), shoveler, gadwall, ruddy duck, geese (cackling, Canada, Ross, snow, white fronted), whistling swan, coot, pied billed grebe, white pelican, great blue heron, egrets (common, snowy), black-crowned night heron, American bittern, common gallinule, dowitcher, greater yellowlegs, avocet, black-necked stilt, black tern, mourning dove, ring-necked pheasant, hawks, owls, and many songbirds. Mammals include muskrat, skunks (striped and spotted), raccoon, red fox, and jackrabbit.
- Motels 7 miles north, in Willows.
- On US 99-W. Nearest airport with scheduled flights at Sacramento, 75 miles southeast.
- A 5-mile self-guided tourist route is the only travel opportunity.
- Open all year; best time mid-October to early January, peak in mid-December, few birds in summer.
- 1 day.
- Free.
- Manager, Sacramento National Wildlife Refuge, Box 311, Route 1, Willows, California 95988/tel: (916) 934–4090.

San Luis National Wildlife Refuge 7,422 acres of marsh and grassland in the San Joaquin valley, providing refuge for 50,000 geese and 500,000 ducks: mallard, pintail, teal, widgeon. Also avocet, black-necked stilt, heron, egret. Skunk, raccoon, coyote. Photography. Near Los Banos. Refuge Manager, Box 2176, Los Banos, California 93635/tel: area code 209–826–3508. Best October to March.

Yosemite National Park 1,200 square miles; 2,000 to 13,000 ft above sea level. The Union Pacific Railroad had not even spanned the continent before some farsighted Americans realized that parts of the country ought to be preserved from exploitation in perpetuity. In 1864 the Yosemite valley and

Snow geese at Sacramento NWR, California (see facing page).

Mariposa Big Tree Grove (of giant sequoias) were granted to California – the first fruits of that realization. Thanks to it the Yosemite valley is today one of the most breathtaking sights in the world. Its sheer walls rise as high as 4,000 ft from the valley floor, their ragged silhouette of domes and peaks broken here and there by plunging waterfalls; the greatest fall is, of course, the Yosemite itself (2,425 ft). Away from the valley extends a wilderness of mountains, forests, and alpine uplands. In winter the park is popular with skiers.

Mule deer, black deer, black bear, more than 7 genera of squirrel including golden mantled ground squirrel, chipmunk, chicharee, and flying squirrel; many amphibians and reptiles. Birds include Steller's jay, black-headed grosbeak, acorn woodpecker, mountain quail, Clark's nutcracker, water dipper, rosy finch.

4 hotels, 4 lodges, 6 camps (5 in the High Sierra), and 1 set of housekeeping units; all vary as to standard of luxury, provision of meals, private baths, self-catering facilities, etc. All are operated by the Yosemite Park and Curry Co, which also offers pack, saddle, and hiking trips of varying lengths as well as all-inclusive guided tours; full details in their 12-page leaflet. Reservations should be made several months in advance. There are public camp-grounds with running water and ablutions, operated on a first come first served basis; only Camp 4, Yosemite Valley, is open all year. There is room for trailers (caravans) but no utilities for them. Camping is permitted only at designated sites. Maximum stay 14 days; 7 days in places. May 5 to September 15.

North from Fresno on Highway 41; east from Merced on Highway 140; east from Stockton on Highway 120 or west from Lee Vining on the same highway. The northern borders of the park abut onto the Stanislaus and Toiyabe national forests.

200 miles of motor road (from which cars may not stray). 700 miles of foot and horse trail. Ski trails in winter. Many filling stations and 20 repair garages.

Whitetail deer at Half Dome in Yosemite NP, California.

☼ Open all year (Glacier Point and area north of Yosemite valley closed in winter); best time spring and late September if you want to avoid the crowds. Winter sports and ski trails at Badger Pass, mid-December to mid-April.

🕐 3–14 days.

✉ $1 per car and occupants per day; or 50c per individual hiker, rider, party tourist.

☞ There is a comprehensive programme of naturalist guided walks, camp-fire programmes, junior rangers, and audio-visual orientation; details are posted on camp bulletin boards and at visitor center.

👁 Giant sequoia groves at Mariposa Grove, Tulomne, and Merced Flat; Pioneer Yosemite History Center at Wawona; largest sub-alpine meadow in high sierra at Tuolumne Meadows; El Portal museum.

⇨ Superintendent, Yosemite National Park, Box 577, Yosemite Village, California 95389.

Hawaii

Haleakala National Park The crater of a dormant volcano $2\frac{1}{2}$ miles wide, $7\frac{1}{2}$ miles long (21 miles round); from 10,000 ft down to sea level. Delicate instruments show that internal adjustments are still happening, but the crater's last volcanic activity was probably several hundred years ago. There is an endless variety of volcanic rock, streaked with ancient flows of black, grey, yellow, and red lava in every stage of erosion.

🐦 Native birds include the golden plover, apapane, iiwi, amakihi, mavii nukupuu (once believed to be extinct), and the reintroduced nene (Hawaiian goose). Species introduced to Hawaii include pheasant, chukar, and skylark. Among introduced mammals are mongoose, goat, and wild pig.

🌿 Silversword plant (unique to the island, except where its seed has been planted). In the rainforest of the recently incorporated Kipahulu Valley, which plunges down to the Pacific, you will find greensword.

🖐 3 cabins, accessible only on foot or horseback; each sleeps 12; free, including blankets, water, firewood, stove, and lamp. Otherwise no overnight accommodation, meals, groceries, filling or service stations within the park. Bookings in advance via the superintendent. Camp-ground and shelters with fireplace, barbecue grills, water, and short nature trail at Grove, near park entrance.

🛬 By plane or ship from Honolulu; 26 miles from Kahului airport via highways 37, 377, and 378. Commercial tours and rented cars from Kahului or Wailuku. Be sure tank is full.

🚐 A motor-road winds through the west of the park, outside the crater. From it run 30 miles of well-marked foot trail, forming a network across the crater floor and linking the cabins. This makes it possible to plan trips lasting from 6 hrs to 4 days. For details of guided horseback trips, contact the superintendent.

☀ Open all year; best time all summer (winters are wet, windy, and cool with occasional snow above 8,000 ft.

✉ By permit only; available on the spot. Minimum 3 hrs, maximum 7 days.

➡ Superintendent, Box 456, Kahului, Maui, Hawaii.

Hawaii Volcanoes National Park 344 sq miles; from coast to 13,680 ft above sea level. The park centres around the still active and spectacular volcano systems of Mauna Loa and Kilauea. Hawaiian lavas are very hot and fluid; they flow up to 20 miles before congealing. So there are no steep, conical mountains here. The land is formed of a succession of eruptions and flows reaching back over millions of years.

🐗 Feral pig, goat, mongoose, native bats and rats. Birds include nene goose, apapane, amakihi, elepaio, iiwi, koae, golden plover, kolea, Hawaiian hawk, pueo, Japanese pheasant, chukar, California quail, and many non-native birds.

🜨 The northeastern slopes of the volcanoes get most of the rainfall. From the crater-rim drive you can see where the rainshadow begins, as lush jungle gives way to sparse semi-desert. Here and there kipukas (islands of ancient soil, untouched by recent flows) support meadows and dense clumps of native trees – koa, ohia, soapberry, kolea, and mamani. The bird park has 40 varieties of native trees.

🖐 Volcano House (hotel) on the rim of Kilauea crater; rates and bookings via Hawaii Volcanoes National Park, Hawaii 96718. The same company operates low-cost cabins. On Mauna Loa there is an overnight resthouse at 10,000 ft and one at the summit – 3 days of arduous climbing; permission from park HQ. The park service maintains 3 camp-grounds: at Kamoamoa (28 miles southeast of HQ), at Kipukanene (12 miles south of HQ), and at Namakani Palo (3 miles west of HQ); open all year.

🛬 Many scheduled daily flights from Honolulu to Hilo (30 road miles away) or Kona (90 road miles). Cars can be rented at both airports.

🚐 18 miles of motor road link the main sites. Many horse and foot trails – but check with rangers or HQ. There is a filling station near the park and a service station 21 miles away.

☀ Open all year; best time all summer, but warm clothing essential for hikers to the summit.

🕐 Half-day–14 days.

Hawaiian nene geese, saved from extinction by Wildfowl Trust (p348).

✉ $1 for car and occupants; or 50c per individual hiker, rider, party tourist.

📖 Full list of publications on natural history of park from Hawaii Natural History Association Ltd, Hawaii Volcanoes National Park, Hawaii 96718.

👁 Museum at park HQ for natural history (daily lectures and shows); museum at Wahaula visitor center for local human history.

➡ Superintendent, Hawaii Volcanoes National Park, Hawaii 96718.

Oregon

Cape Arago State Park 134 acres near sea level. A high promontory projecting $\frac{1}{2}$ mile into the ocean, with fine views of the rocks and waves. Sea lion and common coastal vegetation. 41 picnic sites; no accommodation in park. 12 miles southwest of North Bend on Cape Arago Highway.

Cape Lookout State Park 1,946 acres near sea level. Sand dunes and headland projecting $1\frac{1}{2}$ miles into the ocean. Bear, deer, and other forest mammals, as well as 154 bird species, have all been recorded here – though ornithologists are more likely to notice the variety than is the casual visitor. A numbered nature trail identifies much of the flora, including twinberry, Oregon crabapple, red huckleberry, ferns, conifers, skunk cabbage, and western redcedar. 53 trailer sites ($3), 193 tent sites ($2), 140 picnic sites; open all year. 12 miles south of Tillamook off US 101.

Cove Palisades State Park 4,119 acres; around 1,750 ft above sea level. Located on Lake Billy Chinook in an area of great geological interest. Mule deer. Juniper sagebrush. 87 trailer sites ($3), 94 tent sites ($2), 97 picnic sites. 5 miles west of Culver off US 97.

Crater Lake National Park 250 square miles; 4,824 to 8,926 ft above sea level. In geologically recent times a vast lava plateau that covered much of the far west spawned a series of volcanic peaks; today they form part of the Cascade range. Among the most imposing was Mt Mazama. Later, while streams and glaciers were scoring the mountain's flanks, its molten core drained off through underground fissures, leaving its peak unsupported. It collapsed, forming a caldera slightly over 5 miles east–west, slightly under 5 miles north–south. A final volcanic spurt created a small cone near the western end; the rest is now a tranquil lake: Crater Lake. Its waters are so clear that mosses find enough light to grow over 400 ft below its surface. The entire park is an area of bluffs, creeks, ridges, cones, craters, and springs.

Squirrel, chipmunk, porcupine, yellow-bellied marmot, pika, badger, beaver, coyote, bobcat, mountain lion, fox, black bear, black-tailed deer, mule deer; over 160 bird species include eagles, peregrine falcon, Clark's nutcracker, ravens and many waterfowl.

570 species of trees, flowering plants, and ferns. Trees include fir, pine, quaking aspen, black cottonwood, green-leaf manzanita, and storm-twisted hemlock.

Lodge and cabins at Rim Village; open 15 June to 10 September; rates from $5.50. Reservations through Superintendent. Unbookable camp-sites with space (but no utility connections) for trailers (caravans); open approx 1 June to 15 October, depending on weather; rates subject to change.

From west: US 99, 199, and 101 connect with Oregon 62 and Medford, 69 miles from the park. From south: US 97 connects with Oregon 62 and Klamath Falls, 46 miles from the park. From north: US 97 connects with Oregon 138 and Diamond Lake and Bend – respectively 6 and 92 miles from the park. The north entrance is closed from first heavy snow to mid-June. It is 92 miles SW of Bend via US 97 and Oregon 138 and about 125 miles from Eugene via Interstate 5, Oregon 58, and US 97. From mid-June to mid-September buses of Crater Lake Lodge operate daily from Medford and Klamath Falls. Klamath Falls is served by rail; both towns by air and by transcontinental buses.

Scheduled bus and launch trips around and in the crater. The rim road and its spurs are open only between July and end-September (approx.). Plentiful trails – but, as in all volcanic regions, foothold away from the trails can be treacherous.

Open all year, best time July and August, when weather is like spring at lower altitudes.

2–7 days.

$1 per car and occupants per day; or 50c per hiker, rider, party tourist.

Uniformed park naturalists conduct scheduled park tours.

Superintendent, Crater Lake National Park, Box 7, Crater Lake, Oregon 97604.

Ecola State Park 1,172 acres; near sea level. A rugged coastal park with slide areas, hiking trails, and 2 bathing beaches. Sea lion, elk, deer; common coastal vegetation. 68 picnic sites. 2 miles north of Cannon Beach off US 101.

Hart Mountain National Antelope Refuge 240,824 acres of scenic mountains with aspen groves and desert range of sage bush, juniper, and grass providing fawning grounds, summer and winter habitat for pronghorn, mule deer. Goshawk, mountain bluebird, chickadee, grosbeak. Mammals include mountain goat. Camping facilities. Nearest town is Lakeview. Refuge Manager, Sheldon-Hart Mountain National Antelope Refuges, Box 111, Lakeview, Oregon 97630. Best May to October.

Malheur National Wildlife Refuge 180,795 acres of marshes, meadows, shallow lakes surrounded by sagebrush, juniper uplands. Habitat for nesting and migrating waterfowl (gadwall, teal, redhead and ruddy duck, mallard) and marsh birds including sandhill crane. 51 species of mammals including muskrat, antelope, coyote. Natural Museum, photography. Hotel accommodation at Frenchglen, Oregon. Refuge Manager, Box 113, Burns, Oregon 97720. Best May to November.

Saddle Mountain State Park 3,054 acres; around 1,600 ft above sea level. The second highest mountain in the coastal range. Chief wildlife interest is elk (albino specimens reported); plants include ferns, pines, willows, maples, cypress, lilies, stonecrops, saxifrages, wild roses, honeysuckle, valerian, and sunflowers among many wildflowers. 6 tent sites ($1) May to October. 8 miles northeast of Necanicum Junction off US 26.

Silver Falls State Park 8,259 acres; about 1,400 ft above sea level. Oregon's largest state park, with 14 scenic waterfalls (several over 100 ft) and many hiking trails. Black-tailed deer and grey squirrel among many forest and woodland mammals and birds; Douglas fir, western hemlock, western red cedar, grand fir, western yew, black cottonwood, quaking aspen, maples, elders, and many flowering shrubs. 61 tent sites ($2) mid-April to October, 370 picnic sites. 26 miles east of Salem on Oregon 214.

Tugman State Park 480 acres near sea level. Located on a coastal lake. Elk, deer. 40 picnic sites. 19 miles north of Coos on US 101.

William L. Finley National Wildlife Refuge 5,370 acres in the rich Willamette Valley. Concentrates on protecting the rare dusky Canada goose. Other bird species include wood duck, hooded merganser, mourning dove, pheasant, grouse. Black-tailed deer. Near Corvallis. Refuge Manager, Route 2, Box 208, Corvallis, Oregon 97330. Best March to December.

California sea lion and cormorants on an island off the Oregon coast.

Washington

Columbia National Wildlife Refuge 27,700 acres in arid central Washington state, consisting of eroded and channeled basalt scablands. Irrigation has introduced water into 135 deep lakes and shallow sloughs, now excellent habitat for abundant fauna. 155 species of birdlife include pied-billed grebe, mallard, marsh hawk, chukar, loon. Near town of Othello. Refuge Manager, PQ Drawer B, Othello, Washington 99344. Best April to November.

Mount Rainier National Park 378 square miles; 1,700 to 14,410 ft above sea level. Most of the park, between 2,000 and 6,000 ft, consists of broad meadows interspersed with dense stands of forest timber. At the centre, its flanks scored with 41 named glaciers, stands the ragged cone of Mt Rainier, a dormant volcano and the greatest single-peak glacier system in the US.

⌑ Mule deer, elk, black bear, mountain goat, raccoon, squirrel, chipmunk, porcupine, snowshoe hare, beaver, marmot, marten, red fox, coyote, bobcat, cougar; 130 bird species include white-tailed ptarmigan, pipits, finches, gray jay, Clark's nutcracker, mountain bluebird, raven, woodpeckers, robin, warblers, thrushes, kinglet, chickadee.

❀ Among wildflowers for which the park is famous: Pacific trillium, bunchberry dogwood, three-leaf anemone, calypso, avalanche fawnlily, glacier lily, western pasqueflower, marsh marigold, mountain buttercup, Indian paintbrush lupines, speedwell, valerian, American bistort, cinquefoil; trees include Douglas fir, western hemlock, western redcedar.

⌂ National Park Inn at Longmire (May to October) and Paradise Inn at Paradise (late June to Labor Day); rates from $7–11. Reservations to Rainier National Park Co, Box 1136, Tacoma, Washington 98401. Major camp-grounds, not bookable, at Longmire, Cougar Rock, Paradise, Ohanapecosh, White River, and Sunrise; smaller grounds at Tahoma Creek (no piped water), Sunshine Point, Mowich Lake, and Ipsut Creek; rates subject to change.

From Portland you can reach the southeastern entrance via White Pass (59 miles). Four entrances are between 40 and 58 miles from Tacoma. The east-central and southeastern entrances are 66 to 68 miles from Yakima. All but 2 of these entrances are summer only. Tacoma has rail and air services.

Paved or gravel roads reach most of the camps and visitor centers but do not quite circle the park. More than 300 miles of well-marked trails ring the mountain. The Wonderland Trail is a 90-mile, 10-day hike right around the mountain; you can arrange to be met at each camp-ground with a fresh day's supplies, so all you need carry is a tent and cooking and sleeping gear. Since the trail crosses paved roads at many places, you can also use the trail for short car-based hikes. Guided walks and hikes at Longmire, Ohanapecosh, Sunrise, Ipsut Creek, and Box Canyon.

Open all year; best time July to mid-September.

2–12 days.

$1 per car and occupants; or 50c per individual hiker, rider, party tourist.

Mountain guides, instructors, and equipment available only at Paradise.

Superintendent, Mount Rainier National Park, Longmire, Washington State 98397.

Olympic National Park 1,400 square miles; between sea level and 7,965 ft above. The park is almost a microcosm of the northwestern US. Its Pacific-facing side gets more than 140 inches of precipitation each year; the inland side is as dry as southern California; and between the two you can find the whole geoclimatic cycle – mountains, rainforests of conifers, glaciers, lakes, streams, and wildlife ranging from inhabitants of the foreshore to dwellers above the timberline.

Among 56 species of wild mammals the most visible are: Olympic elk (at 6,000 head the largest remaining herd in the country), black-tailed deer, Olympic marmot, black bear. In summer there are some 140 bird species in the park.

Sitka spruce, western hemlock, Douglas fir, western red-cedar, and numerous wildflowers – especially on the north-eastern side.

Concessioner-operated cabins and lodges at Sol Duc Hot Springs and Lake Crescent (both in the northern part of the park); bookings via National Concessioner Inc, Star Route, Box 9, Port Angeles, Washington 98362; at La Push, on the coast, bookings via Louis L. and/or Helen M. Perkins, La Push, Washington 98350; at Kalaloch, also on the north coast, bookings via Beckers Ocean Resort Inc, Clearwater, Washington 98399 and Carl G. and Isabel Hansen, Route 1, Box 416, Port Angeles, Washington 98362. Rates from $6–17.

The Olympic peninsula has about 3 dozen camp-grounds, most of them in the park; rates subject to change.

Only a handful can take trailers (caravans) but there are no

utility connections. There is a trailer village, with all facilities, on the north of Lake Crescent. Some of the lower-
altitude camp-grounds are open all year.

US 101 circles the peninsula and puts a dozen spurs into the
park; direct access via Olympia and Aberdeen; ferry access
between Victoria (British Columbia) and Port Angeles;
Keystone and Port Townsend; and Seattle and Bremerton.
Daily flights between Seattle–Tacoma and Port Angeles.

Several gravel and paved roads penetrate the park as far as
the camp-grounds and lodges; but most of the trails – some
600 miles of them – are for foot and horse traffic. Consult
rangers or HQ before undertaking anything more than a
short stroll.

Open all year (in part); best time summer and early autumn,
skiing at Hurricane Ridge, late December to March, beaches
remain popular in winter.

3–12 days.

$1 per car and occupants; or 50c per individual hiker, rider,
party tourist.

Summer guided tours offered by Gray Line of the Olympics,
107 E Front, Port Angeles, Washington 98362.

Superintendent, 600 East Park Avenue, Port Angeles,
Washington State 98362.

Ridgefield National Wildlife Refuge 2,483 acres already acquired out of proposed 6,100 acreage; on Columbia River
flood plain, with pastures, shallow marshes for wintering
Canada goose and widgeon. Hawks, coot, blue herons,
killdeer. Photography. Near town of Ridgefield. Refuge
Manager, Box 476, Ridgefield, Washington 98642. Best
March to November.

Turnbull National Wildlife Refuge 17,171 acres of ponds and
marshes with adjacent uplands, on the lava plains of the
Columbia plateau. Primarily a waterfowl habitat, between
5,000 and 6,000 young produced each season. Also the rare
trumpeter swan. Shore and upland birds include ring-necked
pheasant, California quail. Whitetail deer, mule deer, beaver,
coyote, raccoon. Photography, picnicking. Near Cheney.
Refuge Manager, Route 3, Box 107, Cheney, Washington
99004. Best May to October.

Willapa National Wildlife Refuge 9,600 acres on Leadbetter
Point on Long Beach Peninsula, and adjacent mainland of
Willapa Bay. One of the finest salt marshes in the northwest,
which together with the Bay's eelgrass attracts wintering
Pacific black brant and Canada goose. Also shore birds,
grouse, bear, bobcat, deer. Camp-grounds, picnicking. Near
Ilwaco. Refuge Manager, Ilwaco, Washington 98624. Best
March to December.

USA : Mountain States

Colorado

Monte Vista National Wildlife Refuge 13,547 acres around 7,500 ft above sea level – though the surrounding mountains rise above 14,000 ft. This part of Colorado is richly furnished with artesian wells, which have been used within the refuge to create more than 230 small ponds and lakes. The main aim has been to provide habitat for nesting water birds and upland game as well as food and cover for the waterfowl that overwinter here.

- Mallard, gadwall, pintail, widgeon, ruddy duck, blue-winged teal, green-winged teal, cinnamon teal, redhead. Ring-necked pheasant, mourning dove, sandhill crane, avocet, Wilson's phalarope, common snipe, American bittern, black-crowned night heron, great horned owl, marsh hawk, magpie, golden and bald eagles. Mammals include muskrats, skunks, rabbit, coyote, bobcat, badger, weasel.

- Four-fifths of the refuge is wet grassland, sedges and rushes; greasewood on higher ground.

- None within refuge. Hotels and motels in Monte Vista.

- 6 miles south of Monte Vista on Colorado 15.

- One all-weather loop road for cars; closed during hunting season between October and November; elsewhere on foot.

- Open all year; best time November to December for bird-watchers; for general interest April to July.

- 1–2 days.

- Free.

- Refuge Manager, Monte Vista National Wildlife Refuge, Box 511, Monte Vista, Colorado 81144/tel: (303) 852–2934.

Idaho

Camas National Wildlife Refuge 10,535 acres on the lower reaches of Camas Creek. Many wild meadows provide habitat for 155 species of birds including ducks, geese, eagles, hawks, owls, herons, white pelican. Pronghorn, deer, elk, moose, beaver, muskrat, rabbits. Food and lodging in villages of Hamer, Dubois and Roberts, Idaho. Refuge Manager, Hamer, Idaho. Best April to November.

Deer Flat National Wildlife Refuge 11,566 acres two-thirds covered by Lake Lowell, a haven for 750,000 migrating and wintering ducks and geese. Shorebirds include heron, grebe, avocet, pelican, egret. Mule deer, coyote, beaver, porcupine. Limited camping and recreation. Nearest town Nampa. Refuge Manager, Route 1, Box 335, Nampa, Idaho 36581. Best March to May and November.

Minidoka National Wildlife Refuge 25,630 acres along Snake River, includes all of Lake Walcott. Spectacular concentrations of waterfowl during migration periods: geese, mallard, canvasback, ruddy duck. Over 100 species of songbird, also bald eagle, golden eagle, hawks, owls. Mammals include mule deer, pronghorn, bobcat, coyote, marmot. Camping, picnicking, boating. Nearest town is Rupert. Refuge Manager, Route 4, Rupert, Idaho 83350. Best March to November.

Montana

Benton Lake National Refuge 240 square miles of restored prairie marsh and native grasslands. A migration stopover for mallard, teal, pintail, shoveler. Much variety of shore birds. Pronghorn antelope, mule and whitetail deer. Near Great Falls. No facilities provided. Refuge Manager, PO Box 2624, Great Falls, Montana 59401. Best May to October.

Bowdoin National Wildlife Refuge 15,436 acres; about 2,200 ft above sea level. Most of the refuge is taken up with 4 large lakes whose levels are now artificially stabilized, allowing them to support more wildlife than ever before; species, both in variety and absolute numbers, are on the increase. The region is semi-arid, with an average 12 in. annual rainfall. Summer temperatures reach 100°F; winter temperatures can go as low as minus 50°!

⚐ Primary protected species are Canada goose, mallard, pintail, gadwall, American widgeon, blue-winged teal, shoveler, ruddy duck, redhead, canvasback, white pelican, great blue heron, double-crested cormorant, sage grouse. Other visitors include California gull, ring-billed gull, Franklin's gull, black tern, common tern, coot, eared grebe, sora, American bittern, common snipe, yellowleg, dowitcher, ring-neck pheasant, gray partridge, sharp-tailed grouse, yellow warbler, Bullock's oriole, blue grosbeak, redstart. Mammals include mule deer, whitetail deer, elk, pronghorn antelope, muskrat, mink, beaver, coyote, bobcat, badger, skunk, weasel, ground squirrel, jackrabbit, cottontail.

⛩ Hotels and motels in Malta (7½ miles away) or at the American Legion Health Plunge (12 miles).

✈ Highway 2 borders the northwest of the refuge; it links Malta with Saco, which is 20 miles east.

🚐 A single patrol road takes in most of every lakeshore; check with the manager before you set out for the refuge.

☼ Open all year; best time late March to October (rearing season May to July, migratory congregations September to October).

🕐 One day.

✉ Free.

🎫 Not needed.

⇨ Refuge Manager, Bowdoin National Wildlife Refuge, Box J, Malta, Montana. 59538/tel: (406) 654–2863.

Charles M. Russell National Wildlife Range one million acres of prairie, forested coulees, badlands, river bottoms along 125 miles of the Missouri River. Habitat for migrating waterfowl and many endangered species of birds and mammals. Buffalo, elk, deer, pronghorn, bears, wolf, mountain lion, coyote. Camping, picnicking, boating, swimming. Hotel and restaurant accommodations at Fort Peck, Glasgow, Malta, Lewistown and Jordan, Montana. Refuge Manager, Box 110, Lewistown, Montana 59475. Best May to October.

Glacier National Park 1,600 square miles; 3,210 to 10,169 ft above sea level. Glacier is the US section of the Waterton Glacier International Peace Park, which lies across the US–Canada border. It contains over 40 glaciers. In places the terrain is open and park-like, but most of the region is steeply mountainous with wide, glacier-rounded valleys, some of them lake-filled.

Mountain goat, bighorn, black and grizzly bears (dangerous), marmot, squirrels, chipmunk, coyote, porcupine, snowshoe hare, beaver, deer, moose, American elk, marten, wolverine, wolf, otter, northern bog lemming. Among 216 bird species are Lewis's woodpecker, finch, pipit, hawks, eagles, grouse, water ouzel, Clark's nutcracker, osprey, ptarmigan, warblers, nuthatches.

The park has over 1,000 species of trees and wildflowers, among them: beargrass, glacier lily, Indian paintbrush, brown-eyed susan, American false hellebore, western pasque flower, western thimbleberry, cowparsnip, red baneberry, Sitka mountain ash, bearberry, fireweed, aster, fleabane, huckleberry, bearberry honeysuckle, lodgepole pine, Douglas fir, western red cedar, western larch, pines, juniper, black cottonwood, quaking aspen, alder, birch, willow, black hawthorn, pin cherry, common chokeberry, douglas maple.

Glacier Park Inc (May 15 to September 15 at East Glacier Park, Montana 59434; September 15 to May 15, 149 North Stone Avenue, Tucson, Arizona 85701) operate hotels, motels, and cabins (also all-inclusive tours); open mid-June to mid-September; rates from $5; reservation necessary. B. Ross Ludwig, Box 157, Martin City, Montana 59926, operates two chalets accessible only to hikers and riders; open July 1 to Labor Day (1st Monday in September); rates from $4.50. There are 8 large and 9 small public campgrounds, all with fireplaces, tables, and ablutions; 14-day time limit June–September. Rates subject to change.

Glacier is on US 2 and 89 and near US 91 and 93; inquire locally about snow in high passes until June and from September. The Great Northern Railway's main transcontinental line skirts the south of the park; park buses meet the trains. Park buses run from Kalispell, west of the park, and Great Falls, south of it; they also connect with Canadian Greyhound lines from Lethbridge and Ft Macleod. West Coast Airlines serves Flathead County Airport (26 miles from the park) from Spokane and Great Falls; park transport will meet by prior arrangement. Rental cars also by prior arrangement.

One paved road, from West Glacier to St Mary, runs through the centre of the park. Other motor roads circle most of its perimeter, giving rise to short spurs and foot trails. The park has over 1,000 miles of foot and horse trails; trips on them range from short walks to extended overnight trips guided by ranger-naturalists. There is a regular launch service on many of the lakes and rivers. Rental rowboats are available at several sites. Private motorboats are restricted to certain lakes.

Open June 15 to September 15 (to motorists early June

to October 15); best time mid-June to mid-September.

🕐 1–14 days.

✉ $1 per car and occupants per day; or 50c per individual hiker, rider or party tourist.

🗎 Detailed *topographic map* for planning hikes; *Guide to Glacier National Park* by G. C. Ruhle, *The Geologic Story of Glacier National Park* by J. L. Dyson, *Mammals of Glacier Park* by R. R. Lechleitner, *Trees and Forests of Glacier National Park* by D. H. Robinson, *101 Wildflowers of Glacier National Park* by G. W. Sharpe; all on sale in park, or write for full brochure to Glacier Natural History Association, West Glacier, Montana 59936.

⇨ The Superintendent, West Glacier, Montana 59936.

Medicine Lake National Wildlife Refuge 31,457 acres; 1,940 ft above sea level. A waterfowl refuge in the central flyway and an important breeding ground for many water and shore birds. More than half the refuge is put down to pasture and meadow; and about 1,000 acres are cultivated to provide winter feed for this and other refuges. The remainder is taken up by lakes and ponds – including Medicine Lake (8,700 acres) and Homestead Lake (1,280 acres in a separate tract).

🐦 Nesting begins at the end of the thaw, usually late March, and goes on until August; Canada goose, mallards, gadwall, pintail, blue-winged teal, American widgeon, shoveler, redhead, ruddy duck, canvasback. Island nesters from early summer: double-crested cormorant, white pelican, great blue heron, California and ring-billed gulls, common tern. Land and shorebirds: ring-necked pheasant, gray partridge, sharp-tailed grouse (2 dancing grounds in Sand Hills unit), sandhill crane, whooping crane (rare), burrowing owl, Sprague's pipit, lark bunting, Baird's and Le Conte's sparrows, chestnut-collared and McCown's longspurs. Mammals include pronghorn, whitetail deer, mule deer, muskrat, striped skunk, badger, ground squirrel, beaver, porcupine.

🦂 Native grasses, prairie rose, snowberry, chokeberry, buffalo berry, silver berry, sage. Trees (along streams only) include box elder, cottonwood, ash, poplar. Plantations of juniper, Russian olive, caragana.

🛏 None in refuge; motels in the town of Medicine Lake, near its border. There is a recreation area for boating, swimming, and water skiing; it has bath house, earth closets, fireplaces, and tables.

⇨ The HQ is 2 miles east of State Highway 16, 1 mile south of Medicine Lake township. There is an airstrip for light aircraft; no scheduled flights.

🚐 A network of patrol roads and foot tracks crosses the refuge. Individual lengths, however, may be opened or closed at short notice; always check with refuge HQ before entering.

☀ Open all year but winter temperatures in the −50° range have been recorded; strong winds are possible at any time of year; best time May to October.

🕐 1–3 days.

✉ Free.

🗎 Complete birdlist available.

⇨ Refuge Manager, Medicine Lake, Montana 59247/tel: (406) 789–2305.

National Bison Range Nearly 19,000 acres; 3,000 to 4,500 ft above sea level. The refuge was established in 1908 to help save the American bison from extinction. The terrain, which varies from park-like grassland with stands of timber to steep hills and narrow canyons, can support between 300 and 500 bison.

↗   Bison, elk, mule deer, whitetail deer, bighorn sheep, pronghorn, badger, beaver, muskrat, weasel, bobcat, coyote, black bear (occasional visitor), yellowbelly marmot, Columbian ground squirrel, mountain cottontail. Birds include ring-necked pheasant, chukar, grey partridge, blue and ruffed grouse; migratory waterfowl in season.

☘   Bitterroot, paintbrush, clarkia, penstemons, balsamroot, lupine, larkspur, yellowbell, asters, clematis, serviceberry, chokeberry, mockorange, wild rose. The range is noted for the May to June wildflower season.

🛏   None within the range. Nearby motels along US 93.

↱   US 93 and US 10A skirt the borders of the park. On US 10A turn north a mile east of Dixon and take Montana 212 for 5 miles to the HQ at Moiese. Coming from the north on US 93 take Montana 212 about 5 miles south of Ronan and drive 14 miles to the HQ. Nearest air service at Missovla, 50 miles south.

🚗   A self-guiding, 19-mile, automobile round tour through part of the range is available 1 June to 30 September. For organized groups special tours can be arranged in advance. Otherwise visitors are restricted from the open range – a safety measure in their own interest. There is always a display herd in corrals near HQ.

☀   Some roads are open all year, with lower parts of refuge snow-free; best time June to September.

🕐   1–2 days.

💲 $1 per car and occupants for tour route.

➩   Refuge Manager, National Bison Range, Moiese, Montana 59824/tel: (406) 644–2955.

Ninepipe and Pablo National Wildlife Refuge 2,000 acres of water, marsh and upland grass superimposed on Indian irrigation reservoirs in the Flathead Valley. Habitat for 200,000 resting and nesting waterfowl: Canada goose, mallard, redhead, teal, coot, ruddy duck. Mammals include field mouse, muskrat, skunk, badger, porcupine. Picnicking, photography. Nearest towns Moiese and St Ignatius, Montana. Refuge Manager, National Bison Range, Moiese, Montana 59824. Best May to October.

Ravalli National Wildlife Refuge 2,283 acres of the Bitterroot Valley, patches of timber – ponderosa pine, cottonwood – marsh and uplands. Waterfowl refuge, also 163 other bird species including mountain bluebird, hummingbird, blue herons, golden eagle. Near Stevensville. Refuge Manager, 5 Third Street, Stevensville, Montana 59870. Best June to September.

Bison cows and calves. Around the year 1800 there were over 60 million bison in North America; 90 years later there were just 541. Today their numbers have climbed back to over 20,000 – all in reserves.

Red Rock Lakes National Wildlife Refuge 40,223 acres; 6,600 to 10,000 ft above sea level. The refuge lies at the eastern end of the Centennial Valley, near the sources of the Missouri River. To its south and east rise the spectacular walls of the Centennial Mountains; to its north are the foothills of the Gravelly Range. Here in this mountain fastness is the solitude necessary to the trumpeter swan – the species that this refuge was established in order to protect. Snow, melting in these same ranges, also provides the water for the 14,000 acres of marshes and lakes in the refuge.

Trumpeter swan (350-odd – nearly half the population south of the Canadian border); most of the species listed under Medicine Lake National Wildlife refuge are also found here – as well as willet, avocet, and long-billed curlew.

Alpine and sub-alpine flowers bloom in succession throughout spring and summer; best known are windflower, sticky geranium, lupine, and locoweeds.

None within refuge; hotels and motels at Monida, 30 miles west, and West Yellowstone, 30 miles east.

Turn off US 91 at Monida and drive east 30 miles over dirt road; between about 15 May and 1 November you can drive west from West Yellowstone on Montana 191; make local inquiry before attempting either road at any season. Nearest railhead at Monida. No commercial airfield within 150 miles.

A few stretches of patrol track cross parts of the park, most of which is traversible on foot. Access to the areas where the swans nest is restricted.

Roads are snow-free May to October.

1–2 days.

Free.

Refuge Manager, Red Rock Lakes National Wildlife Refuge, Lima, Montana 59739/tel: (406) 276–3347.

113

Nevada

Charles Sheldon National Antelope Refuge 578,109 acres of desert badlands and rolling hills providing habitat for sage grouse, small numbers of waterfowl and shorebirds. Hawks, eagles, owls are common. Pronghorn, mule deer. Camping at designated areas. Visitors should carry extra supplies of food, petrol. Nearest town is Lakeview. Refuge Manager, Federal Building, Lakeview, Oregon. Best June to October.

Desert National Wildlife Range 1,588,379 acres of wilderness where vegetation varies greatly with elevation. Habitat for desert bighorn, mule deer, coyote, bobcat, mountain lion. Migratory and desert birds, hawks. Primitive outdoor recreation. Nearest centre is Las Vegas. Refuge Manager, 1500 North Decatur Boulevard, Las Vegas, Nevada 89108. Best April to November.

Ruby Lake National Wildlife Refuge 37,191 acres of marsh, lake and sagebrush within a hydrologically closed basin. Habitat for trumpeter swan, Canada goose, ducks, sandhill crane, many shore birds including sage grouse. Photography, picnicking. Nearest town Elko, Nevada. Refuge Manager, Ruby Valley, Nevada 89833. Best June to September.

Stillwater National Wildlife Management Area 143,866 acres including a 24,000-acre sanctuary. Alkaline desert land receives water from Newlands Irrigation Project to make 35,000 acres of marsh and ponds, resting and feeding habitat for shore birds, marsh birds and waterfowl: 250,000 ducks, 10,000 geese, 13,000 whistling swan visit annually. Limited camping, boating, photography. Near town of Fallon. Refuge Manager, Box 592, Fallon, Nevada 89406. Best April to November.

Utah

Bear River Migratory Bird Refuge 64,895 acres; 4,200 ft above sea level; surrounding mountains rise abruptly to nearly 10,000 ft. The refuge, sited at the point where the Bear river empties into Utah's Great Salt Lake, is one of the great waterfowl areas of North America and one of the few surviving marsh regions where waterfowl nest in something like their primeval numbers.

Canada goose, gadwall, cinnamon teal, mallard, pintail, redhead, snowy egret, great blue and black-crowned night herons, white-faced ibis, western grebe, yellow-headed blackbird, American avocet, black-necked stilt, long-billed curlew, Wilson's phalarope, Franklin's gull, ruddy duck, green-winged teal, American widgeon, shoveler, canvasback, bufflehead, goldeneye, whistling swan, double-crested cormorant, white pelican, killdeer, Forster's tern, black tern, marsh hawk, willet.

⊨ Hotels and motels at Brigham City.

⇥ By paved road from Brigham City; gates open 8am to 4.30pm. Registration at HQ obligatory.

🚗 You can drive 12 miles around Unit 2, on a gravel road atop the dykes that distribute the river waters; this road is closed during the hunting season, October to December. There are several foot trails around HQ.

⚜ Open all year; best time March to December.

⊕ 1–2 days.

⇨ Refuge Manager, Bear River Migratory Bird Refuge, Box 548, Brigham City, Utah 84302/tel: (801) 723–3577.

Bryce Canyon National Park 56 square miles; 6,600 to 9,105 ft above sea level. Bluffs, gorges, and canyons filled with giant, eroded lipsticks the size of cathedral spires and running the gamut from near-carmine to near-white. Like the higher reaches of the Grand Canyon, 80 miles away to the south, Bryce Canyon embraces several climatic regions, omitting only the low and high desert. At 9,000 ft you may notice slight altitude symptoms.

🐿 Chipmunk, deer, porcupine, golden-mantled ground squirrel, marmot; swallow, white-throated swift, mountain bluebird, Steller's jay, Clark's nutcracker, hummingbird, raven.

🌿 Trees include those listed for the upper regions of Grand Canyon; wildflowers include blue columbine, twinpod, goldenweed, evening primrose, blue flax, painted cup, skyrocket gilia, western yarrow, blue penstemon, segolily mariposa, sagebrush.

⊨ Cabins at the Lodge and Inn on the rim of Bryce amphitheatre, June 7 to September 8; rates from $6–11; reservations through Utah Parks Co, Cedar City, Utah 84720. Non-reservable camp sites (14-day limit per calendar year) from Easter week to November 15. The inn and store near the north camp-ground contain a cafeteria and small shop; open approximately June 10 to Labor Day (1st Monday in September).

⇥ By Utah 12 from US 89. By Union Pacific Railway to Lund for connection with park buses. Main buslines from Salt Lake City and Los Angeles to Cedar City for connection with park buses. Bonanza Airlines from Phoenix to Cedar City, connecting with Salt Lake City. Private aircraft may use Bryce Canyon Airport, 4 miles from park.

🚗 25 miles of paved road run the length of the park. Numerous foot and horse trails. Only the area between Sunset Point and Paria View is open in winter.

⚜ Open all year; best time for birdwatching is spring and early summer.

⊕ Half-day–3 days.

🎫 $1 per car and occupants daily; 50c per individual hiker, rider, party tourist.

☞ Details of guided horseback trips with Jack Church, concessioner, from superintendent.

⇨ Superintendent, Bryce Canyon National Park, Bryce Canyon, Utah 84717.

Fish Springs National Wildlife Refuge 17,992 acres of isolated marsh on the Great Salt Lake Desert, supplied by permanent springs. Nesting and migrating ducks, geese, heron, egret. Primitive camping; access by 75 miles of dirt road. Nearest town Dugway. Refuge Manager, Dugway, Utah 84022.

Ouray National Wildlife Refuge 10,467 acres of isolated bottomlands astride the Green River, bordering the Ouray Indian reservation. Now being developed as a major habitat for Canada goose. Some 75,000 birds during peak migration period. Mountain lion, black bear, antelope, pronghorn. Near town of Vernal. Refuge Manager, PO Box 398, Vernal, Utah 84078.

Wyoming

Grand Teton National Park 485 square miles; 6,400 to 13,766 ft above sea level. The eastern half of the park consists of flattish plains around 6,400 ft altitude, broken here and there by low ridges; the western half is dominated by the Teton range of mountains, caused by a massive uprising of the crust along an ancient fault line. Mt Moran, over the southwest shore of Jackson lake (25,540 acres), still preserves the original rock layers – crystalline, topped by sedimentary, topped by volcanic. The volcanic layer is a dike, formed when hot lava under immense pressure was forced through a geological fault in the sedimentary rock, forcing it apart and solidifying before being exposed to weathering. Elsewhere only the jagged peaks of the crystalline layers remain. The southeastern border of the park is continuous with the National Elk Refuge (page 118).

🏃 Elk, moose, bear, beaver, mule deer, chipmunk, golden-mantled ground squirrel, marmot, cony; trumpeter swan (rare), bald eagle, osprey, Canada geese, great blue heron, water ouzel, magpie, mountain bluebird, western tanager, black rosy finch.

ꗃ Lodgepole pine, alpine fir, Engelman and Colorado blue spruces, cottonwoods, willow, aspen (particularly beautiful in autumn here), sagebrush, silverberry bushes, creeping mahonia, wildflowers.

🛌 Park camp-grounds at Colter bay, Jackson lake, and Jenny lake; trailers permitted but no utility connections; organized groups at Colter bay and Signal Mountain only; rates subject to change. Concessioner operated trailer park at Colter bay village; rates from $3 per day. The Grand Teton Lodge Co operates lodges and cabins at all 3 sites; rates from $7–45 single, daily; reservations to them at Jackson, Wyoming 83001 (in winter: 209 Post Street, San Francisco, California 94108). Scattered throughout the park are many lodges and guest houses, some with housekeeping cabins; many provide horses; write to park administration for full list and prices.

↦ By car: from the east by US 287 and 26 via Togwotee Pass; from the southeast by US 187 and 189 via Hoback Canyon; from the southwest by US 26 and 89 via Snake River Canyon; from the west by US 191, turn off on Wyoming 22 or Idaho 33 near Sugar City (unsuitable for trailers); from the north via US 89 and 287 direct from the south entrance to Yellowstone Park (closed 1 November to 1 May). Rail and bus: Union Pacific trains run to Victor to connect with park buses; scheduled buses connect Jackson and Rock Springs; other services link the Yellowstone and Teton parks daily. By air: Frontier Airlines connect Jackson with Salt Lake City, Riverton, Idaho Falls, Denver, Cheyenne, and Billings.

2 paved roads run north–south through the park, both to the east of the mountains. Over 200 miles of trails – most of them in the mountains – lead from these highways. There are scheduled drives, scenic flights, river-float trips, guided nature hikes, pack trips, and climbing instruction.

Open all year; best time for wildlife in the mountains June to Labor Day (1st Monday in September); but see also National Elk Refuge.

3–12 days.

$1 per car and occupants daily; or 50c per individual hiker, rider, party tourist.

Yellowstone and Grant Teton Wild Flowers by R. J. Shaw; *Teton Trails* (guide); *The Tetons: Interpretations of a Mountain Landscape* by F. M. Fryxell.

The Superintendent, Grand Teton National Park, Moose, Wyoming 83102.

Hutton Lake National Wildlife Refuge 1,970 acres on the Laramie Plains, containing uplands, open water, marshes surrounded by mountains, providing habitat for wintering and migrating ducks: redhead, canvasback. 151 species of birds includes marsh hawk, killdeer, hummingbirds. No recreational activities. Nearest town Laramie. Refuge Manager, PO Box 759, Laramie, Wyoming 82070. Good all year.

The American elk is a race of the red-deer species, found in the temperate zone from Ireland to the Japan Sea. In America it is a western and central-Canadian species. For most of the year males live in separate herds from the females, joining them to carve out personal harems only during the fall rut (usually October). Antlers are shed in early spring and regrown fully by around August.

National Elk Refuge 23,784 acres; about 6,500 ft above sea level. The refuge provides winter feed for the thousands of elk whose ancestors once roamed from the Tetons and other ranges to the flatlands of western and southwestern Wyoming – Jackson Hole among them. As farming consumed their winter grounds it became necessary to provide winter grazing supplemented by harvested feeds. Because the most photogenic concentrations of elk occur during severe winters, when the hay supplement is doled out, the impression has got around that the elk live off handouts and make a beeline for the feedlots. Actually the hay is a poor substitute for the rich diet of grasses and browse plants (and standing crops) in the refuge's 24,000 acres. Nevertheless, the emergency feeding of the elk during January to March is one of the most breathtaking sights in the wildlife of western North America – especially against the majestic backdrop of the Grand Teton Mountains, which rise above 13,000 ft.

🦌 Elk apart there are moose, bighorn sheep, mule deer, bear (occasional), muskrat, beaver, coyote, badger. Birds include trumpeter swan (re-introduced), Canada goose, mallard, pintail, American widgeon, green-winged and cinnamon teal, common and Barrow's goldeneyes, golden and bald eagles, magpie, hawks, osprey, mountain bluebird, savannah and vesper sparrows, yellow-headed blackbird, yellowthroat, Clark's nutcracker, Lewis's woodpecker, Bohemian waxwing, sage, blue, and ruffed grouse.

🛏 None in refuge; hotels and motels in Jackson.

🏞 Jackson abuts on the southwest corner; see also Grand Teton – previous listing.

🚐 US 187 runs along the western border and the Jackson–Kelly road winds through the eastern side.

🌅 Open all year; best time for photography January to March emergency feeding.

🕐 6 hrs to 1 day.

🎫 Free.

⇨ Refuge Manager, Box C, Jackson, Wyoming 83001/tel: (307) 733–2627.

Seedskadee National Wildlife Refuge 916 acres along the Green River, many nesting Canada goose among waterfowl. Also sage grouse, pronghorn, deer, moose, elk, bison. Boating, picnicking, camping. 30 miles from Green River. Refuge Manager, PO Box 67, Green River, Wyoming 82935. Best June to October.

Wyoming State Parks The wildlife of Wyoming – deer, antelope, small game, upland birds, and waterfowl – can be seen in all 8 of the state parks, but not to a greater extent than in the surrounding countryside. For reference the parks are listed below. All have camp and picnic sites, water, and sanitation; all but Hot Springs have boat ramps and most have marinas.

Glendo State Park, concession area and full range of services; Glendo 4 miles, access from Interstate 25 and US 26 and 87.

Guernsey State Park, no concession area, near Guernsey town, access from US 26.

Buffalo Bill State Park, limited concession area, Cody 9 miles, access from US 14, 16, and 20.

Boysen State Park, concession area and full range of services, Shoshone 10 miles, access from US 20 and 26.

Keyhole State Park, limited concession area, Moorcroft 18 miles, Sundance 24 miles, access from Interstate 90 and US 14.

Seminoe State Park, limited concession area, Rawlins 35 miles, access from Interstate 90 and US 30 and 287 at Sinclair.

Hot Springs State Park, no concession area, buffalo herd, world's largest hot springs, Thermopolis walking distance, access from US 20.

Big Sandy State Recreation Area, no concession area, Farson 8 miles, access from US 187.

Yellowstone National Park 3,472 square miles; 5,282 to 11,360 ft above sea level. America's oldest and largest national park. Here at one glance you can see the primeval forces of volcano and glacier that shaped much of the far west – and you can see the final petering out (and even *that* is impressive enough) of one of those forces in the 10,000-plus hot springs, geysers, and mud volcanoes in the park's geyser basins. Most famous of them is Old Faithful, but there are 200 other geysers of various sizes. Away from the well-tramelled thermal areas most of the park is forested and undeveloped. The Grand Canyon of the Yellowstone river, where the falls plunge a sheer 308 ft (twice Niagara's height), is in the north part of the park. In the centre and south is Yellowstone lake, with a 110-mile shoreline – the largest mountain lake in North America at such an elevation.

Black bear, grizzly (rarely seen), mule deer, moose, American elk, pronghorn, bison, bighorn sheep, coyote, marmot, golden-mantled and Vinta ground squirrel, chipmunk; 200 bird species include bald eagle, osprey, white pelican, California gull, mallard, Canada goose, trumpeter swan (rare); western tanager, violet-green swallow, western and mountain bluebirds, Canada jay, water ouzel.

Forest trees include lodgepole, limber, and whitebark pines, Engelmann spruce, alpine and Douglas fir, Rocky Mountain juniper, quaking aspen, cottonwood, mountain alder, willow; shrubs and wildflowers include sagebrush, rabbitbrush, cinquefoil, Indian paintbrush, lupine, columbine, harebell, Rocky Mountain fringed gentian.

16 camp sites, most open June 1 to September 15, operated free of charge on first-come first-served basis; length of stay limited to 14 days between July 1 and Labor Day (1st Monday in September). Hotels, lodges, cottages, cabins, dining-rooms, cafes, boat-, horseback-, and bus-trips – all operated by Yellowstone Park Co, summer address (May 1 to October 1) Mammoth, Yellowstone National Park,

Wyoming 83020. Cabins at Old Faithful, May 2 to October 20; cabins at Old Faithful, West Thumb, Fishing Bridge, and Canyon, May 10 to October 15. Old Faithful Lodge, May 14 to October 6; Lake Lodge, May 9 to September 22; Roosevelt Lodge, June 13 to September 2. Cottages in Canyon Village, May 23 to September 8. Mammoth Motor Inn, all year; Old Faithful Inn, May 14 to October 6; and Lake Hotel open May 30 to September 3; Lake Hotel Cabins, June 13 to September 2.

⇨ By road on half a dozen major highways that run to or near the park's 5 gates. By train to Gardiner, Silver Gate, West Yellowstone, Gallatin Highway, Cody, and Moran. By air to Billings, Bozeman, Cody, Jackson, and Salt Lake City. Park buses connect with trains and major airlines.

🚐 Paved highways connect all major entrances with all camps; camps and highways, in turn, are linked by a rich network of horseback trails. Foot hikers must file routes and times before departure; solo hiking is forbidden. Horses rentable at Mammoth Hot Springs, Roosevelt, Old Faithful, and many dude ranches. Boating opportunities are limited.

☼ Open May 1 to October 31; most facilities operate June 15 to September 15.

🕐 2–14 days.

🎫 $1 per car and occupants daily; or 50c per individual hiker, rider, party tourist.

📖 *Haynes Guide to the Park*, by post from Haynes Inc, 801 North Wallace Avenue, Bozeman, Montana 59715 ($1.50 plus postage); *Yellowstone National Park* by H. M. Chittenden; *Story of Man in Yellowstone* by M. D. Beal; Write to Yellowstone Library and Museum Association, c/o Yellowstone Park, for list of special texts on the park's plants, animals, geology and geysers, and Indians.

📙 Licensed guides available.

⇨ Superintendent, Yellowstone National Park, Wyoming 83020.

Rocky Mountain bighorn sheep at National Bison Range, Montana.

120

USA: The Southwest

Arizona

Grand Canyon National Park 310 square miles; between 2,000 and 9,000 ft above sea level. One of the most spectacular gorges in the world. The chief interest for the naturalist lies in the extraordinary range of climatic zones, ranging from near-equatorial desert at the bottom of the gorge to Canadian-type landscape complete with forests of blue spruce 9,000 ft up on the northern rim. The flora and fauna also reveal this range: from desert spiny lizards, rattlesnakes, chuckwalla, cactus, agave, and yucca on the gorge floor, through regions of pinyon and juniper, of ponderosa pine and, on the South Rim, phlox, blue penstemon, buttercup, spring beauty, mahonia, cliffrose, rabbitbrush, wild sunflower, purple aster, sulfur erigonum, snakeweed, and paperflower, to the forests of the less accessible North Rim. To see the canyon at its most spectacular you should go to the Grand Canyon National Monument on the western boundary of the park. There, from Toroweap point you can look down 3,000 ft into the canyon at a point where it averages less than a mile across. The Colorado River, whose action over the last nine million years (amazingly short by geological standards) has created the vast, 217-mile chasm on whose rim the park lies, is not navigable in the ordinary sense – though several expeditions have managed the awesome rapids along its course. It is also an impassable barrier to the terrestrial fauna of the two rims.

⇌ South Rim: ranges from free NPS camp-grounds, which are not bookable, through concessioner trailer village and hotel; for details of rates and reservations write to Fred Harvey, Grand Canyon, Arizona 86023. Fred Harvey also operates The Phantom Ranch on the floor of the gorge. North Rim: from free NPS camp-ground and concessioner lodge and inn; for details of rates and reservations write to Utah Parks Co, Cedar City, Utah 84720.

⇛ South Rim: US 66 to Williams or Flagstaff, each 2 hrs drive or bus journey from the village; a local train links Williams with the village. US 89 to Cameron then by all-weather scenic highway to the park. Many airlines operate flights to the airport south of the park. North Rim: US 89A to Jacob Lake then by paved road to the park, closed by snow mid-October to mid-May. Buses (mid-June to August) from Cedar City.

🚐 Roads, some paved, some primitive, lead to most of the favourite vantage points. The gorge itself is accessible only on foot or mule and only by well marked trails.

☀ South Rim open all year; best time July and August. North Rim open approximately early May to late September, snow dependent.

🕐 1–4 days.

📧 $1 per car and occupants daily; or 50c per individual hiker, rider, party tourist.

👁 Many Indians live and work in the park.

⇨ Superintendent, Grand Canyon National Park, Grand Canyon, Arizona 86023.

Imperial National Wildlife Refuge 25,764 acres on the Colorado River containing main channel of the river, also lakes, ponds, marshes, desert mountains. Refuge for desert bighorn sheep, beaver, coyote, feral burro. Canada goose, ducks, swans, heron, bald and golden eagles, Harris' hawk. Camping, boating, picnicking; nearby concessions provide lodgings, meals, boat rentals. Near Yuma. Refuge Manager, PO Box 1032, Yuma, Arizona 85364/tel: 725–2619. Good all year.

Saguaro National Monument 98 square miles and 24 square miles (2 sections) between 2,500 and 8,600 ft above sea level. The saguaro is the weirdest and most photogenic of all the large cacti; it can live 200 years, reach 50 ft, and sprout several dozen branches. Even in death its peeling skeleton has a gaunt sort of grace. The older saguaros are in the larger eastern section; the young plantation is in the western (Tucson mountain) section. Desert scenery is not all this park has to offer, for as you climb the trail up the Tangue Verde and Rincon mountains you pass through plant and animal communities typical of every climatic region between Mexico and Canada.

⚲ Mule deer, whitetail deer, javelina, jackrabbit, skunk, badger, coyote, desert tortoise, gopher snake, red racer, rattlesnake, Sonora coral snake, Gila monster (rare), scorpions. Birds include curve-billed thrasher, cactus wren, Gambel's quail, roadrunner, Gila woodpecker, gilded flicker, pyrrhuloxia, house finch, loggerhead shrike, harlequin quail, Mexican jay, Bewick's wren, black-tailed gnatcatcher, red-shafted flicker, hairy woodpecker, Steller's jay, broad-tailed hummingbird.

⚘ Lower desert: needle gramagrass, saltbush, creosotebush. Higher desert: saguaro, prickly pear, cholla, mesquite, ocotillo, paloverde. Grassland: Emory oak, centuryplant agave, gramagrass, curly mesquitegrass. Woodland: scrub oak, pinyon, juniper, sumac, manzanita, mountain mahogany. Forest belt: ponderosa pine, gambel oak, Douglas and white firs, aspen.

⚲ No camping, lodging, food, or gasoline facilities in either section. Hotels and motels in Tucson.

⮞ The Visitor Centre, at the park gate, is 14 miles from downtown via Broadway and Old Spanish Trail. Tucson mountain section: drive west on Speedway Boulevard then out on Gates Pass Road – about 12 miles.

🚗 A 9-mile-loop motor road leads from the Center through the desert section; here and there you can pull out and walk short spur trails. For hardier visitors there are longer trails through the mountains. Horses for hire from nearby ranch owners.

⚜ Open all year; best time May and early June, when the creamy-white Saguaro flower (Arizona state flower) is in bloom.

⏱ 1–3 days.

🎫 $1 per car and occupants daily; or 50c per individual hiker, rider, party tourist.

⮡ Superintendent, Box 17210, Tucson, Arizona 85710.

Young whitetail buck, the most abundant and widespread of North American deer. They prefer mixed wood and meadow to deep forest.

New Mexico

Bitter Lakes National Wildlife Refuge 23,189 acres; 3,500 ft above sea level. The north tract (14,000 acres) is unsuitable for public use and is closed. The refuge as a whole is the most important waterfowl area in the east of New Mexico. It contains 17 impoundments of water along the prehistoric, meandering route of the Pecos river, which has since been straightened and controlled. The two northern impoundments may be visited only with special permit.

⌁ Mallards, American widgeon, pintail, canvasback, geese, sandhill crane, black-necked stilt, snowy plover, American avocet, scaled quail, ring-necked pheasant. Mammals include rabbit, badger, skunk, raccoon, bobcat, muskrat, gray fox, coyote, bridled weasel, mule deer, pronghorn (nearby).

🛏 None within refuge. Hotels and motels in Roswell. Organized youth groups may be allowed to camp overnight.

🛣 By short spur road from US 70 and US 285, about 15 miles north of Roswell.

🚗 A gravel road makes several loops around the southernmost impoundments.

🌤 Open all year; best time April to October.

🕐 1 day.

💲 Free.

➦ Refuge Manager, Box 7, Roswell, New Mexico 88201/tel: (505) 622–6755.

Bosque Apache National Wildlife Refuge 57,191 acres of bottomlands, foothills and mesas along the Rio Grande providing a wintering area for geese, ducks (particularly the endangered Mexican duck) sandhill crane, heron, whistling swan, upland game birds. Mule deer, antelope, beaver, bobcat, coyote. No facilities provided. Near San Antonio. Refuge Manager, PO Box 278, San Antonio, New Mexico 87832. Best April to November.

Carlsbad Caverns National Park 77 square miles of surface area under which are many undeveloped caves; lowest known point is 1,013 ft below the ridged foothills of the Guadelupe mountains. The full extent of the caverns is unknown, as they have not yet been fully explored. The part open to the public is a 3-mile, 4-hour round trip – which you can shorten in a number of ways, either by riding to and from the galleries by elevator or by confining yourself to the big 'rooms' only. The greatest wildlife attraction is the evening bat flight, April to October, when millions of bats (depending on the abundance of food) leave the cave for the night, re-

The evening bat flight at Carlsbad Caverns NP, New Mexico.

turning at dawn. The Guadelupe foothills are cactus desert and grassland with self-guiding nature trails.

🦇 Bats include Mexican free-tailed bats, fringed myotis, western pipistrelle, lump-nosed and pallid bats. Among other mammals: mule deer, pronghorn, black-tailed jack-rabbit, desert cottontail, rock squirrel; spotted, striped, and hog-nosed skunks; raccoon, kit and gray foxes, ringtail, pocket gopher. Birds include black-throated sparrow, ladder-backed woodpecker, scaled quail, mourning dove, cactus and rock canyon wrens, great horned owl, blue grosbeak, black-chinned hummingbird, Scott's oriole, western tanager, Audubon's warbler, white-crowned sparrow, brown towhee, pyrrhuloxia, turkey vulture, golden eagle, common nighthawk, poor-will, cave swallow, road runner. Also many desert reptiles.

🌿 Ocotillo, sotol, creosotebush, agave, sagebrush.

🛏 None within park but approach roads have many hotels, motels, and trailer parks.

🛫 27 miles from Carlsbad via US 285 or US 62–180; 150 miles from El Paso via US 62–180. To Carlsbad via Santa Fe Railroad System or daily flights with Continental Airlines; to El Paso via Texas & Pacific Railway, Rock Island Lines, and Southern Pacific Lines. Carlsbad Caverns coaches serve the park from both Carlsbad and El Paso.

🚗 Parking for 600 cars; elevator; foot.

☀ Open all year; best time summer for bat flights.

🕐 1 day.

🎟 $1.50 (includes guide and elevator fee). Children under 12 and organized school groups, free.

➪ Superintendent, Box 111, Carlsbad, New Mexico 88220.

Oklahoma

Salt Plains National Wildlife Refuge 32,000 acres; 1,000 ft above sea level; about a quarter of the refuge consists of the Great Salt Plains reservoir. The refuge provides habitat for migrating waterfowl of the central flyway.

🦅 Canada, white-fronted, blue, and snow geese, mallard, pintail, green-winged teal, Franklin's gull, avocet, yellowlegs, sandpiper, dowitcher, godwit, white pelican, herons, egret, sandhill crane, whooping crane (rare), bald and golden eagle, Mississippi kite (fairly rare), bobwhite and ring-necked pheasant, wild turkey. Mammals include whitetail deer, raccoon, badger, opossum, squirrels, coyote, muskrat, beaver, bobcat, mink.

🛏 None in refuge. Hotels and motels at Cherokee, a few miles west.

🛫 Refuge HQ is 10 miles north of Jet on Oklahoma 38 (1 mile from the highway), just over 2 miles south of the intersection with Oklahoma 11.

🚗 Mostly on foot. The western border of the refuge can be reached from Cherokee, and via US 64 from Jet; here an observation tower gives a good view of the refuge and the great salt flats (not always safe for cars). Parts of the refuge are temporarily or permanently closed to the public; however, permission to visit there may be granted if the waterfowl concentration is not too heavy.

☀ Open all year; best time April to November.

⏱ 1 day.

◉ 3 miles south of the Cherokee entrance is a selenite crystal area (Saturdays, Sundays, holidays; 1 April to 15 October); visitors may remove up to 10 lb and one crystal; brochure at HQ.

⇨ Refuge Manager, Salt Plains National Wildlife Refuge, Jet, Oklahoma 73749/tel: (405) JET–H015.

Tishomingo National Wildlife Refuge 16,464 acres on the Washita arm of Lake Texoma, a large reservoir on the Red River between Texas and Oklahoma. Fills a gap on the central flyway, provides refuge to numerous geese, ducks, heron, egret. Well equipped picnic areas. Near town of Tishomingo. Refuge Manager, PO Box 248, Tishomingo, Oklahoma 73460. Best April to November.

Washita National Wildlife Refuge 8,084 acres of shortgrass plains on the Washita River. Western Oklahoma's only waterfowl refuge, forming an important link in the central flyway. Some 75,000 waterfowl of 20 different species visit during migration. Sandhill cranes number 15,000 in early December. Boating. Motel accommodation in Butler, Clinton and Elk City Refuge Manager PO Box 488, Butler, Oklahoma 73625/tel: 473–2205. Best May to October.

Wichita Mountains Wildlife Refuge 59,000 acres; 1,600 to 2,467 ft above sea level. Set in what was once rich Indian hunting grounds the refuge was reserved from homesteading in 1901, when the rest of the area was opened to settlement. Most of the animals were re-introduced here after the refuge was created. Excellent boating, swimming, and recreational facilities.

🐾 Buffalo, elk (brought in from Jackson Hole), antelope, whitetail deer, fox squirrel, raccoon, opossum; wild turkey, scissor-tailed flycatcher, bobwhite, roadrunner, great horned owl, bald and golden eagles.

🏕 9 major camp-grounds, none bookable, within the refuge. Nearest hotels and motels at Cache, 6 miles, and Lawton, 30 miles.

🛬 Oklahoma 49 and 115 both traverse the refuge; US 277, 62/281, and 62 all run near by. Nearby towns are Meers, Cache, Indiahoma, and Lawton.

🚗 Paved highway and numerous spur roads. In the southern part of the refuge is a buffer-zone bordering an artillery range; here it is forbidden to leave your car. Elsewhere are plenty of trails. Boating only on Elmer Thomas lake; outboards permitted.

☀ Open all year; best time March to December.

⏱ 1–5 days.

🎫 Free.

⇨ Refuge Manager, Wichita Mountains Wildlife Refuge, Box 448, Cache, Oklahoma 73527/tel: (404) 429–3222.

American alligator at Aransas NWR, Texas. Alligators eat whatever birds, mammals, or fish they can drag from the shore or kill in the water, which they do by vigorous movements that tear their prey limb from limb. They move mainly by swishing their powerful tails.

Texas

Aransas National Wildlife Refuge 54,453 acres; at or near sea level. Consists mostly of tidal sand flats and bays giving way to marshes and higher ground strewn with ponds. The refuge is the main winter ground of the rare whooping crane (mid-October to early-April), of which only 51 birds remained in the wild in 1968. They can be seen from observation towers equipped with telescopes.

Over 300 bird species include whooping crane, ibises, egrets, herons, sandhill crane, roseate spoonbill, mottled duck and many other water and shore birds. Mammals include whitetail deer, javelina, armadillo, raccoon, skunk, squirrel, coyote, bobcat. American alligator is also found.

None in refuge. Nearest motels at Rockport, 35 miles southwest. Tent and caravan (trailer) sites, $1 daily, and open shelters, $2.50, with water, latrines, hot showers, at Rockport; maximum stay 14 days summer, 28 days winter.

Entry daily 8am to 5pm; gates locked at dusk; all entrants must register. The gate is 8 miles south of Austwell on Texas 2040.

24 miles of shell-surfaced roads open to the public; observation points and towers all signposted.

Open all year; best time November to March.

1–2 days.

$1 per car and occupants.

Refuge Manager, Aransas National Wildlife Refuge, Box 68, Austwell, Texas 77950/tel: (512) 748–5611.

127

Bentsen–Rio Grande Valley State Scenic Park 588 acres (5 of water).Favourite spot for birdwatchers: Lichtenstein's oriole, hooded oriole, gray hawk, pauraque, groove-billed ani, long-billed thrasher, green jay, kiskadee flycatcher, red-eyed cowbird. Entrance $1, 77 camp and trailer sites ($1 daily), maximum 14 days May 1 to September 15, 28 days rest of year. The Santa Ana Wildlife Refuge is nearby. 3 miles west of Mission on US 83, then south on Loop 374, then on FM 2062 Spur for 2½ miles, enter on park road 43. Supervisor John T. Mason Jr, PO Box 988, Mission, Texas 78572/tel: 512–585–1107.

Big Bend National Park 1,017 square miles; 1,800 to 7,835 ft above sea level. The southern border to the park is the 107-mile meander of the Rio Grande (and thus also the border of Texas and the USA with Mexico). The river runs in places through canyons over 1,500 ft deep, carved by its passage over hundreds of thousands of years. The centre of the park is marked by the spectacular Chisos mountains. The landscape will look more than vaguely familiar to fans of epic westerns.

↝   You will see few warm-blooded animals during the day. At dusk: desert mule deer, whitetail deer, coyote, ringtail, kit fox, pronghorn, javelina, rock and whitetail antelope squirrels. At night: cougar and gray fox. Over 200 bird species include Mexican jay, Scott's oriole, cliff swallow, cactus wren, roadrunner, poor-will, Colima warbler (rare).

ଞ   Yuccas, agaves, ocotillo, creosotebush, guayacan, strawberry cactus, prickly pear, spiny allthorn, catclaw, lechuguilla, sotol, mesquite, cottonwood. Mountain flora includes Douglas fir, ponderosa pine, Arizona cypress, pinyon pine, oaks, and various junipers.

↜   Cottages with private baths in the Basin; central restaurant; rates from $4–11.50. Bookings via National Park Concessions Inc, Big Bend National Park, Texas 79834. Campgrounds at the Basin and Rio Grande Village; rates subject to change. Trailer park with utility connections at Rio Grande Village and Panther Junction, near park HQ; rates from $1.50 a day. Main supplies and fresh groceries should be brought into the park with you; there are a few small stores in the park.

↦   410 miles from San Antonio via US 90 to Marathon then US 385, via north entrance, 393 miles to Panther Junction; 290 miles from El Paso via Interstate 10 to Van Horn, US 90 to Alpine, then via Texas 118; 353 miles via US 67 to Presidio and Texas Ranch Road 170. Southern Pacific Railway runs to Alpine and Marathon. Continental Trailways buses run east–west through Alpine and Marathon, which are served north–south by Trans-Pecos buses. No regular public transport runs to or through the park.

🚙   110 miles of paved road; many horse and foot trails.

☼   Open all year; best time summer for the mountains, other seasons for the deserts. Midday summer temperatures: 100°F desert, 85°F mountains.

◔   3–12 days.

✉ $1 per car and occupants daily; or 50c per individual hiker, rider, party tourist.

☞ Guides, saddlehorses, and pack animals can be hired; details from Superintendent.

⇨ Superintendent, Big Bend National Park, Texas 79834.

Big Spring State Recreation Park 332 acres (none water). The Big Spring is the only water for 60 miles around and is a magnet for herds of buffalo, antelope, and wild horses. Picnic sites, play area, showers, no accommodation. Supervisor Edward C. Wisenbaker, Box 1064, Big Spring, Texas 79720/tel: 915–263–4931.

Black Gap Wildlife Management Area 102,258 acres in the Big Bend of the Rio Grande on the Texas–Mexico border. Protects the only desert bighorn sheep in Texas; and provides managed (controlled-hunted) habitat for mule deer, javelina, and scaled quail. Camping permitted, screened shelters (25). Just east of Big Bend National Park, 55 miles south of Marathon. Regional Supervisor Robert C. Hauser, Drawer 1590, San Angelo, Texas 76901.

Buffalo Lake National Wildlife Refuge 7,677 acres, one-third Buffalo Lake itself, providing an important sanctuary for 1,000,000 ducks and 25,000 geese; also blue heron, bald and golden eagles, bobwhite, quail. Camping, swimming, boating, skiing; café. Near Amarillo, Texas. Refuge Manager, Box 228, Ombarger, Texas 79091/tel: GY 9–2601. Best March to December.

Chaparral Wildlife Management Area 15,200 ares of brush country – mesquite, black and white brush, and cactus. Habitat for whitetail deer, javelina, bobwhite, scaled quail (all hunted under control) and badger, coyote, turkey, dove, ducks, owls, hawks, feral pig, and raccoon. A centre for research into wildlife-management techniques for the benefit of brush-country landowners. No facilities. 8 miles west of Artesia Wells on the north side of FM Road 133. Regional Supervisor Tom McGlathery, 715 S Brinte St, Rockport, Texas 78382.

Gambill Goose Refuge 674 acres, almost all lake, with up to 2,000 geese between mid-October and March. Parking area, 5 picnic tables and night lights. On Lake Crook, 7 miles northwest of Paris via FM 2820. Regional Supervisor as for Gus Engeling WMA.

Gene Howe Wildlife Management Area 5,821 acres of upper and rolling plains habitat; a centre for studying the ecological effects of various grazing intensities and grain planting for game birds. Deer, turkey, bobwhite, quail, lesser prairie chicken. Field trips by arrangement. 7 miles east of Canadian, Texas. Regional Supervisor as for Black Gap WMA.

Gus Engeling Wildlife Management Area 10,941 acres of post-oak habitat used primarily to study the effects of grazing, brush control, timber clearing, and pasture upgrading on local wildlife, which includes deer, squirrel, upland song-birds, and some waterfowl. Primitive camping facilities but no drinking water. Field trips by arrangement. 18 miles northwest of Palestine on US 287, near Bethel community. Regional Supervisor Harold R. Allums, 530 Beckham, Tyler, Texas 75701.

Hagerman National Wildlife Refuge 11,429 acres on the Red River between Texas and Oklahoma, one-third marsh and water. Habitat for migrating and wintering waterfowl; Canada, snow, blue goose, mallard, diving duck. Meadows and farmland give refuge to reptiles (some poisonous), deer, armadillo, foxes, bobcat. Camping facilities. Nearest town Denison, Texas. Refuge Manager, Route 3, Box 123, Sherman, Texas 75090. Best April to November.

Kerr Wildlife Management Area 6,460 acres of juniper-oak habitat on limestone hills in the Edwards Plateau. A research area devoted to the management of the densest whitetail deer herd in the United States; also home of the yellow-throated warbler and other upland song birds. No facilities. Regional Supervisor Billy J. Smith, PO Box 7653, Waco, Texas 76710.

Laguna Atascosa National Wildlife Refuge 45,147 acres; at or near sea level. Named after the largest of its many lakes (3,100 acres) this is the southernmost refuge in the chain that lies along the central flyway. The landscape is a mixture of desert, marsh, and coastal scrub.

🐾 Redhead, pintail, coots, Canada and snow geese, mottled duck, fulvous tree duck, black-bellied tree duck, white-tailed hawk (rare), white-tailed kite, Harris's hawk; mourning, ground, and white-winged doves; bobwhites – in all some 315 bird species. Mammals include whitetail deer, javelina, raccoon, opossum, cottontail, jackrabbit, striped skunk, coyote, bobcat, jaguarundi, ocelot.

🏕 Camping, limited to 3 days, in the recreation areas alongside the Harlingen Ship Canal, which cuts through the north of the refuge; free. Hotels at Harlingen and San Benito.

🢒 25 miles northeast of San Benito. Airports at Harlingen and Brownsville. Visitors must register at HQ; gates open dawn to dusk.

🚙 1 walk-in, 2 drive-in routes. Maps and tour information at HQ on registration. If you leave your car or enter on foot, watch out for the diamond-backed rattlesnake.

☼ Open all year; best time October to December.

🕐 1–3 days.

🎫 Free.

⇨ Refuge Manager, Laguna Atascosa National Wildlife Refuge, Box 739, San Benito, Texas 78586/tel: (512) 399–2772.

Sandhill crane at Aransas NWR, Texas. Cranes, among the most spectacular of the world's groups of birds, are everywhere in need of protection – none more so than America's sandhills and whoopers.

Lyndon B. Johnson State Historic Park 269 acres on the banks of the Pedernales River. The Parks and Wildlife Department maintains a small herd of buffalo on the park. 20 picnic sites, shower, wildlife display, nature trails. No accommodation. 14 miles west of Johnson City on US 290 toward Fredericksburg. Superintendent Harold C. Woods, Box 201, Stonewall, Texas 78671/tel: (512) 644–2488.

Mackenzie State Recreation Park 542 acres including 15 acres of stream and pond. A public recreation area (bathing, golf, tennis, model airplanes, etc) which has the distinction of containing the only natural cultivated Prairie Dog Town in the United States. Trailer and camp sites; party houses. The park spreads across Yellowstone Canyon, where Double Mountain and Yellowhouse Forks of the Brazos River meet. Superintendent A. C. Mackenzie, City Hall, Lubbock/tel: (806) 763–3481.

Muleshoe National Wildlife Refuge 5,809 acres of shortgrass-rangelands with scattered mesquite, 3 lakes depending on run-off for water and often dry. Important refuge for fall and winter waterfowl including 750,000 ducks, also sandhill crane. Prairie dog, burrowing owl, hawks, coyote. Camping, photography. Near town of Muleshoe. Refuge Manager, PO Box 549, Muleshoe, Texas 79347. Best May to November.

Possum Kingdom State Recreation Park 1,615 acres adjacent to the Possum Kingdom reservoir in the scenic Palo Pinto mountains and Brazos River valley. The park has many deer and houses part of the official herd of pure strain Texas longhorn cattle. 33 tent or trailer sites, 7 cabins. 15 miles east of Breckenridge on US 180 to Caddo, then 17 miles north on Park Road 33. Superintendent Frank Hodge Jr, Box 36, Caddo, Texas 76029/tel: Graham exchange (817) 549–1803.

Santa Ana National Wildlife Refuge 2,000 acres; practically at sea level. The refuge consists chiefly of jungle (elm, ebony, hackberry, ash, anaqua, tepeguaje, guayacon, huisache, and retama) that has vanished from elsewhere along the lower Rio Grande; it thus preserves habitat for birds unique in the USA. It also has three large ponds, combined area over 500 acres, as habitat for waterfowl. Its reputation brings serious students of nature from all over the world.

Over 300 bird species include least grebe, black-bellied tree duck, gray hawk, jacana, chachalaca, red-billed pigeon, white-fronted dove, groove-billed ani, pauraque, buff-bellied hummingbird, rose-throated becard, kiskadee flycatcher, green jay, black-crested titmouse, long- and curve-billed thrashers, black-headed and Lichtenstein's orioles, white-collared seedeater, olive sparrow. Among mammals: raccoon, coyote, skunk, opossum, bridled weasel, armadillo, bobcat, packrat; the ocelot and jaguarundi, though present, are rarely seen.

No overnight stops permitted within the refuge. Nearest motels at McAllen.

$7\frac{1}{2}$ miles south of Alamo and 35 miles west of San Benito. Permit and registration at HQ obligatory. Gates open 8am to 5pm.

Fair weather roads run north–south and east–west through the refuge. More than 15 miles of foot trail criss-cross it.

Open all year; best time September to June.

1–2 days.

$1 per person per day.

The Laguna Atascosa National Wildlife Refuge is near by.

As for Laguna Atascosa.

An armadillo photographed near Santa Ana NWR, Texas.

USA : The Midwest

Illinois

Chautauqua National Wildlife Refuge 4,500 acres of flood plain supporting a population of 1½ million ducks: mallard, black duck, wood duck. Large variety of fish. Usual fauna of the region: squirrels, foxes, woodchuck, beaver. Recreation, picnic areas. Near towns of Havana and Pekin, Illinois. Refuge Manager, Havana, Illinois 62644. Best April to December.

Crab Orchard National Wildlife Refuge 43,000 acres containing 50 ponds, several lakes, habitat for 50,000 geese, 15 species of duck. Turkey, quail, deer. 50 species of trees. Camping, boating, swimming, picnicking. Near Carterville. Refuge Manager, Box J, Carterville, Illinois 62918. Best April to December.

Mark Twain National Wildlife Refuge 21,000 acres extending 250 miles along the Mississippi River, consisting of bottomlands, rich croplands, floodlands, lakes, islands. Reaches into Illinois, Iowa, Missouri. Habitat for waterfowl, 200 species of birds including bald eagle. Beaver, muskrat, deer, mink. Picnicking, boating, photography, primitive camping on La Grange Island, modern camp-grounds elsewhere. Near Quincy, Illinois and Annada, Missouri. Refuge Manager, Box 225, Quincy, Illinois 62302. Best March to May, September to December.

Indiana

Spring Mill State Park 1,280 acres; 500 to 650 ft above sea level. Set in rolling karst hills of south central Indiana and covered with virgin hardwood forest, the park contains a number of caves which provide habitat for some interesting wildlife.

- Blind fish and cave invertebrates.
- White oak, American beech, sugar, sugar maple, hickory, black walnut, tulip poplar; bloodroot, wild ginger, trillium, waterleaf.
- Spring Mill Inn, $6–9 single, $8–12 double. Tent and trailer camp sites $1.50–2.50.
- Nearby Bedford and Bloomington offer road access; both are on rail routes and Bloomington has scheduled air access.
- Surfaced roads; foot and horse trails.
- Open all year; best months, summer.
- 1 day.
- $1.25 per car and occupants.
- Naturalist service at no extra charge.
- There is a restored pioneer village within the park.
- Mr Ray Gaines, Superintendent, RR 2, Box 127, Mitchell, Indiana/tel: (812) 849–4129.

Iowa

De Soto National Wildlife Refuge 7,800 acres; around 800 ft above sea level. The refuge is formed around an oxbow lake, formerly a bend in the Missouri river, now a lake isolated by the construction of a bypass canal. Its chief purpose is to provide resting and feeding areas during the spring and autumn migrations (March to April and 15 September to December); during these months it is closed to the public but available to bona fide naturalists.

🐾 Blue, snow, and Canada geese, many duck and other waterfowl, piping plover, least tern, ring-necked pheasant, bobwhite, whitetail deer, coyote, mink, muskrat, raccoon, opossum, beaver, fox squirrel, cottontail.

🍄 Two good mushrooming areas within the refuge are open during May only.

🛏 None in refuge; hotels and motels at Omaha (30 miles), Blair (6 miles) and Missouri Valley (7 miles). State camping area on Iowa bank by refuge boundary; access from Iowa 29.

🛫 US 73 runs north–south via Omaha and Blair. US 30 runs east–west through Blair and Missouri Valley. Iowa 29 runs from Council Bluffs, next door to Omaha, north to Missouri Valley.

🚐 A good-weather road runs from point to point within the refuge forming a loop; areas open to the public are compact enough to explore on foot.

🌤 Open (except as already noted) daily 4.30am to 10pm; best months May, August, and September.

🕐 1 day.

📧 $1 per car and occupants.

⇒ Refuge Manager, De Soto National Wildlife Refuge, 1B Missouri Valley, Iowa 51555/tel: (712) 2–2036 Missouri Valley.

Forney's Lake, administered by the Iowa State Conservation Commission, is a few miles west of Sidney in the extreme southwest corner of the state. During spring migrations you will see up to half a million blue and snow geese there. The reserve has no public accommodation but there are four nearby State Recreation Areas:

Waubonsie, a few miles south; resident officer, camping, foot and horse trails, shower, shelter, picnics, botanical interest; from Sidney US 275, then Iowa 2 and 239.

Viking Lake, about 55 miles away; resident officer, camping, picnics, swimming, boating, shower; on US 34, 3 miles east then one mile south from Stanton.

Lake of Three Fires, about 65 miles away; resident officer, camping, supervised swimming, boating, shelter, picnics, hiking, shower; on Iowa 49, 3 miles northeast of Bedford.

Lake Manawa, about 47 miles north; resident officer, supervised swimming, boating, hiking; on Iowa 192, 1 mile south of Council Bluffs.

Union Slough National Wildlife Refuge 2,100 acres on a natural slough between two watersheds, once a preglacial riverbed. Habitat for a large variety of ducks, also snow, blue, white-fronted, and Canada geese; pelicans, herons, yellowleg, whistling swan. Whitetail deer, rabbit, mink, raccoon. Swimming, picnicking. Near town of Titonka. Refuge Manager, Box 36, Titonka, Iowa 50480. Best May to October.

Kansas

Flint Hills National Wildlife Refuge 18,546 acres within a floodpool subject to frequent floodings. Refuge for migratory waterfowl, regional fauna, deer. Picnicking, camping, boating, waterskiing. Near town of Burlington. Refuge Manager, PO Box 1306, Burlington, Kansas 66839. Best April to November.

Kirwin National Wildlife Refuge 10,778 acres built on an irrigation and flood control reservoir, half water, half cultivated lands or grasslands. Waterfowl, bobwhite, pheasant, rabbits, blacktail prairie dog, beaver, muskrat. Picnicking, camping facilities; swimming, boating. Near Kirwin. Refuge Manager, PO Box 125, Kansas 67644. Best April to November.

Marais des Cygnes 6,563 acres (1,800 water) containing man-made lakes designed to produce wildfowl habitat and to control public hunting in Kansas. Over 70,000 ducks overwinter here and at times the population reaches 150,000. Blue-winged teal, pintail, mallard, shoveler, widgeon, scaup, gadwall, heron, egret, and shorebirds – about 200 species in all. Also deer, quail, rabbit, squirrel, raccoon, opossum, coyote, fox, muskrat, mink, beaver. No accommodation. Foot travel only. Adjacent to US 69, 5 miles north of Pleasanton and a quarter mile west of Trading Post.

Quivira National Wildlife Refuge 20,860 acres of farmland and marsh, between Rattlesnake Creek and Little Salt Marsh. Autumn flights of Canada goose, mallard, teal, some 75,000 wintering here. Bald and golden eagles, pelican, sandhill crane. Near town of Stafford. Refuge Manager, PO Box G, Stafford, Kansas 67578. Best April to November.

Michigan

Isle Royale National Park The park is an archipelago centred on Isle Royale (210 square miles), the largest island on Lake Superior; it includes 200 small islands and innumerable rocks. Highest point is Mt Desor, 792 ft above lake level, which, in turn, is 602 ft above sea level.

135

⌀ The water barrier keeps out most deer species as well as porcupine, bear, and skunk, but swimmers and non-hibernators (who can cross the ice from the Canadian shore, 15 miles away) can reach the island. They include wolf, moose, red fox, snowshoe hare, red squirrel, weasel, mink, muskrat, beaver. Over 200 bird species include osprey, bald eagle, pileated woodpecker, herring gull.

❀ Bunchberry dogwood, common pipsissewa, twinflower, trillium, pyrola, devilsclub, blueberry, raspberry, strawberry, thimbleberry, sugar plum, sugar maple, yellow birch, white spruce, balsam fir, bigtooth aspen, paper birch, jack pine.

⇌ There are 22 camp sites and grounds fairly evenly spaced along the shores of the 45-mile-long island; most have one or more shelters (3 walls, wood floor, roof, screened front and door), but you must take a tent along in case all shelters are taken; sites on a first-come first-served basis and most carry a 14-day limit; rates variable. Except near Rock Harbour Lodge, which is conveniently close to only 6 camp sites, there are no provisions stores in the park; so you must bring enough for all your needs (including first aid) with you. National Park Concessions Inc operates a lodge, guest houses and housekeeping cabins, inn, open June 18–Labor Day (1st Monday in September); rates from $13.50; reservations to them at Isle Royale National Park, Michigan 49940 (summer) and Mammoth Cave, Kentucky 42259 (winter).

⇢ By boat from Houghton, Copper Harbor, and Grand Portage; day and weekly trips. Air transportation from Houghton.

🚐 A number of privately-owned boats operate scheduled and charter trips from Copper Harbor, Grand Portage, Windigo, and Rock Harbor to a number of shoreside camp sites; also guided excursions and trolling trips. Arrange in advance via Ward Grosnick, Copper Harbor, Michigan 49918, and Sivertson Bros Fisheries, 366 Lake Avenue S, Duluth, Minnesota 55802. On the island there are no roads and no cars.

☀ Open June 18 to Labor Day.

🕐 Day excursion to 14 days. Mosquitos common in moist years in early summer.

✉ $1 per car and occupants daily; or 50c per individual hiker, rider, party tourist.

🛈 Write to Isle Royale Natural History Association, 87 N Ripley Street, Houghton, Michigan 49931, for full list of publications. Maps from Geological Survey, US Dept of Interior, Washington DC 20240. Lake Survey Chart from US Lake Survey, 630 Federal Bldg, 231 Lafayette Blvd, Detroit, Michigan 48226; $1.

⇨ Superintendent, Isle Royale National Park, 87 N Ripley Street, Houghton, Michigan 49931.

Kirtland's Warbler Management Areas The Kirtland's warbler, a bluish-grey bird, streaked with black and with a striking lemon-yellow breast, is one of America's endangered species. Its habitat is sun-scorched, dry, fire-scarred, wind-swept plain; it exists (habitat and bird) only in Michigan. The bird has evolved around fire – the wildfires whose heat pops open the tightly closed cones of the jack pine, spreading the millions of seeds that regenerate the burned area and, incidentally, feed the Kirtland's warbler. With the coming of man and the control of widespread burns, this habitat all but vanished. Then, between 1958 and 1963, local Audubon societies, the state conservation agencies, and the US Forest Service dedicated four areas to the remaining population of about 1,000 birds: the Ogemaw State Forest (4 square miles), the Huron National Forest (6½ square miles), the Thunder Bay River State Forest (3½ square miles), and the Au Sable State Forest (3½ square miles); they lie northwest, south, and south-east of the town of Mio on Michigan 33. In these areas a rotation of controlled burns maintains the barren habitat and the species. A visitor's permit (free) is required during the birds' nesting season (May 1 to August 15). Travel is on foot only, though all the areas can be reached by county roads. There is accommodation at Mio.

Seney National Wildlife Refuge 95,455 acres; around 1,000 ft above sea level. The refuge consists largely of man-regulated lakes and marshes set in the great Manistique swamp on the tongue of land between lakes Superior and Michigan. It exists primarily to support waterfowl.

- Canada, blue, and snow geese; mallard, black duck, ring-necked duck, common and hooded mergansers, blue-winged teal, wood duck, sandhill crane, ruffed and spruce grouse, deer, otter.
- Red and jack pine, sweetfern, Labrador tea, wintergreen, bracken, British-soldier lichen.
- None in refuge. Motels in Germfask and Seney (both on refuge boundaries) also at approx 35 miles distance in Newbury, Manistique, and Munising.
- US 2 to Blaney Park, then Michigan 77 to HQ, just north of Germfask.
- By boat or on foot. Daily 10 miles tour of pools in unit 1; or 1½-mile self-guiding walk from and to the Visitor Center.
- Normally snowed in from November to May; best months June to July, September to October.
- 1–2 days.
- Free.
- Refuge Manager, Seney, Michigan 49883/tel: AC 906–586–6504.

Shiawassee National Wildlife Refuge 8,860 acres on the Shiawassee Flats where several rivers converge, forms a northern link in the Mississippi flyway chain, a main migration crossroads for ducks, geese, whistling swan. Large herd of whitetail deer. Near Saginaw. Refuge Manager, 6975 Mower Road, Route 1, Saginaw, Michigan 48601. Best April to June, September to November.

Minnesota

Agassiz National Wildlife Refuge 61,000 acres; around 1,140 ft above sea level. Established in a bay on prehistoric Lake Agassiz in 1937 as a link in the Mississippi flyway, it provides about 24,000 acres of shallow marsh for migratory and nesting waterfowl and other birds.

🐾 Mallard, blue-winged teal, shoveler, gadwall, ring-necked duck, redhead, ruddy duck, Canada goose; 200 other bird species. Mammals include muskrat, mink, skunk, beaver, moose, whitetail deer, and an occasional black bear.

🌳 Blueberry, wild plum; all varieties of marsh flora, including cattails (raw material for kapok); willows, aspen, green ash, American elm, red oak, white birch, spruce, tamarack.

🛏 None in refuge. Motel at Thief River Falls, 23 miles southwest.

🔜 By car 11 miles east of Holt on State Aid Highway 7.

138

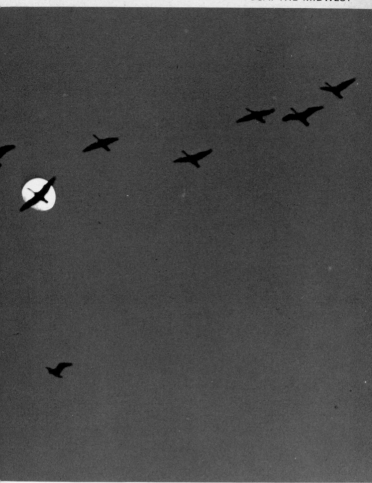

A formation of Canada geese crossing the face of the moon. These were photographed from the shores of Lake Erie.

🚐 By fair weather road from HQ to west and north gates, or on foot.

☼ Open all year; best months June to October.

🕐 1–2 days.

🎫 Free.

⇨ Refuge Manager, Agassiz National Wildlife Refuge, Middle River, Minnesota 56737/tel: (218) 449–2110.

Rice Lake National Wildlife Refuge 17,230 acres; around 1,000 ft above sea level. Established after the droughts of the 1930s to provide a refuge for waterfowl on the Mississippi flyway. The rice grown here, once a staple Indian diet and still an important crop in the local Indian economy, is a great attraction to the birds.

139

⚐ Mallard, ring-necked duck, scaup, white pelican, green and great blue herons, whooping crane, Caspian tern, black-billed magpie, western bluebird, common snipe, American woodcock, sora, Virginia rail, ruffed- and sharp-tailed grouse, ring-necked pheasant. Mammals include whitetail deer, black bear, moose, muskrat, mink, beaver, otter, raccoon.

✿ Wild rice, sugar maple (many scarred by Indians gathering sap for maple syrup).

🛏 None in refuge. Motels at McGregor, 7 miles north.

🚏 On Minnesota 65 about 7 miles south of McGregor.

🚐 Several logging trails are open when dry. The total north–south extent of the park is only 6 miles, so all of it is accessible on foot.

☼ Open all year; best time May to October.

🕐 1–2 days.

🎟 Free.

➡ Refuge Manager, Rice Lake National Wildlife Refuge, McGregor, Minnesota 55760/tel: (218) 768–2402.

Sherburne National Wildlife Refuge 31,000 acres restored from urban overspill to wildlife habitat, mainly for waterfowl. Development planned for southeast portion to provide picnicking, canoeing. Near Princeton. Refuge Manager, 119 Fifth Avenue South, Princeton, Minnesota 55371. Best May to October.

Tamarac National Wildlife Refuge 42,422 acres; around 1,450 ft above sea level. An area of 21 natural lakes, level controlled, with a total area of 9,500 acres. As well there are over 3,000 potholes and hundreds of acres of marsh and slough. Wild rice and other aquatic foods support large flocks of waterfowl.

⚐ Mallard, ring-necked and wood ducks, goldeneye, blue-winged teal, gadwall, scaup, shoveler, ruddy duck, ruffed grouse, herons, Canada goose. Mammals include deer, bobcat, beaver, snowshoe rabbit, muskrat.

✿ White and red pine, clover and alfafa meadows, wild rice.

🛏 None in refuge. Motels at Detroit Lakes, 18 miles southwest. Camp sites for organized youth groups and scouts only.

🚏 From US 59 via Richwood or White Earth or from Minnesota 34 via County Highway 26 or 29. An airport at Detroit Lakes handles charter flights but has no scheduled service.

🚐 County highways 26, 126, 29, and 35 cross the refuge in the north and south; they are linked across the centre by a fair-weather service road. No part of the refuge is more than 2 miles from one of these roads.

☼ Open all year; best months May to November.

🕐 1–3 days.

🎟 Free.

➡ Refuge Manager, Tamarac National Wildlife Refuge, Rural Route, Rochert, Minnesota 55371/tel: (612) 389–3323.

Upper Mississippi River Wildlife and Fish Refuge 194,000 acres of wooded islands, marsh and water, extending 284 miles along the river (the longest inland refuge). Habitat for thousands of waterbirds: mallard, widgeon, teal, wood duck, whistling swan. Also heron, egret, bald eagle. Muskrat, nutria, mink, raccoon, beaver, otter. Boating, camping, picnicking, photography, swimming. Nearest towns Winona and La Crosse, Minnesota. Refuge Manager, 405 Exchange Building, Box 226, Winona, Minnesota 55987. Best April to December.

Missouri

Mingo National Wildlife Refuge 21,700 acres; around 330 ft above sea level. An important waterfowl refuge in the Mississippi flyway. About 16,000 acres are bottomland, bounded east and west by low hills and bluffs. The area was once the bed of the Mississippi river and modern water-control techniques can ensure the flooding of up to 11,000 acres. During the summer this area is partly drained to allow crops to grow in order to support the autumn migrants.

- Mallard, pintail, green-winged teal, black and wood ducks, American widgeon, gadwall, shoveler, Canada, blue, and snow geese, little and great blue herons, cattle and common egrets, cormorant, sora rail, wild turkey. Mammals include whitetail deer, swamp rabbit, bobcat, raccoon, red fox. Three of America's 4 poisonous snakes are found here: cottonmouth, rattlesnake, copperhead.
- Cypress, tupelo gum tree, pin oak, willow oak.
- None in refuge. Motels at Poplar Bluff.
- 1½ miles northeast of Puxico on Missouri 51.
- Marked tour route, 25 miles or 2½ hours long, open every Sunday in October and November. Any organized group of 10 or more can pre-arrange for a conducted tour any day of the week.
- Open all year; best months March to May, October to December.
- 1–2 days.
- Free.
- Refuge Manager, Mingo National Wildlife Refuge, Route 1, Box 9A, Puxico, Missouri 63960/tel: (314) 222–3686.

Squaw Creek National Wildlife Refuge 6,850 acres; 850 ft above sea level. This area, halfway between Kansas City and Omaha, was once a large natural marsh. Attempts to drain it for agriculture were only partly successful, and it has since been returned to marsh under controlled conditions. It is a major resting and feeding area along the Mississippi flyway. This is the best place in the US to see a quarter million blue and snow geese in March and November, with huge concentrations of pelicans and Franklin's gulls in August.

- Blue, snow, white-fronted, and Canada geese, pintail, mallard, American widgeon, blue- and green-winged teals, gadwall, shoveler, wood duck, white pelican, common egret. Mammals include muskrat, whitetail deer, beaver, mink, coyote, fox, raccoon, opossum, skunk.

141

🛏 None in refuge. Hotels and motels in nearby Mound City.

🦅 4 miles south of Mound City along the Bluff Road.

🚗 Some fair-weather tracks lead across the levee tops; otherwise on foot.

🌄 Open all year; best time during spring and autumn migrations.

🕐 1 day.

🎫 Free.

➡ Refuge Manager, Squaw Creek, National Wildlife Refuge, Box 101, Mound City, Missouri 64470/tel: (816) 442–3570.

Swan Lake National Wildlife Refuge 10,700 acres; around 650 ft above sea level. The best refuge in the plains in which to hear the dull roar of thousands of geese feeding; Swan Lake, inaptly named, has the largest autumn concentration of Canada geese in the USA.

🦅 Blue, snow, white-fronted, and Canada geese, pintail, mallard, American widgeon, blue- and green-winged teals, gadwall, shoveler, wood duck, scaup, white pelican, coot, bobwhite, common snipe.

🛏 None in refuge. Motels in Sumner and Brookfield.

🦅 US 36 to between Chillicothe and Brookfield, then south on Missouri 139 to Sumner, whence 1 mile to refuge HQ.

🚗 Fair weather roads on levee tops; otherwise on foot. A gravel road leads to an observation tower near HQ.

🌄 Open all year; best time October to mid-November.

🕐 1 day.

🎫 Free.

➡ Refuge Manager, Swan Lake National Wildlife Refuge, Sumner, Missouri 64681/tel: (816) 856–3323.

Nebraska

Crescent Lake National Wildlife Refuge 46,000 acres of grass-covered sand dunes dotted with lakes, bordering on one of the few remaining undisturbed tall grass prairie regions. Maintains many species of ducks, geese. Prairie chicken, grouse, pheasant, eagle. Deer, coyote, raccoon, badger. Access by a dirt road, no facilities provided. 28 miles from Oshkosh, Nebraska. Refuge Manager, Ellsworth, Nebraska. Best May to October.

Fort Niobrara National Wildlife Refuge 19,122 acres; around 1,200 ft above sea level. Formed out of what was once a military reservation, the grasslands of this refuge have been restocked with buffalo, elk, and longhorn cattle; it is now one of the few places in the US where you can see large herds of these animals in natural surroundings.

🦅 Buffalo, elk, longhorn cattle, whitetail deer, mule deer, beaver, muskrat, mink, striped skunk, weasel, raccoon, fox squirrel, coyote, bobcat. Birds include sharp-tailed grouse, pinnated grouse (prairie chickens), ring-necked pheasant, golden and bald eagles, and many waterfowl.

None in refuge. Nearest hotels and motels at Valentine.

By US 83 or US 20 to Valentine, then by Nebraska 12 to HQ, 3 miles away.

Many miles of auto trail within the refuge; one gravel road leads through the buffalo summer range from HQ.

Open all year; best time spring and autumn.

1–2 days.

Guided tours can be arranged if rangers are available.

The museum at HQ contains, among other exhibits, the fossilized remains of over 20 extinct species that once roamed this part of Nebraska – all dug up within the refuge.

Refuge Manager, Fort Niobrara National Wildlife Refuge, Hidden Timber Route, Valentine, Nebraska 69201/tel: (402) 376–3789.

The North American raccoon, a waterside predator that sits on logs and river banks, dabbing its paw in the water to flip out crayfish, frogs, and other aquatic animals. With these it supplements its diet of nuts, seeds, eggs, and insects. Despite colossal slaughter for the fur trade it is still among the commonest American mammals.

Valentine National Wildlife Refuge 71,000 acres in a sandhill area with lakes, meadows, marshes. Abundant nesting waterfowl. Mammals include pronghorn, coyote, badger. Noted for a great blue heron rookery, and nesting long-billed curlew. Limited camping, picnicking. 17 miles from Valentine. Refuge Manager, Valentine, Nebraska 69201/tel: area code 402–376–1889. Best May to October.

North Dakota

Arrowwood National Wildlife Refuge 15,934 acres; around 1,400 ft above sea level. This long, narrow refuge (15 miles long, maximum width 3 miles) is built around a string of 4 lakes in the James river in eastern central N Dakota. It is one of many refuges on the central flyway. Its development for migrants has also encouraged the growth of habitat for breeding waterfowl, grebes, shorebirds, and upland game birds.

- Mallard, gadwall, American widgeon, shoveler, blue-winged teal, pintail, lesser scaup, redhead, canvasback, ruddy duck, blue and snow geese (pinioned Canada geese are deliberately introduced in a programme to re-establish this species), sharp-tailed grouse, ring-necked pheasant, gray partridge; white-tail deer, pronghorn, mink, muskrat, weasel, red fox, skunk, raccoon, badger, beaver.

- None in refuge; hotels and motels at Jamestown, 14 miles south. Scouts and guides may remain in properly supervised camps overnight.

- North Dakota 9 runs through the northern tip of the refuge; the county road between Edmunds and Kensal runs through the refuge near HQ.

- Public recreation areas are between the two access roads. Other lakes may be visited by car during the waterfowl nesting season.

- Open all year; best months May to October.

- 1–2 days.

- Free.

- Refuge Manager, Arrowwood National Wildlife Refuge, Rural Route 1, Edmunds, North Dakota 58434/tel: (701) 285–4122.

Audubon National Wildlife Refuge 13,500 acres of prairie land on a bend of the Missouri River with two large lakes containing 200 islands. Refuge for mallard, gadwall, teal, pintail, redhead, pelican, cormorant. Pronghorn, whitetail deer. In spring and autumn, Canada goose, blue and snow geese, sandhill crane, grouse. Camping, boating, picnicking areas available. Near towns of Coleharbour, Garrison and Riverdale, North Dakota. Refuge Manager, Coleharbour, North Dakota. Best May to October.

Des Lacs National Wildlife Refuge 18,881 acres; around 1,790 ft above sea level. A long (28 mile) narrow (average

3 mile) refuge around a lake on the Des Lacs (pronounced day lacks) river; running from the Canada border to about 8 miles south of Kenmare. The lakeshore is marshy and tortuous, making a paradise for marsh and waterfowl. Habitats within and bordering on the refuge include short-grass prairie, lowland meadow, and wooded coulee. The area is famous for the courtship display of the western grebe.

🏃 Apart from all the migratory birds of the central flyway (listed under many other refuges in this section) those that stay on to nest in smaller numbers include mallard, pintail, blue-winged teal, American widgeon, gadwall, shoveler, canvasback, redhead, ruddy duck, scaup; sharp-tailed grouse, gray partridge, ring-necked pheasant, Baird's sparrow, Sprague's pipit, chestnut-collared longspur, western grebe (remant of colony); whitetail deer, beaver.

🛏 None within park; nearest hotels and motels are adjacent to the refuge at Kenmare.

🛬 Kenmare, on N Dakota 52, is on the park border; HQ is immediately over the lake from Kenmare.

🚐 Areas are opened or closed as the needs of their wildlife dictate; water levels, too, are varied according to need and season. Both of these factors determine the accessibility of parts of the refuge. Your best course is to call at HQ first and find the best routes and sites for that particular day.

🌞 Open all year; best time April 12–25 app. and October 24–31 (migration peaks are much narrower in northern US). Climate is pleasant and wildlife plentiful May to October.

🕐 1–2 days.

✉ Free.

➩ Refuge Manager, Des Lacs National Wildlife Refuge, Box 578, Kenmare, N Dakota 58746/tel: (701) 385–4468.

Fort Lincoln State Park 800 acres; about 1,000 ft above sea level. Rolling prairie land and river bottom at the junction of the Heart and Missouri rivers.

🏃 Raccoon, squirrels, cottontail, beaver, pheasants, Hungarian partridge, hawks, golden eagle; songbirds include meadowlark, robin, bluebird, woodpeckers; many waterfowl.

🛏 50 trailer sites $1.75 nightly; tent sites $1–1.75 nightly.

🛬 From Mandan on Highway 6, 4 miles; no rail or private air access. Nearest airport at Bismarck.

🚐 Hardtop and gravel roads.

🌞 Open all year; best months for wildlife early spring and late fall.

🕐 2 days–2 weeks.

✉ 50c daily.

◎ Fort Lincoln, site of General Custer's home base, has a museum, blockhouse, Indian mounds, and the exposed foundations of a parade ground. Fort Hancock, in nearby Bismarck, is also open. The North Dakota badlands are within 100 miles, on Interstate Highway 194.

➩ Superintendent, Mandan, North Dakota/tel: 663–3049.

J. Clark Salyer National Wildlife Refuge 59,000 acres; about 1,400 ft above sea level. This refuge is slightly larger than Upper Souris, which is 40 or so miles to the west. It is one of the major stopping sites on the central flyway and the most important duck production area in this part of the US. Yet the droughts of the 1930s and earlier fruitless attempts to drain the land for farming completely destroyed the water habitat. Every acre you see here is the result of careful re-planting, water control and conservation.

Over 250 observed bird species include all the waterfowl of the central flyway (listed under other refuges in this section) plus grebes, white pelican, sandhill crane, lark bunting, longspur; Baird's, Leconte's, and other sparrows; ring-necked pheasant, sharp-tailed grouse, gray partridge; beaver, muskrat, mink, raccoon, weasel, skunk, whitetail deer, coyote, red fox, badger, porcupine, rabbit.

None in refuge; nearest hotels and motels at Minot.

US 2 to Towner, then north on N Dakota 14 via Upham 26 miles to refuge HQ.

County roads parallel and frequently cross the refuge, giving easy access to the best observation points.

Open all year; best time May to mid-November.

1–2 days.

Free.

Refuge Manager, J. Clark Salyer National Wildlife Refuge, Upham, N Dakota 58789/tel: (701) 763–3223.

Lake Ilo National Wildlife Refuge 3,963 acres, once waterless, now an important oasis in the midst of semi-arid land. Refuge to many species of land birds and waterfowl. Mammals include pronghorn, whitetail deer, mule deer, skunk, beaver, badger. Public park for swimming, boating. Near Dunn Centre. Refuge Manager, Dunn Centre, North Dakota 58626. Best May to October.

Lake Metigoshe State Park 800 acres; around 2,500 ft above sea level. A rolling, heavily wooded glacier range strewn with many lakes.

Deer, beaver, muskrat, mink, bobcat, squirrels, chipmunk, snowshoe rabbit, jackrabbit, cottontail, ruffed grouse, sharp-tailed grouse, loons, ducks, geese, swans, and many song-birds including cardinals.

Trembling aspen, balsam poplar, bur oak, green ash, paper birch, American elm.

Trailer camping $1.75 nightly, tent sites $1 nightly. Motel near park $7–14 nightly.

By road 13 miles northeast of Bottineau, which has a private landing field but no scheduled rail or air access.

On foot or by snowmobile; canoeing on lake. Vehicle access to camp sites only.

Open all year; best for camping May to September.

2 days–2 weeks.

50c per day.

👁 The International Peace Garden is 10 miles from the park, and there is good access to Canada and the Riding Provincial Park.

☞ Park Superintendent, Bottineau, North Dakota/tel: 263–4651.

Long Lake National Wildlife Refuge 22,300 acres in the central flyway of which 16,000 acres are water (except during drought); the rest is prairie grasslands, ravines. Developed to control botulism, a disease afflicting ducks. Duck population has exceeded 150,000, including mallard, gadwall, pintail, teal. Sandhill crane often sighted. Photography. Near town of Moffit. Refuge Manager, Moffit, North Dakota/tel: ORchard 3–4403. Best May to October.

Lostwood National Wildlife Refuge 26,750 acres of native grasslands pitted with thousands of small lakes, potholes in the Coteau (hill) country. Noted for waterfowl. 253 species of birds include scaup, teal, shoveler, mallard, widgeon, grouse. Mammals include whitetail deer, pronghorn. Picnicking, boating, swimming. Near towns of Lostwood and Kenmore, North Dakota. Refuge Manager, North Dakota 58754. Best May to October.

Slade National Wildlife Refuge 3,000 acres of rolling prairie, dotted with lakes and potholes formed by glaciation. Shoveler, redhead, teal, mallard; white pelican, heron, sandpiper. Weasel, badger, red fox. Swimming, picnicking. Near town of Dawson. Refuge Manager, Dawson, North Dakota 58428. Best May to October.

Sullys Hill National Game Preserve 1,675 acres of rolling land, timber and meadow. One of four large fenced game preserves where buffalo, elk, deer live in natural conditions. Also muskrat, raccoon, skunk, weasel. Well equipped picnic grounds. Nearest towns Devil's Lake and Fort Totten. Refuge Manager, Fort Totten, North Dakota 58335. Best May to October.

Tewaukon National Wildlife Refuge 7,845 acres of gently rolling prairie with lakes and marshes, excellent waterfowl nesting grounds. Often more than 100,000 blue and snow geese; also mallard, teal, widgeon, gadwall, pintail. Pheasant, partridge, prairie chicken. Photography. Near towns of Forman, Ligerwood and Cayuga, North Dakota. Refuge Manager, Cayuga, North Dakota 58013. Best May to October.

Turtle River State Park 750 acres; about 1,000 ft above sea level. Set on the heavily wooded shoreline of prehistoric Lake Agassiz; a stream runs the entire length of the park.

⚲ Deer, beaver, raccoon, cottontail, squirrels, chipmunk, mink.

⚃ Similar to Lake Metigoshee.

⛺ Trailer sites $1.50–1.75.

✈ On Highway 2, east of Grand Forks. The air terminal is 12 miles east of the park. No rail access.

�foot Foot and horse trails; snowmobiles in season.

☀ Open all year; best for wildlife in early spring and fall.

🕐 2 days–2 weeks.

✉ 50c daily.

👁 Fort Totten, the only intact fort left from the Indian fighting period, is at Devil's Lake, about 60 miles west.

⇨ Superintendent, Arvilla, North Dakota; no telephone.

Upper Souris National Wildlife Refuge 32,100 acres; around 1,600 ft above sea level. This refuge lies between those of Des Lacs and J. Clark Salyer (see previous listings). Habitat and fauna are practically identical. Lake Darling, which occupies most of the refuge, is notable for its two colonies of western grebes and a large rookery of double-crested cormorants and great blue herons. Common shorebirds of interest include the marbled godwit, avocet, willet, and Wilson's phalarope.

⛺ None in refuge; nearest hotels and motels at Minot, about 25 miles southeast.

✈ From Minot northwest on US 52 to Foxholm, then north on County Highway 11; total 25 miles.

🚍 Conducted tours for groups only.

☀ Open all year; peak population mid-April and end October.

🕐 1–2 days.

✉ Free.

⇨ Refuge Manager, Upper Souris National Wildlife Refuge, Foxholm, N Dakota 58738/tel: (701) 468–7912.

Ohio

Ottawa National Wildlife Refuge 4,815 acres of some of the best waterfowl habitat remaining in the Lake Erie marshes, a pivot point for waterfowl populations separating into the Atlantic or Mississippi flyways. 250 species of birds include blue herons, black-crowned night heron. Muskrat, woodchuck, foxes, raccoon. Near town of Oak Harbor. Refuge Manager, Rural Route 3, Oak Harbor, Ohio 43449. Best April to May, September to November.

South Dakota

Custer State Park 72,000 acres; 4,000–6,400 ft above sea level. An area of mountain and wilderness (the famous Black Hills and badlands) traversed by paved roads and a network of unimproved dirt and gravel roads, enclosed by an 8 ft fence. The park houses one of America's largest buffalo herds (1,500) as well as 500 deer, 400 elk, 500 antelope, 25 bighorn sheep, rocky mountain goat, wild turkey, and other animals. Camp sites and a number of concessioner-operated resorts. The Norbeck Wildlife Preserve and the Mount Rushmore National Monument (where the heads of past presidents are carved into the mountainside) are adjacent to the park on its northern boundary. 7 miles east of Custer on US 16 (alt).

Lacreek National Wildlife Refuge 9,482 acres; about 1,300 ft above sea level. The refuge lies on the division between eastern and western US birdlife and so has especial interest to birdwatchers. Its 11 pools are surrounded by the Nebraska sandhills – the dunes of an ancient ocean. On the northern border is the 360-acre Little White River Recreational Area.

   Blue- and green-winged teal, mallard, pintail, gadwall, shoveler, redhead, canvasback, western grebe, pied-billed grebe, goldeneye, common merganser, lesser scaup, bufflehead, willet, American avocet, long-billed curlew, pelican, cormorant, trumpeter swan (being re-established), ring-necked pheasant, sharp-tailed grouse, and eastern–western hybrids of flickers, juncos, orioles. Tree bird species not abundant. Mammals include mule and white-tailed deer, muskrat, mink, beaver, skunk, raccoon, coyote, ground squirrel, mice.

   None in refuge; nearest hotels and motels at Merriman, Nebraska, about 15 miles south.

   HQ is 14 miles southeast of Martin; the last 7 miles over fair-weather road.

   Most of the refuge is accessible by car in fine weather; call at HQ to check what is accessible on your visit.

   Open all year; best months May to October.

   1–2 days.

   Free.

   Refuge Manager, Lacreek National Wildlife Refuge, South Rural Route, Martin, S Dakota 57551/tel: (605) Martin 2651.

Lake Andes National Wildlife Refuge 5,450 acres of which 4,900 acres is the shallow Lake Andes. Habitat for migrating ducks, geese. Wintering area for Canada geese, mallard. 200 other bird species including bobwhite, ring-necked pheasant, grouse. 18 miles from the town of Lake Andes. Refuge Manager, Box 396, Lake Andes, South Dakota 57356. Best May-November.

Sand Lake National Wildlife Refuge 21,451 acres; around 1,270 ft above sea level. More than half the refuge consists of pool and marsh in two big areas impounded behind earth and rock dams; the rest is prairie grassland, planted belts of shelter, and cultivated strips. Its prime purpose is to provide habitat for waterfowl and upland game.

   White pelican, double-crested cormorant, Canada, white-fronted, and blue geese, mallard, pintail, gadwall, American widgeon, green- and blue-winged teal, shoveler, redhead,

149

canvasback, lesser scaup, whistling swan; horned, eared, western, and pied-billed grebes; great blue- and black-crowned night herons, common and Forster's terns, Franklin's gulls, marsh wrens; ring-necked pheasant, gray partridge, pinnated grouse (prairie chicken – rare); white-tail deer, mule deer, mink, muskrat, beaver.

None in refuge; nearest hotels and motels 28 miles from HQ.

From US 12 turn north at Bath Corner and drive 20 miles on County Road 16 via Columbia. From US 281 drive 2 miles north of Barnard then east on S Dakota 10 for 10 miles then south 2½ miles on County Road 16.

Most parts accessible by road in dry weather; call at HQ for maps and advice about the best routes on the day of your visit.

Open all year; peak waterfowl period 10–15 April (when up to 100,000 birds a day can visit the refuge); peak autumn period 20 September to October.

1–2 days.

Free.

Refuge Manager, Sand Lake National Wildlife Refuge, Columbia, S Dakota 57433/tel. (605) 885-3351.

Wind Cave National Park 438 square miles; 3,840 to 3,880 ft above sea level. Named for the whistling cave whose entrance is in the west of the park; it is a sort of natural barometer with a very sensitive response to changes in barometric pressure. The park, in the southeastern reaches of the famous Black Hills, preserves some original Dakotas prairie and its fauna. The two great wildlife attractions are the buffalo and the black-tailed prairie 'dogs' – colonial rodents, relatives of the marmot, whose 'towns' are abundant here.

Buffalo, black-tailed prairie dog, pronghorn, American elk, deer, coyote, badger, raccoon; meadowlark, woodpeckers, warblers, chickadee, sharp-tailed grouse, kingbird, bluebird, magpie.

Bur oak, American elm, yucca, cactus, cottonwood, ponderosa pine, Rocky Mountain juniper, prairie junegrass, needlegrasses, wheatgrasses, pasqueflower, ground phlox, dark-throat shooting star, mariposa, wallflower, verbena.

Camp-ground at Elk Mountain, accessible by gravel road; rates subject to change. Hotels and motels at Hot Springs, Custer, and other nearby towns.

US 385 between Hot Springs and Custer runs through the southwest of the park; S Dakota 87 to Rapid City runs through the west of the park; both are paved. The gravel-surfaced S Dakota 6 runs through the east of the park. Scheduled air services run to Hot Springs. Edgemont is the nearest railhead.

By roads listed above and by self-guiding nature trail to Rankine Ridge lookout.

Open all year (though the cave itself is closed in winter); snow can impede winter travel; all other seasons are pleasant.

1–2 days.

$1 per car and occupants per day; or 50c per individual hiker, rider, party tourist.

The caves may be visited in the company of a ranger-guide

A mother black bear and three cubs at play.

only; rates from $1.50; trips between November and March for organized groups only. The caverns are lined with the world's finest honeycomb-crystal, or 'boxwork', formations.

⇨ Superintendent, Wind Cave National Park, Hot Springs, S Dakota 57747.

Wisconsin

Horicon National Wildlife Refuge 20,924 acres; around 850 ft above sea level. Like so many waterfowl refuges in the US, Horicon owes more to recent man than to millions of years of geological formation, for during the last hundred years the whole region – a peat-filled shallow, honed out by the Wisconsin glacier in the last ice age – was drained, fired, unsuccessfully farmed, and left derelict. Conservationists have carefully restored the habitat during the last 30 years. Now around 100,000 geese are attracted to the vicinity.

🐾 Canada goose, mallard, blue-winged teal, wood duck, coot, gallinule, egret, great blue heron, yellow-headed blackbird; muskrat, raccoon, opossum, whitetail deer.

🛏 None in refuge; hotels and motels at Horicon, Waupun and Mayville.

🛣 More than 20 numbered roads and spurs or loops skirt the refuge or run up to its borders to terminate in observation points.

☼ Open all year; best months April, October and November.

🕐 1–2 days.

🎟 Free.

⇨ Refuge Manager, Horicon National Wildlife Refuge, Route 2, Mayville, Wisconsin 53050/tel: (414) 387–2658.

Necedah National Wildlife Refuge 40,000 acres of open water and marsh separated by sandy ridges and timbered islands, habitat for 30,000 Canada geese, 55,000 ducks, 200 other species of birds including ruffed grouse, sandhill crane. No recreational facilities. Near town of Necedah. Refuge Manager, Necedah, Wisconsin 54646. Best May to November.

USA : The South

Alabama

Eufaula National Wildlife Refuge 11,160 acres, important river and habour habitat for 40,000 ducks, 10,000 geese, also heron, egret, gulls, snipe, bobwhite, turkey. Beaver, fox, raccoon, muskrat, skunk, opossum, squirrels, bobcat, white-tail deer. Picnicking, boating, swimming, water skiing, camping. Near town of Eufaula. Refuge Manager, Box 258, Eufaula, Alabama 36027. Best March to November.

Wheeler National Wildlife Refuge 35,000 acres of swamp, slough, uplands and farmlands on the Tennessee River. Mainly a waterfowl refuge, but also many species of songbird and upland game. Muskrat, squirrels, opossum, raccoon. Boating, picnicking, photography. Near Decatur. Refuge Manager, Box 1643, Decatur, Alabama 35601. Best March to November.

Arkansas

Big Lake National Wildlife Refuge 10,000 acres of wooded earthquake-formed river bottom in flat cotton-growing country. Refuge for 200 species of birds and waterfowl. Mammals include raccoon, mink, rabbits, muskrat, squirrels, deer. The only remaining virgin cypress in the region. Recreation, picnic areas. Near Manila. Refuge Manager, Box 65, Manila, Arkansas 72442. Best March to November.

Holla Bend National Wildlife Refuge 6,352 acres on the Mississippi River, rich bottomlands once subject to floods, now reclaimed and 'farmed' for waterfowl: acres of buckwheat, corn, soybeans grown for wintering ducks, geese. Golden and bald eagle, 140 other species of birds. Deer, coyote, bobcat. Photography, general sightseeing. Near town of Russellville. Refuge Manager, Box 746, Russellville, Arkansas 72801. Best March to November.

Wapanocca National Wildlife Refuge 5,485 acres containing the beautiful Wapanocca Lake, also croplands, hardwood timber, swamps. Habitat for migrating and wintering waterfowl. Raccoon, fox, deer; mink, muskrat, beaver. Photography, boating. Near Turrell. Refuge Manager, Box 257, Turrell, Arkansas 72384. Best February to May, September to November.

White River National Wildlife Refuge 116,099 acres; about 500 ft above sea level. Though its land was once extensively cut for timber it has never been permanently settled. The refuge is about 35 miles long, north–south, and between 2 and

8 miles broad. It extends along the meandering course of the White River, to which are connected its 165 natural lakes and 125 miles of natural stream. In late winter and spring it is extensively flooded, providing habitat for upwards of 200,000 waterfowl.

🏹 Whitetail deer, occasional black bear, swamp rabbit, squirrel, otter, raccoon, mink. Birds include wood duck, hooded merganser, egrets, herons, wood and white ibises, white pelican, wild turkey, chuck-will's-widow, prothonotary and Swainson's warblers, downy and pileated woodpeckers.

🕸 The old cutting scars have vanished and the refuge is now almost entirely timbered with southern bottom land hardwoods such as cypress, tupelo gum, sweet gum, sycamore, bitter and sweet pecan, ash, maple, elm, and overcut, streaked, and willow oaks.

🛏 Overnight camping permitted at designated sites. Jack's Bay on the west side has picnic facilities and river access for boat launching. Other accommodation available at DeWitt (16 miles away) and Stuttgart (40 miles).

🛬 From the north (Memphis) or east (Little Rock) take US 70 to near Hazen, then Arkansas 11 via Stuttgart to DeWitt from where Arkansas 1 leads to St Charles. From the south turn off US 65 either at McGehee or Dumas for Arkansas 1 to St Charles or at Pine Bluff for US 79 to Stuttgart. Nearest rail links are at Snow Lake to the south and at Marianna on US 79. Nearest scheduled air transportation is at Memphis or at Little Rock.

🚐 By road and on foot; always inquire about the roads at refuge HQ in St Charles, they can flood even in high summer.

🔆 Open all year; best time October to May.

🕐 2 days.

🎟 Free.

📋 Birdlist listing 214 species found in refuge is available at HQ.

👁 One of the decisive Civil War battles was fought near the site of the present HQ at St Charles; some of the old gun emplacements have survived. It was here that the northern gunboat *Mound City* was fired on and sunk with 150 hands.

🔲 Refuge Manager, Box 308, 704 S Jefferson Street, DeWitt, Arkansas 72042/tel: (501) 946–1468.

Florida

Chassahowitzka National Wildlife Refuge 30,000 acres of salt bays, estuaries, brackish marshes, hardwood swamps on Florida's Gulf Coast, benefiting wintering ducks and coots. Resident waterfowl include heron, white ibis, bald eagle. Numerous alligators, mink, raccoon, otter, sea cow. Near Homossa. Refuge Manager, Route 1, Homosassa, Florida 32646/tel: Crystal River 795–2201 (AC 904). Good all year.

Everglades National Park 1,400,533 acres of island, sea, mangrove swamp, and sawgrass, at or near sea level. The Everglades are at the most southerly point of the US mainland; they contain subtropical plant and animal communities unique to the country. For instance, two of the three nesting grounds of the wood ibis, America's only stork, are here. The park is well geared to year-round tourism and is a popular vacation resort as well as a wildlife area. Be sure to stop first at Park Headquarters for an Orientation Program, without which it may be difficult to appreciate the subtle ecological systems of the park. There are good Interpretive Programs at Flamingo, Royal Palm, and Everglades City. As this entry goes to press the survival of much of the north of the park is badly threatened by drought (result of drainage schemes) and fire (result of drought); parts will takes decades to recover.

↗ Saltwater crocodile (rare), manatee, alligator, opossum, raccoon, otter, tree snail. Among major bird species are wood ibis, white ibis, anhinga, roseate spoonbill, egrets, great white and blue herons, swallowtail kite (very rare), bald eagle, Everglades kite, white and brown pelicans, laughing gull.

ஃ Mangrove, mahogany, royal palm, sawgrass and hammock.

↤ Camp sites at Long Pine Key and Flamingo operate on first-come-first-served basis; maximum stay 14 days per year. Trailers (caravans) are permitted but there are no utility or sewage links (deposit sewage only at Flamingo). Limited camping on beaches (fire permit necessary) and at other designated sites in the back country. Staple groceries at Flamingo marina; other supplies in Homestead, Florida City, and other nearby towns. Rates from $16–18. Flamingo Inn offers rooms, each with 2 double beds, heating, air conditioning, and private baths; rates from $16–18 ($8–12 between May 1 and December 1); reserve well in advance.

↦ From the east coast (Miami) go south on US 1 and Florida 27 through Homestead to Florida City from where you follow the directional signs to the park. From the west coast there is access to Western Water Gateway (Everglades City) via Florida 29 and to Florida City via Florida 27 – both from US 41. The Shark Valley Loop in the north-central part of the park also leads off from US 41.

↬ The 38 mile paved road between the entrance and Flamingo takes about a day to explore, if you take in the half dozen loops and trails that lead from and back to it. At Flamingo and at Everglades City in the northwest there are regular guided boat trips to the thousands of creeks, islands, and bays that dot the coastline. The Shark Valley Loop, from US 41 has several parking areas convenient for the Otter Cave trail (frequently closed because of high water) and the fire lookout, which gives a panoramic view of the true everglades 'river of grass'. Boats up to 100 ft can berth at the Flamingo Marina; free launching slipway. Small powerboats for rent; airboats and glades buggies are banned from the park.

☼ Open all year; best time December to March (fewer mosquitos and more birds).

◔ 1–14 days.

▨ $1 per car and occupants per day; or 50c per individual hiker, rider, or party tourist.

▽ Boat trips are guided.

◉ Near Everglades City there are shell mounds built around 2,000 years ago by Calusa Indians.

⇥ Superintendent, Everglades National Park, Box 279, Homestead, Florida 33030.

Island hammocks and sea-of-grass in Everglades NP, Florida.

The Florida Keys refuges The Florida Keys, a long, curving chain of scattered islands that reach from the Florida mainland out into the Gulf of Mexico, are the site of three wildlife refuges. The western keys, beyond Key West and out to the Marquesas, form the Key West National Wildlife Refuge (2,019 land acres in 375 square miles). It supports tern, frigatebird, roseate spoonbill, white-crowned pigeon, osprey, great white heron; boats are the only form of transport. The low, mangrove-covered keys to the north of the main chain (that is, to the north of US 1) form the Great White Heron National Wildlife Refuge (1,996 land acres in about 800 square miles); it protects the great white heron, America's largest wader, and other rare species, including the white-crowned pigeon and roseate spoonbill; transport is by boat only. Most of the National Key Deer Refuge (6,745 acres in about 250 square miles) overlaps the central part of the Great White Heron Refuge, though it also includes some of the larger keys, such as Big Pine, Big and Middle Torch, and Cudjoe keys. The whitetail deer found in the keys is markedly smaller than the mainland deer; they thrive in the keys vegetation, which includes red, black, and white mangrove, palmetto, Jamaica dogwood, blolly, gumbo-limbo, pigeon plum, sea grape, red bay, and poisonwood. Silver palm (especially important to the deer), air plants, and orchids add to the tropical variety. Animals include raccoon, alligator, crocodile, and green turtle. Birds, apart from those already listed, include Louisiana heron, reddish egret, double-crested cormorant, least tern, ruddy turnstone, laughing gull, mangrove cuckoo, black-whiskered vireo, boat-tailed grackle.

🚲 Hotels and motels at Key West.

🛫 US 1 runs south of both the heron and deer refuges to Key West. On Big Pine, Summerland, and Cudjoe keys this

155

    highway gives direct access to the deer refuge; otherwise access and internal transport are by boat.

☀   Open and worth visiting on any month of the year.

⏲   3–12 days combined with general vacation.

☞   Locally experienced boatmen are essential to the success of any visit.

⇨   Refuge Manager, PO Box 385, Big Pine, Florida 33040/tel: (305) 872–2239.

Highlands Hammock State Park 3,800 acres of subtropical forest and cypress swamp. Abundant whitetail deer and alligators; turtle, heron, egret, bittern, ibis, anhinga. Tent and trailer camping; picnics, swimming, boating; no vehicles. Guided nature tours. Open 8am to sundown. 6 miles west of Sebring off US 27 (Orange Blossom Trail) by Florida 634. Park Manager, Box 130, Sebring, Florida/tel: (904) 385–0011 or 385–0015.

Jack Island State Park 985 acres of scrub-saltmarsh island on the Atlantic coast, off the shore of the Indian River; with mangrove, sabal palms, gumbo-limbo, buttonwood, pickleweed, and glasswort. Heron and egret roosting area; saltmarsh butterfly, crabs, shellfish, swamp rabbit, raccoon, wildcat, grey squirrel. Accommodation nearby; picnics, swimming, boating. Self-guided foot tours; no vehicles. Park Manager, 327 Harrison Avenue, Coral Gardens, Route 3, Stuart, Florida, 33494/tel: (305) 287–5423.

J.N. 'Ding' Darling National Wildlife Refuge Over 2,500 acres; at or near sea level. The refuge includes the whole of Sanibel Island and the southern tip of Captiva; it lies off Florida's western coast in the waters of the Gulf of Mexico.

🐾   Alligator, otter, sea turtle. Mallard, black-necked stilt, rail, common gallinule, bittern, herons, egrets, white ibis, lesser scaup, mergansers, pintail, American widgeon, brown and white pelicans, gulls, terns, cormorants, frigatebird, blue- and green-winged teals, bobolink, ground dove, roseate spoonbill, scissor-tailed flycatcher, swallowtail kite, glossy ibis, western kingbird.

☘   Salt and freshwater marsh and slough plants.

🛏   In hotels, motels, and houses on the island; details and bookings via Sanibel Business Men's Association, Sanibel, Florida 33957.

☞   Florida 867 from Fort Myers leads 17 miles, part by causeway, to Sanibel Island.

🚗   By car and on foot. Boats may also be rented.

☀   Open and attractive all year.

⏲   1–2 days (longer if combined with general vacation).

🎟   Free.

👁   Each tide brings in masses of shells from the Gulf; this is one of the world's best shell-gathering coasts.

⇨   Refuge Manager, Lighthouse Quarters No 1, Sanibel, Florida 33957/tel: (813) 472–2251.

John Pennekamp Coral Reef State Park 75 square miles of protected ocean waters and a short, developed stretch of shore; part of the only living coral reef formation in North America. Abundant marine fauna. Tent and trailer camping; picnics, swimming, boating (pontoon, motor, sail, canoe and row boats for hire): glass-bottom boat tours; selfguided catwalk through mangrove swamp. 55 miles south of Miami on US 1. Park Manager, PO Box 487, Key Largo, Florida/tel: (305) 852–5350.

Lake Woodruff National Wildlife Refuge 16,227 acres on St John's River, extensive marsh, hardwood swamp, pinelands. The marsh is habitat for wintering waterfowl including ring-necked duck, teal, pintail, scaup. Hardwood swamp and pine lands are habitat for wood duck, also deer, raccoon, bobcat, armadillo. Access only by water. Motels, hotels, boat rentals available at DeLeon Springs and DeLand. Refuge Manager, Box 488, DeLeon Springs, Florida 32028. Good all year.

Great white heron at the Great White Heron Refuge, Florida.

Loxahatchee National Wildlife Refuge 145,562 acres of everglade; at or near sea level. The refuge is a huge freshwater storage area regulated by levees and canals. Like all everglades habitat it was the bed of a shallow sea only 2 million years ago. Today the Loxahatchee bed is around 15 ft above sea level and is overlain by a lush covering of peat and other decayed marsh vegetation. The main purpose of the refuge is to provide nesting for migratory waterfowl over the winter. It is also one of the few remaining nesting areas of the ever-glades kite.

Raccoon, mink, river otter, Florida water rat (a kind of muskrat), bobcat, whitetail deer, rabbit, bobwhite, fresh-water snail, alligator, and many small reptiles. Birdlife includes ring-necked duck, pintail, blue- and green-winged teal, American widgeon, shoveler, mottled and wood duck, coot, everglades kite, limpkin, Florida sandhill crane, ibises, egrets, herons, roseate spoonbill, smooth-billed ani.

Typical everglades country with sawgrass marshes, wet prairie, sloughs, and tree islands; beakrush, white water lily, smartweed.

None in refuge; the whole of Palm Beach and Miami are within easy reach. The refuge is closed from an hour after sunset to an hour before dawn.

From the Atlantic resorts any east–west road leads to US 441, which passes the refuge HQ; it also gives southern access, via the Hillsboro Levee to the S-39 landing, and northern access, via West Palm Beach Canal or Florida 80, to the S-5A landing. The Sunshine State Parkway has interchanges with Florida 802 (for the north of the refuge), 806 (for HQ), and 808 (for the south).

At the S-39 landing there are picnic supplies, guides, and rental boats; details from Loxahatchee Recreation Inc, Route 1, Box 6428, Pompano Beach, Florida 33060. There are also launching ramps and picnic facilities at the S-5A landing and the HQ landing.

Open all year; best time October to May.

1–3 days.

Free.

Refuge Manager, Box 278, Route 1, Delray Beach, Florida 33444/tel: (305) 732-3684.

Merritt Island National Wildlife Refuge 57,996 acres; at or near sea level. The refuge, established as recently as 1963, occupies the 'buffer zone' between the Cape Kennedy launching sites and the John F. Kennedy Space Center. It is composed entirely of shallow areas of fresh water mingled with saltwater creeks and lagoons; here and there are scattered stands of palmetto, oak, slash pine, and cabbage palm. At rocket-launching times, when visitors seek all possible vantage points, most of the refuge is closed.

The official birdlife list records 224 species and 31 casual or accidental visitors. Thousands of waterfowl winter on the refuge. Residents and visitors include mottled duck and 20 other duck species (September to April), lesser scaup, American widgeon, pintail, blue-winged teal, coots, snow and blue geese, brown and white pelican, southern bald eagle (endangered), dusky seaside sparrow (endangered).

Motels in Titusville and other nearby towns.

From US 1 or Sunshine State Parkway via the Port Canaveral road through City Point.

Florida 406 and Kennedy Parkway allow travel over parts of the refuge.

Open all year; best time October to May.

1–2 days.

Refuge Manager, Box 956, Titusville, Florida 32780/tel: (305) 267-2640.

Myakka River State Park 28,875 acres (the largest in the state system) of twisting river, dense woodland, and lake.

Whitetail deer, wild turkey, alligator, feral pig, all abundant. Florida sandhill crane, rare elsewhere, is common. One of the state's largest nesting-roosting areas for heron and egret; 209 bird species. Five rustic cabins; tent and trailer camping; picnics, swimming, boating. Guided foot, boat, and trackless train tours. 17 miles east of Sarasota on Florida 72. Park Manager, Route 1, Box 72, Sarasota, Florida/tel: (813) 924–1027.

Saint Marks National Wildlife Refuge 96,835 acres (31,700 acres closed by Presidential Proclamation); at or near sea level. The refuge includes the only major wintering area for Canada goose in Florida. It lies on Apalachee Bay, some 30 miles south of Tallahassee, and is bisected by the St Marks and Wakulla rivers. Salt water marshes border the bay, giving way to brackish and freshwater marshland; a little farther inland are flatwood and hardwood swamps; the higher land (still only 30 ft above sea level at most) supports pine woods.

↰ Whitetail deer, bobcat, fox squirrel, alligator. Birdlife includes clapper and king rails, willet, marsh wren, seaside sparrow, purple and common gallinules, red-winged blackbird, wild turkey, red-bellied and cockaded woodpeckers, brown-headed nuthatch, bluebird, yellow-throated and pine warblers, pinewoods sparrow, ruddy turnstone, common and snowy egret, great blue, Louisiana, and little blue herons, cormorants, anhingas, night heron, bald eagle, osprey, white and brown pelicans, wood ibis, and, of course, Canada goose.

⅋ Manatee grass; hardwood swamps support oak, bay, holly, southern white cedar, cypress, gum, magnolia, cabbage palmetto, Caribbean pine, myrtle, gallberry, pinegrass; pinewoods include longleaf pine, turkey oak, pinegrass, shrub oak, saw palmetto, and various lugumes.

⇌ Food and lodging available in most of the small bay towns. Cooking and picnicking facilities at the Otter Lake Recreational Area in the park, but no overnight camping.

⇥ From Newport take Florida 30 and then Florida 59 to the refuge entrance. The refuge is open only during daylight hours.

🚐 The Lighthouse Road gives access to nearly all habitats on the refuge.

� Open all year; largest waterfowl concentrations from mid-November to mid-January.

⏱ 1–3 days.

🎟 Free.

📷 Many available in bay towns.

👁 The area has a number of historic monuments: the old Spanish fort San Marcos de Apalachee, dating from 1679; the still working St Marks lighthouse of 1831; and the old seine yards (Florida's oldest) where sea mullet have been seined for over 150 years – here you can buy fish straight from the sea and fry it over open fires.

⇨ Refuge Manager, Box 68, St Marks, Florida 32355/tel: (904) 925–6280.

Georgia

Blackbeard Island National Wildlife Refuge 5,600 acres of oak forest, ponds, salt marshes and windy savannas bounded on one side by the Atlantic Ocean. Habitat for 198 species of birds including ducks, heron, egret, white ibis, chachalaca, turkey, painted bunting. Deer, sea turtle, alligators. Areas set aside for virgin slash pine, hardwood and oak. No facilities provided. Near Townsend, Georgia. Refuge Manager, Savannah National Wildlife Refuge, Route 1, Hardeeville, South Carolina 29927. Best April to December.

Okefenokee National Wildlife Refuge 340,777 acres; 100 ft above sea level. 'Okefenokee' is a paleface rendition of Indian words meaning 'land of trembling earth'. The thick peat deposits that cover the floor of this giant primeval morass are so loose and resilient that in places one can actually set nearby trees trembling by jumping up and down. The giant cypresses, vines, gordonias, other trees, and thick undergrowth are all rooted in this peat crust (20 ft thick in places) – most have no contact with the ground at all. Through the 630 square miles of this unspoiled wilderness thread the rich brown waters of Okefenokee. These twisting waterways finally converge – most at the Suwannee River outlet in the southwest.

- Alligator, bear, raccoon, otter, whitetail deer; sandhill crane, egret, ibis, wood duck, anhinga, limpkin, swallowtail kite, barred owl, wild turkey.
- Cypress, vines, gordonia, cassena, smilax, maple blackgum, white and yellow waterlily, neverwet, pickerelweed, floating hearts, swamp marigold, swamp iris.
- None in refuge; hotels at Waycross and nearby towns.
- Three public use areas: *Okefenokee Swamp Park*, managed by Okefenokee Association Inc, Waycross, Georgia 31501; most of it located outside refuge boundary, 8 miles south of Waycross, just off US 1 and 23; open all year 8am to sunset; no overnight accommodation, guided boat tours. *Camp Cornelia*, on Suwannee Canal; west from Georgia 23 about 7 miles southwest of Folkston; canal and certain areas open to visitors in own small (less than 10 hp) boats without guides; for remoter areas licensed guides are mandatory; information from Camp Cornelia, Suwannee Canal Landing, Folkston, Georgia 31537. *Stephen Collins Foster State Park*, for easiest access to Billy's Lake, Minnie's Lake, and Big Water; boats and guides available as for Camp Cornelia; dormitory and cottage accommodation, restaurant, picnic area; leave US 441 a half-mile southeast of Fargo, follow blacktop road northeast for 15 miles; information from Stephen Collins Foster State Park, Fargo, Georgia 31631.
- No roads in refuge; all transport by boat.
- Open and interesting all year.
- 2–3 days.
- Free.
- Available at all public use areas.
- Refuge Manager, Box 117, Waycross, Georgia 31501/tel: (912) 982–3651.

Piedmont National Wildlife Refuge 33,248 acres of mainly pine forest. Waterfowl and upland game including deer, wild turkey, bobwhite, pileated woodpecker. Photography. Near town of Round Oak. Refuge Manager, Round Oak, Georgia 31080. Best April to November.

Louisiana

Chicot State Park 6,480 acres; 50 to 80 ft above sea level. The park is built around a 2,500 acre lake surrounded by cypress and tupelo gum, mixed pine, and hardwood forest.

⇶ Squirrels, rabbit, deer, fox, opossum, raccoon, nutria, skunk, wildcat, armadillo, and a few alligators. The remoter parts of the park are undeveloped, and there you may see the shyer animals and many upland and shorebirds.

ЯЗ The Louisiana Arboretum occupies 301 acres within the park and has its own separate 32-page guide. Trails lead past 112 different kinds of trees and shrubs.

⇌ Tent ($1.30 nightly) and trailer ($1.80 nightly), campsites; air conditioners $1 extra; 4-berth cabins $7.

⇛ From Ville Platte (nearest city) take Louisiana 3042.

🚗 Hardtop roads, foot trails; hire boats on lake.

🌅 Open all year; fall is best for migratory birds, especially waterfowl, spring is best for the arboretum.

🕐 2–7 days.

☞ Park personnel always on hand with advice and assistance.

⇒ Louisiana State Parks and Recreation Commission, PO Box 1111, Baton Rouge, Louisiana 70821 or Chamber of Commerce, Ville Platte, Louisiana 70586.

Delta National Wildlife Refuge 48,800 acres in the Mississippi Delta: deltaic marshes, shallow ponds, passes, bayous, canals. Blue and snow geese, more than 18 species of duck, brown pelican (Louisiana state bird, rare), skimmer. Whitetail deer, coypu, raccoon, alligator. Accessible only by boat. No facilities. Near town of Venice. Refuge Manager, Venice, Louisiana 70091/tel: Pilottown 3–3232. Good all year.

Lacassine National Wildlife Refuge 31,770 acres; practically at sea level. Less than 40 miles from the Gulf of Mexico, Lacassine is near the southern end of the Mississippi flyway. Its main attraction is the 16,000 acres of man-made pool that fills most of the west of the refuge. It is a major wintering area for waterfowl, housing the largest concentration of white-fronted geese in the flyway and one of the USA's largest fulvous tree duck populations.

⇶ Nutria, armadillo, alligator, otter, mink raccoon, muskrat, skunk, rabbit; Canada, white-fronted, blue, and snow geese; blue-winged teal, pintail, mallard, American widgeon, shoveler, scaup, gadwall; wood, mottled, and fulvous tree ducks; cattle, common, and snowy egrets; white, and white-faced ibises; Louisiana, little blue, great blue, black-crowned and yellow-crowned night herons; purple and common gallinules; roseate spoonbill, anhinga, olivaceous cormorant, eagle, black skimmer.

☃   Chiefly sawgrass and maidencane marsh with a few groves of cypress; planted areas of ryegrass, rye, wheat, and oats for wildfowl grazing.

🛌   None in refuge. Rooms and meals in Lake Arthur (11 miles away). Hotels and motels at Welsh (18 miles) and Jennings (22 miles).

⇌   Refuge HQ is 6 miles west of Lake Arthur on Louisiana 14, then 5 miles south on Louisiana 3056; the refuge can be reached from there only by boat.

🚘   Only by boat; travel on the lake is only by airboat. Boats and airboats may be rented.

☼   Open all year; best time October to April.

⏱   1–2 days.

📩   Free.

🕳   Available and advisable.

⇒   Refuge Manager, Box 186, Route 1, Lake Arthur, Louisiana 70549/tel: (318) 774–2750.

Sabine National Wildlife Refuge 152,845 acres of fresh and brackish marsh, three large artificial impoundments, bordered to the east and west by two large brackish lakes important to wintering blue and snow geese and ducks. A major refuge for the American alligator. Mammals include nutria, mink, otter, deer, foxes, armadillo. Access by boat. Nearest town Hackberry, Louisiana. Refuge Manager, MRH Box 107, Sulphur, Louisiana 70663. Best September to June.

Sam Houston State Park 1,086 acres; 10 to 25 ft above sea level. The park is bordered by the west fork of the Calcasieu river and contains several small lakes. The surrounding forest is chiefly mixed pine and hardwood.

🐇   Squirrel, rabbit, opossum, raccoon, fox, deer (in a large outdoor pen), armadillo, skunk: abundant upland birds and some waterfowl.

☃   Loblolly and longleaf pines, water and red oaks, sweetgum, cypress, tupelo, dogwood, magnolia, ash, hickory, and pecan. Many wildflowers and shrubs.

🛌   As for Chicot State Park.

⇌   Via Louisiana 378 and secondary roads – all signposted. Rail, air, and bus connections to Lake Charles, nearest city.

🚘   Hardtop roads and foot trails; hire boats on the river and one of the lakes.

☼   Open all year; best times spring and fall.

⏱   2–7 days.

📩   Free.

⇒   Louisiana State Parks and Recreation Commission (see Chicot State Park) or Chamber of Commerce, Lake Charles, Louisiana 70601.

One of Louisiana's historic monuments deserves especial mention in this book, for, although it is not especially prolific in wildlife, it is the estate on which in 1821 America's great naturalist-painter John James Audubon painted 32 of his portraits for 'Birds of America'. It is Oakley House, the Oakley Plantation home built in 1799 and since restored and furnished as it was when Audubon was there as tutor to the Oakley children. The Museum, open Monday to Saturday 9am to 4.45pm, Sunday 1pm to 4.45pm, is reached from US 61, 3 miles south of St Francisville via Louisiana 965. There is a small admission charge. Inquiries to PO Box 445, St Francisville, Louisiana/tel: (504) 635–3729.

Mississippi

Noxubee National Wildlife Refuge 45,750 acres of formerly depleted land now reclaimed into woodlands, fields, streams, lakes forming an important multi-purpose refuge for upland game and 115,000 migratory waterfowl. Also 200 species of birds, and deer, otter, beaver, muskrat, bobcat. Picknicking, photography. Near Starkville and Brooksville, Mississippi. Refuge Manager, Route 1, Brooksville, Mississippi 39739/ tel area code: 601, 323–5548. Best February to May, September to November.

Yazoo National Wildlife Refuge 9,836 acres in the bottomlands of the Mississippi valley, habitat for geese and ducks, especially mallard. Also heron, egret. Deer, opossum. mink, bobcat, foxes. Alligators are common. 12 miles from Hollandale. Refuge Manager, Route 1, Box 286, Hollandale, Mississippi 38748. Best February to May, September to November.

A gray squirrel, one of the world's most successful tree squirrels.

North Carolina

Mattamuskeet National Wildlife Refuge 50,177 acres, most of it lake; at or near sea level. In the early years of this century Mattamuskeet Lake bankrupted many companies that tried to drain it and turn its bed into farmland. Then, during the 1930's, the land was acquired for a refuge and the pumping plant was turned into visitor accommodation (its smoke-stack makes a superb observation tower). Today the lake, which is intensively cultivated for wildfowl-preferred food plants, is the winter home of the largest flock of Canada geese on the Atlantic seaboard as well as for a large colony of whistling swans.

- Canada goose, whistling swan, redhead, canvasback, scaup, goldeneye, bufflehead.

- Chiefly aquatic and field waterfowl forage crops, including corn, soybean, and green crops.

- Space for up to 50 people, ranging from singles and doubles with private bath to 4-bed dormitories. During the hunting season (November to January) bookings are heavy and must be made well in advance. Meals in lodge dining room. All inquiries to Concessioner, Mattamuskeet Lodge, New Holland, North Carolina 27885. Motels and rooms in nearby townships.

- US 264 skirts the south of the lake and runs within a half-mile of refuge HQ. North Carolina 94 crosses the lake, linking US 264 with the township of Fairfield on the northern edge of the refuge.

- Being mostly lake, the refuge has few roads; but the trails that lead to the blinds are useful for birdwatching.

- Open all year; few waterfowl but plenty of songbirds in summer; best time for bird watching early autumn and winter and spring, before and after the hunting season.

- 1–2 days.

- Free.

- Available, and required when hunting.

- Refuge Manager, New Holland, North Carolina 27885/tel: (919) 926–4021.

Pea Island National Wildlife Refuge 6,700 acres of beach, dunes, marsh, bounded on one side by Pamlico Sound and on the other by the open Atlantic. A narrow strip of barrier beach offers habitat to thousands of wintering snow geese. 34 species of shorebirds include large numbers of tern. Camping, picnicking, photography. Near Elizabeth City, North Carolina. Refuge Manager, Box 606, Manteo, North Carolina 27954. Best March to December.

Pungo National Wildlife Refuge 12,229 acres dominated by Pungo Lake, also farmland, timber, freshwater marsh. Habitat for wintering Canada goose, duck, swan; migratory stop-over for heron, egret, ibis. Mammals include whitetail deer, raccoon, foxes, black bear. Photography. Near town of Plymouth. Refuge Manager, PO Box 116, Plymouth, North Carolina 27962.

Adult royal terns flying and nesting at a rookery on Gull Island in Pamlico Sound, North Carolina. They are larger than some gulls.

South Carolina

Cape Romain National Wildlife Refuge 60,000 acres stretching along 15 miles of the Atlantic coastline in South Carolina. This is one of the eastern USA's outstanding refuges, comprising sea islands, salt marshes, twisting coastal streamlets, and long sand beaches. Many of the smaller islands are flooded at exceptional tides; others, among them Bulls Island – the most popular and the largest – are always above water. Bulls Island, an ancient barrier reef, measures 6 by 2 miles; its inland woods and ponds provide nesting and feeding habitat for thousands of waterfowl and songbirds.

Alligator, otter, raccoon, fox squirrel, wild turkey, whitetail deer, giant sea turtle, diamondback terrapin; gulls, cormorant, horned grebe, brown pelican, black skimmer, bald eagle, pileated woodpecker, peregrine falcon, black, ring-necked, and ruddy duck, pintail, mallard, gadwall, blue-and green-winged teals, Canada goose, scaup, bufflehead, shoveler, coot, common gallinule, turnstone, sanderling, knot, dowitcher, yellowleg, black-bellied and semipalmated plover, willet, dunlin, long-billed curlew, marbled godwit, American oystercatcher, clapper rail, wood ibis, snowy egret, herons, pine warbler, cardinal, Carolina wren, great crested flycatcher, white-eyed and red-eyed vireo, yellow-throated warbler, chuck-will's-widow, painted bunting, royal and least terns.

Loblolly pine, laurel and live oaks, magnolia, cabbage palmetto, red bay, yaupon, wax myrtle, holly, pine, vines (muscadine, greenbriar, yellow jessamine, supplejack, peppervine, Virginia creeper, and poison ivy), mistletoe, tree fern, banana waterlily, sago pondweed, widgeongrass, giant foxtail, wild millet, smartweed, bullrush, spikerush.

🏠 Dominick House on Bulls Island has space for up to 15 overnight guests. Reservations via Concessioner, Dominic House, Bulls Island, Awendaw, South Carolina 29429/tel: Mobile Unit YJ6–3473, Charleston, South Carolina. Hotels, motels, and rooms in Charleston, McClellanville, and other nearby towns.

🛫 US 17 runs along most of the northwestern border of the refuge. For Bulls Island you turn off it 20 miles northeast of Charleston and take the Sewee Road 5 miles to Moore's Landing where the concessioner's boat (depending on tides) meets you by prior arrangement.

🚗 A small network of improved and dirt roads covers the eastern end of Bulls Island. Boats to nearby islands may be arranged through the concessioner.

🌤 Open all year: best time October to May.

🕐 1–5 days.

📧 Free.

📄 Available.

➩ Refuge Manager, McClellanville, South Carolina 29458/ tel: (803) 887–3211.

Carolina Sandhills National Wildlife Refuge 46,000 acres of sandhills and pine and scrub oak woodland. Emphasis has been on sanctuary for ducks and geese but wild turkey, deer, beaver are plentiful. Mammals include bobcat, foxes, squirrels, cottontail, opossum, muskrat, skunk. Recreation areas, picnic shelters, camp-sites. Near town of McBee. Refuge Manager, McBee, South Carolina 29101. Best April to November.

A long-eared owl. The so-called 'ears' are in fact tufts of feathers used for display; they have nothing to do with hearing. The long-eared species is remarkable for its extremely flexible neck.

Santee National Wildlife Refuge 74,352 acres of marsh with two lakes, on upper coastal plains of South Carolina, refuge for the southernmost major flock of Canada goose. Some 125,000 wintering ducks: mallard, widgeon, pintail, black duck. Raccoon, mink, otter, muskrat, foxes, bobcat. Picnicking, boating, accommodation. Near Summerton. Refuge Manager, PO Box 186, Summerton, South Carolina 29148. Best April to November.

Savannah National Wildlife Refuge 13 acres on the Savannah River, with swamp, marsh, dikes and impoundments. Some 15 duck species, also grebes, rails, ibis, bittern. Whitetail deer. Nearest town Savannah, South Carolina. Refuge Manager, Route 1, Hardeeville, South Carolina 29927/tel: 233–2315. Best March to December.

Tennessee

Cross Creeks National Wildlife Refuge 9,892 acres of rolling hills, rocky bluffs bordering marshy, pool-covered bottomland stretching 10 miles on either side of Barkley Lake. Habitat for 200 species of birds, numerous mammals, reptiles. Wintering refuge for ducks, geese. Picnicking, boating, photography. Near Dover. Refuge Manager, Route 1, Box 113–B, Dover, Tennessee 37058. Best April to November.

Great Smoky Mountains National Park 800 square miles; 1,417 to 6,643 ft above sea level. Named for the smokelike mist that rises from the dense vegetation and forest that covers the Appalachian Highlands along the Tennessee–North Carolina border, the park straddles some of the highest points in the chain of hills and mountains – the loftiest in the eastern USA. Much of this mountain wilderness is unspoiled and virgin; even in days when it was Cherokee country (they have a reservation adjoining the park in North Carolina), it was sparsely settled. White settlers, mainly of British descent, were fewer and lived in virtual isolation until well into this century; some of their buildings, rehabilitated, are preserved within the park.

    Black bear, whitetail deer, woodchuck, flying and other squirrels, muskrat, opossum, bats, moles, shrews, long-tailed weasel, mink, skunk, bobcat. Some 200 bird species include cardinal, Carolina wren, song sparrow, tufted titmouse, eastern phoebe, Carolina chickadee, woodpeckers, scarlet tanager, rose-breasted grosbeak, vireo, saw-whet owl, wood thrush, bunting, flycatchers, Carolina juncos, warblers, raven.

    Over 1,300 flowering species, 2,000 fungus species, 350 liverworts and mosses, 230 lichens. Most extensive stand of virgin red spruce in the eastern US. Yellow buckeye, basswood, yellow poplar, silverbell, eastern hemlock, white ash, sugar maple, yellow birch, American beech, black cherry,

northern red oak, cucumbertree, mountain laurel, blueberry, smilax, sandmyrtle, rhododendron, azalea, clintonia, indianpipe, ladyslipper, Canada mayflower, white baneberry, catawba, Alleghany menziesia, Carolina rhododendron, Fraser magnolia, silver bell, eastern hemlock, trailing arbutus, and many herbs.

8 developed camping grounds, 4 camp sites, and numerous shelter cabins lie within the park or at its entrances; available on first-come-first-served basis, 7-day maximum. There are 56 wilderness camping sites in the park. Trailer facilities (no sewer or electricity) available at some developed camping grounds. Summit Le Conte Lodge, accessible only on foot or horseback (a day's journey, so take lunch); rates from $6; advance reservations (strongly advised) to Concessioner, Herrick B. Brown, Gatlinburg, Tennessee 37738/tel: (614) 436–4473 (winter tel: 615–436–4620). Overnight feeding and care of saddlehorse $5.

More than 2 dozen roads and trails lead into the park from nearby state and national highways, and no part is truly inaccessible. From Knoxville in Tennessee and Asheville in North Carolina there are scheduled Smoky Mountains bus tours; both cities have good rail and air connections.

2 highways run through the park, across the state border. The Appalachian National Scenic Trail, which runs from Georgia to Maine runs for 71 miles (a 6–8 day hike) along the crest of the smokies, through the backbone of the park.

View from Clingman's Dome Road in Great Smoky Mountains NP.

Shelters and camp sites with bunks for 6 people each, are spaced about a day's journey apart. Some 650 miles of foot and horse trail connect the main camping grounds and remoter parts of the park. There are also guided nature walks for groups; details in the *Naturalist Program* posted at visitor centres, ranger stations, and local hotels. Short selfguiding nature trails have also been laid out.

☼ Open all year; best time late spring and autumn.

🕐 2–14 days.

🏕 Under review at time of going to press.

📖 *Land of High Horizons* by E. S. Bowman (Southern Pubs Inc, 1948); *Southern Highlander and his Homeland* by J. C. Campbell (Russel Sage Foundation, 1921); *Our Southern Highlands* by H. Kephart (Macmillan, N.Y.); *The Smokies Guide* by G. M. Stephens (Stephens Press Inc, Asheville); *The Great Smoky Mountains* by L. Thornborough (Univ. of Tenn. Press, 1956).

👁 Pioneer buildings and clearings are chiefly sited at Cades Cove, Tennessee, in the west of the park. Other structures, with a display of tools, household objects, and early hand-made items, are on display at the Ocanaluftee Visitor Center.

⇨ Superintendent, Great Smoky Mountains National Park, Gatlinburg, Tennessee 37738.

169

Hatchie National Wildlife Refuge 1,404 acres of hardwood timbered bottomland on the Hatchie River. Migrating waterfowl, mallard, wood duck. Squirrels, deer, raccoon. Near Brownsville. Refuge Manager, 34 Jefferson Street, Brownsville, Tennessee 38012. Best April to November.

Reelfoot National Wildlife Refuge 11,626 acres including Reelfoot Lake (formed by earthquakes) and uplands. Refuge for wintering waterfowl: Canada goose, mallard, American widgeon, gadwall. Some 230 bird species. Foxes, squirrels, muskrat, mink, beaver. Camping, boating, tourist accommodation. Near town of Samburg. Refuge Manager, Box 295, Samburg, Tennessee 38254. Best April to November.

Tennessee National Wildlife Refuge 51,250 acres on Kentucky Lake, largest and lowermost of Tennessee Valley Authority lakes. Wintering Canada goose, shoveler, gadwall, teal, redhead. Also bald and golden eagles, wild turkey. Squirrels, mink, muskrat, raccoon. Nearest towns Paris and Parson, Tennessee. Refuge Manager, PO Box 849, Paris, Tennessee 38242. Best May to November.

Virginia

Back Bay National Refuge 9,240 acres of barrier beach between Atlantic Ocean and Back Bay; large water areas, marshes, sand dunes, woodland. Dikes provide habitat for wintering whistling swans, geese, varieties of ducks. 250 species of year-round shore birds. Raccoon, opossum, foxes, muskrat, nutria, rabbits. Reached by boat, jeep or beach-buggy. Near Virginia Beach. Refuge Manager, PO Box 6128, Virginia Beach, Virginia 23456. Best August to December, April to June.

Chincoteague National Wildlife Refuge 9,439 acres; at or near sea level. All but 400 acres (which are in Maryland) lie in the Virginia portion of Assateague Island, which shelters Chincoteague Island and Bay from the Atlantic. The refuge is about 13 miles long and about $1\frac{1}{2}$ miles wide; most of it is coastal wetland but man-made dikes protect 7 freshwater pools that hold about 3,000 acres of rainwater whose salinity and vegetation is carefully controlled in the interests of the thousands of waterfowl which inhabit the refuge at various times of the year. Two oddities are the Japanese sika deer, released on the island in 1923, and the Chincoteague ponies, which look like dappled Exmoor ponies and are herded and sold annually in much the same way; they either swam ashore from a wreck or were put ashore to graze – probably since the days of Columbus.

⚑ Ponies, sika deer, red fox, raccoon, muskrat, cottontail, otter. Over 275 bird species include black and sea ducks, blue- and green-winged teal, mallard, gadwall, pintail, American widgeon, shoveler, Canada and snow geese, scoter, oldsquaw, bufflehead, merganser, brant, loon, grebe, sandpiper, plover, curlew, turnstone, oystercatcher, willet, yellowlegs, egrets, herons, ibises, avocet, terns, gulls, black skimmer.

❀ Sago pondweed, widgeongrass, spikerush, bulrush, smartweeds, cordgrass; pines, oak, myrtle, bayberry, sumac, rose, greenbrier; planted crops of millet, ryegrass, and green forage.

🛏 None in refuge; the southernmost part is administered as a recreational area, with store-cafe and other facilities. Motels at Chincoteague.

✈ HQ is 3 miles east of Chincoteague. From Virginia 175 turn left on Main Street, then right on Maddox Boulevard to the refuge.

🚗 The access road leads through HQ and skirts the southern edge of the refuge (ponds A and F) to the concession area. From here and in the refuge itself only foot traffic is permitted.

☀ Open all year; best time March to November.

🕐 1–2 days.

➡ Refuge Manager, PO Box 62, Chincoteague, Virginia 23336/ tel: (703) 336–6122.

Fairy Stone State Park in the foothills of the Blue Ridge mountains has most of the birdlife listed for Seashore State Park as well as others like wood peewee, phoebe, yellow-bellied sapsucker, and pine siskin. Stuart's Knob Trail, within the park, is selfguiding; the brochure identifies 19 trees including sassafras, tulip tree, black or yellow locust, sourwood, shagbark hickory, and cucumber tree. Housekeeping cabins, tent and trailer sites, lakeshore swimming, picnics, boating, horse hire, boat hire, restaurant. Route 57 from Bassett or routes 8 and 57 from the Blue Ridge Parkway. Division of Parks, Suite 501, Southern States Bldg, Richmond, Virginia 23219.

Hungry Mother State Park in southwest Virginia has similar birdlife to the other Virginia parks as well as grosbeak, horned lark, purple martin, and nuthatches; they are best seen from Molly's Knob Natural Area (3,270 ft), which affords a panoramic view of the whole countryside. Facilities as for Fairy Stone State Park. 3 miles from Marion on Route 16 (Exit 16 or 17 from Interstate 81). Division of Parks, address as for Fairy Stone SP.

Parkers Marsh Natural Area on the eastern coast of Chesapeake Bay is an unmanaged swamp wilderness – that is, the ecology is not manipulated by development or controlled hunting. Deer, otter, muskrat, raccoon, red fox, cotton rat; black duck, clapper rail, osprey, marsh wren, sparrows, red-

171

winged blackbird, willet, common and boat-tailed grackles; great blue, green, little blue, and black-crowned night herons; American and snowy egrets, least and American bitterns, mallard, pintail, widgeon, greater and lesser scaups, redhead, canvasback, goldeneye, bufflehead, old-squaw, blue and green-winged teals, greater and lesser yellowlegs, least and spotted sandpipers, least tern, great black-backed, and herring and laughing gulls. Glasswort, bullrush, needlegrass rush, cordgrass, saltgrass, eastern baccharis, bigleaf sumpweed, beach plum, southern waxmyrtle. Foot travel only; access only by boat or with waders. Access to Onacock, nearest town, from US 13 via State 178 and 179.

Pocahontas State Park in a large state forest close to Richmond and Petersburg also has most of the birdlife of the other Virginia state parks; especially common are nuthatches, cardinal, blue jay, tufted titmouse, mockingbird, flicker, quail, and crows. The wildflower area, a natural garden, has bloodroot, trillium, may apple, jack-in-the-pulpit, solomon seal, bellworts, sticktight, joe-pye-weed, goldenrod, sun- and coneflowers, spotted wintergreen, and prince's pine. Campsites, horse trails, boating, swimming; camps for organized groups. 4 miles west of Chesterfield courthouse, Exit 6 from Interstate 95 via State Route 10, or Exit 7 via routes 150 and 10; Route 150 (Chippenham Parkway) connects US 1 and 301, 60, and 360 with Route 10. Division of parks, address as for Fairy Stone SP.

Presquile National Wildlife Refuge 1,329 acres on the James River, tidal swamp and marsh and uplands. Waterfowl include snow and blue geese, black and other ducks. Also 198 bird species including black vulture, yellow-billed cuckoo. Access only by private boat or refuge-operated ferry; notify Refuge Manager before visiting. Refuge Manager, Box 658, Hopewell, Virginia 23860. Best August to November, April to May.

Seashore State Park 2,770 acres; at or near sea level. The park comprises the northern tip of Cape Henry, which guards the southern headland of Chesapeake Bay. It was here, on 26 April 1607, that the first settlers to establish a permanent English-speaking colony in North America first set foot. The park includes a rich mixture of ocean, beach, swamp, saltspray grassland and scrub, and forest.

Apart from numerous reptiles and amphibia; black bear, gray fox, whitetail deer, Virginia opossum, bobcat, eastern cottontail, mink, otter, long-tailed weasel, raccoon, flying, red, and gray squirrels; little brown, silver-haired, red, and evening bats; harbor seal and bottle-nosed dolphin. Over 110 bird species include indigo bunting, cardinal, chuck-will's-widow, mourning dove, ducks, bald eagle, flycatchers, common grackle, pied-billed grebe; hawks, herons, ruby-throated hummingbird, slate-coloured junco, killdeer, kingfisher, mockingbird, common nighthawk, osprey, owls, sparrows, swallows, tanagers, towhee, vireos, vultures, warblers, cedar waxwing, woodpeckers, wrens.

ஃ Dogwood, water oak, partridge berry, loblolly pine, white oak, black oak, holly, beech, southern red oak, baldcypress, hophornbeam, bitternut hickory, white hickory, sweetgum, black gum, red maple, horse sugar, persimmon, water lilies, Spanish moss, and saltspray grasses and shrubs.

⇌ 20 housekeeping cabins; tent and trailer camp sites. Grocery and snack concessions. Camp sites cost $2 per night mid-April to mid-October, $1 rest of year; maximum stay 7 days. Cabins range from $32 per week (capacity 2) to $92 (capacity 6); maximum 14 days (longer if there is no subsequent booking).

✈ On US 60 a few miles north of Virginia Beach. Nearest air and rail access at Norfolk, 7 miles west.

🚐 Vehicle access to camp area, thereafter on foot via marked selfguiding trails and maintenance roads. Public launching ramp.

☀ Open all year; best time summer.

⏲ 1–7 days.

▨ Free, parking fee 40c per car; there are also charges for swimming (40c for adults).

⇨ Division of Parks, Suite 501, Southern States Building, Richmond, Virginia 23219.

Shenandoah National Park 300 square miles; 595 to 4,049 ft above sea level (60 peaks between 3,000 and 4,000 ft). The park, 105.4 miles long, lies along the Appalachian National Scenic Trail, overlooking the Shenandoah River valley. The Skyline Drive, which links this park with the Blue Ridge Parkway and the Great Smoky Mountains National Park, runs along the ridge of the Appalachians, broadly parallel with the Appalachian National Scenic Trail (foot and horse only), through the centre of the park. This region was fairly prosperous in the 19th century, with sawmills, tanneries, and mountain farms. The valley was subjected to Sheridan's Raid during the Civil War – a raid similar in effect to Sherman's 'March through Georgia'. Then with the coming of the railway and larger-scale industry the area was economically blighted. During the 1920's the park was slowly established as the remaining homesteaders were bought out and resettled. The scars of human habitation are still visible – old copper mines near Skyland, for instance, and ancient farmland now being reinvaded by the forests. The park is much more intensively developed and more geared for tourism, especially by car, than the Great Smoky Mountains National Park.

🐾 Whitetail deer, bear, bobcat, fox, woodchuck, chipmunk, gray squirrel, cottontail, flying squirrel (nocturnal), raccoon, skunk. Over 200 birds include buzzard, vulture, raven, indigo bunting, junco, ruffed grouse, wild turkey, towhee, woodpeckers, whip-poor-will, mourning dove, jay, oven bird, red eyed vireo, nuthatch, chickadee, catbird, wrens, brown thrasher, black-throated blue warbler.

Scarlet, red, and chestnut oaks, hickory, black locust, black birch, maple, black gum, ash, pine, birch, yellow poplar, sycamore, basswood, hemlock, red spruce, balsam fir, redbud, dogwood, wild cherry, azalea, mountain laurel, and many wild flowers.

Hotel accommodation at Big Meadows; cabins with baths, restaurants, etc, at Skyland, Big Meadows, and Lewis Mountain – all closed during winter; rates from $10–15; advance bookings through Virginia Sky-Line Co, Inc, Luray, Virginia 22835. Camping grounds and, along the Appalachian Trail, mountain huts with bunks for six – all operated on first-come-first-served basis, limited to 1-day stay. Camp-ground stay limited to 14 days in any one year. Food, ice, fuel, charcoal burners available at Big Meadows Wayside. Locked and equipped mountain cabins bookable in advance through the Potomac Appalachian Trail Club, 1718 North Street NW, Washington 20036, DC.

North Entrance (Front Royal, Virginia) from US 340 and Virginia 55 and 522. Thornton Gap (mile 31.6) from US 211. Swift Run Gap (mile 65.7) from US 33. South Entrance (Rockfish Gap) from US 250 and Blue Ridge Parkway. Buses from nearby towns throughout the year; Virginia Trailways, Charlottesville operate park tours.

The park has over 200 miles of foot and 25 miles of horse trails; horses can be rented by the hour or day at Skyland and Big Meadows. There are many lookouts and parking places along the Skyline Drive and from most of them there are walking-trail circuits. The Dickey Ridge Visitor Center near the north entrance has an orientation display and a colour slide programme that outlines the parks attractions.

Open all year except when weather could make driving hazardous; best time May to October.

1–3 days.

Under review at time of going to press.

In summer, ranger-naturalists conduct daily field trips for groups to places of interest; at night there are campfire programmes at Skyland, Big Meadows, and Lewis Mountains.

Books and maps can be bought in the park or ordered by mail from Shenandoah Natural History Association, Shenandoah National Park, Luray, Virginia 22835. Examples are detailed hiker's guide and maps, *The Mammals of Shenandoah National Park*, *101 Wildflowers of Shenandoah National Park*, and *Skyland, Heart of Shenandoah*, which contains early photographs.

The Superintendent, Shenandoah National Park, Luray, Virginia 22835.

Wreck and Bone Islands Natural Area on the Atlantic coast is another unmanaged saltmarsh wilderness. Otter, mink; gull-bill; least, royal, and common terns; clapper rail, black skimmer, snowy egret, little blue heron, oystercatcher, osprey, willet, geese, loon, black duck, dowitcher, and other shore-birds. Flora similar to Parkers Marsh. Access only by boat from Oyster, reached by State 639 from US 13.

USA: The Northeast

A mute swan, an Old World species widely introduced into North America. It is distinguished from other species by the graceful arabesque of its neck and delicately raised secondary wing feathers.

Delaware

Bombay Hook National Wildlife Refuge 15,111 acres; at or near sea level. The refuge is built on estuarine saltmarshes on the shores of Delaware Bay. These, together with a number of freshwater impoundments, make it an important wintering, resting, and breeding ground for the migratory waterfowl of the Atlantic flyway. There are also many stands of brush and timber as well as about 1,000 acres of planted bird forage.

- Canada goose, black and wood ducks, mallard, gadwall, blue-winged teal – all nest. Pied-billed grebe, clapper rail, common gallinule, coot, willet.
- Salt and brackish marshes, freshwater pools, brush and timbered swamps, croplands and grassy uplands.
- Only picnic areas and observation towers in the refuge. Hotels and motels in nearby towns.

➤ 9 miles southeast of Smyrna; 10 miles northeast of Dover; 45 miles south of Wilmington. The way to the refuge is marked from Delaware 9.

🚐 Foot exploration is possible; a selfguided auto tour route includes all the freshwater impoundments. The refuge is open only during daylight hours.

� Open all year; best time March to November.

🕐 1 day.

✉ $1 per car and occupants.

⇨ Refuge Manager, RFD 1, Box 147, Smyrna, Delaware 19977/tel: (302) 653–945.

Maine

Moosehorn National Wildlife Refuge 22,665 acres; at or near sea level. The refuge lies near the US–Canada border amid rolling hills, with large outcrops of rock, valleys, lakes, streams, and marshes. The tides at the southern Edmunds Unit (6,500 acres) average 24 ft; those at the larger Baring Unit, 10 miles away to the north, are 28 ft – the highest in continental USA. The area was once extensively harvested for its timber, and many logging trails and water flowages still partly survive. It is still harvested on a renewal basis, mature pine giving way to the second growth trees that now cover most of both units. Forest fires (the last one in 1920) made many clearings and open lands now carpeted with blueberries. The chief purpose of the reserve is to provide habitat for the woodcock and the waterfowl of the Atlantic flyway.

🦌 Whitetail deer, black bear, moose, snowshoe hare, red fox, bobcat, muskrat, beaver, mink, otter, fisher, raccoon, skunk, weasel, porcupine; flying, red, and gray squirrels; chipmunk, harbor seal. Nesting birds include black duck, ring-necked duck, green- and blue-winged teals, wood duck, goldeneyes, hooded merganser.

🏕 The Edmunds Unit recreational area has 101 tent and mobile camp sites as well as 49 picnic sites; water and boat-launching ramp. Organized groups may reserve sites but individuals are treated on first-come-first-served basis with a time limit of 2 weeks. Site rent and administration is now handled by the State of Maine. Motels in nearby towns.

➤ US 1 runs through both units. The Charlotte–Calais road and Maine 191 run through the northern Baring Unit. No airport within 150 miles. Except for buses this part of Maine has little public transportation.

🚐 Old logging roads in the woods still provide excellent trails. Township roads reach most open parts of the refuge.

� Open all year; best time June to November.

🕐 2–5 days.

✉ Charged at camp site.

⇨ Refuge Manager, PO Box X, Calais, Maine 04619/tel: (207) 454–3521.

Maryland

Blackwater National Wildlife Refuge 11,216 acres; at or near sea level. An important wintering and nesting area for migratory waterfowl of the Atlantic flyway, Blackwater straddles the tortuous estuarine waterways of the Blackwater River before it flows into Chesapeake Bay. Over 90 per cent of its area consists of marsh, brush, timbered swamp, and freshwater ponds.

- ⌇ Muskrat, fox, raccoon, opossum, skunk, otter, whitetail deer, gray squirrel, Delmarva Peninsula fox squirrel (endangered); Canada goose, black and wood ducks, mallard, pintail, green-winged and blue-winged teals, American widgeon, king and Virginia rails, osprey, gallinule, killdeer, barn owl, loon, grebe, brown-headed nuthatch.

- 🕉 Marsh and swamp flora with stands of sweet gum, red maple, and loblolly pine.

- 🛏 None in refuge; picnic and restroom facilities near HQ. Motels in Cambridge.

- 🚗 County roads traverse the refuge. A guided nature trail can be visited by prior arrangement.

- 🌤 Open all year; best times autumn through spring.

- ◷ 1–2 days.

- ✉ Free.

- ◉ Visitor Center has waterfowl displays and shows wildlife movies to organized groups who give prior notice of visit.

- ⇨ Refuge Manager, RFD 1, Cambridge, Maryland 21613/tel: (301) 228–2677.

Eastern Neck National Wildlife Refuge 2,285 acre island at the mouth of Chester River, contains coves, ponds and marshes providing refuge for migratory and wintering waterfowl. Also whistling swan, Canada goose, black duck, mallard. Mammals include whitetail deer and the endangered fox squirrel. Picnicking, boating. Near town of Rock Hall. Refuge Manager, Route 2, Box 193, Rock Hall, Maryland 21661/tel: (301) 639–7415. Best March to November.

Massachusetts

Parker River National Wildlife Refuge 4,650 acres; at or near sea level. The refuge consists of most of Plum Island, one of the few remaining natural barrier-dunes left in this part of the US, as well as Broad Sound and the mouth of the Parker River, both sheltered from the Atlantic by the dunes. Centuries ago it was intensively grazed and farmed, but now the only commercial use of the island is clam-bed digging and the cutting of saltmarsh hay, which improves the habitat for resident and migratory waterfowl of the Atlantic flyway.

- ⌇ 300 recorded bird species include Canada goose, black duck, blue- and green-winged teal, mallard, pintail, widgeon, bufflehead, scaup, ring-necked pheasant, warblers, and shorebirds; rabbit, deer.

177

⠿ Dune grass, false heather, beach plum, bayberry, rose, willows, aspen, pine, cranberry.

⇦ None in refuge; motels in Newburyport and other nearby towns.

⇥ 32 miles northeast of Boston; the refuge is signposted from US 1 or Interstate 95 near Newburyport.

⛟ Only foot exploration is permitted, except for a single vehicle road on the shoreward side of the refuge.

☀ Open and interesting all year.

⏱ 1–2 days.

✉ Only for parking in connection with recreational use of the beach.

⇨ Refuge Manager, Northern Boulevard, Plum Island, Newburyport, Massachusetts 01950/tel: (617) 465–0961.

New Jersey

Brigantine National Wildlife Refuge 19,412 acres; at or near sea level. The refuge consists mainly of saltgrass-cordgrass marshes and tidal creeks on the Atlantic coast a dozen miles north of Atlantic City. On its inland edge some 1,600 acres have been converted to freshwater impoundment to provide more varied habitat for the 150,000 or more birds that nest or stop here during the spring and fall migrations. On this edge, too, are a number of wooded swamps and uplands.

⇶ Whitetail deer, red and gray fox, red and gray squirrel, striped skunk, opossum, mink, muskrat, cottontail; Canada goose, brant, black duck, pintail, gadwall, shoveler, gulls, terns, rails, black skimmer, seaside and sharp-tailed sparrows, tree swallow, red-winged blackbird.

⠿ Cordgrass, saltgrass, cedar, scrub pine, Japanese honeysuckle, mixed hardwoods.

⇦ None in refuge; hotels and motels in nearby Atlantic City and along New Jersey 9.

⇥ The Garden State Parkway, on which many highways converge near Atlantic City, passes within 6 miles of the refuge. The Intercoastal Waterway runs through the refuge. Rail and air connections to Atlantic City.

⛟ An excellent selfguided auto tour route circuits the waterfowl impoundments; guide leaflet is available. Convenient picnic areas are along the route. Ablutions and WC's at HQ.

☀ Open all year; best time March to December.

⏱ 1–2 days.

◎ Over 30 miles away by road, but less than 5 miles across the bay, stands the 256-acre refuge known as the Holgate Unit. It is managed as a unit of the Brigantine Refuge and offers exceptional habitat for nesting and migrant shorebirds. Parts are closed between May 1 and August 1; all is accessible only on foot.

⇨ Refuge Manager, Great Greek Road, PO Box 72, Oceanville, New Jersey 08231/tel: (609) 641–3126.

The prairie falcon, a native of western North America.

Great Swamp National Wildlife Refuge 5,800 acres (projected); less than 100 ft above sea level. The refuge, which is still under development, is set in natural swamp in northern New Jersey, less than 35 miles from downtown New York. Its chief purpose is to provide wetland habitat for migratory waterfowl of the Atlantic flyway. Its eastern end will be preserved in its natural state, but the western end will be controlled to improve the productivity of waterfowl. In 1966 the Refuge was designated for inclusion in the National Registry of Natural Landmarks, and in 1968 The Congress designated part of the refuge for inclusion in the National Wilderness Preservation System. Morris County has provided a Nature Center on the northeastern boundary of the refuge.

- Whitetail deer, muskrat, raccoon, striped skunk, red and gray foxes, woodchuck, cottontail; Canada goose, black and wood ducks, pintail, mallard, blue- and green-winged teal, shoveler, American woodcock, ruffed grouse, ring-necked pheasant, mourning dove.
- Swamp woodland, hardwood (oak, beach, mountain laurel) ridges, cattail marsh, grassland, rhododendron, and some planted wildlife forage.
- None in refuge; hotels and motels in nearby towns.
- 16 miles west of Newark; 7 miles south from Morristown. US 203 passes less than 2 miles from the refuge; take the New Vernon turnoff.
- 3 roads (Stirling–New Vernon, Meyersville–New Vernon, and Meyersville–Green Village) run through the refuge, most of which is accessible only on foot.

☼ Open dawn-to-dusk all year; best time March to November.

🕐 1 day.

🎫 Free.

👁 The Morristown National Historical Park, George Washington's headquarters in 1779–80 and site of important military encampments during the Revolution, is nearby.

⇨ Refuge Manager, RD 1, PO Box 148, Pleasant Plains Road, Basking Ridge, New Jersey 07920/tel: (201) 647–1222.

New York

Iroquois National Wildlife Refuge 10,784 acres of swamp, wet meadows, open fields, uplands providing habitat for 30,000 migrating Canada geese and many species of duck: mallard, widgeon, pintail. Mammals include deer, raccoon, red fox, beaver. Near towns of Oakfield, Batavia and Medina, New York. Refuge Manager, Basom, New York. Best April to October.

Montezuma National Wildlife Refuge 6,820 acres; between 300 and 500 ft above sea level. The Montezuma Marsh, which was drained almost dry during the early years of this century, is now an important resting, wintering, and breeding area for migratory waterfowl of the Atlantic flyway. It is totally managed to increase waterfowl productivity.

🐾 Deer, red and gray squirrels, red and gray fox, raccoon, opossum, muskrat, mink. Over 250 bird species include herons, terns; Canada goose; blue- and green-winged teals; mallard, wood, black, and ruddy ducks; gadwall, shoveler, redhead, and many shore and songbirds.

🌿 Sago pondweed, wild celery, wild millet, smartweed, bulrush, and plantings of winter wheat, rye, buckwheat, and millet.

🛏 None in park; hotels and motels in nearby towns.

🚲 The Thomas Dewey Thruway crosses the refuge; for access use exit 40 or 41. Many other highway routes pass nearby. The New York State Barge Canal system gives access to the park, the May's Point lock being near the refuge centre.

🚐 Wildlife is best seen from the dike banks. The Main Pool dike is open to vehicles and walkers (weather permitting) all year. All other dikes are closed from the start of the waterfowl hunting season (around October 1 to July 1). Only the Main Pool and May's Point dikes are open to vehicles. Access to all other parts of the refuge (except to the picnic area in the north) is on foot only.

☼ Open dawn to dusk all year; best time March to November.

🕐 1 day.

🎫 $1 per car and occupants for tour route.

⇨ Refuge Manager, RD 1, PO Box 232, Seneca Falls, New York 13148/tel: (315) 568–5987.

Morton Wildlife Refuge 187 acres bordering on a sandy, gravelly peninsula, with wooded bluffs, some brackish water, brush, open fields. Over 200 species of waterfowl, birds of prey, shore and song birds have been recorded. Deer, cotton-tail, grey squirrel, fox, weasel, raccoon, opossum. Hiking, photography. Near Sag Harbor, Long Island. Refuge Manager, RD–359, Noyac Road, Sag Harbor, Long Island, New York 11963, NY. Best May to September.

Pennsylvania

Erie National Wildlife Refuge 5,150 acres of timbered upland, open fields, swamps, marshes supporting geese, ducks, shorebirds, songbirds during migratory periods. Deer, beaver, foxes, muskrat, raccoon, woodchuck. Picnicking. Near Guys Mills, and 40 miles from Erie city. Refuge Manager, Box 13, Route 3, Guys Mills, Pennsylvania. Best May to October.

Vermont

Missisquoi National Wildlife Refuge 4,680 acres of marsh, bog-brush, timber, and open bays on Lake Champlain offer a production and resting area for ducks, specially black and wood ducks. Migrant waterfowl include snow and Canada geese. Deer, red fox, beaver, raccoon, muskrat, mink, otter. Hotels, motels available nearby. Nature trail, boating, photography. Near town of Swanton. Refuge Manager, PO Box 57, Swanton Vermont 05488/tel: (802) 868–4781. Best May to September.

USA : Species List

ALLIGATORS Aransas; Chassahowitzka; Everglades; Florida Keys; Highlands Hammock; JN Ding Darling; Loxahatchee; Myakka R; St Marks; Blackbeard Is; Okefenokee; Chicot; Delta; Sabine; Yazoo; C Romain
AMAKIHI Haleakala; Hawaii Volcanoes
ANHINGA Everglades; Highlands Hammock; St Marks; Okefenokee; Lacassine
ANI, Groove-Billed Bentsen RGC; Santa Ana
— **Smooth-Billed** Loxahatchee
ANTELOPE Malheur; Ouray; all Wyoming State Parks; Bosque Apache; Wichita Mts; Big Spring; Custer
APAPANE Haleakala; Hawaii Volcanoes
ARMADILLO Aransas; Hagerman; Santa Ana; Chicot; Lacassine; Sabine; Sam Houston
AVOCET Havasu L; Sacramento; San Luis; Monte Vista; Deer Flat; Red Rock L; Bear R; Bitter L; Salt Plains; Upper Souris; Lacreek; Chincoteague
BADGER Modoc; Crater L; Monte Vista; Bowdoin; Medicine L; National Bison; Ninepipe; Red Rock L; National Elk; Saguaro; Bitter L; Salt Plains; Chaparral; Crescent L; Valentine; Arrowwood; J Clark Salyer; L Ilo; Slade; Upper Souris; Wind Cave
BATS Hawaii Volcanoes; Carlsbad Caverns; Gt Smoky Mts
— **Evening** Seashore
— **Free-Tailed** Carlsbad

— **Little Brown** Seashore
— **Lump-Nosed** Carlsbad
— **Pallid** Carlsbad
— **Red** Seashore
— **Silver-Haired** Seashore
BEARS Cape Lookout; Willapa; Charles M Russell; Grand Teton; National Elk; Okefenokee; Shenandoah
— **Black** Kenai; Yosemite; Crater L; Mr Rainier; Olympic; Glacier; National Bison; Ouray; Yellowstone; Agassiz; Rice L; White R; Pungo; Gt Smoky Mts; Seashore; Moosehorn
— **Brown** Aleutians; Kenai
— **Grizzly** Glacier; Yellowstone
BEAVER Kenai; Crater L; Mt Rainier; Turnbull; Camas; Deer Flat; Bowdoin; Glacier; Medicine L; National Bison; Red Rock L; Grand Teton; National Elk; Imperial; Bosque Apache; Salt Plains; Chautauqua; Mark Twain; De Soto; Kirwin; Marais des Cygnes; Isle Royale; Agassiz; Rice L; Tamarac; Upper Mississippi; Squaw Cr; Ft Niobrara; Arrowwood; Des Lacs; Ft Lincoln; J Clark Salyer; L Ilo; L Metigoshe; Turtle R; Upper Souris; Lacreek; Sand L; Eufaula; Wapanocca; Noxubee; Carolina Sandhills; Reelfoot; Moosehorn; Iroquois; Erie National; Missisquoi
BECARDS, Rose-Throated Santa Ana
BIRDS OF PREY Morton
BISON *see* **BUFFALO**
BITTERNS Highlands Hammock; JN Ding

181

USA: SPECIES LIST

Darling; Savannah
- **American** Sacramento; Monte Vista;
  Bowdoin; Parkers Marsh
- **Least** Parkers Marsh

BLACKBIRD, Red-Winged St Marks;
Parkers Marsh; Brigantine
- **Yellow-Headed** Bear R; National Elk;
  Horicon

BLIND FISH Spring Mill

BLUEBIRDS Ft Lincoln; Wind Cave; St
Marks
- **Mountain** Hart Mt; Mt Rainier; Ravalli;
  Bryce Canyon; Grand Teton; National Elk;
  Yellowstone
- **Western** Yellowstone; Rice L

BOBCAT Modoc; Crater L; Mr Rainier;
Willapa; Monte Vista; Minidoka;
Bowdoin; National Bison; Desert
National; Bitter L; Bosque Apache; Salt
Plains; Aransas; Hagerman; Laguna
Atascosa; Santa Ana; Tamarac; Mingo;
L Metigoshe; Eufaula; Holla Bend;
Loxahatchee; St Marks; Noxubee; Yazoo;
Carolina Sandhills; Santee; Gt Smoky Mts;
Seashore; Shenandoah; Moosehorn

BOBOLINK JN Ding Darling

BOBWHITE Salt Plains; Wichita Mts;
Buffalo L; Chapparral; Gene Howe;
Laguna Atascosa; De Soto; Kirwin;
Swan L; Ft Niobrara; L Andes; Eufaula;
Loxahatchee; Piedmont

BRANTS Chincoteague; Brigantine
- **Pacific Black** Willapa

BUFFALO Charles M Russell; National
Bison; Seedskadee; Yellowstone; Wichita
Mts; Big Spring; L B Johnson; Ft
Niobrara; Sully's Hill; Custer; Wind Cave

BUFFLE HEAD Bear R; C Romain;
Lacreek; Mattamuskeet; Chincoteague;
Parkers Marsh; Parker R

BUNTINGS Gt Smoky Mts
- **Indigo** Seashore; Shenandoah
- **Lark** Medicine L; Red Rock L; J Clark
  Salver
- **Painted** Blackbeard Is; C Romain

BURRO, Wild Havasu L; Imperial

BUZZARDS Shenandoah

BUTTERFLY, Saltmarsh Jack Is

CANVASBACK Klamath; Minidoka;
Bowdoin; Medicine L; Red Rock L;
Bear L; Hutton L; Bitter L; Arrowwood;
Des Lacs; Lacreek; Sand L; Mattamuskeet;
Parkers Marsh

CARDINALS L Metigoshe; C Romain; Gt
Smoky Mts; Pocahontas; Seashore

CARIBOU Aleutians

CATBIRD Shenandoah

CAVE INVERTEBRATES Spring Mill

CHACHALACA Santa Ana; Blackbeard Is

CHICHAREE Yosemite

CHICKADEES Kenai; Hart Mt; Mt Rainier;
Wind Cave; Shenandoah
- **Carolina** Gt Smoky Mts

CHIPMUNK Yosemite; Crater L; Mt Rainier;
Glacier; Bryce Canyon; Grand Teton;
Yellowstone; L Metigoshe; Turtle R;
Shenandoah; Moosehorn

CHUCKWALLA Grand Canyon

CHUCKWILL'S WIDOW White R;
C Romain; Seashore

CHUKAR Haleakala; Hawaii Volcanoes;
Columbia; National Bison

CONY Grand Teton

COOT Sacramento; Ridgefield; Bowdoin;
Ninepipe; Laguna Atascosa; Swan L;
Horicon; Chassahowitzka; Loxahatchee;
Merrit Is; C Romain; Bombay Hook

COPPERMOUTH Mingo

CORMORANTS Kenai; Klamath; Mingo;
Audubon; Lacreek; JN Ding Darling;
St Marks; C Romain
- **Double-Crested** Klamath; Bowdoin;
  Medicine L; Red Rock L; Bear R; Upper
  Souris; Sand L; Florida Keys
- **OLIVACEOUS** Lacassine

COTTONMOUTH Mingo

COTTONTAIL Bowdoin; Laguna Atascosa;
De Soto; Ft Lincoln; L Metigoshe; Turtle
R; Carolina Sandhills; Chincoteague;
Shenandoah; Brigantine; Gt Swamp;
Morton
- **Desert** Carlsbad
- **Eastern** Seashore
- **Mountain** National Bison

COUGAR see also **MOUNTAIN LION**

Mt Rainier; Big Bend

COWBIRD, Red-Eyed Bentsen RGV

COYOTE Kenai; Modoc; San Luis; Crater L;
Malheur; Mt Rainier; Turnbull; Monte
Vista; Deer Flat; Minidoka; Bowdoin;
Charles M Russell; Glacier; National
Bison; Desert National; National Elk;
Yellowstone; Imperial; Saguaro; Bitter L;
Bosque Apache; Salt Plains; Aransas;
Big Bend; Chaparral; Laguna Atascosa;
Muleshoe; Santa Ana; De Soto; Marais
des Cygnes; Squaw Cr; Crescent L;
Ft Niobrara; Valentine; J Clark Salyer;
Upper Souris; Lacreek; Wind Cave;
Holla Bend

COYPU Delta

CRABS Jack Is

CRANE, Florida Sandhill
Loxahatchee; Myakka R
- **Sandhill** Klamath; Modoc; Malheur;
  Monte Vista; Medicine L; Red Rock L;
  Ruby L; Bitter L; Bosque Apache; Salt
  Plains; Washita; Aransas; Quivira; Seney;
  Audubon; J Clark Salyer; Long L; Upper
  Souris; Necedah; Okefenokee
- **Whooping** Medicine L; Red Rock L;
  Salt Plains; Aransas; Rice L

CROCODILE, Salt-Water Everglades;
Florida Keys

CROWS Pocahontas

CUCKOO, Mangrove Florida Keys
- **Yellow-Billed** Presquile

CURLEWS Clarence Rhode; Chincoteague
- **Long-Billed** Red Rock L; Bear R;
  Valentine; Lacreek; C Romain

DEER Cape Lookout; Ecola; Willapa;
Camas; Charles M Russell; Glacier;
Bryce Canyon; Seedskadee; all Wyoming
State Parks; Big Bend; Buffalo L; Gene
Howe; Gus Engeling; Hagerman; Possum
Kingdom; Crab Orchard; Mark Twain;
Flint Hills; Marais des Cygnes; Seney;
Tamarac; Crescent L; L Metigoshe; Sullys
Hill; Turtle R; Custer; Wind Cave; Big L;
Holla Bend; Wapanocca; Blackbeard Is;
Piedmont; Chicot; Sabine; Sam Houston;
Noxubee; Yazoo; Carolina Sandhills;
Hatchie; Parkers Marsh; Parker R;
Iroquois; Montezuma; Morton; Erie
National; Missisquoi
- **Black** Yosemite
- **Black-Tailed** Crater L; Silver Falls;
  William L Finley; Olympic
- **Desert Mule** Big Bend
- **Mule** Modoc; Yosemite; Cove Palisades;
  Crater L; Hart Mt; Mt Rainier; Turnbull;
  Deer Flat; Minidoka; Benton L; Bowdoin;
  Medicine L; National Bison; Red Rock L;
  Chas Sheldon; Desert National; Grand
  Teton; National Elk; Yellowstone;
  Saguaro; Bitter L; Bosque Apache;
  Carlsbad; Black Gap; Ft Niobrara; L Ilo;
  Lacreek; Sand L
- **Sika** Chincoteague
- **Whitetail** Turnbull; Benton L; Bowdoin;
  Medicine L; National Bison; Red Rock L;
  Saguaro; Salt Plains; Wichita Mts;
  Aransas; Big Bend; Chaparral; Kerr;
  Laguna Atascosa; De Soto; Union Slough;
  Shiawassee Agassiz; Rice L; Mingo;
  Squaw Cr; Ft Niobrara; Arrowwood;
  Audubon; Des Lacs; J Clark Salyer; L Ilo;
  Lostwood; Upper Souris; Lacreek; Sand L;
  Horicon; Eufaula; White R; Florida Keys;
  Highlands Hammock; Loxahatchee;
  Myakka R; St Marks; Okefenokee; Delta;
  Pungo; Savannah; Gt Smoky Mts;
  Seashore; Shenandoah; Moosehorn;
  Blackwater; Eastern Neck; Brigantine;
  Gt Swamp

DESERT BIGHORN Desert National;
Imperial

DESERT BIRDS Desert National

DIPPER, Water Yosemite

DOLPHIN, Bottle-Nosed Seashore

DOVES Chaparral
- **Ground** Laguna Atascosa; J N Ding
  Darling
- **Mourning** Sacramento; William L
  Finley; Monte Vista; Carlsbad; Laguna
  Atascosa; Seashore; Shenandoah;
  Swamp
- **White-Fronted** Santa Ana
- **White-Winged** Laguna Atascosa

DOWITCHER Sacramento; Bowdoin; Salt

Plains; C Romain; Wreck & Bone Is

DUCKS Kern-Pixley; Klamath; Merced;
Modoc; San Luis; Camas; Deer Flat; Ruby
L; Stillwater; Fish Springs; Hutton L;
Imperial; Bosque Apache; Tishomingo;
Chaparral; Chautauqua; Crab Orchard; De
Soto; Union Slough; Shiawassee;
Crescent L; L Metigoshe; Long L; L Andes;
Necedah; Eufaula; Holla Bend;
Chassahowitzka; Merritt Is; Blackbeard Is;
Delta; Sabine; Yazoo; Pungo; Carolina
Sandhills; Santee; Savannah; Cross
Creeks; Back Bay; Presquile; Seashore;
Erie National; Missisquoi

— **Black** Chautauqua; Seney; Mingo;
C Romain; Santee; Chincoteague;
Parkers Marsh; Presquile; Wreck & Bone
Is; Bombay Hook; Moosehorn;
Blackwater; Eastern Neck; Parker R;
Brigantine; Gt Swamp; Montezuma;
Missisquoi

— **Black-Bellied Tree** Laguna Atascosa;
Santa Ana

— **Diving** Hagerman

— **Fulvous Tree** Laguna Atascosa;
Lacassine

— **Mexican** Bosque Apache

— **Mottled** Aransas; Laguna Atascosa;
Loxahatchee; Merritt Is; Lacassine

— **Ring-Necked** Agassiz; Rice L;
Tamarac; L Woodruff; Loxahatchee;
C Romain; Moosehorn

— **Ruddy** Sacramento; Malheur; Monte
Vista; Minidoka; Bowdoin; Medicine L;
Ninepipe; Red Rock L; Bear R; Agassiz;
Tamarac; Arrowwood; Des Lacs; C
Romain; Montezuma

— **Sea** Chincoteague

— **Wood** William L. Finley; Chautauqua;
Seney; Tamarac; Upper Mississippi;
Mingo; Squaw Cr; Swan L; Horicon;
White R; Loxahatchee; Okefenokee;
Lacassine; Hatchie; Bombay Hook;
Moosehorn; Blackwater; Gt Swamp;
Montezuma; Missisquoi

DUNLIN C Romain

EAGLES Crater L; Camas; Glacier; Chas
Sheldon; Crescent L; Lacassine

— **Bald** Kenai; Monte Vista; Minidoka;
Grand Teton; National Elk; Yellowstone;
Imperial; Salt Plains; Wichita Mts;
Buffalo L; Mark Twain; Quivira; Isle
Royale; Upper Mississippi; Ft Niobrara;
Holla Bend; Chassahowitzka; Everglades;
St Marks; C Romain; Tennessee National;
Seashore

— **Golden** Monte Vista; Minidoka; Ravalli;
National Elk; Imperial; Carlsbad; Salt
Plains; Wichita Mts; Buffalo L; Quivira;
Ft Niobrara; Ft Lincoln; Holla Bend;
Tennessee National

— **Southern Bald** Merritt Is

EGRETS San Luis; Deer Flat; Fish Springs;
Salt Plains; Tishomingo; Aransas; Marais
des Cygnes; Upper Mississippi; Horicon;
Eufaula; White R; Everglades; Highlands
Hammock; Jack Is; JN Ding Darling;
Loxahatchee; Myakka R. Blackbeard Is;
Okefenokee; Yazoo; Pungo;
Chincoteague

— **American** Parkers Marsh

— **Cattle** Mingo; Lacassine

— **Common** Klamath; Sacramento;
Mingo; Squaw Cr; St Marks; Lacassine

— **Reddish** Florida Keys

— **Snowy** Sacramento; Bear R; St Marks;
Lacassine; C Romain; Parkers Marsh;
Wreck & Bone Is

ELEPAIO Hawaii Volcanoes

ELK Ecola; Saddle Mt; Mt Rainier; Olympic;
Camas; Bowdoin; Charles M Russell;
Glacier; National Bison; Grand Teton;
National Elk; Seedskadee, Yellowstone;
Wichita Mts; Ft Niobrara; Sully's Hill;
Custer; Wind Cave

FALCON, Peregrine Crater L; C Romain

FINCHES Mt Rainier; Glacier

— **Black Rosy** Grand Teton

— **House** Saguaro

— **Rosy** Yosemite

FISHER Moosehorn

FLICKERS Lacreek; Pocahontas

— **Gilded** Saguaro

FLYCATCHERS Gt Smoky Mts; Seashore

— **Great Crested** C Romain

— **Kiskadee** Bentsen RGV; Santa Ana

— **Red-Shafted** Saguaro

— **Scissor-Tailed** Wichita Mts; JN Ding
Darling

FOXES Aleutians; Crater L; Hagerman;
Chautauqua; Marais des Cygnes; Squaw
Cr; Ft Niobrara; Ottawa; Eufaula;
Wapanocca; Chicot; Sabine; Sam
Houston; Yazoo; Pungo; Carolina
Sandhills; Santee; Reelfoot; Back Bay;
Shenandoah; Blackwater; Morton; Erie
National

— **Gray** Bitter L. Carlsbad; Big Bend;
Seashore; Brigantine; Gt Swamp

— **Kit** Carlsbad; Big Bend

— **Red** Sacramento; Mt Rainier; Isle
Royale; Mingo; Arrowwood; J Clark
Salyer; Slade; Upper Souris;
Chincoteague; Parkers Marsh;
Moosehorn; Brigantine; Gt Swamp;
Iroquois; Missisquoi

FRIGATEBIRD Florida Keys, JN Ding
Darling

GADWALL Klamath; Sacramento; Malheur;
Monte Vista; Bowdoin; Medicine L; Red
Rock L; Bear R; Marais des Cygnes;
Agassiz; Tamarac; Mingo; Squaw Cr;
Swan L; Arrowwood; Audubon; Des
Lacs; Long L; Tewaukon; Lacreek; Sand
L; Lacassine; C Romain; Reelfoot;
Tennessee National; Chincoteague;
Bombay Hook; Brigantine; Montezuma

GALLINULE, Common Sacramento;
Horicon; JN Ding Darling; St Marks;
Lacassine; C Romain; Bombay Hook;
Blackwater

— **Purple** St Marks; Lacassine

GEESE Havasu L; Kern-Pixley; Merced;
Modoc; San Luis; Camas; Deer Flat;
Minidoka; Stillwater; Fish Springs;
Bitter L; Bosque Apache; Tishomingo;
Buffalo L; Gambill; Crab Orchard;
Shiawassee; Crescent L; L Metigoshe;
L Andes; Eufaula; Holla Bend; Yazoo;
Carolina Sandhills; Cross Creeks;
Back Bay; Wreck & Bone Is; Erie National

GILA MONSTER Saguaro

GNATCATCHER, Black-Tailed Saguaro

GOATS Haleakala; Hawaii Volcanoes

— **Rocky Mountain** Kenai; Mt Rainier;
Glacier; Custer

GODWIT Salt Plains

— **Marbled** Upper Souris; C Romain

GOLDENEYES Kenai; Bear R; Tamarac;
Lacreek; Mattamuskeet; Parkers Marsh;
Moosehorn

— **Common** National Elk

— **Barrow's** National Elk

GOOSE, Blue Salt Plains; Hagerman; De
Soto; Forney's L; Union Slough; Seney;
Mingo; Squaw Cr; Swan L; Arrowwood;
Audubon; Tewaukon; Sand L; Merritt Is;
Delta; Lacassine; Sabine; Presquile

— **Cackling** Klamath; Sacramento

— **Canada** Kern-Pixley; Klamath;
Sacramento; William L Finley (dusky);
Ridgefield; Willapa; Bowdoin; Medicine
L; Ninepipe; Red Rock L; Ruby L; Bear R;
Ouray; Grand Teton; National Elk;
Seedskadee; Yellowstone; Imperial; Salt
Plains; Hagerman; Laguna Atascosa; De
Soto; Union Slough; Quivira; Seney;
Agassiz; Tamarac; Mingo; Squaw Cr;
Swan L; Arrowwood; Audubon; L Andes;
Sand L; Horicon; Necedah; St Marks;
Lacassine; Mattamuskeet; Pungo;
C Romain; Santee; Reelfoot; Tennessee
National; Chincoteague; Bombay Hook;
Blackwater; Eastern Neck; Parker R;
Brigantine; Gt Swamp; Iroquois;
Montezuma; Missisquoi

— **Emperor** Aleutians

— **Ross** Klamath; Sacramento

— **Snow** Klamath; Sacramento; Salt Plains;
Hagerman; Laguna Atascosa; De Soto;
Forney's L; Union Slough; Seney;
Mingo; Squaw Cr; Swan L; Arrowwood;
Audubon; Tewaukon; Merritt Is; Delta;
Lacassine; Sabine; Pea Is; Chincoteague;
Presquile; Missisquoi

— **White-Fronted** Klamath; Sacramento;
Salt Plains; Union Slough; Squaw Cr;
Swan L; Sand L; Lacassine

GOPHER, Pocket Carlsbad

GOPHER SNAKE Saguaro

USA: SPECIES LIST

GOSHAWK Hart Mt
GRACKLE, Common Parkers Marsh; Seashore
— **Boat-Tailed** Florida Keys; Parkers Marsh
GREBES Deer Flat; J Clark Salyer; Upper Souris; Savannah; Chincoteague; Blackwater
— **Eared** Klamath; Bowdoin; Sand L
— **Horned** Sand L; C Romain
— **Least** Santa Ana
— **Pied-Billed** Klamath; Sacramento; Columbia; Lacreek; Sand L; Seashore; Bombay Hook
— **Western** Klamath; Bear R; Des Lacs; Upper Souris; Lacreek; Sand L
GROSBEAKS Hart Mt; Hungry Mother
— **Black-Headed** Yosemite
— **Blue** Bowdoin; Carlsbad
— **Rose-Breasted** Gt Smoky Mts
GROUSE William L Finley; Willapa; Glacier; Crescent L; Audubon; Lostwood; L Andes
— **Blue** National Bison; National Elk
— **Pinnated** See **PRAIRIE CHICKEN**
— **Ruffed** National Bison; National Elk; Seney; Rice L; Tamarac; L Metigoshe; Necedah; Shenandoah; Gt Swamp
— **Sage** Klamath; Bowdoin; Chas Sheldon; Ruby L; National Elk; Seedskadee
— **Sharp-Tailed** Medicine L; Red Rock L; Rice L; Ft Niobrara; Arrowwood; Des Lacs; J Clark Salyer; L Metigoshe; Lacreek; Wind Cave
— **Spruce** Kenai; Seney
GUILLEMOT Aleutians
GULLS Kenai; Eufaula; JN Ding Darling; C Romain; Chincoteague; Brigantine
— **California** Klamath; Bowdoin; Medicine L; Red Rock L; Yellowstone
— **Franklin's** Bowdoin; Bear R; Salt Plains; Sand L
— **Great Black-Backed** Parkers Marsh
— **Herring** Isle Royale; Parkers Marsh
— **Laughing** Everglades; Florida Keys; Parkers Marsh
— **Ring-Billed** Klamath; Bowdoin; Medicine L; Red Rock L
GULLBILL Wreck & Bone Is
HARE, Snowshoe Mt Rainier; Glacier; Isle Royale; Moosehorn
HAWKS Kenai; Klamath; Sacramento; Ridgefield; Camas; Minidoka; Glacier; Chas Sheldon; Desert National; National Elk; Chaparral; Muleshoe; Ft Lincoln; Seashore
— **Gray** Bentsen RGV; Santa Ana
— **Harris's** Havasu L; Imperial; Laguna Atascosa
— **Hawaiian** Hawaii Volcanoes
— **Marsh** Columbia; Monte Vista; Bear R; Hutton L
— **White-Tailed** Laguna Atascosa
HERONS Havasu L; Klamath; San Luis; Camas; Deer Flat; Fish Springs; Imperial; Bosque Apache; Salt Plains; Tishomingo; Aransas; Union Slough; Marais des Cygnes; Tamarac; Upper Mississippi; Slade; Eufaula; White R; Chassahowitzka; Highlands Hammock; Jack Is; JN Ding Darling; Loxahatchee; Myakka R; Blackbeard Is; Yazoo; Pungo; C Romain; Chincoteague; Seashore; Montezuma
— **Black-Crowned** Klamath; Sacramento; Monte Vista; Bear R; Ottawa; Sand L; Lacassine; Parkers Marsh
— **Great Blue** Klamath; Sacramento; Ridgefield; Bowdoin; Medicine L; Ravalli; Red Rock L; Bear R; Grand Teton; Buffalo L; Rice L; Mingo; Valentine; Upper Souris; Ottawa; Sand L; Horicon; Everglades; St Marks; Lacassine; Parkers Marsh
— **Great White** Everglades; Florida Keys
— **Green** Rice L; Parkers Marsh
— **Little Blue** Ridgefield; Ravalli; Buffalo L; Mingo; Ottawa; Everglades; St Marks; Lacassine; Parkers Marsh; Wreck & Bone Is
— **Louisiana** Florida Keys; St Marks; Lacassine
— **Night** St Marks
— **Yellow-Crowned Night** Lacassine
HORSE, Feral Havasu L; Big Spring
HUMMINGBIRDS Ravalli; Bryce Canyon; Hutton L

— **Black-Chinned** Carlsbad
— **Buff-Bellied** Santa Ana
— **Broad-Tailed** Saguaro
— **Ruby-Throated** Seashore
IBISES Aransas; Highlands Hammock; Loxahatchee; Okefenokee; Pungo; Savannah; Chincoteague
— **Glossy** JN Ding Darling
— **White** White R; Chassahowitzka; Everglades; JN Ding Darling; Blackbeard Is; Lacassine
— **White-Faced** Bear R; Lacassine
— **Wood** White R; Everglades; St Marks; C Romain
IIWI Haleakala; Hawaii Volcanoes
JACANA Santa Ana
JACKRABBIT Sacramento; Bowdoin; Saguaro; Laguna Atascosa; L Metigoshe
— **Blacktailed** Carlsbad
JAEGER, Long-Tailed Mt McKinley
JAGUARUNDI Laguna Atascosa; Santa Ana
JAVELINA Saguaro; Aransas; Big Bend; Black Gap; Chaparral; Laguna Atascosa
JAYS Shenandoah
— **Blue** Pocahontas
— **Canada** Yellowstone
— **Gray** Mt Rainier
— **Green** Bentsen RGV; Santa Ana
— **Mexican** Saguaro; Big Bend
— **Steller's** Yosemite; Bryce Canyon; Saguaro
JUNCOS Lacreek; Shenandoah
— **Carolina** Gt Smoky Mts
— **Slate-Colored** Seashore
KILLDEER Ridgefield; Bear R; Hutton L; Seashore; Blackwater
KINGBIRDS Wind Cave
— **Western** JN Ding Darling
KINGFISHER Seashore
KINGLET Mt Rainier
KITE, Everglades Everglades; Loxahatchee
— **Mississippi** Salt Plains
— **Swallowtail** Everglades; JN Ding Darling; Okefenokee
— **White-Tailed** Laguna Atascosa
KNOT C Romain
KOLAE Hawaii Volcanoes
KOAE Hawaii Volcanoes
LARK, Horned Hungry Mother
LEMMING, Northern Bog Glacier
LIMPKIN Loxahatchee; Okefenokee
LIZARD, Desert Spiny Grand Canyon
LONGSPURS J Clark Salyer
— **Chestnut-Collared** Medicine L; Red Rock L; Des Lacs
— **McCown's** Medicine L; Red Rock L
LOONS Columbia; L Metigoshe; Chincoteague; Wreck & Bone Is; Blackwater
— **Common** Kenai
LYNX Kenai
MAGPIE Monte Vista; Grand Teton; National Elk; Wind Cave
— **Black-Billed** Rice L
MALLARD Kenai; Havasu L; Klamath; Sacramento; San Luis; Malheur; Columbia; Monte Vista; Minidoka; Benton L; Bowdoin; Medicine L; Ninepipe; Red Rock L; Bear R; National Elk; Yellowstone; Bitter L; Salt Plains; Hagerman; Chautauqua; Marais des Cygnes; Quivira; Seney; Agassiz; Rice L; Tamarac; Upper Mississippi; Mingo; Squaw Cr; Swan L; Arrowwood; Audubon; Des Lacs; Long L; Lostwood; Slade; Tewaukon; Lacreek; L Andes; Sand L; Horicon; JN Ding Darling; Lacassine; Yazoo; C Romain; Santee; Hatchie; Reelfoot; Chincoteague; Parkers Marsh; Bombay Hook; Blackwater; Eastern Neck; Parker R; Gt Swamp; Iroquois; Montezuma
MANATEE Everglades
MARINE FAUNA John Pennekamp
MARMOTS Kenai; Mt Rainier; Olympic; Minidoka; Glacier; National Bison; Grand Teton; Yellowstone
— **Yellow-Bellied** National Bison Range
MARSH BIRDS Malheur; Stillwater
MARTEN Mt Rainier; Glacier
MARTIN, Purple Hungry Mother
MAUII NUKUPUU Haleakala
MEADOWLARK Ft Lincoln; Wind Cave

MERGANSERS JN Ding Darling; Chincoteague
— **Common** Seney; Lacreek
— **Hooded** William L Finley; Seney; White R; Moosehorn
MEW, Glaucous Clarence Rhode
MINK Kenai; Bowdoin; Salt Plains; Mark Twain; De Soto; Union Slough; Marais des Cygnes; Isle Royale; Agassiz; Rice L; Upper Mississippi; Squaw Cr; Ft Niobrara; Arrowwood; J Clark Salyer; L Metigoshe; Turtle R; Upper Souris; Lacreek; Sand L; Big L; Wapanocca; White R; Chassahowitzka; Loxahatchee; Lacassine; Sabine; Yazoo; Santee; Gt Smoky Mts; Reelfoot; Tennessee National; Seashore; Wreck & Bone Is; Moosehorn; Brigantine; Montezuma; Missisquoi
MOCKINGBIRD Pocahontas; Seashore
MOLES Gt Smoky Mts
MONGOOSE Haleakala; Hawaii Volcanoes
MOOSE Kenai; Camas; Glacier; Grand Teton; National Elk; Seedskadee; Yellowstone; Isle Royale; Agassiz; Rice L; Moosehorn
MOUNTAIN LION see also **COUGAR** Crater L; Charles M Russell; Desert National; Ouray
MOUSE, Field Ninepipe
MURRE Aleutians
MUSKRAT Kenai; Sacramento; Malheur; Monte Vista; Camas; Bowdoin; Medicine L; National Bison; Ninepipe; Red Rock L; National Elk; Bitter L; Salt Plains; Mark Twain; De Soto; Kirwin; Marais des Cygnes; Isle Royale; Agassiz; Rice L; Tamarac; Upper Mississippi; Squaw Cr; Ft Niobrara; Arrowwood; J Clark Salyer; L Metigoshe; Sullys Hill; Upper Souris; Ottawa; Lacreek; Sand L; Horicon; Eufaula; Wheeler; Big L; Wapanocca; Lacassine; Noxubee; Carolina Sandhills; Santee; Gt Smoky Mts; Reelfoot; Tennessee National; Back Bay; Chincoteague; Parkers Marsh; Moosehorn; Blackwater; Brigantine; Gt Swamp; Montezuma; Erie National; Missisquoi
MYOTIS, Fringed Carlsbad
NENE Haleakala; Hawaii Volcanoes
NIGHTHAWK, Common Carlsbad; Seashore
NUTCRACKER, Clark's Yosemite; Crater L; Mt Rainier; Bryce Canyon; National Elk
NUTHATCHES Glacier; Hungry Mother; Pocahontas; Shenandoah
— **Brown-Headed** St Marks; Blackwater
NUTRIA Upper Mississippi; Chicot; Lacassine; Sabine; Back Bay
OCELOT Laguna Atascosa; Santa Ana
OLDSQUAW Aleutians; Chincoteague; Parkers Marsh
OPOSSUM Salt Plains; Wichita Mts; Laguna Atascosa; Santa Ana; De Soto; Marais des Cygnes; Squaw Cr; Horicon; Eufaula; Wheeler; Everglades; Chicot; Sam Houston; Yazoo; Carolina Sandhills; Gt Smoky Mts; Back Bay; Blackwater; Brigantine; Montezuma; Morton
— **Virginia** Seashore
ORIOLES Lacreek
— **Black-Headed** Santa Ana
— **Bullock's** Bowdoin
— **Hooded** Bentsen RGV
— **Lichtenstein's** Bentsen RGV; Santa Ana
— **Scott's** Carlsbad; Big Bend
OSPREY Grand Teton; National Elk; Yellowstone; Isle Royale; Florida Keys; St Marks; Parkers Marsh; Seashore; Wreck & Bone Is; Blackwater
OTTER Glacier; Seney; Rice L; Upper Mississippi; White R; Chassahowitzka; Everglades; J N Ding Darling; Loxahatchee; Okefenokee; Lacassine; Sabine; Noxubee; C Romain; Santee; Chincoteague; Parkers Marsh; Seashore; Wreck & Bone Is; Moosehorn; Blackwater; Missisquoi
OUZEL, Water Glacier; Grand Teton; Yellowstone
OVEN BIRD Shenandoah

OWLS Klamath; Sacramento; Camas; Minidoka; Chas Sheldon; Chaparral; Seashore
— **Barn** Blackwater
— **Barred** Okefenokee
— **Burrowing** Medicine L; Red Rock L; Muleshoe
— **Great Horned** Monte Vista; Carlsbad; Wichita Mts
— **Saw-Whet** Gt Smoky Mts
OYSTERCATCHERS Chincoteague; Wreck & Bone Is
— **American** C Romain
PACKRAT Santa Ana
PARTRIDGES Tewaukon
— **Gray** Bowdoin; Medicine L; National Bison; Red Rock L; Arrowwood; Des Lacs; J Clark Salyer; Upper Souris; Sand L
— **Hungarian** Ft Lincoln
PAURAQUE Bentsen RGV; Santa Ana
PEEWEE, Wood Fairy Stone
PELICANS Deer Flat; Union Slough; Quivira; Audubon; Lacreek
— **Brown** Everglades; JN Ding Darling; Merritt Is; St Marks; Delta; C Romain
— **White** Klamath; Modoc; Sacramento; Camas; Bowdoin; Medicine L; Red Rock L; Bear R; Yellowstone; Salt Plains; Rice L; Squaw Cr; Swan L; J Clark Salyer; Slade; Upper Souris; Sand L; White R; Everglades; JN Ding Darling; Merritt Is; St Marks
PHALAROPE, Northern Kenai
— **Wilson's** Monte Vista; Bear R; Upper Souris
PHEASANTS Haleakala; William L Finley; Kirwin; Crescent L; Ft Lincoln; Tewaukon
— **Japanese** Hawaii Volcanoes
— **Ring-Necked** Sacramento; Turnbull; Monte Vista; Bowdoin; Medicine L; National Bison; Red Rock L; Bitter L; Salt Plains; De Soto; Rice L; Ft Niobrara; Arrowwood; Des Lacs; J Clark Salyer; Upper Souris; Lacreek; L Andes; Sand L; Parker R; Gt Swamp
PHOEBES Fairy Stone
— **Eastern** Gt Smoky Mts
PIG, Wild Haleakala; Hawaii Volcanoes; Chaparral; Myakka R
PIGEON, Red-Billed Santa Ana
— **White-Crowned** Florida Keys
PIKA Crater L
PINTAIL Havasu L; Klamath; Sacremento; San Luis; Monte Vista; Benton L; Bowdoin; Medicine L; Red Rock L; Bear R; National Elk; Bitter L; Salt Plains; Laguna Atascosa; Marais des Cygnes; Mingo; Squaw Cr; Swan L; Arrowwood; Audubon; Des Lacs; Long L; Tewaukon; Lacreek; Sand L; JN Ding Darling; L Woodruff; Loxahatchee; Merritt Is; Lacassine; C Romain; Santee; Chincoteague; Parkers Marsh; Blackwater; Parker R; Brigantine; Gt Swamps; Iroquois
PIPISTRELLE, Western Carlsbad
PIPITS Mt Rainier; Glacier
— **Sprague's** Medicine L; Red Rock L; Des Lacs
PLOVERS Clarence Rhode; Chincoteague
— **Black-Bellied** C Romain
— **Golden** Kenai; Haleakala; Hawaii Volcanoes
— **Piping** De Soto
— **Semipalmated** C Romain
— **Snowy** Bitter L
PONIES Chincoteague
POOR-WILL Carlsbad; Big Bend
PORCUPINE Crater L; Mt Rainier; Deer Flat; Glacier; Medicine L; Ninepipe; Red Rock L; Bryce Canyon; J Clark Salyer; Upper Souris; Moosehorn
PRAIRIE CHICKEN Crescent L; Ft Niobrara; Tewaukon; Sand L
— **Lesser** Gene Howe
PRAIRIE DOG Mackenzie; Muleshoe
— **Blacktail** Kirwin; Wind Cave
PRONGHORN ANTELOPE Klamath; Modoc; Hart Mt; Camas; Minidoka; Benton L; Bowdoin; Charles M Russell; Medicine L; National Bison; Red Rock L; Chas Sheldon; Ouray; Seedskadee; Yellowstone; Bitter L; Carlsbad; Big Bend; Valentine; Arrowwood; Audubon; L Ilo; Lostwood; Wind Cave

USA: SPECIES LIST

PTARMIGAN Kenai; Glacier
— **White-Tailed** Mt Rainier
PUEO Hawaii Volcanoes
PUMA *see* **COUGAR** and **MOUNTAIN LION**
PYRRHULOXIA Saguaro; Carlsbad
QUAILS Buffalo L; Gene Howe; Crab Orchard; Marais des Cygnes; Pocahontas
— **California** Hawaii Volcanoes; Turnbull
— **Gambel's** Saguaro
— **Harlequin** Saguaro
— **Mountain** Yosemite
— **Scaled** Bitter L; Carlsbad; Black Gap; Chaparral
RABBITS Monte Vista; Camas; Bitter L; Union Slough; Kirwin; Marais des Cygnes; J Clark Salyer; Upper Souris; Big L; Loxahatchee; Chicot; Lacassine; Sam Houston; Back Bay; Parker R
— **Swamp** Mingo; White R; Jack Is
— **Snowshoe** Tamarac; L Metigoshe
RACCOONS Sacramento; San Luis; Mt Rainier; Turnbull; Bitter L; Carlsbad; Salt Plains; Wichita Mts; Aransas; Chaparral; Laguna Atascosa; Santa Ana; De Soto; Union Slough; Marais des Cygnes; Rice L; Upper Mississippi; Mingo; Squaw Cr; Crescent L; Ft Niobrara; Arrowwood; Ft Lincoln; J Clark Salyer; Sullys Hill; Turtle R; Upper Souris; Ottawa; Lacreek; Wind Cave; Horicon; Eufaula; Wheeler; Big L; Wapanocca; White R; Chassahowitzka; Everglades; Florida Keys; Jack Is; Loxahatchee; Okefenokee; Chicot; Delta; Lacassine; Sam Houston; Pungo; C Romain; Santee; Hatchie; Tennessee National; Back Bay; Chincoteague; Parkers Marsh; Seashore; Shenandoah; Moosehorn; Blackwater; Gt Swamp; Iroquois; Montezuma; Morton; Erie National; Missisquoi
RACER, Red Saguaro
RAILS Klamath; JN Ding Darling; Savannah; Brigantine
— **Clapper** St Marks; C Romain; Parkers Marsh; Wreck & Bone Is; Bombay Hook
— **King** St Marks; Blackwater
— **Sora** Mingo
— **Virginia** Rice L; Blackwater
RATS Hawaii Volcanoes
— **Cotton** Parkers Marsh
— **Florida Water** Loxahatchee
RATTLESNAKE Grand Canyon; Saguaro; Mingo
RAVENS Crater L; Mt Rainier; Bryce Canyon; Gt Smoky Mts; Shenandoah
REDHEAD Malheur; Monte Vista; Bowdoin; Medicine L; Ninepipe; Red Rock L; Bear R; Hutton L; Laguna Atascosa; Agassiz; Arrowwood; Audubon; Des Lacs; Slade; Lacreek; Sand L; Mattamuskeet; Tennessee National; Parkers Marsh; Montezuma
REDPOLL Kenai
REDSTART Bowdoin
REINDEER Aleutians
REPTILES Hagerman; Loxahatchee; Cross Creeks; Seashore
RINGTAIL Carlsbad; Big Bend
ROADRUNNER Saguaro; Carlsbad; Wichita Mts; Big Bend
ROBIN Kenai; Mt Rainier; Ft Lincoln
SANDERLING C Romain
SANDPIPER Clarence Rhode; Kenai; Havasu L; Salt Plains; Slade; Chincoteague
— **Least** Parkers Marsh
— **Spotted** Parkers Marsh
SAPSUCKER, Yellow-Bellied Fairy Stone
SCAUPS Kenai; Klamath; Marais des Cygnes; Rice L; Tamarac; Swan L; Des Lacs; Lostwood; Lacreek; L Woodruff; Lacassine; Mattamuskeet; C Romain; Parker R
— **Greater** Parkers Marsh
— **Lesser** Arrowwood; Sand L; JN Ding Darling; Merritt Is; Parkers Marsh
SCORPIONS Saguaro
SCOTER Chincoteague
SEA COW Chassahowitzka
SEA LION Aleutians; Cape Arago; Ecola
SEA OTTER Aleutians
SEAL, Harbor Seashore; Moosehorn

SEEDEATER, White-Collared Santa Ana
SHEEP, Bighorn Havasu L; Glacier; National Bison; National Elk; Yellowstone; Custer
— **Dall** Kenai
— **Desert Bighorn** Black Gap
SHELLFISH Jack Is
SHOREBIRDS Klamath; Turnbull; Willapa; Deer Flat; Benton L; Medicine L; Red Rock L; Chas Sheldon; Ruby L; Stillwater; Aransas; Marais des Cygnes; Upper Souris; Pea Is; Back Bay; Wreck & Bone Is; Parker R; Montezuma; Morton; Erie National
SHOVELER Klamath; Sacramento; Benton L; Bowdoin; Medicine L; Red Rock L; Bear R; Marais des Cygnes; Agassiz; Tamarac; Mingo; Squaw Cr; Swan L; Arrowwood; Des Lacs; Lostwood; Slade; Lacreek; Sand L; Loxahatchee; Lacassine; C Romain; Tennessee National; Chincoteague; Brigantine; Gt Swamp; Montezuma
SHREWS Gt Smoky Mts
SHRIKE, Loggerhead Saguaro
SISKIN, Pine Fairy Stone
SKIMMER Delta
— **Black** Lacassine; C Romain; Chincoteague; Wreck & Bone Is; Brigantine
SKUNKS Modoc; San Luis; Monte Vista; Bowdoin; Ninepipe; Saguaro; Bitter L; Aransas; Santa Ana; Agassiz; Squaw Cr; Arrowwood; J Clark Salyer; L Ilo; Sullys Hill; Upper Souris; Lacreek; Eufaula; Chicot; Lacassine; Sam Houston; Carolina Sandhills; Gt Smoky Mts; Shenandoah; Moosehorn; Blackwater; Brigantine
— **Hog-Nosed** Carlsbad
— **Spotted** Sacramento; Carlsbad
— **Striped** Sacramento; Medicine L; Red Rock L; Carlsbad; Laguna Atascosa; Ft Niobrara; Gt Swamp
SKYLARK Haleakala
SNAILS, Freshwater Loxahatchee
— **Tree** Everglades
SNIPE Clarence Rhode; Eufaula
— **Common** Monte Vista; Bowdoin; Rice L; Swan L
SONGBIRDS Sacramento; Minidoka; Ft Lincoln; L Metigoshe; Wheeler; Montezuma; Morton; Erie National
SONORA CORAL SNAKE Saguaro
SORA Bowdoin; Rice L
SPARROWS Kenai; J Clark Salyer; Parkers Marsh; Seashore
— **Baird's** Medicine L; Red Rock L; Des Lacs; J Clark Salyer
— **Black-Throated** Carlsbad
— **Dusky Seaside** Merritt Is
— **Le Conte's** Medicine L; Red Rock L; J Clark Salyer
— **Olive** Santa Ana
— **Pinewoods** St Marks
— **Savannah** National Elk
— **Seaside** St Marks; Brigantine
— **Sharp-Tailed** Brigantine
— **Song** Gt Smoky Mts
— **Vesper** National Elk
— **White-Crowned** Carlsbad
SPOONBILL, Roseate Aransas; Everglades; Florida Keys; JN Ding Darling; Loxahatchee; Lacassine
SQUIRRELS Yosemite; Crater L; Mt Rainier; Glacier; Salt Plain; Aransas; Gus Engeling; Chautauqua; Marais des Cygnes; Ft Niobrara; Ft Lincoln; L Metigoshe; Turtle R; Eufaula; Wheeler; Big L; White R; Chicot; Sam Houston; Carolina Sandhills; Gt Smoky Mts; Hatchie; Reelfoot; Tennessee National
— **Columbian Ground** National Bison
— **Delmarva Peninsula Fox** Blackwater
— **Flying** Yosemite; Gt Smoky Mts; Seashore; Shenandoah; Moosehorn
— **Fox** Wichita Mts; De Soto; St Marks; C Romain
— **Golden-Mantled Ground** Yosemite; Bryce Canyon; Grand Teton; Yellowstone
— **Gray** Silver Falls; Jack Is; Seashore; Shenandoah; Moosehorn; Blackwater; Brigantine; Montezuma; Morton
— **Ground** Modoc; Bowdoin; Medicine L;

Red Rock L; Lacreek
— **Red** Isle Royale; Seashore; Moosehorn; Brigantine; Montezuma
— **Rock** Carlsbad; Big Bend
— **Tree** Kenai
— **Vinta Ground** Yellowstone
— **Whitetail Antelope** Big Bend
STILT, Black-Necked Sacramento; San Luis; Bear R; Bitter L; JN Ding Darling
SWALLOWS Bryce Canyon; Seashore
— **Cave** Carlsbad
— **Cliff** Big Bend
— **Golden-Crowned** Kenai
— **Tree** Brigantine
— **Violet-Green** Yellowstone
SWANS Imperial; L Metigoshe; Pungo
— **Trumpeter** Kenai; Turnbull; Red Rock L; Ruby L; Grand Teton; National Elk; Yellowstone; Lacreek
— **Whistling** Modoc; Sacramento; Stillwater; Bear R; Bosque Apache; Union Slough; Shiawassee; Upper Mississippi; Sand L; Mattamuskeet; Back Bay; Eastern Neck
SWIFT, White-Throated Bryce Canyon
TANAGERS Seashore
— **Scarlet** Gt Smoky Mts
— **Western** Grand Teton; Yellowstone; Carlsbad
TATTLER, Wandering Kenai
TEALS Kenai; Havasu L; San Luis; Malheur; Benton L; Ninepipe; Quivira; Upper Mississippi; Audubon; Long L; Lostwood; Slade; Tewaukon; L Woodruff; Tennessee National
— **Blue-Winged** Klamath; Monte Vista; Bowdoin; Medicine L; Red Rock L; Marais des Cygnes; Seney; Agassiz; Tamarac; Squaw Cr; Swan L; Arrowwood; Des Lacs Lacreek; Sand L; Horicon; JN Ding Darling; Loxahatchee; Merritt Is; Lacassine; C Romain; Chincoteague; Parkers Marsh; Bombay Hook; Moosehorn; Blackwater; Parker R; Gt Swamp; Montezuma
— **Cinnamon** Klamath; Sacramento; Monte Vista; Bear R; National Elk
— **Green-Winged** Sacramento; Monte Vista; Bear R; National Elk; Salt Plains; Mingo; Squaw Cr; Swan L; Lacreek; Sand L; JN Ding Darling; Loxahatchee; C Romain; Chincoteague; Parkers Marsh; Moosehorn; Blackwater; Parker R; Gt Swamp; Montezuma
TERNS Florida Keys; JN Ding Darling; Pea Is; Chincoteague; Brigantine; Montezuma
— **Arctic** Clarence Rhode
— **Black** Sacramento; Bowdoin; Bear R
— **Caspian** Klamath; Rice L
— **Common** Bowdoin; Medicine L; Red Rock L; Sand L; Wreck & Bone Is
— **Forster's** Bear R; Sand L
— **Least** De Soto; Florida Keys; C Romain; Parkers Marsh; Wreck & Bone Is
— **Royal** C Romain; Wreck & Bone Is
TERRAPIN, Diamond Back C Romain
TEXAS LONGHORN Possum Kingdom; Ft Niobrara
THRASHER, Brown Shenandoah
— **Curve-Billed** Saguaro; Santa Ana
— **Long-Billed** Bentsen RGV; Santa Ana
THRUSHES Mt Rainier
— **Wood** Gt Smoky Mts
TITMOUSE, Black-Crested Santa Ana
— **Tufted** Gt Smoky Mts; Pocahontas
TORTOISE, Desert Saguaro
TOWHEES Seashore; Shenandoah
— **Brown** Carlsbad
TURKEY, Wild Salt Plains; Wichita Mts; Chaparral; Gene Howe; Crab Orchard; Mingo; Custer; Eufaula; White R; Myakka; St Marks; Blackbeard Is; Okefenokee; Piedmont; C Romain; Carolina Sandhills; Tennessee National; Shenandoah
TURNSTONES C Romain; Chincoteague
— **Ruddy** Florida Keys; St Marks
TURTLES Highlands Hammock
— **Giant Sea** C Romain
— **Green** Florida Keys
— **Sea** JN Ding Darling; Blackbeard Is
UPLAND BIRDS Turnbull; all Wyoming State Parks; Bosque Apache; Gus Engeling; Kerr; Piedmont; Sam Houston; Noxubee

VIREOS Seashore
— **Black-Whiskered** Florida Keys
— **Red-Eyed** C Romain; Shenandoah
— **White-Eyed** C Romain
VULTURES Seashore; Shenandoah
— **Black** Presquile
— **Turkey** Carlsbad
WARBLERS Mt Rainier; Glacier; Wind Cave; Gt Smoky Mts; Seashore; Parker R
— **Audubon's** Carlsbad
— **Black-Throated Blue** Shenandoah
— **Colima** Big Bend
— **Kirtland's** Kirtland's Warbler MA
— **Pine** St Marks; C Romain
— **Prothonotary** White R
— **Swainson's** White R
— **Yellow** Bowdoin
— **Yellow-Throated** Kerr; St Marks; C Romain
WATERFOWL Kenai; Klamath; Crater L; Malheur; Turnbull; Minidoka; Charles M Russell; National Bison; Ninepipe; Ravalli; Chas Sheldon; Stillwater; Seedskadee; all Wyoming State Parks; Aransas; Gus Engeling; De Soto; Flint Hills; Kirwin; Sherburne; Upper Mississippi; Ft Niobrara; Valentine; Ft Lincoln; J Clark Salyer; L Ilo; Lostwood; Tewaukon; Ottawa; Wheeler; Big L; Wapanocca; L Woodruff; Merritt Is; Piedmont; Sam Houston; Noxubee; Hatchie; Reelfoot; Presquile; Eastern Neck; Morton; Missisquoi
WAXWING, Bohemian National Elk
— **Cedar** Seashore
WEASEL Monte Vista; Bowdoin; National Bison; Isle Royale; Ft Niobrara; Arrowwood; J Clark Salyer; Slade; Sullys Hill; Upper Souris; Moosehorn; Morton
— **Bridled** Bitter L; Santa Ana
— **Long-Tailed** Gt Smoky Mts; Seashore
WHIP-POOR-WILL Shenandoah
WIDGEONS San Luis; Ridgefield; Monte Vista; Marais des Cygnes; Upper Mississippi; Lostwood; Tewaukon; Santee; Parkers Marsh; Parker R; Iroquois
— **American** Klamath; Sacramento; Bowdoin; Medicine L; Red Rock L; Bear R; National Elk; Bitter L; Mingo; Squaw Cr; Swan L; Arrowwood; Des Lacs; Sand L; JN Ding Darling; Loxahatchee; Merritt Is; Lacassine; Reelfoot; Chincoteague; Blackwater
WILDCAT Jack Is; Chicot
WILLET Red Rock L; Bear R; Upper Souris; Lacreek; St Marks; C Romain; Chincoteague; Parkers Marsh; Wreck & Bone Is; Bombay Hook
WOLF Aleutians; Charles M Russell; Glacier; Isle Royale
WOLVERINE Kenai; Glacier
WOODCHUCK Chautauqua; Ottawa; Gt Smoky Mts; Shenandoah; Gt Swamp; Erie National
WOODCOCK, American Rice L; Gt Swamp
WOODLAND BIRDS Silver Falls
WOODPECKERS Mt Rainier; Ft Lincoln; Wind Cave; Gt Smoky Mts; Seashore; Shenandoah
— **Acorn** Yosemite
— **Cockaded** St Marks
— **Downy** White R
— **Gila** Saguaro
— **Hairy** Saguaro
— **Ladder-Backed** Carlsbad
— **Lewis's** Glacier; National Elk
— **Pileated** Isle Royale; White R; Piedmont; C Romain
— **Red-Bellied** St Marks
WRENS Seashore; Shenandoah
— **Bewick's** Saguaro
— **Cactus** Saguaro; Carlsbad; Big Bend
— **Carolina** C Romain; Gt Smoky Mts
— **Marsh** Sand L; St Marks; Parkers Marsh
— **Rock-Canyon** Carlsbad
YELLOW BELLY National Bison
YELLOWLEGS Bowdoin; Salt Plains; Union Slough; C Romain; Chincoteague
— **Greater** Sacramento; Parkers Marsh
— **Lesser** Parkers Marsh
YELLOWTHROAT National Elk

Canada

The wolf, a close relative of the domestic dog (with which it can interbreed). They live in families, only forming packs when winters get hard. Their chief diet is small mammals, carrion and fruit.

Algonquin Provincial Park Nearly 2 million acres; rising from 600 to 3,000 ft above sea level. Lying between Georgian Bay and the Ottawa River the park is like a dome with forest, rock, and lake, and rivers flowing off the highland area. Much of the centre is so wild that it can be approached only by canoe or on foot, but the whole area is easily accessible being less than 200 miles from Toronto. Facilities include swimming, with some sandy beaches, trout fishing, and canoeing – particularly since rowboats, canoes and outboard motors can all be hired.

The main attractions are the tame and numerous deer, but timber wolf, red fox, black bear, raccoon, and moose are also to be found. Beavers are common; marten, fisher, otter, and mink are less noticed. Many migrating birds nest in the park, among them the common loon and white-throated sparrow. Ruffed grouse, yellow-bellied sap-sucker, evening grosbeak, red-eyed vireo, and osprey may also be seen.

On the east side are found red and white pine, jack pine, some poplar, white birch, spruce and balsam. On the west side are hardwoods like sugar maple, yellow birch, and beech. Elm, black cherry, and hornbeam also grow, and black spruce and cedar and black ash grow mostly in swampy areas. Sweet gale, leather-leaf, and Labrador tea can be seen on the water's edge. Moss, fern, bracken and orchids are also to be found.

There are camp sites at South Tea Lake, Canisbay Lake, Mew Lake, Pog Lake, Kearney Lake, Coon and Rock Lake, and Opeongo Lake. The cost, $2.50 per day, includes vehicle permit. There are also lodges, holiday cottages, and hotels within this area.

From Huntsville Highway 60 leads to the main west entrance. From Minden and Dorset by Highway Nos. 35 and 60. From Ottawa and Pembroke by Highways 17, 62 and 60. Canadian National Railway runs on the north side between North Bay and Ottawa. There are no buses but non-scheduled float planes land at Kiosk, Brent, Achray, Opeongo, and Smoke Lake.

189

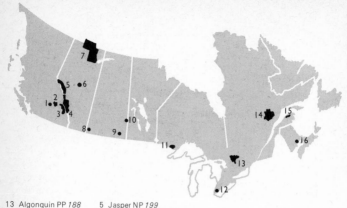

Highway 60 traverses the southern portion of the park, but much of the interior is reached only by canoe or on foot. Many marked walking trails peel off from the highway.

Last Friday in April until 2nd Tuesday in October: best in the high summer months, when days are warm and nights cool.

2 days or a long vacation.

$1 per day up to 4 days or $5 up to 16 days. Vehicle entry permits $10 per season, $1 per day. Boat entry permits $5 per season unless carried on a car.

Fishing guides may be obtained through the lodges or tourist outfitters. Park naturalists lead tours and nature walks during the season.

Museum at Found Lake is open from June to mid-October, and on some weekends in May. A park naturalist is in attendance. Talks, films, and slide shows are given at the Park theatre during the season; at the east gate is a Pioneer Logging Exhibit.

Algonquin Provincial Park and *Canoe Routes in Algonquin Provincial Park* from Department of Lands and Forests.

Department of Lands and Forests, Parliament Buildings, Toronto 5, Ontario.

Banff National Park 1,600,000 acres; from 4,530 ft to 11,902 ft (Mt Forbes) above sea level. Banff is Canada's oldest national park, established in 1887 to cover 10 square miles around a remarkable hot spring at Sulphur Mountain. Now, like its northern neighbour Jasper, it incorporates an enormous stretch of the Rocky Mountains' eastern slopes, and has become an internationally famous resort centre. The town of Banff is the major settlement, with a smaller township at Lake Louise – considered by many to be one of the

Polar bears in Norwegian Bay, Northwest Territories.

most beautiful in all of Canada's lake-strewn landscape. The mountain scenery is breathtaking, especially in its contrast with the softer contours of the forested Bow River valley. Rock climbers are drawn to the granite slopes and peaks of the mountains; fishermen and holidaymakers can take their pick of a whole array of clear mountain lakes; hikers and horseback riders can wander on park trails both here and to the interconnected parks of Jasper, Yoho, and Kootenay. The countryside teems with wildlife (a good starting point is the museum in Banff town). Also worth a visit is the Inglewood bird sanctuary in nearby Calgary.

Mountain goat, bighorn, elk, moose, mountain caribou, deer, black and grizzly bears, beaver, muskrat, marten, Columbian and yellow-mantled ground squirrels, yellow-haired porcupine, cony and snowshoe rabbit, wolverine; over 180 bird species include golden eagle, red- and yellow-shafted flicker, grosbeak, magpie, Canada jay, woodpeckers, hummingbird, western tanager, mountain bluebird, chickadee, redbreasted nuthatch, Bohemian waxwing, horned lark, Townsend's solitaire, and the rarer ruby-crowned kinglet, hermit and Swainson's thrushes, warbling vireo, and winter wren.

Trees and flowers as for Jasper.

Many hotels, motels, lodges, chalets, etc. in and near the two settlements – ranging in price from $24 and up for double room at Banff Spring Hotel (1080 persons) to $10 to $16 double – the average at smaller places. Simpler accommodation is also available at Moraine Lake, Bow Lake, and other remoter places. There are at least 10 campgrounds; Tunnel Mountain (trailers, too), Two Jack Lake, and Johnston Canyon are fully serviced. Many grounds offer nature films. Campgrounds at Lake Louise and Protection Mountain, though lacking electricity, take trailers. Fees as for Jasper.

The red fox occurs from North America, Europe, and North Africa to parts of Asia. Its behaviour is more catlike than that of other dogs – rarely, for instance, does it hunt in packs. In populous areas it adapts well to suburbia, burrowing in railway cuttings and parks.

Banff town is on the TransCanada Highway from Calgary, east of the park, or from Vancouver (over the Rockies) to the west. The highway also passes through Lake Louise. The Banff-Windermere runs from British Columbia Highway 95 through Kootenay National Park to Banff town, providing the best access route from the USA. Regular Greyhound buses on the Banff-Windermere and TransCanada highways. Banff and Lake Louise are regular stops on the main transcontinental line of the Canadian Pacific Railway. The nearest airport is at Calgary.

The Banff-Jasper highway branches from the TransCanada at Lake Louise, winding north through the park. The Banff-Windermere runs south of Banff town through the park. Some good roads radiate out from the two settlements; there are about 700 miles of foot and bridle trails. Regular sightseeing buses; launch trips on Bow River and Lake Minnewanka; snowmobiles operate over the great glaciers. Mountain railway and ski-chair lifts make several peaks accessible. Climbers and hikers off park trails must register with a warden before and after each trip.

Open (except for some mountainous areas of the highways) all year; best times as for Jasper.

7 days to a very long vacation.

⊠ As for Jasper.

☞ Canadian Mountain Holidays operate a guide service within the park (and other mountain areas).

⇨ Superintendent, Banff National Park, Banff, Alberta; or Banff Information Bureau.

Cypress Hills Provincial Park 10,880 acres of park, plus 33,920 acres of adjacent forest; from 3,600 to 4,800 ft above sea level. The park is divided into central and west block and lies in southwest Saskatchewan, about 50 miles north of the border. Consisting mostly of a flat-topped plateau, whose uneven slopes descend sharply to the rolling treeless planes below, it is mainly covered with grass, except for forest on the north-facing slopes and in some of the valleys. Streams and lakes dot the area, and Bald Butte and the Overlook, both at over 4,000 ft, give fine views over the surrounding countryside. Facilities include fishing, boating and swimming, a riding stable, nine-hole golf course, good ski slopes.

⌁ The 58 species of mammals recorded include beaver, bats, prairie dog, marmot, chipmunk, muskrat, porcupine, elk, antelope, moose, Canada lynx, mink, raccoon, Rocky Mountain mule deer and white-tailed deer. Birds include mallards, pintails, Canada goose, grebes, heron, avocet, snipe, curlew, plover, sandpiper, pine siskin, red crossbill, black-capped chickadee, flycatchers, owls, game birds, hawks and falcons.

ဦ Northern wheat grass and spear grass are the dominant grasses. Great woods of aspen grow on the northern slopes of the eastern part of the park, and edge the pine forests elsewhere. Alberta spruce, balsam, poplar, lodgepole pine are also to be found, as are bluebell, crocus, anemone, blue lupin and many other flower species. Fourteen different kinds of orchid have been found along the banks of rivers.

⇌ Maple Creek, to the north of the park, has both hotels and motels. Within the park itself at Beaver, Windfall and the valley of the Windfall there are 41 rental cabins, 5 institutional camps, and 165 cottages. Camping fee: $2 with electricity, $1 without. Rented accommodation mid-May to end-August only.

⇝ 18 miles south of Maple Creek on Highway 21, or 23 miles south from the Trans-Canada Highway. Alternative approach by Highway 21, uniting with route 13. Secondary roads join Cypress Hills to Alberta in the West. By rail and bus to Maple Creek, but from there there is no public transport.

🚘 Foot trails and one gravel access road.

☀ The park is open the year round; best time summer.

🕐 2 days or a vacation.

⊠ $1 daily, $4 season.

☞ Self-guiding nature trails.

◉ Tipi rings can be seen in the Ravenscrag vicinity, on a bench east of Davis Creek near Belanger, and other places. At Chimney Coulee one chimney that gave this place its name remains today.

⇨ The Park Superintendent, Cypress Hills Provincial Park, Maple Creek, Saskatchewan.

Duck Mountain Provincial Park 31,000 acres: from about 1,800 to 2,400 ft above sea level. Most of the park lies above 2,000 ft, the highest part being in the south east. This rolling, hilly terrain is known for the variety of the scenery, for its streams, rivers and lakes, and for the beauty of the Little Boggy Creek valley, which is between one and two miles wide and runs for 15 miles. Set mostly in Western Manitoba, but partly in Saskatchewan too, the western edge of the park divides the Shoal River Basin to the north from the Assiniboine River basin in the south. Facilities include four beaches, a golf course, mooring and launching sites for boats, which can also be hired.

- Bear, deer, moose, beaver, coyote, fox, lynx, mink, muskrat, squirrel and weasel. The park boasts the only colony of turkey-vultures in Saskatchewan.

- White spruce and tall aspens dominate the open plains and bogs.

- Kamsack lies 15 miles west. Duck Mountain Motor Hotel ($7 single, $10 double), Hotel King George ($3.75 single, $6 double), Hotel Russell ($2.75 single, $4.50 double). Within the park itself there are 10 modern and 27 older rental cabin units, 329 cottages, 1 group camp for 100 people, and 4 campgrounds. Camping fees per night: $2 serviced, $1 unserviced.

- By 57 Highway from Kamsack. By Highway 83 from Manitoba. The park is also accessible by some occasionally used trails. Air and rail service to Kamsack.

- Daily bus service through the park by Saskatchewan Transportation Company from Kamsack to Swan River. Some 50 miles of road, and 2½ miles of trails and bikeways lead through the park.

- Open all the year. Best time summer but the distribution of rain among the months June, July and August changes from year to year.

- 1 day to a vacation.

- $1 daily, $4 for season.

- The Park Superintendent, Duck Mountain Provincial Park, Saskatchewan.

Elk Island National Park 48,000 acres; 2,350 to 2,475 ft above sea level. The park was originally designated as a wildlife sanctuary, especially to protect elk and the nucleus herd of prairie bison bought from the USA in 1907 (the species was then nearly extinct in Canada). Now it is a national park it is gaining in popularity as a natural wilderness. It is set in the rolling Beaver Hills some 30 miles east of Edmonton, Alberta, in extensive forest terrain broken by stretches of open prairie. Within the park are a surprising number of small lakes – chief among them being Astotin, 2¼ miles wide, containing more than 20 islands (including Elk Island, from which the park takes its name). Despite its size the park is totally fenced to protect the grazing herds.

- Almost 1,000 plains bison (buffalo to Canadians); elk, moose, mule and whiletailed deer. As a bird sanctuary the park protects mallard, canvasback, coot, black tern, pintail, gadwall, shoveller, bufflehead, ruddy duck, blue-winged teal, scaup, American bittern, Franklin's gull, and a variety of woodland and prairie birds, including grouse, hawks, and owls.

Black and white spruce, willow, paper birch, balsam poplar, trembling aspen, larch, and a wide range of forest and prairie wildflowers. The wild meadow hay, called buffalo grass, is worth noting; it cures where it stands and so provides good year-round fodder.

A group of 17 cabins on the west shore of Astotin lake ($6–$10 for 1–4 persons). Serviced campsite with WC, electricity, etc, at Sandy Beach on east shore of Astotin, Trailer site $1; with electricity $1.50; with water, sewerage. electricity, $2. Also hotels, etc, in Lamont (4 miles north of park) or Edmonton.

Highway 16 east from Edmonton; Saskatchewan Highway 5 west from Saskatoon joining Alberta Highway 16. Bus service from Edmonton. Canadian National Railway to Lamont. Nearest airport at Edmonton.

All-weather road joins north and south entrances and passes through main Astotin recreational area. Secondary gravel roads link with highways near the park. There is a system of trails but walkers are warned not to stroll too casually on the buffalo range.

Open all year; best time May to October, especially high summer and early autumn.

3 days or vacation.

25c per car (50c with trailer). Season ticket valid also in Waterton Lakes, Prince Albert, Riding Mountain, and Point Pelee national parks $2 ($3 with trailer).

Resident park naturalist conducts tours in summer. Parks authorities include superintendent, wardens, Royal Canadian Mounted Police.

Superintendent, Elk Island National Park, Lamont, Alberta.

American elk in Banff National Park.

Gannet colony on Bonaventure Island, Quebec.

Fundy National Park 49,000 acres; from sea level to about 1,000 ft above. The park is on the northern shore of the Bay of Fundy in New Brunswick, between the cities of St John and Moncton. The bay's high tides, which often reach 60 ft, and its wild seas have carved the sandstone cliffs into wonderful sculptured shapes. Fundy is a holiday resort as well as a wildlife sanctuary, so there is plenty of opportunity for seaside sports, golf, and tennis; there is also a handicrafts summer course run by the New Brunswick School of Arts and Crafts – and there is even an outdoor theatre.

⌇ Moose, deer, black bear, beaver, raccoon, lynx, bobcat, red fox, muskrat, weasel, porcupine, rabbit; great blue heron, woodcock, prairie and Connecticut warblers, song sparrows, lark bunting; in their season you can see migrants such as scoter, alcid, razorbill, sandpiper, cormorant, loon, egret, American widgeon, and others. (Such birds also gather in the marshlands 10 miles east of the park, on the coast, and on nearby bird sanctuaries such as Catons Island and Machias Seal Island, in the Bay of Fundy.)

ε3 Spruce, balsam fir, birch, tamarack, ash, beech, poplar, aspen, hemlock, sumach, and the autumnally brilliant maple. Wild flowers and flowering shrubs are plentiful.

⇌ Hotels and motels in the town of Alma just east of the park boundary on the coast; also at or near park HQ at the Alma entrance. The latter have ultramodern chalets ($11 double with kitchenette) and a 20-unit motel ($11 double, $20 for four). Camping facilities include a serviced site at HQ with trailer facilities, all conveniences, swimming pool. There is a serviced site at Point Wolfe and semiserviced grounds at Bennett Lake, Wolfe Lake, Point Wolfe, Micmac, Bogle Farm, and Herring Cove. Some of these have nearby fishing and beaches; rates from 50c per tent per day, $2 per week; 75c per trailer per day (electricity 35c per day extra), $3 per week. Overnight campers must get a (free) fire permit.

➡ From Moncton, east of the park, paved Highway 14 runs 50 miles to Alma and the park entrance. From St John, to the west, Highway 2 through Sussex to Penobsquis (50 miles) then Highway 14 to the park's western entrance at Wolfe Lake. Daily buses link Moncton and Alma.

� Highway 14 cuts 12¼ miles diagonally from Alma to Wolfe Lake; secondary roads link HQ with Herring Cove, Point Wolfe, and other main coastal spots. And a network of nature trails exists throughout the park; plant life along the way is clearly labelled.

🌅 Open May 1 to September 30.

🕐 2 days or vacation.

🎟 Free, including car.

☞ Park naturalists conduct guided tours and nature walks in the summer season. Nature talks, films, slide shows are offered in the park theatre. As in all Canada's national parks, resident wardens and Royal Canadian Mounted Police are on hand to advise visitors as well as to protect the park and its wildlife.

⇥ Park Superintendent, Fundy National Park, Alma, New Brunswick.

Gaspesian Park 3,200 acres; from 500 to 4,300 ft above sea level. The Schick-Shock mountains are the highest east of the Rockies, and two mountains are particularly remarkable. Mont Jacques-Cartier soars to 4,300 ft, while Mont Albert (3,700 ft) is topped by a grassy plateau covering 12 square miles. This is a favourite haunt of the grazing caribou. The rocks at Cap Bon Ami were formerly a great hazard to shipping, but this part of the park has now been developed to give spectacular views. The park which is famous for hunting, fishing, climbing and its interesting flora, also includes the Park of Fort Prevel – with its own inn, golf and tennis – the Port Daniel and also the St John reserve, about 20 miles from Gaspé. A salmon river in Bonaventure County is part of the same domain.

🦌 Caribou, Virginia deer, moose, black bear, squirrel, beaver, wolf, fox, mink, weasel, striped skunk, hare; Canada goose, partridge.

🌼 Particularly rare alpine plants dating from the interglacial age. Also Solomon's seal, cranberry, rosemary, goldenrod, crowberry, cottongrass, chickweed.

🛏 Le Gite du Mont Albert, an inn with 7 cottages (from $14) and alpine in style; rooms $5 single, $8 double. Also in the park are 3 hunting and fishing lodges, several cottages, and one camping ground. At Fort Prevel, the Auberge is known for its French cuisine ($10 single, $14 double). The townships of Sante-Anne-des-Monts, Mont Louis, and Murdockville lie nearby.

➡ By Highway 6 which runs round the coast of the peninsula. The gateways of the park are at Sainte-Anne-des-Monts, Anse Pleureuse, and New Richmond, each with good connecting roads. There is an airport at Gaspé.

🚗 A paved road crosses the park, from north to south, and there are also several dirt roads, foot and bridle paths.

☼ Open June 1 to September 30, which is also the best time to visit.

⏀ 1–4 days.

▧ Free.

☞ Mountain guides are available; no charge.

◎ An interesting hatchery near Gaspé, the oldest in Canada, may be visited.

⇥ Parks Service, Ministère du Tourisme de la Chasse et de la Pêche, Hôtel du Gouvernement, Quebec.

Glacier National Park 330,000 acres; 4,427 to 11,123 ft above sea level. The park is about 10 miles east of Mt Revelstoke National Park, British Columbia, and holds central place in the enormous protected parklands (Banff, Jasper, Yoho, Kootenay, as well as Hamber and Mt Robson provincial parks) of the Canadian Rockies. The park takes its name from the gigantic Illecillewaet Glacier, 10 square miles of ice descending 3,500 ft from its head; it is easily reached from the station. Many spiky but accessible peaks, broad forests, canyons, cataracts, and caves add to the park's features. And it is a limited winter sports centre, with downhill ski runs up to 4 miles long – also within easy reach of Glacier Station.

↬ Black and grizzly bears, mountain goat, mule and whitetailed deer, moose, elk, caribou, beaver, lynx, weasel, marten; birds of prey include golden eagle, hawks, owls; many species of smaller and colourful songbirds and insectivores.

⅋ Typically coniferous forest – cedar, spruce, firs, hemlock – often dense, accessible only on foot. Alpine meadows are rich in pink and white heathers, white dryas, larkspur, lupine, hellebore, Indian paintbrush, and other flowers.

⇌ A motor hotel at Rogers Pass in the park (on the main highway near the eastern entrance) costs $14 double in summer, $9 in winter. Campgrounds near Glacier station offer kitchens, WCs, river water; open July to September at $1 per site – no electricity and no trailers. An Alpine Club hut for skiers and climbers at the Station and another (members only) on Hermit Mountain. Hotels and motels in Revelstoke city cost from $5 single up to $20 double.

⇥ The TransCanada Highway runs through the heart of the park along the lovely Illecillewaet River (in fact, at Rogers Pass there is a striking memorial to the completion of the Highway on September 3, 1962). East of Glacier this main route joins the British Columbia Highway 95 at the town of Golden. Bus services run to and through the park and Canadian Pacific Railway trains stop at Glacier Station.

⇢ The park's section of the TransCanada Highway is the main thoroughfare (kept open through the winter by ingenious avalanche diversions). Hiking trails crisscross the park, mainly following the Beaver River and other large creeks.

☼ Open all year; best time summer and early autumn; winter snowfalls can be very heavy.

⏀ 2–5 days.

▧ As for Yoho.

☞ No mountain guide services in this park.

⇥ Superintendent, Glacier National Park, Revelstoke, British Columbia. Wardens and Royal Canadian Mounted Police in park.

Nesting pelagic cormorant on Mondarte Island near Vancouver.

Jasper National Park 2¾ million acres; between 3,265 and 12,294 ft (Mt Columbia) above sea level. This mountain park contains within its huge area just about everything the Rocky Mountains can offer. Several of its peaks rise above 10,000 ft, with glaciers thrusting between them and river torrents carving canyons at their feet. There are mighty waterfalls, potholes and caves, dense stretches of coniferous forest, and a multitude of mountain lakes. The park offers ample opportunity for camping, riding, boating, and most other sports – including winter sports in their season – in the up-to-date and well-equipped resort area in and around Jasper, which is, in fact, one of Canada's most popular holiday centres. The park also interconnects with Banff National Park to the south, the Rocky Mountains Forest Reserve to the Southeast, and the Willmore Wilderness Provincial Park to the north.

Mountain goat, bighorn, elk, mountain caribou, moose, mule deer, mountain lion, grizzly and black bears, wolf, coyote, hoary marmot, abundant species of squirrel, porcupine, rabbit; ducks, geese, gulls, willow and white-tailed ptarmigans, blue grouse, golden eagle, owls, osprey, and hordes of smaller birds (as for Banff).

White, black, and other spruces; Douglas and alpine firs; alpine larch, lodgepole pine, aspen, balsam poplar, paper birch (used by the Indians for writing, canoes, shelter); heather, larkspur, heliotrope, columbine, fireweed, Indian paintbrush, white dryas, alpine arnica, alpine anemone, glacier lily. Wildflowers are especially thick on the mountain meadows above the treeline.

From luxurious Jasper Park Lodge (just outside the town; 750 beds from· $40 and up for double room with bath) to small but comfortable cabins set in rather wilder spots (Miette Hot Springs Bungalows, Columbia Icefield Chalet, Sunwapta Bungalows, Pocahontas Bungalows, and many others; about $6–$10 double). Between these extremes is a wide range of smaller hotels, motels, chalets, etc, in or near the townsite (between $12 and $16 double). Tents and cabins also available at up to 13 campgrounds, ranging from highly serviced ones like Cottonwood Creek, Whistlers (WCs, electricity, piped water, laundry, showers, nature films) to more primitive grounds where you draw water from the lake or creek. Camp and trailer prices as for Elk Island National Park (trailer services at Cottonwood Creek and Whistlers only).

➣ Alberta Highway 16 west from Edmonton, 200 miles. In summer only, British Columbia Highway 1 over the mountains to join the main all-weather road that links Jasper and Banff. Regular Greyhound buses from Edmonton. The park is on the main transcontinental line of the Canadian National Railways, west from Edmonton. Nearest airport at Edmonton.

🚙 Main route is the Banff–Jasper highway, a branch of the TransCanada Highway as it passes through Banff; it links the scenic centres of both parks, passing many glaciers, lakes, and mountain lookouts on its way from Lake Louise to Jasper townsite. At places this 'Icefield Highway' climbs close to 7,000 ft. In places good secondary roads branch from it. Sightseeing buses run daily through the park from June 15 to September 15. Some wilder beauty spots are accessible only along some of the 625 miles of trails and bridle paths; saddlehorses can be hired. The famous Sky Tram takes 35 passengers 4,000 ft straight up to a lookout on Whistlers Mountain, some 7,000 ft above sea level.

☀ Open all year; best time summer for lakeside holidays, winter for skiing; autumn in the Rockies is spectacular, with much of the park's wildlife preparing for winter.

🕐 7 days to whole vacation.

🎟 Season ticket for fiscal year $2 per car ($3 with trailer).

🗺 Available within park.

➪ Superintendent, Jasper National Park, Jasper, Alberta.

A beaver, among the largest of all rodents. Because of intensive hunting, the beaver is now largely confined to sanctuaries and the remoter parts of the New World where their dams are still to be seen.

Caribou (known in Europe as reindeer), the only deer in which both the male and female carry antlers. They are easily domesticated.

⏚   Grizzly and black bears, mountain caribou, mule deer, moose, elk, mountain goat, and all the usual smaller species of the mountain parks. Birdlife includes golden eagle, varieties of grouse, ptarmigan, magpie, Canada jay, northern pileated woodpecker, bluebird, Clark's nutcracker, hummingbirds.

⬧   Many spruces, Douglas and balsam fir, hemlock, western red cedar, poplar. Wildflowers as for Glacier park.

🛏   No commercial accommodation within the park, but some at Revelstoke at the southwest tip; rates from $5 single up to $20 double. Unserviced campgrounds along the Trans-Canada Highway in the park; rates as for Glacier.

✈   Revelstoke city is on the TransCanada Highway east from Vancouver, west from Calgary. North of the park (but open only in summer) is a drive that follows the 'Big Bend' of the Columbia River – 190 miles of incomparable wilderness scenery. The first 90 miles to Boat Encampment is paved and open all year. Access also from the south via Nelson on Highway 6. Greyhound buses run along the TransCanada daily. Revelstoke is on the main transcontinental line of the Canadian Pacific Railway. Nearest airport at Revelstoke city.

🚐   The TransCanada Highway runs along the southern fringe of the park. A paved all-weather road runs from the main entrance, some 18 miles from Revelstoke city, to Heather Lodge, climbing some 5,000 ft as it does so. There are about 14 miles of hikers' trails, including the main path from the summit of Mt Revelstoke to nearby mountain lakes otherwise inaccessible.

🌅   Open all year, but the road to the park from Revelstoke is open July to October only; best time July to mid-September.

🕐   1–5 days.

🖼   As for Yoho and Glacier.

⇨   Superintendent, Mt Revelstoke National Park, Revelstoke, British Columbia.

Wood Buffalo National Park 11 million acres (17,000 square miles); 100 to 2,500 ft above sea level. Though this is the continent's largest national park, it is primarily a wildlife reserve rather than a vacationland. It lies in the untamed north of Alberta, overlapping into the Northwest Territories, between Lake Athabasca (whose western tip touches the park boundary) and the Great Slave Lake to the north. The terrain is thus typical of the Canadian north: immense forests, broad grasslands, great stretches of marsh and bog (called muskeg,), innumerable lakes, large and small – and a notable lack of human activity. In the park the lakes are mostly watered by the wide Peace River, which flows across it into Lake Athabasca. Initially the area was a sanctuary for the few remaining forest bison, but in 1947 a sizeable herd of plains bison were moved up here and the subspecies have interbred to make a total stock of about 15,000 head – the largest buffalo herd in North America.

⇥ Bison, moose, elk, deer, woodland caribou, black and grizzly bears, and many smaller species, including the elusive wolf, lynx, and wolverine; squirrels, porcupine, beaver, rabbit. Smaller prairie birds abound, also such migrant fowl as Canada, white-fronted, and snow geese, all kinds of wild ducks, coot, grouse, and ptarmigan.

೮ White and black spruce, jack pine, tamarack; black poplar on watercourses; aspen in fire scars. Numerous bogs and muskeg. Patches of prairie with shooting star, bluebell, goldenrod, asters, gentians. Salt plains with cat-tail marshes and sedges. Scattered stands of balsam poplar.

⇖ No accommodation of any kind in park. Limited accommodation in nearby towns: Fort Smith, and Fort Chipewyan on Lake Athabasca. Camping permitted; free fire permit is mandatory.

⇨ Unpaved Highway 5 cuts across the north of the park from Fort Smith to Hay River (township) on Great Slave Lake. Another even less improved road runs south from Fort Smith to Peace Point within the park, on the Peace River. In summer, river steamers connect the Waterways railway terminus at McMurry with Fort Smith in the park. No rail service to park. Small charter aircraft can land at Fort Smith or Fort Chipewyan. A local boom in road construction will soon ensure a link between the park and Pine Point on the Great Slave Lake – rail access thence to Edmonton.

⇙ The Fort Smith to Peace Point road runs from the Point southeast along the Peace River, then cuts north along the park's eastern fringe and back to Fort Smith. There is also limited water transport along the river.

☀ Open all year; best time spring to autumn.

⏱ 3 days.

▣ Free, including car.

⊏⊐ No guides but wardens will help plan trips.

⇨ Superintendent, Wood Buffalo National Park, Fort Smith, Northwest Territories.

Yoho National Park 320,000 acres; 3,685 to 11,686 ft (Mt Goodsir) above sea level. *Yoho* is Cree Indian for 'wonderful' – accurately used if the Indians meant the mountain scenery. These western slopes of the Rockies are especially rich in rivers and gorges, which between them provide some of Canada's most spectacular waterfalls – like the two-pronged Twin Falls at Lake O'Hara or the nearly 1,500 ft drop of the Takakkaw Falls, said to be Canada's highest. Yoho borders eastwards on Banff and southwards on Kootenay national parks, creating a vast and continuous area of protected parkland. Yoho contains the jagged spires of the 'roof of the Rockies' – the continental divide – breached by the Kicking Horse River and the famous Kicking Horse Pass.

- Black and grizzly bears, mule and whitetailed deer, moose, elk, mountain goat, some Rocky Mountain sheep, mountain lion (cougar), lynx, beaver; birdlife as extensive as in Glacier and Banff parks.

- Lodgepole pine, alpine fir, white spruce, trembling aspen, and many other conifers; wildflowers as for Glacier and Banff.

- The park's township is Field, British Columbia; it offers a small hotel (20 beds; $5 and up double) and nearby chalets (50 beds; same rates). Sizeable lodges, chalets, and cabins at Yoho Valley, Emerald Lake, Lake O'Hara, and Wapta Lake (around $10–$15 double; Lake O'Hara Lodge at $28 double room and $35 for double cabin). Campsites include the large Kicking Horse site, fully serviced and taking trailers; the semiserviced Hoodoo Creek ground, and slightly more rugged grounds at Chancellor Peak and Takakkaw Falls. But all have kitchens, WCs, and (except Chancellor Peak) piped water. Fee for site with individual water, sewerage, electricity $2; with electricity only $1.50; site only $1.

- The TransCanada Highway passes through Field in Yoho park, linking the east of the park with the Banff–Jasper Highway. Twice-daily Greyhound buses run east from Vancouver or west from Calgary on this highway. The Canadian Pacific Railway transcontinental main line runs through the park via Kicking Horse Pass. Nearest airport at Calgary, Alberta, 130 miles east.

- Many good main and secondary roads crisscross the park for easy sightseeing by car. One of the most scenic of these leads north from the TransCanada Highway to Laughing Falls; others run to Takakkaw Falls and Emerald Lake. Over 250 miles of trails for hiking and riding; saddle horses for hire at Emerald Lake and other sites. These trails often interconnect with those of Banff and Kootenay parks.

- Open May 15 to October 15.

- 2–5 days.

- 50c per car ($1 with trailer); season ticket at $2 per car ($3 with trailer).

- Some guides are available for mounting climbing. (Note: intending climbers must first register their intention to leave the park trails – as must anybody camping overnight other than on prepared campgrounds.)

- Superintendent, Yoho National Park, Field, British Columbia. There are information stands within the park.

The North American moose, largest of all living deer. The European elk, slightly smaller, is of the same species. Its long legs and short neck make it a poor grazer. In summer (as here) it can browse aquatic plants. In winter, trees and bushes are its main fodder. They are only slightly gregarious in summer, but when the snows come they often form large herds, trampling the snow flat over wide areas known as 'yards'.

Canada : Species List

ALCID Fundy
ANTELOPE Cypress Hills
AVOCET Cypress Hills
BATS Cypress Hills
BEARS Duck Mt
— **Black** Algonquin; Banff; Fundy; Gaspesian; Glacier; Jasper; P des Laurentides; Quetico; Mt Revelstoke; Wood Buffalo; Yoho
— **Grizzly** Banff; Glacier; Jasper; Mt Revelstoke; Wood Buffalo; Yoho
BEAVER Algonquin; Banff; Cypress Hills; Duck Mt; Fundy; Gaspesian; Glacier; P des Laurentides; Moose Mt; Quetico; Wood Buffalo; Yoho
BIGHORN Banff; Jasper
BISON Elk Is; Wood Buffalo
BITTERN, American Elk Is
BLUEBIRD Mt Revelstoke
— **Mountain** Banff
BOBCAT Fundy; Quetico
BUFFLEHEAD Elk Is
BUNTING, Lark Fundy
— **Snow** P des Laurentides
CANVASBACK Elk Is
CARDINAL Point Pelee
CARIBOU Banff; Gaspesian; Glacier; Jasper; Mt Revelstoke; Wood Buffalo
CATBIRD Moose Mt
CHAT, Yellow-Breasted Point Pelee
CHICKADEE Banff; P des Laurentides
— **Black-Capped** Cypress Hills; Moose Mt
CHIPMUNK Cypress Hills; Point Pelee; Quetico
— **Eastern** P des Laurentides
CONY Banff
COOT Elk Is; Wood Buffalo
CORMORANT Fundy
COUGAR *see* **MOUNTAIN LION**
COYOTE Duck Mt; Jasper; Moose Mt
CROSSBILL, Red Cypress Hills
CROW Moose Mt
CURLEW Cypress Hills
DEER Algonquin; Banff; Duck Mt; Fundy; Wood Buffalo

— **Mule** Cypress Hills; Elk Is; Glacier; Jasper; Mt Revelstoke; Yoho
— **Virginia** *see* **Whitetail**
— **Whitetail** Cypress Hills; Elk Is; Gaspesian; Glacier; Moose Mt; Quetico; Yoho
DOVE, Mourning Moose Mt
DUCKS Jasper; Point Pelee; Wood Buffalo
— **Ruddy** Elk Is
EAGLE, Bald P des Laurentides
— **Golden** Banff; Glacier; Jasper; Mt Revelstoke
EGRET Fundy
ELK Banff; Cypress Hills; Elk Is; Glacier; Moose Mt; Mt Revelstoke; Wood Buffalo; Yoho
FALCONS Cypress Hills
FISHER Algonquin; Quetico
FLICKER, Red-Shafted Banff
— **Yellow-Shafted** Banff; P des Laurentides; Moose Mt
FLYCATCHERS Cypress Hills
FOX Algonquin; Duck Mt; Fundy; Gaspesian; P des Laurentides; Moose Mt
GADWALL Elk Is
GAME BIRDS Cypress Hills
GEESE Jasper
GNATCATCHER, Blue-Grey Point Pelee
GOAT, Mountain Banff; Glacier; Jasper; Mt Revelstoke; Yoho
GOLDFINCH Moose Mt
GOOSE, Canada Cypress Hills; Gaspesian; Point Pelee; Wood Buffalo
— **Snow** Wood Buffalo
— **White-Fronted** Wood Buffalo
GREVES Cypress Hills
GROSBEAK Banff
— **Evening** Algonquin
GROUSE Elk Is; Mt Revelstoke; Wood Buffalo
— **Blue** Jasper
— **Ruffed** Algonquin; Moose Mt
GULLS Jasper
— **Franklin's** Elk Is
HARE Gaspesian; P des Laurentides;

Moose Mt; Quetico
HAWKS Cypress Hills; Elk Is; Glacier;
P des Laurentides; Moose Mt
HERON Cypress Hills
— **Great Blue** Fundy
HUMMINGBIRD Banff; Mt Revelstoke
— **Ruby-Throated** P des Laurentides
JAY, Canada Banff; Mt Revelstoke
JUNCO, Slate-Coloured
P des Laurentides; Moose Mt
KINGBIRD, Eastern Moose Mt
KINGLET P des Laurentides
— **Ruby-Crowned** Banff
LARK, Horned Banff
LOON Fundy
— **Common** Algonquin
LYNX Cypress Hills; Duck Mt; Fundy;
Glacier; P des Laurentides; Quetico;
Wood Buffalo; Yoho
MAGPIE Banff; Mt Revelstoke
MALLARDS Cypress Hills; Elk Is
MARMOT Cypress Hills
— **Hoary** Jasper
MARTEN Algonquin; Banff; Glacier;
Quetico
MINK Cypress Hills; Duck Mt;
Gaspesian; P des Laurentides; Moose Mt
MOLE, Eastern Point Pelee
MOOSE Algonquin; Banff; Cypress Hills;
Duck Mt; Elk Is; Fundy; Gaspesian;
Glacier; Jasper; P des Laurentides;
Moose Mt; Quetico; Mt Revelstoke;
Wood Buffalo; Yoho
MOUNTAIN LION Jasper; Yoho
MOUSE, Red-Backed Moose Mt
MUSKRAT Banff; Cypress Hills; Duck Mt;
Fundy; Point Pelee
NUTCRACKER, Clark's Mt Revelstoke
NUTHATCH, Red-Breasted Banff
ORIOLE, Baltimore Moose Mt
— **Orchard** Point Pelee
OSPREY Algonquin; Jasper;
P des Laurentides
OTTER Algonquin; P des Laurentides;
Quetico
OWLS Cypress Hills; Elk Is; Glacier;
Moose Mt
— **Long-Eared** P des Laurentides
PARTRIDGE Gaspesian
PINTAIL Cypress Hills; Elk Is
PIPIT, Water P des Laurentides
PLOVER Cypress Hills
PORCUPINE Cypress Hills; Fundy;
Jasper; Point Pelee; Quetico;
Wood Buffalo
— **Yellow-Haired** Banff
PRAIRIE BIRDS Elk Is
PRAIRIE DOG Cypress Hills
PTARMIGAN Mt Revelstoke; Wood Buffalo
— **White-Tailed** Jasper
— **Willow** Jasper
RABBIT Fundy; Jasper; Point Pelee;
Wood Buffalo

— **Snowshoe** Banff
RACCOON Algonquin; Cypress Hills;
Fundy; P des Laurentides
RAZORBILL Fundy
SANDPIPER Cypress Hills; Fundy
SAP-SUCKER, Yellow-Bellied
Algonquin
SCAUP Elk Is
SCOTER Fundy
SHEEP, Rocky Mountain Yoho
SHOVELER Elk Is
SISKIN, Pine Cypress Hills
SKUNK Moose Mt; Point Pelee
— **Striped** Gaspesian; P des Laurentides
SNIPE Cypress Hills
SOLITAIRE, Townsend's Banff
SONGBIRDS Glacier
SPARROW, Song Fundy
— **White-Crowned** Moose Mt
— **White-Throated** Algonquin;
Moose Mt
SQUIRRELS Duck Mt; Gaspesian; Jasper;
P des Laurentides; Wood Buffalo
— **Columbian** Banff
— **Franklin's Ground** Moose Mt
— **Grey** Point Pelee
— **Red** P des Laurentides; Point Pelee
— **Yellow-Mantled Ground** Banff
SWANS Point Pelee
TANAGER, Western Banff
TEAL, Blue-Winged Elk Is
TERN, Black Elk Is
THRESHER, Brown Moose Mt
THRUSH, Hermit Banff
— **Swainson's** Banff
TURTLES Point Pelee
VIREOS P des Laurentides
— **Red-Eyed** Algonquin; Moose Mt
— **Warbling** Banff
VULTURE, Turkey Duck Mt
WARBLERS P des Laurentides; Moose Mt
— **Cerulean** Point Pelee
— **Connecticut** Fundy
— **Prairie** Fundy
— **Yellow** Moose Mt
WATERFOWL P des Laurentides
WAXWING, Bohemian Banff
— **Cedar** P des Laurentides
WEASEL Duck Mt; Fundy; Gaspesian;
Glacier; Point Pelee
— **Short-Tailed** P des Laurentides
WIDGEON, American Fundy
WOLF Algonquin; Gaspesian; Jasper;
P des Laurentides; Quetico;
Wood Buffalo
WOLVERINE Banff; Wood Buffalo
WOODCOCK Fundy
WOODLAND BIRDS Elk Is
WOODPECKERS Banff; Moose Mt
— **Northern Pileated** Mt Revelstoke
WREN, Carolina Point Pelee
— **Winter** Banff

Mutual attractions: young herring gulls and a visitor at Algonquin PP.

SOUTH AMERICA

Most of the hinterland and quite large areas of the lowlands and coasts of this great continent are barely modified by human influence – a fact that, on the one hand, underlines its fascination for the visiting naturalist, and, on the other, explains why his chances to enjoy the wildlife that undoubtedly exists are so meagre compared with those in most other continents. The paucity of entries for this continent reflects the paucity of places the average tourist can confidently be recommended to visit. However, if you are the kind who regrets not being alive when the great African hinterland was opened to the world, and if, moreover, you are fit, quick at picking up smatterings of alien dialects, have a well-developed sense of humour, and can live rough (all qualities you would have needed in the pioneer-Africa days), then the hinterland of South America has everything to offer you.

For instance there is the Mato Grosso, Brazil, upstream from the Iguassu Falls NP described on page 212. There between the Amambai, Ivinheima, and Pardo rivers, all tributaries of the Paraná, is an almost uninhabited paradise of animals. The giant otter, endangered elsewhere on the continent, is here quite common. So are maned wolves, great anteaters, tapirs, anacondas – all the fauna of the wooded savannahs. The parts near the river banks are accessible by boat from Pôrto São José (road and light-aircraft connection with São Paulo). The hinterland calls for horses and mules, which should be available at Ponto Alegré and Bataguaçu on the São Paulo-Campo Grande road. It must be stressed that facilities are totally absent in this part of Brazil; any trip would be a real expedition. The area is fairly humid, especially in the (not very heavy) March–December rains. Insects are worst in summer.

From Campo Grande you could work south, along the western foothills of the Serra de Maracaju, to Bella Vista on the Rio Apa, which forms Brazil's border with Paraguay. The road goes on to Concepción; between it and the Apa is a wilderness of swamp, river, savannah, and forest. Again the richness of wildlife is quite staggering: black roaring apes, capucins, tapirs, jaguars, pumas, araras, colibris, craw storks, anacondas, caymans, brilliantly coloured lizards, butterflies, fish beyond number ... the whole continent's riches are there. Again, too, it is horse and mule country – though a certain amount of logging takes place and logging trails are negotiable by 4-wheel-drive vehicles (which you can hire in Asunción, and possibly in Concepción, too). The insects are ferocious in summer but are repelled by modern creams. Throughout South America, wherever you leave the beaten track, you should take snake antitoxin with you. Various sera are stocked by all good pharmacists. There is no especial rainy season in this part of Paraguay.

Hoffman's sloth, one of the continent's five species. Sloths rarely leave the trees, where they sleep, eat, mate, and give birth, suspended by their long, powerful claws. Their hair grows counter to the usual mammalian direction, so that the rain runs off. An individual may spend its whole life in a single grove, or even in one tree. Yet, strangely enough, they are also powerful swimmers.

From Concepción or Asunción you could fly north, up the Paraná, to Corumba, on the Brazil–Bolivia border. From there the only road into Bolivia runs through highlands, north and south of its course, teeming with subtropical fauna. In a further 300 miles you come to Santa Cruz, a good centre for horse or jeep exploration of the well watered lands to the northwest. These, too, are prolific in their wildlife.

We would very much like to hear from readers who have experience of travel and wildlife in these and similarly remote parts of South America.

211

Argentina

Iguazu National Park 136,000 acres; around 700 ft above sea level. The park is continuous with the Iguassu NP Paraguay and the Iguaçu NP Brazil. All have the spectacular (however variously spelled) falls: 280 ft cliffs of water on the border between the three countries. The whole area is covered with subtropical forest with some temperate-zone mixtures.

- Jaguar, puma, ocelot, koati, capybara, black howler monkey; herons, ovenbird, trogons; many reptiles.

- There are two hotels, one very near the falls, an old but comfortable building; the other about 14 miles away in the region of Puerto Iguazù; rates between 4,000 pesos single, 5,200 pesos double.

- Best by air; by road Buenos Aires is 1,185 miles – a tedious drive.

◻ᗕ By boat and on foot.

⚶ Open all year; best April to October; during July and August you must book in advance, for accommodation is scarce then.

◔ 1 to 5 days.

⊟ Free.

◺ No guides but information bureau has maps and some literature of doubtful quality.

⇨ Direccion General de Parque Nacionales, Santa Fé 690, Buenos Aires.

Nahuel Huapi National Park 1,930,000 acres; 2,400 to 11,846 ft above sea level. This is one of the premier parks of South America, visited by over 100,000 people each year. Going from east to west there is a surprising contrast in vegetation, beginning with pampas, passing through a mixed zone and ending, on the Andes slopes, with alpine scenery and flora. There is an interesting volcanic region around Tronador ('Thunderer') the highest part of northern Patagonia.

◁ᐣ Pudu deer, guemal, puma, Andean condor, cormorant, brown and grey gallito, kinglet, woodpeckers, flamingo; black swan and some deer species have been introduced.

◿ Several privately owned hotels and some state-run hotels and hostels. They vary from the internationally known Llao-llao (said yea-oh-yea-oh), prices on application, to modest and surprisingly cheap places of good quality. Camping is permitted anywhere provided you tell the warden of the location you choose and the duration of your stay there. Plenty of restaurants, cafes, kiosks and recreation areas.

⇥ Good road, rail, and air (2 hours) access to San Carlos Barriloche, the holiday village on the shores of Lake Nahuel Huapi, within the park.

◻ᗕ By boat on the lake; on foot; or by horse. There are marked trails in the lower parts of the park. Ski-lifts on the Andean slopes. Skiing is the major attraction of the park for most visitors.

⚶ Open all year; winter is difficult for anyone wanting to see the wildlife; best November to April. Humidity is low and the air bracing.

◔ 3 days or whole vacation.

⊟ Free.

◺ No guides are provided in the park but there are several information bureaux where you can get good maps and copious literature (not much of it, however, in English).

⇨ Intendente del Parque Nacional de Nahuel Huapi, Av San Martin 24, San Carlos de Bariloche.

Brazil

Iguaçu National Park 450,000 acres in two blocks; the smaller at about 700 ft altitude contains the falls and the park HQ; it is a mixture of subtropical and temperate forest. The larger, rising to over 1,600 ft has more temperate-zone flora; it is also the western limit of the Brazilian monkey-puzzle pine *Araucaria*. The fauna are as noted under the Argentine section of this park.

🛏 The best sited hotel is the Cataratas, 60 to 140 cr $ single; 70 to 140 cr $ double (booking through Realtur Hoteleira SA, Cataratas, Parque Nacional, 5SOZ DO Iguaçu). Farther away from the falls (6 miles) on the main highway, is the Carima, rates from 60 to 70 cr $ (bookings via Realtur Hoteleira, Carima, BR 469, Parque Nacional, Paraná).

✈ Frequent flights and charter taxiplanes from Rio and São Paulo to the falls. You can also go by road or rail to Presidente Epitacio (Porto Tibiriça) on the Paraná, 250 miles upstream, and then take a small river boat down through virgin tropical forest for 2 days to Guaira, only 4 miles from the falls.

☼ Open all year. Accommodation hard to get in July and August. The rainy season, which is not heavy, is from December to March.

🕐 1 to 5 days.

🏴 Free.

📐 No guides are available.

➡ Sr Administrador do Parque Nacional do Iguaçu, Foz do Iguaçu, Estado do Paraná.

Tijuca National Park (formerly the Rio de Janeiro National Park) 12,350 acres; 328 to 3,350 ft above sea level. Lying a short way west of Rio, the park consists of the city's main catchment area on the slopes of Mt Tijuaca (the third peak inland from the sugarloaf and the highest peak in the ring immediately around Rio). Once there were extensive coffee plantations here, but since 1862 the government has been buying back the land and returning it (or allowing it to return) to primeval forest. Now even experts cannot easily tell the regenerated parts from those that are truly primeval. The wildlife, too, is rich and varied: weeper capucin, black-pencilled marmoset, tayra, Allamand's grison, three-toed sloth, Ingram's tree squirrel; swallow-tailed manakin, channel-billed toucan and naked-throated billbird; jararaca viper, colubrid snake, ground boa; horned frog, Girard's frog, and the frog *Dendrophryniscus brevipollicatus*. The road out to Tijucamar runs south of the park; the branch from this road, to Lagoa da Tijuca, completes the circuit back to Rio via Jacarepaguá; total length of circuit is 18 miles. The park is open, free, all year; best in December–March.

Guyana

Kaietur Falls National Park 27,240 acres; 330 to 1,640 ft above sea level. With a sheer drop of 741 ft, the falls are among the most impressive sights in this part of South America. The surrounding country is a mixture of humid tropical forest, dry forest, and more open savannah. The wildlife is comparably varied and typical of these habitats.

↗ Jaguar, ocelot, capybara, tapir, deer, sloths, opossum, otter; hummingbirds, toucan, parrot, trumpeter, hocco, tinamou.

🛏 Government rest house for 32 people; prices not quoted but said to be 'moderate'. All-inclusive trip is US $95 per person (air, truck, and river boat; 7 days).

✈ It is possible to reach the falls by road; but the 3-day trip is hard going. Guyana Airways, who organize the Falls Tour, operate light-aircraft flights to the falls. Seating is limited so you have to book as far in advance as possible.

🚃 On foot and by boat.

☼ Open all year; best time August to September.

⏱ 1 to 3 days.

▧ Free.

☞ Park staff will act as guides if other duties permit; at any time they are ready with advice.

👁 The Botanical Gardens in Georgetown have a magnificent collection of flowering tropical trees and palms as well as pools of Victoria Regina water lilies, the world's largest aquatic plant.

⇨ Guyana Information Services, 18 Brickdam, Georgetown/ tel: 4460.

Peru

Most South American countries have proved somewhat coy about parting with information likely to interest visitors keen on seeing the wildlife. None more so than Peru. A member of the WWF, who knows the area well, recommends two places in the country to visitors interested in natural history. One is the Pampas Galeras Nature Reserve for Vicuña, 450 miles south of Lima by a good road, near Nasca, where there is a very reasonable hotel. The other is the collection of guano islands and offshore stacks near the coastal resort of Callao on the northern outskirts of Lima. Between September and December these are a fantastic sight, swarming with hundreds of thousands of guanay birds (a kind of cormorant) and other sea birds.

Venezuela

The introduction to the South America section mentions a park in Peru where, with some difficulty and danger, you can see oilbirds. There is a similar reserve in Venezuela. It is a faunal reserve and not open to tourism; but bona fide ornithologists may be interested in applying for a permit. It is the 450 acre Humboldt National Monument, noted for an imposing series of natural caverns, part of which have become rookeries for a colony of guacharos, or oilbirds (*Steatornis caripensis*). There are plans to convert it into a national park. The address of the administering authority is the same as for the El Avila NP.

El Avila National Park 163,563 acres; from sea level to 8,429 ft above. A scenically varied mountainous park, lying between the Caracas valley and the sea. Depending on altitude there is dry semitropical savannah with giant cactus; savannah and deciduous forest; rainforest; and Andean scrub. It is well watered, with many mountain streams and torrents.

🏹 Despite the scenic richness and variety, fauna is not very plentiful. It includes brocket deer, paca, agouti, three-toed sloth, several squirrels and armadillos, crab-eating fox; parrots and small birds are plentiful (and so are reptiles).

🛏 There is a luxury hotel, the Humboldt, in the heart of the park; access by cable from Caracas; room only 45 to 55 bol. a night single, 50 to 60 bol. double. Within the park are free camping areas and mountain huts; and for VIP visitors there is an official guest house. Restaurants are sited at the Humboldt, the cablecar terminal, and in the Los Venados recreation area.

🏹 On foot or by cable car from Caracas.

� On foot. There are numerous well defined hiking trails throughout the park.

🌅 Open all year; best in the driest part of the year, January to May.

🕐 1 to 3 days.

📧 Entry permit costs 1.20 bol.

🗺 Wardens will act as guides if their official duties are not too pressing; no extra charge. And even if they cannot accompany you, they will at any time advise on the best current areas for wildlife viewing.

➡ Ministerio de Agriculture y Cría, División de Parques Nacionales y Incendios, Torre Norte, Piso 9, Centro Simón Bolívar, Caracas.

Canaima National Park Almost $2\frac{1}{2}$ million acres; 400 to 9,843 ft above sea level. Though the area is rich in gold and diamonds it is barely marked by human influence. It is well furnished with rivers and steep mountains, clad in tropical rainforest with extensive stretches of savannah. The Angel Falls, within the park, have a free-fall height of 3,186 ft, the tallest falls in the world. Fauna is extraordinarily rich and varied. The park has only very recently been opened to tourism.

🏹 Jaguar, tiger cat, tapir, peccary, paca, sloths, armadillo; capucin, spider and squirrel monkeys; opossums, capybara, agouti; hummingbirds, cotingas, toucans, tanagers, woodcreepers, flycatchers, ant thrushes, jacamars, puffbirds, tinamous, harpy eagle. Many interesting reptiles, amphibians, and insects.

🛏 Facilities so far developed are not for comfort lovers. There are cheap rustic huts for shelter, but you would be advised to take for all your own needs. A cafe-bar has recently opened in Canaima but we have no reliable word as to its quality.

🏹 There is a poor road from Caracas to Canaima; not recommended. Avensa Airlines run a once-weekly service from Cindad, Bolívar, and Caracas to Canaima (it may be twice weekly by the time this is published).

Horse or on foot. Be ready for hard bargaining as there are no fixed rates. There are charter outboard trips up the two main rivers, one going to the Angel Falls.

Open all year; best December to May. September is the wettest month, March the driest.

At least a week.

Guides are available for trips to Angel Falls; they have no standing within the parks and their rates are not controlled. Bargain carefully.

Ministerio de Agricultura y Cría. Division de Parques Nacionales e Incendios, Torre Norte, Piso 9, Centro Simón Bolívar, Caracas.

Guatopo National Park 228,900 acres; 656 to 4,856 ft above sea level. Set in forested mountains south of Caracas, whose water supply rises in springs within the park. The forest range, from dry, broad-leaved type mixed with savannah down to rainforest, is similar to that of the other parks in the north of the country.

Wildlife is rich and varied: jaguar, paca, peccary, tapir, sloths and armadillos, agouti, puma; hummingbirds, cotingas, toucans, tanagers, woodcreepers, flycatchers, ant thrushes, jacamars, puffbirds, parrots; many reptiles.

Camping areas and mountain refuges within the park, all free and very simple; bring for all your needs except water. VIP guest house. There are also recreation areas and kiosks.

By good road, $2\frac{1}{2}$ hours drive south and east of Caracas.

One road runs through the park, and there are plenty of good hiking trails.

Open all year; best in the dry months January to May; September is the wettest month.

1 to 3 days.

No permit needed.

For study related to the park's purposes (that is, conservation) and for large parties, the keepers acts as guides, free.

Ministerio de Agricultura y Cría, División de Parques Nacionales e Incendios, Torre Norte, Piso 9, Centro Simón Bolívar, Caracas.

Henri Pittier National Park 220,000 acres; from sea level to 7,690 ft above. Like El Avila this is a coastal-mountainous park surrounded by intensively developed land with fair-sized towns and cities. Most of the region is mixed forest-savannah, ranging from the dry broad-leaved type to true rain forest, depending on altitude. Chief plants are mangroves and other aquatic plants in the wetter parts; spiney bush and giant cactus in the drier parts.

The park is reportedly rich in wildlife, especially birds. It is an important refuge for migratory birds. In all some 530 different species have been recorded in the different habitats within the park. Henri Pittier is Venezuela's first park to have a full-time biologist and a strict nature reserve within it – a prototype for the other parks in due course; the research centre is at Rancho Grande.

There is simple overnight accommodation and a swimming pool within the park (rates not quoted), as well as camping and picnic sites. In Maracay, just outside the southern border, there are four hotels at rates ranging from 20 to 70 bol. single (room only) and 23 to 95 bol. double.

The main Maracay-Turiamo highway intersects the park.

There are plenty of hiking trails within the boundaries.

Open all year; best in the dry months Janauary to May. September is the rainiest month.

1 to 3 days.

Entry permit costs 1.20 bol. from Dirección del Jefe del Parque, address below.

The keepers act as guides for parties and for people especially interested in the wildlife – provided their normal duties permit. No extra charge.

Dirección del Jefe del Parque, Región 5-MAC-Maracay, Estado Aragua.

Sierra Nevada National Park 395,000 acres; 1,900 to 11,265 ft (Mt Bolivar, the country's highest peak). Mount Bolivar is one of the peaks of the Sierra de Santo Domingo of the western Andes; the great altitude range makes for three habitats. The hot western edge of the park is covered by tropical forest. Higher up (the majority of the park) is an extensive temperate zone with a rich flora (bush, pines, yellow-wood, etc). The highest, cold zone, below the permanent snows and glaciers, has paramo-type alpine vegetation.

Wildlife is most plentiful in the lowland forests – but nowhere in South America is mountain wildlife at all abundant: it is as good here as you could expect to see it anywhere, except for the absence of vicuñas and chinchillas. The forests have brocket deer, puma, tiger cat, jaguar, and other felines, paca, opossum, parrots, harpy eagle, numerous other birds and reptiles. In the mountains there are various montane rodents, spectacled bear (rare), and Andean condor.

Nearest hotels are in Merida, which is less than an hour's drive from the southwestern corner of the park; rates for single room (room only) from 17 to 45 bol.; double from 28 to 68 bol. per day. Only campsites are available, free, within the park, whose tourist possibilities are still being developed.

By road from Merida.

On foot or horseback; horses and mules are available locally. The network of marked paths is not at all extensive. The remoter reaches of the park are for skilled navigators only – unless you are lucky enough to find a keeper with time to spare. Unofficial guides are also available; do not accept their first quotation.

Open all year; best December to April; May is the wettest month.

At least a week.

Free.

There is skiing in the higher reaches of the park – complete with ski lifts. Cafes are open at both ends of the lifts.

Dirección del Jefe del Parque, Región 2-MAC San Cristobal, Estado Táchira.

The giant anteater, a highly adapted mammal found only between Guatemala and northern Argentina. It lives in grassland and open forest; walks on its knuckles, to keep its claws sharp; rips open termites' nests and licks out the insects with its long, sticky tongue.

South America : Species List

AGOUTI El Avila; Canaima; Guatopo
AMPHIBIANS Canaima
ARMADILLOS El Avila; Canaima: Guatopo
BEAR, Spectacled Sierra Nevada
BILLBIRD, Naked-Throated Tijuca
BOA, Ground Tijuca
CAPYBARA Iguazu; Kaietur Falls; Canaima
CAT, Tiger Canaima; Sierra Nevada
CONDOR, Andean Nahuel Huapi; Sierra Nevada
CORMORANT Nahuel Huapi
COTINGAS Canaima; Guatopo
DEER Nahuel Huapi; Kaietur Falls
— **Brocket** El Avila; Sierra Nevada
— **Pudu** Nahuel Huapi
EAGLE, Harpy Canaima; Sierra Nevada
FLAMINGO Nahuel Huapi
FLYCATCHERS Canaima; Guatopo
FOX, Crab-Eating El Avila
FROG: *Dendrophryniscus brevipollicatus* Tijuca
— **Girard's** Tijuca
— **Horned** Tijuca
GALLITO, Brown Nahuel Huapi
— **Grey** Nahuel Huapi
GRISON, Allamand's Tijuca
GUANAY BIRDS Callao offshore stacks (Lima)
GUEMAL Nahuel Huapi
HERONS Iguazu
HOCCO Kaietur Falls
HUMMINGBIRDS Kaietur Falls; Canaima; Guatopo
INSECTS Canaima
JACAMARS Canaima; Guatopo
JAGUAR Iguazu; Kaietur Falls; Canaima; Guatopo; Sierra Nevada
KINGLET Nahuel Huapi
KOATI Iguazu
MANAKIN, Swallow-Tailed Tijuca
MARMOSET, Pencilled Tijuca

MONKEY, Black Howler Iguazu
— **Capucin** Canaima
— **Spider** Canaima
— **Squirrel** Canaima
— **Weeper Capucin** Tijuca
OCELOT Iguazu; Kaietur Falls
OPOSSUMS Kaietur Falls; Canaima; Sierra Nevada
OTTER Kaietur Falls
OVENBIRD Iguazu
PACA El Avila; Canaima; Guatopo; Sierra Nevada
PARROTS Kaietur Falls; El Avila; Guatopo; Sierra Nevada
PECCARY Canaima; Guatopo
PUFFBIRDS Canaima; Guatopo
PUMA Iguazu; Hahuel Huapi; Guatopo; Sierra Nevada
REPTILES Iguazu; El Avila; Canaima; Guatopo; Sierra Nevada
RODENTS (Montane) Sierra Nevada
SEABIRDS Callao offshore stacks (Lima)
SLOTHS Kaietur Falls; Canaima; Guatopo
— **Three-Toed** Tijuca; El Avila
SNAKE, Colubrid Tijuca
SQUIRRELS El Avila
— **Ingram's Tree** Tijuca
SWAN, Black Nahuel Huapi
TANAGERS Canaima; Guatopo
TAPIR Kaietur Falls; Canaima; Guatopo
TAYRA Tijuca
THRUSHES, Ant Canaima; Guatopo
TINAMOUS Kaietur Falls; Canaima
TOUCANS Kaietur Falls; Canaima; Guatopo
— **Channel-Billed** Tijuca
TROGONS Iguazu
TRUMPETER Kaietur Falls
VICUÑA Pampas Galeras
VIPER, Jararaca Tijuca
WOODCREEPERS Canaima; Guatopo
WOODPECKER Nahuel Huapi

219

Elephant seal in South Shetland. Bulls can weigh up to four tons.

ANTARCTICA

Introduction by Peter Scott

The wildlife of Antarctica is almost entirely oceanic. Of its 5½ million square miles only 3,000 are clear of snow and ice. And, surprising though it may seem, the continent is a *desert*. Even the area of most heavy precipitation, the Antarctic Peninsula, receives the equivalent of only 50 cm (20 in.) a year; elsewhere it is much drier. The presence of so much snow and ice is due not to heavy precipitation but to the fact that whatever does fall can hardly melt – for even in the warmest part (the Peninsula again) at the height of summer, the air temperatures hover around freezing point.

Lack of exposed land, freezing temperatures, and drought . . . the wonder is that any land-based life exists at all. Yet (and again it shows what an astonishing continent Antarctica is) lichens are found within a few degrees of the South Pole! When the sun strikes the bare rock of exposed mountain peaks it quickly creates a temperate-zone a few inches deep, where wind-blown snow melts and lichens, dormant through the long winter night, briefly thrive. Their nutrient comes in part from guano dust blown up from the coastal fringes; so to that extent the lichens are just as dependent on the outer world as the men at the South Pole Station itself.

In general the terrestrial life of the Antarctic makes a meagre list: bacteria, freshwater diatoms, algae, mosses, and lichens – with a few liverworts and just three flowering plants on the north-facing fringe of the Peninsula – these are the complete flora. The largest wholly terrestrial animal is a wingless fly about an eighth of an inch long; for the rest there are about 50 species of springtails, ticks, lice, and mites.

It is fascinating to scientists, of course, for the relative simplicity of the food chains makes it possible to understand the ecology of this continent far more completely than we can yet hope to elsewhere. But to the tourist for whom this book is compiled the fascination of Antarctica certainly lies in its oceanic species and in the awe-inspiring beauty of their habitat.

In numbers, at least, the Antarctic waters are as rich in life as the land is poor. The top layers of the 12 million square miles of Antarctic ocean are the richest oceanic waters in the world, despite their near-freezing temperatures. In fact – and here is another of those shocks that Antarctica deals to our 'common-sense' notions of life processes – the cold is almost entirely responsible for this richness!

First it creates currents that stir up the bottom sediments and make a life-sustaining soup of plankton and krill. And secondly the cold actually slows down the life cycles of all the simpler life forms so that they live about ten times longer than they would in warmer waters. Because their development is not slowed down to the same degree, they mature and breed relatively earlier. And it is this richness which sustains not only the continent's fish but also its birds and mammals (there are no reptiles) in numbers and climatic conditions that astonish every visitor.

Nevertheless, the severely limited number of breeding sites, and the unique adaptations demanded by the Antarctic habitat, have both combined to keep the number of *species* of birds and mammals small. Only 70 species of birds breed in the Antarctic, and only 17 actually on or near the mainland. Many are unique to this icy ocean; all show marked adaptations to it.

Of the 17 species of penguins in the world, for instance, only one is found almost as far north as the Equator (in the Galapagos Islands). Most of the rest live in temperate regions. Yet only four are distinctly Antarctic species. Of these the emperor penguin is the most Antarctic (there are, naturally, degrees of 'Antarcticity' in all the bird and mammal orders found there). When the Adelie penguins, the commonest Antarctic species are heading north to the outer pack ice for the winter, the emperor penguins are heading south to the mainland. There, through the long July-September night, the female lays her single egg, which the parents take turns to incubate between the upper side of the feet and the loose skinfold of the stomach. In this unique way they escape the ravages of marauding seals and skuas, which prey on the rookeries of Adelies and other penguins (the less-Antarctic gentoo and chinstrap penguins, which come no farther south than the islands and the Peninsula, and, still more northerly, the king, magellanic, rockhopper, royal, crested, and macaroni penguins).

The albatrosses and petrels (*Procellariiformes*) also have their exclusively Antarctic forms. Though the 106 species of the order extend to wherever there is salt water, only 18 species breed in the Antarctic and only 6 on or near the mainland: giant, pintado, silver-grey, Antarctic, and snow petrels, and the prions. Competition for available sites is, of course, intense, and in the subantarctic you will often see extraordinary examples of multiple occupation: blue-eyed cormorants and giant petrels nesting on their mounds, interspersed with grassy hummocks that harbour Wilson's petrels, or rocky ledges and clefts where pintado petrels (or Cape pigeons) nest, and in underground burrows the beautiful little dove prion.

Gulls and terns (*Laridae*) number 82 species worldwide; yet only one tern (the Antarctic tern) and one gull (the southern black-backed) breed on the continent. The Antarctic tern breeds right around the coastline and on the islands. It is easily confused with the visiting Arctic tern, which, by migrating from one polar region to the other, enjoys more daylight than any other animal in the world. Two other terns (Kerguelen and South American) are common near subantarctic coasts.

True landbirds are practically nonexistent. The Antarctic pipit and European starling are found within the Antarctic circle though both breed outside it. But there is one non-webfooted bird, the wattled sheathbill, which does breed on the mainland; it lives as a scavenger around seal rookeries, the breeding colonies of cormorants, penguins, and petrels. The bird-predators of those colonies are the southern great skua and McCormick's or the Antarctic skua.

Apart from the huge subantarctic elephant seal, which is found in the islands, there are only four truly Antarctic seals. The leopard seal is a ferocious predator of the Adelie and other penguins, as well as of the cubs of other seals. It is the least Antarctic of the four, living mainly around the outer pack ice and only going south to the fast ice when the Adelie migrates to its rookeries there. Next comes the crabeater, which ought really to be called the krilleater seal, for that is its almost exclusive diet. Its teeth are adapted, like those of the big whalebone whales, to interlock and form a strainer for the krill. One usually sees them basking in small packs on ice floes. The Ross (or singing) seal is the least-studied and much the rarest of all seals. Few men have seen them close to and their breeding habits are still unknown. They live on squid, fish, and krill among the denser pack ice right around the continent. One estimate puts their numbers at only 50,000 – compared with the 5 to 8 *million* crabeaters! The Weddell seal, most Antarctic of all, is closest in habit to the emperor penguin, just as the crabeater is the mammalian competitor of the Adelie (a comparison first made by Edward Wilson, who died with my father on his return from the South Pole in 1912). Like the emperor, the Weddell seal remains on the ice shelf throughout the long winter night. All its front teeth are canine in form, and it swings its head to and fro, sawing and mashing a hole through the ice so that it can reach the 'warm' (30°F) waters below, where it lives most of the winter. Their snorting and huffing as they break back into their ice wells is one of the more eerie sounds of that long and almost lifeless night. Despite the dark, which must be absolute below the ice, it finds enough squid, fish, and bottom invertebrates to live on (probably by echo location). Its pups, born in spring (September–October), are in the water at 3 weeks, still in their woolly coats – the youngest age at which any seal pup takes to the water.

In this introduction I have named almost all the birds and mammals that breed on the Antarctic mainland and its offshore islands! Just over a score of highly adapted species, but with total numbers measured well into millions. As far as they are concerned there is as yet no obvious hazard to their survival – though environmental pollution could at any moment provide one.

Alas, it is quite different among the continent's pelagic mammals. Over 120 years ago Herman Melville in his encyclopedia of whaling *Moby Dick* wrote: 'Whether owing to the almost omniscient look-outs at the mastheads of the whale-ships, now penetrating even through Behring's straits, and into the remotest secret drawers and lockers of the world; and the thousand harpoons and lances darted along all continental coasts; the moot point is, whether Leviathan can long endure so wide a chase, and so remorseless a havoc; whether he must not at last be exterminated from the waters. . . .' Melville was never wrong. Four of the five commercially significant whales of his day, the California grey and the three right whales (southern, black, and Greenland) all of which moved slowly and floated when dead, were hunted almost to extinction by 1890; only the growth of the oil industry and a slump in the whale-oil market saved them. Even today they are rare. Grey whales number only six to seven thousand and no one knows the numbers of the right-whale species. We were fortunate enough to see the characteristic divided spout of one of them in the Ross Sea in February 1971.

The real Leviathan, the blue whale, was too big for 19th-century whalers. At up to 100 ft and 170 tons it is the largest animal that has ever lived. In the single decade 1956-66 we may have reduced its numbers below the recovery level. In this century we have taken more than 325,000 of them from Antarctic waters alone. All the other baleen whales of commercial interest – sei, humpback, common rorqual (the fin whale or finback), lesser rorqual (or minke), Bryde's, and sperm whales – are found in Antarctic waters. All have been hunted below the level at which they can be harvested to give a sustained yield. And, to judge by our experience with the 19th-century whales we so nearly exterminated, it will be more than half a century before we can hope to get back even to the precarious state that led to the first anti-whaling criticisms of the 1950s. And, remembering the recent warnings of Jacques-Yves Cousteau, Thor Heyerdahl, and Jacques Piccard about the severe and world-wide deterioration of marine life, we may wonder if we are not absurdly optimistic to entertain such hopes.

On the mainland itself, the outlook for conservation is, as I say, brighter. On the one hand the severe conditions, and the adaptations they demand, limit the number of species able to survive. On the other, the high productivity of its ocean waters rewards those that have adapted and keeps their numbers high.

The only introduced species is man himself, who now looks like being a permanent visitor. None of the species he usually introduces elsewhere seem likely to survive outside the warm habitat he carries down there with him – not even the hardy husky can survive many winters when it is abandoned.

It would be difficult to overstate the importance of Antarctica. Its remote geological history holds the key to the ancient arrangement of the other continents. Its mineral wealth is unknown but certainly vast. Its plankton-rich waters, properly conserved and harvested, could yet play an important role in a world of starving people. Its simple, prolific ecology offers an unexampled model for study. And the way men have chosen to study all these aspects is, itself, a model to the rest of us: national territorial claims are waived by the Antarctic Treaty making the whole continent a paradigm of international understanding and cooperation – a place where men greet each other as colleagues first and as Russians and Americans, New Zealanders and Australians, Britons and Frenchmen, Chileans and Argentinians second.

For the scientists and support teams – and for a few dozen lucky visitors who come to Antarctica each year – the continent has a more personal and spiritual wealth to bestow. The sight of millions of acres of untrammelled snow and ice . . . the sound of towering ice cliffs groaning at the stress of inconceivable forces as they calve huge icebergs . . . the awe with which you realize that what seem like rocky outcrops are really the peaks of great mountains, thrusting up through a mile-thick mantle of compressed snow . . . the livid pink of melting snow as the red alga within it quickens to its brief, intense life cycle . . . the vast colonies of penguins, standing in haphazard queues on the ice and rocky foreshore, bursting like child acrobats from the fringes of the slick, cold ocean, caught between the leopard seals and the skuas . . . and welding together these unique and diverse insights is the sense of fitness, the *rightness* of it all. Here more than anywhere else on earth we gain once more the certainty that we are at one with the rest of nature – the certainty our early ancestors took for granted and the loss of which has made our species the greatest enemy of the biosphere and of itself. It may be that this insight is Antarctica's greatest gift to us all.

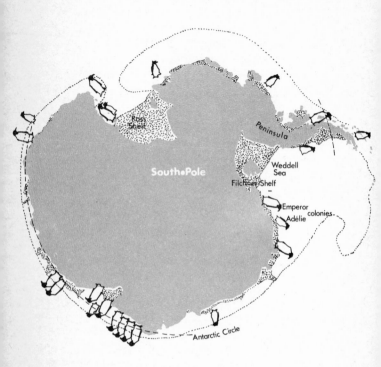

Ross Shelf

Peninsula

South•Pole

Weddell Sea

Filchner Shelf

Emperor colonies
Adélie

Antarctic Circle

The Antarctic To follow the style of other entries in this book one ought to begin: about 5½ million square miles; between sea level and 16,860 ft. Of course, that would be wildly misleading, for, although birds like the skua can overfly the whole continent, most of that giant landmass is devoid of life of any kind. What wildlife there is is dependent on the oceans and so tends to congregate on the fringes of ice and water; and most of those fringes are not yet accessible to tourism. Nevertheless, since 1966, Lindblad Travel Incorporated have been conducting parties of tourists to the Falklands, the Antarctic Islands, the Antarctic Peninsula, and the mainland and Ross Island. From 1970 onwards these expeditions have been in the company's own ship the *Lindblad Explorer*, purpose-built for such tours.

Penguins: king, emperor, gentoo, Adelie, chinstrap, rock-hopper, macaroni, and royal. **Petrels:** giant, pintado, blue, antarctic, white-chinned, great-winged, white-headed, Kerguelen, soft-plumaged, snow, Wilson's storm, black-bellied storm, grey-backed storm, South Georgian diving, and common diving. **Prions:** Salvin's, dove, thin-billed, thick-billed, and fairy. **Albatrosses:** wandering, royal, black-browed, grey-headed, sooty, and light-mantled sooty. **Cormorants:** Kerguelen, blue-eyed, and king. Grey duck, South Georgian pintail, pintail, Stewart Island weka, wattled and lesser sheathbills, great and south-polar skuas, southern black-headed gull, Antarctic and Kerguelen terns, Antarctic pipit, European starling. Among **mammals:** South American sealion, South American furseal, southern elephant seal, Weddell seal, crabeater seal, leopard seal, Ross seal.

The *Lindblad Explorer* is a one-class vessel with 50 outside rooms (100 beds) with private shower and wc, air conditioning, and piped music. Rates between $3,900 and $4,100 per person, excluding air fares to departure port. Tours last just under a month. There are two trips each year during the Antarctic summer, January to February. The organizers have recruited over a dozen leading experts in wildlife, antarctic exploration, and oceanography as lecturers on the tours.

Tour route The original tour went from Montevideo to the Falklands, then to Beauchene Island (2 million black-browed albatross), Drake passage, past the South Shetlands to Admiralty Bay on King George Island (Soviet Station; large penguin rookery), then to Deception Island; from there over the Bransfield Strait to Hope Bay (Argentine Station) at the entrance to the Weddell Sea. The route continued down the Antarctic Peninsula, through the de Gerlache Strait to Paradise Bay (Chilean and Argentine stations), thence via the Neumayer and Peltier channels to the US station Palmer. From Palmer over the polar circle to Adelaide Island (emperor penguin rookery); then north again to Argentine Islands (British station), then north again through the spectacular Lemaire Channel, past Melchior and Smith Islands and back into Drake Passage. The return included a close passage to Cape Horn, a couple of stops at islands rich in wildlife, and the passage of the Beagle Channel with its stupendous glaciers (including the 3,000-ft-long Italia Glacier); and so back to Puntas Arenas on the South American mainland. The 1971 tour went to the other side of Antarctica. Leaving from Hobart it went down via Macquarie Island (fur-seal sanctuary since 1933; king and crested penguin colonies; seabirds), over the polar circle, through the pack ice (penguin and seal colonies) to the majestic and ice-covered Balleny Isles and down to the Ross Ice Shelf and McMurdo Sound. (Large Adelie colony; US-New Zealand base, 12°N of the Pole – the most southerly accessible site; starting point of Scott's ill-fated 1912 expedition; historic Scott and Shackleton huts); then north again via the Campbell Islands (royal and sooty albatrosses, skuas, elephant seals, sealions), Auckland Islands (rabbits introduced by Ross in 1840, shipwreck remains), and so to New Zealand. The 1972 itinerary was not finalized as this book went to press. During March-November the *Lindblad Explorer* tours the Seychelles with parties of naturalists and tourists interested in wildlife.

ASIA

Many national parks and sanctuaries were already well established in Asia before World War II. After the war when most of the countries gained independence, the new administrations took over and extended responsibility for conservation. But poverty and political upheaval have worked against this hopeful trend and have not encouraged the sort of tourism that has made wildlife protection profitable in much of Africa. We have discovered that the same sort of uncertainty extends to the parks themselves; it has proved extremely difficult to come by firm information on the facilities available at parks and on their suitability for the average visitor. Standard references list many parks not included here; those listed in the following pages are ones whose facilities, we are reasonably certain, are likely to meet the average visitor's standards (except for political upheavals since this went to press).

Arabian oryx and calf in Phoenix Zoo, Arizona, USA. With the help of the World Wildlife Fund and the Fauna Preservation Society (London) several wild oryxes were captured in 1962 and sent to Phoenix to establish a breeding-nucleus herd for ultimate return to the wild – where unscrupulous hunting with machine guns from fast cars has brought them to extinction. Today Phoenix has 19 individuals.

Israel

Apart from its richness of biblical associations Israel is blessed with more scenic variety and beauty than any other area of comparable size in the world – from the cool, green, flower-covered hills of Galilee in the north to the dry, hot, southern Negev desert at the other extreme. Most of the outstanding parts are in the north and have been declared national parks or nature reserves; special access roads have been built, and tourism is encouraged.

The Nature Friends of Israel is a nation-wide organization whose chief activity is to organize rambles to places of outstanding beauty and wildlife interest. Every weekend the branches in Haifa, Jerusalem, Nahariya, Kiriyat Tivon, and Tel Aviv organize one-day outings (longer during holiday periods). The going may be strenuous at times but not beyond the powers of the reasonably fit. You should provide proper clothing, footwear, and provisions for yourself. The organization is a nonprofit one and the party leader is himself a volunteer; so costs can be as low as IL7 for a day excursion. Monthly programmes (in Hebrew but with English abstracts) are published in each of the towns named above; parties are well patronized and should be booked as far in advance as possible. Further details from the National Committee, Nature Friends of Israel, PO Box 4142, Haifa.

Hula (or Huleh) Swamp Nature Reserve 750 acres; 435 ft above sea level. Millions of years ago, when the giant East African Rift opened and spread right up through the Red Sea and Syria, it stranded the Hula valley among mountains to the north, west, and east. Then volcanic craters and fissures in the south poured out lava to form a basalt sill sealing off the valley on its only remaining open side – creating, in time, a lake and, in the higher land to the north, a vast swamp. Soon it became the home of migratory birds, who brought, in the mud on their feet, seeds of alien plants from eastern Africa. Thus the valley developed a hybrid European-African flora that persists to this day. Since 1950, however, the swamps have been drained and the fertile land to the north reclaimed. This reserve is the deliberately preserved remnant of that earlier swamp.

⚏ Otter, jungle cat, weasel, nutria (escapee); carp, coombs catfish; Dalmatian pelican, 10 different kinds of heron (including grey and night herons); purple and white egrets; many ducks, including marble duck, moorhen, water rail, coot, sandpipers, plovers, teals, shovellers, tufted duck, flamingo, kingfisher. Near the mouth of the Amoud and Abel, just outside the reserve, is a good site for griffon vulture and kites. There are gazelles in the area.

�£ Papyrus (northernmost site in the world), reed, bur reed, white nymphaea, swamp fern, Jordan tamarisk, sharp-branched willow, hornworts. Spring field flowers in the region include: anemone, cyclamen, crowfoot, salvia, bear's breeches, Syrian thistle, globe thistle, desert spine, sword lily.

⇐ Nearest hotels are in Safad, 15 miles away.

⇥ Good roads from Acre (44 miles) and Tiberias (22 miles).

⇦ There is a good road around the reserve and many paths cross it; but the best way to see it is by boat. Free.

☼ Open all year; best in spring-flower time.

⇨ Hula Nature Reserve, Yissot ha-Maala.

There are 5 nature reserves in northern Israel, all within a 25-mile radius circle:

Wadi Amud (1,700 acres; partly below sea level) Mixture of Mediterranean and steppe vegetation. Nesting raptors, including over a dozen pairs of griffon vulture; also white-rumped swift and rock dove.

Wadi Bezet (1,800 acres; 300 to 1,900 ft) An area of river meanders; slopes are densely covered with northern-Mediterranean maquis; noted for ferns (*Pteris longifolia*, *Dryopteris rigida*). The cliffs hold nesting raptors; stone marten and small-spotted genet roam the maquis.

Wadi Dishon (1,400 acres) Contains an exposed profile of all typical Galilean strata up to middle Eocene, each with its associated flora – many rare. Raptors include griffon vulture, eagle owl, and the buzzard *Buteo ferox*.

Wadi Kziv (1,300 acres) A mountain gorge between bluffs; the floor of the valley has stands of Oriental plane trees, while the slopes are carpeted with maquis, Judas trees, and Syrian maples. Birds of prey, especially buzzards, nest along the bluffs.

Wadi Tabor (1,900 acres; partly below sea level) Exposed ancient geological formations with plenty of gushing springs and streamside vegetation; Arabian gazelle is more common here than elsewhere.

There are two nature reserves in the south of Israel:

Ein Gedi (Dead Sea; 2,100 acres; 1,280 ft above to 660 ft below sea level) An oasis with unique flora, including biblical mustard and helleborine. The fauna is abundant and includes Nubian ibex (no longer a red-listed species), desert partridge, and Tristram's grackle.

Eilat Gulf Coral Reef 247 acres of Red Sea coral reef and its associated flora and fauna; attracted over 100,000 visitors a year in more peaceful days.

Southern Asia

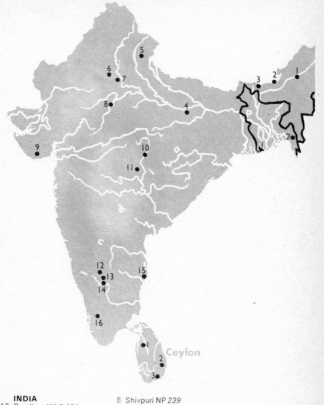

India

Care for wildlife is a tradition in India that dates back to the 3rd century BC Laws of Asoka. Nevertheless, dire poverty and the tremendous pressures of human population have led to a crisis during recent decades. For example the cheetah has been locally extinguished and the lion, tiger, and Indian rhinoceros have all been brought to the verge of extinction. Parks and sanctuaries are now their only immediate hope. The Indian Board for Wildlife, founded in 1952, have greatly improved the conservation and visitor facilities of the national parks, which are now among the best and most attractive in southern and southeastern Asia.

Bandipur Wildlife Sanctuary 310 square miles; 3,200 to 4,000 ft above sea level. This was once the private game reserve of the maharajahs of Mysore; now it forms the inner sanctuary of the Venugopal Wildlife Park. It is noted for its fine herds of gaur and chital. The landscape consists mainly of open stunted forest – chiefly axlewood and sandalwood trees. It adjoins the Mudumalai WLS.

⚲ Gaur, chital, wild elephant, sambar, muntjak, barking deer, common langur, bonnet macaque, wild pig, tiger, leopard, sloth bear, wild boar, panther. Birds include peafowl, grey junglefowl, spur fowl.

🛏 The Public Works Department runs three forest lodges and a guest house; fully furnished, servants; take provisions for a prolonged stay. A motel may have been opened by the time this goes to press. Reservations through the Divisional Forest Officer.

🛬 By road on the main Mysore-Ootacamund road, halfway between the two. Cars and buses available at Mysore. Direct access from Mudamulai WLS. Nearest airport at Bangalore, 136 miles away.

🚚 This sanctuary is more like an African sanctuary in that a good network of roads links most of the waterholes, salt-licks, and grazing grounds. Opportunities for game viewing from cars are better here than at other Indian parks. Truck hire is cheap. Elephants between Rs 10–30 per day.

☀ Open all year; best time June to October.

🕐 1–3 days.
Filming from observation towers costs Rs 7 (120 ft cine), Rs 3 (still).

☞ Local game staff will assist visitors in locating wildlife.

⇨ Divisional Forest Officer, Mysore City, Mysore 5.

Chandraprabha Wildlife Sanctuary 30 square miles; 700 to 1,600 ft above sea level. This small sanctuary in the Vindhayan mountains was established by the Uttar Pradesh government in 1957 as a second home for the rare Indian lion. In that year 1 lion and 2 lionesses, caught in the Gir forests, were released, and the population has since grown steadily.

⚲ Lion, nilgau, wild pig, chinkara, sambar, chital, sloth bear, leopard, wild boar, axis deer, serow. Birds include peafowl, grey partridge, quail, green pigeon.

🛏 Good hotels in Varanasi. Furnished tourist hut at site has cooking facilities (bring your own food); there is also a students' dormitory and two observation towers.

🛬 By good road 43 miles from Varanasi (Old Benares).

🚚 Facilities for elephant riding.

☀ Open all year; best time December to April.

⇨ Chief Wildlife Warden for Uttar Pradesh, Rana Pratap Marg, Lucknow, Uttar Pradesh; Divisional Forest Officer, Varanasi Forest Division, Ramnagar PO, Uttar Pradesh.

Corbett National Park 125 square miles; 1,500 to 3,000 ft above sea level. This was India's first national park, established as the Haily NP in 1935 and renamed in 1957 in honour of Jim Corbett, the famous writer and sportsman. It is, in fact, the locale for his books. It is famous for its tigers, whose extinction (unless conservation was enforced) was predicted by Jim Corbett, and for its gharial (fish-eating crocodiles) and muggers. The park stands in the foothills of the Uttar Pradesh section of the Himalayas. The slopes offer many splendid views across forests of sal; the valleys are particularly beautiful when the trees are in bloom.

⇶ Tiger, leopard, hyena, jackal, wild dog, wild elephant, sambar, chital, hog deer, barking deer, sloth bear, gharial, mugger, mahseer (Indian salmon), trout, goonch (freshwater shark), tortoise, common langur, rhesus monkey. Birds include peafowl, red junglefowl, partridges, and buzzards.

ଓ Flame of the forest, pink bauhinias, kusum trees, sal trees, ferns, orchids, tropical creepers.

⇐ Fully furnished and equipped rest house and annexe at Dhikala; cook; bring own provisions. Rates from Rs 8.50 per party per day including crockery, cutlery, and light. Basically furnished rest houses (bring own provisions) at Sultan, Sarapduli, Boxar, Paterpani, Gaujpani, and Jamunagwar. Cheaper accommodation in tourist hutments at Dhikala. The park has 8 observation towers.

⇥ By road or rail from Delhi, 152 miles. The railhead at Ramnagar is 29 miles from Dhikala.

🚙 70 miles of fair-weather internal roads link all rest houses in the park (impassable during monsoons). Jeep and trailer available for hire. Elephant rides cost Rs 8 per trip.

☼ Open November to May; best months February to May.

⏱ 3–5 days.

◻ Illustrated booklet and folder available from the Chief Wildlife Warden, Lucknow.
Temples, Tigers and Other Stories by J. Corbett (Oxford).
Maneaters of Kumaon by J. Corbett (Oxford and Penguin).
Maneating Leopard of Rudraprayag by J. Corbett (Oxford).
With Camera in Tigerland by F. W. Champion (out of print).
Jungle in Sunlight and Shadow by F. W. Champion (out of print).

◉ Local legend holds that on the day of Makar Sankranti (in January) the gods descend to take their annual bath at Sagar Tal; on that day the park is thronged with pilgrims who come to bathe at the sacred place.

⇨ Chief Wildlife Warden, Rana Pratap Marg, Lucknow, Uttar Pradesh; Wildlife Warden, Ramnagar, Uttar Pradesh.

Gir Wildlife Sanctuary 500 square miles; 300 to 1,400 ft above sea level. This sanctuary is the last natural stronghold of the Indian lion; it was from here that a number were introduced to the Chandraprabha WLS in Uttar Pradesh. In 1880 lions were close to extinction in India; now, thanks to rigid conservation, their number is increasing and has recently passed the 300 mark. The whole sanctuary is forested.

⇶ Lion, wild pig (the lions' chief prey), serow, nilgau, chinkara, sambar, axis deer, chital, four-horned antelope, bear, hyena, peafowl.

ଓ Flame of the forest.

⇐ Forest rest house at Sasan (15 beds); rates from Rs 4 per bed

The tiger originally evolved as a species of the temperate north, and only later moved into tropical forests. It is now either extinct or threatened at all points in its range. The Indian population was recently estimated at fewer than 2,000 animals. The Siberian tiger (a giant race of the species) is verging on extinction.

per day with small surcharge for light and water; catering from Rs 17 per day. Reservations 15 days in advance through Divisional Forest Officer.

- By rail direct to Sasan. By road, 38 miles from Junagadh via Mendarda. By air from Bombay to Kestod (90 minutes), then 42 miles by road to Sasan. Taxis are available but the Forestry Department's jeep or stationwagon (by prior arrangement only) is cheaper.

- Fair weather roads, inaccessible July to October.

- Open November to June; best time January to February (plus March to May if you like it hot).

- 3–5 days.

- Entry fees not quoted. For photographing the lions you need special permission; fees for amateurs Rs 2 (still), Rs 10 (cine); for professionals Rs 20 (still), Rs 800 (cine).

- Arrangements for lion-viewing parties up to 20, including locating, supplying trackers and mazdoors, etc, cost Rs 180; arrange through Forestry Department.

- Divisional Forestry Officer, Gir Division, Junagadh, Gujarat.

Jaldapara Game Reserve 36 square miles; about 250 ft above sea level. A small reserve set up in 1961 specifically for the conservation of the Indian rhino, of which there are now between 50 and 60 head. It is set entirely in riverine forest along the banks of the Torsa in northern Bengal.

- Rhino, gaur, sambar, barasingha, hog deer, barking deer, wild pig, wild elephant (few), tiger, bear. Birds include peafowl and junglefowl.

- Tourist bungalow at Barodabri with self-catering facilities. Reservations and details from Divisional Forest Officer, Cooch Behar Division, Cooch Behar PO, West Bengal.

By rail to Hashimara, just over a mile from the bungalow. By air on twice- or thrice-weekly unscheduled flights from Calcutta to Hashimara airfield, 3 miles from the bungalow. Regular air services from Calcutta to Cooch Behar or Bagdogra, both within easy reach of the reserve by road.

The Forest Department jeep is available for hire; guided elephant rides from Rs 15 per person.

Open all year; best time November to April, particularly toward the end of this period, when new grass is growing.

1–3 days.

Divisional Forest Officer (address above).

Kanha National Park 97 square miles; 2,000 to 3,000 ft above sea level. Formerly the Banjar Valley Reserve, this is one of the best stocked animal sanctuaries in India. The maidan, or open grassy area, resembles undulating English parkland. It is famous for its barasingha (Indian swamp deer). There are watchtowers and observation posts.

Barasingha, blackbuck, chital, muntjak, gaur, sambar, tiger, leopard, sloth bear, wild dog, hyena, fox. Over 90 bird species include peafowl and junglefowl.

Flame of the forest, sal trees, bamboo.

Two well furnished rest houses at camp HQ and Kisli, both within the park; cooks and provisions available.

By road 34 miles from Kanha, 60 miles from Jabalpur. An airfield is planned.

A network of fair-weather roads connects all the important parts of the park. Two elephants available.

Open mid-November to mid-July; best months April to June, when the animals come out to graze on the maidan.

2–5 days.

Available at both rest houses.

Divisional Forest Officer, South Mandla Division, Mandla.

Kaziranga Wildlife Sanctuary 166 square miles; about 270 ft above sea level. This is the main stronghold of the Indian one-horned rhino. In 1908 the area was closed to shooting and made a Reserved Forest; in 1928 it was declared a Game Sanctuary. It lies in flat swampy country on the southern bank of the Brahmaputra river in Assam.

Rhino, wild buffalo, sambar, barasingha, hog deer, pig, wild boar, bear, elephant (wild). Birds include many species of waterfowl, grey pelican, egret, herons, darters, cormorants, brahminy duck, jacana, vultures, eagles.

Water hyacinth.

Fully furnished tourist lodge and bungalow near milestone 135 on main road from Gauhati airfield; inclusive charges from Rs 18 per day. There are also furnished rest houses at Baguri and Arimora, but no catering arrangements.

By road 60 miles from either Gauhati or Jorhat airfields. You can leave Calcutta by morning plane and reach Kaziranga by early afternoon; transport available at both airfields.

A few 4-wheel-drive tracks open December to March; guided elephant rides cost Rs 15 per person.

☀ Open all year; best time November to April.

⏱ 1–4 days.

📧 Sanctuary view-permit costs Rs 8 per person per day. Photography charges: cine Rs 8 per person per day (professionals Rs 20); still Rs 4 per person per day (professionals Rs 10).

📖 Fully illustrated booklet from Assam Tourist Bureau or Divisional Forest Officer, Jorhat.

➡ Tourist Information Officer, Kaziranga Sanctuary, Kohora PO, Sibsagar District, Assam.

Keoladeo Ghana Wildlife Sanctuary 11 square miles; 1,200 ft above sea level. 'The Ghana' in Rajasthan was once the famous duck-shooting preserve of the rulers of Bharatpur state. The sanctuary is a shallow depression sparsely covered with medium sized trees and shrubs. The monsoons turn it into a shallow lake, whose waters are augmented by drainage through an artificial sluice system. It is the best sanctuary in India for seeing waterbirds, which congregate for breeding from July until October. You need special permission to approach the nesting sites. (There is a similar sanctuary at Sultanpur, very close to Delhi; there you can see flamingo, greylag goose, ruddy shelduck, and many northern ducks and waders – 100 species can be seen in a morning. These words are added as we go to press; there will be a more extensive report in future editions.)

🐦 Openbill stork, Asiatic white crane, painted stork, egrets (3 species), darters, white ibis, spoonbill, grey heron, sarus crane, ducks (15 species including comb duck), barheaded and greylag geese, cotton teal, peacock. Mammals include small herds of blackbuck, chital, nilgau, and wild pig.

🛏 Furnished rest house (called Shanti Kutir Hotel); services of cook; either bring own food or give plenty of notice of stay.

🚗 By road or rail, 100 miles south of Delhi or 30 miles west of Agra. The railhead at Bharatpur is 2 miles from the sanctuary.

🚐 Most observation can be done on foot from the many roads and embankments. Small boats with boatmen-guides available by arrangement with Forest Department staff.

☀ Open all year; best during breeding season (at its height in August to September); rest of the year only for migratory birds – duck, goose, pelican, crane.

⏱ 1–2 days.

📖 *The Ghana* (Bombay Natural History Society) free.

➡ Divisional Forest Officer, Bharatpur, Rajasthan.

Manas Wildlife Sanctuary 105 square miles; 270 to 650 ft above sea level. Famous for its wild buffaloes, Manas (also known as North Kamrup Sanctuary) stands at the foot of the Himalayas at a point where the river Manas tumbles through a magnificent gorge and spills out on to a plain. The northern part is mostly forest, which gives way to reeds and grassy stretches in the south.

🐦 Wild buffaloes, rhino, wild elephant, hog deer, tiger. Birds

Barasingha, or swamp deer, are common in the wetter forests and open grasslands. For three months each year the males live in all-male herds, as above, during which time they grow antlers up to 20 points.

include pelican, cormorants, egrets, redbreasted merganser, ibis, pied hornbill, mahseer, bokar.

Furnished rest house and bungalow at Motharguri; bring your own provisions. Campsites available.

By rail to Barpeta Road, which is 45 miles from the sanctuary. By road (closed June to September) 95 miles from Gauhati to Kumgiri, near the boundary of the sanctuary.

Guided elephant tours from Rs 10 per person; inflated rubber boat available for river trips.

October to May.

1–3 days.

Viewpermit costs Rs 8 per person per day. Photography charges: as for Kaziranga WLS.

Divisional Forest Officer, North Kamrup, Barpeta Road, Assam.

Mudamalai Wildlife Sanctuary 124 square miles; 3,000 to 3,800 ft above sea level. The sanctuary stands in undulating country at the foot of the Nilgiri hills. Though it is next door to the Bandipur WLS it is much more thickly forested. The game is thus more difficult to see – though it is, in fact, more plentiful.

Wild elephant, gaur, sambar, axis deer, muntjak, chital, barking deer, mouse deer, four-horned antelope, wild pig, tiger, leopard, sloth bear, wild dog, hyena, jackal, wild cat, wild boar, otter, common langur, bonnet macaque, Malabar squirrel, hare, porcupine, python. Birds include Malabar grey hornbill, grey junglefowl, red spurfowl, grey partridge, peafowl, and many birds of prey.

Three forest rest houses at Kargudi; modern facilities and cook; bring provisions for prolonged stay; rates from Rs 3 per person per day; reservations through Divisional Forest Officer.

By road, 42 miles from Ootacamund on main highway to Mysore; also direct access from Bandipur WLS.

45 miles of fair-weather road; vehicles Rs 8 per day; elephants from Rs 15 per trip.

☀ Open all year; best climate February to June; wildlife at its best in October to November.

⏱ 1–4 days.

📷 No entry fee quoted. Charges for cameras from Rs 14 per day (cine), Rs 4 per day (still).

📖 Illustrated Guide published by Madras Forest Department.

➡ Divisional Forest Officer, The Nilgiris, Ootacamund.

Periyar Wildlife Sanctuary 262 square miles; 3,000 to 6,000 ft above sea level. The sanctuary, as far as the visitor is concerned, is the 10 square miles of the Periyar lake, which was artificially created in 1900 to provide irrigation water for Madras State (though Periyar is just over the border in Kerala). The lake has many lovely creeks and the whole area is noted for its splendid scenery. Accommodation and amenities are among the best in India.

🐾 Wild elephant (very plentiful), gaur, sambar, barking deer, muntjak, wild pig, tiger (few), leopard, sloth bear, monkeys, and many bird species (particularly waterbirds).

🛏 First class modern hotel, Aranya Nivas (64 beds), at Thekkady, within the sanctuary; inclusive rates from Rs 28–50 per day (monthly terms by arrangement). Tourist bungalow (self-catering) at Edapalayam. Reservations for both to the Manager, Aranya Nivas Hotel, Thekkady PO, Kerala. Two rest houses (self-catering) at Thannikudy and Mullakudy.

🚆 On the main Cochin-Madurai road. By rail to Kottayam (72 miles away) or Madurai (88 miles away). By air to Cochin (120 miles away), Madurai, or Tiruchirapalli (145 miles away). Ample bus services from all these places.

🚗 There are plenty of boating facilities on the lake; hire charges Rs 9 per hour plus Rs 12 booking fee. 30-seat boats for 3-hour scheduled cruises. All reservations through Assistant Wildlife Preservation Officer, Thekkady.

☀ Open all year; best months March to May.

⏱ 1–2 days or a whole vacation.

📷 R 1 per person.

🔭 Available at Rs 20 per day.

➡ Wildlife Preservation Officer, Peermade, Kerala.

Ranganthittoo Bird Sanctuary 960 acres; 2,750 ft above sea level. The sanctuary is sited on a number of islands in the Kauveri (or Cauvery) river, which is sacred to Hindus.

🐾 Openbill stork, white ibis, night heron, Indian darter, cormorants, cattle egret, and many other species – all of which establish colonies of breeding birds in summer.

🛏 At hotels in Mysore.

🚆 By road from Mysore, 9 miles, or from Srirangapatna, 1 mile.

🚗 A coracle belonging to the Forest Department will ferry visitors (with prior consent of Divisional Forest Officer).

☀ Open all year; best time during breeding season (June to August for herons).

⏱ Day or half day.

➡ Divisional Forest Officer, Mysore Division, Mysore 5.

An Asiatic lion in the Gir Wildlife Sanctuary.

Sariska Wildlife Sanctuary 80 square miles; 1,700 ft above sea level. Set in one of the most beautiful parts of Rajasthan. The sanctuary has two points of special interest: you can watch (and film) tigers on a tethered kill in a floodlit clearing around which special observation towers have been built; and birdwatchers will be delighted to find that normally wary species (such as partridge) move quite freely and openly.

- Tiger, leopard, sambar, nilgau, four-horned antelope, chinkara, wild boar, Indian gazelle. Birds include partridges, quail, sand grouse, green pigeon, peacocks.
- Flame of the forest, hillsides covered with forests of *Agnoeissus pendula* and *Boswellia serrata*.
- Many well furnished rest houses with electricity and catering; booking must be in advance to the Game Warden.
- By road or rail. The sanctuary is 120 miles from Delhi on National Highway 8 (Delhi–Jaipur). The railhead at Alwar is 22 miles from the sanctuary.
- A network of good roads and paths.
- Open all year; best time February to June.
- No entry fee quoted. Amateurs may photograph the tigers at their kill (each Friday) but professionals must pay Rs 80 for the first 100 ft plus Rs 15 for each subsequent 100 ft or part; for stills Rs 30 per camera.
- Nearby temples of Garsh (10 BC) and Kankwari Fort.
- The Game Warden, Sariska, Alwar.

Shivpuri National Park 61 square miles; 1,300 to 1,600 ft above sea level. This was formerly the game reserve of the rulers of the State of Gwalior; it was designated a national park in 1965. It consists mainly of mixed deciduous forest with lakes and grassy clearings. Birdlife is plentiful near the lakes. There are many observation towers and picnic shelters in the park; good chances for tiger photography.

- Chinkara, sambar, chital, nilgau, serow, axis deer, wild pig, wild boar, sloth bear, hyena, tiger, leopard. Birds include paradise flycatchers and purple sunbird.

↪ Circuit house and dak bungalow belonging to the Public Works Department can be reserved in advance through the Divisional Engineer, Shivpuri, Madhya Pradesh.

↪ The park is 72 miles south of Gwalior on the Agra–Bombay road. A narrow gauge railway runs between the park and Gwalior.

↪ 70 miles of good road run through the park; there are boat jetties on the lakes.

↪ Open and accessible all year; best months February and July.

↪ 2–4 days.

↪ The Conservator of Forests, Shivpuri, Madhya Pradesh.

Taroba National Park 45 square miles; 1,200 ft above sea level. Taroba began as a game sanctuary in 1935 and was designated a national park in 1955. Its focal point is the jewel-like Taroba lake in the middle of the park. Most of the country is mountainous and forested.

↪ Tiger, panther, sambar, chital, deer, buffalo and many birds.

↪ Well furnished rest house and a guest house with modern amenities on the shores of lake Taroba; both have caretaker-cooks, but you must arrange for your own provisions. Two part-furnished rest houses at Moharli and Khandsingi, adjacent to the park. Reservations through the Divisional Forest Officer.

↪ By rail to Chandrapur station, then 70 miles by road. By road from Nagpur, 94 miles via the Jam-Warora road or 123 miles via the Umrer–Naghbir road.

↪ 50 miles of good road; you can hire an observation coach fitted with searchlights.

↪ Open March to May.

↪ 1–2 days.

↪ The Park Officer and Park Guard will assist tourists.

↪ Divisional Forest Officer, West Chanda, Chandrapur, Maharashastra.

Vedanthangal Bird Sanctuary 74 acres; 220 ft above sea level. Vedanthangal is a curiosity among sanctuaries in that it was a commercial success for over a century and a half before it was officially designated; the local villagers protected and valued the birds for their droppings, which made a rich guano fertilizer. Today an artificial lake forms the centrepiece of the park and provides irrigation for local paddies.

↪ Spoonbill, openbill stork, grey heron, darters, cormorants, egrets, white ibis, night heron.

↪ Karunghuzhi rest house (self catering); reservations through District Collector, Chingleput. Many hotels in Madras.

↪ By road 51 miles from Madras. By rail to Karunghuzhi, which is 7 miles from the sanctuary.

↪ Open all year; breeding season December to January.

↪ Day or half day.

↪ State Wildlife Conservator, c/o Chief Conservator of Forests, 81 Mount Road, Madras 6.

Asiatic or water buffaloes live close to water, where they often wallow in the mud. They domesticate easily – the domestic breeds having shorter horns than the wild ones. Wild buffaloes have a fearsome reputation and are dangerous in thick cover. Bulls have often defeated full-grown tigers. In early morning or late evening you are most likely to see them in open grassland, where they come to browse.

Gal Oya National Park 98 square miles; 200 to 300 ft above sea level. The park stands around the fringes of the Gal Oya storage reservoir. About a quarter of the park is dry evergreen forest, the remainder is parklike savannah covered with scattered trees. There is a range of mountains on the outer border.

Elephant, buffalo, deer, leopard, jackal, cobra, and many species of waterbird.

Caravan and campsites within the park. Resthouse at Kalmunai (self-catering); rates from Rs 14–18 per person per day; bookings to the Resthouse Keeper.

By road 28 miles from Kalmunai (215 miles from Colombo).

241

🚐 The park is traversible only on foot and by boat. The River Valley Development Board hires boats at nominal rates.

☀ Open all year; best time April to September.

🕐 1–2 days.

🪧 Visitors must travel with guides, who are provided free of charge.

⇨ The Game Ranger, Inginiyagala.

Ruhuna National Park 92 square miles; 100 to 180 ft above sea level. Ruhuna is the country's premier national park. The landscape is of open parklike plains, scrub jungle with rocky outcrops, and waterholes. The Menik Ganga river runs north–south through the middle of the park. In the southeast high sand-dunes lead down to the sea. In the plains the fruit of the palu tree is a great delicacy to the sloth bears, which are fairly numerous. Proposed extensions will take in the nearby Yala reserve (a strict sanctuary).

🐾 Elephant, sloth bear, leopard, deer, sambar, wild boar, crocodile. Over 200 bird species include waterbirds, hornbills, flycatchers, barbets, orioles, peafowl, and quail.

❀ Yellow ranawara flowers, pink and white amaryllis lilies.

🏠 Two bungalows with keeper-cook, bring own linen and food; servants and drivers free; rates from Rs 6 per head per day; bookings through Department of Wildlife, Echelon Square, Colombo 1. Resthouse (self-catering) at Tissamaharama; rates from Rs 14–18 per day; bookings through Resthouse Keeper. Maximum consecutive stay 6 days.

🛫 By road 6 miles from Tissamahara on the Kirinda road; Tissamahara is 169 miles from Colombo.

🚐 30 miles of jeep track. No foot traffic allowed.

☀ Open all year; best May to July.

🕐 2–6 days.

🎫 80cts per person per day; Rs 3.50 per car; Rs 4.75 for jeeps and vans; Rs 8 for buses and lorries. Permits to photograph at special sites Rs 8 per day.

📄 Pamphlet and map from Department of Wildlife.

🪧 Visitors must travel with guides, who are provided free of charge.

👁 Traces of a 2nd century BC civilization and remains of many Buddhist monasteries in the park.

⇨ Game Ranger, Yala, Tissamahara.

Wilpattu National Park 252 square miles; 280 to 450 ft above sea level. The western part of the park (roughly 100 square miles) consists of sandy tracts covered with shallow pans and straggly forest. These pans hold the monsoon rains and make inland lakes of considerable beauty; most of them support a great variety of waterbirds. The eastern part, mainly of forest crisscrossed with streams, is more verdant.

🐾 Elephant, sambar, buffalo, bear, leopard, monkeys, deer. Birds include storks (4 species), herons (5), egrets, teal, snipe, kingfisher, white ibis, spoonbill, cormorant, sandpiper, woodpecker, parrots, hawk, owl, eagle, junglefowl, hornbill, hoopoe.

🛏 Two bungalows at Maradanmaduwa and Kali Villu, furnished, cook provided but bring own food; linen for hire to overseas visitors; maximum stay 7 days; rates from Rs 5 per person per day (children under 14 half price); maximum stay 7 days; reservations through Department of Wildlife, Echelon Square, Colombo 1. There is a similar resthouse at Puttalam; rates from Rs 14–18; advance booking through the Resthouse Keeper, Puttalam.

🛬 41 miles from Puttalam by road; turn off Puttalam Anuradhapura road at milepost 27 in the village of Timbiriwewa. Puttalam is 81 miles from Colombo.

🚙 200 miles of jeep tracks; jeeps available in park. Alighting permitted only in authorized places.

☀ Open all year; best May to July, between big rains in February to March and August to September. Temperature in the 70–80°F range all year.

🕐 2–7 days.

🎟 R 1.50 (R 0.75 for residents). Use of cameras free if used from within car; special photographic sites from Rs 8 per person.

🗋 Pamphlet and map from Department of Wildlife.

🛆 Visitors must tour park with guide, who is free.

⊚ There are a number of ruins in the eastern section.

⇨ The Game Ranger, Wilpattu, Nochchiyagama.

Axis deer, or chital, are native to India and Ceylon. Sometimes they form herds up to 100 strong but usually live in herds of 10 to 30. The peak mating season is in April and May when the 2 or 3 males in each herd fight for possession of the females. They mate at other times, however. You are most likely to see them near rivers and streams.

Pakistan

Chittagong Hill Tracts National Park 5,093 square miles; 250 to over 3,000 ft above sea level. The park includes a large part of the hills that look down over the mouths of the Ganges and the Bay of Bengal. To the north lies India, to the east and south is Burma, to the west – Chittagong and the coast. It contains a number of large towns, among them Kaptai, Bandarban, Rangamati, and Ramargh; the total population is close on 400,000. The landscape is hilly, with ridges running mainly north-south and divided by river valleys. The river Karnafuli is famous for its gorges. There is also dense bush and teak jungle. The best areas for seeing wildlife are around Ramargh and in the valleys of the rivers Kassalong and Shishak.

- Tiger, deer, wild elephant, buffalo, sambar, leopard, panther, boar, wild dog, wild cat; birds include pheasant, rock pigeon, and junglefowl.

- The VIP rest house at Kaptai has rooms from Rs 24–70 per day; reservations through regional tourist offices in Dacca, Chittagong, or Kaptai. The rest house at Kaptai has beds from Rs 9 per day; reservations through the Administrative Officer, East Pakistan, Wapda, Kaptai. Means from Rs 16 per day. In various centres in the hill tracts there are Forest Department rest houses where tourists can stay by prior arrangement through the Divisional Forest Officer, Chittagong – local tourist offices can also arrange.

- The main highway system of East Pakistan runs to all important locations in the hill tracts.

- As well as the main roads there are many miles of track suitable for 4-wheel-drive vehicles. Launches ply the main rivers.

- Open all year; best time October to March.

- 3 days to whole vacation.

- Free.

- Guided tours can be arranged from Rs 170 per day. Interpreters available from Rs 20 per day.

- *Kaptai* The famous Kaptai lake, site of East Pakistan's principal hydroelectric project, is 38 miles from Chittagong. There is speedboat cruising on the lake from Rs 30–50 per hour or Rs 140–250 per day; also water skiing and rowing. A mile downstream from the dam is the Chit Morong Buddhist Temple, famous for its sculpture. The hill-tribe people are extremely friendly and welcome visitors to join in their communal festivities. *Rangamati*, 20 miles from Kaptai or 50 miles from Chittagong, is a favourite resort; its Chakma Raja's palace is a tribal museum (souvenirs such as homewoven textiles, bamboo handbags, and jewellery for sale). At *Chandraghona* is Asia's biggest papermill. *Ramargh*, 86 miles from Chittagong, is in a tea-growing area with beautiful walks and hikes.

- Regional Tourist Office, Dacca, East Pakistan.

Sunderbans Game Sanctuary 5,400 square miles; at or near sea level. The reserve consists chiefly of evergreen forests cut through by the rich network of rivers that make up the Ganges delta. For miles on end the trees form a tall, almost unbroken canopy through which the sun can barely penetrate. It is not in the part of East Pakistan most severely affected by the 1970 disaster.

🏹 Royal Bengal tiger, deer, monkeys, wild boar, crocodile, python; birds include duck, snipe, heron, coot, and sandpiper.

🏠 Government resthouse in Khulna; rates from Rs 35. Hotels in Khulna; rates from Rs 70. Forest bungalows in Sunderbans; rates from Rs 50. Also luxury launches and houseboats. Bookings through Regional Tourist Office, Dacca.

✈ Khulna can be reached from Dacca by rail, river, road, and air (PIA Helicopter). PIA also operates a service to Jessore, 40 miles by road from Khulna. Daily train service between Dacca and Khulna. From Narayanganj (12 miles from Dacca) there is a leisurely and scenic steamer service to Khulna; the trip takes 19 hours. Private and government launches connect Khulna and the sanctuary.

🚐 By launch or on foot. It is unwise to go without a guide.

☀ Open all year; best time October to March.

🕐 3 days to whole vacation.

✉ Free.

👉 Guides available; rates from Rs 20 per day.

🖐 Regional Tourist Office, Dacca, East Pakistan.

Note: As these pages went to press the political outlook in East Pakistan (or Bangladesh) was extremely uncertain. And though the two sites listed here are away from the main trouble centres, their administration is bound to have suffered – and, as experience in southeastern Asia has shown, when that happens the outlook for the more vulnerable species is grim.

The nocturnal and shy clouded leopard is rarely seen in the wild, and very little is known about its habits. Its range extends from the Himalayas down through the eastern fringes of Pakistan, along the ocean fringes of Southeast Asia and up to China as well as Formosa, Sumatra, Borneo, and Java. It is one of the most strikingly marked of all cats and, despite its name, is not closely related to the leopard. It prefers thick jungle close to river banks.

Southeast Asia

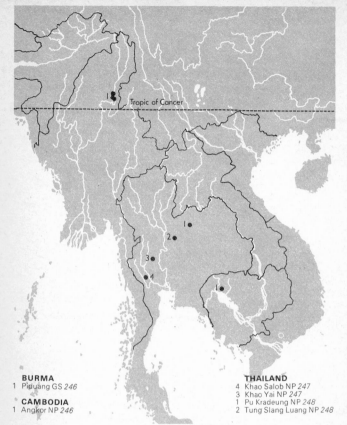

Tropic of Cancer

Burma

Pidaung Game Sanctuary 180,000 acres in four blocks (a large central one of 126,000 acres, a southern extension of 50,000 acres and two small extensions east and west); 2,630–7,250 ft above sea level. The sanctuary is set in the grassy plains of the Irrawaddy river valley and stretches into hilly, evergreen jungle country. Six villages and three tea plantations are within the reserve. Elephant, tiger, leopard, sun bear, banteng, sambar, buffalo, hog-deer, muntjac; numerous peacocks, junglefowl, pheasants. There is a forest resthouse and a two-room mountain hut for tourists at Kasung Hka. There are 45 miles of motor road (including a 20-mile circuit) and 48 miles of footpaths. Nearest town is Myitkyina which is served by rail from Mandalay and Rangoon. Nearest airfield Myitkyina; airport at Rangoon.

Cambodia

Angkor National Park 26,483 acres; about 500 ft above sea level. This area of high forest rich in archaeological remains

The orang-utan of Borneo and Sumatra, the only Great Ape outside Africa. Close to extinction, it now numbers fewer than 5,000.

Philippines

Philippines parks are mapped on page 257.

Aurora Memorial Park 9,084 acres; rising to 8,000 ft above sea level. Set in rolling country broken by rivers, gullies, ridges and strewn with forests. The hills, some of which are gently sloped while others rise steeply, soar to a high point at Camp Labi, the recreational centre, which is set at 8,000 ft and gives spectacular views. As well as this centre there are amenities for camping, picnicking, hiking, and sightseeing in lovely surroundings.

⚔ Deer, wild pig, cimarron or wild caraboo, civet cat, monitor lizard, python, monkeys of various species, hornbill, pigeons, red junglefowl, hawks, rails, quail, parakeet, and owls.

❀ Forest consisting mostly of yakal, guijo, apitong, white lauan, bagtikan, molave, calantas, narra, almasiga, alupag, and pine.

🛏 None within the park. The nearest town with hotels is Cabanatuan, $8.50 single, $11 double.

✈ The park lies 147 miles northeast of Manila, and is accessible by bus.

🚗 The road from Manila to Bengabon-Baler passes through the park, making camp Labi accessible to vehicular transport. Foot and horse trails are plentiful.

🌤 Open all year: best time March and April, although the rainfall is distributed more or less evenly throughout the year.

🕐 2 or 3 days.

✉ Nominal; permit required.

📖 None available.

➪ Pablo C. Rabulan, Aurora Memorial Park, Bongabon, Nueva Ecija.

Bulusan Volcano National Park 7,593 acres; rising 5,113 ft above sea level. The famous volcano – inactive today – dominates the spectacular landscape. But there are also magnificent craters, strange rock formations, cascading waterfalls, and natural mineral hot springs. One of the most lovely features of this verdant park is a lake, beautifully set between hills and mountains, fed by a subterranean stream, so that it has neither visible inlet nor outlet. Other attractions include panoramic views, a dancing pavilion, a charming floating resthouse, bancas (small rowboats), canteen and picnic area. There are also facilities for boating, hiking, and mountaineering.

⚔ Wild pig, deer, junglefowl, monkeys, lizards, kalaws, hornbills, pigeons, parrots and hawks.

❀ Extremely rich flora includes giant ferns, hanging orchids, and thick forest.

🛏 Cottages and an hotel both lie within the park. Further accommodation is available at Legaspie – some 62 miles away.

✈ The park, which is just under 400 miles south of Manila, is reached by train, plane or boat to Legaspie, then by bus or car.

🚗 The roads within the park lead to the accommodation and elsewhere.

🌤 Open all year; best time during the hot season between March and April when the park is cool. Maximum rainfall from November to January.

🕐 3 days or a vacation.

✉ Nominal, a small charge also being made for the entry of vehicles; permit required.

➪ Clemente Ereño, Bulusan Volcano National Park, Bulusan, Sorsogon.

The dugong is an underwater grazer of shallow tropical seas from the western Pacific to the Red Sea. It is closely related to the manatee.

Callao Cave National Park 475 acres. A wild and beautiful place where primeval forest is still found. A hilly region of rivers and streams – some of which flow underground – the land is indented with ravines, caves which lead one into another, and a canyon which is over 300 ft deep. Guano deposits are found in some of these caves, and exploring the natural chambers is one of the great attractions of the park. The terrain also lends itself to swimming, boating, and mountain climbing.

- Wild pig, deer, wild fowl, hornbills, tarictic, doves, pigeon, and bats are all to be found here.
- The primeval molave forest is of particular scientific interest.
- There is none within the park. The nearest is at Tuguegarao; $9 single, $12 double.
- Set a little over 300 miles northeast of Manila, buses run from the capital to Tuguegarao; from there either on hired horses or on foot – a distance of some 15 miles.
- There are no roads, simply tracks to bathing and boating spots; bridle paths lead into the interior.
- Open all year; best time during the relatively dry season from November to April. The park enjoys a cool and healthy climate.
- One day or a vacation.
- Nominal; permit required.
- None.
- Ruperto Gabutan, Callao Cave National Park, Peñablanca, Cagayan.

Caramoan National Park 857 acres; from sea level to 986 ft. above. A rare, undisturbed part of the country, this is the place to visit if you want to see the Philippines in their natural state. Access to this southeast region of Luzon is difficult, and there are no tourist facilities. However, the park's features, its caves, subterranean river, and the panoramic views from its hills are sufficient reward.

⌁ Parrots, parakeets, purple gallinule, pigeons, owls, hawks, and also wild pig, wild fowl, monitor lizard and monkey.

⌁ None within the park. The nearest hotel is at Naga City, some 57 miles away; $8.50 single, $10.50 double.

⌁ Lying some 337 miles southeast of Manila access is by train or plane to Naga City; then by water, horse, bus, or car.

⌁ None save a few tracks.

⌁ Open all year; best time March and April, although there is no dry season. Maximum rainfall can be expected from November to January.

⌁ 2 days or a vacation.

⌁ Nominal; permit required.

⌁ None available.

⌁ Angeles Ternate, Caramoan National Park, Libmanan, Camarines Sur.

Fuyot Spring National Park 2,048 acres. Here the undulating countryside is dotted with wonderful springs, grottoes, caves and other interesting rock formations. The climate is temperate and the scenery varied. As for activities, the park tempts campers, picnickers, hikers and bathers, who can swim in the natural spring waters.

⌁ Quail, doves, pigeons, sambar deer, wild pig, monkeys.

⌁ None within the park. The nearest hotel is at Sitio Marana, a few miles away.

⌁ Just over 50 miles northeast of Manila, the park is reached by taking a bus to Sitio Marana, then by foot or on a hired horse.

⌁ None for vehicular traffic. Tracks for riders and hikers.

⌁ Open all year; best time November to April, when it is relatively dry. The weather varies little throughout the year.

⌁ 1–7 days.

⌁ Nominal; permit required.

⌁ None.

⌁ Demetrio Florendo, Fuyot Hot Spring National Park, Ilagan, Isabela.

Hundred Islands National Park 4,550 acres; at or near sea level. Some 400 little rocky coral islands, enjoying a positively idyllic climate, are scattered over the sea to make up one of the most picturesque areas in the Philippines. Quezon island is especially popular for its shallow sea and wide beach; but there are other wide, soft, sandy beaches. They are backed by caves, perhaps formed by volcanic eruption long ago, and other strange and beautiful rock formations. In the clear waters can be seen myriads of multi-coloured fish, often darting through curiously beautiful coral gardens. Amenities include: a dance pavilion, swimming area, dressing house, and boats for hire.

⌐╝ Indian pygmy goose or cotton teal, coletos, barn swallows, warblers, Philippine bulbul, doves, pigeons, multicoloured fish, and the Philippine nightingale.

ဧ Marine plants of all kinds.

⌐ There is both a National Park resthouse and a restaurant at Barrior Lucap.

⊷ About 250 miles northwest of Manila. Access is by bus to Lucap, and from there on by boat. Inclusive tours from Manila also visit the islands.

🚐 Entirely by motor boat or by bancas (rowboats).

🌞 Open all year; best during the summer, but the change in seasons is here minimal.

⊕ 2 days or a vacation.

✉ Nominal; permit required.

⫐ None official, but the boatmen know the area well.

◎ Roxas Island has a beautiful undersea coral garden.

⇨ Jacinto E. Aquino, Jr., Hundred Islands National Park, Alaminos, Pangasinan.

Mount Apo National Park 190,000 acres; rising to 9,690 ft above sea level. Mount Apo, the highest peak in the Philippines, soars above this park, whose chief attractions are its lake, rushing waterfalls and medicinal hot springs, its dense forests and the volcano. It is an ideal spot for hiking, climbing, riding, or simply for exploring.

⌐╝ Particularly famous as the home of the monkey-eating eagle. Monkeys, deer, wild pig, wild chicken are also seen.

ဧ The mossy undergrowth of the forest is a particular feature. Among trees mayapis, tangile, white lauan, and mangasinuro predominate.

The rare monkey-eating eagle is found only on Mindanao island.

🛏 While there are no hotels within the park itself, there is good family accommodation – but no first class hotel – at Davao City, some 20 miles away.

✈ By plane or boat some 600 miles southeast from Manila to Davao City, then by bus. The road from Davao to Cotabato passes along the park boundary.

🚐 Numerous paths and tracks suitable for cars.

🌦 Open throughout the year; best time: rainfall is more or less evenly distributed throughout the year; during the generally hot months of March and April it is agreeably cool here.

🕐 3 days or a vacation.

🏕 None; permit required.

🏚 None available.

⇨ Ceferino P. Datuin, Officer-in-Charge, Parks and Wildlife Office, Diliman, Quezon City.

Mount Arayat National Park 9,178 acres; rising to 3,564 ft above sea level. Here the legendary mountain of Filipino folklore, a lonely ancient upland, soars above the pastures and remnant forests of central Luzon. To soften its sere outline is a series of springs, rivers, some charming little waterfalls, as well as a natural and a man-made swimming pool. The park also has plenty of facilities by way of a dancing pavilion, bathing hut, a shed and grounds for picnickers, and a parking area.

🐾 Deer, duck, wild pig and wild chicken.

🌿 Cogon pasture, shrubs, and forest trees.

🛏 None within the park, but there is plenty of choice at Manila which is only just over 56 miles away. Here hotel rooms cost from $8 single, and $10 for a double room.

✈ 56 miles by good road northwest of Manila. Manila is connected to the town of Arayat by bus, and from thence taxis are available.

🚐 Tracks suitable for vehicles lead to the swimming pool, dance pavilion, and picnic places. Cars must be parked in the parking area provided and the rest of the park explored on foot.

🌦 Open all year; best time during the dry season between November and April. The park enjoys a temperate climate, but the rest of the year is wet.

🕐 One day.

🏕 Nominal; permit required.

🏚 None available.

⇨ Constancio Buan, Mount Arayat National Park, Arayat, Pampanga.

Naujan Lake National Park 5,374 acres. The park was once famous for both its hunting and its fishing. The hunting is now banned, but the magnificent lake, some 200 ft deep, is still fished commercially as well as for sport. This is the best area in the Philippines for breeding marsh birds and interesting marine life. The park also boasts wonderful panoramic views, a hot spring, boating and swimming, and excellent picnic areas.

🐾 Deer, monkey, wild duck, grebe, coot, gallinule, Oriental darters, rails, heron, bittern, doves, pigeons, owls, song birds of various species, hawks, crows, sail-finned lizards, varied fish life, and crocodiles.

🛏 None within the park limits, but easily found within reasonable reach or at Manila 100 miles away. Prices in Manila range from $10 single, $12.50 double.

🛪 By plane or boat direct from Manila.

🚙 Tracks suitable for vehicles radiate from the lake. Motorized bancas (small boats) for hire.

🌄 Open all year; best time March and April, generally speaking the dry season in the Philippines, although in this park the rainfall is evenly distributed throughout the year.

🕐 2 days to a week.

🎫 Nominal; permit required.

🗂 None.

⇨ Roque Herrera, Naujan Lake National Park, Oriental, Mindoro.

Pagsanjan Gorge National Park 382 acres. A wonderland of caverns, grottoes, rapids and gorges, the park boasts the most beautiful waterfall in the Philippines as well as many lesser cascades and fascinating rock formations. This is the place to visit for boat trips which shoot the rapids, for swimming the beautiful palm fringed natural swimming pools, for mountaineering, hiking, or picnicking.

🐁 Doves, pigeons, wild duck of several species, deer, wild pig, alimos, lizards, bats.

🌿 The vegetation is green and lush, and consists of palms, deep jungle undergrowth, scrub and secondary forest.

🛏 Several privately owned hotels lie within the park including the Rio Vista Lodge which has its own natural spring swimming pool.

🛪 The park lies about 55 miles southeast of Manila, and access is by bus or car on Route 21 to Pagsanjan and then by boat. Inclusive tours – which include a visit to the park – are arranged from Manila.

🚙 Transport is mostly by means of native canoe, but tracks also cross the park. A surfaced road runs to the main falls and the river is navigable to the cauldron at its foot.

🌄 Open all year; best during November to April dry season.

🕐 Day trip from Manila or a vacation.

🎫 Nominal; permit required.

🗂 None.

⇨ Julian Macalintal, Sta. Cruz, Laguna; Lorenzo Brucal, PW Sub-station, Dolores, Quezon; Floro Ayuma, PWS Sub-station Minasawa Game Refuge and Bird Sanctuary.

Quezon Memorial Park 490 acres in the hills and plain near Manila. The park includes a stand of virgin forest, a forest nursery which can be visited, and some of the most beautiful countryside in the Philippines. It is easily visited from the capital; picnic tables, shelters, and drinking water are provided.

🐁 Sambar deer, monkey, wild boar, pigeon, parrot.

🛏 None within the park itself, but there is a choice of hotels at Manila, 7 miles to the west; $10 single, $12.50 double.

- ⇥ By city rail service. Also by asphalt road from Manila.
- ⌷ Footpaths.
- �▩ Open all the year; best during November to April dry season.
- ◔ One day.
- ✉ Nominal; permit required.
- ⌷ None, but there are organized visits.
- ◉ The Montalban Gorge and Bat Caves lie a little to the east and at sunset millions of bats fly out from rock crevices.
- ⇨ Armando Racelis, Quezon Memorial Park, Diliman, Quezon City.

Quezon National Park 4,460 acres; rising to 1,182 ft above sea level. An area of dense virgin forest and picturesque mountains traversed by plenty of cleared walks leading to scenic viewpoints and menadores (observation towers).

- ⇗ Monkeys, deer, wild pig, monitor lizard (bayawak), parrots, tarictic, kalaw, doves, pigeons, jungle fowl.
- ⇌ Resthouse on Pacific coast at Atimonan; hotels and resthouses at Lucena, the provincial capital. There is a dancing pavilion and a natural swimming pool in the park. Temporary snack bars at certain times of year.
- ⇥ By surfaced road 113 miles from Manila; road passes through the park. Nearest railway stations at Pagbilao or Padre Burgos, both nearby. Air access to Lucena.
- ⌷ Foot trails only.
- �▩ Open all year; wettest from November to January.
- ◔ One day.
- ✉ Nominal; permit required.
- ⌷ Not needed.
- ⇨ Eufronio Andalis, Quezon National Park, Zigzag, Atimonan, Quezon.

Tiwi Hot Springs 118 acres. The springs boil and bubble permanently, and are considered medicinal by many. The park is a popular health resort, and pleasant holiday centre; facilities include bathhouses, a swimming pool, picnic areas, and a canteen. The boiling pool is protected by a concrete walk and an iron fence. The country is rich in birdlife.

- ⇗ In this relatively small area can be found rails, red jungle fowls, fish, flowerpeckers, owls, swifts, button-quails, hawks, nightjars, ground doves, insectivorous birds, finches, sparrows, swallows and song birds of various species.
- ⇌ There is a hotel within the park $10 single, $12.50 double. Other hotels at Legaspi, 28 miles away by first-class road.
- ⇌ Situated about 336 miles southeast of Manila, visitors travel to Legaspi by train or plane, and from there to Tiwi by bus.
- ⌷ Footpaths and horse trails.
- �▩ Open all year; best time during the hot season March to May, but the climate is agreeable all year.
- ◔ 1 to 7 days.
- ✉ Nominal; permit required.
- ⌷ None necessary.
- ⇨ Roman Grageda, Tiwi Hot Spring National Park, Legaspi City.

No national parks are listed for the island of
Palawan in the western Philippines and it is
therefore excluded from this map.

PHILIPPINES
 4 Aurora MP *249*
12 Bulusan Volcano NP *250*
 1 Callao Cave NP *251*
10 Caramoan NP *251*
 3 Fuyot Spring NP *252*
 2 Hundred Islands NP *252*
13 Mount Apo NP *253*
 5 Mount Arayat NP *254*
 9 Naujan Lake NP *254*
 7 Pagsanjan Gorge NP *255*
 6 Quezon MP *255*
 8 Quezon NP *256*
11 Tiwi Hot Springs *256*

JAPAN
 1 Akan NP *258*
 2 Fuji-Hakone-Izu NP *260*

Japan

The symmetrical and much-photographed beauty of Mt Fuji, Japan's sacred mountain, the straggling stands of conifers, the carefully made haycocks in the well-trod field – all help to underline the fact that Japan's national parks are places of recreation rather than special wildlife reserves. Even so, they are at least as rich in that respect as, for instance, many of Europe's national parks.

In Japan, more than in most other countries, it is misleading to think of the national parks as especial reserves of wildlife. If there is such a reserve in Japan it is the mountainous-volcanic backbone of each of the islands. Here, where farming barely reaches and industry reaches not at all, is an abundance that other industrialized countries must envy. It is too amorphous a 'reserve' for the usual details of access, accommodation, etc., to be spelled out in detail here. But, to whet your appetite, here is a list of the species you will almost certainly see on any single visit to the Japanese uplands. In winter, contrasting with the white of the snows: Japanese dormouse, Japanese hare, red fox, Asiatic black bear (toward the thaw), giant flying squirrel, hawk eagle, various owls, ptarmigan. At other times you will see all these plus: horse-shoe bat, wild boar, marten, mountain goat, Eurasian badger, Japanese grey heron, night heron, reed warbler, great spotted woodpecker, sandpiper, pheasant, starlings, tree frog. This mountain spine is accessible from most of lowland Japan. Wherever you are, the local tourist bureau will be able to advise on the best way of reaching and exploring this hinterland.

Akan National Park 87,498 hectares; rising from about 300 to over 4,500 ft above sea level. The park is situated in the north east of Hokkaido, the northernmost of Japan's main islands, and the country's most spectacular outdoor playground. The climate is roughly equivalent to that of Northern Europe, and the park is renowned for its scenery, which is both grand and peaceful. Also famous are its beautiful volcanos, lakes and mountains, from some of whose heights, such as O-Akan, Me-Akan and Io, columns of smoke still curl lazily upwards. Three of the lakes are quite outstanding. Lake Mashu is famous both for its setting and beauty. The indigo-coloured water is completely transparent to a unique depth of 25 fathoms. Of the two caldera, Kutcharo is beautifully set amongst mountains, while Lake Akan boasts four islands, lovely inlets and tree-clad shores. Just below the clear surface of the lake floats a beautiful waterweed known as 'marimo'. Parts of the park are still completely unexplored virgin forest, and there are spectacular views from Bihoro Pass, Sempoku Pass and from the Sokodai plateau. Skiing, fishing, water sports, hot spring baths, boating and mountaineering can all be enjoyed in the park.

Brown bear, sable, stoat, Oriental squirrel, white raccoon dog, sika deer, chipmunk; birds include pine grosbeak, great grey shrike, black woodpecker.

Outstanding are rhododendron, azalea, especially yesso azalea, and rare alpine plants. Amongst the trees both birch and maple are to be found, and parts of the park consist of primeval forests of conifers. The most famous plant is the unique spherical waterweed, 'marimo', on Lake Akan, which can be studied at close quarters through box glasses from the pleasure boats.

There are people's lodges and youth hostels within the park itself. Nearby towns also offer a choice of accommodation. Among them are: Kushiro, two hotels (from Y1,500 to 5,500) and also a youth hostel; Tokachigawa Spa, a hot spring resort and a good base for tours of the park, two hotels (from Y2,000 to 3,500); Obihiro also a good starting point has the Hotel Kokkaikan (Y1,300 to 2,000); Kawayu Spa, Misono Hotel (Y2,300 to 5,000); Akan kohan Spa, 3 hotels (from Y2,000 to 5,000).

All Nippon Airways, Japan Domestic Airlines and Japan Air Lines all operate scheduled services between Tokyo and Sapporo, the capital of Hokkaido. There is also a train. Then Kushiro is 40 minutes by plane, and nearly 6 hours by train. Obihiro is 4½ hours by train from Sapporo. Kawayu Spa is reached by train and bus from Kushiro. Bus connects Akan kohan Spa with Kushiro. Tokachigawa is 20 minutes from Obihiro by bus.

Obihiro is the starting point for inclusive tour trips round the park. A rail runs through the park. To see the lakes, pleasure boats may be hired at Y80 an hour. The park is also net-worked by roads, for vehicular traffic, and by tracks for walkers.

Open all year; best time between May and October for general sightseeing, from late September to November to enjoy the crimson foliage, and from December to April for skiing.

None.

Guides will take tours and give lectures particularly July 21 and August 20, a period known as 'Movement for the Communion with Nature', otherwise guides should be hired at Tokyo and big centres.

👁 The Ainus, a hairy, brown skinned aboriginal people, who were the original inhabitants of this whole area, still live hereabouts. In early October, usually the first Saturday and Sunday of the month, they celebrate the Marimo Festival on Lake Akan, when they give prayers for peace, and celebrate the existence of 'marimo'. For visitors in the area it is worthwhile to make the journey to Shiretoko, northeast of Akan, there to see waterfalls cascading from the volcanic coastal range, 600 ft to the sea below.

⇥ The Warden, Kawayu, Teshikaga, Hokkaido, or The Warden, Akan-kohan, Akan, Hokkaido.

Fuji-Hakone-Izu National Park 122,309 hectares; rising from sea level to 12,388 ft above. The whole area really consists of four different parks: Mount Fuji, Hakone, the Izu Peninsula and the seven Isles of Izu. It is a beautiful area of mountain, forest and shore line, but each district has its own special charms. Mount Fuji has long been held to be sacred and this park is easily the most visited in Japan. At the northern base of the mountain are five beautiful man-made lakes where visitors can fish, swim, and boat. The indented coastline of Lake Kawaguchi, the view over the 'sea of trees' from Koyodai (Maple Hill), and the deep blue waters of Lake Motosu are special attractions in the Mount Fuji district. Hakone, which lies between Fuji and the Izu Peninsula is a mainly volcanic district, with 15 hot springs, 7 spas and beautiful woods, hills, mountains, torrents, a lake, and some deep ravines. The Nagao Pass, Mount Koma, and the Jukkaku Pass give particularly spectacular views both of Mount Fuji and the surrounding countryside. The Izu Peninsula, which lies east of Hakone, has some beautiful shores, good swimming, and hot springs. It is favoured for its mild climate and accessibility. Off its shores lie the Seven Islands, which boast volcanic lakes, lava cliffs, and more hot springs. Hachijojuna is the most popular, since it has been specially developed for holiday makers, and offers a great many facilities.

🐾 Sika deer, wild boar, Japanese macaque, Japanese dormouse, monkey, sea birds of many species, sparrow and more than a hundred species of singing birds.

🌿 The lower slopes of Mount Fuji are covered with forests of azalea, cherry and fir. Primeval forest is still found near Lake Motosu. Cherry trees in great abundance are found round Yamanaka – and elsewhere – and look quite beautiful when in flower at the end of April. At Hakone there is a cedar avenue at Hakonemachi and the park, in its entirety, boasts several special gardens. At the Omuro Cactus Park, near Ito on the peninsular, more than 2,500 varieties of cactus are grown under glass. Tropical plant gardens are to be found near Atawaga Spa near Shimoda and on Hatsushima Island.

🛏 *Fuji*: Camping on Laka Kawaguchi and Lake Yamanaka. Hotels: Lake Yamanaka; Fuji New Grand Hotel (Y1,200 to (6,000). Hotel Mount Fuji (Y2,300 to 25,000). Lake Kawaguchi, Fuji-View Hotel (Y2,400 to 4,300). Fuji City, Hotel Grand Fuji (Y2,000 to 8,000) and other Japanese-style hotels.

Hakone: Gora: Gorha Hotel, (Y2,500 to 6,000), Lake Ashi, Hakone Hotel (Y2,500 to 5,000). Miyanoshita, Fujiya Hotel (Y1,500 to 15,000). Kowakidani, Hotel Kowaki-en, (Y2,800 to 20,000). Sengokuhara, Fujiya Hotel (Y1,300 to 3,900) and Japanese style hotels, a motel, and other western hotels.

Izu Peninsula: Atami: Atami has 3 hotels, prices from Y2,500 to 35,000. Kawana: Kawana Hotel (Y2,800 to 25,000). Shimoda, Shimoda Tokyu Hotel (Y2,000 to 15,000). On *Oshima Island*: Oshima Kowaki-en (Y1,500 to 4,000). There are also a great many Japanese style hotels on the peninsula and islands.

Fuji: By rail from Tokyo to Kawaguichiko (2½ hours) via Otsuki. Train from Tokyo to Gotemba, and from there to Lake Yamanaka by bus. By car from Tokyo, by National Highway Route 20 to Otsuki, then by Route 139 to Lake Kawaguchi, other lakes, and Mount Fuji. Buses run from Fuji station to Lake Motosu, and Fuji is connected by train to Osaka and Kyoto. Inclusive bus excursion – one day – visit the park from Tokyo; Y5,400 including lunch.

Hakone: By rail: Tokyo to Odawara (70 mins), from there to Goa by Mountain Railway, and to Sounzan by cableway. Buses also run from Odawara to various parts of the park. By car; Tokyo to Odawara (National Highway Route 1), thence by road to Hakonemachi (8.8 miles), Mount Taikan, and Yugawara Spa.

Izu Peninsula: Train from Tokyo to Atami (eastern entrance) in under 1 hour. From Atami to Ito, and Shimoda by train. By car: from Odawara, good roads along the western coast of the peninsula to its southern tip.

Fuji: Regular buses, especially from early July to mid-August, drive around the park starting from Fuji. Sight-seeing buses take visitors to the 5 lakes at the base of Mount Fuji and up the Fuji Toll Road to the 5th stage of the mountain. From there you must walk. There are six climbing trails on Mount Fuji, and one trail encircles the mountain's waist, a modern road runs round the base of the mountain. The park has good roads.

Hakone: is traversed by various roads, and linked to the other parks by road. The Ashinoko Skyline Driveway gives particularly spectacular views. Bus takes one to the 5 lakes and Mount Fuji. Cable and ropeways take visitors up Hakone mountains.

Izu Peninsula: Buses crisscross the peninsula. A road runs round the peninsula, and the railway runs along the west coast. The Izu Skyline Parkway runs 26 miles from Atami Pass to Arogi Kogen and is spectacular. Sightseeing boats run from Mitohama and Namazu and have special equipment for enjoying marine life. The islands are reached by boat.

Open all the year. Best season May, July, August and then October for the crimson leaves. For skating visit between January and March. For skiing visit from December to April.

One day or a vacation.

Free.

Guides for climbing Mount Fuji may be hired, and generally cost about Y2,000 a day. Other guides for the park may be hired in Tokyo and other big centres, rather than in the park itself.

Fuji National Park Museum on the south shore of Lake

Kawaguchi has exhibits of fauna, fossils, and archaeological remains. There is a Lake Festival during the first week in August, when hundreds of lanterns are set alight to float on the waters of Lake Yamanaka. During the Festival of the Hakone Shrine (July 31 to August 1) at Moto-Hakone there is much the same sort of display on Lake Ashi. On August 16 bonfires, representing a huge Chinese character, are set alight on Mount Myojo. On November 3 a feudal lord's procession parades from Yumoto to Tonosawa and back. At Nittsu Izu Fujimi Lane, near Atami, there is a pleasure ground with tropical plant garden, museum, 'sportland', and a reproduction of the ancient Tokaido Highway, including its 53 stations.

⇨ The Warden, Motohakone, Hakone, Kanagawa. The Warden, Funatsu, Yamanashi. The Warden, Shimoda, Shizuoka.

Asia : Species List

ALIMOS Pagsanjan Gorge
ANTELOPE, Four-Horned Gir; Mudamalai; Sariska
BADGER, Eurasian Japanese Uplands
BANTENG Pidaung
BARASINGHA Jaldapara; Kanha; Kaziranga
BARBETS Ruhuna
BATS Callao Cave; Pagsanjan Gorge
— **Horseshoe** Japanese Uplands
BEAR Gir; Jaldapara; Kaziranga; Wilpattu; Khao Salob; Khao Yai
— **Asiatic Black** Japanese Uplands
— **Brown** Akan
— **Sloth** Bandipur; Chandraprabha; Corbett; Kanha; Mudamalai; Periyar; Shivpuri; Ruhuna
— **Sun** Pidaung
BITTERNS Naujan Lake
BLACKBUCK Kanha; Keoladeo Ghana
BOAR, Wild Bandipur; Chandraprabha; Kaziranga; Mudamalai; Sariska; Shivpuri; Ruhuna; Chittagong Hills; Sunderbans; Khao Salob; Khao Yai; Tung Slang Luang; Quezon; Japanese Uplands; Fuji
BOKAR Manas
BUFFALO, Wild Kaziranga; Manas; Taroba; Wilpattu; Gal Oya; Chittagong Hills; Pidaung
BULBUL, Philippines Hundred Is
BUZZARDS W Kziv; Corbett
— **(Buteo ferox)** W Dishon
CARP Huleh
CAT, Jungle Huleh
— **Wild** Mudamalai; Chittagong Hills
CATFISH, Coombs Huleh
CHICKEN, Wild Mt Apo; Mt Arayat
CHINKARA Chandraprabha; Gir; Sariska; Shivpuri
CHIPMUNK Akan
CHITAL Bandipur; Chandraprabha; Corbett; Gir; Kanha; Keoladeo Ghana; Mudamalai; Shivpuri; Taroba
CIMARRON Aurora
CIVET Khao Yai; Aurora
COLETO Hundred Is
COBRA Gal Oya; Khao Yai
COOT Huleh; Sunderbans; Naujan Lake
CORALS Eilat Gulf
CORMORANTS Kaziranga; Manas; Ranganthittoo; Vedanthangal; Wilpattu
CRANE, Asiatic White Keoladeo Ghana
— **Sarus** Keoladeo Ghana
CROCODILE Ruhuna; Sunderbans; Naujan Lake
CROWS Naujan Lake
DARTERS Kaziranga; Keoladeo Ghana; Vedanthangal

— **Indian** Ranganthittoo
— **Oriental** Naujan Lake
DEER Taroba; Wilpattu; Gal Oya; Ruhuna; Chittagong Hills; Sunderbans; Khao Salob; Aurora; Bulusan; Callao Cave; Mt Apo; Mt Arayat; Naujan Lake; Pagsanjan Gorge; Quezon NP
— **Axis** Chandraprabha; Gir; Mudamalai; Shivpuri
— **Barking** Bandipur; Corbett; Jaldapara; Kanha; Mudamalai; Periyar; Khao Yai
— **Hog** Corbett; Jaldapara; Kaziranga; Manas; Pidaung
— **Mouse** Mudamalai; Khao Yai; Pukradeung; Tung Slang Luang
— **Sika** Akan; Fuji
DOG, Wild Corbett; Kanha; Mudamalai; Chittagong Hills
DORMOUSE, Japanese Japanese Uplands; Fuji
DOVES Callao Cave; Fuyot Spring; Hundred Is; Naujan Lake; Pagsanjan Gorge; Quezon NP
— **Emerald** Khao Yai
— **Ground** Tiwi
— **Rock** W Amud
DUCKS Huleh; Keoladeo Ghana; Sunderbans; Mt Arayat; Naujan Lake; Pagsanjan Gorge
— **Brahminy** Kaziranga
— **Comb** Keoladeo Ghana
— **Marble** Huleh
— **Tufted** Huleh
EAGLES Kaziranga; Wilpattu
— **Hawk** Japanese Uplands
— **Monkey-Eating** Mt Apo
EGRETS Kaziranga; Keoladeo Ghana; Manas; Vedanthangal; Wilpattu
— **Cattle** Ranganthittoo
— **Purple** Huleh
— **White** Huleh
ELEPHANT, Wild Bandipur; Corbett; Jaldapara; Kaziranga; Manas; Mudamalai; Periyar; Wilpattu; Gal Oya; Ruhuna; Chittagong Hills; Pidaung; Khao Salob; Khao Yai; Tung Slang Luang
FINCHES Tiwi
FLAMINGO Huleh
FLOWERPECKERS Tiwi
FLYCATCHERS Ruhuna
— **Paradise** Shivpuri
FOWL, Wild Callao Cave; Caramoan
FOX Kanha
— **Red** Japanese Uplands
FROG, Tree Japanese Uplands
GALLINULE Naujan Lake
— **Purple** Caramoan
GAUR Bandipur; Jaldapara; Kanha; Mudamalai; Periyar; Khao Salob; Khao

Yai; Tung Slang Luang
GAZELLES Huleh; Sariska
— **Arabian** W Tabor
GHARIAL Corbett
GENET, Small-Spotted W Bezet
GIBBON Pu Kradeung; Tung Slang Luang
GOAT, Mountain Japanese Uplands
GOONCH Corbett
GOOSE, Barheaded Keoladeo Ghana
— **Greylag** Keoladeo Ghana
— **Indian Pygmy** see **TEAL, Cotton**
GRACKLE, Tristram's Ein Gedi
GREBES Naujan Lake
GROSBEAK, Pine Akan
GROUSE, Sand Sariska
HARE Mudamalai
— **Japanese** Japanese Uplands
HAWKS Wilpattu; Aurora; Bulusan;
Caramoan; Naujan Lake; Tiwi
HERONS Huleh; Kaziranga; Wilpattu;
Sunderbans; Naujan Lake
— **Grey** Huleh; Keoladeo Ghana;
Vedanthangal
— **Japanese Grey** Japanese Uplands
— **Night** Huleh; Ranganthittoo;
Vedanthangal; Japanese Uplands
HOOPOE Wilpattu
HORNBILLS Wilpattu; Ruhuna; Aurora;
Bulusan; Callao Cave
— **Little Pied** Khao Yai
— **Malabar Grey** Mudamalai
— **Pied** Manas
HYENA Corbett; Gir; Kanha; Mudamalai;
Shivpuri
IBEX, Nubian Ein Gedi
IBIS Manas
— **White** Keoladeo Ghana;
Ranganthittoo; Vedanthangal; Wilpattu
JACANA Kaziranga
JACKAL Corbett; Mudamalai; Gal Oya
JUNGLEFOWL Jaldapara; Kanhà;
Wilpattu; Chittagong Hills; Pidaung;
Khao Salob; Bulusan; Quezon NP
— **Grey** Bandipur; Mudamalai
— **Red** Corbett; Aurora; Tiwi
KALAWS Bulusan; Quezon NP
KINGFISHER Huleh; Wilpattu
KITE Huleh
LANGUR, Common Bandipur; Corbett;
Mudamalai; Khao Yai
LEOPARD Bandipur; Chandraprabha;
Corbett; Kanha; Mudamalai; Periyar;
Sariska; Shivpuri; Wilpattu; Gal Oya;
Ruhuna; Chittagong Hills; Pidaung;
Khao Salob
LION Chandraprabha; Gir
LIZARDS Bulusan; Pagsanjan Gorge
— **Monitor** Aurora; Caramoan; Quezon NP
— **Sail-Finned** Naujan Lake
LORIKEETS Khao Yai
MACAQUE, Bonnet Bandipur; Mudamalai
— **Japanese** Fuji
MAGPIE, Red-Billed Blue Khao Yai
MAHSEER Corbett; Manas
MARTEN Japanese Uplands
— **Stone** W Bezet
MERGANSER, Red-Breasted Manas
MINIVETS Khao Yai
MONGOOSE Khao Yai
MONKEYS Periyar; Wilpattu; Sunderbans;
Angkor; Aurora; Bulusan; Caramoan;
Fuyot Spring; Mt Apo; Naujan Lake;
Quezon; Quezon NP; Fuji
— **Rhesus** Corbett
MOORHEN Huleh
MUGGER Corbett
MUNTJAK Bandipur; Kanha;
Mudamalai; Periyar; Pidaung; Angkor
NIGHTINGALE, Philippines Hundred Is
NIGHTJARS Tiwi
NILGAU Chandraprabha; Gir; Keoladeo
Ghana; Sariska; Shivpuri
NUTRIA, Feral Huleh
ORIOLES Ruhuna
OTTER Huleh; Mudamalai
OWLS Wilpattu; Aurora; Caramoan;
Naujan Lake; Tiwi; Japanese Uplands
— **Eagle** W Dishon
PANTHER Bandipur; Taroba; Chittagong
Hills
PARAKEETS Aurora; Caramoan
PARROTS Wilpattu; Bulusan; Caramoan;
Quezon; Quezon NP
PARTRIDGES Corbett; Sariska

— **Desert** Ein Gedi
— **Grey** Chandraprabha; Mudamalai
PEAFOWL Bandipur; Chandraprabha;
Corbett; Gir; Jaldapara; Kanha;
Keoladeo Ghana; Mudamalai; Sariska;
Ruhuna; Pidaung; Angkor
PELICANS Manas
— **Dalmatian** Huleh
— **Grey** Kaziranga
PHEASANT Chittagong Hills; Pidaung;
Khao Salob; Pu Kradeung; Japanese
Uplands
— **Silver** Khao Yai
PIG, Wild Bandipur; Chandraprabha; Gir;
Jaldapara; Kaziranga; Keoladeo Ghana;
Mudamalai; Periyar; Shivpuri; Aurora;
Bulusan; Callao Cave; Caramoan; Fuyot
Spring; Mt Apo; Mt Arayat; Pagsanjan
Gorge; Quezon NP
PIGEONS Chandraprabha; Aurora;
Bulusan; Callao Cave; Caramoan; Fuyot
Spring; Hundred Is; Naujan Lake;
Pagsanjan Gorge; Quezon; Quezon NP
— **Green** Khao Yai
— **Rock** Chittagong Hills
PLOVER Huleh
PORCUPINE Mudamalai; Khao Yai
PTARMIGAN Japanese Uplands
PYTHON Mudamalai; Sunderbans; Aurora
QUAIL Chandraprabha; Sariska; Ruhuna;
Aurora; Fuyot Spring
— **Button** Tiwi
DOG, White Raccoon Akan
RAILS Aurora; Naujan Lake; Tiwi
— **Water** Huleh
RHINOCEROS, Indian Jaldapara;
Kaziranga; Manas
— **Sumatran** Khao Salob
SABLE Akan
SAMBAR Bandipur; Chandraprabha;
Corbett; Gir; Jaldapara; Kanha;
Kaziranga; Mudamalai; Periyar; Sariska;
Shivpuri; Taroba; Wilpattu; Ruhuna;
Chittagong Hills; Pidaung; Angkor; Khao
Yai; Pukradeung; Tung Slang Luang;
Fuyot Spring; Quezon
SANDPIPER Huleh; Wilpattu;
Sunderbans; Japanese Uplands
SEABIRDS Fuji
SEROW Chandraprabha; Gir; Shivpuri
SHOVELLER Huleh
SHRIKE, Great Grey Akan
SNIPE Wilpattu; Sunderbans
SPARROWS Tiwi; Fuji
SPOONBILL Keoladeo Ghana;
Vedanthangal; Wilpattu
SPUR FOWL Bandipur
— **Red** Mudamalai
SQUIRREL, Giant Flying Japanese
Uplands
— **Malabar** Mudamalai
— **Oriental** Akan
STARLINGS Japanese Uplands
STOAT Akan
STORKS Wilpattu
— **Openbill** Keoladeo Ghana;
Ranganthittoo; Vedanthangal
— **Painted** Keoladeo Ghana
SUNBIRDS Khao Yai
— **Purple** Shivpuri
SWALLOWS Tiwi
— **Barn** Hundred Is
SWIFTS Tiwi
— **White-Rumped** W Amud
TARICTIC Callao Cave; Quezon NP
TEAL Huleh; Wilpattu
— **Cotton** Keoladeo Ghana; Hundred Is
TIGER Bandipur; Corbett; Jaldapara; Kanha;
Manas; Mudamalai; Periyar; Sariska;
Shivpuri; Taroba; Chittagong Hills;
Sunderbans; Pidaung; Khao Salob; Khao
Yai
TORTOISE Corbett
TROUT Corbett
VULTURES Kaziranga
— **Griffon** Huleh; W Amud; W Dishon
WARBLERS Hundred Is
— **Reed** Japanese Uplands
WATERFOWL Kaziranga; Periyar; Gal Oya;
Ruhuna
WEASEL Huleh
WOODPECKERS Wilpattu; Khao Yai
— **Black** Akan
— **Great Spotted** Japanese Uplands

AUSTRALIA

Introduction by Elspeth Huxley

The seeker after paradox does not have far too look in Australia. It is the world's most arid landmass, yet its rivers bring immensely fertile soil down into vast and lush estuaries. It is the world's most thinly populated continent (as though the population of London were to be spread over the whole of Europe), yet many of its species are already threatened and wildlife parks are proving more difficult to establish than you might imagine. Even its wildlife is not all its own but a still unstable amalgamation of native and introduced species.

The native species, especially, are threatened. They include the monotremes – the platypus and spiny enteater (*echidna*), which lay eggs like birds and reptiles yet suckle their young

Kangaroos are often seen leaping in herds across Australia's plains.

like mammals – and the pouched marsupials, which range in size from small mice to kangaroos as big as bears. Introduced European mammals like the domestic cat, the red fox, and the rabbit are superior in cunning and adaptability; by preying on the native species – including ground-nesting birds like bustard and quails – and by grazing down their food, the introduced species have done heavy damage even where men themselves have not yet settled. And in areas where they *have* settled the damage has been even worse. Ploughing, intensive grazing, hunting, and deliberate or accidental bush-fires have altered or destroyed the habitat over millions of acres. Among the threatened species – some of which may, in fact, now be extinct – are the marsupial anteater, certain monitors and the Tasmanian pouched wolf.

Conservationists face a number of problems unique to Australia. First (and surprisingly) geography is against them. The continent has few 'natural' wildlife parks – isolated swamps, inaccessible jungles, remote mountains and table-lands – so that every wildlife area is created in potential competition with other land users. Secondly, Australian animals have a peculiar tendency to make vast and totally unexpected treks – a habit that can make nonsense of setting aside an area to protect a given species. Such treks usually take them into settled areas where they are not at all adapted to survive; hence the particular importance of preserving (and even recreating) virgin areas in Australia. Finally there are such human factors as the country's jealously guarded state autonomy. In the past, and to some extent still, there has been next to no co-ordination of conservation policies in Australia. An animal that is strictly conserved in one state can unwittingly cross a state border and find itself legal prey.

But the picture is not entirely gloomy. The turning point came for most Australians with the saving of the koala. In the late 1920s these endearing little creatures were hunted for their fur almost to extinction; there were probably only a few thousand left when they were put under legal protection. Today their numbers are back to five figures. Since then Australia has created over 60 large protection areas for all kinds of biological communities, as well as several hundred smaller ones, many of them devoted to a single species.

The idea of a large national parks system is only beginning to catch on in Australia. Many of them are actually aimed more at recreation than conservation. There is as yet no cadre of professionally trained rangers, either. Accommodation, too, is patchy; some have luxurious lodges of international standard while others have nothing – or a mountain hut at most. However, the tourist organizations are fully aware of these deficiencies and, with the conservationists, are pressing for urgent up-grading all round; so things could change markedly for the better in the next few years.

The eastern coast, from the tropical north to the cool-temperate south, offers the greatest variety of reserves. Some are in low-lying coastal areas, others, high in the mountains, are sub-alpine. The most unusual reserves are in the Northern Territory, in the deserts around Alice Springs and in the north, near Darwin. The best reserves for birdlife, particularly waterbirds, are in Gippsland, off the eastern part of the southern coast, and near Darwin. Western Australia is better noted to its stupendous range of wildflowers than for its animal and bird life, which is less rich than elsewhere. Unique to Australia, certainly in its easy accessibility, is the Great Barrier Reef.

The Reef is, in fact, a series of reefs and cays (islands composed entirely of coral sand and gravel) stretching 1,260 miles from latitude 24°30′S to the New Guinea coast at 9°15′S. The most southerly (Swain) reefs are 100 miles off-shore; opposite Townsville they are 50 miles closer; off Cairns the distance is down to 20 miles; and in the far north, off Cape Melville, they are a mere 7 miles out. The sea between is, in fact, a shallow channel (20 to 30 fathoms), for beyond the reefs the bed drops sharply to 1,000 fathoms or more in places. In the shallow offshore channel are a number of true islands, the peaks of a submerged mountain chain that was once part of the continent; most have acquired a small fringing reef of their own.

The Reef – one of the greatest biological treasure houses and potential food sources of the world – is now seriously threatened by commercial exploitation, both quarrying and oil drilling. These activities have upset the delicate balance between coral polyps and starfish, each of which is predator and prey to the other at different stages in their life cycles. As a result the polyps have in many places been reduced below the threshold necessary to support renewal. The fight to save the Reef was hampered by legal uncertainty about state and Federal jurisdiction. Meanwhile the quarrying and oil spillage went on – and still goes on. Biologists on the spot now say that large areas of the Reef, especially in the north, are irrecoverably dead.

Efforts to save the rest of the Reef – and, indeed, the whole conservationist effort in Australia – has now reached the highest political levels. There are hopeful signs that senior government members know what is involved. As the Minister of Education and Science, speaking of his country's unique flora and fauna, said in 1969, at the height of the Reef controversy: 'The Prime Minister and other of my colleagues share my view that if we don't preserve this precious and priceless diversity, it will be lost for all time. It is something that can never be replaced.'

Note: Special precautions apply to travel in remote or desert areas (see notes under Tanami Desert Sanctuary, page 273). And since the roads to some of the parks are unsurfaced for at least part of the way, it would be wise to check with local tourist or motoring organizations before starting out.

If you want to leave such worries to others, Australia has some of the most comprehensive tours organizations in the world. They and the scheduled bus services run to or near many of the areas listed in the following pages. The local tourist organizations, the tour operators listed in local guides, and the bus companies will all be glad to advise you.

The parks, reserves, and sanctuaries described in the following pages are listed in groups according to their nearest city; this means that parks in some states inevitably appear grouped with parks in other states; it does not, of course, mean that the parks listed under one city are inaccessible, or even unrewardingly distant from another. In fact, Australia is so well furnished with internal air services that every park is accessible from every city.

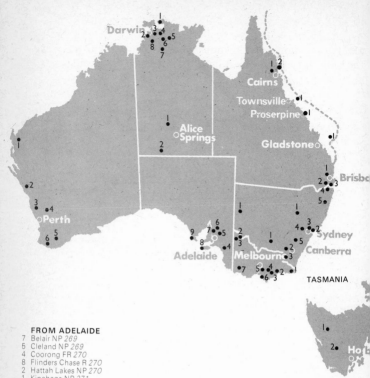

The dingo, a feral dog probably introduced by Aborigines some 12,000 years ago, is a tireless and cunning hunter. Dingoes domesticate well if taken young. In most states there is a bounty on them.

From Adelaide

Belair National Park 2,065 acres, 1,500 ft above sea level. More of an informal park than natural bush, Belair includes recreational facilities and a Victoriana museum (a former viceregal summer residence) as well as a wildlife area. It lies in the outskirts of Adelaide.

- Birdlife includes honey-eaters, parrots, and kookaburras. There are also koalas and echidnas.
- All eucalypts (blue gums, red gums, stringy barks).
- Free.
- National Parks Commission, Belair.

Cleland National Park 1,765 acres, 1,500 ft above sea level. Twelve miles east of Adelaide, in the Mt Lofty ranges, this park has a fairly good range of native animals in a semi-natural setting. The Fauna Reserve covers 65 acres within the park.

- Kangaroo, koala, wallaby, wombat; snakes; brolga, cape barren goose, parrots, waders and waterbirds.
- Acacias, eucalypts, grass trees, wide variety of wildflowers.
- In Adelaide.
- Main highway from Adelaide.
- In Fauna Reserve, on foot only.
- Open all year; best time September to May.
- 1 day.
- Adults 30c, children 10c.
- National Parks Commission, Belair, SA.

Coorong Fauna Reserve 7,800 acres, at or near sea level. One of the best areas in the whole of Australia for seeing water-birds. The Coorong stretches in a wide strip facing southwest over the waters of Encounter Bay.

⚛ A few kangaroos. Birds include pelicans, waders, emus, swans.

ଌ The reserve exists primarily to conserve sand dune vegetation. Creeping spinifex shrubs include current bush spinifex grass.

⇌ No organized camping within the park as yet. Hotels and motels at Meningie, 40 miles away.

⇥ Difficult. Mainly by 4-wheel drive from Kingston, 192 miles southeast of Adelaide.

⇨ Mainly by boat or 4-wheel drive along beach, where conditions are good.

☀ Open all year; best time September to December.

⏱ 1–2 days.

🎫 Free.

⇥ National Parks Commission, PO Box 2, Belair, SA.

Flinders Chase Reserve 135,000 acres at or near sea level. Kangaroo Island, just under 100 miles long by about 40 wide, lies at the mouth of the St Vincent Gulf near whose eastern shore stands Adelaide. The Flinders Chase Reserve covers the western end of the island. Only a small section is opened up for tourism but within it one can see a wide range of native plants and animals.

⚛ Black-faced kangaroo, porcupine anteater, koala, wallaby, emu, black swan, pelican; seals at Seal Bay.

ଌ Eucalypts; open grassland.

⇌ None within the reserve. Hotels and motels at Kingscote, the island's chief town, 50 miles from the reserve; rates from A\$6.00 single. Hotels and motels also at American River and Penneshaw.

⇥ *By air* Kangaroo Island is 40 minutes from Adelaide. *By boat* 6 hours. *By road* from Kingscote.

⇨ By car and on foot.

☀ Open all year; best time September to May.

⏱ 1 day.

🎫 Free.

⇥ South Australian Government Tourist Bureau, 18 King William Street, Adelaide; Fauna and Flora Board, Adelaide.

Hattah Lakes National Park and Kulkyne State Forest 44,000 acres, 200 ft above sea level. In the extreme northwest of Victoria, along the banks of the Murray just before it joins the Darling, the area consists of a number of flood lakes and large tracts of red gum, mallee scrub, and native pine forests.

⚛ Kangaroo (red and mallee grey); lizards; emu, parrots, choughs, cockatoos, mallee fowl, eagles, honeyeaters, ibis, magpipes, ducks, pelicans and other waterfowl.

ଌ Many eucalypts, such as river red gums, black box, mallees, beloh, Murray pine, porcupine (or spinifex) grass; various wildflowers.

⇌ Camping (free) only within the park. Hotels and motels at Mildura (40 miles north) or Ouyen (25 miles south); rates between A\$4.00 and A\$5.00 a day double.

By car from Swan Hill, Ouyen or Mildura. Mildura has rail and air connections with Adelaide, Melbourne and Sydney. Entrance to park 3 miles east of Hattah on the old Murray Valley Highway. 300 miles northwest of Melbourne.

On foot.

Open all year; best time late autumn to spring (or anytime after a good Murray flood).

1–2 days.

Free.

There is a resident ranger.

National Parks Authority, Melbourne or Resident Ranger.

The kookaburra is the world's largest kingfisher. It lives on snakes, frogs, lizards, and young birds. When excited it gives its famous laugh; at dawn or dusk it joins with others in a laughing chorus.

Kinchega National Park 175,000 acres, 200 ft above sea level. This, one of Australia's youngest parks (1967), is a semi-arid grey-soil flood plain crossed by red sand ridges; it was once a sheep station. Within the area are the controlled lakes of Menindee and Cawndilla, which flood widely in wet years, thus providing pasture for, among other animals, red and grey kangaroos and emus. When the lakes are flooded they

271

provide a home to a wide variety of ducks and swans as well as pelicans and silver gull.

☝ Waterbirds in lake system; kangaroos, emus.

🕊 Open country with stunted scrub and grass, mulga, saltbush, and bluebush.

🛏 A number of camp-sites are being developed near the lakes and the Darling river, which runs through the park. Rates at Albermarle Hotel, Menindee, from A$4.80 single.

🚩 Menindee, the nearest town is 2 miles away. It lies on major road and rail routes between Sydney and Adelaide. The park is 405 miles from Adelaide via Broken Hill, 480 miles from Melbourne, and 739 miles from Sydney.

🚗 A network of unsurfaced tracks runs within the park; visitors should consult the resident ranger to plan the day's itinerary. 4-wheel-drive vehicles are essential in wet conditions.

☼ Open all year; best time August to November.

🕐 2 days.

🎫 Free.

🏠 Ranger in park at old homestead.

⇨ National Parks and Wildlife Service, 189 Kent Street, Sydney.

Parra Wirra National Park 3,127 acres, 1,000 ft above sea level.

☝ Grey kangaroo, euros, abundant birdlife.

🕊 All eucalypts (box stringybarks).

🚩 Due east of Elizabeth, 25 miles from Adelaide in Mount Lofty Ranges.

🎫 Free.

⇨ National Parks Commission, Belair.

Lincoln National Park 35,521 acres, sea level to 800 ft. Navigator Matthew Flinders charted the coastline along this point and lost a small boat near Thistle Island. Rough scrubby country with spectacular coastal cliffs.

☝ Scrub kangaroo, emu, white-breasted sea eagle, osprey, Mallee fowl, whipbird.

🕊 Sand dune vegetation and mallee scrub.

🛏 None in reserve. Hotels and motels in Port Lincoln. Rates from A$5.50 single.

🚩 8 miles south of Port Lincoln.

🚗 1–5-mile track through to Wauna Bay and Memory Cove. Rough going.

☼ Open all year; best time September to March.

🕐 1 day.

🎫 Free.

⇨ National Parks Commission, Belair, SA.

Wyperfeld National Park 139,800 acres, 300 ft above sea level. The park is located around some of the terminal lake-beds (dry) of the Wimmera river in northwest Victoria; it consists largely of Mallee scrub.

☝ Mallee fowl, kangaroo, reptiles, emus, parrots and cockatoos.

🕊 Eucalypts (red gum along creek courses, black box, mallee gum), Murray pine, beloh.

🛏 Camping (free) only within the park at Wonga Hut (lava-

272

tories, ablution block). Hotels in Hopetoun and Rainbow.

✈ By road 36 miles from Hopetoun, which has rail links with Melbourne (250 miles) and road links with Adelaide and Melbourne. Rainbow is 30 miles away.

🚗 By car on 2-wheel tracks, and on foot. (Car access is limited by sand ridges but it is usually sufficient.)

☀ Open all year; best time July to November.

🕐 2 days.

🎫 Free.

☞ The ranger is a local farmer who works part-time but who is most helpful.

⇨ National Parks Authority, Melbourne.

From Alice Springs

Ayers Rock/Mount Olga National Park 487 square miles, 2,520 ft above sea level. Ayers Rock is the largest stone monolith in the world. In the midst of thousands of square miles of flat sand plains it rears its great sandstone bulk upward 1,140 ft; its circumference measures 6½ miles. Near by are the 61 weird domes of Mt Olga. Together they create one of the most bizarre landscapes in the whole Pacific area. The park is one of Australia's major attractions. Over 25,000 people visit it each year.

🐾 Kangaroo, euro, parrots, dingo, snakes, lizards.

🌿 Mostly semi-desert vegetation including such drought-resistant plants as mulga, desert oak and many species of grevillia. Also large tracts of spinifex grass.

🛏 Five commercial lodges around Ayers Rock offer accommodation to 200 people; all-in double rates from A\$23 per day. No accommodation at Mt Olga (17 miles away).

✈ Connellan Airways run regular daily services from Alice Springs to the foot of the rock. The road runs about 300 miles from Alice through a number of outback cattle stations. There are a number of 1-, 2- and 4-day tours from Alice, from A\$42 including air travel.

🚗 On foot around Ayers Rock for caves, or by coach tour to Mt Olga. Visitors may climb Ayers Rock up a specified trail.

☀ Open all year; best time April to September.

🕐 1–4 days.

🎫 A\$1.00.

☞ Each chalet has a local guide.

👁 The caves in Ayers Rock have been sacred native grounds for centuries; they are particularly rich in aboriginal decoration.

⇨ Northern Territory Tourist Bureau, Alice Springs.

Tanami Desert Sanctuary 14,490 square miles, 1,750 to 2,000 ft above sea level. This huge sanctuary is about 350 miles northwest of Alice Springs by air. There *is* road access, but because of the aridity of the region only well-equipped and experienced people should even consider making it overland. (The Northern Territory Tourist Guide has several pages of advice and rules for people who want to travel in these remote regions.) Over such a large area there is naturally a great variety in topography. Basically the area is sand plain with dunes. It is traversed by semimountain ranges and here and there you will see 'flood-out' areas (old marsh beds, lakes, and so on). In some areas there are large groups of termite mounds. Vegetation is mainly spinifex with occasional patches of desert timber such as mulga.

🐾 Echidna, fat-tailed marsupial rat and mouse, mulgara, red kangaroo, euro (wallaroo), desert mouse, fox, feral cat, rabbit, leggadina, hopping mice, dingo, wallaby, rabbit-eared bandicoot; geckos (6 species), lizards (2), skinks (7), dragons (3), monitors (6), desert blue tongue, mulga snake, collared brown snake, red-naped snake; emu, bustard, princess parrot, painted finch, flock pigeon, brown hawk, little quail, wrens (2), brown thornbill, crimson chat, little shrike thrush, honeyeaters (2), wood swallows (2). (Bird and mammal census incomplete.)

🏠 Mr and Mrs Bruce Farrand operate a road house south of Tanami Bore. They serve meals and drinks and may, by the time this is published provide accommodation.

🚏 By road from Alice Springs (350 miles; gravel). From April to September Ansett/ANA coaches between Alice Springs and Darwin run through Tanami.

🚌 None.

☀️ Open year round; best time May to October.

🕐 2–3 days.

🎟️ Free.

🔜 Animal Industry Branch, NT Administration, Darwin.

From Brisbane

Lamington National Park 48,870 acres, 800 to 3,806 ft above sea level. Lamington is the best known of all Queensland's national parks. It is an area of mountain peaks and escarpments, scored by deep and winding river gorges. At the border with NSW it forms a 3,000-ft plateau.

🐾 Mammals are not conspicuous – koalas are rare, wallabies uncommon, and most of the others (possums, sugar glider, bandicoots, and rodents) are nocturnal. Platypus and echidna are also rare. The main interest for visitors lies in the number and variety of birds: Albert lyrebird, rufous scrub bird (both unique to the area, which is now their most important undisturbed habitat), brush turkey, satin and regen bowerbirds, currawong, whipbird, catbird, blue wren, finches, and many mountain parrots.

🌿 Mostly rainforest – giant trees, vines, ferns, and orchids. Among the most notable: antarctic beech (whose branches support clumps of staghorn, crow's nest, and elkhorn ferns as well as orchids), shyer beech, king orchids (when they flower in October people drive over 100 miles to see them), pencil orchids, and *Dendrobium kingianum* (which make a coral-coloured fringe at cliff edges).

🏠 Binna Burra Lodge (eastern end); rates from A $5.50 daily or A $35 weekly, full board. O'Reillys Guest House (western end); rates from A $4.70 daily or A $30.80 weekly, full board – both are simple, clean, and unpretentious.

🚏 By car from Brisbane via Pacific Highway, Gaven Way, Nerang. Beechmont to Binna Burra entrance (70 miles); Brisbane via Mt Lindsay Highway, Tamborine Village, Canungra, and Beechmont to Binna Burra entrance (65 miles); also from Canungra to O'Reillys entrance (75 miles).

Brisbane coaches run to Binna Burra (Wed, Fri, Sun; A $4.90 return) and to O'Reillys (Tue, Thur, Fri, Sun; A $4.30 return) for a day trip.

🚐 Some ninety two miles of footpath have been built through the park; picnic sites are well marked and stone firesites provided; detours to waterfalls, of which the park has about 500, lookouts, and other features are all marked. Since the two guest houses are at opposite ends of the park, a popular walk (for the energetic) is from one to the other, then back the next day after an overnight stop.

☀ Open all year; best time May to November.

🕐 2–5 days.

📧 Free.

⇨ Department of Forestry, 388 Ann Road, Brisbane.

Lone Pine Koala Sanctuary 20 acres. The sanctuary stands on the banks of the Brisbane river, 6 miles from the centre of Brisbane. Some 60 to 70 koalas are housed here in enclosures surrounded by a low concrete wall. Visitors may handle the animals under supervision, and lectures are given on the life cycle and habits of these marsupials. There are also enclosures of 3 to 4 acres housing kangaroos, emus and wallabies. Visitors may enter and mingle with the animals and feed them with corn obtainable at kiosk. You can go by city bus or by daily launch from Hayles wharf (depart 2 pm, return 5.30); fares for either route are 70c return; admission 40c extra. Several tours of the city include the sanctuary.

New England National Park 56,400 acres, 1,000 to 5,250 ft. The major national park of northern NSW. Much of it is still unexplored, so many of the biological communities are completely undisturbed. It stands in a huge basin on the northeastern escarpment of the New England plateau; most of it is forested. Towering over the region is the occasionally snow-covered Point Lookout (5,280 ft) below which are the headwaters of the Bellinger river and the tributaries of the upper Macleay and Nambucca rivers.

🦅 Grey kangaroos and several species of *macropods* (smaller members of kangaroo family), lyrebirds, scrub turkey, sub-tropical pigeons (census very incomplete).

🌿 Rainforest of giants such as caribben, bouyong and red cedar; also forests of antarctic beech, ferns, orchids and mosses. Alpine vegetation at higher altitudes.

🛏 A tourist chalet provides motel accommodation for up to six people; A $4 a day for first person plus 50c for each additional person or A $20 a week for first person plus A $2.50 for each additional person. The hiker's cabin provides minimum shelter for up to eight people at A $1 per person per night.

✈ From Sydney (500 miles) turn east off New England Highway at Armidale. Drive of 50 miles leads directly to Point Lookout. On Pacific Highway, turn west at Kempsey.

🚐 By car. Many walking tracks at key points of interest, such as waterfalls.

☀ Fog frequently spoils visits; it is least likely in April to May –

though the climate then is very cold. It is warmer in early spring – but that is when fogs are most likely!

🕐 Minimum 1 day; maximum unknown since much of the park is also unknown.

✉ Free.

☞ Resident rangers will assist visitors.

⇨ Mr P. A. Wright, 'Lana', Uralla, NSW.

Tamborine Mountain National Parks A group of seven national parks, none more than a mile square, grouped closely together on Tamborine Mountain, 1,807 ft above sea level. All are well set out for the visitor, looking more like large landscaped forests than truly wild areas; in fact, roads, walks, and picnic grounds apart, each preserves the virgin landscape. All are notable for their birdlife: lyrebirds, brush turkeys, whipbirds, pigeons, and parrots. Tamborine Mountain is 45 miles south of Brisbane and 20 miles in from the Gold Coast; sealed highway all the way. In clockwise sequence from the north the parks are:

Cedar Creek (412 acres) A picnic area arranged around a spectacular three-section waterfall.

MacDonald Park (30 acres) A mile-long circular walk through rainforest of mixed jungle and hardwood species; picnic area, tables, fireplace, and rainwater tank.

Palm Grove (288 acres) Large piccabeen palm groves mixed with rainforest trees including immense black bean and yellow carbeen, which has interesting buttressed trunks. Picnic area near entrance gates. The grove has the most extensive network of paths, some of which give views to the Pacific coast.

Macrozamia Grove (18 acres) An extensive grove of cycads (*Lepidozamia peroffskyana*, formerly known as *Macrozamia denisonii* – hence the name). At the southern end there is an unusual group of brush cypress.

Witches Falls (324 acres) The cascade falls from a jungle clad ledge down a steep forested hillside; it is, however difficult to view. Between the trees you can see tree ferns, rock gardens, and weirdly shaped fig trees.

Henderson's Knob (198 acres) Open eucalypt forest mixed with dense rainforest and palms around a boulder-strewn creek. Numerous cascades and waterfalls. The two best views from Tamborine Mountain.

Joala (89 acres) Dense rainforest in the centre of Tamborine Mountain. Notable for its arboreal vegetation, which includes elkhorn and staghorn ferns and tree orchids.

Tucki Nature Reserve Anybody who drives down the Princes Highway from Brisbane and who has the interests of wildlife at heart should turn off at Woodburn (140 miles south of Brisbane; 494 miles north of Sydney) and take the road toward Lismore. Some 12 miles along this detour he will reach the twin communities of Tuckurimba and Tucki. These two communities have the rare distinction of having created their own reserve entirely out of local voluntary help and resources. In 1958, when the last virgin eucalypt plantation was dying – and the koalas with it – they established a small food-tree plantation. As it turned out, they were in the nick of time and the koalas were saved from extinction. The plantation has since been extended to 8 acres and many nearby landowners have also planted food trees on their lands. The reserve is a heartwarming sight and a good omen for the future of Australian wildlife.

From Cairns

Atherton Tablelands A number of national parks are dotted throughout the Atherton tablelands, which rise over 2,000 ft in a great escarpment from the coastal plains south of Cairns. The nearest to the coast is Bellenden-Ker, 4 miles inland from Innisfail. In towering, mountainous country it includes Bartle Frere (5,275 ft) the highest peak in Queensland. The remainder are in the rolling open country of the tableland itself. Though the climate is tropical, the altitude makes for cool summer nights and mild winter days. The soil is a volcanic red and extremely fertile. The parks in the tableland are among the most scenically attractive in Australia.

    Striped possum (shy nocturnal), Herbert river ring-tailed possum (nocturnal, found only in rainforest), lemur-like possum (rainforest), green possum (one of the world's few green animals), Lumholtz's tree kangaroo (nocturnal, agile treetop jumpers), cassowary, golden bowerbird, wampoo pigeon, brush turkey (hatches eggs in rotting mounds), king parrot, red-sided parrot, white cockatoo.

    Tropical rainforests, wild orchids, vines and creepers.

    In the north: Mareeba (3 licensed hotels; rates from A $3.65 bed and breakfast to A $8.60 full board); in the south: Ravenshoe (1 hotel; rates from A $3.25 to A $5.95); in the centre: Atherton (4 hotels/motels), Tolga (1 caravan park from A $1.50), Tinaroo (1 motel), Lake Barrine (lodge and motel), Yungaburra (hotel/motel), and Malanda (hotel and motel) – rates between A $2.50 and A $8.60.

    Atherton is 62 miles from Cairns by surfaced road.

    Over 100 miles of surfaced road traverse the tableland; there are also many constructed walks.

    Open all year; coolest months April to September.

    Day tour from Cairns or 3–7 days.

    Free.

    All the major tours of N Queensland include the tableland; all-in rates for 4 days range between A $50 (shared accommodation) to A $63.

    Department of Forests, State Offices, Brisbane; or Queensland Government Tourist Bureau, Brisbane.

Green Island A 30 acre coral atoll, 18 miles northeast from Cairns; part of the Great Barrier Reef. About 17 acres are undeveloped, the remainder holding the guest house, aquarium, underwater observatory, and film theatre. An hour's stroll will take you right around the island. The foreshore is white coral sand but the island has a dense emerald canopy of damson, calophyllum, casuarina, white cedar, and pandanus; coconut palms tower above this canopy, which averages only 50 ft in height. The surrounding reef is exposed for about a mile at low tide, when you can inspect the living coral at close quarters. (Be warned, however: tides and weather can often lead to short-notice cancellation of trips to the reefs.) There are no guides for these trips; a preliminary visit to the underwater observatory and the film theatre will partly compensate for this lack.

A school of free-living mangrove jacks as seen through the observation window of the Underwater Observatory, Green Island.

- The Coral Cay Hotel has accommodation for eighty-six guests in single, twin, and family units at rates from A $6.50 a day. Standards are closer to those of a provincial boarding house than to an international hotel. Visitors seeking such standards should stay at the Great Northern Hotel, the Tradewinds Hotel, or the Lyons Motel in Cairns.
- Daily launch leaves Cairns 9am (returns 3.30pm); fare A $1.30. Extra launches run in the midwinter tourist season.
- 1 day.
- Underwater observatory 40c; marineland aquarium 40c; film theatre 40c; glass-bottom boats 30c.
- Queensland Government Tourist Bureau, Brisbane.

From Cairns or Townsville

Dunk Island National Park 3 miles long, 2 miles wide, about 13 miles in circumference; ranges from sea level to the peak of Mt Koo-tal-oo, 890 ft; other mountain peaks are Tah-loo (790 ft) and Gill-gill (620 ft). Dunk (its aboriginal name is Coonanglebah) is covered with thick tropical rainforest. The coastline is indented with secluded beaches in a jungle setting.

⫯ Small marsupials, reptiles (mostly lizards). Reef herons and Torres Straits pigeons. Insects include bright golden butterflies. Exotic marine life to be found on coral reef.

ꞵ Dense tropical rainforest with palm-fringed beaches. Native flowers include hibiscus and frangipani.

⇌ There is an hotel on the only freehold land on the island (the rest is National Park). Sixty-five beds; twenty-seven in suites for two persons, the rest singles; all with private amenities. There is a licensed restaurant. Rates: A $18 per day single, A $26 double, inclusive of meals.

⇥ By light aircraft from Cairns or Townsville (about 35 minutes). Fare A $14 single. Dunk has an all-weather airstrip.

⊑ No motor transport. Walking tracks are well defined and marked.

☼ Open all year. Best time: April to December.

⊘ 3–5 days.

⊠ Free.

☞ Hotel staff direct visitors to the best points of interest.

⇒ Forestry Department, Brisbane; Avis Rent-A-Car, 214 William Street, Sydney.

From Canberra

Kosciusko National Park 1,314,00 acres, 700 to 7,314 ft above sea level. This huge park, greater than all the other NSW reserves put together, is an area of winter snowfields, mountain ranges, forests, alpine meadows, and swamp plains. It is a roughly 25-mile-wide strip of land running north from the Victoria border to about 30 miles southwest of Canberra. The wide range of altitude and rock type gives a diversity of habitats, including unique alpine areas and extensive snow-gum forests carpeted with snowgrass. The Snowy, the Murray, and the Murrambidgee rivers all rise in these ranges.

⫯ Thirty species of mammal include grey forester kangaroo, brush-tailed rock wallaby, wombat, possum, spiny anteater, and platypus; koalas (now rare) are being encouraged; among 150 bird species are red and sooty gang-gang cockatoo, lyrebird, and emu.

⇌ Camping and caravan facilities within the park. Nearby hotel/motel accommodation averages A $9.00 a day or A $64.00 a week full board. There are also commercial lodges around A $10.00 a day or A $67.00 a week full board.

⇥ The northernmost part of the park, near Brindabella, is only 30 miles from Canberra. But the majority of the park is accessible only from Cooma, 60 miles from Canberra and about 300 from Sydney; or from Khancoban on the Murray river side. Cooma is also the main railhead.

🚗 Car (on highways), 4-wheel-drive (on tracks), footpaths. Special regulations apply to winter travel within the park.

☀ Open all year; for wildlife the best time is from December to early March; peak wildflower time January; skiing season June to October.

⏰ 7–14 days.

🎫 A $1, at main entrance near Jindabyne.

📕 A number of books on the park are available at the Visitors Centre, Sawpit Creek.

🚩 There are guided tours in the south of the park during the December to January school holidays.

➔ The Secretary, Kosciusko National Park Trust, 70 Pitt Street, Sydney.

Pulletop Nature Reserve 358 acres, 720 ft above sea level. This small reserve is devoted exclusively to the conservation of the mallee fowl, which needs dense undergrowth scrub or complete tree canopy, a light sandy soil, and an abundance of acacia shrubs – whose seeds are its principal diet. This is one of the last areas of virgin scrub in NSW; grazing, chiefly by sheep, has drastically altered the habitat elsewhere. Here the mallee fowl and their curious mound-like nests can be seen with little trouble. A visit to the reserve is best combined with visits to the Cocopara and Round Hill reserves near by. The area is some 193 miles from Canberra. The following information applies to all three reserves.

🐦 Mallee fowl, and other small birds.

🌳 Mallee scrub; low, stunted trees.

🏨 Hotels and motels at Griffith and Rankins Springs.

🚆 From Sydney via Bathurst and West Wyalong to Rankins Springs (357 miles from Sydney). Rail to Rankins Springs A $12.22; to Griffiths A $12.22.

🚗 Road from Rankins Springs south to Griffiths (32 miles) runs through reserve.

☀ Open year round; best time August to December.

⏰ 1–2 days.

🎫 Free.

➔ National Parks and Wildlife Service, Sydney.

Tidbinbilla Fauna Reserve 11,500 acres, 2,500 to 5,000 ft above sea level. This horseshoe-shaped reserve is surrounded on three sides by the Tidbinbilla range of mountains. Part of the central valley was cleared in early settlement but over 8,000 acres are still virgin forest. The mountains are occasionally snow-topped in winter.

🐦 Possums (greater glider, ring-tailed, bush-tailed, sugar glider, pygmy glider), kangaroos (grey, swamp wallaby, red-necked wallaby), marsupial mice, tiger cat, common wombat, spiny anteater, koala (very rare), rats, bats, lyrebirds, brush bronze-wing, wonda pigeon, yellow-tailed black cockatoo, gang-gang cockatoo.

🌳 Forest trees in approximate sequence from valley floor to mountain top: candlebark, broad-leaved peppermint, apple box, narrow-leaved eucalypt, ribbon gum, mountain gum, cut-tail eucalypt, alpine ash, snow gum – all of these being various species of *Eucalyptus*.

None in park (Canberra being only 30 miles away). There are picnic facilities within the reserve.

By surfaced road along an attractive route from Canberra.

Walking trails have been constructed through the forest.

Open and interesting at all times of the year.

Day or half-day tour.

Free.

Lands Branch, Department of the Interior, Civic Offices, Canberra City, ACT.

From Darwin

Cobourg Peninsula Reserve 790 square miles, at or near sea level. This reserve, accessible only by sea or air, is more for the scientist and naturalist than for the more casual tourist (who can see the same kind of wildlife and vegetation in more accessible places in West Arnhem Land). Most of the peninsula is open forest interspersed with black soil plains and paperbark swamps. There are small areas of tropical rainforest; the southern coast of the peninsula has some mangrove swamp edges. Apart from the native fauna listed below there are wild herds of banteng cattle, Timor ponies, and deer.

Little northern native cat, fawn marsupial mouse, large northern bandicoot, brush-tailed possum, antilopine wallaroo, agile wallaby, and 9 bat species (all native); brush-tailed rabbit-rat, shaggy rabbit-rat, tunney's rat, fawn-footed melomya, delicate mouse, dingo, buffalo (all introduced); marine turtles (5 species), tortoise, estuarine crocodile,· gecko (6 species), skinks (6 species), lizards, monitors, snakes (18 species, most of them harmless to man). Species lists record 118 bird species including: herons, egrets, geese, ducks, ibises, eagles, falcons, osprey, kestrel, hawks, owls, kingfishers, treecreepers, honeyeaters, finches, orioles, quail, oystercatcher, sandpiper, curlews, tern, pigeons, doves, lorikeets, cockatoos, warblers, flycatchers, bowerbird.

Notable for every type of Northern Territory vegetation except desert. Sand plains to rainforest, mangroves, pandanus, tall eucalypts.

Limited to permit-holders (scientists, naturalists, students, etc) who stay with ranger by invitation.

By air, 125 miles from Darwin; charter flights. *By sea* from Darwin; sailings every two weeks; trip takes 18 hours.

The tracks in the reserve are open only to ranger's 4-wheel-drive vehicle.

May to October.

Animal Industry Branch, Northern Territory Administration, Darwin.

Fogg Dam Protected Area 18,480 acres, 50 ft above sea level. Fogg Dam was built to provide water for and to attract waterbirds away from the nearby Humpty Doo rice project. Over the years it has become a favourite breeding ground and congregating centre for many species of waterbirds. It is very popular with local birdwatchers. To get to it from Darwin you drive 21 miles down the all-weather Stuart Highway, then turn off for Humpty Doo; 18 miles along this road (which is also bitumen surfaced), just past the CSIRO headquarters, you turn left to Harrison Road; the sanctuary is half a mile up this road. Fogg Dam is an easy day trip from Darwin.

Holmes Jungle Protected Area 189 acres, 50 ft above sea level. The jungle is a virgin tropical rainforest traversed by a spring fed stream. It is rich in waterbirds: waders, herons, cranes, ducks, and coots. Animals include native rats, bandicoots, lizards, and snakes. Flora consists of tropical rainforest, with paperbarks and pandanus palms.

Katherine Gorge National Park 56,069 acres, 500 to 700 ft above sea level. Katherine Gorge is a new national park, still being developed. It centres on a rugged gorge in the Arnhem Land Escarpment, 219 miles down the Stuart Highway from Darwin. Katherine, the nearest airport, is 20 miles from the gorge.

- Black rock wallaby. Riverbirds, honeyeaters, fish, reptiles.
- Typical Northern Territory vegetation (eg pandanus, paperbark, eucalypt).
- Katherine Motel. A $12.00 single.
- By car or regular coach tour.
- May to October.
- 1–2 days.
- 10c.
- Animal Industry Branch, Northern Territory Administration, Darwin.

Knuckeys Lagoon Protected Area 294 acres, 100 ft above sea level. Knuckeys 'lagoon' is, in fact, a series of semi-permanent lagoons in the plains about 10 miles south of Darwin. The tracks that lead among them are passable to cars only during the dry season (May to Oct). At other times of the year you have to walk a couple of miles from the Stuart Highway. The best time for visiting is during the dry season, when the water lilies are in flower. At that time the lagoons support thousands of magpie geese as well as brolgas, royal spoonbills, and occasional pairs of jabiru storks. To reach the lagoons go down the Stuart Highway, over the Berrimah crossing, and take the next left turn; the lagoons lie half a mile along the second vehicle track to the right of this side road.

Patonga and Muirella These are two neighbouring commercial lodges in Australia's only government-controlled safari area; hunting is permitted only for the conservation of game and the control of other species. The area is policed by game wardens. The lodges also offer photographic and scenic safaris, which are growing in popularity. Patonga lies on the southern border of Arnhem Land, a region of wide plains and bush dotted with billabongs, paperbark swamps, and mangroves, and broken here and there with richly-coloured rock escarpments.

⚐   Buffalo, dingo, wallabies and other marsupials, crocodile, pig, geese, duck, pigeon, and other northern waterbirds. Many species are subject to strict protection, and shooting is permitted only under local guidance.

⊨   The lodges are colonial style log dwellings with two-bed cubicles, electric light, refrigeration, showers, and septic WCs. Camp-out safaris are only slightly rougher. All-inclusive lodge charge is A $12 per person per day or A $84 per week. Photographic safaris are A $140 per week; hunting safaris (including guide) are A $210 a week.

⇻   Mainly by air. A day air trip leaves Darwin at 9.30am and returns at 6.30pm; A $40 a head for a group of five. The return flight passes low over plains, swamps, and forested savannah teeming with water buffalo and wild geese. Some Darwin tours run to Patonga. Reached by road via Pine Creek from Darwin.

🚚   Only by 4-wheel-drive vehicles, available at the lodge.

☀   Open all year; the wet season lasts January to May, when local transport is severely limited; best time for birdwatching July to September.

🕐   1–14 days.

⇨   Northern Territory Tourist Bureau, Darwin.

Woolwonga Sanctuary 162 square miles, 125 ft above sea level. Woolwonga is the most popular wildlife area in NT; many operators run tours through a section of it. This section includes Goose Camp and Dreaming Waters. Goose Camp is a 5-mile chain of billabongs so thick with burdekin duck, pygmy geese, and magpie geese that it sometimes appears to be one continuous speckled carpet. Dreaming Waters lie at the eastern end of a long chain of lovely clear-water billabongs fringed by pandanus palms; near by, just outside the sanctuary, are aboriginal rock paintings and the burial grounds that give the area its name. The fauna of the sanctuary is similar to that in the Cobourg peninsula, with a greater accent on waterbirds.

⊨   Under-canvas accommodation with communal showers and lavatories for forty guests at Nourlangie; boats available. Cost from A $10 a day.

⇻   Nourlangie is 180 miles by road and water (all but 50 miles being dirt roads); during the December to March rains it is inaccessible by land. Charter aircraft can reach it all year round.

🚚   4-wheel-drive tracks.

☀   May to October.

🕐   2–3 days.

🏴   Free permit from Chief Inspector of Wildlife, Darwin.

☞   Mr Alan Stewart, Nourlangie Safari Camp.

⇨   Animal Industry Branch, Northern Territory Administration, Darwin.

Yarrawonga Flora and Fauna Park 5 acres, 100 ft above sea level. Yarrawonga is rather more contrived than the sanctuaries and protected areas of NT; the animals there are all in captivity; they include buffalo, emu, wallabies, kangaroos, brolgas, dingoes, and (huge) crocodile; there is also a well laid out tropical garden. Admission is 35c. The park is 15 miles down the Stuart Highway from Darwin.

The Australian crane, also known as the brolga or native companion, is the continent's only true crane. It is found in plains and swamps throughout Australia – except in the southwest – and in parts of New Guinea. In the mating season brolgas live in pairs. At other times they congregate in large flocks, in which they are famous for their perfectly timed group-dancing displays (some movements of which have been incorporated into aboriginal corroborees, or dances). Its walk is dignified and it flies with graceful ease. Its trumpeting call can be heard for miles. It eats insects, fish, and some herbage.

From Gladstone

Heron Island Half a mile long, 300 yards wide, Heron Island is one of the most naturally beautiful resorts off the eastern coast. It is a true coral cay of long standing – as its well established trees testify. The centre of the island is a jungle of brittle pisonia trees, which rise up to 60 ft. Around them is a belt of casuarinas and tournefortias. Pandanus is also common. Other plant life includes wild poinsettias and grasses. Throughout the island there are extensive burrows made by mutton birds (wedge-tailed shearwaters) who almost take over the place in October. The pisonias offer good nesting sites for white-breasted sea eagles. Other birds include cormorants, sea curlews, sandpipers, oysterbirds, terns, various gulls – and, of course, herons. The reef is unevenly developed: a mile or less to the west and southwest, 5 to 6 miles on the east. The most beautiful part lies directly out from the settlement, towards the northeast – but even in this small area the fauna can vary widely from point to point. Between Oct–Apr thousands of giant and green turtles come ashore to lay their eggs. Nearby reefs and islands worth visiting are: *Wistari Reef* (prolific and luxuriant growth); *One Tree Island* (the lagoon, with abundant mushroom coral, has some of the most spectacular formations anywhere along the reef); *North West Island* (a good fringe reef); *Tryon Island* (a good example of how cyclones can kill a reef – only the fringes are alive); *Wilson Island* (reef near the end of its natural development – many molluscs, annulates, and echinoderms among its dead coral masses).

- ⇌ Twin, double, 3- or 6-bed units from A\$3.50 per person per day. Fresh water is scarce and is turned on for washing or showering only twice a week – the rest of the time you wash in salt water with special soap. (*Note* Heron Island is not for the elderly nor for those who put comfort at the top of the list.)
- ⇨ Twelve-passenger helicopter service from Gladstone, Mon, Tues, Sat; A\$36 return. Launch service Sats from Gladstone; return fare A\$8.60. The journey can be rough and the transfer to a small boat when going in over the reef can be tricky (and wet).
- ☼ April to November.
- ⏲ 3–7 days.
- ⇨ Queensland Government Tourist Bureau, Brisbane.

From Hobart

Cradle Mountain/Lake Saint Clair National Park 336,000 acres, up to 5,000 ft above sea level. This is the largest of Tasmania's 58 sanctuaries and reserves. It is a well-forested mountainous area, rich in lakes. As with most areas in Tasmania, frequent bushfires have depleted the wildlife and the variety of vegetation.

↶ Opossum, wallabies, and pademelon are numerous in some parts and most of the native species are found in small numbers.

⊗ Mainly eucalypts, although tangled scrub in river valleys, with acacias and creepers. Conifers and alpine vegetation at higher altitudes.

⇦ Hikers huts only. No charge, but they must be left in good order.

⇨ From Devonport or Launceston via Sheffield to Waldheim Chalet for northern approach. From Hobart via New Norfolk to Derwent Bridge in south.

🚐 On foot. Roads at northern and southern ends only.

☀ Open year round; best time November to March.

🕐 1–5 days.

🖾 Free.

🖵 Ranger only.

⇨ Scenery Preservation Board, Davey Street, Hobart.

Mount Field National Park 40,000 acres, 500 to 4,721 ft above sea level. In general the landscape and fauna of Mt Field are similar to those in the Cradle Mountain Park. Variation in altitude affords wide variety of scenery and flora. Rugged mountainous country rich in waterfalls, mountain lakes and rushing streams.

↶ Kangaroo and wallaby on river plains; phalangers and marsupial mice in forested areas; wombats; prolific bird life.

⊗ Giant eucalypts, tree ferns, rich alpine vegetation at upper altitudes.

⇦ National Park Hotel. A $3.75 bed and breakfast.

⇨ By road from Hobart via Derwent Valley. Day tours every day during summer, less frequently at other times of year.

🚐 By road through park. Best scenery can be seen only along walking tracks.

☀ Open year round; best time November to March.

🕐 1–4 days.

🖾 Free.

🖵 Ranger only.

⇨ Mt Field National Park Board, Lands and Surveys Department, Davey Street, Hobart.

From Melbourne

Dowd's Morass State Game Reserve 2,000 acres, 20 to 30 ft above sea level. Like Sale Common, Dowd's Morass is part of the floodplain of the LaTrobe river; it stands at the junction of the river with the Gippsland lakes and is a major rookery for ibises, spoonbills, and egrets. Many of the birds that breed here feed at Sale Common each day.

↶ As for Sale Common.

⇦ As for Sale Common.

⇨ Ten miles from Sale Common; 4-wheel-drive essential in winter.

🚐 Vehicle to the boundaries of the reserve, then on foot.

☼ Open all year; best time September to May.

🕐 6–12 hours – can be combined with Sale Common visit.

⇨ As for Sale Common.

A mother wombat and her newborn offspring. Wombats, the most intelligent of marsupials, are related to koalas. They live in burrows.

Mallacoota Inlet National Park 11,200 acres at or near sea level. The park surrounds one of many large inlets with shoreline of 100 miles in east Gippsland, which is the easternmost part of Victoria. Fine sandy beaches, rugged cliffs.

↝ Wallaby, wombat, possum, native cat. Many varieties of wader and swamp birds, lyrebird, eagles, parrots, many song birds.

❀ Sub-tropical rainforest with many temperate species. Eucalypts, melalencas, acacias, kinzea.

🛏 The motel in Mallacoota charges from A \$4.50 a day.

✈ 334 miles east of Melbourne, 15 miles from the Princes Highway (turn off at Genoa).

🚗 Part accessible by car; parts only by boat.

☼ Open all year; best time December to April.

🕐 1 or 2 days.

✉ Free.

⇨ Secretary, National Parks Authority of Victoria, State Offices, Melbourne.

Phillip Island 1,300 acres of reserves around sea level. Phillip Island is one of Victoria's richest wildlife areas. It comprises a number of reserves, chief among them being Seal Rocks, Cape Woolamai, Penguin Parade, David Forrest Koala, and the Rhyll Sanctuary. It is famous for its penguin parade in which hundreds of penguins come in from the sea to feed their young and march along the beach to their burrows in the sand dunes.

Fairy penguins coming ashore at Phillip Island. Like all penguins the fairy is a powerful swimmer, as perfectly adapted to marine life as are seals and porpoises. Phillip Island is one of the world's best sites for seeing the evening parade of these endearing birds.

Fairy penguin, koala, Australian fur seal, short-tailed shearwater (or muttonbird), many varieties of seabird, ibis and other waterfowl.

There is excellent motel accommodation on the island, at Cowes and Newhaven. Most visitors are day trippers from Melbourne.

By road 70 miles from Melbourne; a bridge connects the island to the mainland. There are regular day tours by coach from Melbourne.

Most of the vantage points for viewing wildlife are accessible by car.

Open all year; most wildlife is more abundant in summer. Main season for viewing penguins is October to May, but they can be seen in lesser numbers all through the year.

1–1½ days. Since the penguin parade is in the evening it is advisable to take rugs and a flask of coffee – even in summer.

To penguin viewing enclosure: 20c.

Victoria Government Tourist Bureau, 272 Collins Street, Melbourne.

Sale Common Game Refuge 800 acres, 30 ft above sea level. This reserve is part of the floodplain of the lower LaTrobe river, the main river in Gippsland. Basically it is a feeding area for waterbirds; some of it is also a suitable breeding environment.

Wild duck, ibis, egret, spoonbill, black swan.

The reserve lies within the township of Sale, which has one hotel (A $6.00 double) and two motels (A $4.50–5.00).

125 miles from Melbourne on the Princes Highway.

By boat or on foot. Most of the reserve's perimeter is accessible by vehicle from outside.

Open all year; best time November to March.

⏱ 6–12 hours.

✉ Free.

⇨ Secretary, Fisheries and Wildlife Department, State Offices, Melbourne.

Sherbrooke Forest Park 2,000 acres, 1500 ft above sea level. The park lies in the Dandenong ranges, the closest mountain forest area to Melbourne. It is chiefly famous for its many lyrebirds and for the ease with which they may be seen; chief among them is the southern lyrebird.

🛏 In Melbourne.

🛫 25 road miles from Melbourne. Electric train to Belgrave (near lower end of park). On many scheduled coach tours.

🚗 On foot only; no vehicles within the park.

☀ Open all year; best time for lyrebirds May to June.

⏱ 6–12 hours.

✉ Free.

⇨ Victoria Government Tourist Bureau, 272 Collins Street, Melbourne.

Sir Colin McKenzie Sanctuary 430 acres, 600 ft above sea level. This small sanctuary stands on a tributary of the Yarra river, 40 miles from Melbourne. It is famous for its display of platypus and other Australian species, including kangaroos and wallabies, koala, reptiles, emu, cockatoos, parrots, lyrebirds, and many waterfowl.

🛏 Hotels in Healesville, 4 miles away, charge from A$5.00 double a day: motels from A$5.75.

🛫 By road 40 miles from Melbourne along the Maroondah Highway; a number of scheduled coach tours take in the sanctuary.

🚗 On foot – no cars allowed within the sanctuary.

☀ Open all year; best time September to April.

⏱ 1 day.

✉ 40c.

⇨ Victoria Government Tourist Bureau, 272 Collins Street, Melbourne.

Tower Hill State Game Reserve 1,600 acres, 200 ft above sea level. The reserve is in an ancient caldera – the remains of an extinct volcano (which may, in fact, have been the most recently active volcano in Victoria). It consists of a large lake and swamp, dotted with islands. From early records and paintings the area is being restored to its wild condition by controlling the water levels and re-establishing native plants. Waterbirds have returned to the area and as the habitat develops, birds and mammals of the forested islands are being re-introduced.

🐾 As yet no animals, but the waterbird population is increasing.

🌳 All destroyed by fire and clearing. Eucalypts, acacias, and casuarinas being replanted.

🛏 None in the reserve but at Warrnambool, 7 miles away, there are two hotels, A$4 to A$6.25 double, and six motels, A$4.50 to A$6.00.

🛫 By car 170 miles along the Prince's Highway, or by rail, from

289

Melbourne. The nearest airport, at Warrnambool, is served daily from Melbourne.

🚐 Most of the crater rim is accessible by road from outside the reserve; inside there is one loop road for vehicles. The main island has a natural history centre.

☀ Open all year; best time October to March.

🕐 6–12 hours.

▥ Free.

⇨ Fisheries and Wildlife Department of Victoria, State Offices, Melbourne.

From Perth

Cape Range National Park 33,171 acres, 500 to 1,500 ft above sea level. Not a well-developed park but containing many insects and animals of scientific interest. On the peninsula of land between Exmouth Gulf and the Indian Ocean. Rugged hilly country with stunted vegetation. Steep gullies with thick scrub and bush. Fast-flowing streams after rains.

🐾 Insects of many interesting varieties. Wallabies. Prolific birdlife.

🌿 Stunted eucalypts. Wildflowers in season.

🛏 None in park. Hotels at Exmouth (expensive).

� *By road* along North West Coastal Highway. Fork east at Mimilya Homestead then 145 miles north to Exmouth. *By air* to Learmonth from Perth A $47.00.

🚐 Four-wheel-drive vehicles only.

☀ Open May to September

🕐 1–2 days.

▥ Free.

📇 Rangers at Exmouth.

⇨ National Parks Board, Perth.

John Forrest National Park 3,646 acres, up to 700 ft above sea level. A popular park for day trips from Perth, 17 miles away. There are many marked walks through the bush, plentiful wildflower displays, picnic facilities, waterfalls, and natural swimming pool. Wildlife is not particularly common but you may see kangaroo and emu.

🌿 The commonest wildflowers are uschananltia and kangaroo paw.

� By road from Perth along Great Eastern Highway.

🚐 Scenic drives of about 4 miles through park.

☀ Open year round; best time September to March.

🕐 6–12 hours.

▥ Free.

⇨ National Parks Board, Murray Street, Perth.

Kalbarri National Park 358,000 acres, up to 400 ft above sea level. 400 miles north of Perth at the mouth of the Murchison river. Impressive limestone gorges rich in colour. Good vantage points are Hawks Head and Ross Graham lookouts.

🐾 Kangaroo, wallaby, and emu are common. Pelicans on the Murchison river. Swans.

⚘   Wildflowers of many different kinds.

⛺   Nearest is in Kalbarri township, which has a motel and accompanying park.

🚆   By road from Perth along the Northwest Coastal Highway past Geraldton and Northampton. Turn west at Ajana for 43 miles.

🚗   Four-wheel-drive vehicle or on foot. One main road only.

☼   Open year round; best time September to March. Wildflowers are spectacular in September and November.

🕐   1–2 days.

✉   Free.

📷   Resident ranger at Kalbarri.

⇨   National Parks Board, Perth.

Stirling Range National Park 269,155 acres, up to 3,640 ft above sea level. In rugged, mountainous country that is also thickly timbered. Excellent lookout points at Eden Peak (3,420 ft) and Bluff Knoll (3,640 ft).

🦘   Kangaroo, wallaby, wombat; emu; many species of birds.

⚘   Wildflowers; tall stands of eucalypt; karri forests.

⛺   None in park. Nearest is at Karri Ban (motel) and Albany. A $6.00. Camping not permitted.

🚆   Take Cranbrook road. Turn off 163 miles south of Perth on Albany Highway. From Albany take Chester Pass road 50 miles north. Air services to Albany A $17,00. Rail service A $11.65 1st Class single. Regular tours from Perth and Albany.

🚗   Two main roads through park.

☼   Open year round; best time October to March.

🕐   1–2 days.

✉   Free.

⇨   National Parks Board, 664 Murray Street, West Perth.

Walpole-Nornalup National Park 32,943 acres, 500 ft above sea level. More of a recreational and floral park than one devoted to wildlife conservation, Nornalup is in the heart of giant karri forest country; its southern border is the Indian Ocean. The karri tree is known as *Eucalyptus versicolor* since the undersides of its leaves are paler green than the upper surface. It is the largest tree in Western Australia, with branch-free trunks reaching 120 to 160 ft before splaying out into a 60-ft crown; their girths at waist height are 24 to 38 ft. Despite their size the leaf canopy they provide is thin, and plenty of sunlight streams through to support a rich undergrowth. On an early morning in later summer, when the sun picks out the pale tangerine of the new bark where it shows through the peeling brown of the older bark, the forest is at its best. In spring the wildflowers turn the more open spaces of the park into a vast herbaceous border.

🦘   As in all forests the wildlife is difficult to see, but you may be rewarded by a sight of kangaroos and wallabies.

⚘   Karri, jarrah, marri (red gum), casuarina (all trees), karri wattle, umbrella plants, crowea, tree kangaroo paws, bracken fern (all undergrowth), bottle brush (many varieties flower in succession), cowslip orchid, star of Bethlehem, *Burtonia scabra*, pink mulla mulla, Sturt's desert pea, scarlet feather-flower (among 7,000-odd species of wildflower and shrub).

⛵ Camping and caravan parking near to Coalmine beach on Nornalup Inlet; laundry, tea room, communal showers, and lavatories; rates from A $1. There is motel accommodation at Walpole, in the park.

✈ By all-sealed road from Perth, 264 miles via Donnybrook, Bridgetown, and Manjimup. The road passes through orchard and dairy country as well as jarrah and karri forests.
By air from Albany 70 miles east of Walpole (A $17 single). Regular tours from Perth take in the park.

🚐 Three surfaced roads – all scenic drives – run through the park.

☀ Open all year; the average rainfall is over 50 inches, most of it falling in October to March. Best time for wildflowers, spring; for forest scenery, late summer.

🕐 1–2 days.

📋 Free.

◎ You can take short trips to Circular Pool, Mt Frankland, The Monastery, Valley of the Giants, and the Petrified Forest – all nearby. The Porongorup National Park (not covered in this book) and the Stirling Range National Parks (see page 291) are a day trip away.

➪ Ranger at Coalmine Beach, or National Parks Board, 664 Murray Street, West Perth.

The spiny anteater, found throughout the continent, is, like the platypus, an egg-laying mammal. It lives on ants and termites.

Yanchep Park 7,000 acres, up to 100 ft above sea level. Yanchep caters for a variety of recreational tastes; conducted tours of caves; swimming, boating, and picnics; conducted wildflower walks in the springtime; golf, tennis, and team games. Within the park koalas, kangaroos, emu, black swan, and other birds are all housed in natural settings. Near by there are sea bathing and camping facilities. There are also a number of hotels and guest houses near the park.

↣ By all-weather road 32 miles north of Perth. Metro Tours tel: 23.4745 or 21.5295 operate tours to the park.

🚌 A short loop road runs around the central area; marked paths and trails lead through the rest of the park.

☀ Open all year; best time September to March.

🕐 1–2 days.

🎫 Free.

⇨ National Parks Board; WA Government Tourist Bureau, 772 Hay Street, Perth; or Superintendent, Yanchep Park, tel: 248.221

From Proserpine

Mandalay Coral Gardens For anyone interested in underwater life this is one of the outstanding attractions of the Barrier Reef area: a fascinating display of coral, collected from the Reef over a period of nine years by Mr and Mrs Basil Keong who are skilled skindivers. Mandalay stands in a tropical garden surrounded by jungle, which abounds in birdlife. The coral collection (over 250 varieties, some very rare, all restored to original colours) is housed in a room overlooking the waters of Whitsunday Passage. On the shore in front of the display-room a reef has been built, with a series of shallow pools into which live coral is transplanted. Concrete walks around the pools provide visitors with the opportunity of studying the coral in any weather, at any tide, and without leaving dry land.

🛏 Within 6 miles of Mandalay there are two modern motels and four caravan parks (two with all modern amenities).

↣ Mandalay is on Pioneer Bay, north of Shute Harbour. Nearest town (24 miles) is Proserpine, 819 miles north of Brisbane, between Mackay and Townsville on the Bruce Highway. To reach Mandalay: *by road* ¾ mile from Proserpine turn right on the sealed road to Shute Harbour; the road to the Gardens is on the left, 1¾ miles past Airlie Beach. *By sea* there is a once-weekly launch service from Shute Harbour to Mandalay; A$5 including lunch and morning afternoon tea.

☀ Best time May to November.

🎫 About 30c.

⇨ Queensland Government Tourist Bureau, Brisbane.

From Sydney

Barren Grounds Nature Reserve 4,390 acres between 1,000 and 2,180 ft above the sea, which is just over 5 miles away. Most of the reserve is undulating heathland plateau atop a circle of sheer sandstone cliffs; parts are swampy. At the cliff edges, on the ridges, and in the gullies are stands of open eucalypt forest and Mallee eucalypt. The surrounding valleys are fertile ancient lava flows, and it is this contrast that justifies the word 'barren'. Right around the edge of the plateau you get superb views of the surrounding country –

particularly of the Illawarra coast to the east and of the Minnamurra valley to the north.

🐦 Swamp parrot, ground parrot, eastern bristle bird, swamp wallaby, lyrebirds.

🛏 Two motels in Kiama. From A $5 single.

🛬 By road 20 miles from Kiama via Jamberoo; Jamberoo is 74 miles south along the Princes Highway from Sydney.

🚐 About 13 miles of open foot trails run through the reserve.

☼ Open year round; best time September to March.

🕐 1 day.

🎫 Free.

⇨ National Parks and Wild Life Service, 189 Kent Street, Sydney.

Blue Mountains National Park 230,000 acres, 2,000 to 3,500 ft above sea level. The chief feature of this park is the deeply-eroded valley of the Grose river, which, with many of its tributaries, runs west-east across the northern section. The Grose river gorge itself cuts a broad 3,000-ft-deep valley through coloured sandstones, shale, and coal seams; it is accessible only on foot.

🐦 Platypus (in the rivers), brush-tailed wallaby, grey forester kangaroo, possums (including phalanger), numerous birds including honeyeaters, lyre birds, and waratahs.

🌿 The fertile valleys support forests of blue gum and turpentine as well as treeferns, maidenhair, bracken, wattle, and mint.

🛏 None in park but many nearby townships (chief being Katoomba) have hotels, motels, and boarding houses.

🛬 The park is 50 miles (2-hour drive) west of Sydney along the Western Highway. The Windsor–Bell road runs through the far north of the park; at Bilpin it splits into two – the direct route through Mt Tomah and a more scenic drive via Mt Wilson. Dead-end spurs off the Western Highway penetrate a little way into the west of the park: at Leura for Mt Hay, at Blackheath for the blue-gum forest near Mt Banks, and at Mt Victoria for the Victoria Falls.

🚐 Apart from the roads mentioned above the rest of the park is accessible only on foot, except for an access road between Woodford and Glenbrook in the southern half of the park.

☼ Open all year; best time in summer.

🕐 3–4 days.

🎫 Free.

⇨ The Secretary, Blue Mts National Parks Trust, Council Chambers, Katoomba.

Ku-ring-gai Chase National Park 35,300 acres, overlooking the sea at Broken Bay about 35 miles north of Sydney.

🐦 Kangaroos and koalas can be seen in enclosures in the centre of the park. Birds include parrots, honeyeaters, kookaburras and native songbirds.

🌿 Many species of wildflowers in spring. Mainly eucalypts of different species, including scribbly gums, water gums, red gums. Acacias and banksias also prolific.

Koalas (the name means 'no drink', for they never drink) feed only on leaves of a certain species of eucalypt. Epidemics and slaughter led to local extinction throughout most of their once-vast range. Now they are found only in Victoria, NSW, and parts of Queensland.

Cabins and camping only. There are eight cabins at The Basin (accessible by ferry from Palm Beach) rates between A $2.50 and A $13.50, depending on cabin and season. Camping in tents at the basin and tents or caravans at Akuna Bay and Illawong Bay: 60c a day or A $3 a week. Also hotels and motels in nearby towns.

By surfaced road from Sydney.

By car and boat.

Open all year; spring months for wildflowers, many of which bloom right into summer; spring and summer months for the animals; the koala sanctuary within the Chase provides a year-round display.

1–7 days.

20c per car.

A large selection of free brochures, including advice on boat hire and motels in the area, at entrances or from National Parks and Wildlife Service of NSW.

☞ Parties of 25–30 are guided free by park rangers.

◉ Immediately north of the park, at Gosford in Broken Bay, is the 14-acre Australian Reptile Park, the creation of author-naturalist Eric Worrell. Here you can see almost every variety of Australian snake and reptile. See page 297.

⇨ The Superintendent, Ku-ring-gai Chase, Bobbin Head Road, Turramurra 2074.

Sir Edward Hallstrom Faunal Reserve 1,986 acres, 200 ft above sea level. The Hallstrom exists mainly to re-establish koalas in this part of NSW. It was established in 1959, thanks to a generous donation from Sir Edward Hallstrom, to breed koalas under simulated natural conditions. The site was chosen because it is within easy reach of Sydney and the Fauna Panel's headquarters; it is also well watered. It consists of a ranger's hut and a fenced-off, 6-acre breeding plantation. There is a fire track along which visitors can walk. Day visitors from Sydney (there is no overnight accommodation) should arrange the visit in advance with the Ranger, c/o Post Office, Cowan, or telephone 610.1246. The drive from Sydney takes about one hour.

Warrumbungle National Park 15,400 acres, 1,500 to 4,000 ft above sea level. The park centres around a series of turretlike peaks and mesas, remnants of ancient volcanoes (now extinct). Toward the end of their lives these volcanoes extruded stiff plastic rock vertically upwards. Millions of years of weathering have removed the more friable cones, leaving these solid plugs of rock which in one place rise 800 ft above the surrounding land. Many are strongly coloured and are especially beautiful at dusk and dawn.

↗ Grey kangaroo, wallaroo, rock wallaby, spiny anteater, koala, possums, thick-tailed gecko, woodgecko, stone adder, white skink, striated skink, parrots and cockatoos (including the Major Mitchell), wedge-tailed eagle, pigeons, finches butcher bird, wagtails, hawks, currawongs. None of these species is very plentiful – especially since the park was gutted by a bush fire in 1966.

⅋ Cypress pine, iron bark, scribbly gum, daisies, asters, guinea flower, heaths, geranium, irises, mint, flax lily, waxlip orchid – and an isolated colony of plants usually found only in coastal sandstone country. It is an offence to pick any flower.

⇦ Converted trams at Canyon Camp take four adults each; electric light, grill, cooking utensils, fridge; beds are railway berths; handbasin and sink; communal ablutions and lavatory; fees A $1.50 per adult, 50c age 15 and under, free age 5 and under, minimum A $2 per night. Book in advance through The Secretary, PO Box 269, Coonabarabran, tel: 420 after 6pm. There is also a caravan site with mains electricity. Camping other than in caravans not allowed. In all cases bring own bedding and cutlery; kiosk sells tinned food. Hotels and motels in Coonabarabran (22 miles away) where rates are around A $9 bed and breakfast double.

⇨ Air connections to Coonabarabran leave Sydney at 10.30 arriving 11.40 every Mon, Wed, Fri, and Sun; return leaves

14.20 arriving 15.25; return fare A$33. The best road from Sydney, much of which is surfaced, is via Mudgee, Dunnedoo, Mendooran, and Coonabarabran, from where the John Renshaw Parkway leads to the park itself.

🚐 The John Renshaw Parkway runs through the north of the park and a short spur runs up to the Siding Springs Observatory (3,823 ft) for a fine panorama. The rest of the park can be seen in a two-day walk along marked trails with an overnight stop in mountain huts (bunks, mattresses, fresh water). Horse riders should not use these trails.

🌄 Open all year; best times spring and autumn; winter is ideal for the serious hiker.

🕐 1–3 days

📧 Cars 20c a day, lorries, caravans, and buses 70c; walking parties 25c per person per week.

🗋 Full description and species list and brochure from North West Tourist Association.

🛏 None provided but could be arranged with Secretary.

⇥ The Secretary, PO Box 269, Coonabarabran.

Australian Reptile Park Eric Worrell's world-famous collection of Australian reptiles and many other native animals, all living in near-natural conditions. Platypus, koala, grey kangaroo, possums, dingo, echidnas, wombat, wallabies;

A termite heap is a complex structure containing food (wood pulp broken down by fungi), walkways, and air-conditioning corridors. The insects block and unblock these corridors so as to keep the temperature in the queen's chamber constant. Heaps may be 50 years old.

taipan (Australia's deadliest snake), rattlesnake, king cobra, adders, vipers, boas, alligator, crocodile; many waterfowl, emu, tuatara. Snakes are milked for venom at irregular intervals all the year; in spring and summer there is a regular milking at 3.30 every Sunday. During the same seasons the crocodiles are fed at 3.30 every Saturday. The park is at Gosford, NSW, 65 minutes by electric train from Sydney, 75 minutes by car, coach, or taxi. Admission is 50c, children half price (with further charges for certain enclosures).

Currumbin Bird Sanctuary At Currumbin in the heart of the Gold Coast holidayland this sanctuary is a popular half-day outing from many nearby resorts. Visitors are given feeding bowls and food and take part in scheduled mass feedings of thousands of lorikeets and other colourful birds. There is a refreshment kiosk in the sanctuary. Admission is free but there is a collection. The sanctuary is 59 miles from Brisbane via Southport. A number of Brisbane tours operators offer day tours at around A$5. Half-day tours from nearby resorts (scheduled ones from Coolangatta and Surfers Paradise) are around A$2.

Fleay's Fauna Reserve Close enough to the Currumbin Sanctuary to be visited in the same day or half-day, this reserve exhibits a variety of Australian birds, mammals, and reptiles in park-like surroundings. It is at West Burleigh, 10 miles from Southport. Tour arrangements and prices as for Currumbin. Admission is 50c.

Australia : Species List

ADDER, Stone Warrumbungle
ANTEATER, Porcupine Flinders Chase
— **Spiny** Kosciusko; Tidbinbilla; Warrumbungle
BANDICOOTS Lamington; Holmes Jungle
— **Large Northern** Cobourg
— **Rabbit-Eared** Tanami
BATS Tidbinbilla; Cobourg
BOWERBIRDS Cobourg
— **Golden** Atherton Tablelands
— **Regen** Lamington
— **Satin** Lamington
BRISTLE BIRD, Eastern Barren Grounds
BROLGAS Cleland; Knuckey's Lagoon; Yarrawonga
BRONZEWING, Brush Tidbinbilla
BUFFALO Cobourg; Patonga; Yarrawonga
BUSTARD Tanami
BUTCHER BIRD Warrumbungle
BUTTERFLIES Dunk Is
CASSOWARY Atherton Tablelands
CATBIRD Lamington
CAT, Feral Tanami
— **Little Northern Native** Cobourg
— **Native** Mallacoota Inlet
— **Tiger** Tidbinbilla
CHAT, Crimson Tanami
CHOUGHS Hattah Lakes
COCKATOOS Hattah Lakes; Wyperfeld; Cobourg; Sir Colin McKenzie; Warrumbungle
— **Gang-Gang** Tidbinbilla
— **Major Mitchell** Warrumbungle
— **Red** Kosciusko

— **Sooty Gang-Gang** Kosciusko
— **White** Atherton Tablelands
— **Yellow-Tailed Black** Tidbinbilla
COOTS Holmes Jungle
CORALS Green Is; Dunk Is; Mandalay
CORMORANTS Heron Is
CRANES Holmes Jungle
CROCODILES Patonga; Yarrawonga
— **Estuarine** Cobourg
CURLEWS Cobourg
— **Sea** Heron Is
CURRAWONG Lamington; Warrambungle
DESERT BLUE TONGUE Tanami
DINGO Ayers Rock; Tanami; Cobourg; Patonga; Yarrawonga
DOVES Cobourg
DRAGONS Tanami
DUCKS Hattah Lakes; Cobourg; Holmes Jungle; Patonga; Dowd's Morass; Sale Common
— **Burdekin** Woolwonga
EAGLES Hattah Lakes; Cobourg; Mallacoota Inlet
— **Wedge-Tailed** Warrumbungle
— **White-Breasted Sea** Port Lincoln; Heron Is
ECHIDNAS Belair; Tanami; Lamington
EGRETS Cobourg; Dowd's Morass; Sale Common
EMU Coorong; Flinders Chase; Hattah Lakes; Kinchega; Port Lincoln; Wyperfeld; Tanami; Kosciusko; Yarrawonga; Sir Colin McKenzie; John Forrest; Kalbarri; Stirling Range; Yanchep

EUROS Para Wirra; Ayers Rock; Tanami
FALCONS Cobourg
FINCHES Lamington; Cobourg; Warrumbungle
— **Painted** Tanami
FLYCATCHERS Cobourg
FOX Tanami
GECKOS Tanami; Cobourg
— **Thick-Tailed** Warrumbungle
— **Wood** Warrumbungle
GEESE Cobourg; Patonga
— **Cape Barren** Cleland
— **Magpie** Knuckeys Lagoon; Woolwonga
— **Pygmy** Woolwonga
GULLS Heron Is
HAWKS Cobourg; Warrumbungle
— **Brown** Tanami
HERONS Cobourg; Holmes Jungle; Heron Is
— **Reef** Dunk Is
HONEYEATERS Belair; Hattah Lakes; Tanami; Cobourg; Katherine Gorge; Blue Mts; Ku-ring-gai Chase
IBIS Hattah Lakes; Cobourg; Dowd's Morass; Sale Common; Phillip Is
KANGAROOS Cleland; Coorong; Kinchega; Wyperfeld; Ayers Rock; New England; Yarrawonga; Mt Field; Sir Colin McKenzie; John Forrest; Kalbarri; Stirling Range; Walpole-Nornalup; Yanchep; Ku-ring-gai Chase
— **Black Faced** Flinders Chase
— **Grey** Para Wirra; New England; Tidbinbilla; Warrumbungle
— **Grey Forester** Kosciusko; Blue Mts
— **Lumholtz's Tree** Atherton Tablelands
— **Mallee Grey** Hattah Lakes
— **Red** Hattah Lakes; Tanami
— **Scrub** Port Lincoln
KESTREL Cobourg
KINGFISHERS Cobourg
KOALA Belair; Cleland; Flinders Chase; Lamington; Lone Pine; Tucki; Kosciusko; Tidbinbilla; Phillip Is; Sir Colin McKenzie; Yanchep; Ku-ring-gai Chase; Sir Edward Hallstrom; Warrumbungle
KOOKABURRA Belair; Ku-ring-gai Chase
LEGGADINA Tanami
LIZARDS Hattah Lakes; Ayers Rock; Tanami; Dunk Is; Cobourg; Holmes Jungle
LORIKEETS Cobourg
LYREBIRDS New England; Tamborine Mt; Kosciusko; Tidbinbilla; Mallacoota Inlet; Sherbrooke Forest; Sir Colin McKenzie; Barren Grounds; Blue Mts
— **Albert** Lamington
— **Southern** Sherbrooke Forest
MAGPIES Hattah Lakes
MALLEE FOWL Hattah Lakes; Port Lincoln; Wyperfeld; Pulletop
MELOMYA, Fawn-Footed Cobourg
MONITORS Tanami; Cobourg
MOUSE, Delicate Cobourg
— **Desert** Tanami
— **Fat-Tailed Marsupial** Tanami
— **Fawn Marsupial** Cobourg
— **Hopping** Tanami
— **Marsupial** Tidbinbilla; Mt Field
MULGARA Tanami
MUTTON BIRD See SHEARWATERS
ORIOLES Cobourg
OSPREY Port Lincoln; Cobourg
OWLS Cobourg
OYSTERBIRDS Heron Is
OYSTERCATCHERS Cobourg
PADEMELON Cradle Mt
PARROTS Belair; Cleland; Hattah Lakes; Wyperfeld; Ayers Rock; Lamington; Tamborine Mt; Mallacoota Inlet; Sir Colin McKenzie; Ku-ring-gai Chase; Warrumbungle
— **Ground** Barren Grounds
— **King** Atherton Tablelands
— **Princess** Tanami
— **Red-Sided** Atherton Tablelands
— **Swamp** Barren Grounds
PELICANS Coorong; Flinders Chase; Hattah Lakes; Kalbarri
PENGUIN, Fairy Phillip Is
PHALANGERS Mt Field; Blue Mts
PIGEONS New England; Tamborine Mt; Cobourg; Patonga; Warrumbungle

— **Flock** Tanami
— **Torres Straits** Dunk Is
— **Wampoo** Atherton Tablelands
— **Wonda** Tidbinbilla
PIGS Patonga
PLATYPUS Lamington; Kosciusko; Sir Colin McKenzie; Blue Mts
POSSUMS Lamington; Kosciusko; Cradle Mt; Mallacoota Inlet; Blue Mts; Warrumbungle
— **Brush Tailed** Cobourg
— **Bush-Tailed** Tidbinbilla
— **Greater Glider** Tidbinbilla
— **Green** Atherton Tablelands
— **Herbert River Ring-Tailed** Atherton Tablelands
— **Lemur-Like** Atherton Tablelands
— **Ring-Tailed** Tidbinbilla
— **Pygmy-Glider** Tidbinbilla
— **Striped** Atherton Tablelands
— **Sugar-Glider** Tidbinbilla
QUAILS Cobourg
— **Little** Tanami
RABBIT Tanami
RATS Tidbinbilla
— **Brush-Tailed Rabbit** Cobourg
— **Fat-Tailed Marsupial** Tanami
— **Native** Holmes Jungle
— **Shaggy Rabbit** Cobourg
— **Tunney's** Cobourg
REPTILES Wyperfeld
RODENTS Lamington
RUFOUS SCRUB BIRD Lamington
SANDPIPERS Cobourg; Heron Is
SEALS Flinders Chase
— **Australian Fur** Phillip Is
SHEARWATER, Wedge-Tailed Heron Is
— **Short-Tailed** Phillip Is
SKINKS Tanami; Cobourg
— **White** Warrumbungle
— **Striated** Warrumbungle
SNAKES Cleland; Ayers Rock; Cobourg; Holmes Jungle
— **Collared Brown** Tanami
— **Mulga** Tanami
— **Red-Naped** Tanami
SPOONBILLS Dowd's Morass; Sale Common
— **Royal** Knuckey's Lagoon
STORK, Jabiru Knuckey's Lagoon
SUGAR GLIDER Lamington
SWALLOW, Wood Tanami
SWANS Coorong; Kalbarri
— **Black** Flinders Chase; Dowd's Morass; Sale Common; Yanchep
TERNS Cobourg; Heron Is
THORNBILL, Brown Tanami
THRUSH, Little Shrike Tanami
TORTOISES Cobourg
TREECREEPERS Cobourg
TURKEY, Brush Lamington; Tamborine Mt; Atherton Tablelands
— **Scrub** New England
TURTLES, Marine Cobourg
WADERS Cleland; Coorong; Holmes Jungle; Mallacoota Inlet
WAGTAILS Warrumbungle
WALLABIES Cleland; Flinders Chase; Tanami; Lamington; Patonga; Yarrawonga; Cradle Mt; Mt Field; Mallacoota Inlet; Cape Range; Kalbarri; Stirling Range; Walpole-Nornalup
— **Agile** Cobourg
— **Black Rock** Katherine Gorge
— **Brush-Tailed** Blue Mts
— **Brush-Tailed Rock** Kosciusko
— **Red-Necked** Tidbinbilla
— **Rock** Warrumbungle
— **Swamp** Tidbinbilla; Barren Grounds
WALLAROOS Warrumbungle
— **Antilopine** Cobourg
WARATAHS Blue Mts
WARBLERS Cobourg
WATER BIRDS Cleland; Hattah Lakes; Kinchega; Fogg Dam; Patonga; Woolwonga; Phllip Is; Sir Colin McKenzie; Tower Hill
WHIPBIRD Port Lincoln; Lamington; Tamborine Mt
WOMBAT Cleland; Kosciusko; Mt Field; Mallacoota Inlet; Stirling Range
— **Common** Tidbinbilla
WRENS Tanami
— **Blue** Lamington

NEW ZEALAND

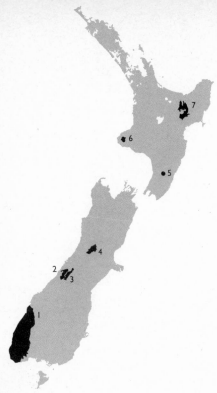

Wildlife protection in New Zealand has the most paradoxical origins. Eminent 19th-century scientists calmly predicted the 'inevitable' extinction of many native species of birds and urged the deliberate introduction of exotic species from Europe and Asia. Acclimatization societies were quickly formed to carry out these aims and protective legislation soon followed.

The tide of opinion turned from 1907 onward, when 29 native birds and the tuatara (a reptile) and the introduced opossum were put under absolute protection. By 1921 no fewer than 180 birds were on the list. And now, in the 1970s, the boot is on the other foot: only game animals, and partially protected animals are listed; all others are totally protected. Thus of native birds only the black shag, kea, and harrier hawk are not absolutely protected; but of the introduced birds only the mute swan is totally protected. The rare Maori rat and two elusive native bats (these three are New Zealand's only native land mammals), the tuatara, and the native frogs are absolutely protected.

Now, too, their habitat is protected by statute. Over 5 million acres, almost a thirteenth of the country's total area, is set aside in 10 national parks. Over a million more acres are set aside as scenic and fauna-protection reserves – often with commendable swiftness. For instance, when in 1948 the takahe, a bird long believed to be extinct, was again sighted in South Island, some 700 square miles of mountain hinterland was immediately declared a sanctuary (not for visitors, note); since then the birds have been extensively studied in their natural habitat. Many offshore islands, uneconomic to exploit commercially, and safe from marauding stoats and rats, have been set up as havens for the most badly threatened native birds. The hub of all this activity has been the Mt Bruce Bird Sanctuary, described on a later page. Here, breeding pairs and groups of several threatened species have been established and studied as a back-up to the attempts to create free-living sanctuaries in islands and remote areas.

Here, before turning to the official parks and sanctuaries are a few notes on species and sites not covered in them.

Most visitors want to see a kiwi, and most are disappointed (except for what they see at Mt Bruce and at Auckland and Wellington zoos). It is nocturnal, almost blind, and extremely elusive. By contrast the tui, a native honeyeater can be seen in brush country throughout New Zealand.

The glow-worms at Waitomo (North Island) and Te-Ana-Au (South Island) are of a species unique to New Zealand; to glide beneath the arching roof of a darkened cavern studded with these tiny creatures is a truly unforgettable experience.

The tuatara is the only surviving species of the reptile order *Rhyncocephalia*; the other members – dinosaurs, ichthyosaurs, and iguanodons – became extinct some 100 million years ago. It exists now only on some offshore islands off North Island, especially Kapiti Island, a strict reserve.

Useful literature includes *Some Birds of New Zealand* (Pamphlet PM 22) and New Zealand Fact Sheets 15 (Flora) and 16 (Fauna) – all free from New Zealand Information Service, PO Box 95, Wellington, New Zealand.

The Government Tourist Bureau publishes a number of itineraries for independent tours of both islands; these are not coach parties or group tours – they allow you to travel independently by coach or rail. So you can select bits from the many itineraries and compile your own route.

Arthur's Pass National Park 242,888 acres; 878 to 7,873 ft above sea level, in a high Alpine region containing the headwaters of the Waimakariri and Otira Rivers. It straddles the Southern Alps between Canterbury and Westland, and has some fine peaks and several small glaciers. The park also contains the famous Otehake Wilderness Area.

🦌 Birds include the mountain parrot or kea, bush hawk, and in remote areas, the kiwi. Red deer, chamois, and opossum have been introduced.

🏕 Includes beech forests, subtropical rain forests and a wilderness area that combines both.

🛏 The Terminus Hotel at Otira is outside the park but on the main highway near the park's border; from $4 single, $6 double. The Perry Range Hotel at Jacksons is also outside the park but on the main highway; from $3 single, $4 double. Additional information from the Tourist Hotel Corporation. The Park Board and Alpine Club provide climber's huts.

✈ Provincial State Highway No. 73 crosses the park. A daily train from Christchurch to the West Coast stops inside the park.

🚐 Highway 73 crossing the park. Numerous tracks for walking. The Temple Basin Track takes only tougher vehicles. Regular rail service from Christchurch to Ross.

☀ Good all year. Highway sometimes closed during the winter by avalanches.

🕐 4–7 days.

👁 Museum in Arthur's Pass township at the park HQ contains mountain and natural history exhibits of the park.

➪ Arthur's Pass National Park Board, Christchurch.

The strangely unbirdlike kiwi, once common in the dense kauri forest, is slowly adapting to life in open woodland near forest borders, as its habitat vanishes. A nocturnal bird, it is rarely seen by day.

Egmont National Park 83,000 acres in a 6-mile radius of Mt Egmont, and including Kaitake Range; maximum altitude 8,260 ft. Rich countryside of gently rolling farmlands and magnificent native bush below the snow-capped Mt Egmont, an extinct volcano and the most beautiful mountain in the North Island. Around the foot of the mountain are public parks and gardens.

🦌 The many indigenous birds include bush hawk, bellbird, rifleman, bush wren, kiwi; introduced species are wild goat and opossum, but no deer.

🚏 *North Egmont:* North Egmont Chalet with accommodation for 28; provides refreshment for visitors. The Camphouse with bunks for 36; cooking ovens, showers. Enquiries to Manager, North Egmont Chalet, Inglewood. *Stratford area:* Stratford Mountain House with full accommodation and camphouse facilities for 52; refreshments provided for visitors. Enquiries to Manager, Stratford Mountain House, Stratford. *Dawson Falls:* Dawson Falls Tourist Lodge accommodates 28. Robson Lodge has bunkroom accommodation for 32. The Cottage accommodates 12. Enquiries to Manager, Dawson Falls Tourist Lodge, Kaponga. Huts are provided throughout the park for climbers.

🛬 A major road circles the park with three excellent secondary roads leading to all three tourist lodges.

🚌 Numerous walking tracks.

☀ Open all year. Best mid-November to April.

⏱ 1–4 days.

🗻 Provided by Tavanaki Alpine Clubs. Party up to three persons, $10 per day; $1 extra per person for larger parties. Information from hostel managers or Public Relations Office, 56 Currie St., New Plymouth.

👁 Koru Pa Historic Reserve, just outside the park. Also the Stony River Scenic Reserve, one of New Zealand's finest beauty spots.

⇨ Egmont National Park Board, New Plymouth, NZ.

Fiordland National Park 3,023,069 acres; sea level to 9,042 ft above. Largest and wildest of New Zealand's national parks, situated in the southwest of the South Island. Includes numerous fiords along the rugged coastline, mountain and forest country, scores of lakes, many beautiful falls like Bowen Falls (540 ft) and Sutherland Falls (1,904 ft). 'The Finest Walk in the World' is the 33-mile-long Milford Track, beginning at the head of Lake Te Anau – largest in the South Island – and ending at the majestic Milford Sound.

🦌 Red deer, wapiti; some flightless and nearly extinct birds: moa, takahe, kakapo. Other birds include penguins, petrels, shags, fantails, parakeets, silvereyes, grey warbler, yellow-breasted tit, cuckoos, bush robin, New Zealand scaup, blue duck, paradise duck, herons, great crested grebe, pukeko, bittern, godwit, and other waders.

🌿 Red and silver beech, miro, kahikatea, totara, kamahi, broadleaf, rata, hebes, toatoa, pink pine. Wild flowers include gentians, eidelweiss, buttercups, violets, orchids.

🚏 *Milford Sound:* Hotel Milford accommodates 75. Southland AA hostel provides 3-bunk cubicles. *Te Anau:* Hotel Te Anau with 86 beds, from $10 single, $13 double; AA motor camp with flats for hire. *Cascade Creek:* AA hostel with 40 beds in 2- and 3-bed huts. *Lake Hanapouri:* guest-house accommodation; camping ground. *Hossburn:* 38 miles from Te Anau. The railway hotel accommodates 27. Enquiries to Tourist Office Te Anau. Huts provided on all tracks and tramping roads; few amenities but free of charge.

🛬 Major roads via Te Anau from Queenstown, Dunedin or Invercargill; regular coach services from these points. Air services to Milford, year-round. Railway as far as Mossburn. Most exciting access is by ocean liners calling irregularly at Milford Sound.

🚐 An all-weather road from Milford Sound through to Manapouri. Good internal system of tracks, closed in winter. Special air flights are available: regular tourist flights over the park and charter flights for special expeditions. Steamer and launch trips available; launches for hire. Excursion coaches available.

☀ Open all year; best December to April.

🕐 4–14 days.

👁 The spectacular Te Anau 'Glow-worm' caves, entered by boat. Beautiful views along guided walking trips up Mount Luxmore and to the Aurora Caves.

⇨ Fiordland National Park Board, Invercargill, NZ.

Mount Bruce Native Bird Reserve Established in 1961, this reserve is aimed at maintaining a breeding nucleus of endangered New Zealand bird species and at re-establishing wild breeding pairs where they have become locally extinct on either island. Among birds currently held there: takahe, eastern weka, saddleback, brown duck, kakapo, blue duck – all rarities. Other birds are also held for research and display: kiwis (displayed 11 am and 3 pm), parakeets, pigeons, scaup, paradise duck, banded rail. Visitors are welcome at weekends, public holidays, and school vacations except during the October to mid-December breeding season. The reserve is in the Wairarapa, on the main road north, 80 miles from Wellington. It is in an area of mixed native forest with natural water supplies suitable for the creation of wetland habitat. The forest is quickly regenerating from former logging and fire damage.

Mount Cook National Park 172,979 acres; maximum altitude 12,349 ft above sea level. The park takes in the Cook, Malte Brun, and Liebig mountain ranges, all having mighty peaks and glaciers. The Tasman glacier, 18 miles long, is the largest outside the Himalayas and polar regions. This vast array of Alpine splendour is dominated by Mount Cook itself – 'aorangi' (Cloud Piercer), as the Maoris call it – and boasts 27 peaks over 10,000 ft.

🐾 All the mammals are introduced species, the most notable being mountain goats and chamois; the indigenous birds include the mountain parrot and bush hawk.

🛏 Hermitage Lodge, with all amenities including tennis, from $10 single, $15 double; Tasman Lodge, from $3 single, $6 double; Sefton Lodge, from $4 single, $8 double.
Further information from the Tourist Hotel Corporation or Mount Cook and Southern Lakes Tourist Company. Camping sites: Hermitage Terrace and a youth hostel. Caravan site at Hermitage Terrace. Shelter and climber's huts provided by the park authorities.

✈ Major State Highway to the park. Railway at Timaru, 132 miles away. An air strip near the Hermitage, and run by Mt Cook Air Services Ltd., provides a regular year-round service. Daily coach services, except Sunday, from Christchurch, Timaru, and points south.

🚐 Excursions to the upper glacier basins from airstrip near The Hermitage. Light Aircraft, including ski planes, for hire (enquiries to Mt Cook Air Services Ltd, P.O. Box 226,

A royal albatross on Campbell Island. Its 9-ft span is only 2 ft shorter than that of the wandering albatross. Like all members of their family they are famous for their awkward courtship antics – bowing, scraping, snapping their bills, and uttering groans in duet. Each pair takes turns to incubate a single white egg for its 77–80-day hatching. Their young take three months to fledge fully.

Timaru, NZ). Numerous tracks. One major road to Hermitage leads to the Ball hut.

☀ Open all year. Heavy snow occasionally closes the highway.

⊘ 1–10 days.

☞ Services provided by Rangers of Mt Cook National Park. $4.50 for half-day; $6.50 for full day. A sliding scale for additional persons. Enquiries to Chief Ranger, Mt Cook National Park, NZ.

◎ Almost year-round skiing and mountaineering.

⇨ Mount Cook National Park Board, Christchurch, NZ or Chief Ranger, Hermitage Terrace, Mt Cook National Park, NZ.

Urewara National Park 493,032 acres; maximum altitude 4,602 ft. A densely wooded park renowned for its Maori history; part of the park is still Maori reserves and settlements. Many beautiful lakes including Lake Waikaremoana with its three falls. The principal falls, Panekiri Bluff, drops 2,000 ft to the waters of the lake. Morere, known for its hot springs reserve, contains 500 acres of beautiful native bush. Many notable caves. In the centre of the park is one of the North Island's last extensive regions of primeval forest.

🗗 Kiwi, kaka, grey warbler, whitehead, tui, bellbird, white-breasted tomtit, parakeet, pigeon, cuckoo, morepork (small owl), grey shoveler, blue duck, black teal.

🙞 Tawa, rimu, matai, rata, red and blue beech, ferns, kahikatea, rewarewa, kowhai, toetoe, and the rare red kakabeak.

🛏 Lake House Hotel at Lake Waikare, sleeps 32; from $4 single, $7 double. Hotel at Murupaea, motor camp at Lake Waikaremoana. Enquiries to Tourist Hotel Corporation. Many huts scattered through park, owned by Park Board and Forest Service.

The New Zealand white heron, or kotuku, is one of several waterbirds found at Westland National Park. Though none of the country's waterbirds is endangered, the steady reclamation of wetlands is bound to reduce their numbers. Another haunt of the heron is the bush-clad Lake Moeraki, quite close to the Haast Highway route.

Provincial state highway between Rotorua and Wairoa across the park. Coach service between these two points Monday, Wednesday and Friday.

Provincial state highway through the park. Innumerable tracks for walkers. Launch cruises on Lake Waikaremoana. North Island main trunk railway nearby.

Open all year.

4–7 days.

Urewara National Park Board, Hamilton; or Manager, Urewera National Park Headquarters, Aniwaniwa, Lake Waikaremoana, NZ.

Westland National Park 210,257 acres; sea level to 11,475 ft above. This park is noted for its amazing variety of scenery that includes mountains, glaciers (the Franz Josef and Fox Glaciers are the most famous); beautiful sandy beaches bordering the Tasman Sea, as well as rugged coastline; innumerable waterfalls and streams; lush green cattle pastures; many lakes including the lovely Lake Mapourika below the Southern Alps, and magnificent forests.

- Wood pigeons, tui, harrier hawk, bellbirds, the kotuku or white heron; red deer and chamois have been introduced.

- Franz Josef Glacier Hotel and Fox Hotel. Both hotels run motor camps. Additional information from Tourist Hotel Corporation. A few huts available for climbers.

- Major access by State Highway 6. The new Haast Pass road provides a scenic circular route round the park. Daily train service from Christchurch to Ross. Regular flights to Hokitika, Fox, and Franz Josef Glaciers. Regular bus service from Nelson to Hokitika, from Hokitika to Fox: in summer, daily from Queenstown to Franz Joseph.

- Tourist flights, one major highway.

- Excellent all year round. Best October to March.

- 4–7 days.

- From the Franz Josef Hotel or from the Mt Cook National Park.

- Two aerodromes, one at the park H.Q. near the Franz Josef Glacier, the other at the Ranger H.Q. near the Fox Glacier. For notable scenery, visit Buller Gorge, the unique Pancake Rocks, and the blowholes of Punakaiki.

- Chief Warden, Franz Josef Glacier or Westland National Park Board, Hokitika.

New Zealand : Species List

EUROPE

Introduction by Paul Géroudet

Small by comparison with other continents, Europe is an occidental extension of Asia, divided from Africa in the south by the Mediterranean and bounded to the west and north by the Atlantic and Arctic oceans. The complex climatic influences that result from this position – together with her equally complex history – have determined the remarkable variety of her plant and animal life. Europe, too, is the home of many past civilizations; for thousands of years human activity has steadily modified nature in almost every corner of the continent. For most of that time the evolution of civilization was slow enough to allow a kind of equilibrium to exist. Until modern times.

Despite these large-scale modifications one can still distinguish four basic natural zones: the Mediterranean basin; middle Europe; the taiga; and the tundra. In each zone we can find most of the seven major habitats: seashore; marshland; lakes; open and wooded plain; mountain; and steppe.

The **Mediterranean zone** is characterized by a mild climate with dry summers and damp winters. Its maritime fringes abound in islands and peninsulas. Its flora is still extraordinarily rich and gives some idea of what a paradise it must once have been for animals, too. But, as the cradle of ancient civilizations, its nature is gravely damaged. Ill-considered deforestation and fires have reduced many areas of one-time evergreen forest, stage by stage, to scrub and low, sparse vegetation whose ultimate fate, when the sheep and goats move in, is erosion and near-sterilization.

Extensive hunting has already practically exterminated the larger mammals and now takes a truly frightful toll of migratory birds, even the smallest of which is considered worth killing. Nowadays the greatest human pressures, tourism and the land speculation it generates, are exerted against the shores. Thus the baleful effects of human exploitation threaten nature from the mountains to the shores and make the Mediterranean zone the weak point of the conservation movement in Europe.

All the surviving large mammals are reduced to small pockets and threatened with extinction: the moufflon and deer in Corsica and Sardinia, the wild goat in Crete, and the monk seal. On the credit side there are still porcupines

The European hare is also found through much of Asia and Africa.

in the Italian peninsula, bears, wolves, and chamois in the Abruzzi, ibex in some Spanish sierras, and jackals in northern Greece. Mediterranean bird life also has its interesting survivors, both in its rare and local species (Corsican nuthatch, Ruppell's warbler, Audouin's gull, Eleonora's falcon, and others) and in its larger birds of prey – vultures and eagles – whose numbers, however, are diminishing alarmingly.

Despite the obviously urgent need for conservation in the Mediterranean, the movement has faced many serious difficulties. Its most remarkable achievement has been the establishment by the World Wildlife Fund of the Coto Doñana biological reserve (1964) and the subsequent purchase (1969) of the nearby marisma of Guadiamar in the Guadalquivir delta. These purchases committed the Spanish government to the establishment of the 135-square-mile Doñana National Park, protecting wildlife of exceptional value including the Spanish lynx, the imperial Spanish eagle, and countless thousands of migratory birds.

(*continued on p. 312*)

Note: The British Isles are
mapped separately on page
333, and Turkey on page 385

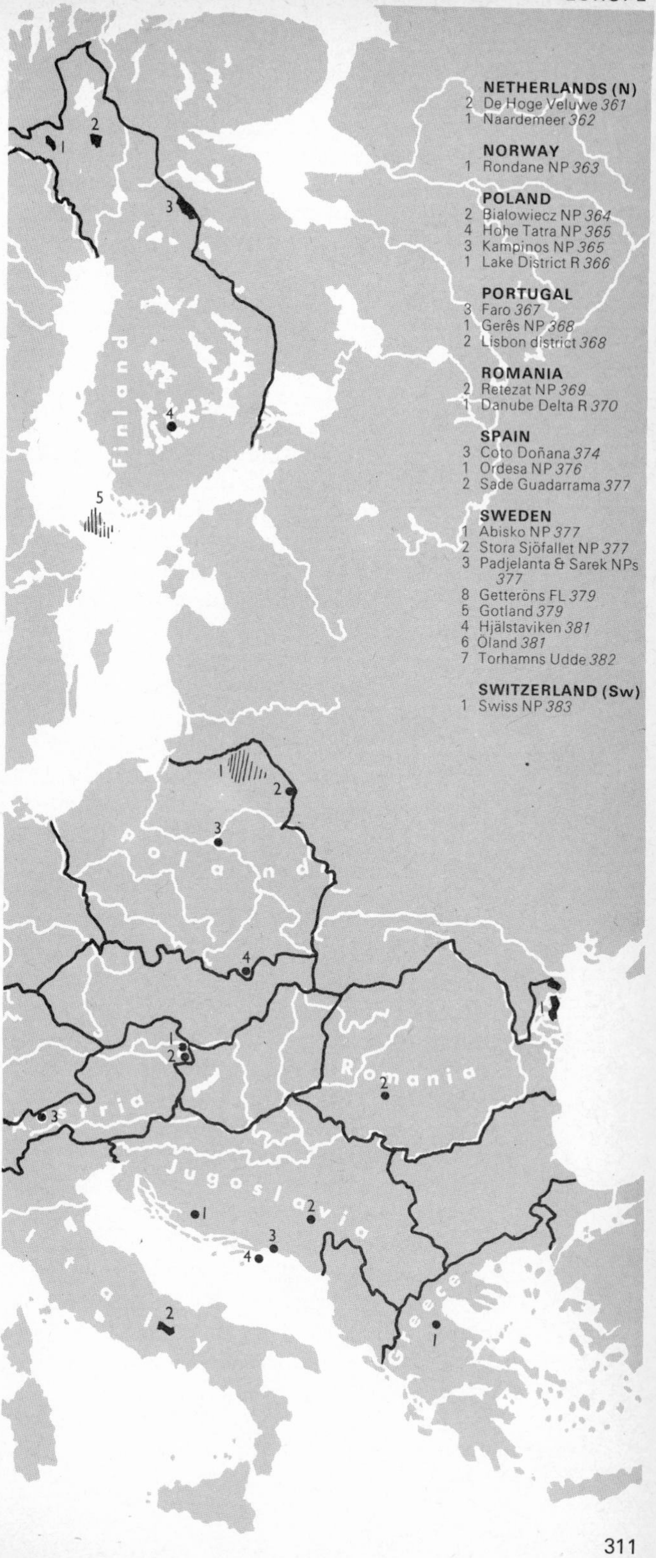

NETHERLANDS (N)
2 De Hoge Veluwe 361
1 Naardemeer 362
NORWAY
1 Rondane NP 363
POLAND
2 Bialowiecz NP 364
4 Hohe Tatra NP 365
3 Kampinos NP 365
1 Lake District R 366
PORTUGAL
3 Faro 367
1 Gerês NP 368
2 Lisbon district 368
ROMANIA
2 Retezat NP 369
1 Danube Delta R 370
SPAIN
3 Coto Doñana 374
1 Ordesa NP 376
2 Sade Guadarrama 377
SWEDEN
1 Abisko NP 377
2 Stora Sjöfallet NP 377
3 Padjelanta & Sarek NPs 377
8 Getteröns FL 379
5 Gotland 379
4 Hjälstaviken 381
6 Öland 381
7 Torhamns Udde 382
SWITZERLAND (Sw)
1 Swiss NP 383
Finland
Poland
Romania
Jugoslavia
Italy
Greece

(*Introduction continued*)

Seven hundred miles away to the northeast the Camargue offers equally important protection to France's southern avifauna, especially flamingoes. Apart from these two places, and a few others of lesser importance, most of the really important parks and reservations of the Mediterranean zone exist only on paper – with little hope of realization in the near future.

Middle Europe, with its temperate climate, was, in general, a zone of deciduous-tree forest that supported a richly varied wildlife. But, in recent centuries, it has become an area of intensive agriculture, booming industry, mushrooming population, and expanding towns between which nature is, as it were, marooned in islands or pockets. The main refuges are the mountains, with their original flora and fauna in a most magnificent setting. Here we find the chamois – in the Alps – the ibex, which has been rescued from near extinction. Here, too, the marmot, favoured prey of the golden eagle, is locally common. The arctic quality of the high summits is marked by the presence of the ptarmigan and mountain hare, as in Scandinavia and Scotland – just as the Alpine chough and the delightful wall creeper remind us of the Himalayas and of Europe's close links with Asia.

Lower down, at the forest level, such birds as the capercaillie, hazel hen, Tengmalm's owl, and three-toed woodpecker preserve ancient relationships between Middle Europe and the taiga.

Unfortunately in our own day even these remote mountain fastnesses of nature are no longer intact. Hydroelectric dams have drowned many valleys while sports and tourism threaten the upper slopes; both have disastrous effects on the delicate balance of mountain ecologies. And though most large reserves and national parks are located in the mountains, they are not necessarily protected from human avarice – as recent distressing experience with the Vanoise has shown.

Down in the plains the nearest approach to virgin nature is found in the larger stretches of woodland and heath, inhabited in general by roe deer, wild boar, and wild cat. Drainage has almost eliminated the marshes, so emergency conservation measures have largely been directed toward preserving the last vestiges of these wetlands. Examples are: Naardemeer in Holland, with its colonies of cormorants and spoonbills; Seewinkel and the Neusiedlersee in eastern Austria; and the last refuges of the pelicans in the Danube delta. In addition, many lake regions (those in Germany, Poland and the Dombes in France are good examples) are known for their ornithological richness. In this connection the Project MAR, carried out by the International Union for the Conservation of Nature, has led to an inventory of the most important wetland habitats and is now directed toward protecting them. Among the most notable are the Atlantic mudbanks, dotting the coast from Denmark to Portugal, especially the Waddenzee, gathering place of large bands of migrating and overwintering waders. Many of these intertidal areas are threatened by reclamation and drainage projects.

Another threat – oil pollution – hangs over every European sea shore and its birdlife; their spectacular colonies, especially in the British Isles, are at constant risk of decimation by this rapidly increasing danger.

The **steppe**, which once stretched through most of southern Russia and part of the Danubian basin, is now almost totally transformed by the expansion of intensive farming. Species characteristic of this region, such as the great bustard, are in danger of vanishing from Europe. Among the last western vestiges of this environment is the Puszta Hortobagy, which the Hungarian government is now considering protecting.

The **taiga**, the northern forest of conifers and birches, stretches from Scandinavia through Russia and Asia and across North America. The severity of its climate and the low productivity of its soil has protected it from much agricultural encroachment, and the population density is still low. So, despite commercial forestry and the tapping of hydroelectric resources, its wildlife is still more or less intact: the elk (moose in North America), the beaver, and even the bigger carnivores such as bears, wolves, lynxes, and wolverines, whose range once extended far beyond the taiga. The vast marshes of this region abound in birds, of which the crane is the most remarkable.

Farther north still the disappearance of trees and the diminishing signs of human occupation herald the **tundra**, which, in Europe, extends through part of Lappland. Though winters there are long, dark, and cold, the short, permanent daylight of summer brings a miraculous upwelling of life. In the peat bogs and around the lakes, ducks, geese, and waders nest in abundance. The gyr falcon hunts in the mountains and the 'domesticated' reindeer roams free. In these vast spaces of the taiga and tundra are found Europe's greatest national parks, pride and honour of the northern countries.

Beyond the continental fringes one must mention Iceland with its harsh volcanic solitudes and glaciers, whose birdlife includes several American species: loon, great northern diver, harlequin, Barrow's goldeneye, and gray phalarope. In the interior live colonies of pink-footed geese and at Lake Myvatan is a paradise for ducks.

This brief panorama makes it clear that Europe still has much to show the enthusiastic naturalist. With around 143 mammal species (not counting sea mammals) and some 600 birds (420 nesting – excluding USSR), the continent is still rich in animal life. During historical times the losses of species have been small, but the recent development of industrial civilization and the demands it makes on the rest of nature are now causing a truly alarming crisis. The bison and ibex have all but disappeared; their remnants have been saved in the nick of time. Improvements in hunting legislation (and the long-term self-interest of hunters) has removed any immediate threat from other ungulate species. But carnivores, especially wolves, bears, and lynxes as well as raptorial bird species, are all diminishing at a disturbing rate. This applies particularly to the lammergeier, vultures, white-tailed eagle, peregrine falcon, and the great horned owl. Threatened, too, are the great aquatic birds, whose habitat is diminishing under the triple pressures of population, pollution, and reclamation.

There can thus be no doubt about the urgency of our efforts to conserve what is left – efforts that must be coupled with more effective education, which alone can bring home to people the need to preserve our balance with nature. Many national and international organizations are working toward these ends; but the critical situation in southern Europe and in the more populous regions elsewhere makes it clear that voluntary and persuasive policies are no longer enough. Government action is needed, and on a fairly large scale.

If such action is long delayed, our continent will lose a natural wealth that can never be replaced; and, by an irony of history, such a loss will come at precisely the time when more people than ever before have the personal wealth, the need, and the will to enjoy those riches.

To restate this in more concrete terms, we still have a Europe in which vultures glide in the skies above Delphos, where lammergeiers soar along the rocky slopes of the Pyrenees, bison graze in the clearings of Bialowieza, where the squat, powerful shape of a bear can be glimpsed in the forests of Croatia, where the curved horns of the ibex stand out against the skies of the Matterhorn or of the Sierra de Gredos, where white-tailed eagles wheel above the Norwegian coast while grey seals sleep on the reefs of the Shetlands, where otters dive in meandering English rivers and pink flamingoes gather in the salty lakes of the Camargue . . . All this was so long before the Parthenon was built or one stone was piled upon another in the lagoon of Venice. Like those places, our wildlife is a part of our heritage. Unlike them it is a living heritage; if part of it is destroyed, no restorer can bring it back. With good management this living heritage can survive for as long as we care to ensure it. This is not really a *choice* that we face; it is a *trust* that we have been given.

Austria

Domestic geese (descended from grey-lags) share habitat with migrant snow geese (left, background) at Austria's Seewinkel Park.

Karwendel Nature Reserve 275 square miles; 1,970 to 8,860 ft above sea level. This magnificently scenic reserve straddles a limestone range of the northern Alps, providing a mixture of living-rock formations, screes, glens, wooded valleys, and large Alpine pastures. A feature of these pastures is the mountain maples, which provide shelter for the cattle. On Grosser Ahornboden, a large pasture, there are about 3,000 mountain maples, some known to be over 600 years old.

⌖ Chamois, red deer, hare; eagles, owls, ptarmigan, wall creeper. There are many insects and molluscs of scientific interest.

🜊 Scots pine, dwarf pine plentiful in the Dolomite areas, beech, firs, and spruce in the limestone areas; in the glens are maple and elm. Above the subalpine forests: heather (*Erica carnea*), alpine rose, striated spurge laurel, and the rare (Dolomite only) ground cistus; higher still are mountain aven, cushion sedge, bear's ear primrose, and many gentians.

🛏 A number of guesthouses and mountain refuges within the reserve can be booked through your local Austrian tourist office or the local Bergwacht. There is only one permanent settlement, with limited accommodation, within the reserve: Hinterriss. But in surrounding towns and villages there are plenty of hotels and inns; rates range between 23 and 45 sch single and 45 to 75 sch double, meals cost between 25 and 30 sch per person. There are campsites at Achensee, Maurach, Buchau, Schwaz, Pill, Volders, Solbad Hall, Absam, Innsbruck, Zirl, Seefeld; fees range between 3 and 12 sch per person per day. Youth hostels at Maurach and Innsbruck. Large guesthouse near the Ahornboden in the Eng.

Local roads more or less follow the reserve boundaries. Only one road through the park (Vorderriss, Riss Valley, to In der Eng) is open to motor traffic. The nearest railway runs along the Inn valley, to the south, and the Mittenwald-Bahn from Innsbruck skirts the western end. A cogwheel railway runs from Jenbach up to Achensee. Cableways from Innsbruck to Hafelekar (Nordkettenbahn) and from Seefeld to Rosshütte.

More than 50 miles of marked paths run through the reserve. You can arrange for baggage to be transported to the mountain huts.

Open all year; best time November to March for skiing, late spring to early summer for wildlife, summer for walking, autumn (especially September) for colour in mountain maples. Other trees remain colourful to October.

3–5 days.

Free.

Lists on application to Fremdenverkehrsverein or Gemeindeamt (town hall service) in local towns and villages, especially the Tyroler Bergwacht in Innsbruck, Telfs, Scharnitz, and Hall.

Austrian tourist offices.

Marchauen Nature Reserve 2,750 acres; around 500 ft above sea level. Almost 8 miles long and between 1½ miles and 600 yards wide, the reserve winds along the western bank of the March river, which is Austria's border with Czechoslovakia (actually the border technically follows an ancient and far more tortuous river line, so that until a new border treaty is made parts of the reserve are nominally in Czechoslovakia!). The reserve encloses one of the last great riverine 'gallery' forests in western Europe; the Reusse valley, Switzerland, has another remnant of this habitat – which was saved by the World Wildlife Fund – and others are found in Hungary, Romania, and Jugoslavia. Marchauen was also saved from the bulldozers by the World Wildlife Fund, working jointly with the nearby village of Marchegg. By a charter dated 1268, Marchegg is actually a city, but its present population is still only 2,000; nevertheless it managed to put up half the £200,000 purchase price, the rest being guaranteed by the World Wildlife Fund. The reserve was originally part of an aristocratic estate, the baroque-style schloss of which is now the entrance and headquarters of the reserve and the home of a splendid hunting museum. Large parts of the reserve are flooded for up to 4 months each year, which – as with the drowned water meadows of yesterday's farms – makes an extremely lush and verdant landscape; many have called it Europe's most beautiful river-forest landscape.

⫞ Red deer (Carpathian race), roe deer, wild boar, hare, pine and beech martens, otter, occasional lynx, and very rare vagrant wolves and brown bears. The chief glory of the reserve is, naturally, its birdlife, which includes Austria's last surviving colonies of cormorants and night herons. Also: 7 woodpecker species (including Syrian woodpecker), 7 owl species (including Ural owl), great white egret, purple and great-white herons, crane, curlew, little bittern, corncrake, black-tailed godwit, black stork, lesser spotted and white-tailed eagles, goshawk, saker falcon, hobby, great bustard, pheasants; river, Savi's, and grasshopper warblers; penduline tit, thrush nightingale and nightingale. Many migrants, such as mallard, gadwall, garganey, common pochard, and greylag goose also use the reserve as an assembly point.

⸿ Oak, elm, willow, poplar, dogwood, elder, wild vine, traveller's joy, guelder rose, wild hop, dewberry, winter cherry, great and lesser reedmace, branched bur reed, marsh spurge, Loddon lily, meadow gladiole, fringed pink, yellow flag, yellow and white water lilies, water chestnut.

⟞ None in reserve but Marchegg and other nearby places have plenty of accommodation at similar rates to those quoted for Neusiedler See.

⇥ Marchegg is 40 miles due east of Vienna and is reached by the road through Markgrafneusiedl.

⟝ On foot by a well-marked network of trails; the denser parts of the reserve are closed to visitors.

☼ Open all year; best time May (tail end of breeding season and start of summer flowers).

🕐 1–3 days.

✉ There is a small entry fee.

⇨ Oesterreichischer Stiftverband für Naturschutz, Colloredogasse 24, Vienna 110.

Neusiedler See and Seewinkel Park 85,400 acres; 362 to 820 ft above sea level. The Neusiedler See is an extraordinary steppe lake, 22 miles long, 5 to 10 miles wide, yet nowhere more than 6 ft deep. The Seewinkel area, to the east of the main lake and close to the Hungarian border (which actually cuts through the southern end of the lake), is a region of shallow marshes, pools, and small salt lakes. It is a haven and breeding colony for more than 300 kinds of waterfowl, including hundreds of herons and spoonbills.

⫞ Great white heron, purple heron, grey heron, great crested grebe, mallard, ferruginous duck, water rail, spotted crake, five species of warbler, marsh harrier, greylag goose, bean goose, white fronted goose, bittern, little bittern, white stork, great bustard, glossy ibis; many small mammals.

⸿ There is a wide variety of soils in and around the park, which thus supports a rich collection of aquatic, marsh, and wetland plants.

⟞ Hotels and guesthouses in Neusiedl, Podersdorf, St Andrä am Zicksee, and other towns and villages; rates vary between 25 and 45 sch single and 50 to 70 sch double; for meals add approximately 25 to 30 sch per person. There is an excellent campground at Podersdorf with parking, bus connection, restaurant, provision store, beach, and all

317

modern conveniences. There is another site, with fewer amenities, at St Andra on the edge of Zicksee. Fees range from 3 to 12 sch per person per day, with reductions for members of FICC, AIT, or FIA. There is a big new youth hostel at Neusiedl.

⇥ There are good roads all down the eastern shore of the main lake, and public transport is plentiful. Rail connections with Vienna and Eisenstadt involve changes and can be slow.

🚗 One of the best ways of getting around is to hire a horse at Illmitz or Apetlon; applications through the Gemeindeamt (town hall service) in each place. The authorities maintain lists of local guides who will take and arrange horseback or boat parties through the park. Boats, too, can be hired.

🌤 Open all year; best time – breeding season April to May (mild weather); plant life May to June, watersports July to August; ice sailing late December to early February.

🕘 1–3 days.

🛣 Some roads are private and charge a toll fee.

🗺 List on application to Gemeindeamt at Illmitz or Apetlon.

👁 There is a museum at Neusiedl and a research station at Illmitz. The research station welcomes ornithologists and entomologists (advance notice needed, of course) and will ferry them out to the best viewing areas. The station maintains a good collection of black and white and colour photos.

⇥ Austrian tourist offices.

Finland

Åland Since the glacial ice sheets melted, some 8,000 years ago, Scandinavia, relieved of their weight, has been rising from the sea. One result of the process has been the emergence of the 6,544 islands (at the last count) of Aland to the west of the Finnish mainland; each century they add an astonishing 3 ft to their stature. There is still a lot of bare rock, especially in the tiny islands toward the east. On the larger western islands are fairly extensive deciduous woodlands mixed with meadow pasture. Many Finns have summer villas here, though surprisingly small islands are often permanently inhabited and cultivated for their hay crops. Since the Baltic is tideless, the reedbeds and rushes are extensive. Nearby waters are rich in fish. As Finland's most easterly point, Åland has some species rarely seen elsewhere in the country: ducks (eider, goosander, velvet scoter, scaup, shelduck), dunlin, thrush nightingale, and barred warbler. The map shows the best birdwatching sites and the key identifies particular species for which each is noted. The summer bird list includes: siskin, nutcracker, willow tit, black grouse, razorbill, black guillemot, Arctic skua, common gull, turnstone, mute swan, greylag goose, eagle owl, goshawk and osprey (both breeding), peregrine, and up to 10 breeding pairs of white-tailed eagle (Finland's best site). Åland is not the place for a day-trip if you are birdwatching; you will see plenty but you would also realize that there is so much more

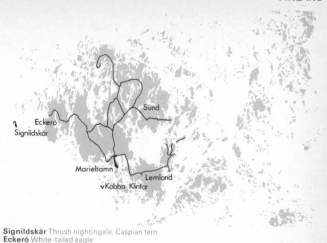

Signildskär Thrush nightingale. Caspian tern
Eckerö White-tailed eagle
Kobba Klintar Razorbill
Lemland Elk
Sund Deer

to be seen. You ought to reckon on spending at least 3 days there. Elk are common in the Lemland Woods; deer in the Sund region. On most islands you will find hare, fox, squirrel, musquash, mink, ermine, otter, mice, and bats. Seals occur in the outer islands.

Access is straightforward and quick: All-year boats and ferries run from Kapellskär in Sweden and Naantali and Turku in Finland; supplemented in summer by services (including hydrofoil) from Stockholm, Norrtälje, and Grisslehamn in Sweden, and Gustavs and Pargas in Finland. Scheduled daily all-year flights run from Helsinki and from Stockholm to Mariehamn, Åland's only town (pop 8,000). Local car ferries connect all the large islands and archipelagoes; and any island can be reached by seaplane-taxi. The lack of tides removes one of the main hazards (or, at least, inconveniences) of birdwatching around more fickle coastlines. Marienhamn has 6 hotels (Fmk15–20 single; Fmk 22–40 double), one motel (Fmk12–14 single; Fmk20–24 double), and 3 boarding houses (Fmk16–26 double). There is a holiday village in Mariehamn with 3-, 4-, 5-, and 6-bed cottages from Fmk130–275/week. Another holiday village at Eckerö has 20 6-bed cottages at Fmk330/week. Bookings for both via Aland Tourist Association, N. Esplanadgatan 1, Mariehamn. The map shows sites of other hotels and hostels in the islands; rates comparable to those for Mariehamn.

Oulanka National Park 26,430 acres; 650 to 1,590 ft above sea level (Rukakunturi Mt). In northeastern Finland, close to the Soviet border, Oulanka shares the character of north and south: fjell-like slopes, tall forests, 50 lakes of varying size, roaring waterfalls, bare sandy banks, gentle-flower-decked water meadows . . . the variety is not surpassed anywhere in

Finland. The north tends to be flat and boggy; the south is more scenic. Cutting right through the park is the Oulanka river, which gives it its name; the canyon carved by the river is the deepest and most precipitous in the country. The park's other main river, Aventojoki, joins the Oulanka at Aventolampi lake. Immediately upstream from the junction is a long series of rapids and falls – home of the rare dipper, which nests only behind or under waterfalls. Below the lake the Oulanka's course is calmer, meandering through ancient meadows cleared by the long-gone Kuusamo people, whose abandoned haybarns can still be seen in groves on the forest edge. The southern edge of the park is marked by the Kiutavaara ridge, rising over 700 ft above the river. Before it reaches the border the Oulanka plunges over the Kiutaköngäs falls, famous throughout Finland.

Reindeer, European elk, fox, hare, squirrel, pine marten: wolverine, wolf, lynx, and bear are all extremely rare. 80 bird species are known to nest in the park, but as this part of Finland is still, ornithologically speaking, being discovered, any knowledgeable visitor still has a good chance to add to the list. The northern swamps have jack snipe, spotted redshank, broad-billed sandpiper, pintail. Among waterside forests: goldeneye, smew, bean and lesser white-fronted geese, whooper swan. The southern species favour the forest groves of the river banks: chaffinch, garden warbler, wren, brambling, song thrush, green sandpiper, hazel hen, ruff, redpoll, little bunting, Siberian jay. Other species: Tengmalm's and eagle owls, raven, buzzard, golden eagle. Oulanka is also the home of the rare red-flanked bluetail (*Tarsiger cyanurus*), which is best seen during midnight-sun conditions in the small hours of the morning.

Pine is the dominant tree, but there is plenty of spruce and birch; also aspen, willow, alder, mountain ash, bird cherry. The Oulanka valley, or gorge, is noted among botanists as an important east-west plant-migration corridor in these parts. More than that, the sunless, north-facing walls and gullies of the gorge, which retain their snow long after the thaw and stay cold and damp all summer, offer a miniature tundra-type climate for Arctic-alpine species – all relics of the last ice age. Alpine butterwort, Irish ciliata, reticulated willow, and *Melandrium affine* flourish here. As a contrast the slopes facing south and the river banks boast: Teesdale violet, clustered gypsophylla, black and rust-red bogrush, calypso, and lady's-slipper orchid.

There is a tourist hotel at Rukatunturi (Fmk23–28 single, Fmk32–40 double; breakfast included). At Kuusamo, about 10 miles from the southern boundary there are 3 hotels (Fmk14 single, Fmk20–27 double), 2 boarding houses Fmk9–10 single, Fmk10–12 double), and a holiday village (4-bed cottage Fmk120/week, 6 bed cottage Fmk160/week). There are simple overnight huts within the park where hikers can stay free (bring for all your needs).

Rail to Taivalkoski then 30 miles on route 20 to Kuusamo. Air to Kajaani then 150 miles on route 5 to Kuusamo.

Marked forest trails lead through the more accessible parts of the park. Route 5 and a byroad from it to Salla give many access points to other parts of the park. Parts of the river are navigable and a boat-hiring concession is on the cards.

☼ Technically open all year; the only feasible season for tourists is May to September.

⊕ 3–5 days.

▨ Free.

☞ None needed where trail is marked. Elsewhere take map and frequent bearings.

⇨ Valtion Luonnonsuojelusualvoja, Unioninkatu 40A, Helsinki 17.

Pallas-Ounastunturi National Park 123,500 acres; averaging 1,600 ft above sea level with peaks rising to 2,695 ft. This is typical Lapp fjell country of mixed peatland and forest. The spruce line runs through the park so there are spruce forests in the southerly Pallastunturi section but only pine to the north. The fjells call for no climbing skill and the view from their tops encompasses not only the nearby lakes but right across the forests and into Sweden, 40 miles away. The upper slopes of the fjells are pure tundra, contrasting with the taiga forest below. Throughout Lappland the mosquitoes can be a pest in high summer.

⇶ Reindeer, red squirrel, occasional bear and lynx, elk, mountain hare, fox, bank vole, stoat, lemming; snow and Lappland buntings, Siberian jay, Arctic warbler; hawk, snowy, and great grey owls; spotted redshank, red-necked skua, smew, greenshank, whooper swan, crane, gyr falcon.

⇐ There is a tourist hotel at Enontekiö, the nearest accessible point outside the park (Fmk24 single, Fmk38 double; breakfast included). A similar hotel inside the park, at Pallastunturi has rooms at identical rates: advance booking for both through Matkaravinto Oy, Helsinki 12, Uudenmaankatu 16–20/tel: 90–662–353 (telex 12–1303).

⇛ Rail and air access to Rovaniemi (overnight sleeper from Helsinki), then bus on routes 79 and 21 to Enontekiö, which is being developed as a winter and summer resort (called Hetta in some literature).

⇌ A byroad to Raatama (off route 79 a few miles before Muonio) has a spur to the Pallastunturi hotel; this is the park's only motor road. The nicer approach is on foot from Enontekiö. The 35-mile trail (marked in difficult places) is described fully in *Hiking Routes in Finnish Lappland* (Finnish Travel Association), which also has useful advice on summer clothing and hiking equipment. There are plenty of rest huts scattered throughout the park.

☼ Open all year (for skiing in winter) but summer (May to September) is best for seeing the wildlife.

⊕ 3–5 days.

▨ Free.

☞ None needed.

⇨ Valtion Luonnonsuojelusualvoja, Unioninkatu 40A, Helsinki 17.

Sompio Natural Park 44,700 acres; rising to a maximum 1,650 ft (Nattaset Mt). At the same latitude as the Pallas-Ounastunturi park, though a hundred miles or so to the east, Sompio has many features in common: fjell, a mixture of taiga forest petering out into pure tundra at higher latitudes.

It is, however, even wilder – without hotels and without roads. Part of the park's boundary is the large northern lake Lokan Tekojärvi, with placid waters and deserted creeks.

🦌   Mammals as for Pallas-Ounastunturi. The marsh outside the park's southern border is a peat-sphagnum bog with desultory scrub in the (relatively) drier parts; this is good for spotted redshank, wood and broad-billed sandpipers, with willow grouse, Siberian tit, and waxwing in the nearby stands of birch and pine. In the park itself: Lappland bunting, shore lark, bluethroat, waxwing, brambling, Siberian tit, willow grouse, capercaillie, spotted redshank, jack snipe, wood sandpiper, greenshank, ruff, ptarmigan, dotterel, broad-billed sandpiper, golden plover, and rough-legged buzzard.

🛏   The nearest hotel is 25 miles away at Laanila (Fmk20 single, Fmk25 double; breakfast included) but there is a tourist hostel offering simple fare at Vuotso, a few miles from the border.

✈   Both Laanila and Vuotso are on route 4, served by regular buses from Rovaniemi, the nearest rail access. There is air access to Rovaniemi and to Ivalo, 25 miles north of Laanila on route 4.

🚐   Route 4, which runs very near the park's western boundary, provides many foot-access points. There are no roads and no marked trails inside the park.

☀   Theoretically open (in the sense that the whole of Lappland is 'open') all year; unless you are particularly interested in the winter ecology, May to September is the best time for wildlife. Mosquitoes can be vicious, though. In the small hours of the morning, when the midnight sun shines, they are less active, and this is the time experienced travellers choose to commune with nature.

🕐   2–3 days.

📧   Free.

🗺   None needed; keep your bearings on Nattaset peak.

➡   Valtion Luonnonsuojelusualvoja, Unioninkatu 40A, Helsinki 17.

Vesijako Natural Park 296 acres; around 350 ft above sea level. This is a rewarding place for birdwatchers to stop on a journey south or north, for a half-day or even a day. It consists almost entirely of spruce forest bordering on several small lakes near the large lake Päijänne. There are all the typical forest species as well as birds that you might not expect to find in such confines: Ural and pigmy owls, osprey; pied, spotted, and red-breasted flycatchers, siskin, goldcrest. Going north on route 4 you look for Arrakoski, 36 miles after Lahti; going south, Arrakoski is 25 miles south of Jämsä, also on route 4. At Arrakoski turn east for just over a mile and you will reach the park. There are 2 boarding houses at Jämsä (Fmk7–10 single; Fmk16 double). Lahti has 3 hotels (Fmk16–24 single; Fmk28–40 double), one motel (Fmk18–25 single; Fmk30–40 double), and one boarding house (Fmk8–10 single; Fmk13–20 double). Nearer than either of these is the holiday village at Padasjoki, with 6-to-8-bed cottages at Fmk90–105/day or Fmk620–720/week.

France

La Camargue The Rhône delta, south of Arles, is one of
Europe's greatest natural treasures and one of the finest
wildlife-viewing areas of the world. Pressure from tourists
and pilgrims has forced the closure of the central reserve
(inside the dotted line on the map); though it is still open to
individual applications for an entry permit: write, stating
your reasons and affiliations, to M. G. Tallon, Directeur des
Reserves Zoologiques et Botaniques de la Camargue,
2 R. Honoré Nicholas, Arles, Bouches-du-Rhône. However
the strict reserve has nothing that cannot be seen – with a
little more effort, to be sure – in the surrounding region.
Actually there are three regions: Camargue, Petite Camargue,
and the large stony plain of La Crau.

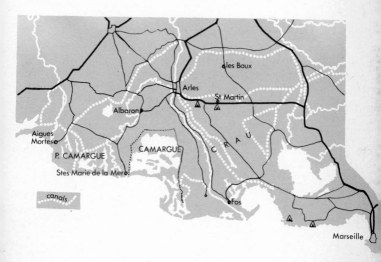

The Camargue and Petite Camargue have a number of
distinct zones; from the sea to the interior: foreshore, dunes,
saltwater and brackish lagoons, freshwater lagoons and
reedmarshes (which are being encroached upon by gradual
extension of cultivated ricefields).

The marshes and reedbeds contain: marsh and Montagu's
harrier, squacco and purple herons, little bittern; Savi's,
moustached, and great reed warblers; spotted, little, and
Baillon's crakes; whiskered tern, black-winged stilt, red-
crested pochard.

The saltwater lagoons, which make up most of the Camargues,
have a highly varied population. The very saline pans near
the sea have the world-famous flamingo populations as well
as large breeding colonies of terns; also avocet, and autumn
waders. There is little life to be seen in winter. The larger, less
salty lagoons with their numerous little islands, house
colonies of larger and smaller gulls (including slender-billed

gull), gull-billed tern, black-winged stilt, red-crested pochard. In the drier parts and along abandoned ditches that have become richly overgrown: Kentish plover, tawny pipit, pratincole, spectacled warbler, crested and short-toed larks, bee eater, roller, great grey and lesser grey shrikes; fan-tailed, Ceti's, Sardinian, and melodious warblers; golden oriole, hoopoe, penduline tit, Scop's owl, black kite. Huge numbers of autumn migrants.

The dunes, which are broadest (almost a mile) in the Petite Camargue, are wooded with stone pine in places: night and squacco herons, little egrets, tawny pipit, short-toed lark.

The foreshore is a breeding ground for Kentish plover.

La Crau is a large stony plain whose chief vegetation is a selection of aromatic herbs, cropped by a few sheep. Here you will see: black-eared wheatear; crested, calandra, and short-toed larks; pin-tailed sandgrouse, lesser kestrel, little bustard.

Apart from birds already listed: oystercatcher, little bittern, spotted and Baillon's crakes, whiskered tern, tawny pipit, woodchat shrike, spectacled, subalpine, and fan-tailed warblers; lesser ketrel. In winter: wigeon, shoveller, gadwall, pintail, teal.

Monotonous and stunted, chiefly made up of saline-loving species dominated by common and shrubby glassworts. Waterlogged but less saline soils support tamarisk. Those still dryer and still less saline are covered by the Camargue 'maquis' – a mixture of mock privet, sea rush, and couch grass. The sand flats grow another glasswort (*Salicornia macrostycha*), while the dunes have a marram-sand couch mixture. The ancient dunes, once sea walls, now grow a specialty of the Camargue: *Juniperus phoenicia*.

Arles is free of the mosquitoes that plague much of the Camargue during high summer; but it is over 20 miles' drive each day. There are 3 hotels with meals and 7 bed and breakfast in or near Saintes-Maries-de-la-Mer (Fr45–88, and Fr28–120 respectively); they are always heavily booked for the festivals on May 24–25 and the Sunday nearest October 22. St-Martin-de-Crau and Fos-sur-Mer each have one hotel (Fr30–35, full board). Albaron has one hotel at similar rates. Campsites are marked on the map.

Nearest airport is at Marseilles. SNCF (French railways) run to Arles, Aigues-Mortes, and Le-Grau-de-Roi; they operate one-day tours of the Camargue from Avignon. Roads are shown on the map.

Car, foot, and horse. You can hire horses in Stes-Maries from: M. Denis Colomb de Daunant, Mas de Carcherel; or M. Laurent Roche, Rue des Léones or Musée Camarguais; or Jean-Marie, Rue Jean Aicard. The firm Camargue-Voyages in the same town hires cars. The SNCF 'Train+ Auto' service operates from Arles.

Open all year. Summers are hot, dry, and very crowded; spring and autumn are the best visiting seasons (especially autumn for waders).

3 days to whole vacation.

Free.

◎ The ruins of the once-powerful Roman and medieval town of Les-Baux-en-Provence provide a superb view over the whole Camargue. There is good birdwatching from the walls – despite the milling throngs of tourists: subalpine warbler, Alpine swift, blue rock thrush, roller, hoopoe. Visitors with botanical interests will certainly want to go on to the Port Cros National Park, 80 miles away, the other side of Marseilles. It is accessible only by launch and has no overnight-stay facilities. Its isolation has protected it from the fires that have raged along this coast from time to time, and so it preserves an original west-Mediterranean flora, especially the Aleppo pine and the very dense undergrowth typical of flintland *maquis*.

Pyrenées-Occidentales National Park 45 miles long by 10 miles wide in uninhabited country in the high Pyrenees against the Spanish border; in fact, part of the park, the former Pic du Midi d'Osseau sanctuary, is continuous with the Ordesa NP in Spain – and shares much of its wildlife.

⚵ Brown bear, wild goat, reintroduced Spanish ibex (*Capra pyrenaica*), northern lynx (Spanish race); Egyptian and griffon vulture; golden, Bonelli's, booted eagles; black and red kites, lammergeier, hobby, goshawk, peregrine, chough and Alpine chough; middle spotted, black, and white-backed woodpeckers; wall creeper, crag martin, rock thrush, Alpine accentor, black-eared wheatear, black redstart, citril and snow finches, rock bunting, red-backed shrike.

⇌ None in the park though a number of refuge-huts are planned. Lourdes has 99 hotels (Fr25–108), Cauterets has 30 (Fr30–58), Luz-St.-Sauver has 6 (Fr23–56), St.-Savin has 1 (Fr40–48), and Gèdre, nearest the roof of the park, has 1 (rates unknown). All rates above are for full board, high-season (out-of-season rates up to 10 per cent lower).

⇥ There is an express train service from Paris to Lourdes 30 miles away, from where N21 winds up to Gavarnie, Cirque de Gavarnie is a short walk beyond the end of the road. There is a 'Train+Auto' service at Lourdes. The road goes up through pine forests to progressively more open wastes of rock, pasture, and scrub.

⤳ Marked and well-defined paths lead through much of the park, from refuge to refuge.

☼ Open all year; summer is best for seeing the wildlife.

◷ 3 days to a whole vacation.

▣ Free.

⇨ There are Syndicats d'Initiative in Lourdes, Cauterets, and Luz-St.-Sauver.

Sept Iles Bird Sanctuary Seven islands (two being mere rock stacks) off the Côtes-du-Nord coast in Brittany. France's premier site for breeding seabirds.

⚵ Gannet, 30,000 puffin (southernmost breeding site for both); 3,000 guillemot, cormorant, 600 razorbill, kittiwake, fulmar, peregrine, raven; herring, greater black-backed, and 5,500 lesser black-backed gulls; storm petrels breed, but because of landing restrictions and rules against disturbance, you are unlikely to see them.

⇌ Lannion has 7 hotels (Fr28–50). There are dozens of resorts along the coast; the two nearest are Perros-Guire with 30 hotels (Fr30–90) and Trégastel, with 12 hotels

(Fr30–80). All rates for full board, high-season; out-of-season rates up to 10 per cent lower.

↦ Nearest airport at Nantes, from where you can take N137 north to Rennes, then west on N12; then you either turn off on N786 – the coast road to Lannion – or go on further along N12 to just beyond Guignamp, where you take N167 north to Lannion.

↦ Boatmen at Perros-Guire run daily boat trips around the islands, and this is much the best way of seeing the birds. Three islands (Cerf, Rouzic, and Malban) are closed to anything but authorized scientific study; the stacks are unsuitable for landing; and on the remaining two islands there are strict rules to prevent disturbance to the birds.

☼ Trips are run only during summer.

⏱ 1 day.

⇨ Union des Syndicats d'Initiative des Côtes-du-Nord, Saint Brieuc.

La Vanoise National Park 52,839 acres of reserve plus a 'touristic buffer zone' of 143,637 acres; from about 3,280 ft to 12,670 ft above sea level. Continuous with the Gran Paradiso NP in Italy. This splendid alpine area, with its high forest and steep, crumbling slopes, snow-clad in winter, was established on 6 July 1963 – France's first and still its major national park. It comprises the whole Vanoise massif, bounded by the valleys of the Isère and Arc. Above the grasslands and forests are glaciers, névés, moraines, and lakes. The highest point is La Grande Casse (12,670 ft). There are two protected nature reserves, one at Tignes, one straddling the Col d'Iséran, to visit which you need a permit from the park authorities. There are also a few small strict reserves not normally open to visitors. At the time of going to press (summer 1971) the scandal surrounding the future of the park has still not been decided. In 1969 the firm owning the holiday village of Super-Tignes proposed lopping off part of the park in order to build a 35,000-bed tourist village at Val Thorens and a 3,500-bed station in Val Polset, both connected by ski lift. The scientific committee of the park vetoed the project unanimously, but, after intense pressure, and by a delegated vote of dubious legality, reversed its decision. In September 1970, after stormy and mounting opposition throughout France, the matter was put to a public inquiry. The decision of the Council of State is expected during 1971.

↝ Chamois, ibex, mountain hare, marmot, stoat, fox. Over 100 bird species include golden eagle, ptarmigan, rock partridge, hazel hen, black grouse, black and three-toed woodpeckers, wall creeper, crag martin, chough and Alpine chough, citril and snow finches, Alpine accentor, crossbill, nutcracker, Alpine swift, Tengmalm's and eagle owls.

ଗ Typical alpine grasslands and forests. Among rarer plants: Alpine groundsel, milfoil, asphodel, sedge, hawksbeard.

↝ Val d'Isère (6,024 ft) has 26 hotels with high-season rates between Fr27–140, full board. Lac de Tignes has 9 hotels (Fr35–100, full board); low-season rates about 10 per cent lower. Camping at Tignes (Le Chantel) June 25 to end-

August, Fr1.60 per person per night plus Fr0.80 per vehicle; water and electricity. This camp also has a few bungalows and rooms to rent. There are 15 huts in the park, accessible to walkers only, where you can stay overnight for a few francs. Those at Félix Faure, Peclet-Polset, le Carro, and Orgère, serve light meals.

➳ From Grenoble take N90 northward until it joins N6, then right on to N6 as far as Lanslebourg, where N202 leads off to the eastern part of the park (the only road in the park); or you can take the Albertville turn off N6 (this is, in fact, the continuation of N90) to Séez where it is joined by the other end of N202. From Geneva come south through Annency to Albertville – N202, N509, N509A, N508, D12, D104.

🚶 On foot or, in winter, ski.

🌅 Open all year; best time May to October (avoiding school holidays if possible, when resorts are crowded and rates high).

🕐 3 days to whole vacation.

🎟 Free.

🎿 There are well-defined paths, which become ski trails in winter, throughout the park. The higher reaches of the park should be explored in company with one of the Guides de Vanoise, Bureaux des Guides de Pralognan-la-Vanoise, Peisey Nancroix, Val d'Isère. Some hotels arrange guided tours of the park, and any of the 40 *gardes-moniteurs* in the park will give helpful advice and directions.

📖 A large-scale map of the park is published at Fr15 by Librarie Didier-Richard, 9 Grand Rue, Grenoble. *Le Parc National de la Vanoise* 179pp, many illustrations, Fr45 from Imprimeries Réunies, 3 rue Lamartine, Chambéry is the definitive book on the park.

➩ Park Director, Parc National de la Vanoise, Boite Postale 105, Chambéry/tel: 34–11–70.

Germany

Königseegebeit 49,000 acres; 1,976 to 8,908 ft above sea level. This is part of a projected Austro-German national park partnership in the Konigsee–Steinernes Meer region a few miles from Berchtesgaden and about 20 miles south of Salzburg. The lake, over 5 miles long and less than a mile wide, nestles between beetling alpine peaks such as Jenner (over 4,000 ft above the lake) and Watzmann (over 7,000 ft above it). The area has many health and winter-ski resorts.

🦌 Roe deer, red deer, chamois, ibex, alpine marmot, snow hare; red-breasted flycatcher, ring ouzel, alpine nutcracker; three-toed, white-backed, and grey-headed woodpeckers; pigmy, Tengmalm's, and eagle owls; crag martin, alpine tit, mountain pipit, alpine redpoll, alpine accentor, wall creeper, snow finch, ptarmigan, rock partridge, alpine chough, raven, lammergeier, and the rare golden eagle.

🌿 Trees include pines (mountain, Swiss, and prostrate), Scots and other firs, beech, larch, sycamore, green alder. Among shrubs: rusty leaved rhododendron, alpine rose, ground cistus, and mountain azalea. Alpine flora includes heathers, liverwort, Christmas rose, wood spurge, pale coralwort, serviceberry, cyclamen, edelweiss, wood goatsbeard, blue sow thistle, Austrian leopardsbane, moonwort, Turk's cap lily, crocus, dwarf primrose, hybrid crowsfoot; dotted, Hungarian, and stemless gentians; lomatogonium, monkshood, alpine ragwort, black orchid, white milfoil, alpine aster, lion's foot, Pyrenean deadnettle and rock beauty, yellow whitlow grass, purple saxifrage, small-flowered columbine, white poppy, Hausmann's rock jasmine.

Königsee has 3 hotels and 8 pensions at prices between DM5 and DM18 (DM12 – DM35 full board), and over 30 bed and breakfast houses (Fremdenheime) at rates between DM5 and DM9 per person per day. Nearby Faseisberg has 1 hotel, 6 pensions, and 9 bed and breakfast houses at similar rates. There are alpine huts (Berghütten) at Jennerhaus and at Kärlingerhaus. There are youth hostels (Jugendheime or Matratzenlager) in Berchtesgaden and between there and Königsee. Rates from DM1.50 – DM6.

A good road connects Königsee with Berchtesgaden, which is, in turn, easily reached from the Munich–Salzburg Autobahn. There is a rail branch line from Salzburg, which also has the nearest large airport.

Mountain railway, ski lifts, foot trails.

Open all year; best time summer.

2–5 days.

Free.

Fremdenverkehrsverband München-Oberbayern 8, München 15, Sonnenstrasse 10/tel: 55 1372.

Lüneburg Heath Naturschutzpark 50,000 acres; 300 to 600 ft above sea level. The park was established during the early years of this century chiefly to protect the heath landscape. Almost all the work done since then has been aimed at effacing signs of industry and restoring old farms and building new ones in traditional style. Ancient crafts such as reed thatching are also encouraged. The park is set amid broad rolling hills clad with heather (some planted but most spread by the moorland sheep) and heavily forested with conifer plantations in places. Since Lübeck, Hamburg, Bremen, Hannover, and Brunswick are all within 50 miles, it is immensely popular with visitors on fine summer and autumn days.

Moorland sheep; red, roe, and fallow deer; wild boar, hare, rabbit, badger, fox, otter, marten, weasel, polecat, squirrel; among 120 bird species are grouse, raven, goshawk, sparrowhawk, buzzard, honey buzzard, barn owl, hobby, kestrel; little, long-eared, short-eared, and tawny owls; Tengmalm's owl (visitor), pallid harrier, curlew, snipe, tawny pipit, house sparrow, stonechat, black woodpecker, stock dove, wryneck.

Many varieties of heather and open moorland plants; junipers, pines, firs, oak, and birch; marsh gentian, bog asphodel, mountain arnica, yellow birdsnest, marsh andromeda, white-beak sedge, and many clubmosses.

Two large villages within the park, Undeloh and Wilsede, offer guesthouse accommodation at rates between DM5 and DM7 per person per bed; full board costs between DM13 and DM16 (all rates plus 10 to 15 per cent service charge). Places like Egestorf and Behringen, just outside the park boundaries, offer similar accommodation at similar rates. Hamburg, with its many hotels, is only 25 miles away. There are youth hostels at Undeloh and at Inzmühlen, on the northern edge. Nearest camping places are at Soltau, 10 miles south of the park (no toilets or running water) and at Bucholz, a few miles north of the park (no provisions).

The Hamburg–Hannover Autobahn skirts most of the east of the park, with access to Hanstedt, Egestorf, Wilsede, and Behringen. Public transport to points within and around the park is abundant.

A good network of roads crisscrosses the park, most of which (except for young plantations) can be explored on foot, too. Many bridle paths have been laid down in the park. The park authority publishes a leaflet listing the 55 people who operate the 76 horse-drawn passenger carts that ply, at very modest rates, within the park; most are 5–seaters but there are some that take up to 20 passengers.

Open all year: best time for moorland flowers late summer.

1 day or vacation.

Free.

Neolithic burial sites and menhirs abound in the Lüneburg region.

Fremdenrerkehrs-Zentrale, Hamburg 1, Bieberhaus am Hauptbahnhof/tel: 24 12 34.

North Sea Coast As Paul Géroudet points out in his introduction to this Europe section, the whole maritime coast of western Europe is a wildlife treasure of inestimable value. The thousands of mudflats, reclaimed lowlands, and small islands of Germany's North Sea coast, from Sylt in the north to the East Friesian islands in the west, offer numerous sites where the seabirds, waders, and waterfowl can be seen with ease, and often in spectacular numbers. Many are reserves of the Deutscher Bund für Vogelschutz (DBV), 6 Frankfurt M-Fechenheim, Steiner Strasse 33. The whole coast is a favourite holiday resort for Germans, so tourist facilities are excellent. For centuries the land has been reclaimed, step by step, from the sea. Several miles inland you may come across ancient dykes surrounding old-established pastures – this, remember, is the homeland of the Friesian cattle breed. Agriculture and fishing are the only industries. The dykes are not the massive affairs you find in the Netherlands, for the reclaimed land is quickly raised above mean sea level; but exceptional high tides often break the dykes and bring widespread, temporary flooding.

The map shows the coastline and the Elbe down as far as the outskirts of Hamburg. Symbols mark the most important DBV reserves and other rewarding birdwatching sites. Here, from north to south, are brief notes on each:

The coast, hinterland, and offshore islands southwest of Husum have three good reserves: Spetinge (recently enlarged to include a nearby reservoir), Westerhever, and the island of Uthörn. Black, little, gull-billed, common, sandwich, and Arctic terns; herring, common, lesser black-backed, and

1 Balje marshes
2 Hamburger Hallig
3 Kleiner Vogelsand & Koogs
4 Knechtsand
5 Südfall
6 Spetinge Staubecken
7 Uthörn
8 Wangerooge
9 Wesel marshes
10 Westerhever

▼ Youth Hostel

canal

black-headed gulls; eider, red-breasted merganser, garganey,
whimbrel, ringed and Kentish plovers, ruff, avocet, black-
tailed godwit, blue-headed wagtail, white stork, marsh
harrier. BDV organize guided tours of Westerhever and
Uthöorn.

North of Husum are two island reserves: Hamburger Hallig
and Südfall, the first connected to the mainland by a dam, the
second accessible at most states of the tide only by boat.
Avifauna similar to the reserves named above; in winter
there is a regular colony of barnacle geese.

The mouth and north bank of the Elbe, though not official
reserves, have a number of good areas. The reclaimed
farmlands (*Koogs*) on the north shore of the estuary, accessible
on foot from the roads shown in the map, are a stopover for
geese on their westward journey each autumn; often they
stay for months. Farther upriver, at Wedsel, are rich marshlands. The southern estuary shore is best around the marshes
near Balje. Greylag, white-fronted, bean, barnacle, and brent
geese; pintail, wigeon, eider, shelduck, mallard, teal, gadwall,
garganey, shoveller, red-crested pochard and pochard,
dotterel, oystercatcher, dunlin; ringed, Kentish, and little
ringed plovers; knot, sanderling, redshank, whimbrel;
wood and broad-billed sandpipers; Temminck's stint.

On the north-facing coast two sites are outstanding:
Knechtsand sanctuary, between the Elbe and Weser estuaries; and the East Friesian island of Wangerooge, which has
4 small DBV sanctuaries. Knechtsand is noted for large

flocks of moulting adult shelduck each July (practically the whole British shelduck population goes there); its vast flocks of migratory waders include turnstone, grey plover, bar-tailed godwit, and knot. Wangerooge – or, rather, the sandflats, mudbanks, tidal marshes, and wet meadows between the island and the mainland – is a good site for waders; it has breeding colonies of black-headed gull and Sandwich, common, Arctic, and little terns; short-eared owl is also recorded.

🖐 This is such a popular holiday coast that there are literally thousands of hotels, inns, pensionen, and hostels to choose among. As a rough guide here are details of three places in the north, centre, and south of the area. List (far north) has 5 hotels (DM9.50–23), 10 pensionen (DM5.50–15), 2 Gasthöfe (DM11), and 3 Fremdenheime (DM3.50–9.50). Husum has 12 hotels (DM8–15), and 9 Gasthöfe (DM5–10). Wangerooge has 12 hotels (DM7–20), 20 Pensionen (DM6–12), and 48 Fremdenheime (DM4–12.50); all prices quoted for bed and breakfast. 36 nearby youth hostels are marked by triangles on the map.

🖐 The map shows the main roads from Hamburg and the south as well as all the seaward roads from these main highways.

🖐 The exposed area of the mudflats is shown on the map. You can walk far out from shore on them between tides – but go prepared to get wet for there are many *Priele* (run-off streams); some are small enough to leap over but many are broad, waist deep, and swift flowing. From most mainland resorts there are 4-wheel horsedrawn carts with extra-large wheels for negotiating the flats and *Priele*.

Naturpark Pfälzer Wald 418,250 acres; 600 to 2,200 ft above sea level. The Pfälzer Wald, near the French border in south-western Germany, is the largest area of unbroken forest in the Federal Republic. It stands on an old Bunter-sandstone plateau marked by deep gullies. There are about 165 villages unevenly distributed throughout the area, more than 75 per cent of which is wooded, some densely. In fact, the only area quite free of woods is the Weinstrasse, where there are many vineyards. The wald is, as yet, hardly touched by tourism from overseas, though it is popular with Germans during school holidays in summer.

🖐 Red deer, roe deer, wild boar, many small mammals, and over 200 bird species. In the enclosed Wildschutzpark Kurpfalz bei Wachenheim (430 acres) there are European bison, moufflon, fallow deer, mountain goat.

🖐 More than 60 per cent of the tree species are conifers (chiefly spruce and Scots pine); beech and oak are the main deciduous trees. These, with typical woodland and forest flora, dominate the landscape.

🖐 Hotels, inns, and guesthouses (totals given in that order) at: Annweiler (3, 7, 12), Bad Bergzabern (12, 3, 5), Bad Dürkheim (8, 8, 3), Neustadt-an-der-Weinstrasse (8, 7, 1), Edenkoben (5, 5, 0); inns and guesthouses at Dahn, Elmstein, Eppenbrunn, Frankeneck, Gleisweiler, Hohenecken, Hochspeyer, Johanniskreuz, and other towns and villages. Hotel rates from DM20 per person per day, bed and breakfast, and DM40 full board. Youth hostels (from DM2) at Annweiler,

Bad Durkheim, Dahn, Hochspeyer, and Neustadt-an-der-Weinstrasse. Camping all year at Bad Bergzabern and mid-March to mid-October at Annweiler; caravan (trailer) facilities at both sites.

The Autobahns E4, E5, and E12 all run near the Pfalz region, which is well serviced, too, by train and bus.

A good network of local roads links the town and villages within the park. Three large valleys intersect the park east-to-west and make it fairly easy for walkers to orient themselves. Car parks with marked foot trails at Annweiler, Bad Bergzabern, Dahn, Edenkoben, and Elmstein.

Open all year; best time May to November.

2–7 days.

Free.

The region is well endowed with medieval and later castles, among them the one at Trifels, near Annweiler (where Richard Lionheart was imprisoned). At Bad Dürkheim there is a huge wine vat (1.2 million litres). Annual grape-harvest festivities and vintage-sampling feasts are worth visiting.

Bezirksregierung der Pfalz, 673 Neustadt/Weinstrasse, Friedrich-Ebert-Str. 14.

Great Britain

Braunton Burrows National Nature Reserve 560 acres at or near sea level. The Burrows form one of the largest sand-dune systems in Britain; only the southern part is a nature reserve; the central part is an occasional military training area. The landscape is virtually treeless – a series of wind-blown sand ridges forming dunes interspersed by dry and wet slacks and, just outside the reserve's northern boundary, some permanent ponds.

The reserve lies on the main west coast migration route. 170 species have been recorded; 60 breeding. But breeding is declining because of military training and low-flying service aircraft – as well as increasing disturbance by visitors. Curlew and redshank colonies are declining, and buzzard, yellow wagtail, lapwing, and black-headed gull no longer breed here at all, though all are visitors.

Marram, sand sedge, and sand couch grass are the common binders of the dunes. Clustered club rush, sharp rush, and sea rush are common. Plants rare elsewhere include water germander, French or sand toadflex (only British site), sea stock, and dune pansy. Other noteworthy plants: sea rocket, prickly saltwort, sea bindweed, sea holly, sea milkwort, marsh helleborine, Argentine dock (introduced), evening primrose (introduced), portland spurge, round-leaved wintergreen, and yellow bartsia.

Hotels at Barnstaple (7 miles), Ilfracombe (7 miles), and Bideford (16 miles).

A361 to Braunton, then B3231 coast road for 1 mile, turn left, free car park 1½ miles. There is then a half-mile walk to the reserve. Foot access from Braunton via Ferry road. Rail access to Braunton.

There are two marked nature trails. The Lighthouse Trail (1½ miles) in the reserve and the Flagpole Trail (1½ miles – closed when the red flag is flying) near its northern boundary.

Open all year; best time spring and summer for plants; autumn and winter for birds.

1 day.

Two self-guiding leaflets, one for each of the nature trails, are available from the warden.

Conservancy staff, part-time, and honorary wardens patrol the reserve and will give advice and guidance.

The north Devon coast has a wealth of picturesque villages.

The Exmoor National Park is about 20 miles away to the east.

⇨ The Warden, Pounds Mean, Hills View, Braunton, North Devon/tel: Braunton 552.

Caerlaverock National Nature Reserve 13,514 acres near sea level. A mixture of saltmarsh and sandy foreshore in the Solway Firth on the east of the mouth of the River Nith. Excellent for its birdlife. In winter up to 3,000 barnacle geese, large numbers of pink-footed and a few hundred greylag geese come to feed and roost. You need a permit to visit the eastern section of the saltmarsh. Access by B725 from Dumfries to Shearington (8 miles) then 1 mile on foot. Nearby attractions include the ruins of Caerlaverock Castle (14th century), the ruins of Sweetheart Abbey (13th century), Ruthwell Church (best-preserved Anglo-Saxon runic cross), and the Burns Mausoleum at Dumfries – all within 10 miles. Nature Conservancy, 12 Hope Terrace, Edinburgh 9.

Cairngorms National Nature Reserve 64,118 acres: 1,500 to 4,296 ft above sea level. This, Britain's largest national nature reserve, takes in part of the central mass of the Cairngorm mountains. Geologically it is an ancient plateau dominated by broad summits, such as Braeriach (4,248 ft), Carn Toul (4,241 ft), and Ben Macdui (4,296 ft); the southern part of Cairn Gorm itself (4,084 ft) is also within the reserve. The plateau runs out to great vertical bluffs, scoured by glaciers to form steep glens and corries (cirques). Only one glen, Lairig Ghru, penetrates right through the range, providing the only easy link between the easily accessible north of the reserve and the less accessible southern parts. The Cairngorms ski resort, on the northern slopes of the mountain, are just outside the reserve boundaries. Since the deer have no natural predators their numbers have to be controlled by shooting, and parts of the reserve are closed in succession between July 1 and February 15. Contact the reserve wardens before entering the reserve during this period.

🐾 Red deer, roe deer, wild cat, fox, badger, otter, red squirrel, mountain hare, and reindeer (imported in 1950 during meat rationing as a possible extra source of meat and now established as a herd). Birds include golden eagle, osprey, peregrine, dotterel, Scottish crossbill, crested tit, greenshank, snow bunting, capercaillie, siskin, black grouse, buzzard, merlin, ring ouzel, and (above 2,000 ft) ptarmigan.

� Many pinewoods in the lower parts of the reserve. Birch, rowan, alder, and willow in Glenfeshie. Shrubby woodland plants and herbs: bilberry, crowberry, ling, creeping lady's tresses, chickweed wintergreen, lesser twayblade, tuberous bitter vetch, common cow-wheat, wood sorrel. Above the natural tree limit: ling, bell heather, cross-leaved heath, red bearberry, trailing azalea, mountain crowberry, cloudberry, dwarf cornel, alpine lady's mantle, roseroot, mountain sorrel, northern rock cress, alpine speedwell. Plants of the high summits: rigid sedge, trifid rush, curved woodrush,

Roe deer do not form herds but live singly or in small families. The male's sudden bark punctuates the rutting season in July and August.

spiked woodrush, starry saxifrage, moss campion, least willow. Mosses, liverworts, and lichens at all levels.

Apart from mountain rescue huts – for emergency use only – there is no accommodation in the reserve. At Loch Morlich, 2 miles from the northern boundary, is a youth hostel and a campsite. Nearby, at Colyumbridge, is another campsite. There is another youth hostel at Aviemore, 3 miles from the northern entrance. To the south there is a campsite (foot access only) at Derry Lodge at the southeastern entrance. Hotels at Aviemore and at Braemar (7 miles).

There are no roads to or within the reserve. To the north and west there are three roads that run from Aviemore and Kincraig to the reserve boundaries – all blind alleys without parking. Your best plan is to walk from either place – 3 and 4 miles respectively, through landscape identical with that inside the reserve. To the south a loop road from Braemar (5 miles) runs around the Linn of Dee, from where three footpaths run to the reserve. All the above towns have rail access.

Footpath only. There is a marked nature trail with a self-guiding leaflet at Loch an Eilein on the northern boundary and easily accessible on foot or by car from Aviemore. From here, too, a footpath leads up Glen Einich to Loch Einich. Another footpath (18 miles and a good day's walk) connects Loch an Eilein with the Linn of Dee via the glen of Lairig Ghru. Other footpaths skirt the eastern and western boundaries.

Open all year; best time spring and summer for plants, fauna at any time.

1–7 days.

Balmoral castle (gardens only open to the public) is about 7 miles east of Braemar. Loch Garten, the famous public-viewing site for one of Britain's successful breeding pairs of ospreys, is about 8 miles north of Abernethy.

A. MacDonald, Chief Warden, Kinakyle, Aviemore/tel: Aviemore 250; D. Holland, Assistant Warden, Achnagoichan Cottage, Rothiemurchus, Aviemore/tel: Aviemore 287. The warden for the southern side is D. Rose, Lilybank, Braemar/tel: Braemar 284.

Coed Llyn Mair Nature Trail A three-quarter-mile trail with self-guiding leaflet in the Coedydd Maentwrog National Nature Reserve (which, in turn, is within the Snowdonia National Park). The trail runs through oak woodlands of a kind that once blanketed much of north Wales. To preserve the woodland the diseased and rotting trees are removed, so nesting boxes have been erected for such birds as the pied flycatcher and coal tit. On the lake of Llyn Mair (Mary's Lake) there are many water birds – breeding mallards, and black-headed gulls in summer; goldeneye, little grebe, and whooper swan in winter. Common butterflies include meadow browns, hairstreaks, and fritillaries. Car access is by B4410 from Beddgelert or Maentwrog; there is a car park near the lake at point 1 of the trail. The outward route has seven stops (1 to 7); the return route 4 (A to D). You can also arrive by the narrow-gauge Festiniog Railway, alighting at Tan y Bwlch; here you start at point A and finish at point 7. Strong boots advisable. Regional Officer, Nature Conservancy, Penrhos Road, Bangor, Caernarvonshire.

Cwm Idwal Nature Trail A 2-mile trail with self-guiding leaflet around the lake of Llyn Idwal in the Cwm Idwal Nature Reserve (part of the Snowdonia National Park). The trail follows a fairly easy path in the Snowdon ranges north-east of the Pass of Llanberris. It averages 1,200 ft above sea level, so warm clothing and strong boots are advisable. On the way you pass across rock faces, pasture, and bog – with views of uplands inaccessible to sheep grazing. The sides of the mountain are frequented by a herd of goats, the wild descendants of early domestic stock. Birds recorded in the area include raven, buzzard, ring ouzel, heron, sandpiper. Whooper swan, pochard and goldeneye are winter visitors. Interesting plants include purple saxifrage, mountain sorrel, and sundew. Access is from the A5 between Bangor and Capel Curig (rail access to Bangor), turning off at Ogwen Cottage Mountain School (limited parking facilities). Regional Officer, Nature Conservancy, Penrhos Road, Bangor, Caernarvonshire.

Exe Estuary National Wildfowl Refuge 1,022 acres near sea level. This is the most important site for wildfowl and waders in southwestern England and has large resident winter populations. Species include wigeon (up to 5,500), teal (up to 2,000), shelduck (up to 1,000), red-breasted merganser, eider, brent goose, avocet, spoonbill. Highlights of the year are brent geese in January and oystercatchers, redshanks, and curlews in September. Access is from the A379 Exeter–Teignmouth road, which skirts the whole western edge of the estuary. Devon Bird-watching and Preservation Society, R. W. C. Elliot (Hon. Sec.), 7 Gordon Road, Exeter.

Glasson Moss National Nature Reserve 143 acres near Port Carlisle on the inner reaches of the Solway Firth. One of the few surviving low-level raised bogs in more-or-less natural condition. Curlew, meadow pipit, skylark. Round-leaved sundew, great sundew, bog rosemary, cranberry, bog asphodel. Wooded fringes to the south contain willow tit, great spotted woodpecker, and some raptorial species. Rockliffe Marsh, a splendid resort for winter wildfowl, and Grune Point, an observation station for migratory birds, are both within 5 miles. Access is from the Carlisle – Port Carlisle road or from the B5307 to Kirkbride. Nature Conservancy, Merlewood Research Station, Grange-over-Sands, Lancashire.

Herma Ness National Nature Reserve 2,383 acres at the northern tip of Unst, the northernmost island of the Shetland group. An important breeding station of the great skua; other species include arctic skua, red-throated diver, red-necked phalarope, gannets, kittiwake, puffin. Whimbrel and snowy owl also breed in the Shetlands. Air access to Baltasound, then 5 miles by road to Burrafirth, then 3 miles on foot. Nature Conservancy, 12 Hope Terrace, Edinburgh 9.

Hickling Broad National Nature Reserve 1,204 acres some 10 miles north of Great Yarmouth. Open water, extensive reed beds, fen, and grazing marshland give habitat for most of Norfolk's plant and animal communities. Bearded tit, bittern, black tern, black-tailed godwit, spotted redshank, Bewick's swan, goldeneye, ruff, garganey, sedge warbler, heron. Swallowtail butterflies are present. Access by A149, 12 miles north of Great Yarmouth, turning right via Potter Heigham; from Norwich 15 miles east on A1151 to Stalham, then 5 miles south on A149 to Potter Heigham. Nature Conservancy, 60 Bracondale, Norwich NOR 58B.

Hope Wood Nature Trail A short walk through wood and gorge in the 101-acre Ebbor Gorge National Nature Reserve, near Wookey Hole, 2 miles from Wells and in the southern Mendip Hills. Buzzard, sparrow hawk, kestrel, chiff chaff, willow warbler, wren, chaffinch, bullfinch, marsh and other tits; badger, fox, grey squirrel. Speckled wood butterfly; greater and lesser horseshoe bats. Ash, pedunculate oak, wych elm, beech, whitebeam, hornbeam, dogwood, spindle, wayfaring tree, buckthorn, blue gromwell, nettle-leaved bellflower, broad-leaved helleborine, bloody cranesbill, greater butterfly orchid. Self-guiding leaflet available. Nearby attractions include Cheddar Gorge, Wookey Hole Caves, and Wells cathedral. Access is by the Wookey Hole road from Wells. There is a car-parking and picnicking area. The Warden, East House, Wookey Hole, Somerset/tel: Wells 3773.

Knockan Cliff Nature Trail A three-quarter-mile walk along an escarpment in the Inverpolly National Nature Reserve. The path goes part-way up the cliff and is quite steep at one point about half way along; less active people can rest at a seat here and turn back to the car park at the starting point. The chief interest of the walk centres on the geology of the cliff and its plant life – trees, dwarf shrubs, herbaceous plants, grasses, sedges, ferns, and mosses. Birds you may see from vantage points along the walk: golden eagle, buzzard, kestrel, raven, hooded crow, jackdaw, red grouse, greenshank, common sandpiper, dunlin, woodcock, pied wagtail, skylark, meadow pipit, snow bunting, robin, wren, ring ouzel, whooper swan, mallard, goldeneye, wigeon, greater black-backed gull, heron, red and black-throated divers. Mammals in the reserve include red deer (500 head), roe deer, badger, otter, pine marten, wildcat, fox, mountain hare. Access is from the A835 road 14 miles from Ullapool. To visit the Drumrunie part of the reserve (not part of the nature trail) in the deerstalking season (mid-July to mid-October) you need a permit from the Assynt Estate Office/tel: Lochinver 203. Hotels in Ullapool. The world-famous Inverewe Gardens of rare and subtropical plants is on the coast near by. Nature Conservancy, 12 Hope Terrace, Edinburgh 9.

Leighton Moss National Wildfowl Refuge 400 acres of arable land, now reverted to fen, reed swamp, and stretches of open water near Warton Sands in Morecambe Bay. The best site for bird watching in Lancashire. From tall wooden hides built up on stilts you can watch bittern, reedwarbler, shoveler, teal, garganey, water rail, grass hopper, lesser redpoll, and mallard. Permits are needed from the Royal Society for the Protection of Birds, The Lodge, Sandy, Bedfordshire, for visiting the hides; but there is a public right of way across the centre of the marsh. The M6 and A6 roads pass within three miles of the refuge. Nearby attractions include Borwick Hall, an unaltered Elizabethan manor, Hornby Castle, and Leighton Hall, with extensive grounds and fine gardens. Royal Society for the Protection of Birds.

Lindisfarne National Nature Reserve 7,387 acres of sand dune and intertidal area sheltered behind the long promontory of Holy Island off the Northumberland coast. A gull roost, migration watchpoint, and a favourite haunt of grey seals. Wigeon, mallard, teal, greylag goose, pink-footed goose, brent goose (only British overwintering site), knot, dunlin, bar-tailed godwit, redshank, mute and whooper swans, occasional Bewick's swan, eider and shelducks. Access is by the A1, 7 miles south of Berwick-upon-Tweed. Nearby attractions include Lindisfarne Priory and Castle on Holy Island. H. Dollman, Chief Warden, The Braes, Hillside Road, Belford, Northumberland/tel: Belford 235.

Red deer belong to the same race as the American elk (page 87). In open country they form large herds, browsing on foliage and grazing among the grasses. The species exists across temperate Eurasia.

Loch Leven National Nature Reserve 3,946 acres (125 being woodland) near Kinross, between the firths of Tay and Forth. The most important freshwater site in Britain for breeding and migratory waterfowl. Mallard, tufted duck, gadwall, teal, shoveler; one of the year's highlights is the arrival of grey geese in October. Access by road is best at a point on the B9097 on the south of the loch, overlooking Saint Serf's Island. Foot access is confined to Kirkgate Park, Findatie, Burleigh Sands, and Castle Island. To visit other parts you need a permit. Nearby attractions include the ruins of Loch Leven Castle (15th century – where Mary Queen of Scots escaped imprisonment in 1568), Burleigh Castle, and Kinross House (17th century – fine gardens running down to the lakeshore). Nature Conservancy, 12 Hope Terrace, Edinburgh 9.

Miners' Track Nature Trail A 2-mile walk from Pen y Pas on the A4068 Llanberis–Beddgelert road up to Llyn Llydaw in the shadow of Snowdon (from 1,180 ft to 1,416 ft). The track takes you through some of the finest mountain scenery in Britain; it was built during the last century to give access to the copper workings around Llyn Llydaw (Lake Brittany), which is still polluted although the workings went idle in 1916. Along the track you pass through poor pasture land and patches of bog where water collects over impermeable hollows in the living rock – which is everywhere near the surface here. Plants include mat grass, sheep's fescue, bent grass, wild thyme, heath bedstraw, and, in boggy areas, cotton grass, bog asphodel, rushes, butterwort, and sphagnum mosses. Birdlife includes raven, wheatear, meadow pipit, ring ouzel, carrion crow, and chough. The track is described in detail in a self-guiding leaflet. From it the energetic can take one of 2 routes, each about 3 miles long, covering the remaining 2,137 ft to the top of Snowdon. Regional Officer, Nature Conservancy, Penrhos Road, Bangor, Caernarvonshire.

Minsmere Reserve 1,500 acres; at or near sea level. There is a bigger variety of breeding birds at Minsmere (almost 100 species) than at any other comparable site in the country; more than 210 species are seen each year. The reserve owes its present form to anti-invasion flooding carried out during the war. Reeds spread from the old network of ditches and made the whole Minsmere Level a superb sanctuary for marsh birds. When the area was again accessible, in 1948, its owner, Captain Oglivie, rented it to the Royal Society for the Protection of Birds, who now administer the reserve. It includes five distinct habitats: a shoreline of one mile; 400 acres of freshwater marsh with some 24 lagoons; 400 acres of old mixed woodland; heathland, birch coppice, and gorse; and 'The Scrape' – a new and unique conservation project consisting of 30 acres of shallow, brackish water whose level is controlled to an inch so as to maintain about 50 islets on which some 1,500 pairs of birds regularly breed. Ten years ago The Scrape was rough grassland supporting about 20 breeding pairs. In 1970 there were (in round figures) 50 pairs of Sandwich terns, 400 of common terns, 16 of avocets (only one other colony in Britain, at Havergate), and 200 pairs of black-headed gulls. Other breeding species in The Scrape: redshank, oystercatcher, ringed plover, and, most interesting of all, 7 pairs of little terns, which are becoming increasingly scarce elsewhere because of growing recreational pressure on their beach habitats. In the reedmarsh there are two or three pairs of marsh harriers, which, since the number of breeding osprey pairs rose to 6, is now Britain's rarest breeding raptor. There are also 40 pairs of bearded tits, 12 of bitterns, scores of water rails, 1,000 pairs each of reed and sedge warblers, and 40 pairs of gadwall (fairly rare elsewhere in Britain) among other ducks. In the woods and hedgerows there are all the common warblers (except wood warbler), woodpeckers, and about 35 pairs of nightingales. Only 4 or 5 pairs of redbacked shrikes now breed, a species that is decreasing throughout Britain. Minsmere is the best of several good coastal marshes in this part of the country.

The numbers on the reserve in any one day is strictly limited, and entry is thus only by permit. Those for escorted visits (Sunday and Wednesday; April to mid-September) cost 75p; for unescorted visits 50p (Monday, Wednesday, and weekends; same months). Leave the A12 just north of Yoxford, turning right on to B1122 for 2 miles to Theberton, then left on a byroad to East Bridge, from were the reserve is signposted. Alternatively, turn off the B1122 before

The return of breeding avocets to Britain, where they were unknown after 1825, is a triumph of post-war bird protection. They are now established at Minsmere and on the Suffolk coast. They winter on the Tamar estuary, the Axe estuary, and the wetlands south of Cork.

Theberton and bear right in Westleton. If you want to approach along the cliff, take the Dunwich road from Westleton and follow the National Trust signs to Dunwich and Minsmere cliffs. There are railway connections from London to Darsham, where you can hire a taxi.

Only on foot; only on the marked paths. All the reserve is visible but only small parts are accessible (hence its success). There are excellent hides throughout the accessible parts. Wear waterproof boots and stout clothing.

Open April to mid-September.

1 day.

Dunwich was once an important East Anglian capital, with 250 churches and religious houses – 249 of which have vanished beneath the sea. There are several ancient buildings and ruins in and near the village (as it now is).

H. E. Axell, Warden, Minsmere Reserve, Westleton, Saxmundham, Suffolk/tel: Westleton 298. Permits from RSPB, The Lodge, Sandy, Beds.

Newborough Warren, Ynys Llanddwyn National Nature Reserve 1,566 acres of foreshore and broad sand dune in southwestern Anglesey. The dunes show every stage of plant colonization, from the beach zone with straggly tufts of marram grass to established pasture at the inland edge; the northern end is a saltmarsh. There are many small mammals,

341

lizards, and toads around the dunes, but they are best known for their birds: large breeding colonies of herring gulls; lapwing, curlew, oystercatcher, skylark, and meadow pipit. Plants of the dunes and slacks include dune pansies, sand cat's tail, mouse-ear chickweed, lady's smock, meadow saxifrage, wintergreen, carline thistle, bird's foot trefoil, wild thyme, several orchids, butterwort, and grass of parnassus. The rocky coast of Ynys Llanddwyn provide breeding grounds for shag and cormorant; the rocks are precambrian – over 600 million years old. In the saltmarsh and Malltraeth Pool to the north you will find shelduck, curlew, redshank, pintail; mute, whooper, and Bewick's swans; goldeneye, black-tailed and bar-tailed godwits ruff and greenshank. Plant life includes sea aster, glasswort, sea arrowgrass, sea rush, sea thrift, and cord grass. Access is from Bangor over the Menai Bridge, then via A4080 to Newborough, then 2 miles by Forestry Commission road to a car park near the foreshore. There are four rights of way through or near the reserve; you need a permit to visit parts away from these paths. Permits from Regional Officer, Nature Conservancy, Penrhos Road, Bangor, Caernarvonshire/tel: STD 0248 (Bangor) 2201. Caernarvon Castle is just across the strait, but 23 miles away by road. Reserve Warden at 'Serai', Malltraeth, Bodorgan, Anglesey/tel: Bodorgan 321.

North Norfolk Coast Reserves These are seven reserves and refuges managed by various authorities and bodies. They form a continuous line stretching 26 miles from the southern mouth of the Wash almost out to Sheringham. From west to east they are:

Holme Nature Reserve (Norfolk Naturalists Trust) 400 acres of foreshore, sand dunes, fresh and salt marshes; habitat for migrant birds and waterfowl; most westerly breeding point of the bearded tit. Access by car from Holme village; car parks are signposted. Foot access along the Thornham sea wall. Visitors should contact the Warden, The Firs, Holme-next-Sea/ tel: Holme 240. The Trust offers limited dormitory accommodation for educational and other parties at The Firs.

Holme Bird Observatory (National Trust) The observatory exists for the systematic recording and ringing of migrant birds. Visitors, who are welcome, should contact the Honorary Warden, Holme Bird Observatory, Holme-next-Sea. Access routes as for Holme.

Brancaster Manor (National Trust) About 1,400 acres of a former manor: foreshore, sand dunes, salt marsh, and reclaimed marshland. Access by road from Brancaster village to the shore car park; flooding in spring tides. Bathing can be dangerous. Warden: R. Roy, Roselands, Brancaster Staithe/ tel: Brancaster 311.

Scolt Head National Nature Reserve (Nature Conservancy) 1,821 acres of island, marsh, and foreshore. Noted for large nesting colonies of sandwich tern and common tern; during May to July you must be accompanied by the warden when visiting these colonies – but elsewhere access is unrestricted. In winter there are large flocks of brent goose and waders. Access by boat only. Boatmen at Brancaster Staithe and Burnham Overy Staithe will row you over; do not be tempted into a foot crossing via the marshes – unless you have a local guide. Warden R. Chestney, Dial House, Brancaster Staithe/tel: Brancaster 330.

Holkham National Nature Reserve (Nature Conservancy) 4,200 acres of sand dune and coastal marsh (some of it grazing pasture) and 5,500 acres of intertidal mudflats and sand. The largest coastal NNR in England; contains one of the country's largest stretches of saltmarsh. Little and sandwich terns breed here; large numbers of winter wildfowl. Access by car from Holkham village; on foot along the sea wall from Overy Staithe or along the beach from Wells. Permits are needed away from the marked footpaths. Nature Conservancy, 60 Bracondale, Norwich NOR 58B.

Blakeney Point Nature Reserve (National Trust) 1,400 acres of shingle beach and sand dunes, with saltmarsh on the landward side. Common and little terns, and occasional sandwich tern, nest on the seaward side. Other breeding species include oystercatcher, ringed plover, redshank, black-headed gull, shelduck. Access (to ternery restricted May to July) from Cley on foot; from Morston and Blakeney by boat and prior arrangement. Warden W. E. Eales, Point House, Morston/ tel: Cley 220.

Cley Nature Reserve (Norfolk Naturalists Trust) 400 acres of partly flooded coastal marsh. Noted for rare migrants. The most southerly fulmar colonies are here; also avocet, black-tailed godwit, ruff, bearded tit, bittern, garganey, pintail, wigeon. Access to the east bank is unrestricted and there is a car park to the west of the main observation hut. But bird-watching facilities are limited to permit holders from April 1 to October 31 (except Mondays and special visiting days). You can apply for permits, a week in advance, to the Secretary of the Norfolk Naturalists Trust, Norwich. Unsold permits for any given day are sold by the warden after 10am on the day in question. Warden W. F. Bishop, Watchers Cottage, Cley/ tel: Cley 380.

Noss National Nature Reserve 774 acres 4 miles east of Lerwick in the Shetlands. With its great cliffs this is one of Europe's most spectacular islands. Nesting and breeding site for gannet, guillemot, fulmar, shag, kittiwake, puffin, herring gull, greater black-backed gull (biggest colony in UK), arctic and great skuas, eider duck. The island is uninhabited and wardened by the Royal Society for the Protection of Birds, with whom arrangements for a visit should be made. Access to Shetlands by air (Sumburgh) or sea (Aberdeen, Leith, or Kirkwall to Lerwick).

Old Winchester Hill National Nature Reserve 140 acres (including 40 of woodland) of rough chalk grassland, yew, and juniper scrub. A marked, self-guiding nature trail, about 2 miles long, visits every corner of the reserve (red trail); for those who cannot negotiate the steep slopes there is a short version (white trail) about 1 mile long. The reserve is equally noted for its plants, birds, and butterflies. Birds: tree creeper, nuthatch, blackbird, robin, tits, great spotted woodpecker, dunnock, bullfinch, chaffinch, yellowhammer, goldcrest, jay, wood pigeon, linnets, stock dove, turtle dove, green woodpecker, mistle thrush, fieldfare, kestrel; little, tawny, and barn owls; occasional buzzard, hobby, and Montagu's harrier. Butterflies: common blue, meadow brown, small heath, small skipper, red admiral, painted lady, peacock, small tortoiseshell, chalkhill blue, green hairstreak, Duke of Burgundy fritillary, clouded yellow, speckled wood, green-veined white; cinnabar and burnet moths. Plants: beech, ash, sycamore, elm, turkey oak, dog's mercury, herb robert, arum, wood aven, coppiced hazel, eyebright, thyme, squinancywort, carline thistle, rampion, stemless thistle, wild mignonette, and a variety of orchids. The reserve also contains a badger sett. Near the end of both trails are the remains of an Iron Age fort (c 250 BC) and some earlier burial mounds. Access is sign-posted from West Meon or Warnford, both on the A32 Alton-Gosport road. Car parking at the roadside; picnic area near the entrance gate. Note: some marked-off areas may contain unexploded bombs – this was once a military training area. Warden J. T. Kennard, Drocheneford, Droxford, Hampshire/tel: Droxford 547.

Pewsey Downs National Nature Reserve 188 acres of chalk downland on the northern scarp of the Vale of Pewsey. 46 bird species include wheatear, stone curlew, quail, tree pipit, whitethroat, nightjar. Chalk-loving plants, such as round-headed rampion, field fleawort, and bastard toadflax. Chalk-hill blue and brown argus butterflies common. Several of the hills in the reserve have historical associations and relics. Knap Hill has a neolithic causewayed camp; Walkers Hill (site of Battle of Wodnesbeorgh, AD 592) has a chambered longbarrow; Milk Hill has the Alton White Horse, cut in 1812. Access from Marlborough via A345, turn right just south of Oare on to byroad to Alton Priors; there turn right on byroad back to Marlborough, which passes by the reserve.

Rhosslli Clifftop Nature Trail A 3-mile walk around the Gower Peninsula (Gower Coast National Nature Reserve) with fine views across to Worms Head. Breeding colonies of guillemot, razorbill, fulmar, kittiwake, cormorant, shag, rock pipit. The clifftops and pastures attract wheatear, stonechat, whinchat, linnet. The steep southerly slopes have long been known to botanists for their rich limestone flora, including some uncommon species. Access is from Swansea via A4118 almost to Port Eynon, bearing right for Rhosslli on B4247. The trail starts in Rhosslli. Warden, Gower Countryside Centre, Old School, Oxwich/tel: Port Eynon 320. Research permits from Nature Conservancy, Regional Officer for South Wales, Plas, Gogerddan, Aberystwyth/tel: Bow Street 338.

Rostherne Mere National Wildfowl Refuge 378 acres (of which 75 are woodland); the finest of the famous Cheshire meres. Rostherne is $\frac{3}{4}$ mile long and nearly $\frac{1}{2}$ mile wide; it lies in a glacial drift of boulder clay. The shoreline is skirted by willow beds, reeds, and mixed woodland. Up to 5,000 mallard and teal in winter; 20,000 gulls gather in their roosts from November on. The best designed observatory in the country is here. Access is by permit only from the Regional Office, Nature Conservancy, Attingham Park, Shrewsbury, Shropshire/tel: STD 0743–77 (Upton Magna) 611. If you wish to use the observatory only, send 25p (5s) and stamped addressed envelope to Mr W. Mulligan, 432 Parrs Wood Road, Manchester 20. Access is from Manchester via A56 to 2 miles beyond Altrincham, then A556 (Watling Street) for $\frac{1}{2}$ mile; the mere is just to the right of the road. Five miles farther south there is access to the M6.

Russland Moss National Nature Reserve 58 acres (of which 10 are woodland). One of the few surviving examples of a Lake District 'moss' – a raised bog (in this case 20 ft above sea level) derived, long ago, from open estuary water. The woodland supports a heronry and there is a small herd of wild red and roe deer in the valley. Access off the footpaths is by permit only from the Regional Officer, Nature Conservancy, Merlewood Research Station, Grange-over-Sands, Lancashire/tel: Grange-over-Sands 2264 & 5. From Windermere take A592 south to Newby Bridge, then A590, 3 miles, to Haverthwaite; thence north on a byway between Windermere and Coniston toward Hawkshead; Rusland is $3\frac{1}{2}$ miles along this byway.

Saint Cyrus Nature Trail A 2-mile walk that takes in most of the 227-acre St Cyrus National Nature Reserve, a coastal reserve some 30 miles south of Aberdeen. Habitat includes rocks (at the northern end), saltmarsh, dunes, dune pasture, and 200-ft cliffs. It is really a botanist's paradise, with over 300 plant species – many at their northern limit. The cliffs and rocks support large bird colonies. Among the birds you may notice: jackdaw, fulmar, herring gull, mallard, shelduck, redshank, oystercatcher, ringed plover, greater black-backed gull, tern, eider, stonechat, yellowhammer, wren. The A92 skirts the western edge of the reserve. Assistant Regional Officer J. Forster, Nature Conservancy, Blackhall, Banchory, Kinkardineshire/tel: Banchory 2206.

Saint Kilda National Nature Reserve 2,107 acres – 1 large and 7 smaller islands and rock outcrops 45 miles west of the Outer Hebrides. The highest sheer cliffs in Britain (several over 1,300 ft). St Kilda has its own races of wren and field mouse and its own sheep, the Soay sheep. It also has far and away the largest gannet colonies in the world (up to 40,000 nests) and a similar number of fulmar nests; also Britain's largest colony of Leach's storm petrel and of puffin. Other species include Manx shearwater and great skua. Access is difficult, but the National Trust for Scotland, 5 Charlotte Square, Edinburgh 2, arranges cruises and research/working parties.

Skomer Island National Nature Reserve 759 acres of island at the southern end of St Bride's Bay in Pembrokeshire, about 1 mile off the mainland. Large colonies of Manx shearwater, puffin, guillemot, chough, and razorbill. A good grey seal breeding colony. The Skomer vole is a larger and tamer race than the mainland vole. Managed by West Wales Naturalists Trust, 4 Victoria Place, Haverfordwest, Pembrokeshire. There is a small landing fee, and access is restricted at certain breeding seasons. Nearby Grassholm has only 10 breeding species but contains one of the 4 largest gannet colonies in the world (15,000 nests); also managed by West Wales Naturalists Trust – access by permit only. (Another nearby island, Skokholm, with up to 20 breeding species, including 20,000 pairs of Manx shearwaters, is limited to members of the WWNT.) From all these islands in October you can see flocks of thrushes and larks bound for southern Ireland. Access is by boat from Milford Haven.

Studland Heath National Nature Reserve 429 acres at the southern entrance to Poole harbour, Dorset. The Heath has resulted from the piling up of sand on the seaward side of the peninsula since at least the year 1600. At its heart is a narrow, tortuous lake, called Little Sea, almost a mile long; the western shore of this lake is the original 17th-century shore-line. The lake and the dunes to the east of it have formed since. Thus within the boundaries are a surprising number of habitats: freshwater lake, reedbed, heath, woodland (chiefly birch), pinewood, marshland, impenetrable wooded swamp, and mature and recent sand dunes.

Woodland: Roe deer, visiting Japanese sika deer, grey squirrel; blackbird, chaffinch, blackcap, chiffchaff, nightingale, whitethroat, willow warbler, long-tailed tit, redpoll, wren, woodcock, starling, sparrow-hawk, merlin. Plants include primrose, cowslip, bluebell, earthnut, three-veined sandwort; wood ant mounds.

Heath: All the British reptiles are found here – smooth snake, grass snake, adder, sand lizard, common lizard, and slow worm (all are protected). Birds include meadow pipit, linnet, stonechat, wren. Heath plants: ling, bell heather, cross-leaved heath, gorse.

Wetlands: Little grebe, herring gull, shelduck, cormorant, mallard, teal, occasional mute swan, wigeon, shoveler, pochard, tufted duck, goldeneye, Bewick's and whooper swans, Canada goose, coot, moorhen; sedge warbler, reed warbler, reed bunting, water rail, hobby, swallow, sand and house martins, occasional harrier. Occasionally you may see an otter – or its tracks. Plants include bog bean, marsh cinquefoil, yellow flag, small quillwort, broad-leaved pond-weed, bog myrtle, royal fern, purple moorgrass, rushes, bog mosses, bog asphodel, marsh orchid, pale butterwort, bog pimpernel, marsh club, the rare Dorset heath.

Dune and foreshore: Oystercatcher, ringed plover, dunlin, sanderling, turnstone, sandwich and other terns, black-necked and great-crested grebes, occasional Slavonian grebe, eider duck, common and velvet scoters; grayling butterfly, lackey moth; fox, pygmy and common shrews, harvest mouse. Plants include marram grass, sand sedge, red fescue, sheeps bit, centaury, sea bindweed, mosses and rosette plants. In the maturest parts there is bracken, birch, sallow, gorse, heather, and lichens. Access is by ferry (cars 20p to 25p, persons 2p) from the northern peninsula, half way between Poole and Bournemouth. Regional Officer, Nature Conservancy, Furzebrook Research Station, near Wareham, Dorset/tel: Corfe Castle 361 & 2.

Semi-natural Collections

Chillingham Wild Cattle Herd This herd of about 40 wild cattle represents the only such species in the world – pure and uncrossed with domestic races. They are thought to descend from the aurochs (*Bos primigenius*). The Chillingham estate has supported the herd for at least 700 years, so the park is, in effect, their 'natural' habitat. The only human management is the feeding of winter hay. The herd is maintained by the Chillingham Wild Cattle Association, Chillingham Park, Alnwick/tel: Chatton 213; a non-profit-making association dependent on public subscription, £1.5 annually. Open every day except Tuesday, 2–5 Sundays, 10–5 other days; adults 13p, children under 14 5p. Access from Alnwick on A1 north 12 miles to B6483 then 6 miles west to Chatton, then 2 miles south on byway to Chillingham.

Norfolk Wildlife Park and Ornamental Pheasant Trust 50 acres of parkland in which British and European mammals and birds are kept in near-natural conditions. Six species of deer found wild in Britain, ibex, moufflon, bear, wolverine, lynx, fox, badger, pine marten, squirrel, otter, seal; ducks, cranes, herons, waders, raptorial species, geese, flamingo. First wheatears, brown hares, and roe deer to be bred in

Britain, first breeding otters since 1880, first breeding European lynx since 1933. Park-bred animals have reinforced declining wild populations: Swinhoe's pheasant to Taiwan, eagle owl to Sweden. The park also has the world's largest collection of ornamental pheasants. Open every day 10.30–6.30 (or sunset if earlier). Adults 25p, children 13p. Parties of 25 and over 13p. Organized school parties, for which there are special educational facilities, 8p. Licensed restaurant; free car park. Membership of Ornamental Pheasant Trust £2 per year. Access from Norwich on A1067 for 10 miles then 2 miles along a byway to Great Witchingham. Director Philip Wayre, Norfolk Wildlife Park and Ornamental Pheasant Trust, Great Witchingham, near Norwich/tel: Great Witchingham 274.

Stansted Wildlife Park 170 acres belonging to Norman House, home of Mr Aubrey Buxton, a Trustee of the World Wildlife Fund. The largest private bird sanctuary in Britain. A former spring-fed lake has been enlarged into a chain of 7 ponds. Flamingoes, cranes, geese, teal, bittern, wigeon, ducks, pintail and many wild visiting birds. Sika deer. Open every day 11 – 6. Adults 25p, children over 5, 13p. Special rates for school parties, societies and associations by arrangement. Membership £2 per year carries free-visiting privileges for member and a guest. Small cinema shows wildlife films. Picnic area and refreshment automat. Open every day 11 – 6 (though members, £2 per year, may visit at any time). Adults 25p children over 5, 13p. School parties 10p, staff free. Special rates for societies and associations. Access is from the A11, turn right about 1 mile north of Stansted Mountfitchet; main gates are on the A11. Warden J. Bunting, Stansted Wildlife Park, Norman House, Stansted/tel: Stansted 3111.

The Wildfowl Trust, Slimbridge A world-famous bird collection of some 160 different species in natural surroundings. The largest and most varied collection of waterfowl in the world (85 per cent of all living species represented). Wild Bewick's swans and 10,000 wild geese roost on the Severn estuary every winter. They can be seen from two observation towers. A further tower gives a view over the decoy, where ducks are caught and ringed for study. There is a tropical house for tropical waterfowl, tanager, hummingbirds, and other species. All six flamingo species now nest here; trumpeter swan, snow goose, paradise duck, Chinese mandarin, Hawaiian nene goose (which was saved from extinction here). Open all year except Christmas Day, 9.30 – 4.30, November–January, and 9.30 – 5.30 other months. Members only on Sunday mornings. Adults 33p, children 18p. Lower rates on Mondays, except Bank Holidays: adults 20p, children 13p. Car park 8p, coaches 25p. Coach parties by arrangement

The spoonbill uses its flattened bill to sift shallow marshy waters for plants, insects, and small fish. Until the 17th century they had many colonies in southern England. Now they are summer visitors to South Devon (Exe estuary) and to the Norfolk-Suffolk coast.

only. Restaurant serves meals and snacks (party booking in advance). Access from Bristol north on A38 for 24 miles to Cambridge (Glos.), then left on a byway 2 miles to Slimbridge. Hon. Director Peter Scott, CBE, DSC, LLD, The Wildfowl Trust, Slimbridge, Gloucester GL2 7BT/tel: Cambridge (Glos.) 333.

Note: In 1971 the Trust established a number of hides on the Wetlands bordering the Caerlaverock NNR (page 334). The chief attraction is the 6,000+ pink-footed and barnacle geese between November and April. Full details from Slimbridge.

The Waterfowl Gardens, Peakirk This is a branch of the Wildfowl Trust, founded by Peter Scott and under his direction. It has about 600 birds of over 100 different species, including Hawaiian nene geese, mandarin duck, red-breasted merganser, paradise shelduck. They are often joined by native British species. Open daily except Christmas Day 9.30 – 5.30 in summer and to $\frac{1}{2}$ hour before sunset at other seasons. Sunday mornings for Wildfowl Trust members only. Adults 20p, children 10p. Parking 5p; coaches by prior arrangement. Tea and snacks from nearby teashop – no parties. Access from Peterborough north on the A15 for 6 miles then right to Peakirk 1 mile along B1443. The decoy at Borough Fen, 2 miles farther along the B1443, is open on certain weekends around Whitsun. The Warden, Waterfowl Gardens, Peakirk, near Peterborough/tel: Glinton 271.

Note: Four more British reserves, side by side in the Ouse Washes, are described and mapped on pages 354-55.

Ireland

Cape Clear Bird Observatory Founded by amateurs in 1959 and kept going by amateurs ever since, this cape on Clear Island, the extreme SW point of Eire, is one of the most fascinating birdwatching sites in Europe. The interest lies not in the migrants, of which the island attracts few, but in the extraordinary off-shore movements of seabirds each autumn. In fact, these migrations – or whatever they are – were first noticed here in the early 1960s, and it is from this site that the habit of 'seawatching' has spread throughout coastal Europe. Every autumn you can join dozens of observers staring across the 4-mile gap towards the Fastnet light and beyond, watching these mysterious movements. The chief birds to watch out for are: Manx, Cory's, sooty, and great shearwaters, storm petrel, great skua, gannet, fulmar, all the usual gulls, sea duck, auk, terns; lucky visitors see little shearwaters, black-browed albatross, and some un-identified (Wilson's?) petrels. Clear Island is reached by boat from Baltimore, which has road links with Cork. There is elementary accommodation for 10 people (30p/night) at the observatory. For details send sae to R D Jackson, 17 The Moorlands, Benson, Oxon.

The Erne Valley Some 300 square miles of water and fertile lowland – mostly below 250 ft altitude – in Co. Fermanagh. The lower end of the valley is filled with the broad expanses of Lower Lough Erne; the Upper Lough, above Enniskillen, is a rolling landscape mottled with small lakes and pools. This water-and-woodland habitat provides excellent breeding grounds for a number of birds. It is the only published breeding haunt of the common scoter in the British Isles; for them the RSPB has created reserves at Horse and Duck islands on Lower Lough Erne. It is also the best of Ireland's few breeding sites for the garden warbler. Other breeding species include common and black-headed gulls and occa-sional Sandwich tern. In winter the waters support whooper swans, several ducks including tufted duck and red-breasted merganser, and occasional geese. The area is best explored from Enniskillen, where there are several good hotels. The town, from its earliest days, dominated the passage between Tyrone and the south; and the whole region is rich in history. Wherever you go you can hardly avoid seeing the 'Plantation Castles' – Protestant castles set up under the Jacobean Plantation Laws that required landowners to build fortifications and bring over a number of Protestant tenants to settle the land. The best one near Enniskillen is at Monea. To the east of the town is a fine Georgian mansion, Castle-coole, now National Trust property.

Wexford Slobs Wildfowl Sanctuary This is not a single definable area of land but a number of refuges on the north and south shores of Wexford harbour, stretching out almost to Rosslare. It is a mixture of saltmarsh, pasture, mud, and dune – all liable to flooding. The southern parts are more marshy, with reeds and patches of scrub giving way to huge dunes at the sea coast. Until recently the northern part, the celebrated home of several thousand Greenland white-fronted geese, was privately owned and inaccessible; but in 1969–70, with the aid of a £10,000 grant from the World Wildlife Fund, the 'Western Refuge' was bought for the Irish Wildbird Conservancy and the Department of Lands, and legal restrictions were put on the 'Eastern Refuge'. There is now an observation tower in this area; details from the Irish Wildlife Conservancy, address below. The South Slob, also privately owned, is more accessible to visitors; take the Rosslare road and follow your nose. The sand spit leading to Rosslare Point is a good starting place. There are several thousand Greenland white-fronts in this southern area, which is also a good place to look for American waders, which are annual rarities. Even in summer this is a good haunt, with terns (3 species), several ducks, sedge warbler and the tree sparrow (one of Ireland's few sites). In autumn there are: black-tailed godwit, ruff, whimbrel, curlew, sand-piper, and spotted redshank. Winter sees: barnacle, pink-footed, brent, greylag, and white-fronted geese; Slavonian grebe, red-breasted merganser, scaup, goldeneye, wigeon and widgeon (USA), whooper and Bewick swans, and black-tailed godwit. The whole south coast of Co. Wexford – all accessible from the city itself – is a paradise for birdwatchers at all seasons. Details from John Temple Lang, Hon. Sec. Irish Wildbird Conservancy, c/o Royal Irish Academy, 19 Dawson Street, Dublin 2.

Britain/Ireland: Species List

ADDER Studland Heath
ALBATROSS, Black-Browed Cape Clear
AUK Cape Clear
AVOCET Exe Estuary; Minsmere; North Norfolk
BADGER Cairngorms; Hope Wood; Knockan Cliff; Norfolk WP
BAT, Greater Horseshoe Hope Wood
— **Lesser Horseshoe** Hope Wood
BEAR Norfolk WP
BITTERN Hickling Broad; Minsmere; North Norfolk; Stansted WP
BLACKCAP Studland Heath
BLACKBIRD Old Winchester Hill; Studland Heath
BULLFINCH Hope Wood; Old Winchester Hill
BUNTING, Reed Studland Heath
— **Snow** Cairngorms; Knockan Cliff
BUTTERFLY, Brown Argus Pewsey Downs
— **Chalkhill Blue** Old Winchester Hill; Pewsey Downs
— **Clouded Yellow, Common Blue, Duke of Burgundy Fritillary, Green Hairstreak, Green-Veined White, Painted Lady, Peacock, Red Admiral, Small Heath, Small Skipper, Small Tortoiseshell** Old Winchester Hill

— **Fritillary** Coed Llyn Mair
— **Grayling** Studland Heath
— **Hairstreak** Coed Llyn Mair
— **Meadow Brown** Coed Llyn Mair; Old Winchester Hill
— **Speckled Wood** Hope Wood; Old Winchester Hill
— **Swallowtail** Hickling Broad
BUZZARD Braunton Burrows; Cairngorms; Cwm Idwal; Hope Wood; Knockan Cliff; Old Winchester Hill
CAPERCAILLIE Cairngorms
CATTLE, Wild Chillingham
CHAFFINCH Hope Wood; Old Winchester Hill; Studland Heath
CHIFF CHAFF Hope Wood; Studland Heath
CHOUGH Skomer Island
COOT Studland Heath
CORMORANT Rhossli Clifftop; Studland Heath
CRANES Norfolk WP; Stanstead WP
CREEPER, Tree Old Winchester Hill
CROSSBILL, Scottish Cairngorms
CROW, Hooded Knockan Cliff
CURLEW Braunton Burrows; Exe Estuary; Glasson Moss
— **Stone** Pewsey Downs
DEER, Chinese Water Norfolk WP

BRITAIN/IRELAND: SPECIES LIST

— **Fallow** Norfolk WP
— **Muntjac** Norfolk WP
— **Red** Cairngorms; Knockan Cliff;
Russland Moss; Norfolk WP
— **Roe** Cairngorms; Knockan Cliff;
Russland Moss; Studland Heath;
Norfolk WP
— **Sika** Studland Heath; Norfolk WP;
Stansted WP
DIVER, Black-Throated Knockan Cliff
— **Red-Throated** Herma Ness, Knockan
Cliff
DOTTEREL Cairngorms
DOVES, Stock and **Turtle** Old Winchester
Hill
DUCKS Norfolk WP; Stansted WP;
Slimbridge; Erne Valley; Wexford Slobs
— **Chinese Mandarin** Slimbridge;
Waterfowl Gardens
— **Eider** Exe Estuary; Noss; Saint Cyrus;
Studland Heath
— **Paradise** Slimbridge
— **Sea** Cape Clear
— **Tufted** Studland Heath; Erne Valley
DUNLIN Knockan Cliff; Studland Heath
DUNNOCK Old Winchester Hill
EAGLE, Golden Cairngorms; Knockan Cliff
FALCON, Peregrine Cairngorms
FIELDFARE Old Winchester Hill
FLAMINGOES Norfolk WP; Stansted WP;
Slimbridge
FLYCATCHER, Pied Coed Llyn Mair
FOX Hope Wood; Knockan Cliff; Studland
Heath; Norfolk WP
FULMAR North Norfolk; Noss; Rhossli
Clifftop; Saint Cyrus; Saint Kilda; Cape
Clear
GADWALL Minsmere
GANNET Herma Ness; Noss; Saint Kilda;
Skomer (Grassholm); Cape Clear
GARGANEY Hickling Broad; North Norfolk
GEESE Norfolk WP; Stansted WP;
Slimbridge
GOAT, Feral Cwm Idwal
GODWIT, Black-Tailed Hickling Broad;
North Norfolk; Wexford Slobs
GOLDCREST Old Winchester Hill
GOLDENEYE Coed Llyn Mair; Cwm Idwal;
Hickling Broad; Knockan Cliff;
Studland Heath; Wexford Slobs
GOOSE Barnacle Caerlaverock; Wexford
Slobs
— **Brent** Exe Estuary; Wexford Slobs
— **Canada** Studland Heath
— **Greenland White-Fronted** Wexford
Slobs
— **Greylag** Caerlaverock; Wexford Slobs
— **Hawaiian Nene** Slimbridge; Waterfowl
Gardens
— **Pink-Footed** Caerlaverock; Wexford
Slobs
— **Snow** Slimbridge
— **White-Fronted** Wexford Slobs
GREBES, Black-Necked and **Great-
Crested** Studland Heath
— **Little** Coed Llyn Mair; Studland Heath
— **Slavonian** Studland Heath; Wexford
Slobs
GREENSHANK Cairngorms; Knockan Cliff
GROUSE, Black Cairngorms
— **Red** Knockan Cliff
GUILLEMOT Noss; Rhossli Clifftop;
Skomer Island
GULLS Rostherne Mere; Cape Clear
— **Black-Headed** Braunton Burrows; Coed
Llyn Mair; Minsmere; North Norfolk; Erne
Valley
— **Common** Erne Valley
— **Greater Black-Backed** Knockan Cliff;
Noss; Saint Cyrus
— **Herring** Noss; Saint Cyrus; Studland
Heath
HARE, Brown Norfolk WP
— **Mountain** Cairngorms; Knockan Cliff
HARRIERS Studland Heath
— **Marsh** Minsmere
— **Montagu's** Old Winchester Hill
HAWK, Sparrow Hope Wood
HERONS Cwm Idwal; Hickling Broad;
Knockan Cliff; Russland Moss;
Norfolk WP
HOBBY Old Winchester Hill; Studland
Heath
HUMMINGBIRDS Slimbridge

IBEX Norfolk WP
JACKDAW Knockan Cliff; St Cyrus
JAY Old Winchester Hill
KESTREL Hope Wood; Old Winchester Hill
KITTIWAKE Herma Ness; Noss; Rhossli
Clifftop
LAPWING Braunton Burrows
LARKS Skomer Island
LINNET Old Winchester Hill; Rhossli
Clifftop; Studland Heath
LIZARDS, Common and **Sand** Studland
Heath
LYNX Norfolk WP
MALLARD Coed Llyn Mair; Knockan Cliff;
Rostherne Mere; Saint Cyrus; Studland
Heath
MARTEN, Pine Knockan Cliff; Norfolk WP
MARTINS, House and **Sand** Studland
Heath
MERGANSER, Red-Breasted Exe
Estuary; Waterfowl Gardens; Erne Valley;
Wexford Slobs
MERLIN Cairngorms; Studland Heath
MOORHEN Studland Heath
MOTHS, Burnet and **Cinnabar** Old
Winchester Hill
— **Lackey** Studland Heath
MOUFFLON Norfolk WP
MOUSE, Harvest Saint Kilda (subsp);
Studland Heath
NIGHTINGALE Minsmere; Studland Heath
NIGHTJAR Pewsey Downs
NUTHATCH Old Winchester Hill
OSPREY Cairngorms
OTTER Cairngorms; Knockan Cliff; Studland
Heath; Norfolk WP
OUZEL, Ring Cairngorms; Cwm Idwal;
Knockan Cliff
OWL, Barn Old Winchester Hill
— **Eagle** Norfolk WP
— **Little** Old Winchester Hill
— **Snowy** Herma Ness
— **Tawny** Old Winchester Hill
OYSTERCATCHER Exe Estuary;
Minsmere; North Norfolk; Saint Cyrus;
Studland Heath
PETREL, Leach's Storm Saint Kilda
— **Storm** Cape Clear
PHALAROPE, Red-Necked Herma Ness
PHEASANTS, Ornamental Norfolk WP
PIGEON, Wood Old Winchester Hill
PINTAIL North Norfolk; Stansted WP
PIPIT, Meadow Glasson Moss; Knockan
Cliff; Studland Heath
— **Rock** Rhossli Clifftop
— **Tree** Pewsey Downs
PLOVER, Ringed Minsmere; North Norfolk;
Saint Cyrus; Studland Heath
POCHARD Cwm Idwal; Studland Heath
PTARMIGAN Cairngorms
PUFFIN Herma Ness; Noss; Saint Kilda;
Skomer Island
QUAIL Pewsey Downs
RAIL, Water Minsmere; Studland Heath
RAPTORS Norfolk WP
RAVEN Cwm Idwal; Knockan Cliff
RAZORBILL Rhossli Clifftop; Skomer Island
REDPOLL Studland Heath
REDSHANK Braunton Burrows; Exe
Estuary; Minsmere; North Norfolk; Saint
Cyrus
— **Spotted** Hickling Broad; Wexford Slobs
REINDEER Cairngorms
ROBIN Knockan Cliff; Old Winchester Hill
RUFF Hickling Broad; North Norfolk;
Wexford Slobs
SANDERLING Studland Heath
SANDPIPER Cwm Idwal; Knockan Cliff
— **Curlew** Wexford Slobs
SCAUP Wexford Slobs
SCOTER, Common Studland Heath;
Erne Valley
— **Velvet** Studland Heath
SEALS Norfolk WP
— **Grey** Skomer Island
SHAG Noss; Rhossli Clifftop
SHEARWATERS, Cory's and **Little**
Cape Clear
— **Manx** Saint Kilda; Skomer Island; Cape
Clear
— **Great** and **Sooty** Cape Clear
SHEEP, Soay Saint Kilda
SHELDUCK Exe Estuary; North Norfolk;
Saint Cyrus; Studland Heath

— **Paradise** Waterfowl Gardens
SHOVELER Studland Heath
SHREWS, Common and **Pygmy** Studland Heath
SHRIKE, Red-Backed Minsmere
SISKIN Cairngorms
SKYLARK Glasson Moss; Knockan Cliff
SKUA, Arctic Herma Ness; Noss
— **Great** Herma Ness; Noss; Saint Kilda; Cape Clear
SNAKES, Grass and **Smooth** Studland Heath
SPARROW, Tree Wexford Slobs
SPARROWHAWK Studland Heath
SPOONBILL Exe Estuary
SQUIRREL, Grey Hope Wood; Studland Heath; Norfolk WP
— **Red** Cairngorms; Norfolk WP
STARLING Studland Heath
STONECHAT Rhossli Clifftop; Saint Cyrus; Studland Heath
SWALLOW Studland Heath
SWAN, Bewick's Hickling Broad; Studland Heath; Slimbridge; Wexford Slobs
— **Mute** Studland Heath
— **Trumpeter** Slimbridge
— **Whooper** Coed Llyn Mair; Cwm Idwal; Knockan Cliff; Studland Heath; Erne Valley; Wexford Slobs
TANAGER Slimbridge
TEAL Rostherne Mere; Studland Heath; Stansted WP
TERNS Studland Heath; Cape Clear; Wexford Slobs
— **Black** Hickling Broad
— **Common** Minsmere; North Norfolk; Saint Cyrus
— **Little** Minsmere; North Norfolk
— **Sandwich** Minsmere; North Norfolk; Studland Heath; Erne Valley
THRUSHES Skomer Island
— **Mistle** Old Winchester Hill

TITS Hope Wood; Old Winchester Hill
— **Bearded** Hickling Broad; Minsmere; North Norfolk
— **Coal** Coed Llyn Mair
— **Crested** Cairngorms
— **Long-tailed** Studland Heath
— **Marsh** Hope Wood
— **Willow** Glasson Moss
TURNSTONE Studland Heath
VOLE, Skomer Skomer Island
WADERS Norfolk WP
— **American** Wexford Slobs
WAGTAIL, Pied Knockan Cliff
— **Yellow** Braunton Burrows
WARBLERS Minsmere
— **Garden** Erne Valley
— **Reed** Minsmere; Studland Heath
— **Sedge** Hickling Broad; Minsmere; Studland Heath; Wexford Slobs
— **Willow** Hope Wood; Studland Heath
WHEATEAR Pewsey Downs; Rhossli Clifftop; Norfolk WP
WHIMBREL Herma Ness; Wexford Slobs
WHINCHAT Rhossli Clifftop
WHITETHROAT Pewsey Downs; Studland Heath
WIDGEON, American Wexford Slobs
WIGEON (European) Exe Estuary; Knockan Cliff; North Norfolk; Studland Heath; Stansted WP; Wexford Slobs
WILD CAT Cairngorms; Knockan Cliff
WOLVERINE Norfolk WP
WOODCOCK Knockan Cliff; Studland Heath
WOODPECKERS Minsmere
— **Great Spotted** Glasson Moss; Old Winchester Hill
— **Green** Old Winchester Hill
WORM, Slow Studland Heath
WREN Hope Wood; Knockan Cliff; Saint Cyrus; Studland Heath
— **Saint Kilda** Saint Kilda
YELLOWHAMMER Old Winchester Hill; Saint Cyrus

A golden eagle visiting a fledgling in its eyrie. Found from the Lake District northwards, they breed only in the Scottish Highlands.

Great Britain: New Reserves

(*Note: Until recently the Washes were open for only a few months in the year, and for this reason we decided to exclude them from this guide. However, in the final month of preparation we heard that the open period had been extended to 10 months a year, and so reversed our decision – too late, alas, to mark the site on the general British Isles map or to include its species in the general species index.*)

Ouse Washes Reserves 1,412 acres; at or below sea level. Here are four reserves, held by the Wildfowl Trust, the Royal Society for the Protection of Birds (RSPB), and the Cambridge and Isle of Ely Naturalist Trust, in one of Europe's most important wildfowl areas. They have support from the World Wildlife Fund. Formerly large stretches of pasture near rivers were drowned each winter as a way of preventing frost damage, improving soil fertility, and gaining an early spring bite. Now that the practice has died out, the Ouse Washes are the largest inland area of flooded grazing marshland in Britain – though the flooding is part of fenland-drainage control rather than a surviving agricultural practice. These Washes have a particular historical interest, too. Early in the 17th century the then Earl of Bedford engaged the Dutchman Cornelius Vermuyden to improve the drainage of the fens. Desultory attempts had been made since Roman times, but this was the first large-scale attempt in modern history. Vermuyden looked at the meandering course of the Ouse, and dug the dead-straight 20-mile dyke known as the Old Bedford River to short-circuit the meander and drain the intervening fen. It worked but proved insufficient; so 20 years later he dug the New Bedford River along a parallel course some half a mile to the south. Today these two dykes form the northern and southern boundaries of the Washes, which become a dump for excess water in time of flood – especially in winter. Most winters the Washes are flooded and it is usually April, and sometimes even May, before cattle can be put on to graze; drainage ditches between the dykes are filled with sluice-controlled water to make a stockproof 'fence'. If heavy rains do not force the river authorities to flood the Washes, some of the pasture is grown on for hay.

When the floods have drained there are a number of breeding habitats for different wetland species. The short-grassed watermeadows hold large numbers of redshank, lapwing, and up to 400 pairs of snipe. The sedge borders and other tussocky parts hold duck such as mallard (200 pairs) and shoveler (about 100 pairs). Small birds breed among the stands of willow, copses, and osier beds. Regular nesting birds include teal, garganey, pintail, tufted duck, black-headed gull, coot, moorhen, yellow wagtail, reed and sedge warblers, reed bunting. Parts of the Washes have the same character as the undrained fen of past centuries. As a result former breeders in such habitat are re-establishing themselves here – black-tailed godwit, ruff, and black tern have all been seen in recent years. In winter the Washes form the only extensive stretches of water in a well-drained countryside and so attract large numbers of waterfowl. The shallowest, grass-mottled areas attract wigeon, mallard, pintail, and teal. In deeper stretches you find pochard, and Bewick's swans (their main British winter area). The fields support golden plover and lapwing. Among 20 other wildfowl species are tufted duck, gadwall, goldeneye, scaup, and goosander. Wild geese are uncommon. Gulls are numerous.

Here are many floral species once common in the fens – floating and aquatic plants, including 16 species and hybrids of pondweed and 4 of duckweed. Other plants include frogbit, fringed waterlily, water parsnip. The pastures are mainly of sweet-grass, foxtail, and reed canary grass; also many rushes, docks, and knotgrasses. In all, the Washes have more than 260 flowering plant species.

The Washes are an easy daytrip from London, but there are plenty of good nearby hotels. The Griffin at March is an old coaching inn. The Rose and Crown at Wisbech is Tudor and 18th century; and there are other hotels there and at Ely – all within the £1.75 to £2.25 b. & b. range.

Entry is by permit only. Application must be made to the RSPB, The Lodge, Sandy, Beds. and not to the reserve itself. Permits are for half days (25p; members of RSPB 15p) or whole days (50p; members 25p; under 17 half price in both cases) on Wednesday, Thursday, Saturday, and Sunday. Permit holders assemble at Purls Bridge at 10.45 am or 1.45 pm; further instructions are displayed there on a signboard to the left of the path, just beyond the small lake.

By boat and path to the hides; indiscriminate and unguided walking is not permitted. Rubber boots are essential; other clothing according to weather.

Open all year except in October and in March. The parts between the reserves are, of course, open and variably accessible (depending on the flooding) all year. However, the nonreserved areas are shot over in winter, so birdlife there is not nearly so rich. The reserve authorities control access to the dyke banks bordering the Washes and to the disused railway line across them.

The two Brinks on the River Nene at Wisbech comprise one of the best-preserved Georgian scenes in England. There are heronries at Denver Sluice (near Downham Market) and at Chettisham (just north of Ely); the gravelpits at Welney and Mepal are also worth a visit.

RSPB, The Lodge, Sandy, Beds/tel: Sandy 551.

Greece

Olympus National Park 9,600 acres; between 2,462 and 9,574 ft above sea level. The park includes the peaks of the Olympus range, including the legendary Throne of Zeus. The rocky slopes, which are deeply eroded to form steep ravines, are lightly forested with pine, beech, and broad leaved evergreens. It exists chiefly as a scenic park, with its strong historical and mythical associations; but it is also a refuge for the rare wild mountain goat.

- ⚐ Wild mountain goat, chamois, hare; golden eagle, raven, hooded crow (southern race), twite, ring ouzel (winter).

- ⌂ Nearest hotels at Litokhoron (2 class C hotels). The nearest town with any choice is Larissa, 50 miles away, where there are 9 hotels at daily rates per person between 75 and 120 drs. There are no organized camps in the vicinity, but ELPA, 6 Amerikis Street, Athens, will supply a list of all nearby sites and facilities. The Hellenic Alpine Club maintains three refuges on the east side of the mountain and one on the south side. Refuge A, at 6,905 ft (Spelios Agapitos is its name), is 7½-hours' walk from Litokhoron (986 ft); it has mattresses for 60, blankets, tank water, stoves, fireplace, kitchen, cooking utensils, and first-aid. The caretaker-guide can supply light meals and drinks. Refuge C, near the summit Profitis Ilias (8,700 ft) is 2 hours from A and 8 hours from Litokhoron; mattresses, etc, for 18. Refuge D, at Stavros (3,283 ft), has mattresses, etc, for 20. Refuge B, on the south face at Vrysopoules (6,220 ft) has accommodation for 18 with dining- and anterooms; near by are ski lifts.

- ⤳ Litokhoron is a few miles off the main Athens–Thessaloniki highway, between Platamon and Katerini. Its railway station is some way from the actual village and is on the main line from Athens. Buses and trains from Athens (7 hours) run daily. The nearest airport is at Thessaloniki, daily flights from Athens; buses connect for Litokhoron, 60 miles away.

- 🚐 The B refuge can be reached from Elasson on the Athens road, by following the Larissa Kozani road, branching off 5 miles beyond Elasson to Kallithea (4 miles) and Olympias (5 miles) and then to Sparmos. From there a military road leads over to refuge B. Elsewhere on foot. Mules may be hired at Litokhoron.

- ☀ Open all year; best time June to October. Nights are cold at these altitudes.

- ◷ 3–5 days.

- ▤ Free.

- ◹ Available at Litokhoron.

- ⇨ The Hellenic Alpine Club, 7 Karageorgi Servias, Athens.

Italy

Abruzzi National Park 73,000 acres; up to 7,325 ft above sea level. Most of the park is in steeply wooded country broken by rocky crags and sheer escarpments. It bears all the signs of ancient glaciation, with gullies, ravines, and glacial cirques. Flora and fauna are alpine in type, though often markedly

Chamois in the dark winter coat that helps protect them when they descend to browse in lower-level forests. In summer they stay high above the reach of predators. They now exist in nine distinct races in the Alps, Apennines, Pyrenees, and Carpathians, as well as in south-east Europe and south-east Asia. Their curved-back horns are unique.

different from their true Alp-dwelling cousins; this is particularly true of the chamois and the bear.

Abruzzi chamois and bear, roebuck (in the park's enormous beech forests), weasel; polecat, marten, and stone marten (all three very rare), wild cat (extremely rare), lynx (perhaps extinct), otter (rare), fox (abundant), badger, and wolf. Nuthatch, marsh tit, blackbird, chaffinch, buzzard, middle-spotted woodpecker, red-backed shrike; at altitude look for blue rock thrush, black redstart, alpine chough, lesser kestrel, crag martin, tawny and water pipit, alpine accentor.

Beech, black and white pines, hornbeam, maple, oak, bitter oak; herbaceous plants include saponarias, alyssums, and members of the ranunculus and rumex families.

The main town within the park is Pescasseroli, which has half a dozen hotels and pensions, with prices between 4,200 and 10,600 lire, per person per day (full board). At many of the villages within or near the park – Villetta Barrea, Alfadena, Civitella Alfadena, Barrea, and Opi – there is comfortable family accommodation at moderate rates. The nearest camping is at Avezzano.

✈ Pescasseroli is served by rail and bus from a number of nearby towns. By car you turn off· Highway 5 (Rome–Pescara) at Avezzano or Popoli. From Naples the park is best reached via Cassino. The nearest main airport is at Rome.

🚐 By car, by funicular railway, or on foot.

☼ Open all year; best time June to September.

⊕ 2–5 days.

▧ Free.

⊙ There is a small zoo and natural history museum at Pescasseroli.

⇨ Ente Provinciale Per Il Turismo (Dell'Abruzzo), Piazza S. Maria di Paganica, L'Aquila, Italy.

Gran Paradiso National Park 140,000 acres; 4,900 to 13,400 ft above sea level. Gran Paradiso is an alpine-zone park at the centre of the great arc formed by the Graian Alps. It contains some of the most extensive glaciers in Italy. The park is inhabited only near the French border, with a few hydro-electric dams and a limited amount of grazing and forestry as the chief forms of employment. It is continuous with the Vanoise NP in France.

⇶ Ibex (3,700; Europe's largest stock), chamois (7,600), ermine, weasel, stone marten, fox, marten, polecat, badger, otter, snow mouse, dormouse, marmot, squirrel, alpine hare; golden eagle, ptarmigan, alpine swift, mountain swallow, wall-creeping woodpecker, wren, water ouzel, alpine blackbird, white grouse, Tengmalm's and eagle owls, snow finch.

❀ The full range of alpine flora is found at Gran Paradiso; also herbaceous plants of artemisia, achillea, hieracium, viola, saxifrage, sempervivum, sedum, campanula, and potentilla families. Trees include European larch, red fir, Siberian pine, and white pine.

🛏 Shelters and campsites within the park. Hotels in nearby villages and towns – Cogne (15 hotels and pensions), Rhême-Notre-Dame-Bruil (2), Rhême-Notre-Dame-Chanavey (2), and Valsavaranche-Eaux-Rousses-Pont (2); rates between 1,500 and 6,000 lire per person per day (full board). There are camping sites at Cogne and Pont Valsavaranche. Three huts of the Italian Alpine Club may also be used.

✈ By road from Aosta to Cogne, or to Pont via Dégioz and Valsavaranche, or to Rhême-Notre-Dame via Chanavey, or from Turin to Ceresole Reale. The nearest railhead is at Aosta for Cogne or at Villeneuve for the other villages. All are served by scheduled buses.

🚐 One local road runs through park territory, but the main way of getting about is on foot along the 250 miles of walking trails within the park.

☼ Open all year; best time June to September.

⊕ 2–5 days.

▧ Free.

⇨ Gran Paradiso Park Management, Torino-Via Bogino 18/ tel: 540.504.

Jugoslavia

Durmitor National Park 80,000 acres; 1,765 to 8,926 ft above sea level. The park lies on rugged, broken ground in the Durmitor mountains in northern Montenegro. It contains 14 lakes, among them the beautiful Black Lake (Crno Jezero). This part of Montenegro is an important winter sports centre and a major summer holiday resort. Near by, the canyon of the Tara river, which rises near the Albania border and flows northwestward through the Durmitor ranges, is one of Europe's most beautiful waterways.

⚮   Chamois, roe deer, bear, red deer; hazel grouse, capercaillie.

🌳   Mixed stands of fir, beech, and white pine with an upper girdle of grassland and pine plantation. Alpine flora.

🛏   Camping ground, rentable bungalows, and 2 hotels at Zabljak. Hotels open all year, with high season from July to September.

🛫   From Titograd (where the Crna Gora is the only hotel of international class) take the road to Niksic for 35 miles, then on to Savnik and Zabljak (4,500 ft). None of these roads is particularly good and night driving, although cooler, is not recommended.

🚐   By car, on foot, and bus excursion.

☀   Open all year; not easy to traverse in winter. The climate is alpine, with hot days and cool nights.

⏱   2–5 days.

✉   Free.

➪   Either Montenegroturist, Titograd, Mose Pijade 19a/tel: 23–763 or Turisticki Savez Crna Gore, Titograd, Gojka Rajkovica 18.

Hutovo Blato Bird Sanctuary 7,680 acres; close to sea level. This sanctuary, sited where the waters of the Neretva and the Adriatic mix, is actually in the middle of Europe's largest waterfowl hunting ground! Because of its closeness to the sea and the admixture of saline waters, it never freezes in winter and so offers ideal nesting sites for thousands of waterfowl and waders, including grey heron, little egret, squacco heron, moorhen, greylag goose, dwarf cormorant, and all kinds of ducks and geese. In all 270 species have been noted. There is a hotel in Kaplinja and a lodge at Karatok near by. Other attractions in the vicinity include Počitelj, a painters' colony, and Vjetrenica Cave, the largest and one of the loveliest of Jugoslavia's big caves.

Mljet National Park 7,750 acres on an island off the south Dalmatian coast. The island has three 'lakes' – actually salt-water bays connected by narrow inlets to the sea – on one of which, Lake Veliko, is a 12th-century Benedictine monastery, now a hotel (Hotel Melita, from the Roman name for the island). The park is covered in rich, evergreen vegetation and well-kept woods of Aleppo pine. The chief wildlife interest in the park is the mongooses, imported centuries ago to control

359

the snakes, and now roaming freely in ecological balance with their prey. The rare monk seal is sometimes seen in the bays. There is private accommodation in Babino Polje (the chief village) and also in the port of Polače. Boats ply regularly between Dubrovnik and Mljet (3½ hours) and there is another regular boat service from the larger island of Korčula (2 hours), where there is plenty of good camping, several hotels, and good underwater fishing facilities. (Korčula, incidentally, is noted for the jackals that roam the island; it is also Marco Polo's birthplace.) Despite the sea breezes, northern Europeans are apt to find July and August rather hot and crowded along this part of the coast; they are also the most expensive months. Even in December to February the average temperature is around 50°F.

Plitvička Jezera National Park 47,930 acres; 1,588 to 2,651 ft above sea level. The Plitzvitzer lakes, 76 in number, lie between the massifs of the Mala Kapela and Liska Pljesevica ranges in Croatia. They were formed by a complex process, part water erosion and part reconcretion of eroded particles by mosses and algae, peculiar to this part of the Adriatic coast. The resulting rock, called travertine, is an extraordinarily beautiful and plastic white, especially near the cascades where the spray nurtures the vegetation that makes the so-called 'living travertine'. The lakes form a lazy double zigzag, just over 4 miles long and dropping from 2,092 to 1,588 ft in that distance. Bathing is permitted only at certain sites.

Brown bear, wolf, fox, wildcat, marten, polecat, badger, otter, roe deer, wild boar, hare, squirrel, small rodents; eagle, hawk, sparrowhawk, Ural and other owls; every European species of woodpecker; crested tit, firecrest, kingfisher, water ouzel, woodgrouse, heathcock, and many kinds of duck and songbird.

The woods of the east (chiefly beech with stands of maple, mountain elm, hornbeam, and yew) descend through moor and meadow (fly honeysuckle, Carniolan buckthorn, holly) to the lakeside slopes, covered with hophornbeam, flowering ash, white beam tree, mossy oak, and wild service tree. The escarpments are covered with such shrubs as cornel cherry, smoke tree, alpine daphne, common chokeberry, cotoneaster, and spring heath. Westwards the land rises again to stretches of virgin forest with giant trees of beech, spruce, and fir. Rare species protected in the park include members of the spirea, astrantia, and senecio families.

4 hotels (total of 310 beds) in Plitvicka Jezera at high-season rates (July to August; room and full board minimum 3 days stay). There are also bungalows for hire at Lake Kozjak. Camping sites at Lake Kozjak and Bihac with food store, restaurant, and ablutions. Reservations, prices, and bookings (well in advance for high season) via Plitvice Enterprise, Plitvice.

To Vrhovine by rail from Zagreb (104 miles), or from Rijeka (115 miles), or from Split (152 miles); then 15 miles by bus to the lakes. To Bihac by rail from Belgrade via Sunja (280 miles) or from Split (134 miles); then by coach (23 miles).

By road from Zagreb via Karlovac and Slunj (91 miles); or from Rijeka via Gorski Kotar (104 miles); or via Crikvenica and Senj (93 miles); or from Split via Sibenik, Obrovak, and Gospic (184 miles); or from Belgrade via Novska, Dubica, and Bihac (269 miles); or from Sarajevo via Jajce, Bosanski Petrovac, and Bihac (235 miles). The nearest railway station is at Javornik, 94 miles from Zagreb, then a 12-mile bus journey through wooded country to Ljeskovac. For the energetic there is a pleasant 4-hour hike along a well-marked trail from the station at Rudopolje, 99 miles from Zagreb.

🚐 A good road skirts the eastern shore of the lake complex. Elsewhere there is a rich network of well-marked paths.

☼ Open all year; the landscape is spectacular in autumn.

🕐 1–3 days.

🎫 Free.

👁 There are organized excursions to nearby peaks, waterfalls, and river sources – also to winter sportsgrounds in season.

⇨ Biro za Turisticku Propagandu, Zagreb.

Netherlands

De Hoge Veluwe 14,000 acres; at or near sea level. Though always intended for the nation De Hoge Veluwe began as a private nature park and cultural centre – the work of the wealthy Kröller-Müller family and now their monument. Its totally fenced area includes three zones, which merge into one another. The northern part contains the museum, most of the road development, the restaurants, the St Hubert's hunting lodge, and the ornamental waters. Here commercial forest, cultivated land and landscape gardening are mingled – except to the east, where some of the original driftsands, now moss carpeted, are still untouched. The central and southern area (most of the park, in fact) is an almost untouched wilderness of heath, grass, birch, and self-seeded conifers. Here and there are ancient groves of oak and beech, remnants of plantations. Only one road and one cycle track run through this part of the park (the Wildbaan, as it is called); to its west is a large reserve of grotesquely shaped junipers. The northeast of the park is unploughed wetland heath, a mixture of marsh, heath, small pools, and drainage ditches.

↗ Red and roe deer, moufflons (wild sheep), wild boar, rabbit, hare, fox, stoat, weasel, squirrel; birds include black grouse, great grey shrike, curlew, hobby, wryneck, long-eared owl, goshawk, buzzard, woodcock; black, green, and spotted woodpeckers; and many small songbirds.

🏨 None in park; first-class hotels in Arnhem and Apeldoorn; rates from fl20 per day. More modest hotels at Hoenderloo, Otterlo (both on park boundaries) and Ede, near by. Camping and caravan sites (trailer parks) in vicinity.

⇥ There are 5 entrance points on the park circumference, giving access from roads to Arnhem and Apeldoorn (to the east) and Ede (to the west).

🚐 Good roads but no through traffic in the northern part; during the rutting season (mid-September to mid-October) it is forbidden to stray from the one road through the Wildbaan.

☼ Open all year and each season has its attractions. Largest crowds in August; almost deserted in mid-winter.

🕐 1 day.

✉ Cars fl1.50, occupants and pedestrians fl0.60; scooter and motorbike riders fl0.90, cyclists and mopeds fl0.75; children under 4 free, between 4 and 16 fl0.30.

👁 The museum has small collections from China, Egypt, and Greece but its chief pride is its painting collection, which reads like a roll of honour of modern art – Corot, Millet, Van Gogh, Pissarro, Renoir, Monet, Sisley, Jongkind, Seurat; Picasso, Braque, Leger, Gris, Mondrian and sculptors Rodin, Lipchitz, Zadkine, Hepworth, and Arp among many others; entry is fl0.50 (fl0.25 for children between 1 and 18), school groups free.

⇨ Stichting Het Nationale Park De Hoge Veluwe, Apeldoornseweg 50, Hoenderloo/tel: 05768–230.

Naardemeer 1,850 acres; at or near sea level. Naardemeer is the Netherlands' oldest nature reserve, formed in 1906 after Amsterdam city council had threatened to make it a rubbish dump. It lies in green belt, mostly of fen and scrub, about 10 miles southeast of Amsterdam. Parts are absolutely reserved, with tree felling and reed mowing prohibited. The reserve is important as the centre of a colony of spoonbills, a bird that breeds nowhere else in northwestern Europe.

🐦 Spoonbill, purple heron, cormorant, marsh harrier, bittern, black tern, mallard, pochard and red crested pochard, tufted duck, reed bunting, warblers (reed, great reed, sedge, and Savi's), bearded tit.

🌿 Typical fen and lake flora – water lily (yellow and white), water hemlock, water soldier, alder, willow, birch, and oak.

🛏 Hotels in Amsterdam at rates between fl10 and over fl20 per person per night, excluding meals.

🚩 By car, about 10 miles along the Amsterdam–Amersfoort road take the Muiderberg road (just before a viaduct over the main road). Drive up the slip road and turn right, then down to a minor road parallel to the main road, turn left and drive about half a mile, then turn right along a small road leading to the fisherman's cottage (*Visserij*). By bus 30, 33, or 38 from Wibaustraat bus station or from NBM bus stop in front of Koninklijk Instituut voor de Tropen (Royal Tropical Institute), 25 minutes to *halte viaduct Googweg*; from there it is 20 minutes' walk following the car route.

🚐 The only way of getting about is by boat under the escort of the fisherman P. Hoetmer or one of his assistants. Since the number of boats, which seat only 4, is limited, it is vital you book as long in advance as possible, allowing four weeks clear of postal time and giving two alternative dates; say also whether you want the 3-hour or the 6-hour trip. Application to Vereneging tot Behoud van Natuurmonumenten in Nederland, Herengracht 540, Amsterdam–C (callers 9–5); open Monday to Friday only.

☼ Open spring to autumn, closed Sundays; best time May to June for birds, July to August for landscape.

🕐 3-hour or 6-hour trips only.

✉ fl5 per hour per boat (boatman's wages).

⇨ Vereneging tot Behoud van Natuurmonumenten in Nederland, Herengracht 540, Amsterdam–C.

Reindeer are the most northerly species of deer.

Norway

Rondane National Park 147,200 acres; 2,968 to 6,443 ft above sea level. This is in one of the loveliest mountain districts in Norway. It is totally unspoiled country, devoid of roads, though there are plenty of roads that run to within a mile or so of the boundary. Because of a dearth of natural predators (wolf and bear are now locally extinct), a certain amount of strictly controlled hunting is allowed at times. The area is extremely rich in birdlife, with over 124 recorded species.

⚞ Elk, reindeer, roe deer, fox, wolverine and lynx (occasional), squirrel, various martens and minks, many mountain and forest rodents; rough-legged buzzard, ptarmigan, snow bunting, meadow pipit, wheatear, shore lark, dotterel, willow grouse, Lappland bunting, red-necked phalarope, dipper, pied wagtail, house martin, willow warbler, wood sandpiper, redshank, snipe, crane, icterine and garden warblers, lesser whitethroat, sand martin, bluethroat, brambling, greenshank, golden eagle, goshawk, sparrow-hawk, osprey, and Tengmalm's, hawk, long-eared, and eagle owls; white-tailed eagle.

ஃ Apart from small stands of birch and evergreens, the vegetation is sparse tundra. Much of it is snow covered between mid-October to the end of May, with a short, frantic flowering season in between the thaw and the following snows (depth 3–13 ft).

⮌ 3 modestly priced tourist chalets within the park: Per Gynthytta (6 beds) near the western boundary; Rondvassbu (70 beds) at the junction of 4 trails in the middle of the park; and Döraalseter (50 beds) just on the northern border. Around the park there are numerous hotels and guest-houses. There is no camping in the park and food is available only at the chalets. Warm clothing is essential on summer evenings.

The main road north from Oslo via Lillehammer (E6) passes close to the park's western edge. Another northbound road (Highway 27) passes close to the park, but the intervening Atna river makes access to the north of the park difficult; the central part can be reached by paths leading up from Straumbuen. A minor east–west road turning off E6 just south of Dovre and winding over to Fallet gives superb views of the Rondane ranges and provides good access to the chalet at Döraalseter. Nearest railhead at Sel.

No mechanized transport of any kind is allowed in the park. Several hundred miles of track thread through the mountains between the roads and villages mentioned above. Compass and map essential.

Open all year; best time late June to mid-September. Skiing is best February to March.

4–14 days, because of the difficulties of the terrain.

Free.

Wardens patrol the parks at varied times and will assist visitors; but they do not routinely act as guides.

Some 25 miles north of the park is Dovrefjell, a popular holiday region with similar but easier terrain. Its chief attraction for nature lovers is the free-roaming herd of musk ox, descendants of a herd imported in 1932 from Greenland (which, with Alaska, is now their only natural stronghold).

Direktoratet for statens skoger, Storgt 10B, Oslo 1.

Poland

Bialowiecz National Park 12,683 acres; less than 600 ft above sea level. The park was established in 1947 (having been protected since 1919) to preserve a unique stretch of virgin lowland forest, which ranges from marshland borders to mixed stretches of hornbeam, pine, lofty spruce, and a huge variety of shrub species, making for thick undergrowth.

European bison (Poland's largest and most accessible herd), elk, tarpan horse, lynx, brown bear, beaver, and small forest mammals; great grey, pigmy, short-eared and eagle owls; white and black storks; spotted, lesser spotted, and short-toed eagles; white-backed and three-toed woodpeckers; red and black kites; collared and red-breasted flycatchers; capercaillie, black grouse, redwing, hoopoe, roller, ortolan bunting, barred warbler, crossbill, thrush nightingale, firecrest.

Hut accommodation for up to 300 people; rates from US $3 per day, full board. First-class hotel at Bialystock, about 40 miles away; rates from US $10 per day, full board.

Road and rail connection with Bialystok, which is about 170 miles from Warsaw. Access, by permit only, through the Director, Bialowieskiego Parku Narodowegu, Bialowiesza, pow Hajnowka, woj. Bialystock.

On guided foot tours only.

Open all year; best time May to September.

1–3 days.

Free.

Visitors must be accompanied by a guide; rates from Zl40 per hour (3 hour minimum).

👁 The park also contains a botanical garden and museum as well as a government research station.

⇨ Polish Travel offices.

Hohe Tatra National Park 53,890 acres; from around 1,600 to 8,260 ft above sea level. The Tatra is set in the highest mountain chain in Poland, about 60 miles south of Krakow and on the Czech border – in fact, it is continuous with the Czech National Park of the same name. It is lush Carpathian landscape, rich in lakes; the terrain is precipitous, forming many caves and pleasant valleys. Higher up the mountain slopes the vegetation is typically alpine.

🦅 Chamois, brown bear, lynx, wolf, marmot; golden and lesser spotted eagles; peregrine, hobby, black stork; Tengmalm's, Ural, and eagle owls; black grouse, hazel hen, capercaillie, nutcracker, wall creeper, rock thrush, willow tit, alpine accentor, crossbill, three-toed woodpecker.

🌲 Some of the valleys and slopes are grazed by cattle and sheep. Elsewhere there are virgin highland forests of fir, spruce, and beech mixed with larch and maple. Higher up is the mountain pine. One species of pine (*Pinus cembra*) is found nowhere else in Poland.

🏨 There are hotels and pensions of all classes in Zakopane, the railhead on the park's northern boundary. Rates (full board) from US $5.50 per day for modest pension to US $10 for first-class hotel. There are also chalets, ski lodges, and tourist huts at 10 sites in the park.

✈ By rail or road to Zakopane; nearest airport at Krakow.

🚗 A few highways thread their way into the park; all but one give out into marked tourist tracks. These tracks form a rich network, linking all the chalets and lodges with lovely scenic walks along or through the mountain ranges.

☀ Open all year; winter is best for skiing (no permanent snow here); best time to see wildlife June to September.

🕐 3–7 days.

🎫 Free.

🚩 Excellent guides in Zakopane; rates Zl 40 per hour (3 hour minimum).

👁 Zakopane has a regional museum, which has good natural history exhibits. The area is a popular health and holiday resort – Poland's premier climbing and winter sports centre.

⇨ Polish travel offices. (Scientific queries to Prof B. Pawlowski, Botany Department, University of Krakow, Lubicz 46.) Permits to visit certain protected areas from The Director, Tatrzanskiego Parku Narodowego, Zakopane, ul. Chalubinskiego 42a, Poland.

Kampinos National Park 101,710 acres (of which 46,250 are totally protected); between 300 and 600 ft above sea level. The terrain of Kampinos consists largely of dune, covered with forests and well watered – in fact it lies in the fork of the Vistula and Bzura rivers. The region has a long history of settlement and there are remains of prehistoric dwellings within the park; even the protected zone contains 30 villages. Thus only a few small areas of the forest are primeval. Elk have been reintroduced into the park and many are now free living. Two rare birds, the grey heron and a crane (*Megalornis grus*) nest in and near the park.

↗ Elk, roe deer, weasel, fox, boar, badger, vole; grey heron, crane, buzzard, rough-legged buzzard, hen harrier.

🎋 Oak and pine woods, alder, birch, bird cherry, and two rare species: durmast oak and black birch. In sphagnum bogs there is chamaedaphne.

🛏 Hotels and pensions of every class in Warsaw.

🚭 By road from Warsaw, 9 miles away.

🚍 By road and on foot.

🌅 Open all year; best time in summer.

🕐 Half to whole day.

🎫 Free.

📑 Couriers and cars available for parties up to 5; rates from US $6 for 3 hours.

👁 There is a museum and an ecological institute within the park.

🔛 Polish travel offices.

Reserves in the Polish Lake Districts The Mazurian and Augustow lake districts lie in a band across northeastern Poland, stretching from the Soviet border to Gdansk and the Baltic. It is a picturesque land of forests and lakes, popular among campers, yachtsmen, canoeists – and sightseers, for the history of the region is long and well attested in churches and castles. The roads are good, making the districts a convenient detour for people travelling through Poland to the USSR. If you happen to be holidaying in the area there are three small reserves worth a visit; and if you happen to be coming by car from East Germany, there is a fourth, not actually in the lake districts but worth a detour on the way. This fourth is the *Osiedle Kormoranow Reserve* (50 acres) in the Rzecznica forest area near Czluchow. It lies near the southern route between Szczezin and Gdansk; but since most travellers take the Baltic route, they can reach it by a 60-mile detour at Koszalin. The reserve, which is in an old beech wood on the banks of the Brda river, protects the largest cormorant colony in Poland – upwards of 150 nests. The nearest airport is at Gdansk and the nearest station Przechlewo.

From west to east the other reserves are: *Kuduypy Beaver Reserve* (8,640 acres, 480 being totally protected), in a stretch of mixed deciduous and pine woods on the Pasleka river. It was set aside in 1958 to protect a colony of beavers now numbering over 40. Gdansk is the nearest airport and Olsztyn the nearest station. *Czerwone Bagno Reserve* (5,440 acres) is a mixture of wooded country and open moorland in which herds of elk roam freely. Warsaw has the nearest airport, Suwalki the nearest station. *Marycha Beaver Reserve* (480 acres) lies near Sejny in the Wigry forest area on the country's northeastern border. The forest is a mixture of pine, birch, aspen, and alder – building materials for several dozen beavers in the Czarna (Marycha) river.

European bison at Bialowiecz NP. The story of how this species was brought back from the verge of extinction is told on page 391.

The lakes are, naturally, a haven for waterfowl. Among species you may see: black- and red-necked grebes; black and white storks; mute swan (world's largest colony, 1,000 pairs, on Lake Lukniary); greylag and bean geese; ferruginous duck, goosander, goldeneye, crane, black kite, goshawk, marsh harrier, white-tailed eagle, peregrine, osprey, quail, ruff, black-tailed godwit, spotted crake, thrush nightingale, ortolan bunting, aquatic warbler, black-headed gull (10,000 pairs on Lake Kruklin), and occasional Caspian tern.

There are ample camping sites and plenty of hotels and pensions within reach of all these reserves. Polish travel offices can arrange all details in advance of your trip.

Portugal

Faro The southernmost point in Portugal is also its largest town. River and sea have combined to build a big complex of dunes that cradle numerous tidal lagoons. Thus it is a good place to see not only the expected birds of passage between Europe and Africa, but also waders and other breeding birds of the shore and dune. Birds of passage include: wood, green, and curlew sandpipers; turnstone, grey plover, ruff, greenshank, little stint, sanderling, terns, gulls, black-winged stilt, avocet. Summer visitors: azure-winged magpie (in pinewoods near the town), Kentish plover, pratincole, white stork, little bittern, buzzard, lesser kestrel, black and red kites. Faro has 4 hotels (1st-A to 2nd class; 210 escudos (written $) to 280$) and 11 pensions (de luxe to 2nd class; 40$ to 135$); all rates plus 10% service and 3.1% tax. Faro is accessible by road and rail from Lisbon.

Gerês The national park at Gerês has no official IUCN recognition as it is not financed up to minimum international standards. However it is one of the best and most convenient sites to visit in the Portuguese hinterland. Animals that were once common here but now locally extinct include bear, wolf, a wild goat or tur that was unique to Gerês, and the imperial eagle. There are still wild boar, deer, including roe deer, and voles. Birds include: golden eagle, hen harrier, raven, rock pipit, rock bunting, chough, crag martin, blue rock thrush, alpine accentor, rock thrush (visitor); citril finch and wall creeper are occasional winter visitors. The park lies between about 2,500 and 5,118 ft, so there are distinct tree ranges: wild cherry, bird cherry, holly, sycamore, strawberry tree, and alder up to about 3,000 ft; oaks end at about 3,300 ft, to be replaced by Pyrenees oak to about 4,000 ft; birch and yew straggle up a further 300 ft or so, but after 4,300 ft there is only bare rock and a variety of heaths. Plants of the lower slopes include: Cretan fern, several kinds of cottongrass, hard-shield fern, narcissus, iris, fragrant orchid, false-flax, rock cress, common whitebeam, Scots pine, several wild berries, common milkwort, wormwood, common butterwort, mountain valerian, small scabious, sheepsbit, aster, hawkweed. There is accommodation in the spa of Caldas do Gerês, at the roof of the park; 4 hotels (2nd and 3rd class; 110 escudos (=\$) to 210\$) and 5 pensions (1st and 2nd class; 85\$ to 125\$); all rates plus 10% service and 3.1% tax. Nearest air (and most convenient rail) access is to Porto. From there you can take the direct route via Braga, then a mountain by road to Soengas, turn left for the spa. Or you can go a more scenic route up the coast to Viana do Castelo, then along the Lima river valley into Spain, cutting back into Portugal through Lovios to the spa.

Lisbon and district For visitors to Lisbon there are two superb birdwatching areas within easy reach: the wetlands of the Tagus and Sado estuaries. The northeastern part of the estuary (opposite the islands on the map) is drained lowland devoted almost exclusively to rearing fighting bulls. Drainage creeks run well into some of the fields, creating small, reedy lagoons. Here you will see Montagu's and marsh harriers, black kite, white stork, little and cattle egrets, great grey shrike, roller, short-toed lark, bee eater, pratincole, and big flocks of waders. In walking through this area do not climb over any fence – there may be fighting bulls on the other side! The southerly shores of the estuary are more varied: vine-yards, stands of pine, and olive groves. The valleys of the smaller tributaries are the most rewarding – between Barreiro and the point where the shore turns northward. Apart from birds named above you will also see: hoopoe, purple heron, bittern, black-winged stilt, rock sparrow, great grey shrike, crested lark, and, during passage, Kentish, grey, and little ringed plovers; curlew sandpiper, black-tailed godwit, whimbrel. The northern (fighting-bull) area is best reached by leaving Vila Franca de Xira southward on N10, taking the Ponta de Erva turn, right, about 5 miles out of town. The other areas are reached by taking the Salazar bridge south from Lisbon and working around the shore through the towns shown on the map. The Sado estuary, 20 miles south, has open shore, salt pans, lagoons, and alkali marshes – as well as cultivated rice fields that support a rich avifauna. The northern shore, east from Setúbal, has marsh, salt pan, mud shoal, and creek. The whole southern shore is similar but there are added habitats of large dunes and woods of pine and cork oak. In winter it attracts thousands of passage waders. Apart from the birds named above you will also find great spotted cuckoo and azure-winged magpie. Records for both estuaries are far from complete; so visiting birdwatchers have a chance here to fill in gaps in our knowledge. There is a hotel at Alcácer do Sal (1st class: 140 escudos (=$) full board); there is a colony of white storks in the citadel here. Setúbal has one hotel (1st-B: 190$ to 240$, full board) and 4 pensions (de luxe and 1st class; 50$ to 250$, full board). All rates plus 10% service; Setúbal rates plus a further 3.1% tax.

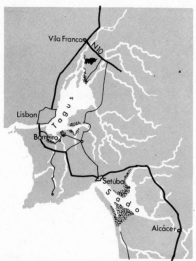

Romania

Retezat National Park 32,500 acres; 1,600 to 8,327 ft above sea level. The park and its surrounding country marks the western end of the Caucasus range. Its highest peak, Mt Pelagra, rises to 8,237 ft; Mt Retezăt itself to 8,166 ft and there are 40 other summits higher than 7,000 ft. Evidence of glacial activity is still marked, with many glacial lakes, cirques, moraines, and scree littered with giant boulders – many still unstably perched. Apart from a little mining and forestry, and, of course, the biological research station in the northern (closed) part of the park, there is little human activity in this region. It has, however, become very popular with tourists in the summer, and you should arrange your visit and make all bookings through your nearest Romanian tourist office well in advance.

Wild boar, wolf, bear (115 at a recent estimate), lynx, marten, chamois (usually visible only in spring on inaccessible and sunlit crags), squirrel, many small rodents; white-headed vulture, cinereous vulture, black vulture, golden eagle, lammergeier (a rare visitor), capercaillie, grouse; two viper species.

The mountain slopes are covered with forests of spruce, pine, and fir, interspersed with stands of rhododendron. Here and there are birches and alders. In more sheltered stretches are flowering ash, walnut, and beech (especially the ancient beech forests on the left bank of the Zlatuia valley at the heart of the reservation). Among a huge variety of shrubs and flowers, including many alpine species, are buttercups, many kinds of aconite, wild raspberries, sedges, orchids, and a number of plant systems unique in Europe.

There are 5 tourist huts in the park. One, the Buta Chalet, is at 5,200 ft; the others are all below 5,000 ft. Price and availability depends on the season and the size of your party. Full details from your local Romanian tourist office.

The park is accessible only from the north. The main Bucharest–Budapest road runs about 40 miles to the north of the park; you turn off towards the mining villages of Petroseni or Sarmizegetusa (the turning is about halfway between Deva and Orastie on the main road). From either of these villages, or from Pui (Petroseni road) or Hateg (Sarmizegetusa road) you can find pathways leading into the park. All these villages, except Pui, are also served by rail. Nearest airport Bucharest.

Foot track only.

Open all year; best time spring to autumn.

3–5 days.

Free.

The book *Nature Reserves in Romania*, published by Meridiane Publishing House, Bucharest, is packed with information at specialist level but is not particularly suited to tourists.

Can be arranged via Romanian tourist offices.

If you arrive and leave by car, from or to Bucharest, you could detour (140 miles, round trip) to Cluj to visit the botanical gardens at Cluj, which rank among the major botanical gardens in the world.

Romanian tourist offices.

Reserves in the Danube Delta The Danube Delta (over $1\frac{1}{4}$ million acres at or near sea level) is one of the most magnificent birdlife regions of the world and certainly the most prolific in Europe. This mixture of marsh, lagoon, lake, river, floating reed islands, and sandbars is a result of a constant struggle between the river Danube, the Black Sea, the rich vegetation – and, in recent years, man. Even in historical times the level and geography has changed out of all recognition. Herodotus, who visited the delta over 2,400 years ago,

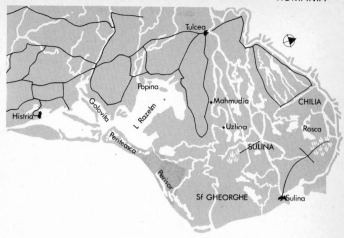

found a huge estuary; its shores were 50 miles farther inland than today's coastline, reaching places like modern Galati, Bráila, and Giurgu. Millions of tons of silt, brought down by the river from distant mountains and plains, have since clogged the estuary, creating a region where, until very recently, there was little chance for human communities to make a living. The spring floods, which last all season (3 to 4 months) and raise the water level as much as 13 ft, still make the going difficult. Nevertheless, cellulose productivity in these marshes is 10 times greater than from forest areas – and a developing country like Romania cannot afford to ignore such wealth. Agronomists, economists, and biologists have worked out a carefully phased programme of development whereby the water levels will be controlled in about half the delta, while leaving the drainage and runoff of the remainder unchanged. As part of the plan about 103,000 acres are set aside as permanent nature reserves, most of them surrounded by buffer zones 1 or 2 km wide. In addition, hunting is restricted throughout the delta (and, naturally, completely forbidden in the reserves); the reed fields and fisheries are visited by only a few fishermen in the summer; and reed burning is carefully controlled by biologists.

The Danube's three main arms divide the delta into its main areas: the Chilia, lying on the country's northern border with the USSR (beyond which lies about a fifth of the delta); the Sulina, the middle arm; and the Sfintu Gheorghe, the most southerly branch. In summer the delta seems to be an endless tract of green reeds, some reaching over 13 ft, interrupted by pools and sandbanks. The roots of the reeds form a thickly woven underwater mat in whose strands collects a mixture of silt and plant and animal humus. In time it may sink to the bottom; but about 250,000 acres are permanently afloat (75,000 acres are actually adrift as floating islands). Between these floating mats, whether anchored or adrift, the silt and gravel piles up into great banks, most of them carpeted with meadow or forest, as well as plantations of hybrid black poplars. Near the Black Sea coast the sandbanks become more arid, turning finally to barren dunes. Almost every European amphibious plant is represented in this complex mixture of environments.

The delta is famous not just·for its birds. The reed mats support large herds of wild boar, as well as mink, otter, ermine, and weasel; fox, wild cat, wolf, muskrat, Enot dog, and nutria also abound. Land tortoises, now rare in the Black Sea littoral, are still common around Lake Razelm and Sfîntu Gheorghe. But birds are its chief glory.

Five important European flyways pass through the delta, making it an important resting place for birds migrating between the Arctic and the Tropics. In addition, many northern birds come here to overwinter, while many others nest here in the summer. The rarer species include pelican; white, red, small white, and yellow egrets; spoonbill, night heron, glossy ibis, dwarf cormorant, crane – all of which exist here in fairly large colonies. Overwintering species include geese (red-breasted, brent, snow, bean, Suskin's and barnacle), great northern and polar divers, black-throated diver, swan and small swan, three sawbill species, and many kinds of duck. Birds of prey include the sea eagle, osprey, black eagle, vulture kite, reed hawk falcon, sparrowhawk, and many owls.

The three large reserves protect the delta's three main kinds of habitat: inland delta, coastal delta, and network lagoon.

Rosca-Buhariova-Hrecisca Reserve (38,050 acres) lies inland in the northern part of the delta. Most of it consists of the Rosca and Buhariova reed-mat marshes, between the western edge of the Letea marine sandbank and the eastern edge of the Chilia continental sandbank. It is crisscrossed by rivulets, most of them draining toward the Chilia in the north. It contains Europe's only large pelican colony as well as mixed colonies of cormorant, glossy ibis, night heron, small white egret, and warblers of many kinds. Occasionally there are colonies of great white egret, spoonbill, and red heron. In the oak forest on the Letea bank there are owls and you will often see the huge nests of the sea eagles. In autumn this is a favourite resting place for migrating woodcock. Mammals include mink, otter, weasel, ermine, muskrat, nutria, wildcat, fox, and boar.

Perisor-Zatoane Reserve (35,200 acres) lies in one of the oldest parts of the delta, south of Sfîntu Gheorghe and east of the Dranov depression and lake; its coastal edge is marked by recently formed parallel sandbars and isolated lakes. It abounds in streams where salt and fresh water mix. The resulting marshes are ideal nesting grounds for mute swans, whose pairs nest in isolation, as well as colonies of white egrets, red and yellow herons, and small white egrets.

The dotterel, whose strange friendliness, succulent flesh, and pretty eggs have helped make it a rarity, now breeds in remote areas only.

Autumn visitors include thousands of cranes from the corn-fields of the littoral. Spring and autumn are the best time to see thousands of migratory fowl, including nesting pairs of stilt, woodcock, crane, avocet, and gulls. Winter species include northern swans, geese, duck, sawbills, and gulls.

Periteasca-Leahove Reserve (9,640 acres) is an area of dry sandbanks and shallow lagoons immediately west of the Perisor-Zaotane Reserve. Like that reserve it is a favourite nesting place for sea-coast birds and winter visitors, who adapt to the varying degrees of salinity in the inland lagoons and marshes.

There are numerous small reserves and protected areas, totalling nearly 20,000 acres, throughout the delta. Mostly they are places of shelter and nesting sites for migratory waterfowl. Among them are mixed colonies at Uzlina and Mahmudia on Sfintu Gheorghe, Popina island on Lake Razelm; Golovita, just south of Lake Razelm (for white egret and spoonbill); Histria, on Lake Sinoie, 30 miles north of Constanta (shelduck). Stilt and avocet nest in the salt marshes between Mahmudia and Uzlina. Temporary sanctuaries are also declared as new migration and nesting patterns create new needs.

The easiest way of seeing the delta, though it affords only glimpses of the reserves, is to take a scheduled 2- or 3-day trip by NAVROM (official tourist) vessels between Tulcea and Sulina or Tulcea and Sfintu Gheorghe. NAVROM can also arrange longer tours, personally conducted by local guides with their own fishing or motor boats; you live en famille with the guides' families.

Only Lakes Razelm, Golovita, and Sinoie are accessible by roads connected to the main highway system – likewise the small reserves at Mahmudia and Histria. The main way of getting about throughout the delta is by boat.

🚐 Boat and foot.

🌦 Open all year; best time for migratory waterfowl early spring or autumn.

🕐 2–14 days.

🎫 Free.

📑 The official guide to the Romanian Black Sea Littoral covers the entire area in the minutest detail.

🗺 Can be arranged through Romanian tourist offices.

👁 The Black Sea coast is one of the finest holiday playgrounds in eastern Europe as well as a popular inland tourist centre. Most local towns trace their history back to Greek and Roman settlements, and their location near the mouth of southeastern Europe's major waterway ensured that there was always some kind of human activity in the area.

⇨ Romanian tourist offices.

Spain

Coto Doñana Reserve About 33,000 acres; at or near sea level. The marshy, many-branched delta of the Guadalquivir river is almost dammed off at the coast by a 45-mile long sand bar stretching from the mouth of the Rio Tinto at Palos to Sanlucar, where the Guadalquivir has its only outlet. The beach and dune is the Coto Doñana proper, but the reserve stretches farther inland over this unusual formation. In fact, there are at least seven important habitats in this mecca for birdwatchers. The *beach* is sandy and almost straight, a breeding site for Caspian tern and Kentish plover; the stone towers, built as fortifications against Barbary pirates, date from the middle ages – peregrines sometimes breed in them. The *dunes and slacks* are mostly still mobile and spreading inland; here and there they are held by pine scrub and marram grass. Stone curlew and thekla lark breed here, and many spring migrants pass through; it is hunted by imperial and short-toed eagles. Farther inland are *woods* of stone pine, quite dense toward Sanlucar; at the other end of the coast, toward Palos, juniper is more common. Mammals here include wild boar and mongoose; birdlife, too, is rich: great grey and woodchat shrikes, red-necked nightjar, great spotted cuckoo; Sardinian, Dartford, and orphean warblers; azure-winged magpie, red and black kites, imperial and booted eagles all breed. The *plain* is halimium thicket dotted with gorse and isolated cork oaks – easy to traverse except where the gorse is dense. Breeding birds, apart from several already mentioned, include heron (heronry at Algaida), white stork, and golden oriole. The *marismas* form a cracked-clay plain covered with glasswort most of the year. Here you will find sandgrouse, calandra, short-toed larks, Montagu's harrier. Dry islands ('vetas') covered with grasses, thistle, and saueda have significant colonies of avocet, black-winged stilt, Kentish plover, slender-billed gull, gull-billed tern, pratincole,

Wild boar in the Coto Doñana snows. Boars grub for nuts and roots, but will also eat worms, insects, and any small animal they can catch.

pintail, pintailed sandgrouse, marbled duck, bee eater. Just over a half mile from the coast, and parallel to it, runs the freshwater channel known as Madre de las Marismas, which irrigates the whole area. In its reeds you will find great reed warbler, purple and night herons, purple gallinule, and spoonbill. Between the channel and open marismas is a rush-filled wet zone, home of ferruginous and white-headed ducks, red-crested pochard, various grebes, marsh harrier, black and whiskered terns, crested coot, Baillon's crake. These wetland birds are also found in the series of *lagoons* between the Palacio de Doñana and the dunes.

- Apart from breeding species listed above, summer visitors include little and cattle egrets, squacco heron, flamingo, spoonbill; griffon, black, and Egyptian vultures; black kite, lesser kestrel, golden and booted eagles, black-bellied sandgrouse, short-toed and lesser short-toed larks, Scop's owl; melodious, Sardinian, Ceti's, Savi's, subalpine, spectacled, and fan-tailed warblers; spotless starling, serin, tawny pipit, woodchat and great grey shrikes.

- Lodging at the Palacio can sometimes be arranged. Camping is permitted only at authorized sites. There are tourist hotels and pensions at Nicola, Almonte, El Rocio, Huelva, Palos, and Sanlucar – all within 25 miles of the coast. No refreshments or food is for sale within the reserve.

- Getting to Coto Doñana is still something of an expedition and should not be undertaken off the cuff. From Seville take the main road to Huelva for 35 miles, as far as La Palma. There take the byroad southward via Bollullos, Almonte, and El Rocio, from where a new road leads to the coast and to the Palacio. The nearest airport is at Seville. Nearest rail access at La Palma.

- Most visitors travel on foot; transport to various sites and on water can sometimes be arranged.

- Open all year; rewarding at all times.

- 1–5 days.

- Permits are necessary and all visits must be arranged in

advance through the Director; give the number in your party, dates of proposed visit, and any other relevant details.

👁 Because the Coto Doñana is so famous, many visitors forget that the whole of southern Andalucia is outstanding for birdwatching. Many of the species listed above can be seen throughout the area. Here is a brief list of other rewarding sites, working south from the Cota area: Sanlucar de Barrameda (black kites); Jerez de la Frontera (sewage farm, breeding stilts); Arcos de la Frontera, a vantage point some 35 miles inland (griffon vultures and lesser kestrels); Cadiz (salt pans, little egret, stilt, short-toed lark, and many waders); Cape Trafalgar (cliff colony of little and cattle egrets); Laguna de la Janda and nearby Sierra de la Plata (herons, stilts, black kite, Egyptian and griffon vultures, woodchat shrike, spotless starling, hoopoe; rufous, olivaceous, and Sardinian warblers; and Europe's only reported breeding white-rumped swifts); Gibraltar (only European site for Barbary partridge). Tarifa, Spain's southernmost point, is a splendid place to see the autumn migrations (storks, raptors, etc) – but the corresponding African coast is even better.

⇒ Dr Jose A. Valverde, Director, Estacion Biologica de Doñana, Paraguay 1, Sevilla, Spain.

Ordesa National Park About 5,000 acres; averaging 8,000 ft with peaks rising to 11,000 ft above sea level. The park is a single valley, part open meadow, part mountain forest, just over the Pyrenean divide from the Pyrénées-Occidentales NP in France. The valley is guarded by steep cliff ramparts – habitat for the mountain mammals and birds.

🐾 Wild boar, brown bear, Spanish ibex, wild goat, northern lynx. Raptors are the chief glory of the park's avifauna; among sites for lammergeier that can be openly acknowledged, this is the best; also: Bonelli's, booted, and short-toed eagles; red and black kites; griffon and Egyptian vultures; Montagu's harrier, goshawk, peregrine, Scop's and eagle owls. Other birds include pheasant, starling, Alpine swift, Alpine chough and chough, hoopoe, great grey shrike, rock thrush, black and black-eared wheatears and wheatear.

🛏 The refugio in the park (June 1 to September 30) has rugged single rooms at 125pta/night, double rooms from 220–280pta/night; meals 290pta extra. There are several hotels at Sallent, ranging from the four-star Formigal to one-star hotels and boarding houses. Only one, the Tirol, is open all year. Rates range from 90–325pta single, 160–515pta double; meals from 240–325pta per day. All the Sallent hotels are modern; the refugio was opened in 1953.

⇨ Leave Jaca eastwards, along the Aragón valley, for about 12 miles, then turn north for the frontier, passing through Biescas and Sallent. This road crosses the frontier and runs almost due north to Pau. It is the only way into the park coming south from France.

�foot On foot and horseback; horses can be rented locally.

❄ Open all year; best in spring and summer.

🕐 3 days.

🎫 Free.

⇒ Tourist Information Office, Coso Alto 35, Huesca/tel: 21 25 83.

Sade Guadarrama Though not an official reserve, the mountain range 35 miles north of Madrid is the best inland birdwatching site in Spain and one of the best in the whole of Europe. All of it is accessible from Madrid – though there are several hotels in superb mountain settings in the Sade itself. The chief flora is thick maquis bush and splendid old pine forest. As with Ordesa NP the raptorial bird species are the great attaction: imperial, golden, booted, and Bonelli's eagles; black and red kites, goshawk, black and griffon vultures, buzzard and honey buzzard, peregrine, lesser kestrel, hobby; also: white stork, woodchat and great grey shrikes, crag martin, rock sparrow, rock and cirl buntings; subalpine, melodious, Dartford, and Bonelli's warblers; crested and calandra larks, roller, bee eater, hoopoe, firecrest, golden oriole.

Sweden

Abisko National Park
Stora Sjöfallet National Park
Sarek National Park
Padjelanta National Park
Because of their similarity of terrain and wildlife these four parks are conveniently dealt with together under most headings. All are in glacial and alpine country north of the Arctic circle. Abisko, being on the direct Sweden–Norway railway line, is the easiest to reach, though some mountaineering equipment is needed to negotiate the remoter foot tracks. Stora Sjöfallet and Padjelanta are slightly more difficult to reach and move around in; while Sarek is really only for climbers. Stora Sjöfallet, Sarek, and Padjelanta are continuous with one another, in that order from north to south, and lie about 80 miles south of Abisko. If you intend staying longer than 3 or 4 days it pays to join the STF (Svenska Turistföreningen) for the sake of the concessions (see ⇦ below) and cheaper boat fares. People under 20 and 2-children families recoup the membership fee even on two nights' lodgings.

Abisko (18,533 acres) consists of the canyon-like valley of the Abiscojokk, part of the lake Törneträsk, and the slopes up to mountains such as Slattatjåkko (3,851 ft) and Nuolja (3,815 ft). The valleys are covered with birch, with occasional stands of pine; vegetation is abundant.

Stora Sjöfallet (31,000 acres) is chiefly mountain and lake; it rises from conifer forest in the east, through alpine country, to the higher mountains of the Norwegian border. The great fall from which the park takes its name is (when hydroelectric demands allow it to flow) the most impressive and beautiful in Lappland.

Padjelanta (504,100 acres) is similar in nature to Stora Sjöfallet but is richer in mountain flora and wildlife.

Sarek (470,490 acres) is western Europe's largest wild area. It is almost inaccessible, with hardly any paths, huts, or bridges (so you need full mountain-expedition equipment and at least 7 days' supply of food); very rich in plant and wildlife.

↗ Mountain fauna include reindeer, wolf, wolverine, arctic fox, lemming, and small rodents; snowy owl, snow bunting, dotterel, long-tailed skua, ptarmigan, golden plover, purple sandpiper, Lappland bunting, meadow pipit, phalarope, Temminck's stint, wheatear, ringed plover, shorelark. Below the treeline you will find elk, bear, hare, weasel, squirrel, otter, marten, lynx, golden eagle, snipe, brambling, redpoll, garden warbler, willow warbler, reed bunting, bluethroat, redwing, fieldfare, raven, wood sandpiper, willow grouse, gyr falcon, rough-legged buzzard, merlin.

✿ In summer the mountain regions are almost a solid mat of colour. Yellow flowers include the globe flower, cinquefoil, buttercup, mountain violet, rose root, and mountain dandelion. White: polygonum, stitchwort, saxifrages, alpine rockcress. Violet: cranesbill, mountain vetches, bartsia. Blue: forget-me-not, gentian, veronica. There are also red campions, mountain and black fleabanes, elegant grasses, many varieties of heath and heather, and, fringeing the barren rock, the glacier crowsfoot. The dominant forests are of birch, freely mixed with mountain ash, dwarf birch, birch cherry and many willow species. The undergrowth is rich meadow-type vegetation. Here and there are stretches of more barren heath and conifer forest, where you will find such flowers as alpine lettuce, northern monkshood, angelica, and King Charles's sceptre.

⌂ Abisko Turiststation, 200 beds, owned by STF; rates from kr23 single, kr42 double (kr62 with bath; up to kr53 for full board per person). Open March 15 to May 2 and June 1 to October 1 (slight variation from year to year); book in advance via STF. There are hotels in Jokkmokk, Kvikkjokk, and Saltoluokta, where full board costs between kr35 and kr40 per person per day. Along the foot trails in all the parks are two-roomed mountain huts (*fjällstuga*, plural *-stugor*) with bunks, mattresses, pillows, blankets, cooking pans, crockery, and fuel wood; they rent for kr6 per night (kr4 to STF members) per person. There are also *kåtor* (singular *kåta; å* is said as the English say 'awe'), conical, turf covered Lapp style huts with dirt floors; reindeer skins, blankets, cooking utensils, axe, and saw. Neither *stugor* nor *kåtor* are bookable in advance nor can they be occupied exclusively by one party as long as there are unused bunks or mattresses. You pay a kr10 deposit for keys to huts and stores at any STF office or mountain station and are then on your honour to pay for whatever use you make of the facilities during your tour since there are no staff at the sites. Except for the tourist station at Vietåsjokk, in Stora Sjöfallet, you have to take your own food; at Vietåsjokk the canteen of the National Power Administration is open to tourists for lunch and dinner; there is also a car park, petrol pump, and camping ground.

⇨ *Abisko* By rail direct from Stockholm or by air to Kiruna and thence by rail. *Stora Sjöfallet* By mail bus or car and ferry up the Lule älv system from Jokkmokk to Saltoluokta and Vietåsjokk, thence by well-marked foot trail. *Sarek* By mountain-climbing routes from the southern footpath between Saltoluokta and Kvikkjokk or from the northern footpath between Staloluokta and Akkå. (Note that *Salto*luokta is in Stora Sjöfallet while *Stalo*luokta is in Padjelanta.) *Padjelanta* By mail bus and ferry from Jokkmokk to Kvikkjokk, thence by well-marked foot trail to Staloluokta.

🚐 In all four parks the only way of getting around is by boat and on foot. The trails are either well marked or obvious. The STF publishes a series of detailed maps covering the area; and their free booklet *Tramping the Swedish Highlands* is essential to proper planning of your visit; it is available from all Swedish tourist offices.

☀️ Abisko is open for skiing in spring; otherwise these parks are open only between late-June and early-September.

🕐 1–2 weeks, though Abisko and Saltoluokta *can* be visited for 2-day trips as part of a general Lappland tour.

📧 Free.

📑 Can be arranged through STF.

🔷 STF, Stureplan 2, Fack, Stockholm 7/tel: 08/22 72 00.

Getteröns fågellokal A peninsula on Sweden's southwest coast, just outside Varberg; it has the greatest variety of birds in Sweden. The southernmost Scandinavian fjord, Kungsbackafjord, is 20 miles away to the north. From there southwards the coast is flat, shallow, sandy-muddy, and almost free of islands – perfect habitat for waders and migratory birds. Recently a proposal to site a motorway close to the shore was defeated, chiefly for the disturbance it would have caused to this birdlife. The foreshore is backed by extensive meadows of sedge and reed. Avocets, black-tailed godwits, marsh harrier, osprey, peregrine (all summer); autumn brings black tern, little gull, red-necked phalarope, numerous waders and, occasionally, such rarities as great white heron, Dalmatian pelican, marsh sandpiper, and black-winged stilt. From Varberg town centre take Östra Hamnvägen north to the edge of town, then Getterövägen westwards; the fågellokal and fågeltorn are signposted from this road. Between April 1 and July 31 birdwatching is confined to the tower, which is never closed. The room below the tower is open only at weekends; on weekdays you can get the key from the Varberg police, Östra Långgatan 5/tel: 18080. Varberg has many hotels; central booking through Rumsförmedling Västra Vallgatan 19/tel: 10168. Other information from Turistbyrån, Brunnsparken/tel: 14370 or 10700.

Gotland The largest Baltic island (80 by 30 miles). The basic rock is limestone, worn by the sea into caves, stacks, and ledges – splendid sites for breeding seabirds. Since the climate is among the mildest in Scandinavia, you will see many birds here at the northern limit of their range. The principal town and the ferry arrival port is Visby. Working outwards from there the best birdwatching sites are:

Allekvie löväng; open grassland crowned by a small area of deciduous woodland. Redwing, collared flycatcher, icterine warbler, thrush nightingale. Take Route 147 east from Visby for 1½ miles, then right on to Dalhem road for 3½ miles; then look for green sign saying Allekvie äng.

Lina myr; an area of reeds, wet meadow, and marsh. Black-tailed godwit, ruff, thrush nightingale, icterine warbler, and sometimes great reed, marsh, and river warblers. Take Route 147 from Visby almost to the east coast, then south on Route 146 for 10 miles then right and, after a mile, right again (both roads signposted Vallstena); soon you come to the river Gothemsån; the marsh road is a mile beyond this. (That is the scenic route. You can also take the Vallstena road from Route 147, bearing left after Vallstena to meet up with the marsh road.)

Gothems storsund; a typical Swedish lake surrounded by pinewoods. Osprey, greylag goose, crane, little gull, Caspian tern, goshawk, green sandpiper, black tern, black woodpecker, and occasional great reed warbler, and white-tailed eagle. Take the scenic route as for Lina myr, above, but stay on Route 146 at the Vallstena turn. A mile past Gothem church bear left to Botvaldevik; look out for a track leading to the car park; from there the birdwatching tower (fågeltorn) marks the sund.

Stockviken; a shallow, marshy lake with surrounding reedbeds and wetlands; only a few miles from Gotland's extreme southern tip. A bird tower gives a good view of most of the marsh, which is noted for occasional visits by such summer rarities as little bittern, greater flamingo, blue-checked bee eater, and black stork. Regular breeders include Caspian tern, greylag goose, ruff, avocet. Take Route 140 south from Visby to Burgsvik, then, just south of the village, take the Hamra road and watch out for the Stockviken (left) sign and then for the birdwatching tower.

Stora and Lilla Karlsöar; two rocky islands a few miles off the west coast; Sweden's only seabird colonies; Lilla Karlsö has a 375-acre nature reserve administered by the Svenska Natur-skyddsförening, Riddargatan 9, Stockholm. Guillemot and black guillemot, red-breasted flycatcher, razorbill, barred warbler, greenish warbler, bluethroat, and scarlet grosbeak. Interesting prehistoric sites and caves are nearby. There is a day tour from Visby by bus to Klintehamn then a 40-minute boat trip, Wednesdays and weekends only; start from Burmeisterhuset 10 am. The ordinary ferry sails from Klintehamn daily at 10 am, returning in the afternoon.

The feral pony, or *russ*, can be seen at many places on the island. The wildest herd is in woodland near Lojsta on Route 142 about 25 miles from Visby.

Visby is rich in prehistoric and mediaeval remains (it was a prosperous Hansa town in the 13th-century). It has many campsites, holiday villages, youth hostels, boarding houses and hotels. The island is reached by ferry from Södertälje,

Nynäshamn, Västervik, Oskarshamn, and Helsinki. The airline Linjeflyg serves Visby from more than 120 places in Sweden; details from any Resebyrå.

Note: The only Swedish breeding site of the roller is on Fårö, which is a military restricted area barred to foreigners. However, under pressure, the military have relented to allow foreign tourists to visit various historic and cultural sites. If enough naturalists pester them, they may relent further. The first approach should be made through the Tourist Office in Slite/tel: (0498) 207 30.

Hjälstaviken One of the best birdwatching sites near Stockholm. It was once an inlet (*vik* means 'bay' or 'creek') on the deeply indented northern shore of lake Mälaren, but now the main highway from Stockholm to Enköping, E18, has more or less turned it into a separate lake, almost entirely invested with sedge and reed. Marsh harrier, honey buzzard, bittern, hobby, osprey, Slavonian grebe; spotted, Baillon's, and little crakes; icterine warbler, and red-backed shrike (summer); autumn visitors include Temminck's stint, green sandpiper, red-throated pipit, ruff, bluethroat, wood sandpiper, and greenshank. Take E18 from Stockholm 39 miles or from Enköping 12 miles. On the Stockholm side of the lake there is a visitors' car park. Good views from nearby Kvarnberget, but during the March 15 – July 15 breeding season visitors must keep to the yellow-blazed path.

Öland 87½ miles long, 10 miles at its widest, Öland lies to the southwest of Gotland and only a few miles from the Swedish mainland. It is basically a long limestone outcrop, high in the west and sloping gradually toward the east. In much of the central plain, where the limestone is covered by only a thin layer of soil, is the unique limestone moorland known as *Alvar*. Smooth and treeless, blessed with several unique plants (particularly orchids), the Alvar has long made Öland a botanist's paradise. It is no less rewarding for the birdwatcher; the collared and red-breasted flycatchers, avocet, and Kentish plover – all found here – are uncommon elsewhere in Sweden. Öland and its small offshore islands are at the northernmost end of the range of a number of species, including barred and icterine warblers, sandwich tern, thrush nightingale, and turnstones. From south to north, rewarding sites are:

Ottenby; close to 'Långe Jan', Scandinavia's tallest (138 ft) lighthouse, dated 1784–85. One of Sweden's best places for birds of passage, especially for Arctic waders in spring and August. Icterine and barred warblers, Caspian tern, short-eared owl, red-breasted flycatcher, avocet, ruff, numerous duck. Nearby is a large established herd of fallow deer. You can stay at the observatory (advance application to Ragnar Edberg, Järnvägsparken 9, Oxelösund. Nearest accommodation at Turisthemmet Solgården, Degerhamn (full-board rates around kr30 per person). Camping sites at Degerhamn.

Möckelmossen; a shallow lake in the Alvar. All the expected marsh birds plus black-tailed godwit and Slavonian grebe. Nearby Resmo church dates from the 12th-century and has interesting Romanesque frescoes. Nearest accommodation Pensionat Sandbergen at Vickleby (full board from kr33 per person) and Hotel Vågen, Mörbylanga (full board from kr30–35 per person). Camping at Vickleby and Mörbylånga.

Beijershamn; reedy, muddy shore south of Färjestaden (ferry-arrival village). Easy day trip from mainland. Migrant ducks and waders, barred and occasional marsh warblers, turnstone, Arctic and little terns.

Kapelludden; not especially rich in birdlife but the best site close to Borgholm, capital of the province and the island's only town. Greylag goose, migrating waders and duck, curlew sandpiper, knot, ruff, dunlin, sanderling. Nearby attractions include the ruined St Birgitta chapel, a fine 13th-century stone cross, and a lighthouse (dated 1872). Borgholm has 5 hotels/pensionats with daily full board rates between kr30 and 55. First-class camping site at Kapelludden.

Betgärdeträsk; a coastal marshland on the east of the island and 10 miles from Borgholm; the bird tower is not conspicuous, being hidden in a stand of pine. Usual marsh birds and marsh harrier, black gull, little tern. Accommodation as for Kapelludden.

Södviken; shallow dunes and meadows near the shore; breeding marsh birds. Black-tailed godwit, ruff, avocet, Arctic tern, shelduck, occasional Kentish plover (world's northernmost point).

Torhamns Udde A bird station at the extreme southeast of the Swedish mainland and one of the best places to watch the migrations. Barnacle and brent geese; Caspian, Arctic, common, and occasional Sandwich terns; rough-legged buzzard, white-tailed eagle, osprey, long-tailed and many other ducks, occasional barred warbler. From Karlskrona take Route 15 to Jämjö church then right to Torhamn; the last 1½ miles is rough. Buses run daily to Torhamn from Karlskrona. Nearby campsites at Kristianopel, which is also a holiday village; apply Herr Wolfgang Lohmann, Fågelmara/tel: (0455) 64229; and at Björjenäs, Jämjöslätt/tel: (0455) 42482. Blekinge, the province containing Torhamns Udde, is among Sweden's less-crowded holiday lands – though it is growing increasingly popular with German visitors. The beaches are as good as anything elsewhere in the country, and inland there are many pretty stretches of deciduous woodland.

Switzerland

The Alpine marmot, found only in the Alps and western Carpathians.

The Swiss National Park 45,500 acres; 5,000 to 10,414 ft above sea level. The central Alps in this region (Lower Engadine, on the Swiss–Italian border) are extremely rugged and picturesque. The region was chosen, in 1914, because it was practically untouched by modern man; today, apart from a few rangers' huts and a laboratory, it remains that way. Only one road runs through the park, and, though there are plenty of trails, it is forbidden to leave them and wander at will.

⚲ Red and roe deer, chamois, ibex (reintroduced), marmot, fox, badger, pine marten, weasel; mountain cock, moorhen, white grouse, golden eagle, raven.

⚭ The timber and snow lines are high in this corner of Switzerland (7,190 ft and 9,810 ft respectively – another reason why it was an ideal location for a national park). There is the complete primeval range of alpine flora.

🛏 Park hotels on the park's only road at Il Fuorn and Süsom Givé. Other hotels and pensions at Schanf (4), Bad Scuol (21), Tarasp (5), Vulpera (4), Zernez (9), and Zuoz (8) – all within easy reach of the park. Summer (cheaper) rates for bed and breakfast, room, and bath from Fr17 to Fr70. Campsites at Scuol (class 2) and Zernez (class 2); both have car and caravan (trailer) parks (trailer utilities at Zernez only), showers, shaver sockets, food stores, restaurants; swimming at Scuol site. Rates from Fr2.50 per person per night, children under 6 free, between 6 and 12 at half rates; cars Fr1; cycles/scooters Fr0.50.

✈ The road from Zernez to the Italian border via the Ofen pass leads through the park. Railway at Zernez. Nearest airport at Samedan, 15 miles from Zernez.

🚐 Footpath only – from which you must not stray; this is a strictly protected park.

☀ Open all year; best time summer and autumn. In winter the deer often wander to lower altitudes and so are not to be seen in the park.

🕐 1–2 days.

✉ Free.

⇥ Grisons Tourist Office, CH 7000 Coire, Switzerland.

The white stork is the stork that has a legendary role in human obstetrics – a tradition that has played an important part in saving it from human depradation (witness France, where there is no such tradition – and no stork, either). Originally, it was said that a couple on whose house the stork nested would be blessed with children; the baby-ferrying role was tacked on later. Nevertheless, throughout many parts of Europe people still build platforms for storks to nest on as bringers of general good luck. All the storks from eastern and southern Africa as well as many from Arabia and the Indian subcontinent pass through the Bosphorus and Black Sea area.

Turkey

Lake Manyas Bird Paradise 125 acres of the northeastern shore of Lake Manyas, near the Sea of Marmara. The reed-beds and shallows have been protected for a long time – privately before 1959, officially since. Over the years they and the nearby woodlands (part of which are also in the sanctuary) have come to support a large variety of birds in astonishing numbers; it is also a major stopover for migrants.

    Little bittern, dwarf cormorant, egret, spoonbill; night, grey, and purple herons; Savi's and great reed warbler, roller, black-headed bunting, bee eater, penduline tit, Spanish sparrow, Kentish and spur-winged plovers, lesser kestrel, Scop's owl. Migrants include: squacco heron, glossy ibis, white-winged black and Caspian terns, mallard, teal, gadwall, ferruginous duck, garganey, white pelican.

Bursa is centrally placed for all three lakes, though at 56 miles from L. Manyas, it is a little far for a day trip except for the most casual birdwatcher. Bursa has 3 hotels (total 245 rooms) at rates per room from 55–70 lire per day. Erdex, 25 miles from L. Manyas, and on the Sea of Marmara coast, has 4 hotels (total 183 rooms) from 100–110 lire full board. Many people camp freely on the sea coast. There is a cheap BP campsite at Bursa.

The sanctuary is 100 miles by road from Istanbul, across the Bosphorus and around past lakes Iznik and Apolyon (both of which have bird populations worth detouring to see). There is a daily ferry from Istanbul to Bandirma, from where you can take a taxi to L. Manyas.

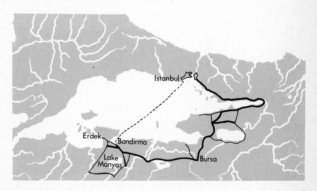

On foot.

Open all year; best in summer and during migrations (especially late August to early October).

1–2 days.

Istanbul itself is a wonderful place to watch the autumn and spring migrations between Europe and the eastern side of Africa. Migratory birds, looking for thermals, obviously prefer to fly over land wherever possible – and in the region of the Bosphorus that doesn't leave them much choice. In order of numbers you are likely to see: white stork, buzzard, honey buzzard, Levantine sparrowhawk, lesser spotted eagle, black kite, and short-toed eagle. Also reported, though in lesser quantities: spotted, booted, and imperial eagles; griffon and Egyptian vultures; red kites, falcons, goshawk, hobby, harriers, crane, lesser kestrel. Black kites and white palm doves scavenge the markets.

Ministry of Tourism & Information, Directorate General of Information, Cebeci Caddesi No. 2, Sihhiye, Ankara; information bureaux in Istanbul at: Maritime Station, Galata; Hilton Hotel, Harbiye; and Yesilköy Airport.

Europe : Species List

ACCENTOR, Alpine Pyrenées-
Occidentales; la Vanoise; Königseegebiet;
Abruzzi; Hohe Tatra; Gerês
AVOCET Camargue; North Sea Coast;
Faro; Danube Delta; Coto Doñana;
Getterön; Gotland; Öland
BADGER Lüneburg; Abruzzi; Gran
Paradiso; Plitvička Jezera; Kampinos;
Swiss NP
BATS Åland
BEAR, Brown Marchauen; Oulanka;
Pallas-Ounastunturi; Sompio; Pyrenées-
Occidentales; Abruzzi; Durmitor;
Plitvička Jezera; Bialowiecz; Hohe Tatra;
Retezat; Ordesa; Abisko
BEAVER Bialowiecz; Polish Lakes
BEE EATER Camargue; Lisbon District;
Coto Doñana; Sade Guadarrama;
L Manyas
— **Blue-Cheeked** Gotland
BISON, European Pfälzerwald;
Bialowiecz
BITTERN Neusiedlersee; Naardemeer;
Hjälstaviken
— **Little** Marchauen; Neusiedlersee;
Camargue; Faro; Lisbon District;
Gotland; L Manyas
BLACKBIRD Abruzzi
— **Alpine** Gran Paradiso
BLUETAIL, Red-Flanked Oulanka
BLUETHROAT Sompio; Rondane; Abisko;
Gotland; Hjälstaviken
BOAR Marchauen; Lüneburg; Pfälzerwald;
Plitvička Jezera; de Hoge Veluwe;
Kampinos; Gerês; Danube Delta;
Retezat; Coto Doñana; Ordesa
BRAMBLING Oulanka; Sompio; Rondane;
Abisko
BUNTING, Black-Headed L Manyas
— **Cirl** Sade Guadarrama
— **Lappland** Pallas-Ounastunturi;
Sompio; Rondane; Abisko
— **Little** Oulanka
— **Ortolan** Bialowiecz; Polish Lakes
— **Reed** Naardemeer; Abisko
— **Rock** Pyrenées-Occidentales; Gerês;
Sade Guadarrama
— **Snow** Pallas-Ounastunturi; Rondane;
Abisko
BUSTARD, Great Marchauen;
Neusiedlersee
BUZZARD Oulanka; Lüneburg; Abruzzi;
de Hoge Veluwe; Kampinos; Faro;
Sade Guadarrama
— **Honey** Lüneburg; Sade Guadarrama;
Hjälstaviken
— **Rough-Legged** Sompio; Rondane;
Kampinos; Abisko; Torhamns Udde
CAPERCAILLIE Sompio; Durmitor;
Bialowiecz; Hohe Tatra; Retezat
CAT, Wild Abruzzi; Plitvička Jezera;
Danube Delta
CHAFFINCH Oulanka; Abruzzi
CHAMOIS Karwendel; la Vanoise;
Königseegebiet; Olympus; Abruzzi;
Gran Paradiso; Durmitor; Hohe Tatra;
Retezat; Swiss NP
CHOUGH Pyrenées-Occidentales;
la Vanoise; Gerês; Ordesa
— **Alpine** Pyrenées-Occidentales;
la Vanoise; Königseegebiet; Abruzzi;
Ordesa
COCK, Mountain Swiss NP
COOT, Crested Coto Doñana
CORMORANT Marchauen; Sept Îles;
Naardemeer
— **Dwarf** Hutavo Blato; Danube Delta;
L Manyas
CORNCRAKE Marchauen
CRAKE, Baillon's Camargue;
Coto Doñana; Hjälstaviken
— **Little** Camargue; Hjälstaviken
— **Spotted** Neusiedlersee; Camargue;
Polish Lakes; Hjälstaviken
CRANE Marchauen; Pallas-Ounastunturi;
Rondane; Kampinos; Polish Lakes;
Danube Delta; Gotland
CREEPER, Wall Karwendel;
Pyrenées-Occidentales; la Vanoise;
Königseegebiet; Hohe Tatra; Gerês
CROSSBILL la Vanoise; Bialowiecz;
Hohe Tatra
CROW, Hooded Olympus

CUCKOO, Great Spotted Lisbon District;
Coto Doñana
CURLEW Marchauen; Lüneburg;
de Hoge Veluwe
— **Stone** Coto Doñana
DEER Åland; Gerês
— **Fallow** Lüneburg; Pfälzerwald; Öland
— **Red** Karwendel; Marchauen;
Königseegebiet; Lüneburg; Pfälzerwald;
Durmitor; de Hoge Veluwe; Swiss NP
— **Roe** Marchauen; Königseegebiet;
Lüneburg; Pfälzerwald; Durmitor;
Plitvička Jezera; de Hoge Veluwe;
Rondane; Kampinos; Gerês; Swiss NP
DIPPER Rondane
**DIVER, Black-Throated, Great
Northern, & Polar** Danube Delta
DOG, Enot Danube Delta
DORMOUSE Gran Paradiso
DOTTERELL Sompio; North Sea Coast;
Rondane; Abisko
DOVE, Stock Lüneburg
DUCKS Plitvička Jezera; Danube Delta;
Öland; Torhamns Udde
— **Eider** Åland; North Sea Coast
— **Ferruginous** Polish Lakes;
Coto Doñana; L Manyas
— **Long-Tailed** Torhamns Udde
— **Marbled** Coto Doñana
— **Tufted** Naardemeer
— **White-Headed** Coto Doñana
DUNLIN Åland; North Sea Coast; Öland
EAGLES Karwendel; Plitvička Jezera
— **Black** Danube Delta
— **Bonelli's** Pyrenées-Occidentales;
Ordesa; Sade Guadarrama
— **Booted** Pyrenées-Occidentales;
Coto Doñana; Ordesa; Sade Guadarrama
— **Golden** Oulanka; Pyrenées-
Occidentales; la Vanoise;
Königseegebiet; Olympus; Gran
Paradiso; Rondane; Hohe Tatra;
Gerês; Retezat; Coto Doñana;
Sade Guadarrama; Abisko; Swiss NP
— **Imperial** Coto Doñana; Sade
Guadarrama
— **Lesser Spotted** Marchauen;
Bialowiecz; Hohe Tatra
— **Sea** Danube Delta
— **Short-Toed** Bialowiecz; Coto Doñana;
Ordesa
— **Spotted** Bialowiecz
— **White-Tailed** Marchauen; Åland;
Polish Lakes; Gotland; Torhamns Udde
EGRETS L Manyas
— **Great White** Marchauen; Danube Delta
— **Cattle** Lisbon District; Coto Doñana
— **Little** Camargue; Hutavo Blato;
Lisbon District; Coto Doñana
— **Red, Small, & Yellow** Danube Delta
ELK (European) Åland; Oulanka;
Pallas-Ounastunturi; Sompio; Rondane;
Bialowiecz; Kampinos; Polish Lakes;
Abisko
ERMINE Åland; Gran Paradiso;
Danube Delta
FALCON, Gyr Pallas-Ounastunturi; Abisko
— **Peregrine** Åland; Pyrenées-
Occidentales; Sept Îles; Hohe Tatra;
Polish Lakes; Coto Doñana; Ordesa;
Sade Guadarrama; Getterön
— **Reed Hawk** Danube Delta
— **Saker** Marchauen
FIELDFARE Abisko
FINCH, Citril Pyrenées-Occidentales;
la Vanoise; Gerês
— **Snow** Pyrenées-Occidentales;
la Vanoise; Königseegebiet;
Gran Paradiso
FIRECREST Plitvička Jezera; Bialowiecz;
Sade Guadarrama
FLAMINGO Coto Doñana
— **Greater** Gotland
FLYCATCHER, Collared Bialowiecz;
Gotland; Öland
— **Pied** Vesijako
— **Red-Breasted** Vesijako;
Königseegebiet; Bialowiecz;
Gotland; Öland
— **Spotted** Vesijako
FOX Åland; Oulanka; Pallas-Ounastunturi;
Sompio; la Vanoise; Lüneburg; Abruzzi;

Gran Paradiso; de Hoge Veluwe;
Rondane; Kampinos; Danube Delta;
Swiss NP
— **Arctic** Abisko
FULMAR Sept Îles
GADWALL Marchauen; Camargue;
North Sea Coast; L Manyas
GALLINULE, Purple Coto Doñana
GANNET Sept Îles
GARGANEY Marchauen; North Sea Coast;
L Manyas
GEESE North Sea Coast
GOAT, Mountain Pfälzerwald; Olympus
— **Wild** Pyrenées-Occidentales; Ordesa
GODWIT, Bar-Tailed North Sea Coast
— **Black-Tailed** Marchauen; North Sea
Coast; Polish Lakes; Lisbon District;
Getterön; Gotland; Öland
GOLDCREST Vesijako
GOLDENEYE Oulanka; Polish Lakes
GOOSANDER Åland; Polish Lakes
GOOSE, Barnacle North Sea Coast;
Danube Delta; Torhamns Udde
GOOSE, Bean Neusiedlersee; Oulanka;
North Sea Coast; Polish Lakes;
Danube Delta
— **Brent** North Sea Coast; Danube Delta;
Torhamns Udde
— **Greylag** Marchauen; Neusiedlersee;
Åland; North Sea Coast; Hutavo Blato;
Polish Lakes; Gotland; Öland
— **Red-Breasted, Snow, & Suskin's**
Danube Delta
— **White-Fronted** Neusiedlersee;
Oulanka; North Sea Coast
GOSHAWK Marchauen; Åland; Pyrenées-
Occidentales; Lüneburg; la Hoge Veluwe;
Rondane; Polish Lakes; Ordesa;
Sade Guadarrama; Gotland
GREBES Coto Doñana
— **Black-Necked** Polish Lakes
— **Great Crested** Neusiedlersee
— **Red-Necked** Polish Lakes
— **Slavonian** Hjälstaviken; Öland
GREENSHANK Pallas-Ounastunturi;
Sompio; Rondane; Faro; Hjälstaviken
GROSBEAK, Scarlet Gotland
GROUSE Lüneburg; Retezat
— **Black** Åland; la Vanoise; de Hoge
Veluwe; Bialowiecz; Hohe Tatra
— **Hazel** Durmitor
— **White** Gran Paradiso; Swiss NP
GROUSE, Willow Sompio; Abisko
— **Wood** Plitvička Jezera
GUILLEMOT Sept Îles; Gotland
— **Black** Åland; Gotland
GULLS Camargue; Faro; Danube Delta
— **Black** Öland
— **Black-Headed** North Sea Coast;
Polish Lakes
— **Common** Åland; North Sea Coast
— **Greater Black-Backed** Sept Îles
— **Herring, & Lesser Black-Backed**
Sept Îles; North Sea Coast
— **Little** Getterön; Gotland
— **Slender-Billed** Camargue; Coto Doñana
HARE Karwendel; Marchauen; Åland;
Oulanka; Lüneburg; Olympus; Plitvička
Jezera; de Hoge Veluwe; Abisko
— **Alpine** Gran Paradiso
— **Mountain** Pallas-Ounastunturi;
Sompio; la Vanoise
— **Snow** Königseegebiet
HARRIER, Hen Kampinos; Gerês
— **Marsh** Neusiedlersee; Camargue; North
Sea Coast; Naardemeer; Polish Lakes;
Lisbon District; Coto Doñana; Getterön;
Hjälstaviken; Öland
— **Montagu's** Camargue; Lisbon District;
Coto Doñana; Ordesa
— **Pallid** Lüneburg
HAWK Pallas-Ounastunturi; Plitvička Jezera
HEATHCOCK Plitvička Jezera
HEN, Hazel Oulanka; la Vanoise;
Hohe Tatra
HERONS Coto Doñana
— **Great White** Marchauen; Neusiedlersee;
Getterön
— **Grey** Neusiedlersee; Hutavo Blato;
Kampinos; L Manyas
— **Night** Marchauen; Camargue;
Danube Delta; Coto Doñana; L Manyas
— **Purple** Marchauen; Neusiedlersee;
Camargue; Naardemeer; Lisbon District;
Coto Doñana; L Manyas

— **Red** Danube Delta
— **Squacco** Camargue; Hutavo Blato;
Coto Doñana; L Manyas
— **Yellow** Danube Delta
HOBBY Marchauen; Pyrenées-
Occidentales; Lüneburg; de Hoge
Veluwe; Hohe Tatra; Sade Guadarrama;
Hjälstaviken
HOOPOE Camargue; Bialowiecz;
Lisbon District; Ordesa; Sade Guadarrama
HORSE, Tarpan Bialowiecz
IBEX la Vanoise; Königseegebiet;
Gran Paradiso; Swiss NP
— **Spanish** Pyrenées-Occidentales; Ordesa
IBIS, Glossy Neusiedlersee;
Danube Delta; L Manyas
JAY, Siberian Oulanka;
Pallas-Ounastunturi
KESTREL Lüneburg
— **Lesser** Camargue; Abruzzi; Faro; Coto
Doñana; Sade Guadarrama; L Manyas
KINGFISHER Plitvička Jezera
KITE, Black Camargue; Pyrenées-
Occidentales; Bialowiecz; Polish Lakes;
Faro; Lisbon District; Coto Doñana;
Ordesa; Sade Guadarrama
— **Red** Pyrenées-Occidentales; Bialowiecz;
Faro; Coto Doñana; Ordesa;
Sade Guadarrama
— **Vulture** Danube Delta
KITTIWAKE Sept Îles
KNOT North Sea Coast; Öland
LAMMERGEIER Pyrenées-Occidentales;
Königseegebiet; Retezat; Ordesa
LARK, Calandra Coto Doñana;
Sade Guadarrama
— **Crested** Camargue; Lisbon District;
Sade Guadarrama
— **Shore** Sompio; Rondane
— **Short-Toed** Camargue; Lisbon District;
Coto Doñana
— **Lesser Short-Toed, & Thekla**
Coto Doñana
LEMMING Pallas-Ounastunturi; Sompio;
Abisko
LYNX Marchauen; Oulanka; Pallas-
Ounastunturi; Sompio; Pyrenées-
Occidentales; Abruzzi; Rondane;
Bialowiecz; Hohe Tatra; Retezat;
Ordesa; Abisko
MAGPIE, Azure-Winged Faro;
Lisbon District; Coto Doñana
MALLARD Marchauen; Neusiedlersee;
North Sea Coast; Naardemeer; L Manyas
MARMOT la Vanoise; Gran Paradiso;
Hohe Tatra; Swiss NP
— **Alpine** Königseegebiet
MARTEN Lüneburg; Abruzzi; Gran
Paradiso; Plitvička Jezera; Rondane;
Retezat; Abisko
— **Beech** Marchauen
— **Pine** Marchauen; Oulanka; Swiss NP
— **Stone** Abruzzi; Gran Paradiso
MARTIN, Crag Pyrenées-Occidentales;
la Vanoise; Königseegebiet; Abruzzi;
Gerês; Sade Guadarrama
— **House, & Sand** Rondane
MERGANSER, Red-Breasted
North Sea Coast
MERLIN Abisko
MICE Åland
MINK Åland; Rondane; Danube Delta
MONGOOSE Mljet; Coto Doñana
MOORHEN Hutavo Blato; Swiss NP
MOUFFLON Pfälzerwald; de Hoge Veluwe
MOUSE, Snow Gran Paradiso
MUSKRAT Danube Delta
MUSQUASH Åland
NIGHTINGALE Marchauen
— **Thrush** Marchauen; Åland; Bialowiecz;
Polish Lakes; Gotland; Öland
NIGHTJAR, Red-Necked Coto Doñana
NUTCRACKER Åland; la Vanoise;
Hohe Tatra
— **Alpine** Königseegebiet
NUTHATCH Abruzzi
NUTRIA Danube Delta
ORIOLE, Golden Camargue; Coto
Doñana; Sade Guadarrama
OSPREY Åland; Vesijako; Rondane; Polish
Lakes; Danube Delta; Getterön;
Gotland; Hjälstaviken; Torhamns Udde
OTTER Marchauen; Åland; Lüneburg;
Abruzzi; Gran Paradiso; Plitvička Jezera;
Danube Delta; Abisko

EUROPE: SPECIES LIST

OUZEL, Ring Königseegebiet; Olympus
— **Water** Gran Paradiso; Plitvička Jezera
OWLS Karwendel; Marchauen; Plitvička
Jezera; Danube Delta
— **Barn** Lüneburg
— **Eagle** Åland; Oulanka; la Vanoise;
Königseegebiet; Gran Paradiso; Rondane;
Bialowiecz; Hohe Tatra; Ordesa
— **Great Grey** Pallas-Ounastunturi;
Bialowiecz
— **Hawk** Rondane
— **Little** Lüneburg
— **Long-Eared** Lüneburg; de Hoge
Veluwe; Rondane
— **Pigmy** Vesijako; Königseegebiet;
Bialowiecz
— **Scop's** Camargue; Coto Doñana;
Ordesa; L Manyas
— **Short-Eared** Lüneburg; North Sea
Coast; Bialowiecz; Öland
— **Snowy** Pallas-Ounastunturi; Abisko
— **Tawny** Lüneburg
— **Tengmalm's** Oulanka; la Vanoise;
Königseegebiet; Lüneburg; Gran
Paradiso; Rondane; Hohe Tatra
— **Ural** Vesijako; Plitvička Jezera; Hohe
Tatra
OYSTERCATCHER Camargue; North Sea
Coast
PARTRIDGE, Barbary Coto Doñana
— **Rock** la Vanoise; Königseegebiet
PELICAN Danube Delta
— **Dalmation** Getterön
— **White** L Manyas
PETREL, Storm Sept Îles
PHALAROPE, Grey Abisko
— **Red-Necked** Rondane; Getterön
PHEASANTS Marchauen; Ordesa
PINTAIL Oulanka; Camargue; North Sea
Coast; Coto Doñana
PIPIT, Meadow Rondane; Abisko
— **Mountain** Königseegebiet
— **Red-Throated** Hjälstaviken
— **Rock** Gerês
— **Tawny** Camargue; Lüneburg; Abruzzi;
Coto Doñana
— **Water** Abruzzi
PLOVER, Golden Sompio; Abisko
— **Grey** North Sea Coast; Faro; Lisbon
District
— **Kentish** Camargue; North Sea Coast;
Faro; Lisbon District; Coto Doñana;
Öland; L Manyas
— **Little Ringed** North Sea Coast; Lisbon
District
— **Ringed** North Sea Coast; Abisko
— **Spur-Winged** L Manyas
POCHARD, Common Marchauen; North
Sea Coast; Naardemeer
— **Red-Crested** Camargue; North Sea
Coast; Naardemeer; Coto Doñana
POLECAT Lüneburg; Abruzzi; Gran
Paradiso; Plitvička Jezera
PRATINCOLE Camargue; Faro; Lisbon
District; Coto Doñana
PTARMIGAN Karwendel; Sompio; la
Vanoise; Königseegebiet; Gran Paradiso;
Rondane; Abisko
PUFFIN Sept Îles
QUAIL Polish Lakes
RABBIT Lüneburg; de Hoge Veluwe
RAIL, Water Neusiedlersee
RAVEN Oulanka; Sept Îles; Königseegebiet;
Lüneburg; Olympus; Gerês; Abisko;
Swiss NP
RAZORBILL Åland; Sept Îles; Gotland
REDPOLL Oulanka; Abisko
— **Alpine** Königseegebiet
REDSHANK North Sea Coast; Rondane
— **Spotted** Oulanka; Pallas-Ounastunturi;
Sompio
REDSTART, Black Pyrénées-
Occidentales; Abruzzi
REDWING Bialowiecz; Abisko; Gotland
REINDEER Pallas-Ounastunturi; Sompio;
Rondane; Abisko
RODENTS Plitvička Jezera; Rondane;
Retezat; Abisko
ROEBUCK Abruzzi
ROLLER Camargue; Bialowiecz; Lisbon
District; Sade Guadarrama; Gotland;
L Manyas
RUFF Oulanka; Sompio; North Sea Coast;
Polish Lakes; Faro; Gotland;

Hjälstaviken; Öland
SANDERLING North Sea Coast; Faro;
Öland
SANDGROUSE Coto Doñana
— **Black-Bellied** Coto Doñana
— **Pintailed** Coto Doñana
SANDPIPER, Broad-Billed Oulanka;
Sompio; North Sea Coast
— **Curlew** Faro; Lisbon District; Öland
— **Green** Oulanka; Faro; Gotland;
Hjälstaviken
— **Marsh** Getterön
— **Purple** Abisko
— **Wood** Sompio; North Sea Coast;
Rondane; Faro; Abisko; Hjälstaviken
SAWBILLS Danube Delta
SCAUP Åland
SCOTER, Velvet Åland
SEALS Åland
— **Monk** Mljet
SERIN Coto Doñana
SHEEP Lüneburg
SHELDUCK Åland; North Sea Coast;
Danube Delta; Öland
SHORELARK Abisko
SHOVELLER Camargue; North Sea Coast
Shrike, Great Grey Camargue; de Hoge
Veluwe; Lisbon District; Coto Doñana;
Ordesa; Sade Guadarrama
— **Lesser Grey** Camargue
— **Red-Backed** Pyrénées-Occidentales;
Abruzzi; Hjälstaviken
— **Woodchat** Camargue; Coto Doñana;
Sade Guadarrama
SISKIN Åland; Vesijako
SKUA, Arctic Åland
— **Long-Tailed** Abisko
— **Red-Necked** Pallas-Ounastunturi
SMEW Oulanka; Pallas-Ounastunturi
SNIPE Lüneburg; Rondane; Abisko
— **Jack** Oulanka; Sompio
SPARROW Lüneburg
— **Rock** Lisbon District; Sade Guadarrama
— **Spanish** L Manyas
SPARROWHAWK Lüneburg; Plitvička
Jezera; Rondane; Danube Delta
SPOONBILL Naardemeer; Danube Delta;
Coto Doñana; L Manyas
SQUIRREL Åland; Oulanka; Lüneburg;
Gran Paradiso; Plitvička Jezera; de Hoge
Veluwe; Rondane; Retezat; Abisko
— **Red** Pallas-Ounastunturi; Sompio
STARLING Ordesa
— **Spotless** Coto Doñana
STILT Danube Delta; Coto Doñana
— **Black-Winged** Camargue; Faro; Lisbon
District; Coto Doñana; Getterön
STINT, Little Faro
— **Temminck's** North Sea Coast; Abisko;
Hjälstaviken
STOAT Pallas-Ounastunturi; Sompio; la
Vanoise; de Hoge Veluwe
STONECHAT Lüneburg
STORK, Black Marchauen; Bialowiecz;
Hohe Tatra; Polish Lakes; Gotland
— **White** Neusiedlersee; North Sea Coast;
Bialowiecz; Polish Lakes; Faro; Lisbon
District; Coto Doñana; Sade Guadarrama
SWALLOW, Mountain Gran Paradiso
SWANS Danube Delta
— **Mute** Åland; Polish Lakes; Danube Delta
— **Small** Danube Delta
— **Whooper** Oulanka; Pallas-Ounastunturi
SWIFT, Alpine Camargue; la Vanoise;
Gran Paradiso; Ordesa
— **White-Rumped** Coto Doñana
TEAL Camargue; North Sea Coast;
L Manyas
TERNS Camargue; Faro
— **Arctic** North Sea Coast; Öland;
Torhamns Udde
— **Black** North Sea Coast; Naardemeer;
Coto Doñana; Getterön; Gotland
— **Caspian** Polish Lakes; Coto Doñana;
Gotland; Öland; Torhamns Udde;
L Manyas
— **Common** North Sea Coast; Torhamns
Udde
— **Gull-Billed** Camargue; North Sea Coast;
Coto Doñana
— **Little** North Sea Coast; Öland
— **Sandwich** North Sea Coast; Öland;
Torhamns Udde
— **Whiskered** Camargue; Coto Doñana

— **White-Winged Black** L Manyas
THRUSH, Blue Rock Camargue;
Abruzzi; Gerês
— **Rock** Pyrenées-Occidentales; Hohe
Tatra; Gerês; Ordesa
— **Song** Oulanka
TIT, Alpine Königseegebiet
— **Bearded** Naardemeer
— **Crested** Plitvička Jezera
— **Marsh** Abruzzi
— **Penduline** Marchauen; Camargue;
L Manyas
— **Siberian** Sompio
— **Willow** Åland; Hohe Tatra
TORTOISE, Land Danube Delta
TURNSTONE Åland; North Sea Coast;
Faro; Öland
TWITE Olympus
VIPERS Retezat
VOLE Kampinos; Gerês
— **Bank** Pallas-Ounastunturi; Sompio
VULTURE, Black Retezat; Coto Doñana;
Sade Guadarrama
— **Cinerous** Retezat
— **Egyptian** Pyrenées-Occidentales; Coto
Doñana; Ordesa
— **Griffon** Pyrenées-Occidentales; Coto
Doñana; Ordesa; Sade Guadarrama
— **White-Headed** Retezat
WADERS Camargue; Hutavo Blato; Lisbon
District; Coto Doñana; Getterön; Öland
WAGTAIL, Blue-Headed North Sea Coast
— **Pied** Rondane
WARBLERS Neusiedlersee; Danube Delta
— **Aquatic** Polish Lakes
— **Arctic** Pallas-Ounastunturi
— **Barred** Åland; Bialowiecz; Gotland;
Öland; Torhamns Udde
— **Bonelli's** Sade Guadarrama
— **Ceti's** Camargue; Coto Doñana
— **Dartford** Coto Doñana; Sade
Guadarrama
— **Fan-Tailed** Camargue; Coto Doñana
— **Garden** Oulanka; Rondane; Abisko
— **Grasshopper** Marchauen
— **Great Reed** Naardemeer; Coto Doñana;
Gotland; L Manyas
— **Icterine** Rondane; Gotland;
Hjälstaviken; Öland
— **Marsh** Gotland; Öland
— **Melodious** Camargue; Coto Doñana;

Sade Guadarrama
— **Moustached** Camargue
— **Olivaceous, & Orphean** Coto Doñana
— **Reed** Naardemeer
— **River** Marchauen; Gotland
— **Rufous** Coto Doñana
— **Sardinian** Camargue; Coto Doñana
— **Savi's** Marchauen; Camargue;
Naardemeer; Coto Doñana; L Manyas
— **Sedge** Naardemeer
— **Spectacled** Camargue; Coto Doñana
— **Subalpine** Camargue; Coto Doñana;
Sade Guadarrama
— **Willow** Rondane; Abisko
WATERFOWL Hutavo Blato
WAXWING Sompio
WEASEL Lüneburg; Abruzzi; Gran
Paradiso; de Hoge Veluwe; Kampinos;
Danube Delta; Abisko; Swiss NP
WHEATEAR Rondane; Abisko
— **Black** Ordesa
— **Black-Eared** Pyrenées-Occidentales;
Ordesa
WHIMBREL North Sea Coast; Lisbon
District
WHITETHROAT Rondane
WIDGEON Camargue; North Sea Coast
WOLF Marchauen; Oulanka; Abruzzi;
Plitvička Jezera; Hohe Tatra; Danube
Delta; Retezat; Abisko
WOLVERINE Oulanka; Rondane; Abisko
WOODCOCK de Hoge Veluwe; Danube
Delta
WOODPECKERS Marchauen; Plitvička
Jezera
— **Black** Pyrenées-Occidentales; la
Vanoise; Lüneburg; de Hoge Veluwe;
Gotland
— **Green** de Hoge Veluwe
— **Grey-Headed** Königseegebiet
— **Lesser-Spotted** de Hoge Veluwe
— **Middle-Spotted** Pyrenées-
Occidentales; Abruzzi; de Hoge Veluwe
— **Syrian** Marchauen
— **Three-Toed** la Vanoise; Königseegebiet;
Bialowiecz; Hohe Tatra
— **Wall-Creeper** Gran Paradiso
— **White-Backed** Pyrenées-Occidentales;
Königseegebiet; Bialowiecz
WREN Oulanka; Gran Paradiso
WRYNECK Lüneburg; de Hoge Veluwe

Flamingoes photographed by floodlight in the Camargue.

USSR

Female musk deer and calf. This species' lack of horns gives it a kangaroo-like head. The male has sharp, projecting incisors instead.

The vast plains that make up most of the present Soviet Union and the former Russian Empire are separated from the rest of the world by natural barriers of mountains, marsh, and ice. The mountains form a contorted tangle in the southwest, south, and southeast; the marsh creates a belt that separates it from Poland and the Baltic republics; and the Arctic tundra and ice complete the enclosure – a rare accord of political and geographical limits. With most of it cut off from the influence of warm seas, its most obvious feature is the regularity of its vegetation lines, which broadly speaking follow the lines of latitude; even the mighty Urals deflect them only slightly to the south.

Below the Arctic Circle the desert tundra gives way to the taiga, that enormous coniferous Eurasian forest which is the world's largest reserve of timber. Southward, between latitudes 58° and 55°, is a mixed forest zone in which deciduous trees become more numerous the farther south you go. However, this zone does not extend east of the Urals, the soil there being poor in quality and lacking body at the surface. Below the forests is a belt of rich and extremely fertile wooded steppe that extends 1,500 miles from the Carpathians into Siberia. Men have cleared out so many of its wooded islands that trees now account for only about 5 per cent of the total area; so the zone merges imperceptibly into the black-earth zone proper – the true steppe, which reaches southward to the Black Sea and eastward into Siberia and Kazakhstan. The steppe becomes drier and drier until it blends with the desert steppe. Generally speaking the rivers flow longitudinally; in Siberia they flow unhelpfully away from the dry interior toward the Arctic seas.

It is this abundance of forest and river which made Russia traditionally the land of furs; and it was naturally enough the depredations of the hunter which threatened many of the fur-bearing species. It was largely to counter this danger that reserves have been created; here not only is hunting forbidden but intensive breeding and ecological adjustment have been actively managed. The most dramatic of these has been on behalf of the aurochs, the European bison. Though once abundant in every forest in Europe, by 1900 it was to be found only in the forests of eastern Poland and along the upper reaches of the river Kuban in the north Caucasus. By 1920 the last Caucasian animal had been killed, and soon afterwards the Polish remnant, too, had been systematically hunted to extinction. In the whole world at that time there existed only 96 head – all in zoos. In 1923, at the instigation of the Polish naturalist Jan Stoleman, an International Society for the Protection of the Aurochs was formed. They decided to refresh the species by crossing the European beast with the American bison, a close relative. The descendants of the cross were mated successively with the captive strain until a large herd was developed which could scarcely be distinguished from the original species. It was introduced into the Caucasus Reserve in 1938, the Byelovezhskaya Pushcha in 1940, and into the Oka Terrace somewhat later. In the Oka reserve artificial salt springs were constructed and planted with stands of willow and poplar undersown with wild grasses for fodder. Among the reserves there is a yearly exchange of stock.

The beaver, prized for its silky fur and valuable musk glands, had become so depleted that by 1900 only a few hundred were left in the vast lands now known as the USSR. There was no improvement until in 1938 beaver hunting was banned; today the population numbers about 40,000. Deliberately introduced to the Oka reserve from the Voronezh it rapidly multiplied, encouraged by the planting of willow and poplar. Very soon their dams were a common sight and the animal now has spread far beyond the reserve territory.

Sable and marten were saved by protection and intensive breeding, and in the north Urals (Pechoro-Ilychsky Reserve) a hybrid developed as a result of cross-breeding; it has since flourished vigorously.

The list of dying species saved by reservation work is too large to give in full, but one must mention the Saigak antelope and the spotted deer, both of which were almost hunted to extinction for the supposed medicinal properties of their antlers. Other rarities include the Ussuri tiger (totally protected), Asiatic wapiti, roe deer, and the shy Asiatic wild ass.

It is to protect such species and to promote scientific research that the USSR now has 86 reserves covering a total of 17.5 million acres. By special legislation they are excluded from the agricultural economy. All are open to parties of visitors, who are generally restricted to fixed itineraries, as a rule under the guidance of a warden. The following list, chosen to exemplify the great diversity of wildlife in the Soviet Union today, describes 10 of them.

The editor is deeply indebted to Professor A. G. Bannikov of the Soviet Academy of Sciences, whose learned and most thorough essays on the 10 parks listed (private communication) form the basis of these entries. He is also grateful to the staff of the Natural History Museum, South Kensington, for their generous help in correctly rendering the names of the plants and animals listed in Professor Bannikov's papers. By contrast, he is in no way indebted to Intourist, which stolidly refuses to admit the existence of any reserve other than Askaniya Nova.

As a private tourist you are at the mercy of Intourist and can have little hope of visiting 8 of the 10 parks listed here (Byelovezhskaya Pushcha and Oka Terrace ought to yield to ordinary persistence). To see the others there are two basic stratagems. The best is to get to know someone who has been on a visit to any Soviet reservation, find out how he did it, get the names and addresses of any contacts he made over there, and ask them to pull the necessary strings. The next best is to work through official channels – use the resources of western organizations (such as your national World Wildlife Fund, local fauna-preservation and ornithologists' societies, Audubon clubs, and so on) and through them contact the relevant Soviet Academy of Science (usually the most powerful body in this field). It always helps to arrange for a *party* to visit the USSR; even Soviet citizens visit the parks on organized tours rather than in individual visits. Hope, it must again be stressed, is slim; but if enough potential tourists exert enough pressure, the bureaucracy will ultimately yield a little. (The editor would welcome accounts of individual and group experiences in gaining access to any Soviet parks and reservations. Future editions could then be more specific on this point.)

For these reasons, the usual tourist details are given only sparsely in the following entries; while the fauna and flora are listed somewhat more formally than elsewhere in the book.

8 Altai R *393*
5 Astrakhan R *394*
7 Axu-Jabagly R *394*
6 Badkhyzsky R *397*
9 Barguzinsky R *398*
1 Byelovezhskaya Pushcha R *399*
4 Caucasian R *400*
2 Oka Terrace R *401*
3 Pechoro-Ilychsky R *402*
10 Sikhote-Alinsky R *402*

Altai Reserve 2,160,000 acres in the northeastern part of the Altai mountains. The reserve generally slopes upward to an alpine-type zone in the south, where the treeline is between 5,900 and 6,200 ft. The moist northern fir forest gives way to mixed cedar and fir, then cedar, then cedar and larch, and finally just larch. In the cedar forest on the Kyigi river there are spectacular giant umbels; in the most southerly larch forests there is no undergrowth at all – creating a cathedral-like atmosphere. Lake Teletskoye, in the centre of the reserve, is up to 4 miles wide and some 50 miles long. In the rest of the reserve are many salt-springs rich in minerals where mammals come to lick and drink. The southerly parts are dry, with less than 20 in. rainfall per year; the north is wetter, with up to 34 in. The lake freezes in winter.

꒯ 60 mammals, 300 birds, and 10 amphibians and reptiles include: argali, Mongolian gazelle, reindeer, European elk, musk deer, Siberian ibex, squirrel, long-tailed souslik, Asiatic chipmunk, northern and Altai pikas, sable bear, snow leopard; Altai snowcock, willow grouse, and demoiselle crane.

393

🪺 Anemone, Oriental globeflower, rhododendron, and typical steppe grasses on the drier southerly slopes.

🏹 By car on a well-maintained road from Beesk to the village of Yäilo on the northern shore of the lake; reserve HQ is in this village.

Astrakhan Reserve 100,000 acres; below (world) sea level. The reserve, whose area has increased enormously in recent years thanks to the fall in level of the Caspian Sea, is at the sea end of the Volga Delta – a gigantic system of twisting streams, islands, mud creeks, and silt banks. Even 8 or more miles out from the ragged shoreline the water is often less than 3 ft deep; but this can change dramatically when the much-feared Moryany wind chases the sea and delta water inland, drowning whole islands and even killing fairly large animals such as boar. Certain creeks called *Kulturki* are well sheltered from the Moryany and here huge flocks of waterfowl congregate. Underwater meadows of *Vallisneria spiralis* with patches of potamogeton grow amid rushes and support migratory colonies of duck and swan. The water is clearer the nearer you get to the Volga.

🐾 In meadows: hare, fox, badger, Asiatic polecat. In the *Kulturki*: hybrid tern, black tern. On open sandbanks: herring gull, common tern, coot. On reedy islands: greylag goose, whooper swan, Dalmatian and white pelicans. When floods abate many species of heron feed in the creeks. During migrations food is scattered for: white-fronted and other geese, ruff, curlew, sandpiper, godwit. During summer moulting the creeks are dense with: grey and other ducks, pintail, mallards, teal, wigeon. In better drained woodland: cormorant (nests at creek shores), spoonbill; great white, night, and squacco herons; little egret, glossy ibis; kite, rook, white-tailed eagle, osprey, raven (main predator); penduline tit. Nathusius's bat. Among the reeds: purple heron, great reed warbler, bearded tit, marsh warbler, reed bunting. Reptiles include grass snake, pond tortoise (*Emys orbicularis*); the commonest amphibian is the marsh frog (*Rana ridibunda*).

🪺 Reeds, reedmace, holly-leaved naiad, lesser naiad, flowering rush, water chestnut, water lily, yellow water lily, woody nightshade, water fern, fringed water lily, *Nelumbo nucifera*.

Axu-Jabagly Reserve 182,500 acres; rising to 6,600 ft above sea level. The reserve consists of the foothills, terraces, and peaks of a number of mountains. Most of it is in the Talassky-Alatau range, the remainder being in the Uramsky range. (There is also a sub-reserve of 320 acres in the Boroldaisky range but its function is more paleontological – being connected with finds at Karabastau – than conservational.) The summits of the Talassky-Alatau lie above the snow line and stretch in a magnificent panorama for over 150 miles to the upper reaches of the Axu and Jabagly rivers for which the reserve is named. The northern slopes are gently terraced; the southern ones precipitous. The reserve has no real forest, but occasional stands of juniper cling in the mountain clefts.

Brown bears, once common in temperate lands, have now been driven into northern coniferous forests, where they eat roots, berries, nuts, birds, small (and even ailing large) mammals. Though not ferocious they are more aggressive than black bears and should be avoided.

Geologically these mountains are young, so the river valleys are steep clefts that begin as mountain amphitheatres and form glacial troughs. Where they run out into the foothills the troughs form deep, narrow canyons. The Axu canyon, for instance, averages 1,640 ft depth for over 19 miles of its length, during which it is never more than a half mile wide. And the River Baldabrek runs over 330 ft deep though rarely more than 26 ft wide. In April and again in July it floods, spreading havoc over its plain. None of the rivers ever freezes.

The foothill zone is typical Asian steppe; the terraces are Himalayan and boreal meadow (between 5,900 and 6,600 ft above sea level). Reserve HQ is at Vannovko, Chikmyenskaya Oblast, Khazakhstan.

In steppe zone: jerboa, Asiatic polecat, hedgehog, corsac fox; skylark, calandra lark, eastern calandra lark, common myna. On steep slopes: fox, badger, booted lynx, weasel, stone marten, Siberian ibex, argali, snow leopard, wolf, deer, moose; Siberian deer (maral) deliberately introduced. In the subalpine zone: brown Isabel bear, marmot. Birds nest predominantly on steep slopes: mistlethrush, blackbird, rufous-bellied crested tit (black-crested race), orphean warbler, barred warbler, whitethroat, spotted flycatcher, wood pigeon, oriental dove; rock headed buntings; Stewart's, corn, and red-nightingale Siberian rubythroat. In meadows: partridge and rock partridge, quail, black-eared wheatear. On cliffs: mountain finches, eastern rock nuthatch, house martin, swift, rock thrush and blue rock thrush. Close to mountain streams: dipper and brown dipper, penduline tit, golden oriole, paradise flycatcher, blue whistling thrush. Among the rocks above the subalpine zone are Himalayan snowcock, snow finch, red-fronted sevin, water pipit, Alpine and Himalayan accentors, shore lark, black redstart, Buchan's bunting, wall creeper, Hodgson's and Brandt's mountain finches. One snake (*Ankistrodon halys*); one lizard (*Ablepharus alaicus*).

At meadow-steppe level are juniper forests of two species (*J. seravschanica* and *J. semiglobosa*). They are tallest on the gentle northern slopes, where also grow: honeysuckle, cotoneaster, berberis, wild rose, clustered bellflower, goatweed, *Asyneuma argutum*. Thick grasses abound on the high terraces. In boreal-type meadows grow: couch grass, awnless brome, meadowgrass, fescue, bindweed, knotgrass, meadow foxtail, cocksfoot, Turkestan sedge, slender-leaved vetch,

The Asiatic wild ass was domesticated in Sumerian times but was replaced by the horse. Nowadays it is rare throughout its range (Central Asia, Persia, West Pakistan) and is threatened with extinction. It can tolerate dehydration up to 30% of its body weight; on reaching water it can gulp down up to a quarter of its own weight.

Agropyron trichophorum, *Alopecurus songaricus*, *Geranium collinum*, betony, pinks, mountain St. Johns wort, and *Hypericum* elongatum. On Himalayan-type meadow: wild barley (*Hordeum bulbosum*), *Prangos pabularia*, *Ferula tenuisecta*, *Rheum maximoviczi*; other meadow plants include oriental cinquefoil, nulk vetch, hairlike feathergrass, vipergrass, thyme, *Ixiolirion tataricum*, *Schrenkia golickeana*. The rocky slopes of the gorges abound in: columbine, Albert's bellflower, Albert's saxifrage, dropwort, sandwort, wild garlic, Turkestan sanicle, burnet (*Sanguisorba riparia*), alpine and great burnet, round-leaved wintergreen, *Ephedra equisetina*, *Atraphaxis*, *Allium karataviense*. Other subalpine plants include: cranesbill, bindweed, forget-me-not, anemone, globeflower, white cinquefoil, sainfoin, *Thymus dmitrievae*, *Ziziphora pamiroalaica*, *Gentiana tianschanica*, *Onobrychis*.

Badkhyzsky Reserve 215,000 acres; between 2,600 and 3,940 ft above sea level. Badkhyz is a vast hilly area in the Turkmen Republic (extreme south of USSR, on border with Afghanistan and Persia). The word *badkhyz* means 'wind getting up'; the area is noted for an almost constant, strong, dry wind. The reserve slopes upward toward the west, where the northward-running gorges of the Gez-gedyk range cut through it. The east is more plateau-like with wide, pleasant valleys. Northward lie the ranges of the Duzen-kyr and Elli-bir mountains. To the south the plateau dips down into a wide hollow, Er-Oilan-Duz, 1,600 ft deep and about 6 miles by 12; in its centre is a saline lake. The north wall of the hollow is cut through by the huge ravine Kyzyl-Dzhar, 11 miles long, whose upper slopes are dominated by sheer red walls of sand that tower 100 ft in places. The most rewarding areas for viewing wildlife are in the water meadows of the river Tedzhen and the waterholes of the river Kushka; just east of the ravine Kzyl-Dzhar there is a large (75,000 acre) tract where gazelle and wild ass gather to give birth. Reserve HQ is in the village of Morgunovka near the town of Kushka, Turkmenian Republic.

40 mammals, 250 birds, and 35 reptiles include: Asiatic wild ass (or kulan) – the USSR's only reserve to have this rare species (700 head), Persian gazelle, Siberian ibex, wild goat, wildcat, ratel, porcupine; striped hyaena (rarely seen though traces are fairly common), Afghan vole, jird, Afghan mole-vole. Short-toed, pimaculated and crested larks, great grey, lesser grey, and bay-backed shrikes; rose-coloured starling, isabelline wheatear, red-headed bunting, bee eater, roller, eastern rock nuthatch, Lichtenstein's desert finch, Korshun kite, long-legged buzzard, Egyptian vulture, kestrel, saker falcon, short-toed, and pennate eagles. Reptiles include Horsfield's tortoise, lizards (*Agama sanguinolenta* and *A. erythrogastra*), Schneider's and yellow-bellied mole skinks, desert lacertid lizard, Brandt's snake-eyed skink, desert monitor (*Varanus griseus*), mountain racer (*Coluber ravergieri*), cliff racer (*C. rhodorachis*), *Vipera lebetina*, carpet viper (*Echis carinatus*), gamma snake (*Boiga trigonata*), steppe ribbon snake (*Psammophis lineolatus*), 3 species of sand boa (*Eryx*), and the Oxus cobra (*Naja naja oxiana*).

USSR

✿ Unique Asian steppe of meadowgrass (*Poa bulbosa*), sedge
(*Carex pachystylis*), poppies, malcolmia, tulips, irises, star-
of-Bethlehem, flowering kale, wormwood, Mastich tree
(*Pistacia vera*) which reaches over 20 ft on hill slopes, tanace-
tum, cousinia, salsola, ferula, dorema, *Merendera robusta*. In
gorges you will find the small Afghan fucus, Turangi poplar,
and occasional almond. The black saksaul tree flourishes in
the most arid reaches of Er-Oilan-Duz.

Barguzinsky Reserve 620,000 acres on the east bank of Lake
Baikal; 700 to nearly 10,000 ft above sea level. The reserve
includes a large part of the Barguzinsky mountain range, as
well as the lake, where aquatic studies are an important part
of its programme. The mountain peaks rise to nearly 10,000 ft
above sea level and enclose natural amphitheatres that are
either dry or formed into mountain lakes, which empty
through steep waterfalls. Half the reserve is alpine-zone habitat. Here and there are hot springs surrounded by giant
grasses, salix, and betula. Around the rivers are water
meadows, and peat bogs dotted with larch and cranberry. The
Baikal ices over between January and May; the mean winter
shore temperature is −6°F (min −22°) rising to 50° in summer. Inland the temperatures average 5° below those of the
shore falling to −35° (min) in winter. On the heights the snow-
fall lets up only in July; shoreside falls average 40 in. a year
rising to 80 in. on the heights. In autumn there are severe SW
winds (called *Sarma*) which gust to over 90 mph and raise
fantastic and beautiful ice grottoes on the lake shore. Reserve
HQ is in Davsha, the steamboat disembarkation point.

⌁ Sable, ermine, Siberian marten, weasel, alpine marten,
wolverine, otter; largest concentration of bears in Siberia;
reindeer, European elk, Siberian red deer, musk deer,
Asiatic chipmunk, flying squirrel, Kamtchatka marmot,
northern pika; northern, northern red-backed, large-
toothed red-backed and Sayan mountain voles; wood lemming. Lake Baikal is the only home of the Baikal seal; up to
100,000 of them share the waters with their close relatives,
the ringed seal. Ringed seals are also found in Arctic waters,
but Baikal seals are the only exclusively freshwater species
in the world. Both are menaced by the increasingly polluted
waters of the lake. Birds include: willow tit, nuthatch, yellow-
browed and greenish warblers, red-flanked bluetail, crossbill and two-barred crossbill, nutcracker, three-toed woodpecker, jay; white, grey, and pied wagtails; common sandpiper, yellow-breasted and pine buntings, scarlet rosefinch,
Pacific and needle-tailed swifts, bean goose, whooper swan,
white-tailed eagle, capercaillie and Siberian capercaillie,
hazel hen, willow grouse, ptarmigan, Japanese quail,
Siberian jay, pine grosbeak.

✿ Cobresia, carax, anemone, aquilegia, geranium, Asiatic
globeflower, dryas (incl. *D. octopetala*), cladonia, centaurea,
lichens; larch, pine (incl. *P. pumila*), balsam poplar, wild red
and black currant, chosenia, padus, spiraea, honeysuckle,
ash, elder, thelicrania, potentilla, and wild roses.

⇨ By air to the town of Ust-Barguzin or by steamboat from
Irkutsk to the village settlement of Davsha.

Desert monitor at Badkhysky Reserve. They can reach 5 ft in length, are carnivorous, and can survive in extremely high temperatures.

Byelovezhskaya Pushcha Reserve 340,000 acres; averaging 500 to 560 ft above sea level. Some 185,000 acres are in the USSR, 155,000 acres are in Poland, but the organization is cooperative. Much of the reserve is primeval forest that floods in autumn; about 7 per cent of the area is permanently flooded bog. In the south a range of small hills forms the watershed of the Niemen, Bug, and Pripet rivers. Within the reserve boundaries are the rivers Narev and Narevka (to the Baltic) and the Lyesna (a tributary of the Bug, which flows into the Black Sea). There are two artificial lakes, one of 875 acres was filled only recently, the other, of 50 acres (near Pererov) is old. On raised sandy areas are stands of giant pine that reach 100 ft and grow to exclude all undergrowth. In well drained parts where the soil is richer there are 130-ft alders where thick undergrowth makes for impenetrable virgin forest. Winters are short and mild; summers heavy and close.

⌑ 55 mammals, 204 birds, 11 amphibians, and 7 reptiles include: European bison (famous in this reserve), roe and other deer (which have driven the European elk, a poor competitor, out of the reserve and into the Pinsk marshes to the SE), thousands of boar; badgers, bear (very rare nowadays), fox, wolf, lynx, raccoon-like dog, weasel, stoat, polecat, pine marten, muskrat, dormouse and edible and forest dormouse, many squirrels; yellow-necked, harvest, northern birch, and long-tailed wood mice; bank, common, short-tailed, and northern voles and vole rat; many shrews including Mediterranean water shrew. Birds include red and Korshun kites, Ural owl, scarlet rosefinch, bullfinch, serin; three-toed, green, white-backed, and middle-spotted woodpeckers; great reed and barred warblers. In raised-pine dry zones: Peregrine falcon and short-toed eagle. Among spruce: buzzard, spotted and lesser-spotted eagles, goshawk, sparrowhawk, kestrel, honey buzzard, hazel hen, black grouse, capercaillie, woodcock, snipe, ruff, great snipe, black and white storks. Amphibians include: common, moor, edible, and European tree frogs; common, green, natterjack, spadefoot, and fire-bellied toads; crested newt. Reptiles: slow worm, sand lizard, adder, grass snake, common lizard, smooth snake, European pond tortoise.

By good road, 20 miles from Brest-Litovsk.

Thick forests make foot travel the only practical way of getting around.

The sable inhabits coniferous forests from the Urals to the Japan Sea.

Caucasian Reserve 655,000 acres in the west Caucasus; rising to 11,028 ft above sea level. There is a small subsidiary station, the Khostinskaya Yew-Box Coppice, measuring 78 acres, close to the Black Sea shore. The high-Caucasus range cuts the reserve into two unequal parts, the larger of which lies to the north; at the western end the range is not high and the distinction between north and south is less marked. Three notable peaks toward the eastern end are Fishta (8,395 ft), Chugush (10,625 ft), and Smidovitch (11,028 ft). The whole range shows signs of extensive glacial action, though now only the tributaries of the Trogi form glacial amphitheatres (glacier, lake, and disintegrated rock formation); above them are sharp unweathered peaks whose shade holds permanent snow. To the east the rivers Bolshaya Laba and Byelaya run north to feed the river Kuban, which runs down to the Sea of Azov. From the southern slopes the rivers Mzymta, Sochi, and Shakhe flow down to the Black Sea. The range thus separates the damp Black Sea climate from the drier regions of the Caspian and trans-Kuban. The northern climate is the more continental; in the south, and in the northern lowlands near the sea, the snow does not settle in winter. Mountain passes are open only between June and September. Autumn is dry and clear. Reserve HQ is at Maikopo.

A mixture of south-European, northern, and Asiatic-mountain species; once the Caucasus was an island and the influence of that era is still notable: Caucasian tur, long-clawed mole vole, Mlokosiewicz grouse, Caucasian snow-cock, Kasnakowi viper. This is also one of the chief centres for the re-introduction of the European bison; already the species here (about 500 head) is longer-legged than those of the Byelovezhskaya Puscha. Other species now flourishing here: deer (9,000 head), chamois, moose, occasional bear, leopard (very rare now but common earlier this century), wildcat, pine and beach martens. Birds include rock pipit, whinchat, snowfinch, alpine accentor, red-tailed rosefinch, Alpine chough and chough, buzzard, griffon and black vultures, lammergeier, golden eagle. Frogs include European tree frog and *R. macronemis*.

Many plants are Tertiary relics. Caucasian fir, oriental beech, oriental spruce, Spanish oak, Caucasian lime, and *Castanea*. In the undergrowth is *Rhododendron ponticum*, *Laurocerasus officinalis*, *Ilex colchica*. On the SW slopes up to about 3,000 ft are forests of oak with Caucasian hornbeam, pear, apple, *Prunus divaricata*, common and Norway maples, lime, ash. Beech dominates where shade is moist. In the forest: oxalis, wintergreen, *Ranunculus grandiflora*, *Pachyphragma macrophyllum*, and – especially over fallen trees – *Hedera colchica*. Farther east, tight up against the treeline: spruce, rowan, birch, mountain maple. In clearings: wild lilies and campanula. In subalpine meadows: purple and wood small-reeds, white anemone, aquilegia, globeflower, polygonum, baneberry, betony, centaurea. Above the treeline: matgrass, fescues, and hairgrasses.

Oka Terrace Reserve 15,000 acres on the left bank of the Oka river; between 390 and 590 ft above sea level. This is the nearest reserve to Moscow and an easy day trip from the capital. The area is basically pine forest with a mixture of spruce, oak, and lime. It also contains a small peat bog where sundew, cranberry and Iceland moss give the landscape a typical north Russian appearance. Just above the river's water meadows is an island of pure steppe. From the northern edge is a marked nature trail leading 5 miles through ancient pine forest down to steppe grass whose flora is special to the Oka. The river itself marks the boundary between wooded steppe and mixed forest; there is some overlap, so you will find southern plants like *Veronica incana*, *Koeleria grandis*, and genista growing alongside northern mosses. Artificial salt springs provide a nursery for the aurochs. Reserve HQ is at the village of Donki near the town of Serpukhov.

Elk, roe deer, beaver, marten, squirrel, hare, woodhen, grouse, capercaillie; when the water meadows flood you may see otters in transit.

Though the river shore is never more than 7 miles wide you will find examples of steppe, wooded steppe, deciduous forest, and south and middle taiga. Commonest species: heath anemone, feathergrass, fritillary, purple vipergrass, elegant St John's wort, fescues, *Cerasus fruticosa*, *Tulipa biebersteiniana*.

Hotels in Moscow.

Suburban train (*Elektrichka*) from Moscow's Kursk station to Serpukhov, then an 8-mile taxi ride.

Only on foot.

Pechoro-Ilychsky 1.8 million acres in the mesopotamia of the rivers Pechora and Ilych; 300 to 600 ft above sea level. Set in extreme northeast Europe, the reserve is almost entirely covered by black taiga conifer forest, with occasional islands of scrub and subalpine meadow. The distant Ural mountains form steep escarpments that look like medieval castles, on whose ramparts bare mountain tundra clings precariously. The area has one of the heaviest snowfalls in Europe, with mean January temperature at $-1°F$, falling as low as $-67°$; summer temperatures are between $52°$ and $57°$ on average, with peaks in July of $91°$. The park headquarters are in the small village of Yaksha on the Pechora river, Kormi Autonomous Republic.

Reindeer, European elk, lynx, wolverine, badger, weasel, stoat, otter, European beaver, Asiatic chipmunk, red squirrel, mountain hare, northern pika, sable, pine marten, harvest and northern birch mice, bank and northern red-backed voles, numerous shrews. Capercaillie, black grouse, hazel hen, willow grouse, ptarmigan, nutcracker, crossbill, Siberian jay. Common lizard, ground frog, common toad.

Pines (including *P. sylvestris and P. sibirica*) spruce, and firs.

By air from Syktykvar (the capital of the Kormi Autonomous Republic, within whose borders the reserve lies) via Troitsko-Pechorsk.

The reserve contains some interesting limestone caves; one, called *Myedvezhy* (Bear), has a large collection of stone age relics.

A raccoon-like dog in the Sikhote-Alinsky reserve. It is nocturnal and may partly hibernate in cold winters, coming out on warm days.

Sikhote-Alinsky Reserve 775,000 acres; between sea level and 5,244 ft above sea level. This reserve, in the extreme southeast of the Soviet Union, has about 30 miles of coast along the Sea of Japan. Almost all of it is mountainous, with a central mountain range dividing the reserve southwest to northeast.

Three folds of this range point seaward, one inland; their eastern slopes are more sheer than those facing westward. The three main rivers (Sankhobe, Belimbo, and Iodzike) flow into the Ussuri, on the disputed China-USSR border, and so northward via the Amur to the sea; they are rich in waterfalls. The reserve also contains the Shandunsky system of mountain lakes (connected underground) between 1,600 and 2,600 ft above sea level; they are used by moose to rid themselves of bloodsucking insects, and they also provide habitat for migratory waterfowl. Climate is best in autumn, though, apart from the thin coastal strip, there are often cold winds off the Siberian landmass. Winters are frosty and usually cloudless. Summers are cooled by onshore winds. The monsoons come in late summer and there is an occasional typhoon. Reserve HQ is in the village of Ternyei, Vladivostock.

⌿ Sable antelope, musk and roe deer, moose, boar, lynx, Ussuri tiger, wapiti, Asiatic black and Arctic bears, raccoon-like dog, Siberian weasel, yellow-throated marten, northern pika, sika deer, Manchurian wapiti, leopard cat, Japanese and mountain hares, goral, East Siberian mole. Birds: hawfinch; great-spotted, lesser-spotted, white-backed, grey-headed, and three-toed woodpeckers; masked and black-tailed grosbeaks, white-tailed eagle, osprey; eagle, long-eared, and Japanese scops owls; grey-faced buzzard-eagle; harlequin duck, Gould's merganser, Temminck's cormorant, black-tailed gull, sooty guillemot, ancient auklet. Reptiles and amphibians: Adder, *Elaphe schrenki*, *Natrix tigrina*, *Rana rugosa*.

ɞ There are distinct vertical zones in the reserve: oak from the coast up to 1,000 ft; cedar and angiosperms from 650 to 1,600 ft; mixed cedar-spruce from 1,300 to 2,300 ft; and fir-spruce mixture between 700 and 4,500 ft. Above this there is stunted cedar and sparse birch. In the lower woods the undergrowth is rich in broad-leaved ferns, polypody, epiphyte lichens, and mosses. There is more variety along the narrow coastal strip: wild roses, crataegus, spindle tree, viburnum, French maple, burnet, meadow rue, angelica, hogweed, hazel, stunted oak, Korean pines, *Lespedeza*, *Syringa amurensis*. *Larix gmelinii* abounds in the dunes. In the forests: chrysanthemum honeysuckle, ladyferns, *Sorbaria sorbifolia*, *Matteucia struthiopteris*. On high northern slopes: yew, Korean cedar (often towering to 160 ft), *Picea jezoensis*, *Abies nephrolepsis*.

⇨ By boat 375 miles on the Sea of Japan from Vladivostock to the village of Ternyei.

USSR: Species List

— **Arctic** Sikhote-Alinsky
— **Asiatic Black** Sikhote-Alinsky
— **Brown Isabel** Axu-Jabagly
BEAVER Oka Terrace
— **European** Pechoro-Ilychsky
BEE-EATER Badhyzsky
BISON, European Byelovezhskaya
  Pushcha; Caucasian; Oka Terrace
BLACKBIRD Axu-Jabagly
BLUETAIL, Red-Flanked Barguzinsky
BOA, Sand Badkhyzsky
BOAR Byelovezhskaya Pushcha; Oka
  Terrace; Sikhote-Alinsky
BULLFINCH Byelovezhskaya Pushcha
BUNTING, Buchan's Axu-Jabagly
— **Corn** Axu-Jabagly
— **Pine** Barguzinsky
— **Red-Headed** Axu-Jabagly; Badkhyzsky
— **Reed** Astrakhan
— **Rock** Axu-Jabagly
— **Stewart's** Axu-Jabagly
— **Yellow-Breasted** Barguzinsky
BUZZARD Byelovezhskaya Pushcha;
  Caucasian
— **Honey** Byelovezhskaya Pushcha
— **Long-Legged** Badkhyzsky
BUZZARD-EAGLE, Grey-Faced Sikhote-
  Alinsky
CAPERCAILLIE Barguzinsky;
  Byelovezhskaya Pushcha; Oka Terrace;
  Pechoro-Ilychsky
— **Siberian** Barguzinsky
CAT, Leopard Sikhote-Alinsky
CHAMOIS Caucasian
CHIPMUNK, Asiatic Altai; Barguzinsky;
  Pechoro-Ilychsky
CHOUGH Caucasian
— **Alpine** Caucasian
COBRA, Oxus Badkhyzsky
COOT Astrakhan
CORMORANT Astrakhan
— **Temminck's** Sikhote-Alinsky
CRANE, Demoiselle Altai
CREEPER, Wall Axu-Jabagly
CROSSBILL Barguzinsky; Pechoro-
  Ilychsky
— **Two-Barred** Barguzinsky
CURLEW Astrakhan
DEER Axu-Jabagly; Byelovezhskaya
  Pushcha; Caucasian
Musk Altai; Barguzinsky; Sikhote-
Alinsky
— **Roe** Byelovezhskaya Pushcha; Oka
  Terrace; Sikhote-Alinsky
— **Siberian** Axu-Jabagly; Barguzinsky
— **Sika** Sikhote-Alinsky
DIPPER Axu-Jabagly
— **Brown** Axu-Jabagly
DOG, Raccoon-Like Byelovezhskaya
  Pushcha; Sikhote-Alinsky
DORMOUSE Byelovezhskaya Pushcha
— **Edible** Byelovezhskaya Pushcha
— **Forest** Byelovezhskaya Pushcha
DOVE, Oriental Axu-Jabagly
DUCKS Astrakhan
— **Grey** Astrakhan
— **Harlequin** Sikhote-Alinsky
EAGLE, Golden Caucasian
— **Lesser Spotted** Byelovezhskaya
  Pushcha
— **Pennate** Badkhyzsky
— **Short-Toed** Badkhyzsky;
  Byelovezhskaya Pushcha
— **Spotted** Byelovezhskaya Pushcha
— **White-Tailed** Astrakhan; Barguzinsky;
  Sikhote-Alinsky
EGRET, Little Astrakhan
ELAPHE SCHRENKI Sikhote-Alinsky
ELK, European Altai; Barguzinsky; Oka
  Terrace; Pechoro-Ilychsky
ERMINE Barguzinsky
FALCON, Peregrine Byelovezhskaya
  Pushcha
— **Saker** Badkhyzsky
FINCH, Brandt's Mountain Axu-Jabagly
— **Hodgson's Mountain** Axu-Jabagly
— **Lichtenstein's Desert** Badkhyzsky
— **Mountain** Axu-Jabagly
FLYCATCHER, Paradise Axu-Jabagly
— **Spotted** Axu-Jabagly
FOX Astrakhan; Axu-Jabagly;
  Byelovezhskaya Pushcha
— **Corsac** Axu-Jabagly
FROG, Common Byelovezhskaya Pushcha

— **Edible** Byelovezhskaya Pushcha
— **European Tree** Byelovezhskaya
  Pushcha; Caucasian
— **Ground** Pechoro-Ilychsky
— **Marsh** *(Rana ridibunda)* Astrakhan
— **Moor** Byelovezhskaya Pushcha
— *Rana macronemys* Caucasian
— *Rana rugosa* Sikhote-Alinsky
GAZELLE, Mongolian Altai
— **Persian** Badkhysky
GEESE Astrakhan
GOAT, Wild Badkhyzsky
GODWIT Astrakhan
GOOSE, Bean Barguzinsky
— **Greylag** Astrakhan
— **White-Fronted** Astrakhan
GORAL Sikhote-Alinsky
GOSHAWK Byelovezhskaya Pushcha
GROSBEAK, Black-Tailed Sikhote-
  Alinsky
— **Masked** Sikhote-Alinsky
— **Pine** Barguzinsky
GROUSE Oka Terrace
— **Black** Byelovezhskaya Pushcha;
  Pecho-Ilychsky
— **Mlokosiewicz** Caucasian
— **Willow** Altai; Pechoro-Ilychsky
GUILLEMOT, Sooty Sikhote-Alinsky
GULL, Black-Tailed Sikhote-Alinsky
— **Herring** Astrakhan
HARE Astrakhan
— **Japanese** Sikhote-Alinsky
— **Mountain** Pechoro-Ilychsky; Sikhote-
  Alinsky
HAWFINCH Sikhote-Alinsky
HEDGEHOG Axu-Jabagly
HEN, Hazel Byelovezhskaya Pushcha;
  Pechoro-Ilychsky
HERON, Great White Astrakhan
— **Night** Astrakhan
— **Purple** Astrakhan
— **Squacco** Astrakhan
HYAENA, Striped Badkhyzsky
IBEX, Siberian Altai; Axu-Jabagly;
  Badkhyzsky
IBIS, Glossy Astrakhan
JAY Barguzinsky
— **Siberian** Barguzinsky; Pechoro-Ilychsky
JERBOA Axu-Jabagly
JIRD Badkhyzsky
KESTREL Badkhyzsky; Byelovezhskaya
  Pushcha
KITE Astrakhan
— **Korshun** Badkhyzsky; Byelovezhskaya
  Pushcha
— **Red** Byelovezhskaya Pushcha
KULAN *See* ASS, Asiatic Wild
LAMMERGEIER Caucasian
LARK, Calandra Axu-Jabagly
— **Crested** Badkhyzsky
— **Eastern Calandra** Axu-Jabagly
— **Pimaculated** Badkhyzsky
— **Shore** Axu-Jabagly
— **Short-Toed** Badkhyzsky
LEMMING, Wood Barguzinsky
LEOPARD Caucasian
— **Snow** Altai; Axu-Jabagly
LIZARDS Badkhyzsky
— **Common** Byelovezhskaya Pushcha;
  Pechoro-Ilychsky
— **Desert Lacertid** Badkhyzsky
— **Sand** Byelovezhskaya Pushcha
LYNX Byelovezhskaya Pushcha; Pechoro-
  Ilychsky; Sikhote-Alinsky
— **Booted** Axu-Jabagly
MALLARDS Astrakhan
MARAL *See* DEER, Siberian
MARMOT Axu-Jabagly
— **Kamtchatka** Barguzinsky
MARTEN Oka Terrace
— **Beach** Caucasian
— **Pine** Byelovezhskaya Pushcha;
  Caucasian; Pechoro-Ilychsky
— **Siberian** Barguzinsky
— **Stone** Axu-Jabagly
— **Yellow-Throated** Sikhote-Alinsky
MARTIN, House Axu-Jabagly
MERGANSER, Gould's Sikhote-Alinsky
MOLE, East Siberian Sikhote-Alinsky
MOLE-VOLE, Afghan Badkhyzsky
— **Long-Clawed** Caucasian
MONITOR, Desert Badkhyzsky
MOOSE Axu-Jabagly; Caucasian; Sikhote-
  Alinsky

MOUSE, Harvest Byelovezhskaya Pushcha; Pechoro-Ilychsky
— **Long-Tailed Wood** Byelovezhskaya Pushcha
— **Northern Birch** Byelovezhskaya Pushcha; Pechoro-Ilychsky
— **Yellow-Necked** Byelovezhskaya Pushcha
MUSKRAT Byelovezhskaya Pushcha
MYNA, Common Axu-Jabagly
NATRIX TIGRINA Sikhote-Alinsky
NEWT, Crested Byelovezhskaya Pushcha
NIGHTINGALE Axu-Jabagly
NUTCRACKER Barguzinsky; Pechoro-Ilychsky
NUTHATCH Barguzinsky
— **Eastern Rock** Axu-Jabagly; Badkhyzsky
ORIOLE, Golden Axu-Jabagly
OSPREY Astrakhan; Sikhote-Alinsky
OTTER Barguzinsky; Oka Terrace; Pechoro-Ilychsky
OWL, Eagle Sikhote-Alinsky
— **Japanese Scops** Sikhote-Alinsky
— **Long-Eared** Sikhote-Alinsky
— **Ural** Byelovezhskaya Pushcha
PARTRIDGE Axu-Jabagly
— **Rock** Axu-Jabagly
PELICAN, Dalmatian Astrakhan
— **White** Astrakhan
PIGEON, Wood Axu-Jabagly
PIKA, Altai Altai
— **Northern** Altai; Barguzinsky; Pechoro-Ilychsky; Sikhote-Alinsky
PINTAIL Astrakhan
PIPIT, Rock Caucasian
— **Water** Axu-Jabagly
POLECAT Byelovezhskaya Pushcha
— **Asiatic** Astrakhan; Axu-Jabagly
POND TORTOISE *(Emys orbicularis)* Astrakhan
PORCUPINE Badkhyzsky
PTARMIGAN Pechoro-Ilychsky
QUAIL Axu-Jabagly
RACER, Cliff Badkhyzsky
— **Mountain** Badkhyzsky
RAT, Vole Byelovezhskaya Pushcha
RATEL Badkhyzsky
RAVEN Astrakhan
REDSTART, Black Axu-Jabagly
REINDEER Altai; Barguzinsky; Pechoro-Ilychsky
ROLLER Badkhyzsky
ROOK Astrakhan
ROSEFINCH, Red-Tailed Caucasian
— **Scarlet** Barguzinsky; Byelovezhskaya Pushcha
RUBYTHROAT, Siberian Axu-Jabagly
RUFF Astrakhan; Byelovezhskaya Pushcha
SABLE Barguzinsky; Pechoro-Ilychsky
SANDPIPER Astrakhan
— **Common** Barguzinsky
SEAL, Baikal Barguzinsky
— **Ringed** Astrakhan
SERIN Byelovezhskaya Pushcha
SEVIN, Red-Fronted Axu-Jabagly
SHREWS Byelovezhskaya Pushcha; Pechoro-Ilychsky
— **Mediterranean Water** Byelovezhskaya Pushcha
SHRIKE, Bay-Backed Badkhyzsky
— **Great Grey** Badkhyzsky
— **Lesser Grey** Badkhyzsky
SKINK, Brandt's Snake-Eyed Badkhyzsky
— **Schneider's** Badkhyzsky
— **Yellow-Bellied Mole** Badkhyzsky
SKYLARK Axu-Jabagly
SLOW WORM Byelovezhskaya Pushcha
SNAKE, Gamma Badkhyzsky
— **Grass** Astrakhan; Byelovezhskaya Pushcha
— **Smooth** Byelovezhskaya Pushcha
— **Steppe Ribbon** Badkhyzsky
SNIPE Byelovezhskaya Pushcha
— **Great** Byelovezhskaya Pushcha
SNOWCOCK, Altai Altai
— **Caucasian** Caucasian
— **Himalayan** Axu-Jabagly
SNOWFINCH Axu-Jabagly; Caucasian
SOUSLIK, Long-Tailed Altai
SPARROWHAWK Byelovezhskaya Pushcha
SPOONBILL Astrakhan
SQUIRREL Altai; Byelovezhskaya Pushcha;

Oka Terrace
— **Flying** Barguzinsky
— **Red** Pechoro-Ilychsky
STARLING, Rose-Coloured Badkhyzsky
STOAT Byelovezhskaya Pushcha; Pechoro-Ilychsky
STORK, Black Byelovezhskaya Pushcha
— **White** Byelovezhskaya Pushcha
SWAN, Whooper Astrakhan; Barguzinsky
SWIFT Axu-Jabagly
— **Needle-Tailed** Barguzinsky
— **Pacific** Barguzinsky
TEAL Astrakhan
TERN, Black Astrakhan
— **Common** Astrakhan
— **Hybrid** Astrakhan
THRUSH, Blue Rock Axu-Jabagly
— **Blue Whistling** Axu-Jabagly
— **Mistle** Axu-Jabagly
— **Rock** Axu-Jabagly
TIGER, Ussuri Sikhote-Alinsky
TIT, Bearded Astrakhan
— **Penduline** Astrakhan, Axu-Jabagly
— **Rufous-Bellied (Black-) Crested** Axu-Jabagly
— **Willow** Barguzinsky
TOAD, Common Byelovezhskaya Pushcha; Pechoro-Ilychsky
— **Fire-Bellied** Byelovezhskaya Pushcha
— **Green** Byelovezhskaya Pushcha
— **Natterjack** Byelovezhskaya Pushcha
— **Spadefoot** Byelovezhskaya Pushcha
TORTOISE, European Pond Byelovezhskaya Pushcha
— **Horsefield's** Badkhyzsky
TUR, Caucasian Caucasian
VIPERA LEBETINA Badkhyzsky
VIPER, Carpet Badkhyzsky
— **Kasnakowi** Caucasian
VOLE, African Badkhyzsky
— **Bank** Byelovezhskaya Pushcha; Pechoro-Ilychsky
— **Common** Byelovezhskaya Pushcha
— **Large-Toothed Red-Backed** Barguzinsky
— **Northern** Barguzinsky; Byelovezhskaya Pushcha
— **Northern Red-Backed** Barguzinsky; Pechoro-Ilychsky
— **Sayan Mountain** Barguzinsky
— **Short-Tailed** Byelovezhskaya Pushcha
VULTURE, Black Caucasian
— **Griffon** Caucasian
— **Egyptian** Badkhyzsky
WAGTAIL, Grey Barguzinsky
— **Pied** Barguzinsky
— **White** Barguzinsky
WAPITI Sikhote-Alinsky
— **Manchurian** Sikhote-Alinsky
WARBLER, Barred Axu-Jabagly; Byelovezhskaya Pushcha
— **Great Reed** Astrakhan; Byelovezhskaya Pushcha
— **Greenish** Barguzinsky
— **Marsh** Astrakhan
— **Orphean** Axu-Jabagly
— **Yellow-Browed** Barguzinsky
WEASEL Axu-Jabagly; Byelovezhskaya Pushcha; Pechoro-Ilychsky
— **Siberian** Sikhote-Alinsky
WHEATEAR, Black-Eared Axu-Jabagly
— **Isabelline** Badkhyzsky
WHINCHAT Caucasian
WHITETHROAT Axu-Jabagly
WIGEON Astrakhan
WILDCAT Badkhyzsky; Caucasian
WOLF Axu-Jabagly; Byelovezhskaya Pushcha
WOLVERINE Barguzinsky; Pechoro-Ilychsky
WOODCOCK Byelovezhskaya Pushcha
WOODHEN Oka Terrace
WOODPECKER, Great-Spotted Sikhote-Alinsky
— **Green** Byelovezhskaya Pushcha
— **Grey-Headed** Sikhote-Alinsky
— **Lesser-Spotted** Sikhote-Alinsky
— **Middle-Spotted** Byelovezhskaya Pushcha
— **Three-Toed** Barguzinsky; Byelovezhskaya Pushcha; Sikhote-Alinsky
— **White-Backed** Byelovezhskaya Pushcha; Sikhote-Alinsky

MARINE AREAS

Bermuda

To the oceanographer the waters around Bermuda are the equivalent of a land desert (which is why they are so clear). This means that fish and squid are not numerous, though the number of species is vast. And the scarcity reacts right up the ecological chain. Most visitors comment on the startling scarcity of shore-birds; and even those breeding birds that settle temporarily must range over wide areas in search of food.

The best single site is Spittal Pool, a 60-acre government sanctuary on the neck between Harrington Sound and the Atlantic; it has more waterfowl than all the other Bermuda marshes combined. In fact you can expect to see practically every bird in the *Checklist and Guide to the Birds, Mammals, Reptiles and Amphibians of Bermuda*, published by the Bermuda Audubon Society. Other good waterbird areas are the mangrove swamps at Hungry Bay and Pilchard Bay, especially for waterthrushes, kingfishers, and yellow-crowned night herons. Resident common gallinules and coots are best seen at Pembroke Marsh and in the ponds on the Mid-Ocean Golf Course, Tucker's Town.

The spring and autumn migrations can disappoint the short-term visitor. One day you can scour the islands and not see a single migrant; next day you can see dozens. From late July to September you may see all the common arctic species on their way down to South America, from golden plovers to white-rumped sandpipers. Throughout the winter you will find ducks, herons, ibises, egrets – almost all the eastern North American waterfowl species. Among landbirds you may expect to see over 30 different warblers from August to October; the blackpoll warbler often turns up in large numbers. The spring migration is even more of a trickle – at least on land. You can expect to see purple gallinule and indigo bunting and even an occasional painted bunting. But the really spectacular springtime movements are out at sea – in marked contrast to autumn and winter, when the sea is virtually birdless. From March to June you may see the northward migrations of shear-waters and the southward migrations of the northern species – jaegers (even small flocks of the rarely seen long-tailed jaeger), terns, Leach's petrel, and so on.

Hamilton Aquarium houses one of the world's finest tropical marine collections. About 5 miles away, in Hamilton Sound, is a splendid natural aquarium called Devil's Hole. The main pool, 35 ft deep, is flanked by two shallower ponds. Here you can see the massive green turtle, grouper fish, moray eels, shovelnose sharks, trigger fish, blacktail bream, Scotch porgies, and cowfish (among 400 species).

In the 400 square miles to the west, north, and east of Bermuda is an area of sunken islands, reclaimed by the sea at the end of the last ice age. The waters average a mere 2 fathoms and are rich in corals. You can take 2-to-3 hr trips in glass-bottomed boats at rates around £1 an hour.

Further information from the News Bureau, 50 Front St, Hamilton.

Dominica

The main sanctuary for wildlife (particularly birdlife) in Dominica is provided by the forest-clad mountains of the interior, which reach above 4,000 ft – even though the coastline is nowhere more than 5 miles away. Many of the montane landbirds listed under Grenada-St Vincent (below) also occur here; in addition you will see the sisserou or imperial parrot, the rammier or blue pigeon, and the agouti (a rabbit-sized rodent). The two obvious mountains are Morne Trois Pitons (easily accessible by road) and the Diablotin (accessible by a 2,000 ft climb from the end of the Pointe Round road). Here, too, you may see the black-capped petrel, known locally as the diablotin (confusingly enough the same name as is given to Audubon's shearwater in Grenada!).

There are 9 hotels, rates between US$10 to US$40 single, US$14 to US$75 double (summer rates up to 50 per cent lower); 4 guest houses between US$11 single and US$15 double. Seaside cottages are available at around US$10 and US$12.50 daily. The leading local tours organization is Dominica Safaris, PO Box 176, Roseau, Dominica.

Grenada to St Vincent

This stretch of the Windward Isles is especially rewarding and convenient for the birdwatcher. The two main islands, Saint Vincent to the north and Grenada to the south, are well enough developed to provide the visitor with every reasonable comfort and amenity, but not so well developed that the wildlife is severely affected. And in between are some two score of small islands and cays – the Grenadines – all accessible and all rich in birdlife.

Sea birds At most times you can expect to see: yellow-billed tropicbird (St Vincent – sites named thus in brackets are the best, not necessarily the only ones), brown pelican (western Grenada), brown booby, American frigatebird; royal tern (from Point Salines northward). The commonest winter migrants are Leach's petrel (flying southward) and Wilson's petrel (northward), both seen well off shore; summer migrants include gull-billed and sooty terns and occasional least terns. Among summer visitors: Audubon's shearwater (breeds April–May, Green and Sandy islands), red-billed tropicbird (breeds April–May, Les Tantes and Isle de Rhonde), roseate tern (April–September, west and north coast of Grenada and on other islands), and bridled tern (breeds April–August, Green Is, Les Tantes, and elsewhere). Laughing gulls are common, March–August.

Water and shore birds Pied-billed grebe (on ponds at Levera, River Antoine, I. de Rhonde), great blue heron (Union I., Carriacou), little blue and green herons (both common), black- and yellow-crowned night herons (Point Salines, Carriacou), purple gallinule (rare, I. de Large), Florida gallinule (common); greater and lesser yellowlegs are commonest in winter. Off shore you can expect to see osprey and, during spring and autumn passages, willet. Winter migrants and visitors include blue-winged teal (common), sora rail (rare and the group's only rail); northern ring-necked, Wilson's and killdeer plovers; golden plover (but here in non-nuptial plumage), black-bellied plover, ruddy turnstone and spotted sandpiper (both common), sanderling (Petit Martinique), belted kingfisher (common).

Landbirds Broad-winged hawk, black crab hawk (mountains on St Vincent), peregrine, red-necked pigeon (some cays, a wary bird), violet-eared dove (Point Salines, Levera, Petit Martinique), ground dove (common), St Vincent parrot (mountain woodlands), mangrove cuckoo and smooth-billed ani (both common); hummingbirds include hairy hermit and Antillean crested (both common) and emerald-throated (Grenada); yellow-bellied elaenia (common); also many swifts, swallows, wrens, thrashers, thrushes, vireos, honeycreepers, and tanagers.

The most comprehensive guide is *Birds of Grenada, St Vincent and the Grenadines*, a highly personal and absorbing checklist by Fr Raymund P. Devas, published by Carenage Press, Grenada.

There are several dozen hotels and guest houses in the two main islands as well as on Bequia, Union Is, Prune Is, and Petit St Vincent. Rates range from US$5 to US$50 single (incl 2 meals) to US$6 to US$60 double. Further information from ATBEC, Room 238, 200 Buckingham Palace Road, London SW1.

Jamaica

Virgin Jamaica – the original forest that Columbus must have seen rising from shore to the 7,400 ft peaks of the Blue Mountains, broken only by a few Arawak Indian clearings – is probably non-existent today. Something close to it may survive at Point Rhoades (appropriately near to Discovery Bay) and high in the Blue and John Crow mountains. The rest is a fascinating mixture of Indian, Spanish, and later introductions. The Arawaks brought arrowroot, maize, sweet potatoes, and cassava. With the Spaniards came bananas, coconut, sugar cane, and citrus fruits. The English and later visitors brought mangoes, ackees, poinciana, cassia, tulip trees, logwood, cashew, guango trees, pasture grasses, rats (by accident), mongoose (to get rid of rats), and other animals named below – now a well-balanced variety. This richness of flora and fauna is matched by an enormous variation in the type of landscape, from the savannah-like grasslands near the Old Harbour to the weird cloudforests of lichens, ferns, and mosses high in the Blue Mountains.

The chief glory of the island is its birdlife – though the visitor who stays close to Kingston is likely to be impressed only by the general drabness of the birds he will see: nightingale or mockingbird, petchary, grassquit, loggerhead, savanna blackbird, turkey buzzard (known as John Crow), kingfisher, and hopping Dick (a thrush); even the hummingbirds (streamertail, Jamaican mango – both unique – and vervain, no bigger than the bumble bee) are less coloured than most of their kind. The saffron finch, introduced around 1923, is a colourful exception. So are the black- and yellow-billed parrots and the parakeet – all destructive and on the pests list. And the unique Jamaican tody, green, white, and cherry red, is worth a whole reel of colour film.

Far more elusive are the unique crested quail dove and the rufous-throated solitaire – both found (with a lot of luck and persistence) in the deep upland forests. Other all-year residents include the Greater Antillean (or tinkling) grackle, whitebelly pigeon, pea and ground doves, and bananaquit. The starling was introduced in 1903 and the Guiana parrotlet in 1918; both are now seen in big flocks over most of the island. A curious self-introduction (1951) is the cattle egret; each autumn they turn up by the thousand and feed on the insects and ticks around the cattle estates. To watch them turn their night-time roosting trees white with their plumage is quite a sight.

Other migrants, which add that wanted note of colour, include: bobolink (September and October onward), indigo bunting (from December, especially near Montego Bay), American redstart (which is actually resident here – despite its name – from August to the following May), and black and white and many other warblers. Summer visitors include grey kingbird, nighthawk, and black-whiskered vireo.

Jamaica's other animals are a more impressive lot than you will find on many of the smaller Caribbean islands and cays. There are 25 bat species, including a fish-eater often seen at dusk around Kingston harbour. Other mammals include the manatee and porpoise. Crocodiles (here called 'alligators') abound in the southern swamps. Other reptiles include the ground lizard, the croaker (a gecko often seen at night, clinging with its sucker feet to vertical walls and other surfaces), galliwasp (wrongly believed to be poisonous – the island has no poisonous reptiles), and the anole lizard (who often displays his colourful throat fan at his less brilliant mate). There are three snakes, two constrictors and a burrower, all rare near habitations. And most visitors treasure memories of the fireflies and other colourful insects.

There are several dozen hotels, inns, and guest houses at prices to suit every pocket. Leading tours operators are Jamaica Tours, PO Box 227, Montego Bay/tel: 2887 and Martins Jamaica/tel: Kingston 85011; both will take care of all bookings, car hire, and travel arrangements within the island.

Netherlands Antilles

The southernmost group of islands (Aruba, Bonaire, Curacao) lies only 80 to 100 miles off the South American mainland. The birdlife is extremely rich. On all of them you are likely to find: brown booby, brown pelican, Brazilian cormorant; royal, Cayenne, and least terns; magnificent frigatebird; great blue, Louisiana, little blue, yellow-crowned night, and green herons; American and snowy egrets, southern mockingbird, black-faced grassquit, ground dove, bananaquit, emerald and ruby-topaz hummingbird, yellow warbler, golden oriole, bare-eyed pigeon, white-fronted dove, kestrel, sparrowhawk, groove-billed ani, tropical kingbird; in less settled areas you may also see Audubon's caracara, blue pigeon, and white-tailed hawk. And if that isn't enough to send you straight to the nearest travel agent, the individual islands have these specialities to offer:

Aruba This least verdant of the three islands has: rufous-collared sparrow, troupial, crested quail, the rare burrowing owl; the local race of the yellow-winged parrot died out in the 1940s. *Best sites*: Spanish Lagoon, Frenchman's Pass, Paarden Baai and Lagoon, Malmok and Westpunt, Boca Prins, Savaneta old Salina, Rooi Takki, Jamanota district and Bubali district.

Curacao Least grebe, Bahama pintail, black-necked stilt, snowy plover, Caribbean elaenia; the local race of barn owl is the smallest and palest in the world; the crested quail, rufous-collared sparrow, and troupial are found here, too. *Best sites*: Knip Estate, St Michiel's Lake, St Joris Bay, Mt Christoffel, Jan Thiel Lagoon, Malpais, Tefelberg, and many lagoons around the always-rewarding shoreline.

Bonaire This, the most unspoiled island of the three, has the world-famous breeding colony of up to 2,000 flamingos at Pekelmeer (also excellent for shorebirds); also gray kingbird, yellow-winged parrot, and pearly-eyed thrasher. As on Curacao you may also see Bahama pintail, black-necked stilt, Caribbean elaenia, snowy plover, and least grebe. *Best sites*: Bronswinkel (especially for blue pigeon) and Mt Brandaris; Lac (shorebirds and herons); Onima (grebes, parrots, hawks, and other landbirds); and all salt pans and shores.

The northernmost group of islands (Saba, St Martin, and St Eustatius) lie at the pivot of the Antilles, where the chain turns abruptly westwards. The largest, St Martin, is only 9 × 8 miles in extent – and much of that is lagoon; the other two are less than half that size. Nonetheless, they too are quite unspoiled and have a great deal to offer the visiting birdwatcher. All have: ground dove, red-billed tropicbird, banana- and grassquits, emerald-throated and Antillean crested hummingbirds, Antillean bullfinch, pearly eyed thrasher, and zenaida dove.

St Martin is best for shorebirds. *Best sites*: coastal drive; trails to Mt Sentry, Pt Blanche, Ft Amsterdam; and the Cul de Sac Experimental Station.

St Eustatius has a lush tropical rainforest inside the extinct Quill crater; its birdlife specialities are similar to Saba's.

Saba Steep and rugged, with its tree ferns and cloud forest, its remote cliffs, rich in bird colonies, is far and away the most rewarding of the three. Noteworthy birds include: brown booby, yellow-billed tropicbird (Ft Bay), bridled quail dove, garnet-throated hummingbird, trembler, green euphonia, scaly-breasted thrasher. *Best sites*: Diamond Rock, Green Is, Booby Point Cliffs, Spring Bay Gut, and Mt Scenery. The best guide is *Birds and Fish of the Netherlands Antilles* by Henry H. Collins Jr; Caribou Press, Bronxville, NY.

There is ample accommodation on Curacao and St Martin; visitors' facilities are undergoing considerable development as this goes to press; for latest details contact Dutch Antilles House, Badhuisweg 175, The Hague, Netherlands.

Trinidad

Trinidad is the southernmost link in that long chain of islands which sweeps up from the South American mainland to form the Lesser and Greater Antilles. Ten miles off the Orinoco delta in Venezuela, it is roughly 50 miles north-south by 37 east-west, with two great arms stretching westward to the mainland.

As with the other islands, the chief attraction is the birds. Trinidad is well furnished with bays, inlets, marshes, pasture, woodland, and upland forest – habitat for most of the birds named in the section on Grenada-St Vincent. The most rewarding site is the famous Caroni Swamp near the island's western shore: scarlet ibis, egrets, white, blue, and other herons, spoonbill, kingfisher, honeycreepers, vireos, wood and Old World warblers, tanagers, cardinals, buntings, American sparrows, thrushes, thrashers, dippers, hummingbirds, owls, pigeons, parrots, gulls, terns, oystercatchers, limpkins, rails, osprey, hawks, eagles, New World vultures, frigatebirds, cormorants, gannets, boobies, tropicbirds, grebes; there are also a number of families that extend no farther up the chain than Trinidad – cotingas (also in Jamaica), manakins, ovenbirds, motmots, ant thrushes, toucans, jacamars, oilbirds, jacanas, tinamous; guans and curassows have been introduced; and birds of paradise have been introduced into nearby Tobago.

Part of the swamp's 10,000 acres is an official sanctuary. To visit you need a pass from the Chief Game Warden, Forestry Department, Long Circular Road, Port of Spain/tel: 24521 or through the Tourist Board, 56 Frederick St, Port of Spain/tel: 38299. The swamp is best explored by boat; individual or group conducted tours can be arranged through Hub Travel, 44 New St/tel: 54266, Battoo Bros, 67b St Vincent St/tel: 32571, Oudit Nahan/tel: 638 3033, and David Ramsahai/tel: 638 4174.

Fiji

Like most of the other island and marine areas discussed in this section, the 300-odd islands of the Fiji group are as rich in birdlife as they are poor in mammals and interesting reptiles. But with their soft, palm-fringed beaches and coral reefs, their fertile volcanic soil, wooded mountains, palm groves, and generally unspoiled character, they offer as congenial and rewarding a birdwatching ground as even the most jaded ornithologist could wish for.

Shoreline Sooty rail (Beqa, Taveuni, and other mongoose-free islands), mongolian dotterel, turnstone, Pacific golden plover, wandering tattler, banded rail and purple swamphen (mongoose-free islands), little mangrove heron (larger islands), bar-tailed godwit, whimbrel, reef heron (especially along Nasese coast road near

Suva), and Australian grey duck (Fiji's only duck since the local extinction of the whistling tree duck).

True forest Pink-bellied parrot-finch (only on Nadrau Plateau on Viti Levu above 3,000 ft), Fiji warbler (several subspecies), blue-crested broadbill (3 main islands; 3 subspecies), red-throated lorikeet (Viti Levu, Ovalau, Taveuni), Fiji shrikebill (several subspecies), Polynesian starling, golden whistler (10 subspecies), island thrush (5 subspecies), giant forest honeyeater (3 main islands), friendly ground dove (actually a very shy bird – larger islands only).

Lowland bush Pacific pigeon (Lau group), long-tailed New Zealand cuckoo (April–September), and feral domestic fowl (mongoose-free islands).

Mixed town/country habitat White-rumped swiftlet (Polynesia's only swift), orange-breasted honeyeater (Fiji's smallest bird), red-headed parrot-finch, strawberry finch (larger islands), Pacific swallow, Vanikoro broadbill (4 subspecies), Java rice sparrow (introduced 1930 to Viti and Vanua Levu), Polynesian triller (several subspecies), wattled honeyeater, collared lory, red-vented bulbul (introduced 1903 to Viti Levu and neighbours), jungle mynah (introduced 1900 to larger islands), Indian mynah (introduced 1890 to larger islands), Malay turtle dove (larger islands), Fiji goshawk, swamp harrier.

Mixed country/bush habitat Grey-backed white-eye, white-collared kingfisher (except some Lau-group islands), fan-tailed cuckoo (larger islands), white-throated pigeon.

Mixed bush/forest Scarlet robin (larger islands), Layard's white-eye (3 large islands), slaty flycatcher, spotted fantail (3 subspecies, 3 main islands and Ovalau), many-coloured fruit dove, orange dove (Vanua Levu, Taveuni, Rabi), golden dove (Viti Levu, Ovalau, Bequ, Gau), velvet dove (unique to Kadavu), Peele's pigeon (larger islands), red-breasted musk parrot (3 subspecies), yellow-breasted musk parrot (Viti Levu).

There are a certain number of birds of limited range: silktail (Taveuni, Vanua Levu), Kadavu fantail (only Kadavu), and versi-color (only Ogea). Among 21 recorded **seabirds**: Gould's gadfly petrel, tropicbirds, black-naped, crested, and bridled terns, and white-capped noddy.

The best birdwatching areas near Suva are: Suva gardens, when the figs are in fruit; Nasinu Caves; Rewa Delta (duck, waders, little mangrove heron); Colo-I-Suva village (parrots, honeyeaters); and the Wailoku Valley road. The best guide is *A Field Guide to Fiji Birds* by Robin Mercer; published by the Fiji Museum.

Calling the turtles This ancient ceremony is still sometimes performed by the flower-garlanded men of the craggy island of Koro; at certain times they exhibit their skill at calling up the giant sea turtles and bringing them ashore. Details from the Visitors Bureau.

There are hotels at Suva and around much of the southern and western coastline of Viti Levu; daily rates from 50s single and 100s double, meals about 50s extra. There are many cruises and excursions to the other islands. Further information from Fiji Visitors Bureau, cnr MacArthur St and Victoria Parade, Suva/tel: 22867.

Galapagos

Among naturalists the group of volcanic islands 500 and more miles off the coast of Ecuador (of which country they are a part) hold a special place. For it was after his visit to the islands in *HMS Beagle* in 1835 that Charles Darwin first formulated the ideas that were to culminate in his monumental *On the Origin of Species by Means of Natural Selection* in 1859. For there, among those 16 major islands, he found a fascinating group of finches. There are 13 well-defined species and many subspecies. There were clear differences among them, especially in the formation of their beaks; but just as clearly they had derived from a common ancestor – at least that was the most obvious explanation for their marked similarity. The same sort of variation from a common ancestor had happened among the giant land turtles that were then found on every island in the group. Those on the lush-vegetation islands of Chatham, Santa Cruz, Floreana, and southern Albermarle had domed shells and short necks; while those on the more arid islands of Duncan, northern Albermarle, and Abingdon had saddleback shells and long necks adapted to reaching up to browse on cactus pads. Pondering such differences led Darwin to think of how variations might arise and how they would suit or unsuit an animal for its environment – and so, over two decades of painstaking work, to his famous theory.

The same process of species formation is still going on, especially among the marine iguanas, unique to the islands. So Galapagos still has plenty to teach us.

The islands were first discovered by the Spanish bishop of Panama in 1535; it was he who gave them their Spanish names. In the following century they were repeatedly colonized and stocked by British pirates, who gave them their English names – only two of which (Charles for Floreana and Indefatigable for Santa Cruz) have failed to catch on. Thanks to them there are more than 75,000 head of wild cattle on Albermarle alone, and many other islands have cattle, pigs, and goats. To prevent a further spread (for the ecological damage done by such introductions is irreversible) the Ecuador government has established the Charles Darwin Research Station at Academy Bay on Santa Cruz and it maintains regular patrols of the straits between the islands in the group.

Since 1965 Lindblad Travel Inc, New York (who also operate the Seychelles and Antarctica cruises described elsewhere in these pages) have offered cruises with the accent very strongly on wildlife and conservation to these islands. The route may vary slightly from year to year, but not its scope or purpose. Here, for example, is the list of islands visited in 1971:

James Sealions at Sullivan Bay; nesting great blue heron along shore; flamingo colony at Crater Lake; red crab at James Bay.

Tower Huge colonies of oceanic seabirds – red-footed booby and swallow-tailed gull (200,000), frigatebirds (many thousands), storm petrel (over a million), swallow-tailed gull (several thousand; also South American furseal, here fighting back from its recent near-extinction).

Narborough Thousands of marine iguana; flightless cormorant; Galapagos penguin; sea lion; penguin; there is a still-active volcano, which spews out lava as black as pitch.

Albermarle Nesting flightless cormorant at Tortuga Point; Galapagos penguin; furseal.

Duncan Giant land tortoise (saddleback species unique to this island).

Champion Champion mockingbird (unique to the island).

Hood Punta Point for a big colony of blue-footed and masked boobies, tropicbirds, shearwaters; Hood Island marine iguanas; Hood mockingbird; sealions.

Santa Cruz Study the work of the Charles Darwin Foundation Research Station.

Plaza Land guana; sealion; swallow-tailed gull.

Each cruise is led by at least two naturalists who have specialized in studying the ecology of the Galapagos group.

The two 1971 cruises, which were in April–May (13 days each) cost from \$1,000 to \$1,500 depending on cabin size and location (excluding fares to and from Ecuador).

Further information from Lindblad Travel Inc., Lindblad Travel Bldg, 133 E 55th St, New York NY 10022/tel: 212 PLaza 1–2300; London Agents: Houlders World Holidays, 53 Leadenhall St, London EC3/tel: (01) 481 2020.

Sealions, a marine iguana, and a flightless cormorant – the last two being unique to Galapagos. The cormorant is larger and heavier than any other member of its family. The iguana's long tail enables it to swim – and even to crawl along the sea bed, where it browses on seaweed. It also eats shrimps, worms, crickets, and other meat.

Kenya Coast

The stretch of coast between Malindi and Mombasa is now being developed – or perhaps one should say 'carefully undeveloped' – so as to provide the best facilities for visitors while producing the least disturbance to the environment – the coral reefs, the bright sandy beaches fringed with casuarinas, and the warm and brilliantly coloured waters of the Indian Ocean. That, after all, is what most visitors will come in order to enjoy. To this end the Government has declared 15 miles of coastline south from Malindi to be a marine reserve, within which two marine national parks have been organized. Malindi Marine Park, in the north of the reserve lies off Casuarina Point, at present accessible only after a bumpy but short car ride; the magnificent coastal scenery and coral gardens make it worthwhile. There are no officially organized boat trips or other facilities here, yet, but local hotels (see below) will arrange visits. The Watumu Marine Park and Mida Creek (within the park) is more accessible. At its northern end, overlooking Turtle Bay, are two hotels, Seafarers and Ocean Sports (rates from 60s per person per day). Here you can hire glass-bottomed boats (10s per head plus fee of 10s) except during the May–June long rains. Species lists for these areas are still in preparation.

Still farther south, about half way between Malindi and Mombasa, is a water-bird area that no birdwatcher should miss: Kilifi Creek. Here you will see: grey, reef, black, and night herons, woolly-necked and yellow-billed storks, little and great white egrets, fish eagle, osprey and 7 other raptors, curlews and sandpipers (including Terek sandpiper), plovers (including Mongolian sand plover), gulls, terns, silvery cheeked hornbill, kingfishers (including mangrove kingfisher), sunbirds, pink-backed pelican, drongo, Peter's twinspot, pale flycatcher – to name just a few of the

127 species so far recorded. The Mnarani Club (a hotel) is right at Kilifi Creek; rates from 90s single to 180s double per day, children 50s, plus 10s daily or 200s annual membership; facilities for boat hire, aqualung hire and instruction, goggling and sailing. Guided visits to the creek cost 60s an hour for parties of 6; best season February–March.

Seychelles

Until the volume of traffic through the new airport builds up, the Seychelles are not readily accessible to ordinary tourism – and its rich and unique wildlife therefore remains largely hidden. But since 1970 Lindblad Travel Inc in association with BOAC have operated the MS *Lindblad Explorer* (see also Antarctica) on a series of 14-day cruises – not just of the Seychelles, but of Aldabra, Grand Comoro, and Zanzibar, too. The Seychelles are a tiny group of islands (total 150 sq miles) some 900 miles east of Africa, between 4° and 5°S. They are unique in being the only oceanic islands to be composed of continental rock; in fact, 180 to 135 million years ago, they, like Madagascar, were part of the African mainland – both bits of land having since drifted to their present positions. As a reminder of their continental past the Seychelles have a whole group of archaic, legless amphibians that have survived only as rare relics in the outside world. Only specialists are interested in these survivors, but the bird life is rich enough and rare enough to excite even the most casual visitor. Nine species are on the red list of endangered species, though, thanks to enlightened management and strict enforcement of the regulations, the danger lies more in the fact that their populations are small than in any specific threat directed against them. The islands themselves come close to most people's idea of the original Eden; in fact, General Gordon (of Khartoum fame) narrowed the choice down to the Vallée de Mai on Praslin island (described below). All have steep beaches of brilliant white coral sand, fringed by palms and tropical shrubs, bathed by some of the clearest and most limpid waters in the world – all under a sky of bluest azure (at least, during the period of the tours: end-March to mid-November). The 1971 tour went from Mombasa via Mahé, Frigate, Cousin, Mahé (again), Bird, La Digue, Praslin, Desroches atolls, Aldabra, Grand Comoro, Zanzibar, and so back to Mombasa. And since the Desroches atolls and Aldabra are of coral origin, and Comoro is volcanic, passengers have a chance of seeing the three main types of island to be found in the world's oceans. From London by BOAC the inclusive round trip cost between £598 (3-bedded room on B Deck) to £840 (single-bed room on A Deck), plus optional safari tours en route: to Serengeti NP, Tanzania (1 day, £14) or Tsavo NP, Kenya (3 days, £32). Comparable figures for US tourists from Lindblad (address at top of page 413).

A brief description of each of the islands and its wildlife:

Mahé The largest of the Seychelles at 55 square miles – 17 miles north-south, $3\frac{1}{2}$ to 5 miles east-west, with a central granitic spine rising to 3,000 ft. Only home of the Seychelles scops owl (red list).

Frigate Only home of the very rare magpie robin (world population estimated at 2 dozen; often called the rarest bird in the world), and of the Seychelles fody – both red listed.

Cousin Recently declared a bird sanctuary; home of up to 20,000 fairy tern, and of the Seychelles fody (red list). Only home of the colony's finest songster, the Seychelles brush warbler (red list).

Bird An atoll, northernmost of the Seychelles group. Home of over 2 million sooty and noddy terns, whose eggs are commercially exploited during a short open season; also shearwater, which nests in holes, booby, and frigatebird.

La Digue Only home of the rare Seychelles black paradise fly-catcher (estimated 40 birds; red list), which was understandably but mistakenly reported extinct in 1958.

Praslin The Vallée de Mai Nature Reserve, mentioned earlier, is unique for its giant double coconut, known as coco-de-mer. For a long time it was known only by its fruit, specimens of which were washed up on the Indian coast. No one could believe that a tree capable of bearing such fruit existed anywhere on earth and its origin was placed in some mythical lost continent below the waters. In fact, it has the largest fruit and the largest leaves of any plant in the world; some specimens reach over 150 ft. Also in the reserve you will see the black parrot (actually slate-grey) and the red-listed lesser vasa parrot. For both species the island is the only known habitat.

General Apart from the species listed above you will find, throughout the islands: swiftlet, bulbul, scarlet fody (or cardinal, the islands' most colourful bird), Indian mynah, barred dove, turnstones (which here catch crickets during their stay!), whimbrel; and you may be lucky enough to see the three endangered species: Seychelles kestrel, Seychelles white-eye, and the Seychelles turtle dove. One of the most colourful sights is the aerial display of the Dutch pigeon, named for its red, silver-white, and blue colouring, which reminded locals of the Dutch flag. The only mammal – apart from man and the rats and dogs he has brought with him – are the fruit bats or flying foxes. There are plenty of colourful lizards and geckoes, as well as frogs, which you are more likely to hear at night than to see. Giant tortoises are now extinct in the wild, though there are plenty kept in gardens; as long as their eggs are protected from the rats they thrive and multiply. Green and hawksbill turtles are protected in Seychelles waters. Fish you will see on any underwater dive include: black, blue, and yellow angelfish; coral-eating parrot fish, striped sergeant majors; and while walking along the shore you will see mud skippers and dozens of different kinds of shells.

Aldabra A coral atoll with 60 square miles of solid land; 21 by 9 miles. Its large lagoon, filled with living coral, is dry at low tide. Only 20 people, fishermen and their families, live on Aldabra. It is most famous for its 100,000 or 120,000 giant tortoises – being the only home of this species, which man has eliminated from every other island between Madagascar and the Seychelles. Here also live over a million frigatebirds and thousands of red-footed boobies (in the mangrove swamps). The island is the only home of the Aldabra kestrel (red list), the white throated rail, the Aldabra fody (a small red and yellow finch), and the Aldabra drongo.

Comoro A volcanic island once famous for pirates, now an Arabic trading town better known for its fruit, vanilla pods, and spices. The Comoro group has three endangered species on the red list: the Comoro blue pigeon, the Moheli green pigeon, and the Anjouan sparrow hawk. On Grand Comoro itself, most of the avifauna peculiar to the region is found in the evergreen forests some way up the slopes of the 8,070 ft Mt Karthela: greater vasa parrot, spine-tailed swift, courol, cuckoo shrike, Comoro thrush, yellow white-eye, and two sunbird species.

Acknowledgements

Apart from those mentioned on pp 6–7 we must record our gratitude to Rennie Bere, Paul Géroudet, Elspeth Huxley, Peter Scott, and Roger Tory Peterson – all of whom, despite heavy personal commitments, agreed to provide introductory essays for the book's major sections. Peter Scott and his wildlife assistant, Jane Fenton, were early and constant encouragers of the whole project; their help at many crucial moments was invaluable. Thanks also to Ian S. MacPhail, (former Director-General of the WWF British National Appeal), without whom the book might not have got off the ground; to Arnold Thorne (Administrator, British National Appeal, WWF), Kay Partney Lautman (Associate Director, WWF Inc., Washington), and Fritz Vollmar (Secretary General, WWF, Morges) for help at many different stages. Most of the photographers and archives listed on this page reduced their fees when they heard that the book was to benefit the WWF. Gratitude to Professor Bannikov (USSR) and the staff of the Natural History Museum, London, is recorded on page 392, and to Jeffrey Boswall on page 18. Thanks also to Prof. Helmut Gams, Vienna, for information on Austrian and Polish sites. Space does not permit a record of the dozens of administrators in tourism and conservation agencies around the world whose help is nonetheless greatly appreciated. Without all this generous dedication of time and professional service such a book could certainly not have been compiled.

Picture credits

The cover picture shows a black swan, a native of Australia (courtesy Australian Tourist Commission).
The frontispiece shows a reticulated giraffe (courtesy World Wildlife Fund, London; Donald Paterson/Bruce Coleman Ltd).

We are grateful to the following for the pictures that illustrate the main body of text; sources are listed in alphabetical order, pictures from each source in page order:

AUSTRALIAN TOURIST COMMISSION 264–97
AUSTRIAN STATE TOURIST DEPARTMENT 315, 349 (Harrandt)
Professor A. G. BANNIKOV 399, 402
CANADIAN GOVT TRAVEL BUREAU 151, 191, 195, 203, 205, 208, 209
EAST AFRICAN RAILWAYS & HARBOURS 12/13
FINNISH TOURIST AUTHORITY 363
FRENCH GOVERNMENT TOURIST OFFICE 389
JAPAN NATIONAL TOURIST ORGANIZATION 258
JOHN KARMALI 27
LINDBLAD TRAVEL 220 (George Holton)
MALAWI MINISTRY OF TOURISM 45, 69, 71, 85
NATIONAL FILM BOARD OF CANADA 138–9, 143, 166, 175, 179, 188/9, 192, 196, 198, 200
NEW ZEALAND HIGH COMMISSION 302–306
NORMAN MYERS 25
NOVOSTI PRESS AGENCY 390, 401

OREGON STATE HIGHWAY DEPARTMENT 86–7, 105
PORTUGUESE INFORMATION OFFICE 56 W. RASHEK 396
SATOUR 35, 51, 66, 77, 81
JOHN SAVIDGE 59
US DEPT OF THE INTERIOR/BUREAU OF SPORT, FISHERIES, AND WILDLIFE 99 (Peter J Van Huizen), 100 (Ralph H Anderson), 102 (Rex Gary Schmidt), 113 & 117 (both E. P. Haddon), 120 (Joe Mazzoni), 123, 127 & 131 (both Luther C. Goldman), 132 (W. P. Taylor), 157 (Howe Sadler), 163, 165 (Jack F. Dermid)
US DEPT OF THE INTERIOR/NATIONAL PARKS SERVICE 96 (Adolph Murie), 124 (M. Woodbridge Williams), 155 & 168–9 (both Jack E. Boucher)
ROGER WHEATER 33, 62, 82
WOMETCO MIAMI SEAQUARIUM 251
WORLD WILDLIFE FUND, LONDON 245 (E. Hosking), 309, 335 (J. Behnke/Bruce Coleman Ltd), 353 (Werner Haller/Bruce Coleman Ltd), 383 (Fritz Polking/Bruce Coleman Ltd), 395 (APN)
WORLD WILDLIFE FUND, MORGES 65 (Norman Myers), 75 (J. F. Ormond), 211 (P. Schauenberg), 219 (James Hancock), 228 (Sally Anne Thompson), 234 & 237 (both E. P. Gee), 239 (F. Vollmar), 241 (E. P. Gee), 243 (F. Kurt), 249 (Mrs B. Harrisson), 253 (F. Vollmar), 339 (Franz Antonicek), 341 (W. Fendrich), 357 (C. A. Vaucher), 367 (P. Géroudet), 373 (J. P. Strijbos), 375 (C. A. Vaucher), 384 (F. Vollmar), 413 (Heinz Sielman)